D. S. Mirsky
A Russian–English Life, 1890–1939

For BARBARA, *again*

D. S. Mirsky
A Russian–English Life, 1890–1939

G. S. SMITH

OXFORD
UNIVERSITY PRESS

OXFORD
UNIVERSITY PRESS

Great Clarendon Street, Oxford OX2 6DP

Oxford University Press is a department of the University of Oxford.
It furthers the University's objective of excellence in research, scholarship,
and education by publishing worldwide in

Oxford New York

Athens Auckland Bangkok Bogotá Buenos Aires Calcutta
Cape Town Chennai Dar es Salaam Delhi Florence Hong Kong Istanbul
Karachi Kuala Lumpur Madrid Melbourne Mexico City Mumbai
Nairobi Paris São Paulo Singapore Taipei Tokyo Toronto Warsaw

and associated companies in Berlin Ibadan

Oxford is a registered trade mark of Oxford University Press
in the UK and certain other countries

Published in the United States
by Oxford University Press Inc., New York

© G. S. Smith 2000

The moral rights of the author have been asserted
Database right Oxford University Press (maker)

First published 2000

British Library Cataloguing in Publication Data

Data available

Library of Congress Cataloging in Publication Data
Smith, Gerald Stanton.
D. S. Mirsky : a Russian–English life, 1890–1939 / G. S. Smith.
p. cm.
Includes bibliographical references and index.
1. Mirsky, D. S., Prince, 1890–1939. 2. Critics–Soviet Union–Biography. I. Title.
PG2947.M53 S63 2000   801′.95′092–dc21   [B]   00-025130

ISBN 0-19-816006-2

1 3 5 7 9 10 8 6 4 2

Typeset by Best-set Typesetter Ltd., Hong Kong
Printed in Great Britain
on acid-free paper by
Biddles Ltd.
Guildford and King's Lynn

Acknowledgements

WHEN I began work on the life of D. S. Mirsky, a number of people still survived who had known him personally or shared his various environments. I would like to express my gratitude to three of them in particular: Dorothy Galton (1901–92), Gleb Petrovich Struve (1898–1985), and Vera Traill (1906–87). I was also fortunate enough to receive eyewitness testimony to various episodes in Mirsky's life from Sir Isaiah Berlin, E. H. Carr, Michael Florinsky, Salomeya Halpern, Dame Elizabeth Hill, Janko Lavrin, Hugh MacDiarmid, Roy Pascal, and Mirsky's elder sister, Sonya Pokhitonova.

For sharing with me their private knowledge of Mirsky and his doings, I would like to thank particularly Tania Alexander, Edward J. Brown, James Klugmann, Marina Ledkovsky, Sir Dmitri Obolensky, and Francis J. Whitfield. For generous assistance with particular problems I am grateful to James O. Bailey, Birgit Beumers, Neil Cornwell, A. G. Cross, Martin Dewhirst, Paul Dukes, Francis Greene, Olga Kaznina, Vadim Kozovoï, Nina Lavroukine, Yury Davidovich Levin, Ekaterina Lubyannikova, Peter Mackridge, M. V. Mikhalkov-Andronov, Vladimir Perkhin, Andrew Reynolds, Thomas J. Shaw, and Emily Tall. Among the many librarians and archivists who have helped me at various times I would like especially to thank Elizabeth Inglis, Carole Menzies, June Pachuta, Mary Stuart, Gregory Walker, Jackie Willcox, Elizabeth Yeo, and the staffs of the Bakhmeteff Archive at Columbia University, the Harry Ransom Humanities Research Center, University of Texas at Austin, and the State Archive of the Russian Federation, Moscow.

The award of a Research Fellowship at the University of Liverpool, through the good offices of Arnold McMillin, who was then Bowes Professor of Russian, made it possible for me to get to grips with the subject, and I am deeply grateful to them. A John Simon Guggenheim Memorial Fellowship at another particularly critical stage enabled me to devote some time wholly to this project.

I am happy to express my gratitude for financial support for various aspects of the work on this book from the Curators of the Taylor Institution and the Faculty of Medieval and Modern Languages, University of Oxford. David Howells and his colleagues in the Slavonic Section of the Taylor Institution Library, University of Oxford, have been unfailing in their courteous and painstaking professionalism.

The wit, erudition, and meticulous scholarship of Richard Davies have been an inspiration to me for many years.

Galin Tihanov gave my manuscript a scrupulous reading and shared his unique expertise in Continental literary theory. Dominic Lieven offered some valuable correctives to my ideas about pre-revolutionary aristocratic life. Catriona Kelly's acerbic but benignly constructive critique immensely improved the broad balance and also the detailed coherence of the final result.

Robert Wiebe's big books on big issues in American history stand a long way away from my own subject, but they have taught me many lessons. His immaculately professional scrutiny of my manuscript gave me exactly the outside perspective I needed.

D. S. Mirsky lived his adult life without a constant companion. I have been fortunate enough to live much of mine with Barbara Heldt. She has coped (to risk a complacent British understatement for the male approval of conventional female behaviour) with forbearance spiked with her own unique iconoclastic intelligence. The impress of her mind is so pervasive in this book that to make adequate formal acknowledgement of it is impossible.

Contents

Russia's rulers and Russia's ruled—Bureaucracy and constitutionalism—The Svyatopolk-Mirskys—Mirsky's mother—The family—Home tuition and home cooking—'*Si l'Empereur vous demande quelque chose . . .*'—'Where shall I go to school now?'

Languages—Literary debut—Mikhail Kuzmin—Intellectual currents—Undergraduate to guardsman—Mirsky the poet—Poetry circles

The Great War—The revolutions—White versus Red—The defeat of Denikin—Poetry and politics—Leaving Russia—Anthem for doomed youth

The bread of exile—Passports and visas—Russians in London—The Williamses and others—*The London Mercury*—Bernard Pares and the School of Slavonic Studies—Miss Harrison—Bloomsbury—The *Décades* at Pontigny—Roger Fry—Mirsky observed—Mirsky and the English—Writing books—The *History*—After the *History*—Liberal values

Russia outside and in—Boiled lettuce—'The poetry of will and reason'—*A Little Anthology*—The *émigré* press—*The Well-Intentioned*—Mirsky and conservatism—The Eurasian movement—'A man without convictions'—Aleksey Remizov—Marina Tsvetaeva—Finding funds—'The Ambience of Death'—*Vyorsts*—Vladislav Khodasevich—Cooling to Tsvetaeva—More *Vyorsts*—Mirsky and religious faith

List of Illustrations

Transliteration and Conventions

I HAVE translated all the quotations from Russian in this book; in the annotation I have retained transliterated Russian in referring to such items.

In transliterating Russian Cyrillic in the body of the text I have followed the *Oxford Slavonic Papers* conventions, but I have omitted the equivalent of the soft sign, thus producing such forms as 'Babel' and 'Gorky'; I have used 'i' where the soft sign comes before a vowel, as in 'Prokofiev'. I have represented Cyrillic 'ë' as 'yo'. In references and bibliography, I have retained the strict *OSP* convention. In referring to dates before 1917 I have retained the original Old Style without comment for documents such as letters, but I have given both Old and New Style dates for events not mentioned in this way.

I have made liberal use throughout the book of my interviews with Vera Traill. These interviews were conducted almost entirely in Russian, which I have translated here into English. I have indicated this material with such phrases as 'Vera Traill said to me' when introducing quotation and paraphrase. I have followed the same procedure in citing my interviews with Dorothy Galton, Janko Lavrin, and Roy Pascal.

When referring to Mirsky's letters in publications by myself, a list of which is given in section 2 of the Bibliography, I have simply indicated in the body of the text the addressee and date of the letter concerned.

When referring to Mirsky's published writings in the endnotes, I have cited reprints whenever they are available, and supplied details of the original publication in the Bibliography.

Introduction

> There are two ways of writing history, which I may call the mythological
> and the novelistic. The mythological way is to work in generalizations, to
> simplify history into a formula, to think in types and moulds. The other
> method rejoices not in the potential simplicity, but in the actual
> complexity, of Nature, appears later in history and is displayed more
> seldom. Periods, nations, civilizations are too much of a generalization for
> a historian of this disposition; but a biographer, of course, if he pretends
> to be anything but a mere recorder or anecdote-monger, must have
> something of this quality. (D. S. Mirsky, 1923)

How best to refer to the hero of this book is not a straightforward matter. He
was born and brought up as 'Prince Dimitry Petrovich Svyatopolk-Mirsky'—
a title, a given name, a patronymic, and a double-barrelled surname. When he
simplified his name to 'D. S. Mirsky' for his English readership after emigrating from Russia, he retained a reference to the more resonant element in his
original surname, and eliminated the patronymic. In his Russian publications
outside Russia, though, the double-barrelled form was usually still preferred.
After he returned to Russia, 'D. S. Mirsky' was the name he continued to
employ. The full form has never been obliterated; some English and American
editors remained attached to the man's title, and post-Soviet Russian commentators have tended to return not only to this but also to the double-
barrelled form of the surname. 'D. S. Mirsky', though, is the name he unambiguously came to prefer himself in formal circumstances. He will usually be
referred to here simply as 'Mirsky'.[1]

Mirsky is familiar to all students of Russian literature outside Russia,
amateur and professional, as the author of what is still generally regarded as
the best history of their subject from the beginnings to 1925. This masterpiece
was originally published in two volumes, and reissued in a one-volume abridgement.[2] It has held its place in the English-speaking world for over seventy years,
which may well be a record for this kind of book. Translations into German,
Italian, and French have consolidated its status in Western Europe.[3] Meanwhile, in his native country, Mirsky's *History* was accessible before 1991 only
to the privileged few who held passes to the restricted holdings of the metropolitan libraries, since it was written in English, published in Great Britain and
the USA, and was ideologically unacceptable. When the book was eventually
translated into Russian, it was published in London like the original,[4] and it
has still not been published in Russia.

Mirsky's other principal books have also had curious fates, for different reasons. His *Russia: A Social History* (1931), a unique attempt to give an account of the subject on a geopolitical basis, has been strangely neglected; its value as an introduction to Russian history has only increased as other meta-narratives have come and gone. *The Intelligentsia of Great Britain* was written in Russian and published in Moscow, but like most non-fiction published in the early 1930s it is dismissed by the few Russians who know it as politically expedient hack-work; the English translation (1935) had a brief *succès de scandale* and was then forgotten, its hard-line Marxism too much to take except for the most intransigent comrades. Finally, Mirsky's last major book, his Russian-language *Anthology of Modern English Poetry* (1937), was published under somebody else's name after Mirsky was arrested; it is still revered by poets and quarried by Russian students of English literature, but to this day not many of them know that it is his work.

The reasons for this situation, which would be bafflingly anomalous in the context of any modern European culture other than Russian, lie in the political and cultural travails that afflicted Mirsky's homeland during the twentieth century, and in his uncompromising responses to them.

Mirsky wrote no memoirs, and his multitudinous publications avoid the personal. In fact, he published only two autobiographical statements, and they partially overlap. The first was the self-serving account of his ideological evolution that he wrote after joining the Communist Party of Great Britain and setting out to earn a Soviet passport. The original version of this testament was published in French,[5] and shorter versions of it appeared in English and Russian.[6] Here, Mirsky makes hardly any reference to the physical events of his life. The other autobiographical statement appeared on the dust-jacket of *The Intelligentsia of Great Britain*. In macro-Communist style, it uses the third person:

Dmitri Mirsky was born in 1890 in the neighbourhood of Kharkov (Ukraine) as the son of General Prince (Svyatopolk) Mirsky, who was for a short time Russian Minister of the Interior (1904–5).

Studied Chinese, Classics and History at the University of St. Petersburg, graduating in 1914. During the war was an officer in the Foot Guards. In 1919–1920 served in Denikin's White Army, after the collapse of which he emigrated, and settled in England.

From 1922 to 1932 was Lecturer in Russian Literature at King's College, London. In 1920 he began writing for the English literary press.

In 1931–1932 he took an active part in the work of the Friends of the Soviet Union, and spoke in various parts of England several times weekly, and also in Holland and Ireland. He took part in the Amsterdam Anti-War Congress (1932). In the autumn of 1932 he returned to Russia. Since then he has specialised more and more in literary criticism.

This account reduces Mirsky's life to its extremes. Several important elements have been prudently omitted from it; and when it was written, Mirsky had over five years of eventful life remaining. Inevitably, there is nothing here to give the reader a sense of the various contexts of this individual life and the reasons for the subject's actions, much less any sense of nuance; everything is seen in categorical terms.

In fact, Mirsky's life was riven with contradiction. After his privileged boyhood and schooling, he was inducted into two professions that in terms of contemporary social norms were deeply incompatible with each other, if not indeed antagonistic—academic philologist and historian on the one hand and Guards officer on the other. He was also a minor poet, and a precocious participant in the vaunted cultural revival that took place in St Petersburg in the first years of this century. Mirsky then spent the best part of a decade serving in the armies he mentions. He was forced into emigration along with most of his surviving comrades-in-arms on the White side. Whatever his political views may have been at the time, he had practically no option but to leave Russia: men of his social situation were in principle marked down for physical extermination by the new regime, especially if they had taken up arms against it.

Mirsky spent ten years in England and France, and achieved greater international eminence than any other *émigré* Russian literary intellectual of his time. For a decade he was accepted on equal terms by his peers in the British, French, and Russian *émigré* literary worlds. His role in the increasingly politicized Eurasian movement was particularly important. Mirsky then abjured his past, and joined the Communist Party of Great Britain in 1931 before going back to what had become Stalin's Russia. He was arrested in 1937 during the Great Purge, and died in the GULag before he was 50 years old. He thus fell victim to the most sustained episode of democide—murder by the state—that has ever been known. In what sense, if at all, Mirsky can properly be regarded as an innocent victim of this crime is one of the most disturbing problems posed by a consideration of his life.

Mirsky belonged to the most talented and tragic generation in Russian history. In early adulthood these people had to decide whether to cast their lot for the Revolution or against it, and then to remain in their native country or to leave it. They included a sainted quartet of poets—two men and two women, two Jews and two Gentiles, two from Moscow and two from Petersburg: Anna Akhmatova (1889–1966), Boris Pasternak (1890–1960), Osip Mandelshtam (1891–1938), and Marina Tsvetaeva (1892–1941). Akhmatova, who once defined herself as 'born in the same year as Charlie Chaplin, Tolstoy's *The Kreutzer Sonata*,[7] the Eiffel Tower, and (I think) T. S. Eliot'—she was one year out on the last item—stayed in Russia with defiant resolution, and suffered appallingly as a result. Pasternak came back from Berlin in 1923 after a brief experiment with emigration, leaving his parents and sisters abroad. Tsvetaeva left Russia in 1922 to rejoin her husband, Sergey Efron, who had fought in the White army, and eventually followed him back to Russia. Mirsky had already been arrested by the time his friend Efron arrived in Moscow, and he died twelve days before Tsvetaeva, who had also been his friend, arrived in Leningrad by boat on 18 June 1939. She hanged herself just over two years later. Mandelshtam stuck it out in Soviet Russia, and his life ended in a transit camp near Vladivostok on 27 December 1938. Mirsky had passed through this camp fourteen months earlier and then travelled one long 'stage' further along the route Mandelshtam was destined for had not death intervened, by sea to Magadan.

The lives of these four great poets have become world-famous; it is mainly from accounts of them that the horrendous circumstances faced by their generation of Russian intellectuals have been brought home to the non-Russian world. Mirsky's career as a critic was spent in the aura of their lives and work. He confidently and consistently proclaimed the stature of all four of them in print before anyone else; he was the first person to write anything substantial in English about any of them, and he did so about all four. He was the only major contemporary critic who accepted and championed Tsvetaeva's mature poetry. But his changed loyalties intervened. After he went back to Russia, Mirsky toed the official line and kept silent about Akhmatova, Mandelshtam, and Tsvetaeva, all of whom had by then become *personae non gratae* in the USSR. He did what he could, though, to bolster the position Pasternak was trying to establish as a poet acceptable to Soviet power.

The public events contemporary with Mirsky's life are no mere backdrop to it, significantly less so in fact than they are to the lives of the great poets who shared his worlds. On both sides Mirsky's family was highly visible and politically active. From boyhood he was trained for public service, and later he was educated as a historian, ancient and modern. Throughout his life he paid careful attention to international current affairs, and he wrote multiple successive accounts of the social and political history of his times. In his literary studies, although he was profoundly averse to theorizing, he constantly examined the relationship between *Dichtung* and *Wahrheit*, and between the public and private realms; he was thoroughly sensitive to, though never overawed by, the complexities of these relationships. Though he did not play a leading part in shaping public events, Mirsky's personal actions were directly influenced by his interpretation of them. And so, if the narrative line of this book switches away from Mirsky's individual experience to incorporate broader questions, it will do so in order eventually to trace and comprehend that experience with greater clarity—not as background, but as a constituent element of the experience itself.

If Mirsky was reticent about the personal aspect of his public life, he was completely silent about his private life, which as a result has become wreathed in myth and legend. It would be appropriate for a biographer to respect Mirsky's own attitude and also remain silent on this subject, were it not for the fact that at several crucial points in his life the private sphere had a decisive impact on the public one. In particular, the decision Mirsky made to go back to Russia was partly conditioned by the fact that he lived alone and had no dependants. I have allowed myself to speculate about what lay behind this preference in Chapter 2, after my account of Mirsky's childhood.

Apart from the psychological significance of the adult Mirsky's solitary mode of life, the result of it was that he left nobody behind to occupy themselves with what might be called his material memory. Even after many years of searching by many people in many places, no significant amount of private papers that belonged to Mirsky has ever turned up. Whether or not he brought with him any kind of archive when he left Russia in 1920 is unknown, but it is almost certain that he did not. When Mirsky went back to Russia in 1932 he either took his personal papers with him or—which is more likely—he destroyed them, as potentially incriminating. This means that almost all the letters he received—from Maurice Baring, T. S. Eliot, Pasternak, Aleksey Remizov, and Tsvetaeva, to name but a few—have been lost; the letters from Jane Ellen Harrison form the only significant exception.[8] The situation is more helpful with regard to letters written by Mirsky; the substantial series to Dorothy Galton and P. P. Suvchinsky are particularly important. Mirsky's letters to Salomeya Halpern and Vera Suvchinskaya (Traill) stand as eloquently fragmentary testimony to two other important relationships. In general, though, for most of his life Mirsky was in easy reach of his relatives, friends, and business acquaintances, and there was no need for written communication apart from the most elementary practical information about his comings and goings. Also, the telephone was coming into common use during his lifetime. When Mirsky was arrested five years after he returned to Russia, his papers were seized by the NKVD; their fate is unknown for certain, though Vitaly Shentalinsky was once given an official assurance that they had been destroyed.[9] The greater part of the files kept on Mirsky by the NKVD does survive, though, and through the good offices of the Memorial Society (Moscow) I have been able to make use of them thanks to the new dispensation in Russia after the collapse of the USSR.

The secondary sources concerning Mirsky's life are surprisingly scanty in view of the number of people he encountered, and the fact that he spent most of his adult life in a literary and intellectual environment. Notwithstanding his involvement in the public affairs of the Russian emigration and his frequent public statements as a Soviet critic, after 1920 he remained essentially a solitary and compulsive worker, reading and writing. It is worth emphasizing that in Mirsky's case, unlike those of several other prominent Russian literary men of this century, there was no devoted woman whose widowhood was dedicated to nurturing the legend of her late husband's life. The student of Mirsky therefore has to glean what can be found among the scattered reminiscences of colleagues and acquaintances. Here again, though, the fact that Mirsky turned against his English acquaintances and was for many years an 'unperson' in his native country meant that on the one hand people tended to write him off as an ex-White Guard turned blackguard, and on the other were very circumspect even about recording the fact that they had known him.

Mirsky's writings began to be substantially published again in Russia nearly forty years after his death,[10] and since then interest in him has continued to rise. Unfortunately, though, he is still known there mainly through republications of his Soviet-period work rather than for what he wrote in English. Long after most of the present book was researched and written, V. V. Perkhin published some invaluable archival documents,[11] and he was also the first Russian scholar to incorporate Mirsky into a history of literary criticism of the Soviet period.[12] Olga Kaznina's study of the Russians in England has now furnished a useful context for Mirsky's life in emigration.[13] The republications of Mirsky's writings in Russia continue to accumulate, but they still do not include his best work. Mirsky's life, too, has remained obscure for many years in all but the broadest outline, both inside and outside Russia. The pioneering efforts of Lavroukine and Tchertkov made the first substantial stride towards an account of it.[14] I have gratefully made use of their materials, though I cannot resist mentioning that I had completed my own fundamental biographical and bibliographical foundation before they appeared.

In my account of his life, I have privileged Mirsky's literary activity. He was first and foremost a man of the published word, and his writings about literature stand as his principal monument. Despite the enormously unpropitious circumstances of his life and times, Mirsky did manage to give adequate expression to his talent, unlike so many others among his Russian contemporaries. After he had finished his *History*, he went on responding to literary developments for another decade, touching on practically everything that he considered important in this sphere. This leads to the biggest difficulty of all in putting together an adequate account of his significance in this central respect.

When Mirsky started writing for the English-speaking reader, the amount of worthwhile secondary literature in his subject was disappearingly small. In the years since his death, this secondary literature has become monstrously large, many times more than any single individual can encompass. A great deal could and should be said about the impact of Mirsky's work on this subsequent scholarship; but even to register the documentary evidence of it, let alone critically assess the evidence, even in the case of one major author (Pushkin, say), would easily fill a substantial book by itself. The unacknowledged impact of Mirsky's work has also been very substantial. His *History* was thoroughly assimilated by the first generation of professional Russianists in Britain and the USA after the Second World War, and formed the basis of the teaching given to the generation of academics now occupying senior posts in these countries. It was internalized by them largely unattributed; partly as a result of this, Mirsky's wheels are still constantly being re-invented and elaborated. Also, to trace the relationship between what Mirsky wrote and the anterior tradition of literary scholarship in Russian would fill an even more substantial book. And so, since my main purpose here is to give an account of the man's own life and writings, I have offered only the most impressionistic views of these matters.

Generations of undergraduates have answered examination questions quarried by their grateful teachers from 'Mirsky'; generations of graduate students have used the book as their first port of call. However, before he was canonized in the appropriate volume of René Wellek's already obsolescent history,[15] Mirsky was not granted a place in the accounts of Russian criticism that have been written outside Russia.[16] Inside Russia there has been an even more profound silence. Setting aside the circumstances of Mirsky's life and his political evolution, this neglect has come about largely, one suspects, because he was a supremely practical critic who did not care to flaunt his theoretical assumptions and principles, and he was read by the educated public as much as if not even more than by academics. The contrast between Mirsky's academic reputation and those of some of his Russian contemporaries is very instructive. Chief among these contemporaries are the Russian Formalists Mirsky left behind in Russia, and apart from them, the spectacular individual case of Mikhail Bakhtin (1895–1975).[17] By natural inclination Mirsky was not some sort of philosopher *manqué* like Bakhtin; nor was he a belletrist (not so *manqué*) like Shklovsky and Tynyanov, nor yet an academic literary scholar like Eikhenbaum, Tomashevsky, and his schoolmate Zhirmunsky. Mirsky merits attention as a practising literary critic—a supremely intelligent, perceptive, well-informed, polyglot interpreter of printed literary texts who had a clear sense of priorities and values and a fearless directness in expressing them.

Mirsky's writings have not been, and indeed cannot be, used as a blueprint for constructing a social, moral, or ethical world-view. For him, the aesthetic dimension was always paramount—though he repressed it more and more as time went on. Like all the best literary criticism, what Mirsky has to say sends the reader back to the texts that he happens to be discussing rather than away from them into other domains of knowledge, understanding, and pleasure. This is not to say that the contemplation of what Mirsky wrote and did may not lead to some far-reaching conclusions about how literary interpretation might best be approached and theorized, or how the intellectual life should or should not be lived, and what such a life might mean.

There is no detailed account of what Mirsky did and where he did it, much less a sustained enquiry into why and how he did it. The present book is an attempt to bring together and interpret such reliable information about Mirsky as can be recovered at the time of writing. Its primary purpose is to portray

Mirsky as an individual in his time, resisting the categorization of him as representative of this or that broad historical trend or social type. He merits this treatment because he was a remarkable human being who left a distinctive intellectual legacy that has stood the test of time exceptionally well, and also because no other prominent person was involved in and reported on quite the same combination of the critical events and sites in the life and culture of Europe in their time.

PART I

In Russia, 1890–1920

1   *Two Names*

It seems to be Russia's fate that the man with understanding will never
work, and all the work will be done by those who have none. (D. S. Mirsky,
1920)

RUSSIA'S RULERS AND RUSSIA'S RULED

The Russia in which Mirsky grew up, between the recovery from the Crimean
war and the war against Japan in 1904–5, was a mighty world power.[1] Formally,
the country was an absolute monarchy, and as such widely held by natives and
foreigners alike to be an embarrassing anachronism. Mirsky's father and several
close male relatives on both sides of his family were highly placed members of
the tiny élite that governed it, and his mother moved in Court circles; their son
was inevitably brought up to follow in his father's footsteps. Mirsky's sense of
his country's status was fundamental to his mentality; and he was never allowed
to forget his origins even if he wished to himself.

The basis of Russia's status was its sheer size, territorial and human. The
population of the Empire shot up from about 117 million in the year of
Mirsky's birth to about 175 million by 1914. Only just over half of these people
were Great Russians, and increasing ethnic diversity represented one of the
government's thorniest problems during this time. His father's career in the
Ministry of the Interior continuously confronted Mirsky with the problems of
multi-culturalism; the family papers suggest that such matters were discussed
at home rather than being left behind at father's office. Nationalism—and in
particular the vexed questions of the proper place of the Great Russians in
their empire, before and after 1917, and the proper place of Russia in the
world—was to be a constant factor among Mirsky's intellectual concerns. His
Oriental eyes and black hair, the first things mentioned by everybody who
described his appearance, bore witness to his country's complicated ethnic
history.

Aristocratic Russians born about 1890, the year Mirsky came into the world,
formed the pointed head on a social torso that was very broad at the bottom.
This organism is usually said to have consisted of three elements: the few rulers
and the many ruled, who on the whole did not talk to each other, and those
between them—the unruly intelligentsia—who talked to neither but told the
world about both.[2]

The princely families of ancient lineage such as Mirsky's formed a tiny
enclave intertwined with but separable—in their own minds especially—from

the ruling class (for want of a better term) of pre-revolutionary Russia, the *dvoryanstvo*. Usually called the 'gentry' in English and sometimes, just as mis-leadingly, the 'nobility', this group was by no means homogeneous. It consisted of several sub-sets distinguishable from each other in terms of wealth and lineage. The *dvoryanstvo* derived its status from state service, which provided a non-hereditary entrée into it. A helpful account of the *dvoryanstvo* in Mirsky's time was set down by an Englishman who came to know him well, who spent a lot of time in Russia, and who—a rare accomplishment at the time—had an active command of spoken Russian, the Hon. Maurice Baring (1874–1945). Attempting to explain who ruled Russia, Baring comments: 'Any one can get into the governing class, that is true; but nobody who is not in it can check its action, and at one period nobody could even criticize it. The result is the triumph of bureaucracy at the expense of any kind of democracy or of any kind of aristocracy; while the only thing that profits by it is arbitrary despo-tism.'[3] Mirsky was born into this 'excluded' aristocracy. But his father and grandfather both rose to the top of the triumphant bureaucracy. As for democ-racy, Mirsky never seems to have had any respect for what Western European liberals like Baring understood by this concept, much less its more novel mani-festations (women's suffrage, for example). Mirsky died at the hands of a suc-cessor despotism that he consciously chose to serve, but which operated in a manner more arbitrary and unchecked than anything Baring could ever have imagined.

Next below the *dvoryanstvo*, and partly overlapping with it, came a social group that Mirsky did more to make familiar to the English reader than any other commentator, and about which more is commonly known than about any other Russian social group, because of its function as the engine of high culture. This was the intelligentsia, a highly diversified body of people even more difficult to define precisely than the *dvoryanstvo*. Maurice Baring offered his readers of 1914 a well-informed chapter on this subject too, dwelling on the complexity of the phenomenon.[4] For Baring, the intelligentsia meant first and foremost 'the representatives of the liberal professions—lawyers, doctors, professors, literary men, agricultural experts, statists [i.e. statisticians], school-masters, journalists'. In the two fields listed here that boasted the most women at the time in Russia, literature and schoolteaching, Baring's language unthink-ingly emphasizes men only. Harold Williams (1876–1928), the shrewdest foreign observer of Russia at the time and a mentor of Mirsky in London, was married to an outstanding female from the Russian intelligentsia, and he was much more inclusive in speaking of the intelligentsia's practical social work: 'Women worked side by side with men on a basis of complete equality, and fre-quently were leaders in organisation; in fact, one of the remarkable features of the intelligentsia was the number of strong and able women it brought to the front.'[5]

Baring also represented the intelligentsia as 'the intellectual middle class', and saw it as divided into the 'educated' and the 'half-educated'. From the half-educated majority of the Russian intelligentsia, asserted Baring, came the revolutionaries, and about them he makes an observation that has direct relevance to Mirsky's views and conduct:

They were as simple and as natural in their assassinations and their martyrdom as they were in the rest of their behaviour. [They exhibited] no mockery, no irony, but an inverted and inflexible logic which leads people to disregard all barriers and to carry out what they preach in theory, though they should cause the pillars of the world to fall crashing to the ground.[6]

However much he might have denigrated the radical intelligentsia and denied his kinship with it, Mirsky came to share this characteristic maximalism; the combination of this tendency with the tradition of public service in the families of his parents went a long way towards making him what he was.

Writing about Russian literature for the English reading public in 1925, Mirsky himself spoke of 'the current and superficial idea of Russia as a peasant country'.[7] However, it would be difficult to deny the validity of this idea in quantitative terms when speaking of the country in which he grew up. In the book he devoted to Russian society, Mirsky gave a cogent account of the changes in the sociological composition of the peasant masses as industrialization and urbanization went forward.[8] But peasants engaged in agriculture still made up about three-quarters of the empire's population during Mirsky's childhood; the intricately handcrafted Fabergé eggs commissioned by the rich were paid for more than anything else by exporting grain produced by mass peasant toil, which like that of the egg-makers was performed largely without benefit of machinery. Mirsky hardly encountered any of these toilers personally, except as servants and rank-and-file soldiery, and he never spoke of them in anything other than abstract terms, as an undifferentiated mass.[9] To his credit, unlike so many other intellectuals he never posed as one of the common people or attributed wonder-working wisdom to them. Saintly long-suffering and endurance, identified *ad nauseam* as the supreme virtue of the Russian people both by their own apprehensive rulers and by fascinated foreigners, were for Mirsky despicable. He called Platon Karataev, the peasant guru in *War and Peace*, 'difficult to put up with': 'He is an abstraction, a myth, a being with different dimensions and laws from those of the rest of the novel.'[10] The only person of indisputably humble social origins whom Mirsky dealt with as anything but servant or soldier before he moved among the proletarian intelligentsia of the USSR fifteen years or so after the revolution was Maksim Gorky (1868–1936), who had emerged from a provincial family of artisans. As one of the few members of the intelligentsia who really knew what he was talking about in this respect, Gorky heartily detested such people, along with the 'dark' Russian peasantry as a whole.

BUREAUCRACY AND CONSTITUTIONALISM

Vladimir Nabokov, who was born nine years later than Mirsky, created in his autobiographical writings about his childhood an influential myth of nostalgia for paradise lost; the Russians themselves now tend to favour this myth over the one of paradise gained that was promoted in Soviet ideology.[11] Neither the peasants nor Russia's upper classes had good reason to enjoy that sense of idyllic stability and prosperity that Nabokov evoked, and which is frequently ascribed to their contemporaries in Western Europe before the calamity of 1914 began to overthrow the old order. Rather than being a long, leisurely, golden holiday, the childhood of these Russians is more adequately understood in retrospect as a time of wrenching social and economic change, the 'transition to modernity' of accelerated urbanization and industrialization. Some large-scale natural disasters stretched the social fabric, chief among them the catastrophic famine of 1891–2.[12] In its wake came yet another of the cholera epidemics that had regularly scourged Russia since the eighteenth century.

What we now sometimes call 'the transition to modernity' in its political aspect was summed up by Harold Williams as a power struggle between bureaucracy and constitutionalism,[13] the former frequently articulated as police repression and the latter as subversion, with both often involving physical violence. The violence was due partly to acts of terror by individuals or small groups, as when Prime Minister Stolypin was assassinated in 1911, and partly to popular risings, as in the events of January 1905 that had direct consequences for the Svyatopolk-Mirsky family. The violence that gave the word 'pogrom' to the English language led to the emigration of two million Jews from the Russian Empire in the period immediately before 1914. At the same time, millions of Russian peasants emigrated internally, eastwards along the newly built railway to Siberia and the Pacific. This railway was later put to a more sinister use, of vital political and economic importance: Mirsky became one of the millions of prisoners who made a one-way journey along it to the eastern extremity of the GULag during the 1930s.

When the Russians born around 1890 were in their middle teens, their country went through the traumatic war with Japan. Having in mind mainly the military technology of the two sides, another of Mirsky's English mentors, Bernard Pares (1867–1949), asserted that 'European Japan defeated Asiatic Russia', and pointed out that the Japanese were fighting for their lives, whereas the Russians were fighting for a political purpose few could believe in—the acquisition of an eastern empire to compensate for the expansion in Central Asia that the British had stymied since the mid-nineteenth century.[14] Military failure on the Pacific precipitated the inconclusive but destabilizing revolution of 1905.

Under the premiership of Stolypin between 1906 and 1911—he began by restoring order in a fairly unceremonious way with knout and noose—the country seemed to be pulling itself together. The three successive Dumas introduced a tentatively representative element into government, and the country groped its way towards reforms that would bring about some sort of social reconciliation based on private rather than collective ownership of land by the peasants. If there was ever any golden age, it was enjoyed during these few years, when Mirsky was in his late teens and early twenties. The economic boom they saw was underwritten in a way that led Mirsky, always nationally conscious, to assert in 1929, just before the Wall Street crash reinforced his nascent Marxism:

The banks [after 1905–6] came under predominantly foreign control. The heavy industries were likewise mainly owned by foreign shareholders. By 1914 Russia had gone a good part of the way towards becoming a semi-colonial possession of European capital. The prevalence of French, Belgian, and English over German capital in Russian investments was such that quite apart from the imperialistic appetites of her bourgeoisie, Russia had no choice but to fight on the side of the Entente.[15]

The president of one of the biggest of these banks, the Anglo-Russian, was an uncle of Mirsky's on his mother's side of the family, the immensely rich Bobrinskys. What seems to have mattered more to Mirsky at the time he was actually living through this period, though, was the high cultural scene in St Petersburg. Several factors combined to inject new vitality into it during his teenage years after the decline—a phenomenon of the kind that Mirsky was fond of referring to as a 'falling line'—that had followed the demise of the great novelists in the 1880s. Russian culture opened itself up both to foreign influences and to its own ancient past. Poetry reasserted itself after having been sidelined by prose since the early 1840s. A temporary erosion of censorship relaxed the watch on the gates[16] at the same time as the mass production of reading matter and other commodities was challenging élitist assumptions about what culture was and by whom it should properly be 'consumed'.[17] The Orthodox Church seemed to be losing what little was left of its authority, although its rituals were still widely observed.[18] Under the last Tsar there was indeed a marked rise in religiosity in public life, promoted by the imperial couple and their various unsavoury advisers.[19] Among the intelligentsia, though, experimentally unorthodox ethical teachings and practices gained ground. All this made Mirsky fairly unshockable and uncensorious with regard to the private lives of the people he knew, though he did retain an aristocratic touchiness about personal honour.

A series of cataclysms began in August 1914, and went on for almost a decade. For the Russians, the Great War against Germany was a humiliating disaster, and apart from immense physical suffering it led to revolutionary social discontent, the downfall of the monarchy, the Bolshevik seizure of power, foreign intervention, and one of the most savage civil wars in history. As a result, the social torso of Russia was beheaded. The upper-class survivors who managed to get out of the country were left with their wits, their cosmopolitan education, and their connections—plus the proceeds from the Fabergé eggs and such that they might have succeeded in smuggling out on their persons. Very few of the *émigrés* managed in fact to retain much of their money, possessions, and influence. A knowledge of at least one modern language other than Russian was the only negotiable advantage that most of them derived from their upbringing. The professions of the men were rarely marketable outside Russia,[20] and they were reduced to bartering their bodies rather than their minds to earn their daily bread. For the women, this situation was business as usual, of course, but in an unfamiliar social context.

Argument will never cease about whether what happened in Russia was—for example—inevitable, foreseeable, comprehensible, desirable, reversible; argument will never cease about the kind of Russia that would have resulted if events had taken a different turn.[21] The ultimate reasons for the Russian plunge into extremism remain inscrutable; the obsessive search for such things as ultimate reasons is perhaps itself a manifestation of this accursed extremism. But there can be no doubt that the feature pinpointed by Maurice Baring—the purblind exclusion of all but a tiny élite from political authority and the process of government—was an underlying reason for the disaster. The result of the events following 1914 was that from the standpoint of Europeans and Americans born fifty years or more later than them (apart from the citizens of the former Yugoslavia), people who on the whole have not had to make any life-threatening political decisions, Mirsky's Russian generation of 1890 was faced by an unimaginably categorical series of choices and risks, as their country made the transition from seemingly solid but in the event fragile stability through anarchic violence to the tormented birth of a radically new order.

THE SVYATOPOLK-MIRSKYS

The Svyatopolk-Mirskys were one of the most ancient princely families of Russia, claiming descent from the ninth-century Varangian prince Ryurik, conventionally recognized as the founder of the Russian state. At the end of the nineteenth century there were twenty-three clans whose members could with some justice claim to be 'sons of Ryurik' (*Ryurikovichi*). Even after the seventy years of Soviet effort to erase their memory, many of these clans still have instant name recognition and inherent glamour among ordinary Russians, in some cases helped by the perfect-pitch variations Tolstoy played in naming his fictional characters: the originals were such as Dolgoruky, Gagarin, Kropotkin, Obolensky, Shcherbatov, and Volkonsky. In these families, the men bore the title 'Prince' (*knyaz'*), their wives that of 'Princess' (*knyagínya*), and their unmarried daughters had their own special grammatical form (*knyazhná*). They were properly addressed as, literally, 'Your Radiance' (*Vashe Siyátel'stvo*).

They were outranked only by the junior members of the ruling Romanov family, who had the adjective 'Grand' (*Velíkii*) added to their *knyaz'*. There were a dozen of these latter in 1917, of whom only half survived the next two years. The title *knyaz'* went so far back into the country's history that its Scandinavian origins (cognate with English 'king') were forgotten. It was considerably senior to the title *tsar'*, which had been introduced to designate the Prince who was pre-eminent over the others—and the Romanovs were distinctly parvenus, a family which after all celebrated a mere tercentenary on the throne in 1913, coming out of virtual seclusion for a prodigal feast before the time of plague, presided over by the last of them to sit on the throne of Russia.

Compared with the tribe of Ryurik, the families who had been ennobled for services to the Tsar relatively recently—since Peter the Great's attempts to extirpate medieval (or perhaps primeval) Russia in the early eighteenth century—bore foreign-sounding titles: 'Count' (*Graf*), and the loathsomely meritocratic (commerce and wealth!) 'Baron' (*Barón*). True, these families included some recognizably ancient Russian lineages who had been slighted during earlier turns of the wheel, such as the Tolstoys. It is not accidental (as the Russians tend to say, earnestly upturning an index finger) that Dostoevsky's Prince Myshkin is noble and unworldly, even a genuine idiot, while Chekhov's Tuzenbakh is a petty little fellow, baron though he is. The prince has a surname that derives unmistakably from the homely Russian word for 'mouse', while that of the baron is a Teutonic abomination.

The name 'Svyatopolk' was borne by the eldest son of St Vladimir of Kiev, who brought Russia into Christianity in 988, and into history along with this son's name went his sobriquet *Okayánnyi*, 'The Accursed'. He earned it because he murdered his half-brothers, two of whom, Boris and Gleb, were later canonized as Christian martyrs. Svyatopolk 'The Accursed' seized their appanages, and made common cause with the Poles and Pechenegs against Yaroslav the Wise to seize the throne of Kiev. One of the fratricide Svyatopolk's descendants was Prince Mikhail Yaroslavovich Svyatopolk (1050–1113), Grand Prince of Kiev. In the thirteenth century came the invasion of Russia by the Mongols, and the Svyatopolk family disappeared into relative obscurity in Poland-Lithuania for several centuries. Svyatopolk 'The Accursed' was never forgotten, though; the tag was still used on occasion to taunt D. S. Mirsky.

At least as early as the sixteenth century one branch of the Svyatopolk family had settled in the district of Mir, near the town of Nowogródek in what is now Belarus; the second element of the surname refers to this place, and was added to it less than a century before the October Revolution abolished titles of nobility in Russia. The princely title and compounded surname of the Svyatopolk-Mirskys were 'recognized', as the genealogies put it, with reference to Poland by a Senate decree of 1821 and with reference to Russia by one of 1861, the first holder of the title being Thomas-Bogumile-Jean (1788–1868). Poland had become a Congress Kingdom of the Tsar of Russia, a vassal state, in 1815; and Thomas-Bogumile-Jean was a high government official who represented the Polish Diet in St Petersburg. This was D. S. Mirsky's great-grandfather. He made his career at a time when most of the other sons of Ryurik no longer went in for high office; like the intelligentsia that was emerging at about the same time, they looked down on the state-serving bureaucracy.

The two Svyatopolk-Mirsky sons were entirely Russian in respect of upbringing and education, and they followed their father into high-flying service careers. They bore the patronymic Ivanovich, formed from the Russianized last element of the father's Christian name. The elder was D. S. Mirsky's grandfather and namesake, Prince Dmitry Ivanovich (1825–99), a fighting soldier who rose spectacularly to become chief of staff to a great general, the conqueror of the Caucasus, Field Marshal Prince Aleksandr Ivanovich Baryatinsky (1815–79), who was also of the tribe of Ryurik. Dmitry Ivanovich eventually became an aide to the Emperor. He also served for a while as Governor-General of Kharkov in Ukraine, and this seems to be the reason for the family's connection with that region. D. I. had a connection with Tolstoy, whom he had met during the Crimean War; in the 1880s, like hundreds of other Russians, he wrote the great man some letters (and a poem!) about religious matters.[22]

Dmitry Ivanovich's younger brother, Nikolay Ivanovich Svyatopolk-Mirsky (1833–98), was also a professional soldier; he became ataman of the Don Cossacks and also commanded the élite Semyonov regiment of the Guards. Nikolay Ivanovich had eight sons. The eldest, Ilya, died in infancy, as did the sixth and seventh, Vasily (1877–9) and Pyotr (1881–2); the second, Mikhail (1870–1938), never married. But the other four all had children, and the extant Svyatopolk-Mirskys are their descendants. By 1917, the Svyatopolk-Mirsky clan immediately related to the two Ivanovich patriarchs was very extensive, and widely intermarried with its fellow aristocrats. In emigration, the descendants married non-Russians and their children assimilated, so that in familiar *émigré* fashion there are American, British, French, and Swiss citizens who continue to bear the family name but are Russians in no other respect.

D. S. Mirsky traced some of his family history in one of his youthful poems, a sonnet to which he attached such importance that he placed it last when he collected them. The word 'glory' (*slava*) crops up in it three times. When he comes to his own generation, with modest propriety Mirsky strikes an elegiac but still patrician note, having in mind the fact that he was one of four children, and that therefore the 'clan' would likely continue to reproduce and go on doing good works. How wrong he turned out to be, about this and so much else.

> Our Clan
>
> Where did you spring from, bareboned little princes,
> Whose clan declined in Batu's heady days?[23]

As newcomers or simple Polish gentry
You found no glory, nor a Senate seat.

No Lithuanian magnate's crown awaited,—
A different kind of exploit came to you,
For it was snowy mountain peaks that crowned you
With the stern glory of the Russian knight.

Unknown by both Chodkiéwicz and Sobiéski,[24]
Your glory with Baryátinsky ascended,
And now grows ever higher and more proud,

In bounteous summer brilliance comes to manhood,
Thenceforth with easy stateliness in autumn
To be dispersed over the fecund lea.[25]

In discussing Pushkin's aristocratic ancestry when writing in English, incidentally, Mirsky sometimes used the word 'race' as the equivalent of the Russian word *rod* that appears in the title of his poem, and sometimes also 'stock';[26] both are as useful as the word 'clan' in understanding what he is talking about.

The elder son of Dmitry Ivanovich Svyatopolk-Mirsky was Prince Pyotr Dmitrievich,[27] who was born at Vladikavkaz on 6/18 August 1857. He was educated at the Corps de Pages. This was the social summit of the Russian education system. Entry into it was open only to the sons of men in the top two categories of the Table of Ranks; and out of it a gilded high road led directly towards the inner circles of the Imperial Court. Prince Pyotr Dmitrievich graduated in 1874 with first-class honours, upon which he was appointed Page of the Chamber.

Mirsky's father was about the same age as, and would have been at the Corps de Pages with, Tolstoy's fictional Count Vronsky, and *Anna Karenina* stands as the most indelibly memorable portrayal of the way these people lived—or perhaps one should say, with the kind of sensitivity to Tolstoy's agenda that Mirsky displayed, of the ways Tolstoy represented some of them living rightly and others living wrongly. One matter of particular significance in this connection is that the upper-class characters in *Anna Karenina*, which is set in the 1870s, use English as their preferred polite language, where those of the Napoleonic period in *War and Peace* had used French. The turn to English in the *beau monde* of his parents' generation and the persistence of this preference until 1917 was of profound significance for everything Mirsky was later able to achieve as a critic and historian of literature.

Svyatopolk-Mirsky senior, unlike Count Vronsky, served as a front-line officer in the Caucasus rather than going off as a volunteer to seek an honourable death, and he seems never to have done anything drastic in his personal life. Instead, he conducted himself more like Anna's unbending husband Karenin, first on the military side of the career ladder, going by natural succession into the army and becoming a cornet in the Empress's Life Guards

Hussars in 1875. He saw active service in the war against Turkey in 1877–8, and was decorated for his conduct at the battle of Kars (the 'snowy mountain peaks' of his son's poem). Pyotr Dmitrievich's military career then took a turn that was fairly unusual in the case of a man as high-born as he was: selection for the Academy of the General Staff. He passed out in 1881—the year, as we remember, when the 'Tsar-Liberator' was assassinated—and was then appointed to the Imperial Suite; shortly afterwards he was 'nominated to be present for special purposes on the staff of the VII army corps'. He continued his career in the army; by 1884 he was acting commander of the staff of the 31st Infantry Division, and by 1887 commander of the staff of the 3rd Grenadier Division.

To have been both a Guards officer and a graduate of the Academy of the General Staff in late imperial Russia, like P. D. Svyatopolk-Mirsky, was a fairly rare combination. On the one hand, Guards officers formed a self-conscious élite who despised other officers and closed ranks against them. Their status and privileges were 'based on the principle of birth, incompatible with the necessities of a modern army'.[28] The reforms introduced by Milyutin in the wake of the Russian defeat in the Crimea attempted to institute education and character rather than birth as criteria for promotion; the Academy of the General Staff was established to foster this change. Guards officers soon became inferior in power and prestige to graduates of the Academy, who were referred to in army slang as *genshtabisty*. Admission to the Academy was by competitive examination after recommendation following four years of commissioned service. P. D. Svyatopolk-Mirsky was thus both an aristocrat and a military meritocrat; and the system that made him such survived just long enough for his son to follow in his footsteps. It is worth noting here that the unwillingness of the *genshtabisty* to stand up for the Tsar and his government was one crucial factor that led to the downfall of the regime in February 1917. During the Civil War that soon followed, D. S. Mirsky served on the staff of the *genshtabist* Denikin, one of the most outstanding non-aristocratic commanders the Academy system had produced.

With that easy transferability between military and civil careers that was understandably suspected and resented by ordinary Russians, and not only by them,[29] P. D. Svyatopolk-Mirsky was appointed Governor of Penza in 1895. He moved on to become Governor of Ekaterinoslav in 1897. Penza is a south-central province of European Russia, Ekaterinoslav on the Dnepr in the Ukraine. The office of governor was immensely important in pre-revolutionary Russia; as the local representative of the Tsar, a governor wielded almost absolute power over the people in his district. Such was the nature of the Tsar's trust in these men that those who abused this power were hardly ever brought to book, because the Tsar stood by them when they got into difficulties, understanding that his own absolute power was potentially at issue.

Svyatopolk-Mirsky returned to the capital in 1900 as Deputy Minister of the Interior and Commander of the Corps of Gendarmes—head of the secret police. He now held the rank of lieutenant-general, the third from the top of the Table. His son once gave an incisive account of the Gendarmes, which had been created by the reactionary Nicholas I, the first years of whose reign in the 1820s

saw the institution of a new body of secret police—the Corps of Gendarmes, whose head was the Emperor's most intimate friend, and which became the most real and omnipresent force in the country. The gendarmes saw to it that no one spoke, thought, or wrote against the established order; they did their work of suppression conscientiously (they were, perhaps, the only incorruptible branch of the administration) and efficiently. The Corps survived till 1917 [when, as Mirsky does not say, but was soon to learn at first hand, it was replaced by a series of much more efficacious bodies].[30]

Of the twelve ministries that formed the uppermost layer of the Tsar's government, Interior was the largest and most widely tasked, being responsible for public order in all its aspects. Its Minister was consequently the most vulnerable, and one succeeded another almost as often as the Russian seasons, and with similar abruptness.[31]

Meanwhile, as we already know, Prince Pyotr Dmitrievich's father died and he became head of his branch of the family. A document in P. D.'s archive, drawn up on 31 July 1898, makes the following provisions from his father's estate, and affords some idea of who was closest to him outside his immediate family. To his sister Nina Dmitrievna Den [Dehn] was assigned 30,000 roubles. This woman, who is referred to in the Mirsky family papers as 'Aunt Nina', was born in Tiflis in 1853; in emigration, she lived in Rome. Her husband Vladimir was an official in the department of state for Finnish affairs. He would seem to have been a close relative of 'Lili' Dehn, one of the Empress's closest friends.[32] The same amount went to Dmitry Ivanovich's niece Princess Olimpiada Aleksandrovna Baryatinskaya; and 40,000 roubles to 'my father's wards Nadezhda, Pavel and Sergey Mirsky together with their mother, the widow Aleksandra Semyonovna Kasnenskaya'.[33] These were very substantial amounts of money. Some idea of what they represented may be gained from the fact that Svyatopolk-Mirsky's annual salary as Minister of the Interior in 1905 was 18,000 roubles; Maurice Baring once estimated that to maintain a middle-class lifestyle in late imperial Russia cost about 1,000 roubles per annum. But the bulk of the wealth, it would seem, was in land and property rather than money; the family holdings in the Kharkov district amounted to 900 dessyatins (about 2,400 acres) and in the Oryol province, 500 dessyatins (about 1,350 acres).[34] In terms of combined inherited and earned wealth, and of hereditary and service-derived social prominence, the family may not have been plutocrats and of the blood royal, but they were comfortably off and highly respectable.

The political views of Prince P. D. Svyatopolk-Mirsky were widely known to be on the 'liberal' side, to use the literal equivalent of the Russian adjective that was current among the ruling classes to designate someone who thought that perhaps a few important things needed to be reformed. His standpoint was demonstrated when on 17 September 1902 he accepted appointment as Governor-General of the Vilna, Kovno, and Grodno provinces, an area then officially known as the North-Western Territory; it corresponds to present-day Lithuania and the western and northern parts of Belarus. This was a backward step in Svyatopolk-Mirsky's career, and he took it rather than continue in the Ministry of the Interior in the capital under the new Minister, the reactionary V. K. Plehve. The situation in Lithuania at this time was explosive: revolutionary and nationalist movements were combining to foment disobedience against Russian rule. Svyatopolk-Mirsky's governorship was civilized and humane, and he gained a popular reputation as a fair administrator in an extremely difficult situation. He certainly had a sympathetic attitude towards the Jews, a rare quality in Russians of his background, and as far as he dared, he blamed Russian administrative measures for the difficulties faced by the Jews during his period of office.[35]

Among Svyatopolk-Mirsky's papers is a passport issued in Vilna on 20 January 1904 which includes his wife and children; it states that he left Russia on 22 January 1904 and returned on 11 March 1904, but it does not state where the family was in the meantime. Apparently, he was granted leave on finishing his term in Vilna. He was promoted adjutant-general on 30 July 1904, and a month later he was appointed Minister of the Interior.

MIRSKY'S MOTHER

Mirsky's sonnet about his ancestors concentrates, characteristically, on descent in the male line. And when he said that in Russia 'the man with understanding will never work, and all the work will be done by those who have none' Mirsky undoubtedly meant 'males', but by default; there is no evidence that it ever crossed his mind to include women among those who 'work' in any public capacity. It goes without saying that males controlled the world of public power and authority.[36] Patriarchy is the most substantial respect in which Russian society has remained the same since 1917 as it was before, despite a commitment to abolish it on the part of the triumphant revolutionaries, who included a greater proportion of women in their leading ranks than there was in any other calling.[37] Mirsky never knew personally anyone remotely resembling what fifty years after his death would come to be understood as a professional woman, unless he chanced to come across one of the small but influential number of women doctors in Russia, many of them foreign-educated.[38] Despite their growing prominence in life, he probably only ever saw a female teacher on the stage—Irina in Chekhov's *The Three Sisters*.[39] The actress who played her belonged to the most visible group of professional women of Mirsky's time.[40] Instead of teachers in state schools, Mirsky knew personally another type of female pedagogue: foreign middle-class governesses. He might well have set eyes on some of the 7,000 or so professional women of a different kind who walked the streets of St Petersburg in his youth;[41] as far as is known, he never engaged the services of one.

Women—except for the revolutionaries—hardly ever actively participated in activities that involved potentially fatal physical violence; and they were not usually privy to nor openly influential in what the men considered to be the most serious dimensions of their political and intellectual existence.[42] Though his writings on Russian literature by no means neglect women writers—if anything, he seeks them out wherever they can be found—in speaking of one of the greatest of them, Zinaida Gippius (1867–1945), Mirsky innocently betrays his fundamental attitude: 'The most salient feature in all her writings is intellectual power and wit, things rare in a woman. In fact there is very little that is feminine in Mme Hippius, except a tendency to be over-subtle and a certain wilfulness—the capriciousness of a brilliant and spoilt coquette.'[43]

Though it by no means went unquestioned, the gendered demarcation of social functions was the norm during Mirsky's time at all levels of society. To speculate about which side benefited or suffered more from this demarcation is futile, of course, but it is the principal factor among several that caused Russian women to live longer lives than their men, and still does. On the whole, the women settled for control of the private sphere; and they survived to bear witness to the lives of their men. Politicians and soldiers aside, if a Russian man's life was lived without a real or fictional constant wife or a devoted alternative to one, and after it ended there was no widow or fictionalized muse to hoard the testimony and shape the legacy, the man concerned would not be well remembered. Many of the women concerned in fact defined themselves in terms of their spouse, as did Mirsky's mother, rather than recording their lives on their own account. The legends about Russian men tend to be articulated through a Lara or a Margarita, or commemorated by a Nadezhda Yakovlevna.[44] D. S. Mirsky never fantasized a Lara, nor fictionalized a Margarita, nor cohabited with a Nadezhda Yakovlevna.

The dominant presence during Mirsky's childhood, though, was certainly his mother. At some time in the mid-1880s, Prince P. D. Svyatopolk-Mirsky married Countess Ekaterina Alekseevna Bobrinskaya (1864–1926), who came from another of Russia's most eminent aristocratic families, though not one of ancient lineage: the founder of it was Aleksey Grigorievich Bobrinsky (1762–1813), the illegitimate son of Catherine the Great and Grigory Orlov. The Tula branch of the Bobrinskys, from which Ekaterina Alekseevna came, had made a fortune in sugar manufacturing, and this was the main source of the combined Svyatopolk-Mirsky wealth. Ekaterina Alekseevna was born in Moscow, and her mother was a Pushkin.

High politics ran in the mother's family. Her father, Count Aleksey Pavlovich (1826–94), was a friend and neighbour of Tolstoy. The most prominent Bobrinsky in the next generation was his son Count Vladimir Alekseevich (1868–1927, the 'Volodya Bobrinsky' of Mirsky's childhood letters). He had been a Guards officer, but then he went as an undergraduate to the University of Edinburgh. Bernard Pares, who knew him as a Tula delegate to the 2nd Duma and brought him back to Britain on an official visit in 1909, said that this Bobrinsky 'talked public-school English without a flaw, and generally, even in the lobby of the Duma, he had a pipe in his mouth'.[45] Pares regarded him as 'quixotic and chivalrous'; he was happily married to a peasant woman, and he had at one time considered entering the Church.

Of particular interest for what it implies about Mirsky's own family background is the following passage, written in connection with the centenary of Tolstoy's birth in 1928 at a time when a passing interest in Freudianism made itself felt in his writings shortly before being ousted by his Marxism.

In Tolstoy's actual attitude to his wife there was, as in all his experiences [sic] an inherent contradiction. Tolstoy's attitude was, to begin with, essentially patriarchal. . . . In Russia by the second half of the nineteenth century it was almost obsolete among the upper classes. It was (and is) prevalent among the peasants. . . . Socially, Tolstoy's attitude to his wife was that of a peasant. Psychologically and sexually, the patriarchal view corresponds to an attitude to the wife as a possession, but a possession that is in very truth part of the owner, 'the same flesh', a limb rather than a chattel. Tolstoy was too sophisticated, too educated emotionally, to give a naïve expression to this view. Like everything in him it was big with a contradiction. Hence, moments when he believed in and *lived* the complete identity and union of flesh and mind with his wife alternated with others where he *saw* her living an independent life of her own, escaping his hold, being a person with her own will, not his limb but a detached human being with head and soul complete.[46]

In this passage Mirsky is leading up to a discussion of the diary of Countess Tolstoy, recently published in English, with its revelations about her husband's mental cruelty, which led to some shocked discussion among English reviewers. One wonders if Mirsky ever read the diary his own mother kept for several months during 1904–5 when her husband was at the peak of his career.[47] The diary gives a powerful impression of 'division of work between the sexes' in this social circle where the son apparently held patriarchy to be a bygone, and has far-reaching implications about the sense in which the author actually was or ever could have been 'a detached human being with head and soul complete'.

The diary shows Ekaterina Alekseevna to have been a person of considerable political acumen. Her husband seems to have confided in her completely. He would evidently come back home from his working day (the Tsar sometimes summoned him at awkward times), tell her what had happened, and at some time later she would set down her record, often including in it what purport to be verbatim exchanges between her husband and the Tsar. On 22 November 1904 she states: 'I'm writing all this down in bits, because P. has told it me at different times when we've been talking, and it's coming out disjointed, but P. doesn't know I'm making notes, and I don't want him to know, I'll tell him later.'[48]

During the Russo-Japanese war, Mirsky's mother did volunteer work from time to time at a Red Cross depot in Petersburg, sometimes taking in clothing and footwear for the troops. Her charity work was not entirely an example of the behaviour automatically expected of women of her social circle; she was manifestly religious. In her diary she sometimes gives mild expression to her faith, which was obviously a consolation to her. But much more often she says how much she wants to get away from the stresses of public life and retreat to the country. As early as 14 November 1904 she writes: 'All this time there's been too much worry. I'm beginning to realize that my thoughts are becoming confused, I've lost sight of what matters, I feel I must get close to nature, for nature always brings one towards truth.'[49]

THE FAMILY

When she referred to 'nature', Ekaterina Alekseevna was thinking first and foremost of the Svyatopolk-Mirsky country estate in Ukraine, about 4 miles from the small manufacturing town of Lyubotin, which is about 15 miles away from Kharkov on the railway line that runs westwards towards Poltava. The family's postal address on the letters of Mirsky's childhood is usually given as 'Lyubotin Station, Southern Railway, Giyovka village'. This is where Mirsky was born.

Kharkov was and remains the metropolis of the heavily Russianized eastern part of Ukraine. With the coming of the railway age to Russia in the mid- to late nineteenth century it assumed great importance as the crossing-point of the principal north–south and east–west main lines, and it became a major manufacturing centre, specializing in transport vehicles and agricultural machinery. It was inhabited by a volatile mixture of Russians, Ukrainians, and Jews.[50] The city possessed a university of international standing, especially in philology. The Kharkov area was fought over heavily in the Russian Civil War, and even more destructively during the Second World War, but the rebuilt Svyatopolk-Mirsky house survives with its pond (though its church is in ruins), and is used as a boarding-school.

The fact that his birthplace was in Ukraine did not mean, of course, that Mirsky was Ukrainian by language and culture, any more than being born into the aristocracy in Scotland, say, means that the person concerned is identifiably Scots by language and culture.[51] What Mirsky thought of the place can be gauged from a sly quotation from Chekhov's *A Dreary Story* (1889) that he once used as an illustration of 'the Chekhovian state of mind':

'Let us have lunch, Kátya.'
  'No, thank you,' she answers coldly.
  Another minute passes in silence.
  'I don't like Khárkov,' I say; 'it is so grey here—such a grey town.'
  'Yes, perhaps. . . . It's ugly. . . . I am here not for long, passing through. I am going on to-day.'
  'Where?'
  'To the Crimea . . . that is, to the Caucasus.'[52]

The country lifestyle of the class to which the Svyatopolk-Mirskys belonged has been described many times; the accounts of foreigners are particularly revealing. Maurice Baring stayed with the Svyatopolk-Mirsky family at Giyovka in the autumn of 1907,[53] and recorded the following impression:

Prince Mirski lived in a long, low house, which gave one the impression of a dignified, comfortable, and slightly shabby Grand Trianon. The walls were grey, the windows went down to the ground, and opened on to a delightful view. You looked down a broad avenue of golden trees, which framed a distant hill in front of you, sloping down to a silver sheet of water. In the middle of the brown hill there was a church painted white, with a cupola and a spire on one side of it, and flanked on both sides by two tall cypresses. There were many guests in the house: relations, friends, neighbours. We met at luncheon—a large, patriarchal meal—and after luncheon, Prince Mirski used to play Vindt in the room looking down on to the view I have described.[54]

Pyotr Dmitrievich and Ekaterina Alekseevna had four children. Dmitry was the second of them, born on 9 September (28 August OS) 1890.[55] The eldest child of the family was a daughter, Sofya, born at Kuskovo near Moscow, the country seat of the Sheremetevs, on 18/30 May 1887 (some sources say 30 May/11 June). Like her mother before her, in 1910 Sofya became a Lady in Waiting, but to the last Tsar's wife, the widely detested Empress Alexandra. Sonya married—apparently before she left Russia for emigration—an engineer called Nikolay Pokhitonov. The third Svyatopolk-Mirsky child was another son, Aleksey, born in April 1894. He was a pupil at the Corps de Pages in 1908–10; he was killed while serving in the White army in 1920.[56] The fourth and youngest child was another daughter, Olga, named after her mother's mother, Olga Pushkina; she was born at Ekaterinoslav on 18 February/2 March 1899. The mother and children existed as a close-knit unit until 1914, their most stable base being the country estate at Giyovka, where they spent the summers. At other times of the year they sometimes moved with their father to his various places of appointment, but they spent the winter in St Petersburg, and apparently continued to do so after the father came to the end of his career early in 1905. Their town house was at No. 24 Sergievskaya, one of the streets near the centre of the city that runs into Liteiny prospekt on the right as it heads towards the river; after the revolution their street was renamed in honour of Tchaikovsky.

None of the four Svyatopolk-Mirsky children replicated this pattern of family life when they became adults. The reasons stemmed only partly from the abolition of their titles and the expropriation of their property and income in 1917; as far as it is possible to tell, they are to be found mainly in the individual personalities of the children. Sofya, the only one of the four who formed a long-lasting heterosexual relationship, gave birth to a daughter, but she died in infancy in January 1927. Olga was married to a person called Agishchev for about six months, at what time and under what circumstances I do not know. The sisters lived with their mother until she died in 1926, finally separating soon after that. Like many other older *émigrés*, Sonya and Olga went back to Russia from France after the Second World War, notwithstanding the fate of their elder brother; with them as with him, patriotism was a powerful factor. 'This is my motherland, after all,' said Sonya when I met her in Moscow not long before her death on 4 September 1976. Her younger sister had died there on 3 July 1968. The four children of Pyotr Dmitrievich and Ekaterina Alekseevna thus constituted the last generation of their branch of the Svyatopolk-Mirsky family.

Through all the vagaries of his adult existence, though, D. S. Mirsky did manage to keep up two very significant elements from the pattern of life he was born to. First, he was almost always based in capital cities (St Petersburg, Athens, London, Paris, Moscow—even Magadan was a capital city of a sort), and he lived near the heart of them. Also, he always went away for the summer from these cities—except the last-named!—to various resorts. But the most fundamental respect in which Mirsky lived his entire life in the manner to which he was born was that he never looked after himself in respect of what the Russians call *byt*, everyday chores.[57] The classic lifestyle of the Russian male intellectual aims to eliminate demeaning involvement in *byt* through the exploitation of dependent wives and servants, and leave him free to pursue intellectual and other forms of self-gratification, justified and rationalized through all sorts of variously pretentious moral and ethical excuses. Nabokov was as accomplished at this art as at any other. As for Mirsky, he managed to eliminate *byt* more completely than most for the entire duration of his life, remaining in many respects a baby, both physically and emotionally. He grew up with servants to see to his material needs, and during his peacetime military service he was an officer in the phenomenally cosseted Guards. In emigration he never lived with a family for which he was responsible, never bought a house but instead lived in lodgings and hotels or with relatives, and ate in restaurants. Back in Soviet Russia this pattern continued, but in more straitened circumstances. Mirsky never learned to do anything mechanical or practical. The very idea of his typing his own writings, much less doing his own laundry or sweeping the floor, is risible. Almost as risible is the idea of Mirsky gardening, say, or taking an interest in sport, or doing anything at all (apart from eating) for the sheer pleasure of it. This is to say nothing of sharing his adult life with somebody else, and perhaps bringing up children.

Mirsky's letters to Dorothy Galton, larded as they are with ritual male wheedling ('I want you to be an angel once more . . .'), show just how accustomed he was to getting women to fetch and carry for him. In May 1935 he even managed to get her to order him a pair of trousers in London and have them brought to Moscow. In his 40s he had put on weight: 'The measurements are rather dreadful: waiste [sic] to ankle 102 cm; round the belly 104 cm! I have tried to reduce the centimetres into inches, but suppose that will be done in London by more competent brains.'[58] When she visited Mirsky in London in 1926, Marina Tsvetaeva prevailed on him to buy three expensive shirts; he would not have taken such a step on his own, apparently. Vera Traill told me:

He used to go around wearing God knows what. He was completely uninterested—he was always very badly dressed, everything falling apart, and there was no elegance at all. I think I remember once persuading him to buy a jacket or something, but this was a complete exception, I don't know who actually bought it, maybe nobody did, maybe Dorothy [Galton] did; after all, I never lived with him, I used to see him when so to speak we lived together (not together in bed, but together in the same house, as you might say . . .)

From cradle to grave Mirsky managed to be served, as were most other males of his time and class, and as indeed were women born to the station of his mother before the Second World War. Even when he landed up in the GULag there were cooks and cleaners to service the inmates; true, their situations were envied and fought for, sometimes to the death, by the ordinary prisoners. In all likelihood Mirsky never shopped for, let alone cooked and cleaned up after, a single meal in his entire life. Asked if Mirsky could cook, Vera Traill sputtered with bemused astonishment: 'N-n-n-o, he couldn't at all. There was nothing he could make, even tea and coffee, nothing. He was a completely helpless man.'[59]

This aspect of his existence gave rise to what became a well-worn taunt, probably attributable originally to an Italian journalist,[60] to the effect that Mirsky succeeded in being a parasite under three regimes: a prince under the Tsars, a professor under capitalism, and a professional writer under communism. In his defence it should be added immediately that if the first was an unearned accident of birth, the second and third were paid for by unremitting intellectual labour, and the third was no sinecure, but a perilous adventure that eventually cost Mirsky his life. If he was indeed in some sense a parasite, he was one of the most productive there has ever been; he was always active, and he always gave back much more than he took.

HOME TUITION AND HOME COOKING

A certain amount of evidence about the family's life before 1905 survives among the papers of Prince P. D. Svyatopolk-Mirsky.[61] The earliest is a very substantial batch of letters to the head of the family written between 1895 and 1912 variously from Giyovka, Moscow, Ipswich, and Yorkshire by an Englishwoman, Mrs Clara Sharp. She had been the governess of Svyatopolk-Mirsky's wife, and she continued to live with the family from time to time even after her former charge had a family of her own.[62] Addressing the Brontë Society in Leeds on 3 March 1923, Mirsky spoke of her, without mentioning her name: '[We] had in our family an English governess who came from Bingley, which, I take it, is a place almost next to Haworth. She had, however, little local feeling for the Brontës, I am afraid. The Brontë novels were among the few English novels my sisters were not allowed to read: they were brought up on Miss Yonge.'[63]

There are forty-eight letters to the father from the elder son; the earliest was written on 8 December 1896 from Mount Pleasant, Devon. It is replete with inverted letters, phonetic spellings, and grammatical mistakes; the boy writes in Russian, but uses English for the personal and place-names and the phrase 'Christmas pudding'. This would appear to be the earliest surviving example of Mirsky's writing:

Deer Papa,
Mummy was in Teignmouth anb Torquay. Weve not been for a walk for two days now. Papa [sic; Mirsky is actually addressing his father] gave me some bricks with the Inglish alphabet on. We can go to Torquay too if I dont cry for a whole month. Mummy went to Teddington and brote me a [illegible word] boat. Ellen gave Sonya some mother-of-pearl beads. In Dalish is a mountain called Backlake Hill. We just went to Dawlish and then Exeter on the way back. We stirred the Christmas pudding. Mrs Sharp and Jack were here. Alyosha and Sonya kiss your hand Miss Trenb sends you greeting. Goodbye I kiss you Dim.
8 December 1896[64]

The contraction of his Christian name with which Mirsky signs this letter is pronounced in Russian with the equivalent of a long 'i', something like 'Deem'; this was the form of address his intimates used throughout his life.

By far the most substantial set of letters to survive in the archive was written by the elder of the Brontë-deprived girls, Sonya (to use the familar form of her name). There are more than 350 of them; the earliest was written on 29 September 1896. For obvious reasons, both Sonya and Dim write when the father is not with the family, but away at his bureaucratic duties. The regular reports on the family by the two eldest children end in the summer of 1905; the father was now retired, and the family was together, except when the elder son was away at school.

The evidence of the letters implies that from late September 1896 to early March 1897 the mother and children were in England, at Mount Pleasant, near Exeter in Devon. In May and June 1897, May and June 1898, and July 1901, they were at a country estate called Pokrovskoe. From the mother's diary it is clear that on the way back to Petersburg from Giyovka they would stay in or near Moscow with their relations the Sheremetevs; they were there in February 1898 (when Dim reports seeing *Prince Igor* at the Bolshoi), and again in January and November 1900, and also in December 1902. On a few occasions, the family was based where the father was serving as governor, and apparently he was away in St Petersburg: Sonya and Dim write from Penza in January and March 1896 and January 1898, from Ekaterinoslav in February 1900, and Vilna in December 1903. All the other letters are from Giyovka: the family (minus the father, who would evidently join them later) would go there in May and stay until late September. We may assume that for the rest of the year they were in St Petersburg.

On 7 June 1901 Dmitry reported to his father from Pokrovskoe. He refers to a visit to the estate at Mikhailovskoe, where the Russian national poet had written some of his greatest work in 1824–6 and close to which he was buried:[65]

Dear Father, We had a very jolly time at Mikhailovskoe. There's a botanical garden and museum there. We visited the Saburovs at Voronovo and Pleskovo, where Uncle Pyotr[66] lives but he wasn't there. Uncle Dmitry and Auntie Ira came with their family the day before we left. At Mikhailovskoe when Grandad Sergey Dmitrievich comes they run up the flag. On the way to Pokrovskoe at Golitsyno we met the Golitsyns. Uncle Volodya has bought a white house and is going to move it to Boturovo.[67] Auntie Maya Romanovna, Varya and Volodya arrived the day after us. . . . The Pushkins have a troika, a pony, and a donkey, and the children have a hammock and a tent. . . .[68]

The Golitsyns made a reciprocal visit to Giyovka in October 1900, and in September 1904 Dim made a trip to Sarov and Nizhny Novgorod with them. This would have been a pilgrimage to the shrine of St Serafim (1760–1833) in Tambov province. He had been canonized only the year before, with enormous pomp, after intense lobbying by the Empress. The shrine was visited by thousands of Russian military men before they left to do battle in the Russo-Japanese war. The war was eight months old when the Golitsyns and Svyatopolk-Mirskys made their journey there.[69]

From late in 1896 (to judge from the letters; possibly in fact earlier) a permanent presence is Miss Trend, the English governess.[70] Soon after that a French governess appears whose surname was Baumanne, but who is usually referred to simply as 'Madame'; she teaches her native language and also piano.

Miss Trend was a piano player too. On 6 October 1896 Sonya reported to her father that at Mount Pleasant 'We study French in the evenings after tea, and after the lesson Mama speaks French with us'. From September 1900 a tutor appears called Ernst Sigizmundovich; his duties comprised teaching Dmitry Latin, Greek, fencing, and riding, the latter including hunting. From 1903 another teacher appears in the letters, one Feliks Moiseevich, who coaches Dim in German; in August 1904 he was reading *Faust* to his pupil. Occasionally, the servants are referred to: at least two, Katya and Dunyasha, were with the family in England, and Dunyasha even learned to speak some English. In June 1902 at Giyovka one of the carpenters was beaten up, and in July there was trouble with a drunken cook called Vasily.

Sonya pays special attention to the progress of the eldest son. She reports on his childhood infirmities: in January 1897 at Mount Pleasant he had a pain in the stomach; in June 1897 at Pokrovskoe he had a bad ear and throat.[71] On 16 February at Teignmouth Uncle Alyosha bought Dim a shotgun and also presented him with 'a real bow and arrows'; later that month Dim was taken to Exeter to buy boots. On 2 March at Mount Pleasant 'Dim went riding and Potter is going to teach him and Dim's saddle is being made into a ladies' one and [perhaps] I will go riding too . . .'. On 30 May at Pokrovskoe Dim took communion; and also bought himself some toy soldiers. In May 1900 one Vladimir Aleksandrovich Fuchs visited Giyovka and taught Dim to play chess and draughts. For the boys there were various games: skittles (*gorodki*), tennis, football, swimming, skating, and—much more serious than games—riding and shooting (for snipe from Giyovka on 28 September 1901, for wolf from there on 5 October 1901). For Dim's thirteenth birthday at Giyovka in 1903 there was a fireworks display.

On 2 February 1900 Dim tells his father from Ekaterinoslav that he and his mother are going to fast that week; but for the rest of the time, indulgence seems to have been the order of the day. Dim reports on 1 June 1900 from Giyovka that lunch that day consisted of green cabbage soup with eggs, kasha and kulebyaka, lamb, baked potatoes, and a pie. Supper was meatballs in sour cream, and curd fritters (*syrniki*). In between these blow-outs, the boys and their tutor made an expedition to Lyubotin. On Dim's 10th birthday in August 1900 at Giyovka for lunch there was green cabbage soup again, chicken, corn, and ice cream; and for supper, meatballs and baked potato again. On 17 July 1900: 'Today we're going to Lyubotin for the whole day. I've been riding 7 times now; my horse is called Moroz ['Frost'], he's a very good horse. The day before yesterday we had a picnic and I ate too much.' This interest in food foreshadows the adult Mirsky's gourmandise. Similarly, the future poet and critic relishes the baby names his younger sister Olga gives to the other members of the family, reporting them twice to his father.

The family occupied themselves, naturally, with polite literary pursuits. In May 1899 at Giyovka they were reading Pushkin aloud. It was an experience such as this that lay behind a passing remark Mirsky made in arguing that Pushkin's tale *Tsar Saltan* is among the poet's greatest achievements:

It is just because of the absence in it of all 'human significance' that *King Saltan* is the most universally human of Pushkin's works. For it is pure form, and as accessible to all those who understand Russian as pure ornament is to all those who have eyes. The child (I speak from personal experience) is as admiringly absorbed in the process of narration and in the flow of rhyme as is the sophisticated critic in the marvellous flaw-lessness of the workmanship and the consistency of the 'style'.[72]

'Pure form' it may be; but the content of Pushkin's tale is not without a certain interest. The story is not centrally about the Tsar Saltan of the title, but about his son, Prince Gvidon. The Tsar is deceived into sending the newborn prince and his mother into exile. But the Prince grows up protected by a magic swan, who grants his cherished wishes before transforming herself into a beautiful princess who becomes his bride and bears him a son. There is a blissful happy ending, with everyone reconciled, much feasting, and the Prince a hero. The story was made into a ballet by Rimsky-Korsakov, and it is from there that 'The Flight of the Bumble-Bee' comes; in the course of the story, the Prince is thrice turned into an insect, and he flies back to his father's court, stings one of the jealous deceivers, and makes good his escape. Any young prince would revel in it all, whether or not he appreciated the 'flawless-ness of the workmanship'.

In June 1900 Madame read to the children Jules Verne's *Vingt mille lieues sous les mers*. And in the same month there were amateur theatricals at Giyovka in honour of the father's name-day. Sonya was excited: 'We are going to play a comedy called '*La Vieille Cousine, ou: Il ne faut pas juger l'arbre d'après l'écorce*', it's from the book you bought us, *Théâtre de la Jeunesse*. In this comedy will appear Madame Baumanne, Olimpiada, Dim and I, and we want to invite one of the Novosiltsevs; Olimpiada is going to be the hunchback.' In July 1903 Mama read *War and Peace* to the children. In July 1904 she read them *Les Misérables*.[73]

At the centre of attention in the family, a more serious business than anything else that went on, was the education of the elder son, an education that was obviously meant to steer him in his father's footsteps; we have noted the toy soldiers, the weapons, and the riding. Dim was tutored at home until he was going on 13. Sonya reports from Mount Pleasant in October 1896 that Dim 'has learned how to hawk and spit', but also that 'Dim has started to have classes'. The presents he received, and which he reports in his dutiful birth-day letters to his father, show clearly the direction his life was supposed to take. At Giyovka on 7 May 1900 one Vasily Nikolaevich Lukomsky gave him *A Survey of Russian Wars from Peter the Great to Our Times*. For his birthday in 1900 he got *The History of Suvorov* from his mother (also some soldiers and a notebook), *A Survey of Russia's Wars* from Olimpiada ('about the war in the Caucasus', he adds, mindful of his grandfather's and father's exploits), another notebook from Mrs Sharp, and more soldiers from Yury. A month later he reports that he is reading one of the military histories and has learned some soldiers' songs. In Moscow on 5 December 1902 his mother gave him *The History of the Caucasian War*. In 1903 he was given *Africa* and a history of the Middle Ages by his mother, and by others *The History of Assyria*, *Governors and Thinkers*, *Martyrs of Science*, and *Through Deserts and Wastelands*.

In his later writings, as we have seen, Mirsky occasionally allowed himself a reference to his childhood reading. In his discussion of Pushkin's predecessors in prose, he speaks of 'the first complete Russian novel in the manner of Scott, Zagoskin's *Yurii Miloskavski, or the Russians in 1612 . . .* It was still a household book when I was young and was the first novel I read.'[74] In actual fact there were very few Russian households in which such a book could be found; but that Mirsky should have had put into his young hands a story about an episode of Russian military triumph over foreign foes—he also speaks of its 'crude nationalism'[75]—is entirely characteristic of the education he received at home. By contrast, Dim reports his sister Sonya's innocuously decorative birthday presents for her 13th birthday in 1900: a medallion from Mummy, a paperweight from Yury, a book (no title stated) from Olimpiada, a bouquet from younger sister Olga, mint cakes (*pryaniki*) from Katya, and a box for stamps from himself.

Writing from Giyovka on 8 October 1900, the son describes his routine:

Dear Father, These are the lessons we're having every day now: at 8.30 I have music, from 9 to 10 Latin, and then half an hour of gymnastics, from 11.30 to 12.30 either Russian language or arithmetic, from 12.30 to 4 there are no lessons, then from 4 to 5 there is calligraphy, then German until 6.

Even some of the family games had a serious purpose: Dim writes on 13 August 1903 from Giyovka: 'Lately we've been playing football, tennis, and a new game where you have to write down in 5 minutes the names of as many great persons as you can beginning with the same letter.'

On 28 August 1903 Dim writes: 'On the 26th Feliks Moiseevich, Alyosha and I rode to the place where the Imperial train crashed. We rode 30 versts there and back along the railway.' After that they played football by moonlight. This train crash had happened fifteen years earlier, on the morning of 17 October 1888 at Borki, just along the line from Kharkov. Tsar Alexander III and his son Nicholas, the future Tsar, who were on the train, escaped with their lives, but twenty people were killed and sixteen injured. Alexander was apparently only bruised; but by the beginning of 1894 this injury had transmogrified into the kidney disease that killed him on 20 October that year, just short of his 50th birthday.

On 5 July 1904, when he got back from riding, Dim expressed great sorrow at the news that Chekhov had died. He was later to treat Chekhov with considerably less courtesy, in an attempt to disabuse the gullible English of their inflated idea of this writer's status. Twelve days later Sonya writes: 'All of us yesterday were terribly shocked by the murder of Plehve.' But she immediately continues with her usual prosaic information: 'Yesterday the weather was good . . .' Dim writes on 18 July with a similar switch from high politics to child's play:

It rained all night yesterday. Who will be appointed to replace Plehve, do you think? Mummy wants it to be Prince Obolensky (not the Finland one). Here they've found a wild goat, still quite young. Emma has simply fallen in love with it, keeps running up to it and calling it a little angel. Au revoir, Your son Dmitry Svyatopolk-Mirsky.

On 31 July there is good news; Sonya exults: 'An heir apparent at last!' This long-awaited and much prayed-for baby boy, of course, was the doomed haemophiliac Tsarevich Aleksey.

'SI L'EMPEREUR VOUS DEMANDE QUELQUE CHOSE . . .'

The murder of Plehve in July 1904, which shocked 16-year-old Sonya, was a political act by a bomb-throwing revolutionary, and the Tsar faced a dilemma in appointing a successor. There was a right-wing choice in B. V. Sturmer. But the Tsar chose P. D. Svyatopolk-Mirsky, apparently—in this matter as in many others—in deference to the urgings of his mother, the Dowager Empress Mariya Fyodorovna (1847–1928), widow of Alexander III. Ekaterina Alekseevna Svyatopolk-Mirskaya had been a lady-in-waiting to the Dowager Empress, and retained her confidence. Ekaterina Alekseevna summed up the circumstances in the opening entry of the invaluable diary she kept in 1904–5. She sensed that her husband was going to be involved in something of historic significance, and that in fact he was about to be handed a poisoned chalice. Her very first entry gives a very good idea of this remarkable woman's mentality. Her contemptuous attitude towards Nicholas II, and towards the inner circles of St Petersburg and all they stood for, is palpable here and continues throughout her diary; elsewhere she calls the whole epicentre of power in late Imperial Russia 'a moral morass'. Her writing is as crisp as her elder son's was ever to become. She refers to her husband by his pet name 'Pepka', or simply as 'P'. On 10 August 1904 she writes:

Two days ago I had a letter from Pepka in which he says that the sovereign, when P. was presented to him on the occasion of his promotion to adjutant general, told him he needed to see P. on business . . . On that day when he was presented to Mariya Fedorovna she said: 'Si l'Empereur vous demande quelque chose, je vous supplie de ne pas refuser'[76] and also added a good deal that was very flattering to P. Evidently the issue is the Ministry of the Interior. P., to judge from his letter, is very embarrassed, and says that after two ministers have been murdered it is hard to refuse, but all his views are diametrically opposed to the existing state of affairs. He told Mariya Fyodorovna that if the sovereign were to say something to him, he would have to voice his view of things. I hope that happens. I think the Tsar wouldn't like it. But if this is what we are fated for, we will trust in God. I am beginning this diary so that if this unfortunate thing comes to pass and P. is appointed minister, then the truth will be recorded. In the present state of Russia, with a sovereign like the one we have, it seems to me that no minister can do anything; and besides, all that Petersburg squabbling can ruin the reputation of a saint, let alone an ordinary mortal. P. never thinks about what people will say of him, and he's too simple-hearted to battle against intrigue, and so if only for the sake of our descendants I want to record things accurately.

The distinguishing feature of P. is his benevolence, both in private life and in his public activity, and also his good nature and simple-heartedness. He has a highly developed sense of duty and legality, and this is why he is so concerned about the current direction the government is taking, which exhibits neither legality nor benevolence, but only malicious arbitrariness.[77] At the same time, traditional devotion to the sovereign is too deeply rooted in him for it to be easy for him to go directly against the sovereign's wishes.[78]

As this passage suggests, the diary is indeed something of a whitewash, the story of a sensitive and decent man with an impossible job to do who is frustrated at every turn by fools and knaves motivated only by vanity and ambition.[79] Anyway, studiously patient Svyatopolk-Mirsky senior came down from Petersburg to his country estate, Giyovka, on 17 August, and five days later received the expected telegram from the Tsar. He was appointed Minister of the Interior on 11/24 August 1904, with the rank of general, second from the top of the Table, the highest ever achieved by all but the most extraordinary individual men.

It was the most unpropitious of times, if not yet the worst. The new minister was faced with mounting social unrest at the same time as Russia was engaged in the war that Japan had initiated without a declaration in January 1904. On taking office, Svyatopolk-Mirsky stated that he intended to cooperate with dissident elements in society rather than repressing them. His attitude was summarized by his wife:

If liberal reforms are not made and if the entirely natural wishes of everybody are not satisfied, then there will be changes, but in the shape of revolution. As I understand it, the wish of the overwhelming majority of well-intentioned people is the following: without affecting the autocracy, to institute in Russia the rule of law, broad religious toleration, and participation in the work of lawmaking.[80]

Svyatopolk-Mirsky's brand of earnest, loyal liberalism may have earned him a good press at the time in Russia; but it was not viable as a political doctrine even before the revolutionary events of 1905. Most participants and commentators agree that the Tsarist order was already too far gone to be ameliorated, and the proportion of 'well-intentioned' people in the population prepared to act on their fundamental sense of loyalty turned out to be pitifully small when moments of extreme crisis came. Bernard Pares commented: 'The appointment of Prince Mirsky after the murder of Plehve had lent colour to the popular idea that bombs were the only argument to which the Government would listen.'[81] Moderation was shoved aside with what seems like contemptuous ease in the ensuing years by extremism of various kinds. Again, it must be said that Minister Svyatopolk-Mirsky's elder son never seems to have written or done anything to suggest that he inherited or absorbed from his father any attachment either to moderation or to participatory democracy, much less toleration in matters of religion. Like his mother, he had no respect for the vacillating and 'well-intentioned' Nicholas II; and he came to have a lot of respect for the single-minded, ruthless, and utterly unscrupulous Lenin.

In office, Svyatopolk-Mirsky senior tried his best according to his lights. He sacked Plehve's closest associates from the Ministry, and called for a spirit of mutual trust in the ways his officials were to deal with the population. He ordered the release of many prominent dissidents from imprisonment and internal exile; one of them was Maksim Gorky, who was a member of a delegation that came to see Svyatopolk-Mirsky on 9 January 1905 to try and persuade him to listen to the representatives of the workers.[82] Gorky may well have recalled this act many years later when he facilitated the return of the Minister's son to Russia from emigration. The result of such acts of mercy was a remarkable expression of public support.

Under Svyatopolk-Mirsky's aegis, various steps were taken towards the introduction of some sort of national assembly, and also towards the organization of professional unions. He permitted the National *Zemstvo* Congress[83] to meet in St Petersburg in November 1904, with an agenda calling for the discussion of previously smothered issues such as freedom of speech and of the press. The Congress made an eleven-point resolution, which Svyatopolk-Mirsky persuaded the Tsar at least to receive. And the Minister made his own proposals parallel to those contained in the eleven points. The Tsar set up a select committee to examine them. Svyatopolk-Mirsky's most important proposal was that the elected *zemstvo* members be included in the Council of State. This was rejected on the advice of Count Witte. Svyatopolk-Mirsky offered to resign in favour of Witte, but the Tsar declined. For the remainder of the minister's tenure the Tsar played a cat-and-mouse game with his proffered resignation that infuriated the Minister's wife.

On 18 November 1904, after her husband comes home and reports yet another squabble in the presence of the Tsar, Ekaterina Alekseevna writes:

I don't care two hoots about all this. On the whole I'm convinced now that P. possesses an amazing character. I would have long since strangled one of them, but even though they pester him all day long and he gets terribly tired, he is always kind and welcoming with everybody and almost always cheerful—just once in a while despair comes over him; and after all he's bored stiff with everything.[84]

This last remark is worth noting. The Minister's elder son took after his mother rather than his father and had an extremely low threshold of boredom, and he certainly did not manage to be 'kind and welcoming' all the time; rather, he was impatient and could be abrasively rude. He was never circumspect. Igor Vinogradoff, the son of Sir Paul, knew several members of Mirsky's mother's family, and their gossip suggested that 'his unbalanced side probably came from his Bobrinskoy mother'.[85] He added: 'Mirsky's Bobrinskoy mother was of the Tula branch—a sister of the well-known Duma member—much more excitable people, under the surface, than the Petersburg branch. His (Mirsky's) sister was also, I believe, capable of astounding fits of rage.'[86]

Svyatopolk-Mirsky's patience was sorely tried. Only the least controversial proposals he made were adopted by the Tsar, in an *ukaz* published on 12/25 December 1904, but they were vitiated by another *ukaz* two days later that called on officials not to step outside the narrow limits of their duties.

The military disasters in the Far East gave an additional edge to the unrest in the capital. There were further street demonstrations as the year 1905 began, and they were more violent, culminating in the 'well-intentioned' demonstration that ended up as Bloody Sunday, 9/22 January 1905, when troops fired on the demonstrators and about 150 people were killed. Svyatopolk-Mirsky was at last allowed to step down a week later; his final act of service was to act as the Tsar's scapegoat for these events. His son was later to translate the Marxist historian Pokrovsky's view of what happened, a view endorsed by Lenin. Here, 'Bloody Sunday' is presented as a premeditated provocation by the government. Discussing these events, Pokrovsky cites the British newspaper correspondent Dr Dillon, and the Minister's son adds a parenthesis for the English reader: 'The governor of the city, Fullon, knew about it, so did the Assistant Minister of the Interior, the Minister, Svyatopolk-Mirsky, Witte, Muraviev (The Minister of Justice.—*Tr.*)—in a word several days before the massacre everyone was informed of what was being prepared.'[87]

On 18/31 January 1905 Svyatopolk-Mirsky was granted eleven months' leave with retention of salary; but he was not made a member of the State Council, as would normally have been the case. The autocracy staggered on into the 'Duma period', soon afterwards technically no longer an absolute monarchy but one which was slightly limited, its 'most august' head apparently believing to the end that if only there were not such a shortage of sound men for the key posts, he could govern the country firmly and effectively.

Pyotr Dmitrievich Svyatopolk-Mirsky took no further part in public life after he resigned his Ministry, and he died in St Petersburg after close on ten years of retirement, on 16 May 1914, three years short of 60. Such a decade of tranquillity never came the way of his eldest son; when he died, D. S. Mirsky was about the same age as his father when P. D.'s public career ended. On the father's death, his estate passed to his four children, with the mother retaining possession for the remainder of her lifetime. The Russian revolution thus cost Mirsky, as it did Vladimir Nabokov, personal wealth and possessions enough to last a comfortable lifetime.

'WHERE SHALL I GO TO SCHOOL NOW?'

The time eventually came for the eldest son to be put to formal schooling. On 14 May 1903 the V St Petersburg *gimnaziya* certified that after being educated at home, the boy had taken the third-form examination and achieved the following marks (all out of 5, as consistent a feature of pre- and post-revolutionary Russia as patriarchy): Scripture 5, Russian 4, Latin 5, Mathe-matics 3, History 5, Geography 5, Natural History 5, and French 5. The order in which the subjects are named is not accidental; it reflects the priorities according to the official view of the school curriculum. The almost complete absence of natural science from Mirsky's subjects is indicative, as is his excel-lent performance in geography; he knew such things as the capital of the Sand-wich Islands, as we shall soon see, and he remained fascinated by maps and terrain for the rest of his life.

On 29 August 1904, after an evening of music-making at home, Dim tells his father, 'Your biography is in all the papers and they all say that you were born in 1859. Tomorrow Mama is arriving. . . . Where shall I go to school now? Tomorrow I'll probably start studying seriously with Feliks Moiseevich . . .'. His mother notes in her diary on 20 January 1905, after her husband had resigned his ministry but before it was clear whether or not he would remain in the capital: 'I'm looking forward to spring in Giyovka, it's very nice, I'd like P. to go into retirement and for us to be free citizens; the only problem is Dim— where should we place him?'[88]

The family got back to Giyovka on 7 February 1905 and started seeing their neighbours. The mother notes one particular encounter that confronted the youthful Mirsky with the antagonism that existed in Russia between the mili-tary and the intelligentsia:

A. L. Velichko came round, he's the Marshal of the Gentry for Lebeda now, a most loyal and conservative man, a retired Hussar who recognizes only military service because that's the only area where discipline still exists. I think he shocked Dim because he said that the universities only spend their time on foolishness.[89]

This 'lack of discipline' turned into rioting and then revolution in the ensuing months. On 8 February 1905 Dim went to Kharkov with his mother and they saw some groups of striking workers. This is one of the last entries before a long gap in her diary. On 9 October she notes:

I havn't written anything for nearly 8 months. So many things have happened that it's hard to keep track of them. The battle of Tsushima and the loss of the fleet, the mani-festo of 6 August, peace, the autonomy of the universities—they're the most outstanding facts. But there are so many others, the death of Kolya Den in particular;[90] in social life all the *zemstvo* congresses, the disturbances, the manifesto on religious toleration, too much to count it all. In short, Russia last February is almost a different country from Russia now. And there's no ray of light to be seen. What a calamity for Russia was the death of S. N. Trubetskoy![91]

Prince Sergey Nikolaevich Trubetskoy (1862–1905), the historian of ancient philosophy, was elected Rector of Moscow University after winning his long fight for university autonomy, but died just after his appointment. As the most widely respected intellectual in Russia, he had written a letter to P. D. Svyatopolk-Mirsky on 28 November 1904 pleading for reform. He was the father of D. S. Mirsky's friend, the great linguist Prince N. S. Trubetskoy, the future leader of the Eurasian movement. Sergey Trubetskoy was an exception to Mirsky's maxim asserting that in Russia only those do who can't think. Mirsky's mother commented on 8 February 1905:

We have a lot of well-intentioned people, but few who are strong in spirit and capable of sensible activity. There is nothing to give joy and much that is sad. The *Potemkin*, the *Baku*—it's been hard to live through all that in the course of one year. What will happen next? The railways have gone on strike now . . .[92]

It is clear from the following few entries that the elder son was not in Giyovka when the disturbances reached their climax in October 1905; he had in fact started school in Moscow. His mother managed to exchange several telegrams with him as communications broke down in October and November. On several occasions, the Svyatopolk-Mirsky estate at Giyovka was threatened by marauding bands; they were diverted by simple bribery and on one occasion by the gift of a barrel of vodka. Eventually, the death toll at the barricades in Kharkov reached 200. On 18 October Ekaterina Alekseevna records:

We've lived to see a constitution, may God only grant that Russia calms down. I was still drinking my tea this morning when Pepka came in with a telegram in his hand and a serious look on his face. I was alarmed, but then I noticed that his face was relaxed, and those of Sonya and Alyosha were joyful. It turns out . . . that a manifesto has come out granting freedom of the person, speech, assembly etc.—in short, what we've been trying to achieve for so long and so hard, and at first I was astonished rather than glad. At first when I get something I've wanted for a long time, I always wonder whether it's for the better.

May God grant that we can make good use of our freedom! At last Russia is a free country. But I'm afraid that the revolutionaries will not stop at this. Of course, the vast mass of the intelligentsia will be satisfied, but now the revolutionaries can seduce the ordinary people with their socialist propaganda, and they'll see that this freedom won't make much immediate difference to them, and the revolutionaries will tell them they've been hoodwinked, and so on.

Ekaterina Alekseevna was not fantasizing here, for it was the fear that the people would settle for gradualism that had motivated the revolutionaries of the People's Will to assassinate the 'Tsar-Liberator' Alexander II in 1881 when it was known that he was on the point of granting a constitution. The ex-Minister's wife continues:

And the only thing that can work against this is a sense of property. If the perverted principle of communal landholding isn't done away with, Russia will never be at peace. In order to settle the peasants on their own land one could even resort to such a measure as infringing property rights—the mandatory purchase of a certain part of the country squires' land, once and for all.[93]

Here, Ekaterina Alekseevna adumbrates what was to be the central plank in the reforming policy of Stolypin in the coming years, aimed to reform the most vexing problem besetting the Russian countryside. Ekaterina Alekseevna's diary breaks off on 21 October 1905 with the following exasperated comment: 'There's another lull, but no hope of getting away. The leaders [of the rail-waymen] are just revolutionaries—what more do they want? This means they want anarchy.'[94] What 'they' wanted was to be expressed to devastating effect a dozen years later.

Just as his country emerged from the abortive revolution of 1905 that terminated his father's career, the adolescent prince was set to follow in his footsteps and be trained for public service. Imperial Russia was entering the final phase of its existence.

2 Two Callings

[The 1905] Revolution was defeated, the intoxication passed, and a wave of disillusionment in public ideals swept the *intelligentsia*. Personal enjoyment and freedom from morality became the order of the day, and sexual licence, often on a definitely pathological foundation, spread like an epidemic. (D. S. Mirsky, 1925)

LANGUAGES

On the reverse of the certificate Mirsky received after being examined in 1903 is the following annotation: 'Was accepted into the *gimnaziya* division of the Lycée into the VI form by entrance examination and departed from same according to the wishes of the parents, concerning which a special certificate was issued on 31 May 1906.' The lycée concerned was the Imperial Lycée in Moscow, known as the 'Katkov lycée'; the youth attended it for the academic years 1905–7. What this meant was explained to his English contemporaries by Harold Williams:

Quite apart from the other educational institutions stand the schools of the privileged classes, the Lyceum, the School of Jurisprudence, and the Corps of Pages, as well as the various schools for the training of officers. The two former institutions represent the closest parallel that Russia possesses to English public schools, only that the higher classes of the Lyceum and the School of Jurisprudence have a University character. . . . They are boarding-schools with resident masters, and a conventional system of discipline in which the English public school ideas are modified by the habits of wealthy Russian families.[1]

The nurture lavished on the eldest son of the Svyatopolk-Mirsky family shaped the youth observed by Maurice Baring on a visit to Giyovka in the autumn of 1907:

I was staying in the South of Russia at the house of a gentleman who had played no unimportant part in Russian politics . . . when the son of my host, a boy at school, only seventeen years of age, yet familiar with the literature of seven languages, a writer, moreover, of both English and Russian verse, fired up and said: 'In fifty years' time we Russians shall blush with shame to think that we gave Tolstoy such fulsome admiration, when we had at the same time a genius like Dostoievsky, the latchet of whose shoes Tolstoy is not worthy to unloose.'[2]

It may seem impudent to suggest that Baring may have misunderstood what Mirsky said on this occasion, but despite all the other changes in his literary views as they evolved, Mirsky's preference for Tolstoy over Dostoevsky remained constant. Be that as it may, of more interest here is Baring's assessment of Mirsky's linguistic ability. To judge from the family letters and the references in Mirsky's earliest publications, the seven literatures Baring alludes to here were Russian, English, French, German, Italian, Latin, and Ancient Greek. Nothing has ever surfaced of the English verse that the boy was writing at this time (or later); but Mirsky published several specimens of Russian verse dated to 1906 and 1907, which we will come to in a moment.

The linguistic attainments that so impressed Baring were the foundation-stone of Mirsky's achievements. His first language was unambiguously Russian, and there is plenty of evidence that demonstrates his virtuoso command of it across a broad spectrum of registers. Mirsky lived in the golden age of the gramophone, and a sample of his spoken Russian happens to have been preserved, in the recordings he made in London for the Linguaphone company just before he went back to Russia. Even in these inhibiting circumstances he spouts on with bubbling energy, in an upper-class accent that now sounds almost comic but is at the same time strangely glamorous. There is always a touch of haughty impatience in his voice as he runs through dialogues such as 'The Restaurant'; after all, this is an aristocrat who has spent the last ten years doing systematic fieldwork in the best eating-places in France:

(Mirsky) 'Is this table free?'
　'No, it's taken.'
'Then we'll take this one. Give me the menu, please. What do you have today?'
　'Cabbage soup with kasha, lamb, and kissel.'
'What are the appetizers?'
　'Sardines and salted cucumber.'
'Shall we drink vodka? I think we should have a decanter.'[3]

As for Mirsky's English, it was as accurate as that of any non-native ever gets, and infinitely more resourceful than that of most native speakers. His active command of the written language was astoundingly good. He never wrote any fiction, so no direct comparison with Vladimir Nabokov is possible. But Nabokov, and his academic-journalistic contemporary Gleb Struve, were the only literary Russians of Mirsky's time who could hold a candle to him in terms of all-round mastery of English. Other Russian intellectuals of the age who spent time in England but who as children did not have the benefit of English nannies, such as Boris Anrep, Korney Chukovsky, Nikolay Gumilyov, and Evgeny Zamyatin, seem to have been able to read straightforward English with (often misplaced) confidence, and to speak it just about well enough to make themselves understood in everyday situations, but unlike Mirsky they had no active command of the written language.

Mirsky's written English, though, was manifestly inferior to his Russian.

Astounding though his competence is, he does not seem to feel 'the resistance of the material' in his second language, even though like Nabokov he started learning it from a native speaker simultaneously with Russian. The reason, of course, is that his primary informant was his nanny, a genteel Englishwoman, and that Mirsky was over 30 years old before he used English as a working language on its home ground. The difference can be sensed acutely by comparing the vivid Russian of his letters to Suvchinsky with the stiffish English of those to Jane Ellen Harrison. The fact that in the first instance Mirsky is addressing a male compatriot and contemporary and in the second a foreign female elder obviously accounts for the difference in general tone, but not for the difference in Mirsky's command of the idiom appropriate to each. That there are no letters to speak of to an English male contemporary, incidentally, says something very important about Mirsky's acquaintanceship among English people.

The vast bulk of Mirsky's published writing in English went through the hands of the punctilious copy-editors, compositors, and proofreaders of the 1920s and was as a rule purged of serious errors. But it could not have been brought to the high standard it displays if the original copy had not been exceptionally sound. When Mirsky came to edit some translations of English poetry into Russian in the mid-1930s, even though by then he had been away from the living language for several years, his unaided comments still demonstrate an impressive sensitivity to the nuances of the originals.[4] However, the examples we have of Mirsky's unedited writing in English show that some idiomatic features always evaded him. His principal linguistic mentor, Jane Ellen Harrison, ticked him off on one occasion: 'You will go to yr grave misusing our prepositions.'[5] Mirsky ruefully admitted that the reader would easily be able to tell which chapters of his history of Russian literature had been weeded by Harrison, and he was right. Here, for example, is an unweeded passage—admittedly the worst of its kind—where the syntax especially is embarrassingly full of Russianisms:

Korolenko's last work is an autobiography, which seems to be even a singularly exact and truthful account of his life but which for some supersensitive scruple he called the history not of himself, but of his contemporary. . . . He gives a delightful picture of life in yet semi-Polish Volynia—of his scrupulously honest but wilful father. He records his early impressions . . . of the great events he had to witness. . . .[6]

Vera Traill told me that Mirsky spoke English with an accent and could never have been taken for a native speaker; but she also said that when she spoke Russian with him, she always felt that his English was better. There again, though, Vera's English had originally been learned from a Petersburg governess,[7] and she spoke it with what was to my ear stiff and archaic upper-class intonation and phraseology. Mirsky's French and German, written and spoken, both seem to have been almost as fluent as his English; again, he was instructed in both these languages at home from a very early age by native speakers, but there is much less evidence by which to judge the results. All this is to mention only the principal modern European languages.

Mirsky was a voracious reader with a polyglot verbal memory whose capacity astounded people who met him—even such as Maurice Baring, who was no slouch himself in this respect. Mirsky's linguistic ability was a case quite different from the Russian propensity for spouting reams of schoolroom Pushkin and quotations from the anthology of 'winged words', part of a mystique which still sometimes leaves Anglo-Saxons awed. Mirsky tended to spout Dante and Virgil, and not in Russian translation. Incredible though this may seem in view of the amount of ground Mirsky covered, he does actually seem to have read what he wrote about, and to my knowledge he has never been caught out bluffing.[8] What is more, he read everything *in the original*. In this respect he remains utterly exceptional among Russian literary intellectuals, even those of his own privileged class and generation, who grew up before foreign travel was rigidly controlled and cultural cosmopolitanism equated with treason. All this goes to make up one fundamental reason why he has been impossible to surpass as a practical critic and historian of European literature of the period up to and including his own times. The intervening century between his youth and our times has destroyed both the old obligatory groundwork of the humanities in the classics that was vouchsafed the few and also the competence in modern languages that was once supposed to replace it for the many. Meanwhile, Mirsky had both, and also a confident working knowledge of the canonical literature that went along with them.

LITERARY DEBUT

When he left the Moscow Lycée, Mirsky transferred to another élite school, but this time one in which the arts and humanities were strong. Evidently, his literary proclivities had made his parents doubt the wisdom of his following exactly in his father's footsteps and going straight from the Moscow Lycée into the army at the age of 18. Whatever may have been the case, there was a profound discontinuity between these two callings.

Mirsky was sent to one of the outstanding secondary schools in the capital, the I Petersburg *gimnaziya*.[9] This was one of a group of private institutions that are commonly referred to as 'the Gurevich *gimnaziya* of the Tenishev College (*uchilishche*)'; to judge from the academic records of Mirsky's fellow students, they shared a literary circle and some teachers. The star literature teacher was Vladimir Vasilievich Gippius (1876–1941), whose father was one of P. D. Svyatopolk-Mirsky's underlings in the Ministry of the Interior. V. V. Gippius had been one of the pioneering literary decadents in the 1890s, an atheist and cynic who cultivated a pose of world-weary indifference. With new-found dedication to positive thinking, he started as a schoolmaster at the Tenishev in 1906, becoming Director in 1917. Mandelshtam and Nabokov were among the pupils who never forgot him.

Viktor Zhirmunsky, who became one of Russia's greatest literary theorists and historians, was at the school from 1900 to 1908. Another schoolmate, who seems to have become Mirsky's closest friend during their childhood and again during the last years before Mirsky's arrest, was Aleksey Mikhailovich Sukhotin (1888–1942); unlike Mirsky, he carried on with Oriental languages in his professional life and eventually became a premier Soviet specialist in this field.[10] His father, Mikhail Sergeevich Sukhotin (1850–1914), was a landowner in the Tula region and a friend of Tolstoy; in 1899 he took Tolstoy's beloved daughter Tatyana (1864–1950) as his second wife, and his children became frequent visitors to Yasnaya Polyana in the last years of the great man's life.

A schoolmate bound for lesser glory was the precocious Lev Pumpyansky (1891–1940), a classicist who became a recognized Soviet literary theorist and historian. There was also Vasily Vasilievich Gippius (1890–1942), the brother of the teacher, who was at the VI *gimnaziya*. He too became a Soviet academic, and as a time-serving Pushkin specialist he was to be involved in an ill-omened clash with Mirsky in 1935 when the latter made one of several visits to what had become Leningrad, renewing contact with a number of his former schoolmates who had stayed on in Russia and survived the de-gentrification of academic life.

The literary circle that included Zhirmunsky, Pumpyansky, Sukhotin, and Mirsky put together a miscellany under the title *Links* (*Zven'ya*, as of a chain; several later Russian periodicals have used the same title). Two issues were published, in 1906 and in 1907, and it was here that Mirsky made his literary debut as critic, poet, and translator.[11] His contributions to the 1906 issue are signed 'Eleutheròs'.[12] His contribution consisted of three original poems, a translation of Rossetti's sonnet on Keats, and an extraordinary piece of rhetorical prose, the like of which—fortunately—Mirsky was never to attempt again:

The time has passed when with constant trust we heeded the word of Reason. The worship of Utility is gone by, and Art has ceased to consider itself the slave of Truth. We have lost faith in the Wisdom of our fathers, we have cursed the paths they broke for us and with trembling heart, abashed by the majesty of the Possible we await a new revelation. The crowd still believes in its gods. And who knows? Perhaps it is right, perhaps Universal Satiety will indeed become Universal Happiness. But we have lost our faith, we are seeking the new, the insane and the false perhaps, we love our future with our passionate natures, with our hopeless and disenchanted Love. We believe, we want to believe! We shall go on believing, and through the power of our belief mountains will move, the sun will stand still, and the dead will rise from their graves. . . .

Mirsky continues in the same vein for another paragraph, and then comes a grand finale:

It is not the darkness of slavery nor the running sores of Debauchery that we promise, but an eternal unfading kingdom of unlimited Freedom and divine Beauty. Then the individual personality will cast off the chains of the past and shake the dust from his feet, the dust of the millennia. And to this he will be led by Art that is free like God and eternally new like Nature, self-sufficient and pre-ordained for all. We, the younger generation, dedicate ourselves to this struggle, a struggle long and stubborn, but radiant and infinitely beautiful. And our happiness, our joy in Beauty will be the prototype of the great joy that will envelop the world when that longed-for morning breaks.[13]

This effusion is followed by a prim note: 'From the editors. This article about Art is a personal opinion, and alternatives will be accepted with great pleasure.' With regard to the general attitude expressed in this youthful article, it has sometimes been argued that the entire spectrum of schools and movements in early twentieth-century Russian culture shared an eschatological and messianistic view of themselves.[14] Mirsky's schoolboy article on Art in fact provides the only serious evidence in his work that he ever entertained this attitude; and it was a short-lived phase in his development. He entertained no transcendental view of himself as Poet or God-Man or whatever, much less of his age as big with messianism. Instead, he writes with the acute historical awareness and eschewal of metaphysics characteristic of his straight-thinking contemporaries, among them Zhirmunsky and Trubetskoy (to name but two of the scholars), and Kuzmin and Komarovsky (to name but two of the poets). Paradoxically, an eschatological note appeared in Mirsky's attitudes only when he became a Marxist-Leninist in the late 1920s.

Mirsky's contribution to the second collection put out by his schoolmates is considerably more restrained. Under the general heading 'Reflections' come two prose poems, 'Venice' and 'Florence', dated '15 XII 1906'; a translation of Verlaine's 'Dans l'interminable ennui de la plaine', from *Romances sans paroles*; and finally, Mirsky's first piece of published criticism, a review of Sergey Gorodetsky's collection *Yar*.[15] Mirsky sees this book as a breaking away from flaccid decadence and a reconnection with primeval strength, a demonstration that symbolism really can have genuine Russian roots. But, Mirsky points out, such primitivism is a conscious pose. This is a topic that he was to return to again and again as a critic.

The pupils at the Tenishev *gimnaziya* attempted to involve themselves actively in current Russian literature. Mirsky acted as their spokesman when they made an approach to Aleksandr Blok, universally acknowledged to be the greatest living Russian poet, who was then at the height of his powers. On 11 February 1907 Mirsky wrote to Blok:

My comrades have instructed me to inform you that if it is convenient for you we will expect you at our *gimnaziya* (Ivanovskaya Street, corner of Kabinetskaya) tomorrow,

Monday, at 8 in the evening. I saw M. A. Kuzmin yesterday and he promised to give me the music for *Balaganchik*. . . .[16]

Blok evidently obliged, but the plan to put on his play did not come to fruition. On 14 February 1907 Mirsky wrote to Blok again:

I am obliged to inform you of a very unpleasant and sad circumstance. Yesterday, the 13th, those opposed to staging *Balaganchik* demanded that this question be re-opened. The first time, with open voting, only an insignificant minority, about 7–8 people, were against *Balaganchik*. But when there was a secret vote all the lack of culture of our public was exposed, which is of course not surprising. There were only 12 votes for *Balaganchik* and 20 against.[17]

Mirsky later explained for the English reader that Blok's play,

a 'pierrotic' comedy, was produced in 1907 and had a fairly long run. On those who saw it, *Balagánchik* produced an unforgettable impression. It contains much of Blok's very best lyrical manner, but it is in essence a satire, a parody, and a piece of grim blasphemy. It is a parody on Blok's own mystical experience and a satire on his mystical hopes and aspirations. . . . The lyrical charm and capricious symbolism of *Balagánchik* may obscure from most readers its terrible pessimism, but it is in essence one of the most blasphemous and gloomiest things ever written by the poet.[18]

Produced by Meyerhold, the play had opened on 30 December 1906 and had caused a sensation in the febrile intellectual circles of Petersburg.

MIKHAIL KUZMIN

In his first letter to Blok, Mirsky mentions seeing Mikhail Alekseevich Kuzmin (1872–1936),[19] who composed the music for *Balaganchik*. Mirsky's relationship with Kuzmin is the most intriguing episode from his schooldays that has so far come to light. The relationship is attested in the poet's diary, one of the most revealing of all sources about St Petersburg culture during the modernist period. The diary is in fact so revealing that its survival is something of a miracle. It could not even be referred to publicly in any objective way until after the fall of the USSR and its attendant literary controls, and it has still not been published in full.[20]

Before 1905–6 Kuzmin had led a varied life.[21] In his early teens he became a vigorously active homosexual. He made several long trips to Western Europe and the Middle East, accompanying various older lovers. He then spent two years at the Petersburg Conservatoire, studying among others with Rimsky-Korsakov and Lyadov; and he dabbled in various religions. In the years just before Mirsky met him, he had been seen wearing Russian national costume and consorting with merchants who professed the Old Believer faith.

In 1906 Kuzmin began to appear at the 'Tower', the apartment Vyacheslav Ivanov and Lidiya Zinovieva-Gannibal had settled into when they came back to Russia the year before; it soon became *the* meeting-place for the aspiring modernists in the Petersburg literary intelligentsia, as it was intended to. Kuzmin moved in with the Ivanovs for a while the next year. Like Russian Symbolism in general, the Tower is hard to take seriously if one has any sense of humour at all, let alone a sense of the absurd, but in Kuzmin's diary the Tower comes over as not much more than a drunken, garrulous, poseur-ridden orgy.[22]

In July 1906 Kuzmin made his literary debut in *The Scales*, the leading Symbolist journal, edited by Valery Bryusov in Moscow. Bryusov made a selection from what eventually became *Songs of Alexandria*, a set of poems in free verse that was once thought to draw heavily on Pierre Louÿs's *Chansons de Bilitis*, but more recently has been ascribed to less obvious sources.[23] The penultimate issue of the journal for the same year was entirely devoted to Kuzmin's novella *Wings*. At about the same time, Kuzmin switched to Western clothes, with special emphasis on embroidered waistcoats; this was probably less sensational than has sometimes been assumed, to judge from a remark by Harold Williams, who was admittedly a sober son of the manse: 'About the years 1907 and 1908 the display of dress in theatres and concert-halls was simply barbarous in its crude ostentation.'[24] At about this same time Kuzmin started consorting with two of the most prominent homosexuals in the artistic and theatrical avant-garde of Petersburg, Konstantin Somov and Sergey Sudeikin. Somov (1869–1939) was Kuzmin's lover in the autumn of 1906; his portrait of Kuzmin is reproduced in just about every publication that has anything to do with the latter. With Sudeikin (1882–1946) Kuzmin had an affair that flowered between October and December 1906 and ended when Sudeikin devastated Kuzmin by marrying one of the most famous women in Petersburg bohemia, the ballerina and actress Olga Glebova (1885–1945), a great friend of Anna Akhmatova.[25]

Published as a separate book in 1907, *Wings* is the earliest work in Russian high literature that is explicitly homoerotic. Kuzmin instantly became a scandalously famous figure in St Petersburg society.[26] The book brought him avid fan mail, and rumours started to spread alleging that Kuzmin was the ringleader of a secret society dedicated to sexual debauchery. In the autumn of 1907 Kuzmin several times records in his diary the idea of setting up such a circle, with himself as the guiding spirit, along the lines of the homoerotic 'Hafiz' group that coalesced from the antics in Vyacheslav Ivanov's Tower.[27]

On 1 October 1907, out of the blue, Kuzmin received a telegram from four *gimnaziya* boys, expressing their gratitude to 'the sweet author of the Songs of Alexandria and the plays'.[28] The telegram was signed, but there was no return address; Kuzmin found it out from the main post office the next day, and noted in his diary: 'That's where the Svyatopolk-Mirskys live.' On 6 October Kuzmin saw his current lover, Viktor Andreevich Naumov.[29] He notes: 'Before he arrived there were 6 *gimnaziya* boys here, talking, smoking, eating sweets. Each more ugly than the next, only Pokrovsky's all right, a bit of a fattyface [*mordal'on*] but pleasant and lively.' On 10 October he writes: 'I saw my *gimnaziya* boys, soon they're going to visit me.' They did visit him in a group on 15 October. Mirsky visited Kuzmin on his own on 28 October, and then the group visited again on 2 November, when Kuzmin noted: 'They keep wanting to bring me various young men; all well and good; they described the candidates to me: handsome, from a good family, etc. We sat there for a long time. I ought to invite them one at a time.' Then, on 6 November: 'They tried to drag me along to the Vienna [restaurant], but Somov, Nuvel,[30] the *gimnaziya* boys and I went to Palkin's [restaurant]. It was very nice indeed and my friends liked Svyatopolk-Mirsky very much.' The next day: 'We were at [Nuvel's], he was delighted with the evening yesterday, with Mirsky, the young ones—aren't I good to do all this for my friends . . .' And the day after that: 'I received a letter from Mirsky, very nice, asks me to invite him very soon, he misses me already, etc. . . . It's flattering that the young ones aren't bored by us,—they search us out, they come to see us, and it's something they want to do.'

Soon the idea arose of putting on an amateur performance of Kuzmin's musical play *The Seasons of Love*, which Mirsky was soon to describe for his English readers without mentioning anything about his first-hand knowledge: 'the whimsically exquisite "eighteenth-century" pastoral *The Seasons of Love* (1907), in which his wonderful, almost acrobatic skill in handling rhyme is at its best. (The music to the pastoral is also by Kuzmín.)'[31] On 19 November Kuzmin notes: 'The schoolboys were here, [also] Dmitriev, Seryozha,[32] Somov, Nuvel, and unexpectedly Bakst, who'd just arrived [in Petersburg]. Somov is an awful slowcoach and didn't say two words to Mirsky. . . . Seryozha [Auslender] annoyed me with his snorting in the presence of the young ones, his familiarity, and maybe because Mirsky likes him.'

Rehearsals began of Kuzmin's play. In the next mention of his name in Kuzmin's diary, on 21 November, Mirsky acquires a sobriquet: '*Il principino* came and we sat nicely for an hour.' The performance of *Seasons* took place on 30 November and was a disaster, though Kuzmin made the best of it:

It began very late, the audience was upset, there were masses of people I knew. Somov and Mirsky sat next to me. . . . Afterwards five of us went to Palkin's; the young people are getting positively tame. I invited them for Monday. They're very nice, they joked and drank and chattered freely; they would make charming friends apart from everything else. On the way back I even linked arms with Kornily [Pokrovsky]. Remizov asked me to introduce the schoolboys to Serafima Pavlovna, and she invited them to come and see her.[33] An evening very well spent.

A newspaper review of the performance, very condescending, records that the evening was supposed to begin with a lecture by Andrey Bely—but he left for Moscow on 18 November after his famous quarrel with Blok's wife and did not turn up.[34] As a divertissement, there were readings by Remizov, Blok, and Sergey Gorodetsky, and various singers performed.

On 2 December Kuzmin writes:

A note from Pokrovsky that it is not to be. . . . Somov didn't turn up, there were only Nuvel, Mirsky, and Poznyakov. Mirsky left early. The student [Poznyakov] said, stamping his foot, that he needed to be loved if only by Satan, that nothing was working for him, and finally lay down on the divan. He abused Mirsky and said that Pokrovsky liked prostitutes . . .

After this, Nuvel tried to win the schoolboys away from Kuzmin; on 8 December '[Nuvel] got tickets to the ballet for himself and the *Principino* . . . [Nuvel] thrust himself at Naumov, and now he's doing it at the *Principino*, as if he hadn't got much of his own'. The schoolboys are not mentioned again individually until 26 January 1908: 'I did some work with Seryozha, then Poznyakov came, the three of us went to Remizov's, complete misery there. The schoolboys and [Nuvel] were there. . . . Poznyakov and Nuvel went somewhere else, and with Mirsky and Pokrovsky I wended my way home. Something's gone wrong.' On 19 March Kuzmin had a letter from Pokrovsky suggesting they break off relations.

All this raises the subject of Mirsky's adolescent, and subsequently (or consequently) adult, sexuality.[35] There is no unambiguous evidence of a physical relationship with the 17-year-old Mirsky in Kuzmin's diary, which tends to be unboastfully explicit about the occasions when such relationships did take place; among the schoolboys, Kuzmin clearly went for Kornily Pokrovsky, and Mirsky if anything seems to have become closer to Nuvel.

Mirsky had a brief marriage in 1916; later, he proposed to Vera Suvchinskaya. Vera told me that she once compared notes with Marina Tsvetaeva about Mirsky on the basis of the fling he had with the poet in 1926, and was confirmed in her own view that he had little physical interest in women. The only unambiguous statement that the adult Mirsky was if anything homosexual was made by his sometime friend Konstantin Rodzevich to Veronika Losskaya, in the context of a discussion of Tsvetaeva:

Before he met [Tsvetaeva] personally, Mirsky spoke ill of her. Then they met. He wanted to do something for her. People say they had an affair, but after all Mirsky didn't especially care for women—he was sooner a man of other inclinations [*on byl skoree drugikh naklonnostei*]. She thought him clever, but she said 'He's defective, like all princes.'[36]

Dorothy Galton spoke about her sense of Mirsky's underlying homosexuality as openly as propriety permitted once when I was talking to her about Mirsky as she knew him in London between 1929 and 1932. Miss Galton saw Mirsky in many different situations, public and private, and she summed up: 'I can't believe that he really enjoyed life very much anywhere; he was a psychological problem to himself, you see.' I asked her what she thought might be the root of this 'psychological problem', and she spoke about Mirsky's childhood:

[They] made a fuss of him . . . [He] was surrounded with too many girls and women and so on, and this did him harm. I wouldn't know what was the basis of it, and his sister[37] didn't elucidate any problems for me very much; but certainly he had some kind of twist-up inside himself which one can't define; this must be so because of his inability to make any contact with people . . .

Miss Galton added an afterthought to this in a letter: 'I also forgot an important side of DSM in an area to which I could not accompany him. He was fond of *erotica*, and one of his interests was in Mario Praz.'[38] She then went on to speak about D. H. Lawrence, and concluded: 'This interest in the erotic and the "queer" undoubtedly affected DSM's attitude to Gide, for instance, and probably to many others.'[39]

There is some evidence of this interest in Mirsky's published writings, but it is unavoidably oblique. Shortly after he left Russia, Mirsky mentioned that Kuzmin 'has a great liking for refined and perverted vice'.[40] This phrase is as near as Mirsky ever came in his published writings to actually naming homosexuality. In the course of his brilliant pages discussing the life and works of Konstantin Leontiev (1831–91) Mirsky mentions that 'he was always in some love affair—and confided them to his wife. She did not like it, and it would seem that these confidences were the cause of her mental illness . . .'.[41] On 22 November 1924, close to the time he wrote this, Mirsky said in a letter to Suvchinsky: 'I've been struck by two biographical discoveries: the first is that Leontiev was a pederast[42] (see Strakhov's letters to Rozanov), and the second is that in 1861–3 Rozanov's first wife Apollinariya Suslova was Dostoevsky's mistress! There's an amazing connection for you!' The contrast between public and private is manifest, but of course in no way surprising, given the legal risks involved. Mirsky obviously assumes that Suvchinsky knows what he is talking about when he refers to the letters of Strakhov to Rozanov; writing for the English reader, he makes what is inevitably an enigmatic reference to this subject:

Apart from these books [*Fallen Leaves*] his most remarkable utterances are to be found where one would least expect them—for instance, in footnotes to other people's letters. Thus, one of his greatest books is his edition of Strákhov's letters (*Literary Exiles*, 1913) to himself; the footnotes contain passages of unsurpassed genius and originality.[43]

These footnotes do indeed contain such passages; and the most remarkable of them all is the one that mentions Leontiev, perhaps the most subtle discussion of same-sex love in Russian modernist writing.[44] This one small example points, however, to something characteristic of Mirsky, and important: he may have considered his own sexuality to be something to be ashamed of, as conventional teaching of the time insisted, but in his private writings, as in his life, there is no evidence that he thought of discussing anybody's sexuality in terms of anything but personal ethics and aesthetics; the moral condemnation of others, much less condemnation on religious grounds, does not occur to him.

Such interest in bodily functions as Mirsky had was centred above the neck, and primarily involved oral gratification for the purpose of filling his stomach. But although it may not have concerned him very much in physical terms, sexuality was very important as a part of his mental furniture, albeit usually sublimated in various metaphorical modes. In his mature critical writings, one of the most frequently used concepts, always positive, is *muzhestvo*, which cannot be translated by any single English word, unless that be 'manliness'. The root of it is *muzh* ('man', in the sense of 'a male person'), but the derivative is the normal Russian word for 'courage'. Writing in 1922, Mirsky observed:

There is a great injustice in the word *muzhestvo*: the property it indicates is by no means the monopoly of our sex, and that same *muzhestvo* that there is in Gumilyov and Mandelshtam (a *muzhestvo* that does not exclude femininity) we also find in Anna Akhmatova.[45]

What mattered most for Mirsky in his meetings with Kuzmin was mental rather than physical: the thrill of consorting with the most innovative Russian writer of the time. Mirsky had started writing poetry the year before he met Kuzmin, and in Kuzmin he found a professional who was responsible for the latest stride that Russian poetry had taken. When the *principino* and his school chums made their move on Kuzmin, they might not have realized fully that Kuzmin himself had only just entered the big-time literary world; he was in his mid-30s, after all. By dint of relentless self-fashioning—which involved music, reading, learning languages, travelling, and apprenticing himself to various talented mentors (all enabled by an allowance from his widowed mother)—Kuzmin burst upon the Petersburg scene in 1906 with a repertoire of aesthetic values that challenged the received Russian Symbolist agenda. The nodal points of it were: early Christianity; Plotinus; Italian mysticism of the fourteenth and early fifteenth centuries; *Sturm und Drang*, especially Hamann and Heinze; the thought and faith of the Russian Old Believers; and Leskov.[46] This repertoire must have been irresistible for Mirsky; the traces of it, especially its last two—Russian—ingredients, show up strongly in his literary-historical writings of the 1920s.

Kuzmin was the epitome of that abnegation of sentimentality, overt emotion, and self-conscious philosophizing that Mirsky was to value positively throughout his critical career. Mirsky the mature critic hailed Kuzmin as the first Russian writer to 'abandon philosophy', perhaps the most succinct way that has ever been found of formulating what is seen in standard Russian literary historiography as Kuzmin's most important contribution: that he 'overcame Symbolism' and laid the conceptual basis for what has unavoidably to be referred to as Acmeism.[47]

INTELLECTUAL CURRENTS

Writing to Suvchinsky on 29 January 1924, Mirsky described his outlook at about the time of the first revolution, just before he met Kuzmin. Alas, since Suvchinsky's letters to Mirsky have never been found, we do not know what led up to the following assertion, which begins with banter and then becomes serious:

'Cosmic pessimism' is even closer to me and I'll even say specially close. 'What party do you belong to?' 'I'm a cosmic pessimist'. This reminds me of . . . my father as well, who was very worried about me when I was an SD and an SR,[48] but calmed down when I announced that I was a mystical anarchist (1906).[49] But joking aside, cosmic pessimism is very close to me, and that's why I so despise Goethe and so love Pushkin and K[onstantin] Leontiev.

Svyatopolk-Mirsky senior obviously took the two political parties seriously, but viewed 'mystical anarchy' as the babblings of a handful of harmless literary intellectuals; if his son's 'article about Art' of 1907 is a specimen of mystical anarchy, as would seem to be the case, the former Minister's judgement was sound.

Writing in the early 1930s after he had become a Marxist, Mirsky once implied that his serious education began in the year of the relationship with Kuzmin:

Like all bourgeois intellectuals of my generation, I had undergone an idealist education since 1907. I used to like to apply to myself the celebrated *mot* of Pestel[50] which was noted by Pushkin: '*Mon cœur est matérialiste, mais ma raison se refuse à l'être*'. My 'reason', in fact, tormented by the aesthetic and mystical ideology of post-1905, had accepted the axiom that the modern mind was incarnated in Dostoevsky, Nietzsche,[51] Bergson[52] and *tutti quanti*, and that Marxism was a primitive doctrine that an informed intellectual could only look down on.[53]

The most immediate consideration behind the last clause of this sentence is without doubt Mirsky's contemporary reaction to the publication in 1909 of *Landmarks* (*Vekhi*). In this collection, three prominent figures in particular made public their intellectual transition from youthful Marxism into middle-aged idealism and reconciliation with Orthodox Christianity—exactly counter to that of Mirsky twenty years later: Nikolay Aleksandrovich Berdyaev (1874–1948), Sergey Nikolaevich Bulgakov (1871–1944), and Pyotr Berngard-ovich Struve (1870–1944).[54] All three opposed Lenin's revolution and went into emigration, but true to their temperamental opposition-mindedness they remained 'left of centre', and never became reactionaries. Mirsky knew them all personally in the middle 1920s, just before his own evolution brought him to a new version of the commitment they had abandoned, and he was the first critic to present them in an informed way to the English-speaking public, though as literary figures rather than as serious religious and social philosophers. Mirsky never completely abandoned his admiration for these 'older brothers'. In a somewhat bitter essay published under Mirsky's editorship nearly twenty years after *Landmarks*, Berdyaev acknowledged that his pre-revolutionary activity had been an ignominious failure because it had no broad support; but he also declared that he could not hope for support among Mirsky's 'betrayed' generation in any case, because 'The children usually destroy the fathers—such is the law of our sinful life in time.'[55]

Like Mirsky, but for different reasons, the *Landmarks* men detested the Russian radical intelligentsia; and like Mirsky, they were committed to ceaseless intellectual toil. More important, they seemed to have shared an idea of Russia—or rather an ideal of what Russia might become—which transcended the transition from Imperial to Soviet statehood. Their commitment to Orthodoxy and Mirsky's to Marxism were both revisionist acts of reconciliation with the current ruling ideology of Russian imperial power.

With regard to Dostoevsky, Nietzsche, and Bergson, the 'axiom' Mirsky refers to in 1931 was articulated above all in the works of two thinkers whom Mirsky was to discuss with great insight and respect before he became a Marxist, but after that simply dropped. We have already encountered Vasily Rozanov; the other was Lev Shestov (1866–1938), of whom Mirsky saw a good deal during their early days in emigration. The writings of Rozanov and Shestov had already started to get through to the English reader before Mirsky arrived in London, but he provided the first really up-to-date, contextualized discussion of them.[56]

Whether Mirsky actually ever read Bergson and Nietzsche is not clear, but like many other contemporary intellectuals he felt himself entitled to assume familiarity with them, and on occasion summarize them. Writing about the original Eurasians in 1922, he said that 'most of the authors of the "Exodus" have well studied their Bergson. This is tantamount to saying that they do not believe in a predestined future, and that all depends on will and effort.'[57] Mirsky here formulates precisely the voluntarism that was characteristic of his own thinking in the 1920s, and which may have developed during his schooldays.

UNDERGRADUATE TO GUARDSMAN

The next formal stage in Mirsky's 'idealist education', which like the preceding stage seems to have been anything but a torment to Mirsky's reason and/or heart at the time, came when he went up from school to St Petersburg University in 1908, and spent three years studying Oriental languages. On 13 October 1908 he reported to his father that 'Professor Ivanov (Chinese language) and Postyshev (Japanese) . . . are awfully boring. Japanese is pretty easy. But Chinese is extraordinarily strange. Their grammar has a completely different conception of everything.'[58] It has been asserted that during these years Mirsky was also taught by members of the great linguistics department of the university, including V. V. Bartold, V. M. Alekseev, and the most distinguished of them all, the dissident Polish professor of linguistics Baudouin de Courtenay.[59] The work he did as an undergraduate left relatively little trace in Mirsky's later writings, but it was of profound importance for his mental habits. Of the Russian intellectuals of his generation, very few could match Mirsky's knowledge of Western European languages and cultures, but there was nobody else of any stature who combined this knowledge with an awareness of the cultures of Asia based on first-hand linguistic study. The result was more negative than positive, but of immense value for the quality of Mirsky's thinking, where it is manifested as a much greater reluctance to claim universal significance for any of the Russian cultural phenomena he discussed than was customary among his contemporaries. The most striking example of this concerns Dostoevsky, who was promoted in Mirsky's time, first among Russians and then among foreigners, as a thinker whose psychological insight attained some sort of universal humanity. Mirsky's enhanced awareness of alternatives never led him into complete relativism in cultural values, as it did N. S. Trubetskoy (who always made an exception of his commitment to Orthodox Christianity), but it kept him back from the kind of chauvinistic exaggeration based on ignorance that bedevils the historiography of Russian literature.

In 1908, his first year at the university, Mirsky participated in an academic enterprise that is regarded by some as the high-water mark of pre-revolutionary Russian academic scholarship, the Pushkin seminar run by Professor Semyon Vengerov. It was here that the first generation of professional Pushkinists in Russia was trained. The list of participants in the seminar, published in 1914, does not mention that Mirsky delivered a paper; it describes him as a poet.[60] Later critics have tended to denigrate Vengerov as the epitome of the nineteenth-century approach to academic literary studies, a positivist compiler of data. Mirsky was one such critic. Not long after he had attended the seminar, writing for the English reading public, Mirsky spoke with scorn about Vengerov, and the attitude he expresses strongly implies by contrast the aims that drove his own approach as a literary critic:

The most curious of all editions [of Pushkin] is the Brockhaus–Efron Edition (1907–1916) in six large quarto volumes edited by the late Prof. S. A. Vengerov. It is a monument of infinite industry and infinite bad taste. . . . The edition contains a great mass of prefatory, commentary, and biographical matter, most of which is more or less worthless, though some of it is indispensable to every student of Pushkin.[61]

Without completing his course, Mirsky left the university in 1911 and went into the army as a 'volunteer' or, more literally, 'free self-determiner' (*vol'noopredelyayushchiisya*), that is, a person in the ranks, but having secondary education, and therefore entitled to certain privileges rather than being completely subject to the military discipline of the ordinary troops—a kind of sampler for middle- and upper-class boys considering a military career.[62] His regiment was the Emperor's Own IV Life Guards Rifles. He told his father in September 1911 that many of his acquaintances were going into the army on the same terms. In 1912 he took the officers' entry examination and was commissioned as a 2nd lieutenant. He served a total of two years and three months in the peacetime army, mainly in and around the capital, carrying out duties that were as much social as military.

One person who knew Mirsky socially at this time was Hélène Izwolsky (Elena Izvolskaya), whose father served as the last Tsarist ambassador to France. She obviously had a lot of time for Mirsky, but his private opinion of her, expressed in a letter to Suvchinsky of 25 February 1926, was that she was 'not stupid, but tragically ungifted'. Izvolskaya's memoirs were written after she renewed contact with Mirsky in emigration; they offer a useful introduction to the Petersburg high society that Mirsky inhabited as a Guards officer in the years before the First World War:

Though I submitted obediently to all the rites and customs of these grand affairs, I remained an outsider in this closed, clannish Petersburg. I had little in common with it, having tasted the sophistication of Paris and known its intellectual ferment. The men I danced with were absorbed with their own affairs, mostly pertaining to the military, or to horses and the hunt. They seemed unaware of all that was going on outside this narrow world. Politics, at that time hotly discussed by the Russian intelligentsia, were ignored by them. They felt secure in their 'status' or 'way of life', and the idea that it could ever be upset never entered their minds. As to their cultural interests, they were no less limited and conventional.

However, I am wrong to generalize. Some of my dancing partners were highly educated and brilliant young men. My most interesting friend was Prince Dimitri Sviatopolk-Mirsky, an erudite scholar. He was a close friend of my brother, Grisha, and therefore we met on familiar terms. He was a black-bearded man with strange, Mongol features and a sardonic smile. A revolutionary at heart, he scarcely tried to hide his convictions. Soon after my debut, he was demoted from his rank as officer for refusing to drink to the Tsar's health at a regimental dinner.[63]

The Guards regiments of Imperial Russia were noted for two types of accomplishment, neither of them much to do with making war. The first, in Mirsky's time long in the past, was political activity, and kingmaking in particular. It was they who had put Catherine the Great on the throne in 1762, a coup that incorporated assassinating her husband Peter III. In 1801 they assassinated Emperor Paul I, but then in 1825 they were on the losing side as leaders of the Decembrist revolt, when five of the six ringleaders to be hanged were

Guards officers, one of them Pavel Pestel, a man profoundly admired by Mirsky, as we have seen. The second vaunted accomplishment of the Guards was dissipation among the aristocrats who officered them. The tone had been set just before Mirsky's time by the bisexual Grand Duke Sergey Alexandrovich; the uncle of Nicholas II and at one time his regimental commander, he was a titanic drinker who expected the officers' mess to follow him in ritualized debauchery. It was probably during his stint in the peacetime army that Mirsky's drinking became habitual.

It must be said, though, that this side of the Guards officers' activities has been exaggerated.[64] These men were as a group no more debauched or bone-headed than, say, the literary intelligentsia, the clergy, or the peasantry; there is no evidence apart from accumulated hearsay to suggest that their cultural level was any lower, and a good deal to suggest that it was if anything higher. The most influential view of all this in Russia outside military circles was articulated by Tolstoy in a characteristic tirade in his last big novel, *Resurrection* (1899):

Military service in general depraves men, placing those who go in for it into conditions of complete idleness, that is, the absence of rational and useful work, and freeing them from common human obligations, in place of which it holds out the conventional honour of the regiment, the uniform, and the colours, and on the one hand unlimited power over other people and on the other slavish deference to superior officers. But when to this depravity of military service in general, with its honour of the uniform and the colours, and its permissive attitude towards violence and murder, are added the depravity of wealth and close relations with the Tsar's family—as happens in the élite Guards regiments, in which only wealthy and exalted officers serve—then in men who are subjected to it this depravity attains a condition of total egotistical insanity.[65]

Tolstoy himself was a great aristocrat, of course, and he had been on active service as an officer in the Crimea; but the view of the military he puts forward here as a veteran was standard among literary circles, Nikolay Gumilyov being the only well-known exception in Mirsky's time.[66] The most trenchant expression of it in the period after the Japanese war was Kuprin's novel *The Duel* (1905), 'when all radical Russia was united in exulting over the defeats of the Imperial Army'.[67]

In 1913, Mirsky retired to the reserve, and went back to university; in his own words, he 'began to prepare for the state examinations in the Faculty of History and Philology (Department of Classics), having obtained permission to take the examination as an external student. In May 1914 I passed the examination and received a proposal from Professor Rostovtsev to stay on at the University.'[68] This was the customary way of becoming a university teacher in Imperial Russia, and Mirsky would doubtless have done so if the First World War had not intervened. The professor concerned was Russia's greatest ancient historian.[69]

Mirsky was to spend ten years of his life as a professional university teacher, but unlike his mentor Vengerov and his schoolmate Viktor Zhirmunsky he was never a professor, nor even a specialized academic, much less an Academician. He never published any textual, bibliographical, or philological work; he was always a practical critic with a primary interest in current literary events.

MIRSKY THE POET

Mirsky was based in or near St Petersburg from the autumn of 1907 until the outbreak of the First World War.[70] He evidently moved in literary circles at this most complicated and creative of times, and he published a collection of lyrics in 1911, the year he left the university for the army. In terms of the received version of the history of Russian poetry, as first authoritatively set out for English readers many years ago by Mirsky and restated many times since, this year is on the cusp of the transition in Russian modernist aesthetics from Symbolism to Acmeism and also Futurism, a shift in poets' aspirations from striving for the infinite to capturing the finite, from neo-romanticism to neo-classicism, from aspiring to the condition of music to exploiting the wordiness of words, from obsession with the metaphysical to concentration on the physical.[71]

Mirsky's collection bears the simple title *Stikhotvoreniya 1906–1910*, 'Shorter Poems 1906–1910'.[72] On the title-page the author is given the abbreviated form of his title and his full double-barrelled surname, 'Kn. D. Svyatopolk-Mirsky'; the place of publication is given, 'S.-Peterburg', but no publisher. To say that Mirsky's book was a private publication is not to denigrate it; practically all the collections published in Russia at this time by living poets (apart from absolutely the most eminent, like Blok) were financed by one well-wisher or another and appeared in tiny print runs.

Mirsky must have felt enough confidence in the book to send out review copies of it; one of them came into the hands of Nikolay Gumilyov. Still in his middle 20s, only four years older than Mirsky, Gumilyov was in the process of establishing himself as the leading critic of current poetry, and his pushiness was resented by older figures such as Vyacheslav Ivanov, Valery Bryusov, and Aleksandr Blok. Gumilyov was one of the principal driving forces behind the launch of the monthly journal of the arts *Apollo* in October 1909; it was to last until 1917 as the premier literary periodical of Mirsky's youth.[73] Looked at nowadays, it appears much less glamorous than it must have seemed at the time. It was printed on stoutish paper in a page size unusually broad for its height, and from the start it featured abundant illustrations, at first monochrome; from about the middle of 1911 it blossoms into genuinely glorious colour. Gumilyov's contributions are placed right at the back of the issues they appear in, coming after the informative surveys of the cultural scene all over Europe (with particular attention to Germany). Gumilyov used the general rubric 'Letters on Russian Poetry'. In the eighteenth of them, the first part of which appeared in the April issue for 1911, on the very last page opposite the contents list, Mirsky's little book is mentioned. Gumilyov deals with twenty books in this piece. He dismisses Modest Druzhinin and K. E. Antonov as non-starters, and then divides the rest of the batch into the amateurs, the insolent, and the real writers. Mirsky comes under the first category:

As one reads [Prince Svyatopolk-Mirsky's poems] one begins to wonder whether the author really intended to narrow his horizon to this extent, to reject all piquant emotion and stimulating images, and to select only the most inexpressive epithets so that nothing might divert his mind from the smooth succession of finely chiselled and full-sounding stanzas. It's as if he is still afraid to admit to himself that he is a poet; for the time being I have no desire to make more bold than he does.[74]

This sort of superior attitude will appear in Mirsky's own critical writing in Russian. Anyway, Gumilyov eventually gets to the 'real writers'. Among others about whom most later canon-makers would agree, they include Igor Severyanin, Vasily Kamensky, Velemir Khlebnikov, Benedikt Lifshits, Ilya Erenburg—and Marina Tsvetaeva; Gumilyov here discusses her first collection, *Evening Album*, self-published like Mirsky's. This was the first time that their names were linked on the record.

Mirsky never listed his book of poems among his publications. Oral legend says that soon after he had published his review, Gumilyov met Mirsky on the street in Tsarskoe and observed, echoing the conventional literary man's contempt for the soldier: 'Not bad for a Guards officer.' At that Mirsky is supposed to have sent one of his father's footmen round the bookshops to retrieve any copies that might have escaped the attention of the reading public, and commit them to the flames.

Mirsky was steeped in a culture where graphomania is almost as besetting a disease as alcoholism, and manifests itself more often than not in iambic tetrameter quatrains with alternating rhyme. But he had the critical self-knowledge to understand that he was not a poet 'by the will of God', as the Russians say; since he could never stand the second-rate, he stopped writing the stuff altogether, unlike countless thousands of his countrymen. He really did merit the tribute Marina Tsvetaeva paid him fifteen years later when she singled him out as a shining exception among the dolts who broke her rule: 'The first obligation of the critic is not to write bad poetry himself—or at least, not to publish it.'[75]

Mirsky's collection is actually a polished, thoroughly accomplished performance. Its seventy-four pages are exquisitely typeset and printed on thick creamy paper. The poems are divided into three sections: first come 'Elegies', of which there are twenty-eight; then 'Miscellaneous Poems', of which there are eleven; and finally, there are five 'Odes'. Nothing is reprinted from the poems published in the school almanacs of 1906–7, but four previously unpublished poems in the book are dated to these years, and they are the only pieces that carry a date. It remains a mystery, therefore, as to whether Mirsky was writing poetry steadily between then and the date of his collection, or whether the bulk of the collection is the result of a burst of creativity, around 1910 or any other year; the content of the poems gives no clue, floating as it does above chronological time, and sited for the most part somewhere in abstract space. The poems employ a wide array of forms, never using exactly the same metrical structure twice, except in the case of the half-dozen sonnets; this is the hallmark of Mirsky's indebtedness in matters of form, shared with every other Russian poet (real and would-be) of his generation, to the reigning Moscow magus, Bryusov, a ruthlessly systematic devotee of formal experimentation.

The themes of Mirsky's poetry, and particularly the elegies in the first section, stand as a copybook example of belated second-rate Symbolist verse, almost a parody of it, especially the aspect of it that aims to recapture certain aspects of Romanticism after the Realist domination of Russian literature of the mid- to late nineteenth century. The very first poem in the book strikes the keynote: self-indulgent contemplation of misunderstood personal emotions. It is a lament about the futility of writing, since nobody will understand or take notice, and the poet will therefore be doomed to nurse his melancholy (*toska*) as he suffers alone, baited by the philistine crowd. There are some poems in the book about being in love with love itself (including 'I pine, but for whom I know not, / I love, but I know not whom'). When an object for the poet's yearning is found, she—the object is always grammatically female—soon leaves him, and the teenaged Mirsky responds with a series of moping complaints about lost love; nobody can be surprised to discover that the beloved was only ever glimpsed from afar as an incarnation of divine beauty.

It would not be difficult to poke fun at the entire book in similar vein, but there are some things in it apart from the formal polish that indicate the author's precocious literary awareness and self-confidence. In his critical writings Mirsky pointed out several times that, among other things, the late nineteenth-century revival of poetry in Russia brought with it a renewed cosmopolitanism, and his own collection bears ample witness to this tendency. It comes as no surprise to find epigraphs from Ariosto and Dante; less standard is Millevoye; but nobody now remembers the Pole Niesecki, from whom Mirsky takes an epigraph for the last poem in the book. All these epigraphs are given, needless to say, in the original languages. Shamelessly for a teenager, Mirsky also takes epigraphs from Baratynsky and Pushkin. But he goes further afield. His study of Oriental culture, however strongly refracted through Bryusov it may be, is reflected in a neat series of tankas, in the lyric invoking Buddha (complete with epigraph in Sanskrit), and in the impressive sonnet to India that stands as the penultimate poem in the book.

The poem about Mirsky's family history that was cited earlier is not the only one where he seems to be taking things very seriously. Two other poems merit attention. 'Narcissus' is a plangent declaration of the essentially self-sufficient nature of Mirsky's personality, the contentment with solitary aesthetic contemplation that was evident for much of his life; its final stanza asserts:

> I shall not tarry here for nymph or goddess;
> Alone, and happy with myself, I'll love
> Naught but the play of line, so magic-pure,
> In underwater mirror depths.[76]

The other poem that is of particular significance presents the earliest expression in Mirsky's writings of an attitude that seems to underlie the crucial events of his life. He aspired to be a person for whom thought and action were one, and the poem illuminates his motivation for taking the particular sides he did, with the momentous and ultimately fatal consequences that flowed from them. The poem is sub-Lermontovian in its juvenile rage and pity about a world lapsed from ancient grandeur and heroism. The epigraph is from *The Fountain of Bakhchisarai*.

> I regret that in the forgotten chamber
> Grows the desert grass. (Pushkin)

> I do regret—the Throne once lofty
> We neither dread nor worship now,
> That earth possesses no Great Mogul,
> That shallowness has won the day;
> Regret there is no limping Timur,
> That Macedonian phalange
> Will not repeat its puissant deeds;
> That once attained, accomplishment
> Leads not to other victories,
> That to our age, sober and frigid,
> Our fathers' course is risible,
> Our grandsires have no path to show,
> The wood of prejudice has been felled,
> That limits are there none, nor closures.
> And I regret that dust of greatness
> Sleeps on in unregarded urns,
> That in the buskin of the tragic
> The ancient player does not stride,
> That Zeus is gone, and gone Isida,
> That pyramids we build no more,
> That Iliads we write no longer,
> That common sense and sober view
> Have cracked the elemental spell,
> That plough can turn up naught but dust
> Where once the steppe grass used to grow.
> That up from Nineveh's cold ashes

> Will not arise amidst a tempest
> The unthroned shadow of the kings.[77]

The young poet is plaintively looking for something big enough to be worth serving. Eventually, he found it; and paid the price.

POETRY CIRCLES

For most of the time he was in the peacetime army, Mirsky was stationed in Tsarskoe Selo, where Pushkin had been one of the first intake of pupils in the lycée that had been opened in a wing of the imperial palace in 1811. Pushkin and the other poets who were his schoolmates and friends, the principal one among them Delvig, founded the tradition of 'Tsarskoe poetry': elegant, classically poised, and often elegiac musings in the setting of equally elegant palaces and parks, the latter dotted with reflecting ponds on which white swans glide, but all this intermingled with a genuine rusticity where cows crossed the path of cuirassiers. After the events of 1905, the imperial family spent hardly any time in the Winter Palace, preferring the safe seclusion of Tsarskoe; they only emerged on any significant scale for the Romanov tercentenary celebrations in 1913.

In Mirsky's time the local literary tradition was being renewed and extended by some poets who had come to live there.[78] First to take up residence was the classicizing—but described by Mirsky as 'quite disconcertingly free from any kinship with antiquity'[79]—Innokenty Annensky (1856–1909), who was headmaster of the *gimnaziya* at Tsarskoe before he moved on to become an inspector of schools. Nikolay Gumilyov lived in Tsarskoe with his family from 1887 to 1896, and was a pupil at Annensky's school from 1903; afterwards he stayed put, except for his Sorbonne period (1903–6). Anna Akhmatova's family settled in Tsarskoe in 1890, and the poet lived there until she was 16, when her parents divorced and she spent two years in Ukraine with her mother, returning then to Tsarskoe. She lived there as Gumilyov's wife from 1910 to 1916, with time out in Paris in spring 1911 and Italy in spring 1912, and made return visits for the rest of her long life.

Mirsky was observed in Tsarskoe by Sergey Makovsky, the editor of *Apollo*, the journal that had printed Gumilyov's review of his poetry. Makovsky saw him as 'a stately and handsome dark-haired man in the raspberry-red shirt and kaftan of His Imperial Majesty's sharpshooters'. He would amaze people with displays of his phenomenal memory for geographical facts and the biographies of famous people (the fruit of his youthful reading and the game of writing down the names of great persons):

He would be stubbornly silent, and then suddenly for no reason he'd blurt out: 'When was Ivan Moneybag born?'[80] 'What is the capital of the Sandwich Islands?'[81] He made an argumentative display of his monarchist views. Once when he was having dinner with me and some military men, every time the Sovereign's name was mentioned, Svyatopolk-Mirsky would leap up from his chair and stand to attention, and then silently lower himself back into his seat. . . . After dinner I had to put in a friendly plea with him to desist in future from these protestations of loyalty.[82]

In this episode, as in so many others in Mirsky's life, it may be suspected that the accompaniment of alcohol to his extravagant behaviour is more than incidental.

Makovsky's memoirs attest that Mirsky was often in the company of Count Vasily Komarovsky (1881–1914), who was considered by many authoritative observers to be the most talented writer of his generation (which included Blok and Bely, both born in 1880), and to epitomize the renewed Tsarskoe tradition in poetry. Like Mirsky, he was the son of a high-ranking official from an aristocratic family with roots in Poland and had been at the lycée in Moscow. Since the late 1890s, after the death of his father, Komarovsky had lived quietly in Tsarskoe with his aunt; like Mirsky he left the University of St Petersburg without taking a degree. He published a slim volume of poetry in 1913. Komarovsky was mentally unstable. He committed suicide in a Moscow mental hospital a month after war broke out, on 8/21 September 1914. Mirsky later wrote that 'he died from the nervous shock produced by the outbreak of the war'.[83] For the tenth anniversary of his death Mirsky published a memorial article about him.[84] It includes an eloquent passage in which Mirsky could almost entirely be talking about himself:

It is not difficult to explain Komarovsky in terms of cultural and literary history. He came from a different milieu from all the other literary and cultural figures of the last sixty years. The scion of an ancient Moscow–Petersburg noble dynasty with extensive kin and a strong family tradition, he was absolutely unmarked by intelligentsia culture. His cultural soil was compounded from family legends, an old-fashioned upbringing that was more French than Russian, his grandfather's ancient library that he talks about so well in his dying poem 'Raksha', and finally and very likely most important, a fund of anecdotes concerning diplomacy, high society, and the court, with a sturdy genealogical basis, and all heard at first hand—an unmediated tradition going right back to the eighteenth century.

Komarovsky is known to have taken some part in the meetings of the most serious literary-academic grouping in prewar Petersburg, the Society of Enthusiasts of the Artistic Word (*Obshchestvo revnitelei khudozhestvennogo slova*), which brought together mainly contributors to *Apollo*, and met at the editorial office of the journal overlooking the Moika. This grouping is sometimes known colloquially as 'Vyacheslav Ivanov's Academy of Verse', partly because it was a formalized development of some private lectures Ivanov delivered in his apartment in 1909 (the 'Pro-Academy'). The original audience consisted of three poets who had asked Ivanov (and also Annensky and Voloshin) to instruct them in verse technique. They were all a bit older than Mirsky, and their later lives exemplify the post-revolutionary options: Count Aleksey Niko- laevich Tolstoy (1882–1945), Pyotr Potyomkin (1886–1926), and the poet we last met as a critic, Nikolay Gumilyov. Tolstoy emigrated, then 'changed land- marks' and made a spectacular return to Russia in 1923, becoming the most high-born figure in the Soviet literary establishment; he remained inviolate, a shocking exception to the rule about 'former' people in the new society. There are many anecdotes about him, such as the one where his servant tells a caller that 'His Highness has deigned to depart for the Supreme Soviet'. He is remembered now, if at all, for once having his face slapped by Osip Man- delshtam. From the many references to his work in Mirsky's critical writings, it is clear that Mirsky despised Tolstoy as a talented but brainless opportunist. Potyomkin was the leading satirical poet of prewar Petersburg; he emigrated and died in Paris. Gumilyov returned to Russia from his military service abroad in 1918, and was shot for counter-revolutionary activity three years later.

For a short time in the spring of 1909, Vladimir Alekseevich Pyast (Pestovsky, 1886–1940) was involved in the group. In his indispensable memoirs, Pyast recorded that 'Many beginning poets came to these meetings'.[85] Andrey Bely presented his statistical analysis of the Russian iambic tetrame- ter (which he had devised as an antidote to insomnia) to the Society on 18 Feb- ruary 1910.[86] And most resoundingly, it was to a meeting of the Society that Vyacheslav Ivanov delivered his keynote paper on the 'crisis of symbolism' on 26 March 1910.[87] The precise membership of this group and its proceedings have not been investigated in detail; there are only fragmentary accounts.[88] Mandelshtam attended some meetings, and so did the prose writer Remizov.

The most serious activities of the society were dominated by younger men who were by calling literary scholars rather than writers; there was a certain amount of cross-membership with Vengerov's Pushkin seminar. Nikolay Vladimirovich Nedobrovo (1882 or 1884–1919), like Mirsky, came from Kharkov; he shook off the stigma of the provinces and made himself into the epitome of suave Petersburg stylishness after he came up to the university. When he graduated he took a job in the office of the Duma; and he became a member of the 'Presidium' of the Society. He was a close friend of Akhma- tova and was the dedicatee not only of several of her best-known early lyrics but also of the Tsarskoe selo section of her *Poem without a Hero*. He died of tuberculosis rather than meeting the violent end that his date of death would suggest. Two of Nedobrovo's Kharkov schoolmates are of particular interest from the point of view of Mirsky's acquaintanceship. One was Boris Anrep, who consolidated their friendship when he entered the Faculty of Law at St Petersburg University in 1905. Nedobrovo several times invited to Petersburg another Kharkov schoolmate, Aleksandr Ivanovich Beletsky (1884–1961), who was to become a Soviet academician.

Of the other known members of the Society, we have already encountered

Sergey Auslender as one of Kuzmin's *gimnaziya* boys. Mirsky's schoolmate Viktor Zhirmunsky was also headed for the Soviet Academy; Vasily Gippius was never so prominent after 1917. And there were two other friends of Akhmatova in the Society, the verse theorist Valerian Chudovsky (18??–19??), and the art historian Nikolay Punin (1888–1953), who published a serious essay about Komarovsky in *Apollo*. Punin eventually became Akhmatova's third husband, in which capacity he was arrested; like her son by Gumilyov, he survived the camps. By the time the war came the Society had fifty-seven members, and in view of his links with so many of them, it is almost impossible to believe that Mirsky was not one of them. Indeed, in the latter phases some of the sessions were chaired by Mirsky's teachers F. F. Zelinsky and M. I. Rostovtsev. However, no precise information has yet been made public about Mirsky's contribution, if any, to the activities of this group,[89] which was one contributory element in what later became the Petersburg wing of Russian Formalism. When he wrote a concise c.v. for Sir Bernard Pares before taking up his job at the School of Slavonic Studies, Mirsky stated that he had written a work on Russian versification, which he described as 'unpublished and lost in the Civil War';[90] a concern with this subject was prominent among the younger literary intellectuals of the capital at this time, and the text of this lost work would have provided important evidence of Mirsky's ideas and literary allegiances during his formative period.

It has also been asserted[91] that Mirsky took part in the activities of the first 'Guild of Poets' (*Tsekh poetov*) which was founded by Gumilyov and Gorodetsky. According to Anna Akhmatova, who served as secretary, the Guild had about fifteen meetings between November 1911 and April 1912, when the Gumilyovs left for Italy; and then about ten meetings between October 1912 and April 1913.[92] No documentary evidence of Mirsky's participation has ever come to light.[93] Mirsky stopped being a poet precisely when the Guild began, no doubt at least in part because of Gumilyov's review. But there can be equally little doubt that Mirsky's critical stance was shaped by Gumilyov to a greater degree than by any other single contemporary.

In 1929, without mentioning himself personally, Mirsky once pinpointed the mentality of the post-symbolist generation to which he belonged, and which had found its pioneering self-definitions in the attitudes of Kuzmin and Gumilyov:

On the eve of the Revolution a second generation of 'modernists' was growing, more bohemian than bourgeois, less sophisticated and freer from the influence of Dostoevsky, free also from all *fin-de-siècle* æstheticism, and, for the most part, from all ideas and philosophies. This younger generation was only to come to maturity after 1917.[94]

These post-symbolist 'freedoms from' were the basis of that liberal and humanitarian agnosticism that among other things enabled Mirsky to write, in emigration, a history of Russian literature that has lasted so many years. But in due course he came to believe that, in clearing away the enthusiasms and false gods of the preceding generation, he and his contemporaries had left a vacuum at the centre where some sort of comprehensive and integral world-view used to be sited, a space they filled with various kinds of what Mirsky eventually referred to as 'formalism'. For him there was no way forward (or backward) to the refilling of this vacuum with a view based on Christianity or any other idealist system. In the late 1920s Mirsky constructed his Marxism in this space. He had a long way to go before he got to this point. In the last few years before war broke out, he managed to combine soldiering with his literary interests. And then in 1914, literature, culture, and agonizing about world-views were forced into the background for seven long and eventful years.

3 Two Armies

One should have become a Bolshevik in 1912, or else have been born ten years later. (D. S. Mirsky to P. P. Suvchinsky, 1929)

THE GREAT WAR

In 1928, just before he revised his intellectual values and declared himself a Marxist, Mirsky set down the most trenchant version of several assessments he expressed in print about Russia's part in the war of 1914–18:

[The 1914–18] War passed over Russia almost unnoticed by the Russian mind. Russia did not live the War; she only submitted to it until, weary of submission, she ended by revolting against it. The War, in the case of Russia, is of importance only as the immediate cause of the Revolution. It was neither a national nor a popular war. It was imposed on the nation by an irresponsible minority. The professional soldier, in so far as he survived the first hecatombs, though incompetently led, fought, as he had always fought, heroically, and the mobilised peasant, under the pressure of ancestral traditions of obedience, showed much passive heroism, accepting conscription and the War as an inevitable calamity of the natural order. But the bourgeoisie excelled only in the art of avoiding the front, while a large part of the intellectual élite were conscientious objectors and *défaitistes*.[1]

This is a considered view that so far as it goes would command a good deal of general assent among historians of all factions writing in the late twentieth century.[2] Writing elsewhere at the same time, Mirsky also said that the upper classes at first accepted the war with enthusiasm '(which, except in the case of families with military traditions, was not accompanied by any readiness for self-sacrifice)'.[3] What Mirsky thought in 1914, as an upper-class man from a military family who was simultaneously one of the professional soldiers facing the hecatombs and a member of the intellectual élite, was probably more complicated.

Mirsky rejoined his regiment as soon as war was declared.[4] In an official context he once stated that he had spent a total of three years eight months in the Imperial army and ended up as a captain.[5] Germany declared war on Russia on 1 August 1914, so this would mean that Mirsky served in his first fighting army until the end of March 1918.

The most widely documented incident Mirsky was involved in during this time took place away from the front: his short-lived marriage, which came about as a result of his being wounded. No information has yet come to light about what kind of wound it was and where and how it was sustained. But it cannot have been very serious. Mirsky's death certificate in his GULag file indicates that he carried a scar, but that it was on his right thumb. However, as a result of being wounded Mirsky did apparently spend some time in hospital, and during that time he married one of the nurses. The only particulars that seem to have survived about this woman, astonishingly, are in Mirsky's NKVD file, and there only her name and date of birth appear. She was called Vera Flerinova and she was born in Kharkov in 1891; so perhaps the acquaintance was struck up on the basis of the Kharkov connection, or Mirsky was sent back home to convalesce and was nursed by local women. Vera Traill related what she knew about Mirsky's marriage:

Yes, when he was drunk during the war—he was a young officer, and he got married to some nurse or other, and later he couldn't remember it at all—he said she was called Natasha or Pasha or something . . . they lived together for a fortnight, then they got divorced and he had nothing further to do with her, and he never got married again.

That Mirsky had once been married was known to his closer friends. Mirsky told Baron Meyendorff about it in London, and Meyendorff repeated the story to Beatrice Webb, who summarized:

According to Meyendorff Mirsky is a born rebel and fanatic. As a young officer in the Guards he refused to drink the Czar's health and was dismissed the regiment; had an interval of university life, joined up in the war and distinguished himself for bravery . . . During the war he was married for six weeks; but separated from his wife, and 'forgot to mention his marriage to his mother'—altogether a strange character with a Russian strain of mysticism and romance.[6]

In what order the principal events related here actually occurred is hard to disentangle. In his autobiographical statement of 1936 Mirsky offers some detail: 'mobilized at the beginning of the imperialist war and was on the German front until the summer of 1916, then on the Caucasian front, where I remained until demobilization in the spring of 1918. In the winter of 1916–17 I underwent preparatory training at the military academy in Petrograd.'[7]

Not surprisingly, Mirsky says nothing here about being disgraced. This incident, whatever it was, probably took place in August 1916, and this was the reason why Mirsky was sent to the Caucasus.[8] Edmund Wilson recorded two versions of what happened, without giving any source for his information. In the first, Mirsky refused to drink the health of the Tsar, declaring that he never drank to people he did not know; and in the other he is supposed to have declared: 'I refuse to drink to that idiot!'[9] In his book of 1927 Mirsky gave a crisp account of the political circumstances in which his act of disrespect, if any, would have taken place; it was clearly more than an isolated personal outburst:

[Under] the influence of the tremendous reverses of 1915 [the upper classes] grew uneasy and began to demand responsible government. They obtained at first a few concessions, but when the German advance was stopped the policy of reconciliation was discontinued. The Government had no confidence in the administrative qualities of the upper classes, and these definitely assumed an attitude of opposition. At the same time, the imperial household began to emancipate itself from the Goverment. The Empress Alexandra, obsessed by the idea of the right divine of the autocrat, urged her husband to display his autocracy with more energy. Both the Emperor and Empress were totally incompetent persons, and were easily influenced by various sinister personages, first of whom was the Siberian hypnotist, Rasputin, whom they regarded as a saint. In these conditions their personal policy, opposed by all the more or less sensible and responsible members of the bureaucracy, soon began to verge on insanity. The upper classes were terrified and began to consider the possibility of a *coup d'état.*[10]

So there would appear to be nothing unusual among people of Mirsky's social circle in a disrespectful attitude to the Tsar. And it seems quite clear that at Makovsky's table in Tsarskoe before the war he was deliberately guying his real views, unless he was simply drunk. Whatever Mirsky actually said about the Tsar, and whatever punishment might have resulted, he was soon reinstated, and he went on to the Academy of the General Staff like his father before him, passing out in January 1917.

Mirsky was thus one of the very last staff officers to qualify before the fall of the monarchy, which took place when Nicholas II abdicated on 2 March 1917. The Academy had been closed on the outbreak of war in 1914, to the dismay of the *genshtabisty,* and reopened in the summer of 1916, when the shortage of staff officers became acute. It now offered only accelerated courses, but as in the case of Mirsky's father, selection for them came in recognition of outstanding ability and promise, and a reward for distinguished service.[11]

THE REVOLUTIONS

The majority of the military élite were opposed to the old regime and not prepared to fight for it, notwithstanding their oath of allegiance. Otherwise, the House of Romanov would not have fallen. After the February revolution Mirsky seems to have been well away from the military actions that followed, which took place on what for the Russians was their western front. First came the offensive against the Germans initiated by Kerensky as a token that post-revolutionary Russia was not going to pull out of the Great War, which ended up in the rout of the Russian army at Tarnopol on 15 July 1917; then came the attempted *putsch* by General Kornilov in August; and finally, the dis-integration of the army's morale in the late summer and autumn of 1917, fertilizing it for the Bolshevik agitation that encouraged the peasant soldiers to desert and make their way home to claim the land.

The most explicit statement Mirsky ever made about Lenin's seizure of power in October 1917 was written for an anti-Bolshevik publication in England in 1922, one of numerous disdainful passages on this subject in his writings at about this time; characteristically, it appeals to literary sources as a representation of contemporary thinking:

The immediate reaction of the Bolshevik Revolution on [sic] the great majority of thinking Russians was a feeling of disgust and despair. Most of us then sympathised with Voloshin when he prayed that Russia should cease to exist, divided between the Germans and the Japanese, and with Merezhkovsky when he exclaimed in his usual hysterical way: 'We are children cursed by our mother and ourselves cursing her.'[12]

Mirsky changed his mind about this during the course of the 1920s; by 1927 he referred to the Bolsheviks as the 'logical end' of the Revolution, adding that 'the Left-wing Socialists, the Bolsheviks, the only party who promised the people what they wanted, were also the only party led by men who understood the nature of revolutionary government'.[13]

In his autobiographical statement of 1936 Mirsky asserted that when in June 1918 he went back to Kharkov it was from Transcaucasia. The clearest statement he ever made for publication about what happened to him after Staff College occurs in a context so obscure that it has gone completely unnoticed. Here, Mirsky says that he spent the winter of 1917–18 in 'the Turkish town of Erzerum', adding: 'It was a terrible time; the Russian front had already collapsed, and we, the remainder of the Russian Army in Armenia, were waiting in suspense and inactivity for the inevitable end.'[14] When the army finally did disintegrate, Mirsky made his way back to Giyovka. Though he went there from Armenia, in making for the south of Russia he was part of a mass exodus as the upper classes of old Russia fled from the Bolshevik-dominated north. He was very lucky to have had somewhere to go to beyond the precarious but decidedly inimical jurisdiction of the new government.

Soon after he emigrated, Mirsky published an account of the political situation of the Ukraine at this time which includes a lucid explanation of the long-term history that led up to it. This is the most impressive piece of expository prose on a non-literary subject that he ever wrote, especially in view of the labyrinthine complexity of the issues involved. The crisp style and precise military detail, and the thoroughly top-down approach—with outstanding men making considered decisions on big strategic issues that lead rationally to the intended consequences or are thwarted by the superior designs of yet more outstanding men or the failures of those men who are not up to leadership—suggest that behind it lies Mirsky's training as a staff officer, or at least the qualities that commended him for training as such. Here is his account of the events just before he went back to Giyovka:

The Ukrainian Rada was upheld by a certain number of enthusiastic Ukrainophiles, by a few adventurers who were playing an anti-Bolshevik card, and by non-political officers who thought it their duty to oppose Bolshevism at all costs. . . . The campaign was very short. In the beginning of February 1918, after ten days' bombardment, Kiev was taken by the Bolsheviks, the Ukrainian Rada and their staffs escaping to Zhitomir. There ensued a terrible massacre, the victims of which were mostly officers of the Russian army who had taken no part in the hostilities. Similar events occurred in all the other provinces of South Russia (the massacres were especially horrible in the seaports of the Crimea), and all the local Governments were swept away. In Bessarabia alone the Bolsheviks were unsuccessful; the Rumanians, with the connivance of the Austro-Germans, seized the opportunity of laying hands on this province. The Rada, on escaping to Zhitomir, turned for help to the Germans; and a treaty was signed, by the terms of which the Central Powers recognised the independence of Ukraina and pledged themselves to support the Rada in its struggle against the Bolsheviks. In return for this the Rada was to submit to a military occupation of the whole Ukrainian territory, and the Germans received the right to export as much grain and other products as they required. The Bolsheviks had also, by the treaty of Brest, recognised the independence of Ukraina. But they had instituted an Ukrainian Soviet Government, nominally independent, which continued hostilities against the Rada and their allies, the Austro-Germans. The campaign of General Eichhorn against the Soviet Ukrainians was very short and easy. In the beginning of March 1918, Kiev was occupied by the Germans, and by the end of April the whole territory of Ukraina was clear of Red troops. In this campaign all the work was done by the Germans, the Ukrainian troops playing a purely ornamental part; from a military point of view they were negligible. Thus did 'Independent Ukraina' come into existence.[15]

This was the situation, with the Reds temporarily in abeyance, that enabled Mirsky to make his way back to the family estate.

Typically, he did not waste his time there. In the autumn of 1918 Mirsky took some sort of degree in history at Kharkov University; by his late 20s he had thus acquired formal academic qualifications in classics and history, neither of which subjects he ever taught. A few references in his writings reflect the short penultimate period he spent near or in his birthplace. During 1918, the city of Kharkov—'so grey' for Chekhov's dreary characters of 1889 but soon to become stark Red, then White, then Red again—was, albeit always in second place to Kiev, an important cultural centre, as people crowded into it from the north. In particular, it was a focus of Futurist activity in literature and the arts. At some time in 1918 Ilya Erenburg was there.[16] Mirsky knew about the 'Poetry Studio' that was started in Kharkov in 1918 by Erenburg and Georgy Shengeli,[17] and he knew Erenburg's novel *The Face of War* before it was published; he can only have seen it in Kharkov in 1918.[18] It must also have been at this time that Mirsky saw the manuscript of Beletsky's book on nineteenth-century women writers in Russian literature.[19]

Mirsky gave the following account of what caused him and his family to move on:

Petlura and Vinnichenko [the heads of the 'Directory' that succeeded the Rada as the government of independent Ukraine] were now nominally in control of all Ukraina, but their position was precarious. The Russian White Armies of Denikin and Krasnov did not recognize them, and were extending over the south-east, occupying the mining country and North Taurida. The policy of the French, who had occupied Odessa, was ambiguous. In the fight between the Ukrainians and Whites, which gave Odessa to Denikin, they remained neutral. Makhno and other 'banditti' were independent and unreliable. But the principal danger was from the north; the Bolsheviks were steadily advancing on the heels of the Germans, not molesting these, but always victorious (if one can be victorious over an enemy that never accepted battle) over the Ukrainians. They had occupied Kharkov by New Year 1919, and restored the puppet Government of Soviet Ukraina under Rakovsky.[20]

WHITE VERSUS RED

During his first interrogation after he was arrested in 1937 Mirsky made the following statement about his service in the White Army:

I served in the Kubansk Cavalry Corps. With this Corps I took part in the following battles against the Reds: in the Rovenkov region in March and April 1919, then in the Zadonsk steppe, the Velikoknyazheskaya region, and towards Tsaritsyn in May and April of that year. After these battles I was transferred to May-Maevsky's Corps, continuing to serve on the staffs of the 1st and then the 3rd Divisions during the battles in the Lgov and Oryol areas.

The only person I have ever talked to who mentioned discussing with Mirsky his service in the Civil War was Janko Lavrin, and it was this last episode that he remembered Mirsky talking about; Lavrin said Mirsky was the Chief of Staff at the battle of Oryol. Mirsky's account to his NKVD interrogator 1937 continues:

In October 1919 I was transferred to the staff of the 9th Division, located at Nezhin, and I took part in battles near Nezhin and on the retreat to Cherkassy. In Cherkassy I contracted typhus. After recovering I went to Tiraspol, where I joined up with the staff of the Division, with which I retreated to Gusyatino (the Polish border). In Gusyatino, General Bredov's detachment, of which the 10th Division was a part, was disarmed and by agreement with the White Army command was directed to a concentration camp in Poznań prior to the dispatch of the detachment to Vrangel's army.[21]

The fact that Mirsky joined Denikin's army in March 1919 means that he was not by any means one of the original volunteers for the armed struggle against the Bolsheviks, which had been going on in earnest for over a year by the time he joined up. And he was equally not part of the first efforts in the emigration to mobilize public opinion against the new regime in Russia, which was undertaken by people like the Williamses who emigrated as soon as the Bolsheviks took power. Internal and external counter-revolution had taken shape during the winter of 1917–18, while Mirsky was still in the Caucasus.[22]

The generals who had been detained after the Kornilov affair escaped and made their way south, believing that the best place to organize an army against the Bolsheviks would be the territory of the Don Cossacks.[23] General Alekseev, who had been Supreme Commander of the Russian army under the Provisional Government, arrived in Novocherkassk on 2 November 1917. General Denikin, who had commanded the western and south-western fronts, arrived there at the end of November. General Kornilov arrived on 6 December. Volunteers continued to arrive, running the Bolshevik gauntlet, drawn south by the presence of their former commanders on the Don.

The relations between these quarrelsome fighting generals were not easy, and their relations with the leading anti-Bolshevik politicians who turned up on the Don were also frustrating and counterproductive. Organizing and equipping a new army in the context of the hostility of the vast majority of the surrounding population, of whom a bare majority were in any recognizable sense Russians, was difficult from every point of view. If at the start the Volunteers had some idea about what they were going to fight against, they never could agree about what they were fighting for. The British and French military missions arrived in the south from Moscow in late December, their task to try and ensure that at least some Russian troops stayed in the war against Germany. By Christmas Day 1917 Kornilov had emerged as overall commander. But by February 1918 his army numbered no more than 4,000 men. The fundamental attitude among them as this army coalesced was that Bolshevism and the Germans were equally detestable, and that the former were in the pay of the latter. But the Whites had nothing like the strength necessary to engage the German army, which almost casually expanded its zone of occupation into the Crimea and the Ukraine while armistice talks with the Bolsheviks were going on at Brest-Litovsk.

Mirsky seems to have lain low for as long as he decently could after he got out of the old army. His move south in December 1918 from Kharkov to the Crimea was part of a further mass exodus by the old upper classes before the oncoming Reds. Mikhail Bulgakov's play *Flight* offers a terrifying but also grotesque picture of these events. Vladimir Nabokov's family took the same way out as Mirsky's, and in his *Speak, Memory* the novelist gave a rose-tinted account of the situation in the Crimea at the time Mirsky was there. But Mirsky, who was nine years older than Nabokov, was of an age then to participate in some of the critical actions of the war; and in fact, he was on hand when the 'rising line' of counter-revolution peaked.

In 1925 Mirsky gave the following dispassionate summary of the events he was involved in:

The civil wars, which lasted almost exactly three years (from the 'October'—old style—Revolution on November 7, 1917, to the fall of Wrangel in the middle of November, 1920), reached farther and wider into Russian life than the Great War did. The greater part of the Russian territory saw actual fighting. From the parts that did not, all the young men were enrolled in the Red Army. The civil war was also a much more terrible business than the war with Germany. On all sides—White, Red, and Green—it was accompanied by nameless cruelty. Epidemic diseases (over ninety per cent of the armies that fought in South Russia went through typhus) and the breakdown of all material civilizations [sic] increased the horror produced by war.[24]

General Denikin's was the first army in the field in the armed struggle against the Bolsheviks, and it had been active in the intermittent fighting that had been going for over a year when Mirsky joined up with it. What Mirsky witnessed can only be inferred from the assessments he subsequently published of literary representations of these campaigns. The earliest such assessment opens with coolly detached aestheticism:

The Russian Civil War bids fair to become an important stimulator of literary inspiration. It is certainly worthy of it. Its poetical value is in many ways superior to that of the great war. It lacks the most inhuman features of the great war—it is less machine-like, less hard-and-fast, and certainly richer in adventure. On the other hand, no international war has ever been such a hotbed of cruelty.

The literature produced by the civil war is already considerable. Certain aspects of the war have been dealt with in foreign literature, even in fiction. . . . But the foreigner, of course, can have no intimate understanding of the moods and motives of the Russian civil strife, and it will appear to him necessarily as a chaotic maze of meaningless bloodshed.[25]

The events of 1918–19 on the Don are recounted from the point of view of the Cossacks in Part IV of Mikhail Sholokhov's *The Quiet Don*; when Mirsky reviewed Sholokhov's literary career in 1934 he stated quite flatly—without mentioning, of course, that he was writing as an eyewitness to the latter part of these events, having been a combatant on the White side—that this novel contained the best description of the Civil War in Soviet literature.[26] The impact of its scenes of mass executions, usually clumsily carried out, its clinical recording of the effect of the sabre as the preferred weapon for close combat and execution, and of the rape of women as the ever-present accompaniment to the violence males were doing to each other has not been dimmed by all the years of increasingly explicit descriptions of violence in literature and the graphic arts. The same is true of Babel's stories, which Mirsky was the first critic to bring to the attention of the English readership. Mirsky was on the other side of the shifting front that is described in *Red Cavalry*, and it is with the same retreat into aestheticism that he welcomes Babel's manner, 'to treat the worst horrors and cruelties as a matter of course'.[27] Mirsky also pointed to the authenticity of Babel's language in these stories, appealing directly to his own experience in a way that is rare in his writing: 'I have, myself, a certain familiarity with the latter form of speech ['the Russian of the (originally Ukrainian-speaking) Cossacks of the Kuban, as modified by badly digested Red journalese'] and can testify to Babel's extraordinarily truthful rendering of it.'

Mirsky several times singled out 'Salt' and 'A Letter' as the greatest of Babel's stories; in them 'the horror and filth are without residue distilled into what I cannot call anything but poetry'. Mirsky himself made an attempt at cauterization; he had seen enough of the horrors both of brutality and refinement, and he was looking to literature for something quite apart from its value as a testimony to historical events.

The White equivalents to Bulgakov, Sholokhov, and Babel in Russian fiction are much less well known outside and especially inside Russia, but they are powerful works nonetheless; and as a historian of émigré literature Mirsky made several positive references to the principal book that was published about the part of the Civil War he was involved in, V. V. Shulgin's *1920*, on one occasion calling it 'one of the freshest and most genuine books ever written';[28] unfortunately, it was never translated into English.

Harold Williams, who was soon to be Mirsky's colleague in London, arrived in Ekaterinodar, HQ of Denikin and the Kuban Cossacks, on 30 May 1919 as correspondent for *The Times* and the *Daily Chronicle*. Williams described the HQ in wonderment:

Imagine half the War Office, half Westminster and Fleet Street huddled together, say, in Taunton, sleeping three to a room, wearing all sorts of costumes and uniforms, working for the liberation of England. Superficially it suggests for a moment a muddled epitome of Petrograd and Moscow on a Cossack background. In reality it is the centre of a crusade. . . .[29]

As an adjutant on Denikin's divisional staff, Mirsky was nearer to the sharp end of political power at this point than at any other time in his adult life, notwithstanding his father's ministerial tenure. On 24 May 1919 in Paris the Allies resolved to nominate Admiral Kolchak as Supreme Governor of Russia.[30] Harold Williams commented: 'Denikin's officers showed no eagerness to concede seniority to their Siberian comrades. But Denikin acted nobly and recognised Kolchak as Supreme Governor.'[31] The main fighting army, though, was Denikin's, the army in which Mirsky was a staff officer. It captured Kharkov on 25 June 1919 and remained there until 11 December.

Denikin's army was at the height of its success in mid-October 1919. C. E. Bechhofer reported that 'another few weeks, it seemed, and the Bolshevists would cease to rule in Moscow, and Russia would be free again'.[32] On 22 September General Kutepov took Kursk, and then on 14 October he took Oryol, only 270 miles from Moscow (Mirsky was Chief of Staff for this action, as we know). But on 15 November Kutepov had to evacuate Oryol; he could not hold it because part of his force had to be detached to fight the anarchist-cum-Ukrainian nationalist forces of Makhno and Petlyura.

Attached to Denikin's army as a member of the British Military Mission was H. N. H. Williamson, a professional artilleryman who survived the war in Flanders and volunteered for service in Russia at the end of it. Williamson's account of Denikin's campaigns gives a vivid impression of what the Civil War was like in the field, with its armoured trains making unsupported forays along the railways, whirling cavalry skirmishes in the featureless steppe, mutinies, mass desertions, looting, reprisals, drunken revels, and constant improvisation. It is also a compendium of British attitudes towards the Russians, all the more interesting because of the absence of literary contamination in the mentality of the observer, who was an excellent writer with a rigid upper lip and a talent for dry understatement. The Englishman goes by the book and never forgets there is a war on, while the Russians play at soldiers, dropping everything for a vodka-soaked party at the least opportunity. In one of Williamson's photographs he stands easy with folded arms while General Sidorin, carrying a sabre as long as his leg and almost as beefy, addresses the troops; Williamson is wearing a pith helmet to go with his British tunic and Sam Browne, while the Russians wear stubby-peaked 'pancakes' and belted kaftans. Williamson's first impression of the White Army emphasized the fact that the strength of its rank and file was always unstable, because the 'awkward country youths' it recruited, 'with a tendency to tie wild flowers to their rifle barrels on the march and gape at the unfamiliar brick buildings', would melt away back to their villages as soon as they could. Their officers, says Williamson,

were an extraordinary crowd, dressed in a mixture of uniforms, their badges of rank sometimes marked on their epaulettes with blue pencil. Some of them wore spurs with rowels as big as half crowns that jingled like marbles in a tin, and for the most part they knew nothing at all about what was going on. If they did, they gave only vague answers and, when pressed, took refuge behind the language barrier. . . . They were lazy, arrogant, ignorant, and often cowardly, chiefly because they knew their men had no heart for fighting their fellow countrymen and because they had already once seen them desert and mutiny, and were firmly—and rightly—under the impression it could easily happen again.[33]

Though it scored some spectacular victories in the spring and summer of 1919, Denikin's army advanced too fast, and failed to consolidate any of the positions it had won. The Volunteers began to be harassed from the rear by the anarchist Greens; and the Reds executed a series of brilliant flanking movements. By Christmas 1919 the Volunteer army was back in Rostov on the Don, where it had started. 'Exhaustion, disease, and corruption had destroyed their discipline and morale', commented Bechhofer.[34] The land policy of the Whites was the main reason for their failure to win the loyalty of the peasant masses; they dithered about long-term policy, but at the same time they amply demonstrated that they wanted not only restitution but also revenge on those who had expropriated their property. Whether or not the Svyatopolk-Mirsky estate was restored to the eldest son when the Volunteer army captured Kharkov, near where Giyovka lay, we do not know. Mirsky himself once summarized what went on soon after the event; understandably, he is euphemistic here, specifying nothing about the forms taken by White indiscipline—which included mass murder, bloody reprisals, and vicious pogroms:

Denikin's Government failed to satisfy any one. The White troops were everywhere (especially in the south and east) welcomed at first, but everywhere in two or three months they were heartily hated. The looseness of their discipline and their contempt for human life and property made them a pest to the population.[35]

Just over ten years later, forced collectivization in the Ukraine would nationalize the land, leading to many more casualties than in the Civil War, especially when the ensuing famine is taken into account. The Communist Mirsky of that time, however, would find no words of condemnation for this tragedy, but would instead stick to the Party line of political and economic inevitability.

Brigadier Williamson gives a brusque professional assessment of Denikin as his White armies were pushed back. He thought Denikin resolute and not lacking in courage, but without charisma. Denikin had difficulty with men such as Mirsky; he was, according to Williamson,

morbidly sensitive against aristocrats, courtiers and officers of the ex-Imperial Guard . . . Many of the men who surrounded him didn't like fighting, and these men, dressed in absurd uniforms, all spurred and laced, took great pains to avoid work. But though Denikin was strong-willed and inflexible himself, he showed an inexplicable lack of resolution with them. While a real soldier himself, he did not seem to dare to ask anything of his subordinates.[36]

THE DEFEAT OF DENIKIN

Panic commenced in Rostov in December 1919. Kharkov fell without being successfully evacuated. The Whites retreated in confusion, and attempts to escape from Russia began, in three main directions: towards Ekaterinodar by rail; across the Don and into the steppe; and south towards the sea. The front collapsed when it was realized that the Allies, and especially Great Britain under internal political pressure, now regarded the war in Russia as no more than a civil war, and certainly not an extension of the Great War—which is how many of the White officers and their men conceived of it, Mirsky included. Lloyd George made speeches on this theme in November 1919. Brigadier Williamson states that 'The final blow was the report of Lloyd George's speech at the Guildhall in London on November 9th, which, summed up, told the struggling Russian Loyalists that they had failed to do what was expected of them, and could now stew in their own juice!'[37] Asquith described Denikin as 'an adventurer'. As will soon become apparent, Mirsky regarded this kind of talk as treachery.

An additional complicating factor arose when in January 1920 war broke out between Lenin's Russia and Poland. The Poles moved east into the Ukraine, joining up with Petlyura and the Ukrainian nationalist forces. On 7 July the Red army was winning the war against the Poles, but not for long; the allies supported the Poles against the Bolsheviks, but as we shall soon see, the Poles would not help the Whites.

Taganrog fell on 6 January 1920; Novocherkassk, the seat of the Don Cossacks, on 9 January; and Rostov fell on 11 January 1920. At the end of January the Whites held only Odessa and its environs. General Denikin had succeeded Admiral Kolchak as Supreme Ruler of Russia after his victories, but the failure of the winter campaign sapped his authority, and in March 1920 he proclaimed General Wrangel his successor. In April 1920 Denikin left Russia for ever, to begin a wandering life in exile that ended in Ann Arbor, Michigan, in 1947. Although they provided a destroyer to take Denikin himself to Constantinople, and shortly afterwards offered to set him up as leader of a Russian government in exile—which he declined—the British could not provide sufficient ships to evacuate Denikin's army, and the White navy was too poorly supplied to be of service in this operation. The British ferried some of the soldiers to the Crimea.

Some other units of Denikin's army, under General Bredov, started a march towards Bessarabia. However, the Romanians did not allow the Russians to cross their border, and the exhausted soldiers had to fight their way northward to anti-Bolshevik Poland, where they were interned. Captain Prince D. P. Svyatopolk-Mirsky was a member of this group, which is referred to in the military histories as 'the Bredov detachment'. He was interned with it from February to June 1920.[38] This experience of a concentration camp was not to be his last. However, the camp where he sojourned in Poland, unlike the GULag, was relatively porous. Mirsky escaped from it, he later said, because there was talk of the internees being sent to fight with Wrangel in the Crimea. When he was interrogated in 1937, he said that in April 1920 he escaped from the camp and went to Warsaw, where he was given shelter by his relative Mikhail Nikolaevich Svyatopolk-Mirsky. After a few days there, Mikhail Nikolaevich helped him to get to Austria, and from there he went to Greece.

Mirsky had participated in some of the most cruel and crucial episodes of the Civil War. Soon after he liberated himself, he wrote a letter to Maurice Baring, from Athens on 5 September 1920, and gave vent to some of his feelings. The first part of the letter seethes with a sense of honour betrayed, expressed in the language of an officer and gentleman:

I have been in the army since 1914 and left it only 3 months ago, after running away from a concentration camp, where the Polish dogs had treacherously interned a portion of our army and where, I am sorry to say, the British representatives would not move a finger to help us. I have been in Armenia and other funny places. . . . These years have been dreadful years of losses (my brother was killed in February 1920 and all my friends, with two exceptions)[39] and still more of disillusions. Russia came first with Rasputin, Kerensky, the bolsheviks and all, and Europe followed close behind with the infamous treaty of Versailles, that damned humbug Wilson, that despicable coward Lloyd George and those traitors the French.[40]

Of this list of the detested, the only item Mirsky later changed his mind about, at least for public consumption, was 'the bolsheviks and all'. In 1929–30 in his book on Lenin he summarized the history of the Civil War from the now patriotic official Bolshevik point of view, and delivered a series of categorically simplistic interpretations of what it all meant:

The issue in the Civil War was whether the Communist Party, with the working class behind it, was to retain the power and thus (incidentally) to preserve the country from subjection to foreign Imperialism; or whether the White Armies were to restore the bourgeoisie to power as the agent of Allied Capitalism.[41]

Occasionally, in the writings Mirsky published after he emigrated, and especially after his political views had evolved towards an acceptance of the Bolshevik revolution, there is a reference to military matters that draws on his inside knowledge. For example, he once wrote a review of General Wrangel's memoirs, objecting to the publisher's claim that Wrangel commanded the last Russian national army, on the grounds that this army in fact allied itself with the Poles and the French against the overwhelming majority of the Russian people. The condescending attitude to his former superiors is entirely characteristic:

Wrangel was no doubt the ablest of the leaders of the White armies, but that is scarcely high praise. He was a good cavalry leader, quite capable of commanding an army corps or even a small army, but his political understanding (though superior to that of General Denikin or Yudenich) was not above the level of an average colonel of the Guards.[42]

And so Mirsky ended the Civil War in the eyes of his fellow émigrés still a prince and also a heroic veteran, but in the eyes of the winning side he was a criminal—not only an ex-prince but also a belogvardeets, an ex-White Guard officer. The latter two attributes came together in one of the stock figures in caricatures of the inter-war Russian emigration. All Mirsky needed to do to complete the picture was drive a Paris taxi or play the balalaika in a cabaret.

POETRY AND POLITICS

The oscillation between the military and literary worlds in Mirsky's youth and early manhood was very significant for his attitudes in later life. Despite his immense linguistic and literary competence, from the beginning Mirsky was not typical of Russian literary society. He always despised the intelligentsia, and notwithstanding what he was later to say on this subject, he was never genuinely part of it. His thinking is always that of a man of action rather than a man of reflection. This disposition is reflected in such things as his enduring preference for the front-line officer Tolstoy over the non-combatant military doctor's son Dostoevsky; the fundamental lack of sympathy with Chekhov, the most anti-heroic of great Russian writers; the rejection not only of Orthodox Christianity but also of any of the transcendental alternatives to it; and the eventual embracing of a regime that seemed to embody ruthless action and disdain for the intellectual niceties. In these respects he was by no means alone among the men of his class who had gone through the Civil War on the White side.

Mirsky, though, never made common cause with those of his politically conscious contemporaries who after 1917 agitated to get back their property and privileges, perhaps even to restore the monarchy, and who formed a shabby new establishment in the social and political life of the emigration. Of all the men that he came across in pre-revolutionary Russian literary society, Mirsky was temperamentally most akin to Gumilyov, who was the only significant Russian poet, indeed almost the only Russian literary intellectual, to see action in the First World War, a fact for which Mirsky frequently expressed his admiration.[43] However, Mirsky never dreamed of or hankered after a world ruled by poets, as Gumilyov did after 1917; and his notion of the ruling ideocracy of the Eurasians seems to have had no room for poets either, as we shall see.

Mirsky had grown up in close touch with the real world of political power in the person of his father, his mother's relations, his élite schools, and his service in the Guards, and he was much better informed about it than any other prominent literary intellectual of his time. Concluding his account of the meetings of the 'Poetic Academy' in the offices of *Apollo* just before the First World War, Vladimir Pyast mentions the fact that these premises were shared by the editorial offices of *Urban Affairs*, and that the highly professional staff of this serious civic journal would sometimes pause on their way to work and listen in disbelief to the airy-fairy babbling of their literary neighbours. Pyast observes: 'Indeed, at that time "society as a whole" was separated from "poetic society" as if by the Great Wall of China.'[44] This separation did not hold in the life of Mirsky, at this time or later.

In 1931, Mirsky's contemporary Osip Mandelshtam formulated his alienation from the realm of political power in one of his greatest poems; at the time, this question was becoming one of life and death for the whole of Russian literature:

> With the world of authority linked in but infantile fashion,
> I was scared to eat oysters, at guardsmen looked only askance,
> Not one speck of my soul is obliged to all that in the slightest,
> Howsoever I tortured myself to assume an alien mien.[45]

We will shortly hear of the ex-Guards officer Mirsky eating oysters, and negotiating to enter the world of political power. This was not in St

Petersburg, though, but in London and Paris. And we will come across some evidence that it was a desire to reconnect with 'the world of authority'—into which he had been born and in which he grew up—that brought him back to Russia.

LEAVING RUSSIA

Mirsky's mother and sisters probably left Kharkov for the Crimea at the same time as he did. From there the women went to Athens. They may have been exploiting their long-standing connection with the Imperial Court, although there is no absolutely firm evidence of this. The Queen of the Hellenes, Olga Konstantinovna (1851–1925), was a Romanov. She had married George I of Greece in 1867; he was, ominously, a Prince of Denmark, and Mariya Fyodorovna, the mother of Nicholas II and now the Dowager Empress, was his sister. The Queen of the Hellenes remained very Russian; she spent the First World War in Petersburg busy with her medical charities. She got out of Russia in a Red Cross train in May 1918, and was allowed back into Greece in 1920. She seems to have arranged to take in a number of Russian *émigré* aristocrats, though her own situation in Greece was not altogether rock-solid.[46]

Mirsky joined his mother and sisters in Athens after escaping from the concentration camp in Poland. Soon after, he described his situation and prospects to Maurice Baring, in the letter mentioned once already. Apart from the first-person statement it makes about Mirsky's position and the way he saw his prospects as he went out into emigration, this letter gives an excellent idea of the state of his unaided English. It is quite remarkably fluent, accurate, and idiomatic, but there is awkwardness with prepositions. The arch tone is surely unintentional:

And now I am . . . in Athens, all the better for contemplating the Erechthaeon, the Saronic gulf & the evening purple on the Hymettos, perspiring to my heart's content, reading the *London Mercury* & [*La*] *Nouvelle Revue Fran[ç]aise* & not reading the news. . . . If it were not for the two reviews I just mentioned and all what [*sic*] they stand for, I should not have the inkling of a doubt that England's and France's case was [*sic*, induced by the subjunctive, a gallicism this time] worse even than Russia's. Still as long as you have men like Claudel and Chesterton & there [*sic*] like there is a hope for recovery. And it is a great gratification after 6 years of seclusion to come again into touch with the wide world.

Mirsky was to become a contributor to the two journals he speaks of reading in Athens: the *London Mercury* was one of his staple sources of income throughout the *émigré* period, and it was in the *NRF* that he eventually published his account of his conversion to Communism. The judgement comparing post-war France and England with post-revolutionary Russia is a characteristic piece of Mirsky *épatage*. But seeing in the anti-establishment religiosity of Claudel and Chesterton a hope for recovery was to be a short-lived attitude. Besides telling Maurice Baring about his reading matter at this time, three years later Mirsky told a different English audience:

'Wuthering Heights' I first read in Athens. I had it lent to me, together with 'The Mysteries of Udolpho' by Mrs Radcliffe. The lady who lent me the two books said, 'If you like sensational blood and thunder stories, here you have them.' I have often wondered at this association of the stern genius of Emily with the tawdry and mawkish sentimentalism of the clever Mrs Radcliffe. Evidently, however, to some people it seems natural.[47]

Mirsky continues his letter to Baring in more personal vein:

You probably know that my idea was always to do literary work, but literary work in Russia now is a pure impossibility, & God knows when this state of things may change. So I have come to think whether I might not be capable of literary work abroad in England or France. I remember your flattering though anonymous mention of my person in your Landmarks.[48] And I thought you could give me definite advice, as to whether it were possible to try something of the sort. I have begun a book in French on French Poetry as it strikes *un barbare* (as you know we are barbarians). But it is damned difficult writing without definite hope and without encouragement. I am preparing also (in my mind as yet) a series of essays on Russian writers, the less known ones, and these could be written in English. . . . I would be very glad to hear from you and also to see you if possible. I may be turning up in Paris some time before next spring, or in London for the matter of that. Athens, with due respect to the remains of [the] V century, is *à la longue* an exceedingly dull & out of the way place. I have mastered some modern Greek. They have got some excellent poetry, Solomos, Valaoritis, but especially their unique folk-songs.

One of the last books I reread in Giofka before I saw the last of it [was] your Landmarks. And I have often meditated on the opening chapter which I think is the standard passage on Russian Poetry as a whole.

I see that Chehov is getting popular in England. It is certainly sublime art (though is he really greater than Euripides?) but is it very sound mental food? The writer I should like to see more widely read in the West is Leskov. There is Russia [Mirsky uses a Russianism; he intends an emphasis on the first word], not Stephen Graham's, nor Lenin's Russia, but the Russia of the black soil &c. I shall never stop divagating about all this. So I am

Yours very sincerely
D. Sviatopolk Mirsky

This was the last letter I have seen that Mirsky signed with the full form of his surname, which he writes without a hyphen. Shortly afterwards, he set down an opinion of Leskov that amplifies its last sentence and says a good deal about his own general values, about the revisions he was soon to make when writing for the English about Russian literature, and even points forward to his eventual commitment to Stalinism:

Leskov, the man who knew Russia better than any other man and who found in her depths not the 'superfluous men' of Turgenev, or the Freudian characters of Dostoyevsky, but men with inflexible wills, unbending passions, knowing not what it is to repent, men like the Italians of Stendhal, and also good strong saints of the cast of Adam Bede . . .[49]

Alas, Baring's response to this letter, like almost every other letter received by Mirsky, has never come to light; but Mirsky's actions may be deduced from the date 'November, 1920' standing under his first contribution to the London periodical press, the first of the 'Russian Letters' series that appeared in the *London Mercury*. Two letters written by Baring to other people at about this time record that he gave Mirsky money to get him started; they suggest that he had arrived in London by late July 1921.[50]

ANTHEM FOR DOOMED YOUTH

Discussing Pushkin's *The Feast in Time of Plague* in one of the first books he wrote for the English reader, Mirsky quotes a passage from it that might be seen as an epitaph for his youth. He explains that the attitude it articulates was popular a generation earlier, when 'Symbolism, the cult of the Dark and Nietzschean individualism, were the order of the day':

> All, all that menaces with ruin
> Contains for the heart of Mortals
> Ineffable delight;
> The token maybe of immortality.
> And happy he, who in the midst of excitements,
> Was able to discover and to know it.[51]

Soon after he had become a Marxist in the late 1920s, Mirsky wrote another sort of epitaph for his youth; it forms a footnote to the title of his account of how he achieved 'liberation' from the class and milieu into which he had been born:

For the sake of simplicity I here identify myself with the bourgeois intelligentsia, even though, since I come from a noble family, I do not entirely have the right to do so. The Russian nobility was an essentially feudal class (in the economic sense of the word, i.e., it lived on inherited privilege and not investment capital). But this nobility, which remained the social base of tsarism until 1917, had by the end of the nineteenth century reached such a degree of decadence and cultural sterility that it was incapable of producing even intellectuals who would remain within its bosom. The very fact of being an intellectual, in touch with the movements of ideas of the time—such as they were—made one déclassé. This automatic déclassement perhaps played a part in my subsequent development.[52]

Very little in what we know so far of Mirsky's life supports this view. Apart from the obvious political agenda he is following here, his thinking is coloured, surely, by the humiliations attendant upon a decade in emigration. Before 1917 he showed no real sign of dropping out of the class he was born into, but if anything remained in remarkably close touch with his family and relations. His fluency in English and direct contact with an English literary intellectual like Maurice Baring, in particular, marked him out as an aristocrat. There was almost nobody in the rank-and-file Russian literary intelligentsia of Mirsky's time who shared this orientation, and lower social circles were still by and large catching up with French. Mirsky's education and his involvement in literature brought him into contact with people who were not all that different from him in social terms; and in any case, he spent at least as much time in the company of Russia's highly aristocratic officer corps of the Guards as he did in literary circles. To speak of these people as exhibiting 'decadence and cultural sterility' is the sort of treacherous double-think that Mirsky was always quick to condemn in others—an attitude that reflects his continuing adherence to the officer-and-gentleman code of honour he was brought up with. It is as well that Mirsky's deeply civilized and perceptive mother never lived to read this passage, to say nothing of his long-suffering father.

Mirsky's thirty years of privileged existence in imperial Russian society did not go to waste. In view of his later accomplishments it is quite astonishing to realize that he only ever made peripheral use of the formal training he had undergone in Oriental languages, ancient history, and military science, and that essentially he made his living from and became a world authority in his hobby, Russian literature. It is hard to think of another Russian literary intellectual in this century whose upbringing gave them the same breadth of competence. Whereas most literary historians of the twentieth century can 'do' either poetry or prose, Mirsky could 'do' not only both of them, but also ancient and modern history, and with equal competence. And his knowledge was by no means only bookish: he had grown up during one of the most innovatory and fertile periods in the history of Russian culture, but through his father and family he had also grown up in touch with the real world of political power, and he had then been involved as an officer on active service during the most traumatic period in Russian history. Mirsky parlayed this experience into books for the English reader that have served us ever since as nobly and prominently as any of his ancestors served the Tsar.

PART II

Out of Russia, 1921–1932

4 Writing English

The wine of the English poets comes no stronger than madeira, and for us, used to bootleg vodka, it can seem wishy-washy. (D. S. Mirsky, 1920)

THE BREAD OF EXILE

Mirsky spent nearly twelve years outside Russia. He had lost for ever the affluent security of his boyhood and youth, and also his élite social status, but in emigration he was never actually indigent or driven very far down the social scale. From 1921 to 1929 he prospered in every way. The first five of these years were Mirsky's best from the point of view of enduring intellectual endeavour. The peak came in 1926–7 with his English-language history of Russian literature. Before this, he was establishing himself in the London literary and intellectual world. His publishing in English also paid due attention to the USA, where interest in Russian literature in some ways anticipated and surpassed what was going on in Britain.[1] After toying with the idea for several years, he crossed the ocean for the first and only time on an academic visit in the summer of 1928.

The pattern of Mirsky's life during these years was absolutely consistent. He spent the three ten-week university terms in London, teaching, but mainly writing. As soon as vacation began, he left for France. He evidently minimized the loss of working time by making the journey overnight. His letters to Suvchinsky record, for example, that he gave his last lecture of the autumn term in the afternoon on Thursday, 13 December 1928, then caught the night boat to Dunkirk and arrived at the Gare du Nord at 10 the next morning, which he describes as 'very early', perhaps having in mind Suvchinsky's habits rather than his own. While his mother was still alive, her house just west of central Paris provided a convenient base for operations; after her death in April 1926 Mirsky stayed mainly in hotels, but occasionally spent time with his elder sister, Sonya, and her husband, first in Pont de Briques and later in Grenoble. Mirsky's activities in France included his intellectual and social life in the Russian cultural emigration, a wider involvement with the literary intelligentsia of France, and also a substantial amount of carefully planned and apparently solitary gastronomic tourism. The actual bread of exile seems to have tasted anything but bitter to Mirsky. It was probably the main thing he had in mind when he wrote to Suvchinsky on 29 April 1925, shortly after they had been discussing Oswald Spengler: 'When are you going to move to Paris for good? When all's said and done, no matter what attitude one takes towards

Abendlandia, first-rate is always better than second-, and in Europe, first-rate can only mean France.'

To live in the way Mirsky preferred required funds, and he set about acquiring them with an acumen somewhat surprising in a man of his background. He was far more successful at day labour in the Western literary world than anybody else in the Russian emigration before Nabokov in the 1950s,[2] and as a money-maker he was surpassed only by people whose chosen media did not necessitate translation, such as a few of the painters, dancers, and musicians. The getting of daily bread was much more problematical for literary intellectuals, and among Mirsky's fellows in the Russian emigration there were very few for whom it was not a primary concern.

The key to Mirsky's success was, obviously, his superb active command of English, which opened up opportunities far more varied and lucrative than those available to the Russians who could only manage French or German. And that key was turned by Mirsky's driving intellectual energy and ruthlessly disciplined work habits. He was always 'thinking to some purpose'. After his youthful book of poems, he never wrote anything speculatively or out of self-indulgence, apart from a few bits of occasional verse in English. Even his private letters are goal-oriented. Indeed, Mirsky said to Suvchinsky on 4 December 1922, at the very outset of his continuous career as a publishing critic, that he was incapable of working without some sort of 'external compulsion'. One particularly telling episode took place in 1925. That summer Mirsky had undertaken to write an article for the literary almanac being put together at the time by another émigré prince, the dilettante poet D. A. Shakhovskoy (1902–89). On 19 October 1925 Mirsky wrote to Shakhovskoy to say that he had been so deluged with work since he made the undertaking— the proofs of two books and the start of the academic year—that he had had no time to get the piece done. But then he adds, with characteristic briskness: 'when I got your letter I remembered that I'm an officer of the General Staff and that for this corporation of ours there are no excuses for lack of time, knowledge, or ability, so I sat down and wrote it'.[3]

The most revealing remark of all that he made about himself in this connection is an aside in the letter he wrote to Vera Suvchinskaya (later Traill) on 12 March 1930, when he was hard at work on the book that he came to regard as a turning-point in his life: 'I've just received the typed version of the first chapter of my *Lenin*. This gives me great moral satisfaction, like anything that is clarified and set in order.' The letters to Suvchinsky—an occasionally startling source of information about Mirsky's private life in emigration for which there is no equivalent in the pre- and post-emigration periods—are full of itemized listings of things for Suvchinsky to get done, and relentless badgering calculated to bring issues to a head. This lust for closure, this gratification from getting things cleared up and out of the way, coupled with Mirsky's dissatisfaction with any kind of status quo, was unmistakably one of the fundamental features of his personality and may well have been the principal driving force behind the eventually fatal choices he made in life.

Mirsky's total continuous writing career spanned not much more than a decade and a half, from late in 1920 until half-way through 1937.[4] In view of the brevity of this period—especially taking into account the fact that it was preceded by a long separation from literary circles and a major relocation, that it was broken by another major relocation when Mirsky went back to Russia, and that before this he held a full-time teaching job (however untaxing it might have been)—Mirsky's sheer productivity is imposing, to put it mildly. He published a total of something like 400 separate items during his career, which represents about one publication per fortnight, a strike rate maintained fairly consistently over sixteen years. Among them are six substantial books: *Pushkin* (1926); the two-volume history of Russian literature (1926–7); *Russia: A Social History* (1931); *Lenin* (1931); and *Intellidzhentsia* (1933), all but the last originally written in English. There are then three smaller books: the anthology of Russian poetry (1924); *Modern Russian Literature* (1925); and *A History of Russia* (1928). Mirsky's Russian-language anthology of English literature, published after he was arrested in 1937, is about 450 pages long, and represents a massive feat of editorial labour. The two volumes of Pokrovsky's *Brief History of Russia*, published in Mirsky's translation—out of, not into, his native language—in 1933, make up a total of well over 600 pages, and contain an abundance of interpolations from the translator. Mirsky's translation, again from Russian into English, of Vladimirtsov's *The Life of Chingis-Khan* (London, 1930) consists of about 170 pages of dense argument, involving many arcane terms and concepts. Hardly any of Mirsky's publications are perfunctory items such as one-page summarizing reviews, and a high proportion of them involve some sort of dual-language mental manipulation.

Mirsky never really repeats himself, even though he wrote about certain major authors and themes many many times; it is enough to compare his various treatments of Tolstoy, say, to realize that each is tailored to the format and audience specified by the particular task. And the point of view from which the subject is approached evolves over time. Almost everybody who has discussed Mirsky's literary criticism has condemned him for inconsistency; this is still a ritual gesture particularly among Russians, most of whom have read few or none of his writings in English. A more justifiable view of the matter is that, unlike most of his critics, he never stopped assimilating new material, and his point of view evolved in a reasoned series of responses to what he had read and to the evolution of events.

PASSPORTS AND VISAS

When he left Russia in 1920, Mirsky was a single individual among what is conventionally estimated at one million human beings who did the same

between November 1917 and March 1921.[5] As an unmarried ex-officer in early
middle age, he was a typical phenomenon in the sociological profile of the
Russian emigration. Nothing else about Mirsky or what happened to him,
though, was standard for the first-wave Russian *émigré*.[6] To begin with—unlike
Sergey Efron, for instance—he did not spend months languishing in the
typhoid-ridden refugee camps that had been set up near Constantinople while
international negotiations went on about what could be done about him and
tens of thousands of other ex-combatants of the White army.[7]

On 15 December 1921 the Soviet government decreed that several categories
of former Russian citizens were henceforth summarily deprived of their civil
rights. They included those persons who had left the country before the establishment of Soviet power on 7 November 1917, those who had left since that
date without government permission, and those who had served in the White
armies or any other organization deemed to be anti-Soviet. This left the
refugees stranded, and a commission of the League of Nations headed by the
famous explorer Dr Fridtjof Nansen was charged with sorting out the consequences. The Russians formed a majority among stateless persons in Europe
at this time, but they were by no means the only ones; a century of mass human
deracination and attendant heartbreak and misery was not yet a quarter run.
The 'Nansen passport' was introduced in 1922. This document was held by
the majority of the stateless Russian *émigrés*, but even when they had armed
themselves with one, they had to face endless bother about securing visas in
order simply to enter the major European countries, let alone settle in them.
By the end of 1924 most principal powers had recognized the Soviet government, and the Nansen passport became the only form of identity document
available to the refugees, creating a powerful incentive for assimilation. By the
same year also most principal powers, including the USA, had also introduced
immigration quotas or other forms of restriction, and the idea of moving on
became highly problematical.

Mirsky's NKVD file reveals that in 1921 he came to England via Rome and
Paris, and that he held a travel document allowing multiple entry into France.
He evidently did not need to acquire the Nansen passport. Once again,
Mirsky's connections must have been put to good use. The international lawyer
A. J. Halpern is the obvious link between Mirsky, Baring, and the British Home
Office.[8] Mirsky was to turn to Halpern several times during the 1920s for help
in passport matters, but always in connection with other people. As for himself,
he seems to have had no problems with the dozens of journeys he made
between England and France in the 1920s, but he did have difficulties when
other countries were involved. In 1922 he considered making a return trip
to Germany, but decided against it because of difficulties with visas. In
March and again in May 1926 he planned a trip to Belgium to visit Prince
Shakhovskoy, on the first occasion accompanying Marina Tsvetaeva; again, the
passport problems proved too awkward for the journey to be arranged. When

Mirsky organized his trip with Suvchinsky to Italy at the end of 1927 to see Maksim Gorky he had to pull some personal strings to get a visa for them both. Eventually, it was the problem of his right to work in England that caused Mirsky really serious trouble, and the nub of the matter was then above all a matter of personalities, because he needed an annual testimonial from his sponsor, Sir Bernard Pares, who by this time had fallen out with him on political grounds.

RUSSIANS IN LONDON

By the time Mirsky arrived in England, the country had played host to several distinct types of refugee Russian. The most prominent individuals among them in the second half of the nineteenth century were three. The most famous of them was the socialist Alexander Herzen (1812–70); he came to London in 1853 and stayed until 1864. The second was another Russian prince, who was educated at the Corps de Pages and had served as an army officer, the anarchist Pyotr Kropotkin (1842–1921); he came to London in 1886 and wrote his *Memoirs of a Revolutionary* (1899) in English. Kropotkin lived long enough to return to Russia in 1917 and disapprove of Lenin's revolution. The third was the ex-terrorist Sergey Stepnyak-Kravchinsky (1851–95), who in 1878 took part in the murder of General Mezentsov, one of P. D. Svyatopolk-Mirsky's predecessors as chief of gendarmes; like Kropotkin, Stepnyak-Kravchinsky wrote one of his most important books, *The Career of a Nihilist* (1889), in English.

Kropotkin delivered a series of lectures on nineteenth-century Russian literature in 1901 at the Lowell Institute in Boston, and out of them came an important antecedent to Mirsky's history, *Ideals and Realities in Russian Literature* (London, 1902; 2nd impression, 1905). Jane Ellen Harrison hit the nail on the head when she wrote to Mirsky on 30 April 1925 to acknowledge receipt of his little *Modern Russian Literature*, a pilot version of his two-volume masterpiece: 'Yr book ought to take the place of Kropotkin's. I never knew him but he leaves me with the impression of a man who had no real first hand reaction to literature.'[9] No doubt thinking of the next two book-length treatments of the subject after Kropotkin, Maurice Baring's *Landmarks in Russian Literature* (1910) and *Russian Literature* (1914), Harrison adds, betraying one of her ineluctable prejudices: 'Mr Baring who does care & writes with such charm has the eternal drawback of being utterly an Englishman & they're eternally incapable of real literary judgement.' Mirsky did not share this view; he repeatedly recommended Baring's two books to the English readership, and referred to them as 'classics'.[10]

In the late 1920s Mirsky made a telling remark about the personality of Prince Kropotkin in the context of his characterization of Jane Ellen Harrison:

This combination of a Radical intellect with Conservative tastes and manners cannot fail to remind one of those Russian revolutionaries born in aristocratic families who espoused and developed with the greatest sincerity the boldest revolutionary doctrines, but were never able to throw off the habit of behaviour, the tone, and the sensibility of the class into which they were born. Their hatred of the past and of their social roots was thorough-going and sincere, but their every word and movement betrayed their antecedents. The completest type of this kind—and the best known in this country— was Peter Kropotkin.[11]

It was not only outstanding individuals such as Herzen, Kropotkin, and Stepnyak-Kravchinsky who had taken refuge in England before 1914, though. Three congresses of Russian revolutionaries had been held in London: in 1903, removed from Brussels, when the historic Bolshevik/Menshevik division came about; in 1905; and in 1907. When the February Revolution unseated the Romanovs in 1917, the Russian revolutionaries were scattered across the globe, and it has been estimated that there were between 300 and 400 of them in London.[12] One group among them soon formed the embryo of the Soviet foreign service. Maksim Litvinov (1876–1951), who had met Lenin for the first time in the Reading Room of the British Museum in 1903, came back to London in 1908 after working for the revolution in Petersburg. He had a job with the publishers Williams and Norgate, wangled by Maksim Gorky through Sir Charles Hagberg Wright (1862–1940), the Secretary and Librarian of the London Library, who had been educated partly in Russia, and whose acquisitions were a godsend to Mirsky when he started work in London.[13] In London Litvinov married Ivy Low (1889–1977), who might well have coined the sobriquet that has stuck with Mirsky more enduringly than any other, 'Comrade Prince'.[14] Maksim Litvinov has been credited with devising the master-plan that turned a very significant number of upper-class (if not princely) Englishmen into comrades.[15] Among the other highly placed cadres of the future Narkomindel (People's Commissariat of Foreign Affairs) was a school classmate and close friend of Mikhail Kuzmin, G. V. Chicherin (1872–1936); during his time in London he contributed articles to Orage's The New Age on political prisoners in Russia, polemicizing with another person we encountered as a journalist in what he called 'Denikin's Russia', C. H. Bechhofer.

There had been relatively few Russians in England before 1914 whose sojourn was neither politically nor socially motivated. Just before the First World War, two young Russian poets spent some time in England; the knowledge they acquired was called on when they became the founders of Soviet poetry for children in the 1920s. Samuil Marshak (1887–1964) is now best remembered for his translations of Burns and Shakespeare's sonnets; Korney Chukovsky (1882–1969) made one of his many major contributions as a pioneering translator of Walt Whitman. Before Mirsky returned to Russia in 1932, Marshak and Chukovsky were the leading Soviet experts on current English literature; however, their taste never moved beyond the Georgian figures who were dominant during the time they spent in England before the First World War. Evgeny Zamyatin was in England designing and building icebreakers in 1916–17, and he had very little to do with metropolitan literary circles, spending almost all his time at his job in Newcastle. He became deeply interested in the British and dissected them in several literary works, notably *Islanders*. Zamyatin's movements mirrored those of Mirsky; he went back to Russia in 1917 and with Stalin's permission left the USSR for France in 1931. Mirsky had played a key part in introducing Zamyatin's work to the English reader; whether or not the two men saw each other during Mirsky's last sojourns in Paris in 1931–2 is yet another open question.[16]

The most important intermediary between the literary cultures of England and Russia before 1917 was Constance Garnett (1862–1946).[17] Beginning in 1892, by the early 1920s she had single-handedly given the English reader practically the entire high canon of nineteenth-century Russian prose. Her industry was prodigious almost beyond belief: a seventeen-volume Turgenev; thirteen volumes of Chekhov short stories, a two-volume translation of his plays, and another single-volume edition of his letters; a twelve-volume Dostoevsky; the major works of Gogol; *War and Peace*, *Anna Karenina*, and other works by Tolstoy; Goncharov's *A Common Story* (she was pipped on *Oblomov* by C. J. Hogarth's abridged version); Herzen's *My Past and Thoughts*; and Ostrovsky's *The Storm*. Nothing remotely like the cumulative impact of Garnett's achievement has been seen before or since; she was not, after all, churning out pot-boilers. She brought about a profound modification in the sensibility of the English reader and that of many English writers too. She is on the whole splendidly accurate; her late Victorian English has ceased to seem quaint, and instead has a captivating period charm, 'little fathers' and all. Meanwhile, Tolstoy's acolytes had been toiling too. Aylmer Maude did another *War and Peace* and *Anna Karenina* to set by Garnett's, and added *Resurrection*, much of Tolstoy's short prose fiction, and the crucial later essays, including the massively influential 'What Is Art?'

Mirsky's direct predecessor in mediating between English and Russian culture was the feminist Zinaida Vengerova (1867–1941), the younger sister of the St Peterburg professor in whose seminar Mirsky developed his distaste for source-heavy academicism. Vengerova spent several periods in London in the 1890s, and she was a pioneer in reporting current literary developments for the Russian press, fostering that new cosmopolitanism that Mirsky was later to point to as a distinguishing feature of the post-Realist literary process in Russia; she also wrote on Russian literature for a wide range of Western periodicals. When war broke out in 1914, Vengerova had published only the first of her projected ten-volume collected works, *English Writers of the Nineteenth Century*, and the project remained stalled at that point, as consequently did her reputation. Vengerova lived in England during the First World War, went back to Russia in 1917, and then left again in 1922. She married the poet Nikolay

Minsky in 1925; they lived mainly in England until his death in 1937, when she moved to New York.

After the fall of the Russian monarchy, the political exiles started making their way back to Russia, and the *émigrés* started leaving the country.[18] There were never very many first-wave Russian *émigrés* in England, compared with France, Germany, and other centres. It has been estimated that their total number was 9,000 in 1922, declining through re-emigration and naturalization by 1930 to about 4,000.[19] This figure may represent the residue of a much larger number of Russians who had passed through Great Britain or been resident in one way or another since 1917, and may include some from before that date. Among them was the old diplomatic corps, which was left high and dry when the Bolsheviks took power in October 1917; its leading lights formed the backbone of the Russian presence in London during the interwar years. One other distinct component was made up of the people from Arkhangelsk who had supported the British intervention and had to be evacuated. The Russian colony soon set up a characteristic network of social and charitable organizations and began organizing a corporate life.[20] But the efforts of the post-revolutionary Russian *émigrés* in London to galvanize opinion and action against the Bolsheviks had already passed their peak by the time Mirsky arrived in 1921; by then the Civil War was lost, Allied intervention had been reconsidered, and Lenin's government was a fact of life.

There were several reasons for the way in which the Russian *émigré* presence was distributed between the countries of postwar Europe. To begin with, for the first few years after the Civil War some influential *émigrés* continued to believe that there would soon be a change of government in Russia and they would be able to go home. The belief that Bolshevik intransigence had softened was encouraged by the introduction of what looked like a return to capitalist values with the New Economic Policy in 1921. It was not until the mid-1920s or even later that this optimism faded, and the Russians outside Russia finally admitted to themselves that they were unlikely to go back, be restored in their property rights, or obtain compensation for their losses. Before this, many of them felt it advisable to take up what they thought of as temporary residence as close to Russia as possible. The break-up of the Russian empire had given rise to the independent Baltic states (Latvia, Estonia, and Lithuania) and to independent Poland; in 1922 there were 230,000 Russians in these countries, falling to 127,000 by 1930 as hopes faded and people moved on. Yugoslavia and Czechoslovakia had significant Russian minorities, encouraged by governments that were friendly towards the 'has-beens' (*byvshie lyudi*) who, like Mirsky, had lost everything; these countries provided the nearest thing to a home from home for them. The Czech government in particular, guided by its Russophile President, Thomas Masaryk (1850–1937), gave grants to Russian refugee writers and students; Mirsky's friends Marina Tsvetaeva, Sergey Efron, and Konstantin Rodzevich were among the beneficiaries. In the non-Slavonic countries, the economic situation made Berlin a very attractive place to settle in the early 1920s, and it became the centre of *émigré* cultural activity until about 1925,[21] with an estimated total of 250,000 Russians in 1922, which had gone down to 90,000 by 1930. As soon as he could after he got to England, Mirsky visited Berlin in order to find out what was going on in Russian literature.

And then there was France, an immensely more sympathetic refuge among the non-Slavonic nations than aloof England or the recent enemy Germany.[22] As we have seen, there was widespread knowledge of French and a benevolent attitude towards that country among the Russian aristocracy and upper bourgeoisie. What is more, the devastated industries of France were crying out for able-bodied male labour to replace the hands lost during the Great War. There were an estimated 70,000 Russians living in France in 1922; contrary to the situation in all other European countries, that number rose, to 175,000 by 1930.

In contrast to the countries of Continental Europe, there was a much smaller degree of cultural identification among the Russians with England—except, as we have seen, among the aristocracy, Mirsky's own social group. At the time of the post-revolutionary Russian emigration, the threat of unemployment and labour unrest, which made the British government delay with demobilization in 1918–19, meant that immigration was actively discouraged.

Despite this fundamentally antagonistic situation, however, some prominent families did settle in England. The Benkendorffs, friends of Maurice Baring and also of the Svyatopolk-Mirskys, naturally came to England because the father had been the last Ambassador to the Court of St James. There was also the Golitsyn family, who settled at Chessington near London. Mirsky's social connections with the Benkendorffs and Golitsyns, which went back to his childhood, seem to have withstood the stress caused by the evolution of his political views, and he continued to see them until he went back to Russia. Apart from Mirsky's old friends, the Golitsyn entourage included a person who was to become one of Mirsky's close associates, Pyotr Semyonovich Arapov.

The England to which Mirsky came in 1921 was undergoing an upsurge in interest in Russia, spiced now in the post-revolutionary situation by even sharper factionalism than had been the case in the liberal/revolutionary debates before 1914. There had never been any strong support in Britain for the Russian monarchy, which being absolute rather than constitutional was commonly regarded as hopelessly reactionary; and Russia had been an obstinate imperial rival in the Caucasus, the Middle East, and northern India. Russia had frequently been condemned for 'bullying' her European neighbours, the main recipient of Britain's rather suspect sympathy, then as later, being Poland. When Mirsky arrived, four years after the revolutions, the postwar coalition led by Lloyd George was in its last year in office. Lloyd George had practically torpedoed the Intervention and was thought by the anti-Bolsheviks to have sold them down the river, as witness Mirsky's words about him in his letter to Maurice Baring from Athens. The first step towards the recognition of the Bolsheviks had been taken with the Anglo-Soviet trade agreement of March 1921.

THE WILLIAMSES AND OTHERS

The most prominent group of post-revolutionary Russian *émigrés* in London when Mirsky arrived were the anti-Bolshevik liberals grouped around Ariadna Tyrkova-Williams (1869–1962) and her husband, Harold Williams (1876–1928). The Williamses constituted the most substantial personal nexus between the Russian- and English-speaking political and intellectual worlds that had been formed before 1917. Ariadna Tyrkova-Williams was a journalist; after the revolution she was to become an important novelist and biographer (though she was hardly ever translated and her work consequently remained within the Russian *émigré* ambit). She had been a politically active dissident since her youth, and had inevitably spent several periods in exile in Western Europe; it was during one of them, in 1904, that she had first met Harold Williams, at the home of the exiled P. B. Struve in Stuttgart. She worked steadily in the cause of constitutionalism, and eventually became a member of the Central Committee of the Constitutional Democratic Party, the most eminent woman in Russian politics of her time. She came into post-revolutionary emigration with her husband in 1918.

Harold Williams[23] was a New Zealander by birth who was widely reputed to be the greatest practical linguist of his time. He had espoused the cause of the liberation of Russia as a result of reading Tolstoy.[24] Williams lived in Russia as correspondent of various newspapers from December 1904 until March 1918. During this time he was the principal intermediary between the Russian world and the English-speaking public, more prominent in terms of the continuity of day-to-day events even than Maurice Baring and Bernard Pares.[25] Williams first met Pares in Moscow in 1905,[26] and they found themselves fundamentally in agreement about what they saw as the mission of their lives: to work for a constitutionally governed, liberalized, but still godly Russia acting in concert with Great Britain against the threat of German militarism. Shortly after his return to England from reporting on the Civil War, Williams began writing for *The Times*, and in May 1922 he became its Foreign Editor. Williams held this position until his premature death. He was a staunch anti-Bolshevik, and was saddened by the recognition that the new regime increasingly commanded in Britain.

Mirsky met the Williamses soon after he arrived in England, and their relations were cordial. He called on their contacts when arranging for a reading by Marina Tsvetaeva in London in 1926, but the relationship seems not to have

survived Harold Williams's death in 1928, just before Mirsky made his decisive move to the left. There were only two anglophone foreign experts on
Russia of whom Mirsky consistently spoke well. One was Baring, perhaps
because he felt he owed him too much for the gentleman's code to permit
otherwise; the other was Williams, perhaps because he died so soon.

Immediately after their return to London from Denikin's Russia, the
Williamses organized the Russian Liberation Committee in an attempt to
mobilize British public opinion and government policy against the Bolsheviks.
It was funded by one of the very small number of *émigré* Russians who was
seriously rich, the businessman Nikolay Khrisanforovich Denisov. The Committee included two prominent members of the old embassy personnel: E. V.
Sablin, who was to remain at the centre of the Russian community in London
until his death in 1947, and Konstantin Dmitrievich Nabokov, the novelist's
uncle, who ended up teaching Russian at Cambridge. The other three members
of the Committee were very distinguished personages indeed. One was the
most eminent intellectual of all those who came into emigration, and an
Anglophile of long standing, Professor Pavel Nikolaevich Milyukov (1859–
1943). He had served as Foreign Minister in the Provisional Government; after
British-based resistance to the Bolsheviks collapsed, he moved to Paris, where
he edited the *Latest News*, the nearest equivalent the Russian *émigrés* had to
The Times. Then there was Mirsky's old teacher from St Petersburg University, the ancient historian Mikhail Rostovtsev, who left London for the USA in
1921, apparently just before Mirsky arrived; and finally there was the doughty
old revolutionary-turned-loyalist in whose home the Williamses had met, P. B.
Struve. The Committee had an office at 173 Fleet Street; it published a broad-
sheet, the highly informative *Russian Life*, and a series of pamphlets. Mirsky
became actively involved in this enterprise, which was, however, on its last legs
by the time he came on the scene; his participation leaves no room for doubt
that at this early stage his political views were firmly anti-Bolshevik. He never
moved further to the right of this position.

One other Russian who was close to Mirsky in his early days in London,
and with whom he never broke relations, despite their disagreements, was
Mikhail Timofeevich Florinsky (1894–1981).[27] Florinsky was born and educated in Kiev, where he studied law. His father, an eminent academic historian,
was murdered in 1919. Florinsky served as an artillery officer in the First World
War, and emigrated to London after the Revolution, bringing his mother out
with him, but leaving his brother and sister behind in Moscow. He told part of
his story in a letter he wrote to me on 2 March 1974:

I came to London in 1920 as research secretary to Sir Paul Vinogradoff who was
working on a major revision of the [*Encyclopaedia Britannica*] article on Russia.[28] As
Vinogradoff's assistant I had a desk in the North Library of the British Museum. . . .
Mirsky, and the late Baron A. F. Meyendorff . . . worked regularly in the Reading
Room and we met frequently for frugal meals at a near-by ABC tea-room in New

Oxford Street.[29] . . . Vinogradoff died in December 1925 and early in 1926 I went to New York.

In New York Florinsky soon found a job at Columbia University. He became Mirsky's principal American contact, and eventually opened the gate to one of the most important roads that Mirsky did not take, a permanent academic post in the USA.

Mirsky's closest personal relationship of all in London may well have been with the Slovene Janko Lavrin (1887–1986) rather than with any fellow Russian. Lavrin had worked as a journalist in St Petersburg before the war; among other acquaintances of particular interest to Mirsky, Lavrin had known Rozanov, Khlebnikov, and Sergey Gorodetsky. Finding himself in London on his way back to Russia in 1917, Lavrin decided that the situation there was too uncertain for it to be wise to continue his journey. He started working as a journalist in England, making a wide variety of contacts, particularly with A. R. Orage. Like Mirsky, Lavrin was steered into a university teaching post by Bernard Pares, but this time at Nottingham, and he taught there from 1919 until he retired in 1953. He invited Mirsky to lecture, and saw a good deal of him on his visits to London. Their relationship lasted from 1922 until Mirsky went back to Russia. As we will see, his testimony is particularly valuable on the question of why Mirsky took this step.

Another distinctive set of Russian men came to England immediately after the Revolution; they were born about the turn of the century, the sons of prominent public figures. They included Sergey Konovalov (1899–1982), Vladimir Nabokov (1899–1977), Gleb Struve (1898–1985), and Eugene Vinaver (1899–1979). All of them had connections that led to funding to attend Oxford or Cambridge immediately after the war, and they all went on to illustrious careers as writers and scholars. It is characteristic of him that with this younger generation, who arrived in emigration at about the age of 20, Mirsky had little in common and apparently had no dealings.

Mirsky's overlooking or ignoring Nabokov's writing is perhaps the most surprising negative feature of his works on current Russian literature to the retrospective observer, until we reflect on how rarely it is that anybody genuinely cares for the work of the generation that is succeeding their own. Similarly, and despite his political development, Mirsky also seems not to have paid any attention to Nabokov's greatest contemporary among Soviet writers, Andrey Platonov (1899–1951). Though they were ten years younger than he was, both Nabokov and Platonov were sufficiently well established in his time for Mirsky to have discussed them had he wished to. Gleb Petrovich Struve, Nabokov's earliest discerning critic, replaced Mirsky at the School of Slavonic Studies in 1932; to Mirsky, Struve was not much more than one of the sons of his illustrious father Pyotr Berngardovich, while to Gleb Petrovich, Mirsky was an unprincipled and irresponsible mischief-maker.

THE LONDON MERCURY

Mirsky secured his first foothold in London by activating his acquaintance with Maurice Baring. His debut publication in English, the first instalment of the 'Russian Letters' series, which is dated 'October, 1920', was sent to the *London Mercury* before he left Athens. The founding editor of the *Mercury* in 1919, Sir John Squire (1884–1959), was still in charge when Mirsky made his last contributions in 1931.[30] It was in this same year that Squire edited the book for which he is best (albeit faintly) remembered, *If, Or, History Rewritten*, with contributions from G. K. Chesterton, Winston Churchill, and H. A. L. Fisher, among others; their attempts to imagine 'counter-factual' historical events contrast strongly with the Marxist determinism that begins to appear definitively in Mirsky's historical writing at this same time.

The *Mercury* was to be a mainstay for Mirsky as a literary journalist all through his London years. Dorothy L. Sayers (1893–1958), whose first contribution to the *Mercury* was made the year before Mirsky's, described it to her mother as 'a particularly swell sort of monthly, run by tip-top people . . . I believe they pay very well'.[31] Back in Russia, when as a neophyte Soviet Marxist he cauterized everything he had been involved with while he was in England, Mirsky turned on the *Mercury* when launching his discussion of 'highbrowism':

It was during the 'twenties that the esthetising intellectuals saw their best days and had the greatest general influence on the intelligentsia as a whole. On the right wing was the motley crowd round the petty middle-class *London Mercury*—people far removed from any kind of amoral esthetic extreme, and eminently suspicious of all foreigners, yet none the less completely assured that literature and art correspond to absolute values situated somewhere above the stratosphere and quite unhampered by the transitory trifles of political life. . . . True highbrowism at least demands a knowledge of Freud, a cult of Proust, and a respectful recognition of the superiority of *la cuisine française* over a pudding diet. True highbrows make frequent trips to Paris. True highbrows admit no barrier in sexual matters between what is permissible and what is not. . . .[32]

Apart from contributing a number of solid articles, Mirsky became the first-call reviewer of foreign books and works of literary criticism for Squire's monthly throughout the 1920s. A typical effort, under the standard rubric 'Recent Foreign Books', appeared in the *Mercury* in September 1926, that is, just after Mirsky had proofread the second volume of his history of Russian literature and when he was in the thick of getting together the second issue of the Russian almanac *Vyorsts*. The review begins with positive assessments of four recent French novels. First comes *Bernard Quesnay*, the latest effort by André Maurois. Mirsky then deals with two novels by Georges Duhamel, *La Pierre d'Horeb* and *Lettres au Patagon* ('And as M. Duhamel's irony is free from the bitter grimness of Voltaire, so is his sympathy from the irresponsible superiority of Chekhov'). The fourth novel is *Paulina 1880*, a novel by Pierre-Jean Jouve that was much praised in its time and seriously compared to *Madame Bovary*; here, Mirsky particularly relishes the portrayal of the heroine: 'The account of Paulina's life in the convent of the Visitandines at Mantua [after she has killed her lover] is especially remarkable, and, I think, goes very deep into the understanding of the sexual mainsprings of Western (as opposed to Eastern) mysticism.'

From this Mirsky passes to works of literary history and criticism. First comes Mario Praz's *Secentismo e Marinismo in Inghilterra: John Donne–Richard Crashaw*; Mirsky pays some gracious compliments to one of the few contemporaries whose linguistic versatility could rival his own, even allowing, 'I am particularly impressed by his intimate acquaintance with seventeenth-century Dutch poetry.' Mirsky then considers Herman Bahr, *Notizen zur neueren spanischen Literatur*, where among other things 'One is also pleased to find a wholesome (if qualified) contempt for the writings of Blasco Ibáñez'. Two more items are listed in the heading of the review, both by one E. Pons, *Le Thème et le sentiment de la nature dans la poésie anglo-saxonne* and *La Jeunesse de Swift*, but Mirsky's remarks on them seem to have dropped off the end of his contribution, or else he deemed the two books not worthy of further mention. The variety of languages and literatures represented in this single review is entirely typical of Mirsky's efforts for the *Mercury*. In almost every one of these reviews some scintillating aphorism sparkles in the stream of urbanities.

Besides opening the way to the *London Mercury*, Maurice Baring also gave Mirsky an introduction to Lady Juliet Duff, one of his closest friends, in August 1921, and asked her to be kind to him, adding: 'He is a very nice man and very intelligent and trying to get literary work in London.' Baring also gave Lady Duff a warning: 'remember that he is penniless and don't suggest anything that will entail expense, such as a trip on an aeroplane or a good feed at the Ritz'.[33] Baring may have had in mind here a rather more intimate connection than simply an entrée into British high society, since Juliet Duff had lost her husband in the First World War, and was the passive and decorative kind of upper-class woman he considered ideal. But his introduction was wasted on Mirsky, who apart from anything else seems to have had time for aristocrats only when they were Russians he had first met back home. He never belonged to any 'smart' social set, holding all forms of mental and physical high fashion in disdain. In Paris he eventually came to know Lucien Vogel (1886–1954), the socialist pioneer of fashion journalism;[34] and one of his closest friends was Salomeya Halpern, who worked for Vogel. But Mirsky's personal contempt for the vestimentary values of such people is apparent from all the descriptions of his physical appearance, which consistently stress the shabbiness of his clothes. During his time in London, Mirsky consorted not with the nobs of Mayfair, but with the snobs of Bloomsbury.

BERNARD PARES AND THE SCHOOL OF SLAVONIC STUDIES

To Mirsky's foothold in the London literary world was soon added a foothold in the academic world, which was in its infancy as far as Russian studies were concerned. A start had been made before the First World War in two principal places. In Oxford, William Morfill (1834–1909) had spent a lifetime pleading the cause of the Slavonic languages, cultivating contacts with eminent native scholars and writers, and tirelessly publishing study aids. Morfill's articles on Russian literature for the *Encyclopaedia Britannica*, first published in the 9th edition in 1886, updated for the 10th (1902) and 11th editions (1911), are the pioneering professional surveys of the subject published by an English person; they were eventually superseded in the 1920s by entries written by Mirsky.

The most active academic pioneer in Britain was Bernard Pares. With his School of Russian at Liverpool University, founded in 1907, Pares pioneered what was eventually called area studies, the multidisciplinary approach to a particular country or countries. After the war and his experiences in post-revolutionary Russia, Pares transferred his operations to London and set up the School of Slavonic Studies, initially as a department of King's College of London University, where Russian was already on the curriculum. Lloyd George's government commissioned Sir Stanley Leathes to produce a report on modern language teaching; when it came, in 1919, it put the case—mainly on political grounds, of course—that Russian was an important modern language. In 1922 the University Grants Committee earmarked £2,000 per annum for the School of Slavonic Studies, and Pares set up shop. Instruction in the Slavonic languages other than Russian was funded by the appropriate governments, with Masaryk's Czechoslovakia the leading donor.

With no hope of support from Lenin's government—apart from anything else, Pares had actively opposed the Revolution, and he remained *persona non grata* until the middle 1930s—Pares used his money to hire new Russianists, and the post-revolutionary situation put at his disposal some superb scholars. One of them was Harold Williams, who was used mainly in an advisory capacity. The next most senior was the man with whom Mirsky and Michael Florinsky would repair to the ABC teashop from the British Museum, Baron A. F. Meyendorff (1869–1964), who had been a lecturer in peasant land law at the University of St Petersburg and a Vice-President of the Third Duma; in 1918 he left St Petersburg for Riga, and he was brought to England on a British warship in 1919. Pares 'found him drudging at language teaching in London'[35] and hired him as Reader in Russian Laws and Institutions. Meyendorff's principal post was at the London School of Economics, where from 1922 to 1934 he served as Reader in Russian Institutions and Economics.[36]

In the spring of 1922 Pares invited Mirsky to apply for the position of Lecturer in Russian. He was given excellent references for the job by the retiring teacher of Russian, Robert L. Smith, and by Harold Williams. Both were written on 26 April 1922.[37] On 14 May 1922, evidently having been asked by Pares to show what he could do, Mirsky told him that he would be happy to deliver 'the three public lectures you speak about', and suggested as topics Pushkin, Leskov, and Blok. He also informed Pares that he was writing some book notices. These too would have been a nominal qualifying examination; they were to be the first of a large number of reviews Mirsky contributed to the School's house journal, the *Slavonic Review*, which began publication in June 1922 and continues to this day. The academic standard of this journal during the 1920s was very high, and it is a unique source of information about Russian studies in Britain.

When he was appointed at the School, Mirsky became the first and only full-time academic specialist in Russian literature in the country. In a letter he wrote to Pares on 19 October 1922 he reported his teaching hours: Wednesday 11–1 and Thursday 2–4 (Russian literature for advanced students) and Thursday 12–1 ('same for beginners'). This five-hour teaching load, tucked into two days to leave Mondays, Tuesdays, and Fridays free, seems to have been Mirsky's basic norm during his years at London. His duties also included a certain amount of language teaching; in particular, the School arranged language instruction for War Office personnel, and this aspect of Mirsky's activities attracted the particular interest of his interrogators after he was arrested in 1937. He also did some language examining for the Foreign and Commonwealth Office; in the summer of 1926 in one of his letters to Florinsky he testily mentions the possibility that he might have to return from France to carry out this duty, but in the event there turned out to be no candidates and he was 'stood down'.

The number of students at the School during Mirsky's time was very small. After giving his first lectures, Mirsky wrote on 11 October 1922 in his first letter to Suvchinsky: 'There's not much here that's good. ... I'm giving lectures and have all of five in the audience!' Dorothy Galton makes one of her characteristically tart remarks in this connection, referring to

one of Pares' most obvious, although rather endearing, faults: his inability to distinguish fact from fiction where his favourite ideas were concerned. Sometimes, hearing him talk, one would gain the impression that the School was a hive of industry, with many students playing an important part in the life of the nation and empire; alas, the degree lists for the period (1922–39) tell a different story, and most of the staff were engaged in teaching of an elementary kind more appropriate to a secondary school.[38]

However illusory the great enterprise may have been in fact, Mirsky showed himself willing to pitch in on a slightly broader front than simply delivering his lectures. Suvchinsky started pestering him for a Eurasian-inclined article soon after he and Mirsky met in 1922, but Mirsky put him off; on

22 February 1923 he informed Suvchinsky—using numbered points for the first but by no means the last time—

At the moment I haven't enough peace and mental clarity to write anything serious; I could write either a purely informative article (which nobody needs) or some sort of glossolalia[39] that I'd have to disavow a week later. But I can't do either, so snowed under am I with work: 1) I'm giving a course on Russian literature of the mid-19th century and have an awful lot to read; 2) I'm giving Russian lessons, 8 hours a week; 3) there is work on the University's Slavonic journal, purely mechanical; 4) there's a whole lot of public lectures coming up soon and I've got to prepare for them.

Some information was published about these 'public lectures' that Mirsky gave in addition to his duties at the School. The lecture he delivered on 3 March 1923 to the annual meeting of the Brontë Society at Leeds is a suave performance that culminates with a grandiloquent display that must have swelled the bosoms of Mirsky's Yorkshire audience:

The country that produces great people has to pay the penalty—it forfeits the exclusive right to such eminent children. Shakespeare belongs to mankind as much as to England. Charlotte and Emily belong to England as much as to the West Riding; and I venture to claim them for the world. If the world at large has not yet realized what it is losing in failing to accept the Brontës as its common property, I cannot afford to do without them; and if it is impossible to tear them away from the West Riding, well, I must have the West Riding as well.[40]

In London there were regular meetings of the Anglo-Russian Literary Society, which had been founded in 1893 by a group of British Russophiles who included Donald Mackenzie Wallace.[41] Its meeting-place and the home of its library had been the Imperial Institute, but with the emergence of the School of Slavonic Studies at King's College, the Society's meetings were transferred to the latter institution. On 6 February 1923 Mirsky spoke on 'The Vitality of Russian Literature Today'. Mirsky's talk was the first given at the new meeting-place, and was reported quite extensively.[42] As it is natural to expect, the main points he made are broadly the same as those found in his published writings of the same period: that privations and hardships had afflicted individuals but not brought the literature to a halt; that poetry currently predominated, but a 'young prose' was developing. These ideas run through Mirsky's writings of the time, and are pitched directly counter to the standard *émigré* charge that Russian literature worthy of the name had been murdered by the revolution.

The *Slavonic Review* also gives some details of the discussion that followed Mirsky's paper, dwelling on the contribution made by his colleague Roman Dyboski, an eminent Polish scholar who had been brought to London by Pares, about the current situation of the Russian drama. The notice of Mirsky's lecture concludes with a summary of a talk given by Harold Williams on

6 March, the topic being 'Russian Ideas and Russian Politics'; among those contributing to the discussion was the American Charles R. Crane, who had recently crossed the Continent by rail, and who told his audience about 'the complete bankruptcy of the Soviet attempt to impose an alien centralisation upon the mass of the people, whose passive resistance has made its success impossible'. No comments from the floor are recorded.[43] On 6 May 1924 Mirsky gave a lecture to the Anglo-Russian Literary Society on 'English Poetry in Russia'.[44]

After Mirsky's initial flurry of contributions to Russian literary life in London, his involvement became sparse, to judge by the published accounts. On 3 May 1927 he made a speech on Tyutchev at the Anglo-Russian Literary Society, following Miss M. Parkhurst Webb's lecture.[45] In the Lent term of the academic year 1927–8, Mirsky gave the lecture devoted to Russian literature as part of a series on the modern European literatures arranged at King's College by Professor Rose.[46] The year 1928 was the centenary of Tolstoy's birth, and Mirsky was appropriately active in London, among other things editing a special issue of the *Slavonic Review*.

Mirsky's post at the School provided him with a steady income during his decade in emigration. But in the last analysis he evidently regarded his university salary, which Dorothy Galton said 'never exceeded £350', as no more than a pittance, and the duties for which it was paid as an inconvenience, even a tiresome chore. Mirsky felt completely free to market his talents, and consistently gave a good deal of his energy to paid work that was supplementary to his professional academic activities.

MISS HARRISON

Bernard Pares set Mirsky up in the London academic world, as Maurice Baring had set him up in London literary journalism. Mirsky's link to the broader literary world, in London and on the Continent, was Jane Ellen Harrison (1850–1928).[47] She had been an undergraduate at Newnham College, Cambridge, in the 1870s, and she returned there as College Lecturer in Classical Archaeology from 1899 to 1922 after living in London doing the research for her ground-breaking books. In 1922 she moved to Paris with her companion Hope Mirrlees,[48] and stayed there until 1926. By 1914 Harrison had become an international authority in historical anthropology because of her work on ancient religion. And she had a much wider reputation because in these books she had made a crucial contribution to the post-Darwinian erosion of the intellectual respectability of Christianity in British polite society. Her most attractive quality to Mirsky seems to have been that, while her intellectual curiosity and 'progressive' attitude never abated, her manners remained conservative—a characteristic she shared with Kropotkin:

While her mind was busily destroying the rotting structure of Victorian ideas, while she was conjuring up out of the past the Demons of Sex and Change, welcoming Freud and the Russians, lending a sympathetic ear to Joyce and refusing to say a word against the Communist Revolution, her manners, her bearing, her talk, preserved the dignity and the delicacy of a more aristocratic age.[49]

Mirsky once formulated his view of Harrison's significance with a degree of respect for which it is hard to find an equivalent in his other writings, except perhaps for the way he sometimes spoke of Tolstoy, and later of Lenin. Mirsky evidently regarded their fusion of the personality with the times, of consciousness with being, as the supreme attribute of the human individual, and aspired to live in this way himself:

At any rate the historical rôle played by the science of anthropology and comparative religion in undermining Victorian security was at least as great as that of Russian literature, and the real salt and zest of the great age of English Anthropology seems to me to have resided precisely in the heterodox and unacademic Miss Harrison rather than in her more famous and canonised fellow-workers. . . . she was more than a scholar, she was a *contemporary*, a human being who *lived her age*, and for whom science was not divorced from contemporary life in general. When (and if) the theories of *The Golden Bough* cease to be up to date and actual, that great work will remain a landmark of primary importance in the history of science, but the ideas of Jane Harrison, inseparable from her personality and her time will live as part of a more human history, for they are an unremovable part of her age, which she expressed in a way that was unmistakeably hers and no one else's, but which enters as one of the brightest threads into its living texture. The way walked by her from the study of Greek vases through that of primitive religion to Freud and Tolstoy will be recognised as one of the most illuminating expressions of the intellectual evolution of the English mind at the turn of two historical epochs.[50]

By the time Mirsky met her, Harrison had been fascinated with things Russian for some years; indeed, she was the daughter of a Yorkshire timber factor who traded with Russia. Her *Ancient Art and Ritual* (1913) contains two passages on Tolstoy's theory of art that Mirsky regarded as exemplary. In 1915 she had published 'Russia and the Russian Verb', and she expanded it in 1919 into *Aspects, Aorists, and the Classical Tropos*, arguing for the admission of Russian into the Cambridge syllabus on an equal footing with Ancient Greek. Russia's significance for what Harrison and like-minded intellectuals thought of as the played-out Western European mind, desiccated by commercialism and materialism, is formulated in a postcard she wrote to her mentor and great friend, Gilbert Murray, in 1914: 'Yes, that is just what I longed to have said— that whatever sort of a wild beast Russia makes of herself she still cares more than any other nation for the things of the spirit, and that is priceless (though as you say dangerous).'[51] In 1919 Harrison declared: 'The Russian stands for the complexity and concreteness of life—felt whole, unanalysed, unjudged, lived into. . . .'[52] Mirsky apparently ventured an objection to this sort of thing early in his relationship with Harrison; her reply, written on 14 May 1924, is firm: 'O yes I know full well there is another side to the Russian character but then that is a side that we English & the Germans & French possess too so it does not interest me. It gives me nothing fresh to live by.'

It would seem that Mirsky and Harrison first met in Paris, at some time in the winter of 1923–4. The earliest surviving letter by her to him dates from the first week of April 1924, and the correspondence was intense before their close relationship petered out in 1926. During this time, as the letters show, Harrison style-edited at least three of Mirsky's books. Whenever Mirsky was in Paris, she would invite him round for tea, and she set up meetings not only with such Anglo-Saxon worthies as Gilbert Murray, David Garnett, Logan Pearsall Smith, and the Woolfs, but also with key French intellectuals such as Jacques Rivière, Jean Schlumberger, Charles du Bos, and perhaps—the evidence of the letters is not conclusive—Paul Valéry.

It would seem to have been through Harrison that Mirsky made personal contact with some of his fellow Russian *émigrés*, among them the most eminent being Lev Shestov. In return, Mirsky put Harrison and Mirrlees in touch with the Remizovs and Marina Tsvetaeva. The two Englishwomen were inspired by Mirsky and Remizov to translate the autobiography of Avvakum, and Mirsky supplied a brilliant preface, one of his best pieces of historical writing.[53]

There was obviously a profound personal bond between Mirsky and Harrison, significantly greater than with any woman of his own age where a sexual dimension was potentially present. Soon after she met Mirsky, Harrison wrote to Gilbert Murray: 'I have lost my aged heart to a Bear Prince—why did I not meet him 50 years ago when I cld have clamoured to be his Princess.'[54] Mirsky's sense of indebtedness to Harrison is enshrined in the dedication to her of the first volume of his *History of Russian Literature*. After she died in 1928, Mirsky was accorded the signal honour of giving the second of the memorial lectures in her name in Cambridge in 1929; the first was delivered the year before by Gilbert Murray.

BLOOMSBURY

Mainly because of her Cambridge connection, Jane Harrison had known most of the people who formed the 'Bloomsbury' of Mirsky's time since they were children.[55] Postwar 'New' Bloomsbury inherited and developed an idea of Russia that had been shaped by the translation of Russian fiction and theorized before the Great War by Maurice Baring and partly by Harrison herself—her notion about Russia caring more for the things of the spirit is central to it. Mirsky clearly had some idea of how matters stood before he arrived in London. In his letter to Baring from Athens, he sarcastically referred to himself and his fellow Russians as 'barbarians', people from outside the cultured world.

He was caricaturing what he knew to be the essence of the believer Baring's view, a view that has been influential ever since. Virginia Woolf eventually remarked that 'it is no longer within the power of the English mind—the gift may be enjoyed perhaps in Russia—to see fur grow upon smooth ears and cloven hoofs where there are ten separate toes'.[56] This idea of Russia as apart, different, preserving primordial spiritual values that had been lost in the West, was completely unacceptable to Mirsky, and his major writings stand as a denunciation of it.

Mirsky met the Woolfs in Paris in the spring of 1924.[57] They moved to their definitive Bloomsbury address in Tavistock Square, very close to the School of Slavonic Studies, in March of that year. Mirsky continued to see them until he went back to Russia. By 1924 their shoestring Hogarth Press had been operational for seven years, and the Russian-adviser slot had been bagged by S. S. Koteliansky.[58] There is no conclusive evidence that Koteliansky and Mirsky ever actually met. Although Mirsky never seems to have recorded anything negative about Koteliansky in public print, as someone who had recently emerged from the thick of the Petersburg literary scene he must inevitably have regarded 'Kot' as a provincial amateur—which is essentially what he was. For his part, Koteliansky once gave Esther Salaman a copy of Mirsky's *Lenin*, describing it and the author as 'rotten . . . he was prepared to tell any number of lies, to humiliate himself to any extent, just to be allowed to return to Russia: he needed not anger but our prayers. . . .'.[59]

Notwithstanding Koteliansky's presence, Mirsky had a hand in two elegant little Russia-related books published by the Hogarth in 1925. The first was the excellent Harrison–Mirrlees translation of Avvakum's autobiography, and the second, a more idiosyncratic but fascinating compilation that brought together Harrison's interest in totemism with her Russophilism, the jewel-like *Book of the Bear*, which retains great value because of the literary quality of the translations. The two tales in it by Remizov are particularly noteworthy, and so is the facsimile of a sample of his calligraphy.[60]

The only culturally prominent Russian besides Mirsky who spent time in both prewar St Petersburg and postwar Bloomsbury was the mosaicist Boris Anrep (1883–1969).[61] There are so many obvious links between Mirsky and Anrep that it is inconceivable that they never met, but there is no evidence that they ever did. Besides Anrep there was one other Russian denizen of 'new Bloomsbury', but she had not moved much in Petersburg literary circles before 1914. This was the ex-Diaghilev ballerina Lidia Lopukova (1892–1981), who married John Maynard Keynes in 1925; Mirsky certainly knew them.[62]

In 1927 Mirsky commissioned, translated into Russian, and published an important article by E. M. Forster (1879–1970) for his journal *Vyorsts*. Despite his close connections, T. S. Eliot is not usually regarded as part of Bloomsbury; Mirsky knew him at least *in* Bloomsbury, and wrote a good deal about his work for the Russians.[63] Besides his *London Mercury* link to 'mainstream' literary journalism, Mirsky thus had a line to the contemporary avant-garde, the people who were to bring into English culture that French-oriented modernism whose absence Mirsky had derided when he first arrived in the country.

THE *DÉCADES* AT PONTIGNY

Mirsky's involvement with the Continental literary scene was never confined to Russian-speaking circles. In this respect he was yet again somewhat different from the majority of his fellow *émigré* intellectuals.[64] Symptomatically, Mirsky's connection with the cultural milieu of France was made through his English acquaintances. In August 1923, Jane Harrison was invited to the '*décades*' at the former Cistercian abbey at Pontigny, in the *département* of Yonne, in Burgundy, which were conducted under the general supervision of the owner of the estate, the philosopher and critic Paul Desjardins (1859–1940), Professor at the College de Sèvres.[65] These colloquia took place every year from 1910 until 1939, except for suspension during the First World War. They were organized in three series of ten days each (hence the term '*décades*'), which were concerned respectively with religion, literature, and politics. A general theme was proposed for each session. The subject for the literary *décade* of 1924, for example, was '*Y a-t-il dans la poésie d'un peuple un trésor réservé?*' Breakfast was at 8.30, the mornings were left free for private study and writing, lunch was taken at 12.30, and the actual 'conversations' took place during the remainder of the afternoon. The participants sat down to a sumptuous dinner according to a *placement* fixed by Desjardins, with a switch every three days; after dinner came intellectual party games.

Thanks evidently to a recommendation by Jane Harrison, who attended from 1923 to 1925, Mirsky first took part in the literary *décade* in August 1924, and it is certain that he went back in 1925 and 1927. Whether or not he attended in 1926 is not entirely clear; this was when he was unusually busy even for him, among other things writing the second volume of his history of Russian literature.

The dominant figures at these gatherings during Mirsky's time were André Gide (1869–1951) and the critic Jean Schlumberger (1877–1968), who in 1909 had been co-founders of the journal Mirsky had perused in Athens, the *Nouvelle Revue Française*. The chief organizer, and from some accounts the life and soul of the party, was the critic Charles du Bos (1882–1939). Mirsky took a particular shine at Pontigny to two other prominent French intellectuals, highly esteemed in their day but never well known in the English-speaking world, the philosopher Bernard Groethuysen (1880–1946) and the literary critic Ramón Fernández (1894–1944). He eventually translated and reviewed their work in the Russian periodical press. These two men both added lustre to their reputations during the 1930s, but during the Occupation they went different ways: Groethuysen kept to the left and took part in the Resistance, while Fernández was a collaborator.

To be invited to Pontigny was to be recognized as a member of the European intellectual aristocracy, and Mirsky was the second Russian to receive this accolade, being preceded by Shestov in 1923. The only other Russians besides Mirsky who were later invited on a regular basis were Nikolay Berdyaev and Alexandre Koyré.[66] Mirsky flaunted this mark of distinction to his boss: on 20 August 1924 he wrote to Pares that he had just returned from Pontigny, where he had spent 'a very agreeable fortnight in the company of many eminent people, French, Russian, English, Spanish, German and others'.

Mirsky was by no means overawed at Pontigny; he maintained his customary lack of piety. After his visit in 1925 he told Prince Shakhovskoy that he had returned from Pontigny, where 'the French occupy themselves in clever conversation and where it is very difficult to get anything done'[67]—a remark that comes from the core of Mirsky's personality. Jane Harrison's private attitude was similar; she had written to Mirsky on 23 August 1924, after he left the colloquium: 'The *entretiens* are becoming horribly metaphysical & to me their main interest now is the study they present of French mentality.'

The second *décade* of 1926 was held from 15 to 25 August on the theme '*L'empreinte chrétienne: à quoi reconnaissable?*' Mirsky wrote a letter to Suvchinsky from Pontigny on 21 August, saying absolutely nothing about what was going on in the formal part of the meetings. This is the only piece of evidence to suggest that he attended in the summer of 1926; that there is no record of a contribution at this time is particularly unfortunate, because this was the period immediately following the death of his mother when he seems to have abandoned any lingering allegiance he might have still had to the Russian Orthodox Church. He went to Pontigny again in 1927, when Berdyaev was also present, but after that Mirsky either dropped out or was not re-invited. The *décades* had evidently served their purpose, and from them Mirsky retained his acquaintanceship with Gide and a few other key intellectuals, Bernard Groethuysen particularly, who moved to the left as the 1920s went on. It was probably through Gide that Mirsky became involved with the most enduring of his non-Russian Continental activities, the journal *Commerce*. After 1927 Mirsky's dealings with it in some ways filled the gap that had been left by Pontigny.

ROGER FRY

On 9 September 1925 at the Hôtel de l'Étoile in Chablis, Mirsky ran into a key Bloomsbury figure, the artist and critic Roger Fry (1866–1934), who had also just been at Pontigny. The two men dined together, and at some point afterwards Fry reconstructed their conversation, the only time someone has purported to reproduce Mirsky's conversation in English.[68] Fry represents himself as making much longer speeches than Mirsky. Both men were no doubt well oiled at the time, and in that condition, by all accounts, Mirsky tended to be even more laconic than usual. They begin by discussing one of the papers they had heard at Pontigny, and by contrast with it Fry praises the precision of 'the scientific method'. This produces the first of Mirsky's blunt responses: 'Well, all I can say is I don't believe in science and I don't think it can contribute anything of value for thought. To tell the truth I get far more from Theology.'

The two men then turn to a discussion of Ramón Fernández's paper on Cardinal Newman's *Grammar of Assent*, decide that Fernández is a Pragmatist who envisages action, and of Pragmatism Mirsky says that 'just now when speculation and thought have rotted the educated classes of Europe it is most salutary'. Fry makes a speech about the nature of Action, and Mirsky responds that Europe is in for a period of violent convulsion:

FRY. Like several thinkers at Pontigny you anticipate a new Dark Ages.

MIRSKY. Yes, and I'm impatient to see them.

FRY. Impatient? That does astonish me. You want to see all the slowly piled up achievement of European thought perish?

MIRSKY. I'm not interested in Europe, it's done for. I'm interested in Russia.

FRY. But surely Russia has come into the orbit of European thought?

MIRSKY. No, never really, and it is freeing itself and is going to create new conceptions of life and that's what I care for.

When Fry asks Mirsky about the nature of these Dark Ages in Russia, Mirsky tells him that 'Russia will not want Science; it will have Theology', which, he says, has the great advantage of being irrational; 'I should really like to believe in the theology of the Ancient Greeks, but still Christianity will do for me, only it must be the Christianity of the Orthodox Russian Church, not the Roman. It seems to me on the whole the best explanation of the world.' He soon becomes even more categorical: 'The only truths of any value are the truths that come directly revealed to man by the necessities of his life. It is by finding what he can live by that he discovers what is inevitable and therefore true.' Fry objects that in disagreeing, Mirsky and he don't try to strangle each other because they are guided by reason; to which Mirsky replies that he does not do so because 'my nervous system is too sensitive. Violence to another is repugnant to my nerves, that's all. I have no moral objection to violence and even to cruelty, but it shocks my nerves.' Fry speculates that 'like all Russians', Mirsky suffers from 'hypertrophy of the soul'. Mirsky responds: 'No, I don't know at all that I have a soul, and really I doubt if I can throw more light on my Theology. [Its] unreason is its great attraction, its opposition to Science.'

The discussion is now back where it started, and Fry closes it by reiterating his belief in 'the method of Science'.

There is nothing in Mirsky's words that is inconsistent with attitudes that he expressed elsewhere or implied in print at the time concerned. By science, he and Fry mean natural science, in which field Fry had qualified brilliantly at Cambridge; for Mirsky the scientific attitude was of little interest, until he fell into Marxism and became 'scientific' in a fatally fundamentalist sense. The idea of the imminent 'New Dark Ages' was a commonplace among Russian intellectuals at the time; it had recently been the subject of a book by Berdyaev. After the mention of it, we find practically the last recorded evidence for the vestiges of Mirsky's boyhood indoctrination into Orthodox Christianity. Here, though, Mirsky may be twitting the self-consciously atheistical Fry, who at the *entretiens* that had just been held at Pontigny had 'just now and again put a spoke in the Christian prayer wheel which would otherwise go buzzing around ever so merrily', as he later boasted to Helen Anrep. But Mirsky's claim that he lacks any supra-personal scruple is the most arresting assertion he makes here; his words about having no moral objection to violence seem to announce his acceptance of the most repugnant facet of Stalinism.

MIRSKY OBSERVED

The photograph of Mirsky with the teaching staff of the School of Slavonic Studies in 1925 has been said by several people who knew him well to be the best picture of him that they know to have survived, especially because of the quizzically inclined head and the narrowing of the already slitted eyes. A number of people set down their impression of Mirsky's appearance after he reached manhood. Men and women, Russian and English, all invariably emphasize that he was tall, bald, bearded, dark, with Oriental or 'Tartar' eyes and bad teeth. I have not found a single picture of Mirsky where he shows these notorious teeth.[69] The most vivid of all the verbal portraits of Mirsky comes from Leonard Woolf, and in it, teeth are the most important attribute:

Sometimes when one caught in a certain light the vision of his mouth and jaw, it gave one that tiny little clutch of fear in the heart. . . . I have known only a very few people with this kind of mouth; its sinister shape comes, I think, from the form of the jaw and arrangement of the teeth. There is always the shadow of a smile in it, but it is the baleful smile of the shark or crocodile. Mirsky had this kind of smile. It may have had no psychological significance and he may well have had nothing cruel or sharklike in his character. In all our relations with him he seemed an unusually courteous and even gentle man, highly intelligent, cultivated, devoted to the arts, and a good literary critic. He had, at the same time, that air of profound pessimism which seemed to be characteristic of intellectual Russians, both within and without the pages of Dostoevsky.

Certainly Mirsky would have found himself spiritually at home in *The Possessed* or *The Idiot*.[70]

Vera Traill said that the first things one noticed about Mirsky were his black beard, Mongolian eyes, and bald head; but being a woman who was interested in men's bodies, she added: 'he had a bad figure,—I mean he was tall, but he was, you wouldn't say fat, but somehow everything was unattractive'. She said she could not remember his going grey, and his beard remained black; she summarized by saying: 'He had no hair at all, but a great deal of charm.' Dorothy Galton, speaking of the time she got to know Mirsky in the autumn of 1928, took a less sinister view than Woolf and a less intimate view than Traill; writing as she was forty years after the time in question, her visual memory was perhaps coloured by the group photograph of 1925:

He was a painfully shy man whom it was difficult to get to know. He could not easily converse with others, and his silences sometimes rendered them equally dumb. With his shaggy beard and long pale face, he presented an agreeably ugly appearance. When speaking he used to lean his head to one side with a quizzical grin.[71]

Vera Traill said that Mirsky never spoke simply out of politeness, and had no small talk. This was not from shyness, she explained; he was simply 'a wild man' who would speak when he felt like it and be silent when he felt like it. Janko Lavrin took a less sympathetic view of this:

As far as his personal character was concerned . . . I would say that Mirsky was one of the most *dogmatic* or dogmatically self-sure people I have ever met. When you talked with him, you soon noticed that he was not quite able to talk, but only to argue. And he argued only to assert his own position, his own idea and so on, and his own idea, of course, like everybody's ideas, very frequently changed too. But I noticed one thing,— that he was particularly inclined to argue a thing, d'you know, in such a way as to become offensive, really.

MIRSKY AND THE ENGLISH

The English people Mirsky knew well make an odd collection. After his nanny, Miss Trend, his mother's nanny, Mrs Sharp, and the odd groom and butler at Mount Pleasant in the 1890s, he got to know Maurice Baring and Bernard Pares, two upper-class late Victorian men whose obsession with Russia and social slumming there says something about their attitude towards their own society, notwithstanding Pares's hearty devotion to the songs he had learned at Harrow, Gilbert and Sullivan, the annual Varsity cricket match, and Chelsea Football Club.

Both Pares and Baring were practising Christians, Pares an Anglican and Baring a convert to Catholicism. Pares translated the fables of Krylov, using Russian peasant soldiers as his linguistic informants. During his visits to Russia

Baring was fond of pretending to be someone other than he was and getting into conversation with peasants and private soldiers. His writings on Russia abound with comments on what he saw as the unspoiled perception of God among the common people in Russia, such as: 'The churches are still crowded in Russia, and they have that attribute without which a Church is not a Church—they smell of the poor.'[72] This sort of attitude—that poverty corre-lates with spirituality, and that the innocence and authenticity supposedly lost by the over-civilized West can be recaptured through mental copulation with the 'Russian idea'—was common among foreign Russia-lovers before 1917, and it seems to be indelible. It stemmed in large part, of course, from never having nor choosing to go near the vast tracts of England that 'smelled of the poor'; after all, the Russians concerned were still on the whole picturesquely rural rather than swarming together as a nasty urban industrial proletariat. This atti-tude towards Russia was without doubt one of the things that drove Mirsky to distraction when he was an *émigré*.

After Baring and Pares, into Mirsky's ken came the atheist Jane Ellen Harrison, a 74-year-old intellectual Englishwoman whose entire life was spent denigrating Englishness and looking for alternatives to it. Then came the Bloomsburyites. To these quintessentially English oddities was added in 1928 Dorothy Galton, the daughter of the Secretary of the Fabian Society, who, as she primly declared in her account of her friendship with Mirsky, 'made no secret' of her own Socialism. It is little comfort to reflect that Mirsky's social acquaintance in his own country was almost equally restricted; before he emi-grated, he was a prince and a Guards officer who moved in Court circles; after he went back, he lived in the well-serviced ghetto of the Writers' Union. There is no evidence that Mirsky, obsessionally busy as he was with his writing, ever did anything to broaden his familiarity with the people of his new country, for example by 'listening in' to the wireless, which revolutionized public commu-nications during the 1920s; even under the Reith conventions he could have heard something about the world outside his intellectual and sociological cocoon.[73] He seems never to have done anything for the sake of entertainment or relaxation—except take to the bottle.

During the 1920s Mirsky seems never to have gone far afield even in London. Apart from his visits to the Golitsyns at Chessington, he remained an insular Bloomsburyite from the beginning to the end of his time in London. His earliest surviving series of letters from London, from May 1922 to February 1923, were written from 24 Gordon Square, the address of the School of Slavonic Studies. From January 1924 through to May 1926 Mirsky addressed most of his letters from 15 Torrington Square, in the middle of Bloomsbury. Writing to Michael Florinsky on 16 May 1926, Mirsky refers to 17 Gower Street, London WC1, as his 'new adress' (to retain his habitual Franco-Russian spelling), and almost all the remaining letters that he wrote in London are from there. This was the premises of the London University Club, just round the corner from what soon became the Senate House site. Whether or not Mirsky actually lived in this building, or simply used it as an office, is not clear. In one early letter to Dorothy Galton he referred to a 'housekeeper' at this address, and so he may have resided there. Janko Lavrin recalled visiting Mirsky several times in a room at the top of a house in Montague Street, which runs along the east wall of the British Museum from Russell Street to Russell Square. The School was housed on the other side of the Museum, in 'a former army hut on Malet Street', which had two rooms;[74] it moved to 40 Torrington Square in 1929, and there at last the seven members of staff had 'a room of one's own', something one of their Bloomsbury near neighbours considered rather important. Vera Traill remembered Mirsky eating at Lyons Café and the further downmarket (but still 'respectable') ABC tea-rooms because 'there isn't anything appetizing in England anyway', and saving up his money for vacations in France.

The most significant factor in Mirsky's confrontation with England was that he had grown up in a cultural and intellectual atmosphere in which many people had felt the apocalypse to be imminently at hand—and they had not been deluded.[75] In 1917–20 he had lived through events that had fundamentally changed the circumstances of his own life, those of his country, and the history of the world. And then he came to a country where, as it seemed to him, nothing momentous had yet happened, and what Akhmatova in her *Poem without a Hero* (1940) called 'the real twentieth century' had yet to begin. In the one piece he published in Russia while he was in emigration, Mirsky asserted:

For England the war was not a great national tragedy such as it was in France and Germany, but only a series of small, personal family tragedies, it did not revive, nor give a second birth to, nor yet cripple the English soul, and notwithstanding the rise in income tax and unemployment, England still remains the same almost in everything as it was in 1913.[76]

Writing here for the neophyte Soviet Russian readership, he could not mention Russia along with France and Germany in this context, as it seems blindingly obvious that he should have done. Mirsky made this statement before many of the monuments to the dead of the First World War were put up all over the country, but it is doubtful that even they would have altered his attitude. The only Englishman of his own generation he came to know at all well in London seems to have been his exact contemporary and School colleague, the shy and retiring unmarried bookworm Norman Jopson (1890–1969), like Harold Williams a prodigious linguist; because of his knowledge of 'obscure' languages Jopson was used in London in intelligence during the Great War, and he was never on active service.

Mirsky arrived in England in the year of the first London performance of *The Rite of Spring*, the year in which Yeats in 'The Second Coming' descried his 'rough beast' slouching towards Bethlehem to be born. The following year, he read *The Waste Land* and *Ulysses*, and changed his mind about England's cultural backwardness. As did T. S. Eliot at the time, in postwar England Mirsky discerned an ideological aridity that for him was the true sign of decline and fall in a nation's history. But Mirsky's way out was the opposite of Eliot's; writing as a Marxist in 1929, Mirsky said, using the language of vitalism that permeates his early writings:

For it is one of the main differences between the 'healthy,' 'constructive,' industrial and ascendent capitalism of the nineteenth century and the decadent, openly preda-tory and senescent capitalism of the twentieth that the former was and the latter is not capable of creating a system of ideas that might justify its existence.[77]

The full fruit of this negative attitude, expressed now with a good deal of scornful personal malice, was to be put on display in Mirsky's *The Intelligentsia of Great Britain*. To most people outside Russia who commented on it when the translation was published in 1935, this book seemed to be an unfair, unwar-ranted, and unforgivable outburst that had been made purely for the sake of political accreditation; this itself is evidence of the political polarization that was taking hold in England at the time. There is very little evidence before 1929 that Mirsky did anything but enjoy and profit from the cultural delights of Bloomsbury; but in *The Intelligentsia* he breached one of the fundamental tenets of the Bloomsbury code, which was to value and be loyal to friends above all else, including country. Mirsky the Marxist decisively placed friendship second to the demands of political ideology. But in view of his lack of real friends in London, there cannot have been much of a struggle.

WRITING BOOKS

Mirsky's literature lectures at the School of Slavonic Studies were a test-bed on which he developed, in an amazingly short time, what were to become his most important books. As early as 19 March 1924, less than two years after he had started delivering these lectures, Mirsky asked Pares for help in pub-lishing them in America and undertaking an associated lecture tour.[78] On 20 August he told Pares that he had decided not to go to America in 1925 be-cause he was 'too full up with work', having signed contracts to write no fewer than four books before the end of the summer of that year. Instead, Mirsky proposed to visit America in 1926.

The four books Mirsky has in mind here came out in rapid succession. In 1925 Oxford University Press published his *Modern Russian Literature* in the 'World's Manuals' series, a highly compressed account in about 120 small-format pages that ends its story at the outbreak of war and was soon overtaken by Mirsky's own lengthier treatments, but which retains its value as a short-compass survey. Besides the aphorisms that glitter throughout the book, it includes such things as arguably the best brief comparative summary in any language of the significance of Dostoevsky and Tolstoy, a splendid page on the differences between the Russian and English poets of the Victorian age, and a highly instructive (and original, one of the earliest such summaries) supplement listing translations of Russian literature into English. In February 1925, Mirsky finished the first volume of his big history, *Contemporary Russian Literature 1881–1925*, which he dedicated to Maurice Baring.

In September and October 1925 Mirsky proofread not only this book, a matter of over 350 printed pages, but also a monograph that he had managed to write simultaneously with it, *Pushkin*, about 250 printed pages long.[79] This biographically structured introduction to the Russian national poet, the first serious monograph on his work in English, had been heralded in 1923 by Mirsky's first article for the *Slavonic Review*, which remains to this day the best short introduction to the subject. It makes no reference whatsoever to secondary sources, and sustains from beginning to end a level of incisively expressed insight that is exemplified by the following passage contrasting Pushkin and the Russian intelligentsia, a subject that Mirsky was to return to often. Mirsky is defining himself here; his character contained both the sides that he contrasts, and in his intellectual development he moved from the Pushkin side towards that of the intelligentsia:

Perhaps even the easiest way of describing Pushkin would be to enumerate the characteristics of the Russian intelligentsia—and then to say that Pushkin is just the opposite. In politics, for instance, the intelligentsia stands for equality, anarchy, radicalism; Pushkin for liberty, law and tradition. The intelligentsia abhors all established forms of religion, but would be very glad to institute a compulsory irreligious creed of its own: it is fanatical without faith; Pushkin had an intelligent respect (I use the word this time in its true English meaning) for the time-honoured and efficient institution of the Christian Church, but had no need of a religion for himself. The intelligentsia has no interest in discovering the essential laws that rule the moral universe, but it is very anxious to impose on its fellow-creatures laws of its own making. Pushkin has no strong personal views on what is right or wrong in other people; but he has an almost uncanny knowledge of the moral laws that actually do govern this world of ours. The intelligentsia has a profound respect for the profession of letters and a deep contempt for the craft; Pushkin thought little of the profession, and much of the craft. This series of antitheses might be prolonged indefinitely.[80]

The Pushkin book of 1926 has been reprinted several times, and remains particularly valuable for the author's compelling account of Pushkin's class sensibilities, a topic that was to return to haunt Mirsky in the 1930s. In June 1926, Mirsky also finished the second volume of his *History*, which covers from the beginnings to 1881.[81] The English and American editions were published simultaneously on 22 April 1927.

In the course of three years of intense work, writing in his second language, still only in his mid-30s, and after a severance of many years from major libraries and the centres of literary life, Mirsky had thus produced what for most people would have been more than enough to rest on as a lifetime's achievement. At the same time, as we shall see, he had been vigorously publishing in Russian as well. And the spring of 1926 was also the time when Mirsky's involvement with Marina Tsvetaeva was at its height.

THE *HISTORY*

When it appeared in 1926–7, Mirsky's history of Russian literature was neither the earliest nor the most comprehensive treatment of the subject, in English or in any other major European language. There is no mystery about the materials that Mirsky had to hand, because he supplied a pithily annotated 'working bibliography' for each of his two original volumes. These bibliographies provide a list of translated works, not only into English but also into French and German. Mirsky's task in writing the history was made feasible by the toil of the translators. The result was that when he was dealing with Russian prose from before about 1910, he did not have to waste space summarizing plots.

Mirsky seemed to feel that his predecessors had written not out of an admiration for the subject but out of various kinds of inferiority complex, with an agenda that began either from finding chimerical alternatives to the culture of their own first language on the part of foreigners or from apologias for their backwardness and imitativeness on the part of Russians. Mirsky wrote as someone who was quite sure that he had grown up during one of the great periods of his nation's literature and that he possessed first-hand inside knowledge of it. At the time he wrote his *History*, he was keeping company with the European intellectual élite of his day, especially at Pontigny, and he knew he had nothing to fear. After all, he had read all their literatures in the original and could communicate with them in their own languages. None of them could say the same of themselves with regard to him. Perhaps most important of all, Mirsky was writing out of a conviction that his country had actually gone and committed what the Dostoevsky-crazed foreign Russophiles had seen as the most distinctive potential *acte gratuit* and behaved like Raskolnikov or even Stavrogin, self-destructing out of a metaphysical fascination with sin. But Russia, Mirsky thought, had then come out on the other side, and he wrote his *History* partly out of fierce national pride: 'We may affirm that Russian literature—and with it the soul of the Russian nation—has stood the test and passed the ordeal. The invincible freedom and courage of the human soul has emerged victorious from its Purgatory, and purified by its fires.'[82]

In terms of critical writing for the general public, British appreciation of Russian literature followed in the footsteps of France; Mirsky had a very high opinion of the key pioneering work, Melchior de Vogüé's *Le Roman russe* (1886), though he did lay at its door the creation of 'that cheapest and vulgarest of French inventions, "the Slav soul"'.[83] Maurice Baring's books picked up from there. All in all, in terms of both translation and critical writing, English (and, on the whole, American) knowledge of Russian literature when Mirsky began writing reflected something like the literary-historical situation as it had existed in Russia up to and including the year 1910; for example, the cult of Dostoevsky, which began in Russia in the 1890s, took off in England in 1912.[84] For Mirsky, however, the year 1910 in many respects marked the beginning of a new age that for him had killed the reputations of some previously well-regarded writers (foremost among them Merezhkovsky, Andreev, and Artsybashev) and utterly changed the perspective from which others (such as Gorky) needed to be approached.

If the educated English readership knew something about Russian prose, even belatedly, very little Russian poetry had been translated into English, and even less had been expertly discussed. In fact, within living memory only two substantial books had been specifically devoted to the subject. The first is well informed and contains some exceptionally good translations, but ends with Nadson (1862–85);[85] the second is by a rank amateur whose knowledge was risibly superficial and out of date.[86] For Mirsky, writing when he did for the English public—beginning as late as 1922—the English reader has to be given elementary information even about Blok, who had died the previous year.

Just before Mirsky published his *History*, the situation in England was improved by the appearance of an anthology whose preface he regarded as entirely praiseworthy so far as it went, Maurice Baring's *Oxford Book of Russian Verse* (1924). Baring's selection was in all likelihood influenced by Mirsky's Russian anthology of the same year, or at least by discussions of it with the compiler; at the end of his preface, Baring recommends Mirsky's work. Like Mirsky's *History*, this book has held its place since its first publication, and Mirsky's notes have remained in print at the back of it, though shorn of an attribution to him since the expanded edition of 1946. But Baring's anthology contains only one post-revolutionary poem, by Voloshin, whereas Mirsky's anthology ends challengingly with Pasternak and mentions his name in its subtitle.

Mirsky's very earliest articles in English aimed primarily to inform the reading public about the hitherto unknown poets of the period after 1910. Outstanding among them, besides Blok and Voloshin, were Akhmatova, Gumilyov, Mayakovsky, Pasternak, and, later, Mandelshtam and Tsvetaeva. This created an enduring legacy: with the exception of Mayakovsky and Blok, and to a certain extent Pasternak, these poets were soon subjected to severe misrepresentation in their own country, or not mentioned at all. For the English-speaking world, Mirsky's books and articles placed them firmly on the map, and they stayed there.

In the opening sentence of a piece dated 'May, 1924', just before he signed the contract to write his *History*, Mirsky was blunt: 'The English reading public knows next to nothing of contemporary Russian literature.'[87] Like all worthwhile books, Mirsky's history was undertaken because the author felt strongly that what had been said before was either misleading or incomplete, or both, and that he had the knowledge and talent to put things right. The misleading element was the interpretation of Russian literature current in the West:

Western histories of Russian literature are in the habit of telling their readers, to begin with, that Russian literature is different from every other literature in the world in that it is more closely linked with politics and social history. This is simply not true. Russian literature, especially after 1905, is almost surprisingly non-political, considering the colossal political cataclysms it witnessed. Even when treating 'political' subjects, modern Russian writers are in substance non-political; even when they write propaganda, like Mayakovsky, propaganda in their hands is a means, and not an end.[88]

Fighting talk indeed; and it has to be said that in this respect Mirsky has remained on the whole a voice crying in the wilderness, especially after the experience of the Stalinist literary system. It is evident from this statement that Mirsky shared an idea the Russian Formalists were fetishizing at the time—that of the autonomy of the literary process: 'Literature has a life of its own which goes its way undeviated by political and social revolutions.'[89]

This principle is manifested widely in Mirsky's literary-historical writings, most obviously in the ways that his work is subdivided into topics and in the way periodization is conceptualized. Within the autonomous literary process, Mirsky sees the literary genres as both inter- and intra-acting: periods when prose is dominant alternate with periods when poetry is dominant, prose strong in narrative alternates with 'ornamental' or self-referential prose, and so on. Only once does Mirsky actually name a driving force behind this ceaseless movement, in speaking of Russian prose in the early 1920s, and he makes a reversion to Bergsonism: 'But the novel [Erenburg's *Julio Jurenito*] is frankly cheap and second-rate, and it is quite evident that the *élan vital* of Russian prose is concentrated in the formless and baroque productions of the aggressively Russian and "Eastern" ornamentalists.'[90]

When he wrote his *History*, Mirsky seems to have had no hesitations about what constituted his proper object of concern. Print culture was supreme, and Mirsky's work celebrates it. In actual fact, it celebrates not print culture in general, but *books*, and in particular, novels and collections of poetry. Further, Mirsky had a 'traditional' view of the genre hierarchy within literature; his occasional remarks about popular reading are almost all by way of being contemptuous or indulgent asides about something that he does not hesitate to write off as second-rate. Mirsky never doubted the legitimacy of 'the canon', and his comparative rankings and placings are made with endless self-confidence, and with no tincture of relativism:

symbolism was an aristocratic poetry, which appealed, all said and done, only to the elect. Akhmátova's poetry is more universally interesting, but if it does not require any intellectual preparation, at least it demands from its reader a finer sensibility than that of the average newspaper-reader and picture-goer. But the picture-goer and newspaper-reader aspired to have his own poetry, and the great widening of poetical taste allowed by the symbolists permitted the inclusion within the pale of poetry of much that was not allowed by the 'Victorians'. The moment came when vulgarity claimed a place on Parnassus and issued its declaration of rights in the verse of Igor Severyánin (pseudonym of I. V. Lótarev, 1887–1942).[91]

The *History* was written at a point of equilibrium in Mirsky's unquiet intellectual development, and it shows him at his best. The bedrock of its enduring merit is the series of superb summaries it presents of the literary achievement of the major authors in their chronological and generic sequence. Mirsky chose to deal separately with the poetry and prose works of several authors, rather than breaking the genre continuity of the book. The summaries have never been surpassed. One candidate for the masterpiece of summarization must surely be the account of Herzen's work in Mirsky's chapter on 'The Age of Realism: Journalists, Poets, and Playwrights'. As elsewhere, it leads off with a sure-footed chronological account of the author's life. Mirsky then confronts the principal problem he faces in assessing Herzen: his rival claims to attention, as political thinker versus literary figure. Inevitably deciding that in the context of his history of Russian literature he must privilege the latter, Mirsky nevertheless proceeds to characterize Herzen's political thinking with a confidence and authority that very few literary historians can match, in three packed paragraphs, of which the third is the epitome of judiciousness:

What makes Herzen, however, much more than a mere teacher of revolutionary doctrines, and conciliates with him even those who are least inclined to share his aspirations, is his intellectual fairness and capacity for detachment. In spite of the extremeness of his views, he could understand his enemies and judge them by *their* standards. His historical intuition, his ability to see history in broad outline, to understand the significance of details and to *relate* them to the main lines, is marvellous. His thought is mainly historical, and the way he understood history as a spontaneous, unpredestined, incalculable force continuing the equally spontaneous and unpredestined evolution of nature makes him, like Grigóriev, akin to Bergson. He saw the 'creativeness' of the process of becoming, the novelty of every future in relation to every past, and the pages he devotes to the confutation of all idea of predestination, all notion of an extrinsic *idea* guiding human history, are among the most eloquent he wrote.[92]

Mirsky then goes on to give a brilliant thumbnail sketch of each of Herzen's major works. The significance of his third introductory paragraph goes far beyond the immediate subject with which it is concerned, of course; it is an ideal definition of the stance from which Mirsky's masterpiece itself was written, but with history substituted for literature. This enlightened liberalism was soon to be abandoned under the pressure of political developments by Mirsky himself, and also by the subsequent historiography of his subject. The 'Herzen attitude' was largely brushed aside, except by Isaiah Berlin, who treated it as tenable even in the face of the political horrors that drove others towards the extremes of right or left. Berlin's endorsement of the one-volume edition of Mirsky's history is one of the most eloquent tributes to its value.[93] Mirsky's analysis of Herzen's enlightened liberalism surely played its part in shaping Isaiah Berlin's own interpretation of him, the keystone of Berlin's interpretation of Russian thought.

It would betray the spirit in which Mirsky's great history of Russian literature was written to treat it as somehow set in stone as the last word on its subject. It does, after all, end in 1925. But apart from this, in Mirsky's day, to use Chekhov as an example, the English reader had available in translation a fairly full repertoire of the short stories and plays, and a small number of critical accounts; and Mirsky could set about countering these writings in the knowledge that his reader could encompass everything he was talking about. Since then, innumerable alternative translations have been made, and the plays have accumulated a rich stage history; and all this has been discussed by people who do not necessarily have any knowledge of the original texts. Also, an army of professional Russianists have been at work, in Russia and abroad, and they have drawn on a body of primary and secondary materials whose extent Mirsky would have been hard put to imagine. Innumerable variations in perspective on all the classic authors have been brought about by the accumulation of another seventy years' worth of Russian creative writers who have continued to orient themselves on them and rewrite the history of their reception. The value of Mirsky's contribution has been if anything enhanced by this situation; the present-day specialist, especially the beginner, needs primary, uncluttered, and authoritative orientation and guidance more than anything else, and again, in this respect Mirsky has not been bettered. His facts are almost all right, his sense of priorities is acute, and he always gives his reader—the expert as well as the beginner—something to think about and build on.

Mirsky's history originally came out in two volumes. The book dealing with the later period, *Contemporary Russian Literature, 1881–1925*, was written first, and published in 1926. *A History of Russian Literature from the Earliest Times to the Death of Dostoevsky (1881)* came out the following year. Both books were reissued several times in Britain and the USA, but by 1945 they were out of print. They took on a new lease of life just over twenty years after their first appearance, when Francis J. Whitfield edited and abridged them into one volume, with the simple main title *A History of Russian Literature*. This is the book, several times reprinted, that generations of students and teachers have known simply as 'Mirsky'. Whitfield conscientiously and honestly explained how he had set about his editorial task in his Preface. The abridgement brought

Mirsky's text down to a total of just over 500 pages. In the original books, the entire history of the subject up to 1881 was dealt with in just under 400 pages, while the modern period, the following forty-five years to 1925, was allotted only twenty or so pages less. In the one-volume abridgement, the balance is quite different, roughly three-fifths to two-fifths. The missing parts, unfortunately, deal with exactly those authors and subjects where what Mirsky had to say was at its most immediate and original, but where his vision was inevitably foreshortened by the fact that most of the writers were at the time in mid-career.[94]

Two particularly unfortunate victims of the abridgement are Remizov and Tsvetaeva. The account of the history of Russian prose in the one-volume abridgement ends with Remizov's work up to 1920, while the discussion of his subsequent work represents Mirsky's most original contribution to the history of contemporary Russian prose (and not just for the English reader). Tsvetaeva is represented in the one-volume edition by a single paragraph, which takes up three-quarters of one page, mentions only one specific work (*The King-Maiden*), and contains a good deal of negative comment, such as 'At her worst she is painfully pretentious (as in her prose) and obscure'. This judgement was set down just before Mirsky met Tsvetaeva personally and published the earliest and most percipient accounts of her mature poetry. Although Mirsky never saw the mature autobiographical prose Tsvetaeva wrote in the 1930s, his judgement of 1925—based on the small number of violently partisan essays she wrote before that date—has often been mistaken as a judgement on her prose as a whole.

Almost all the translations that adorn the original two volumes are missing from the abridgement; understandably, they come from the chronological extremes of Mirsky's coverage, with at the one end the extensive extracts from the *Lay of the Host of Igor* and Avvakum's epistles, and at the other some inspired selections from Rozanov and some superbly judged prose versions of Akhmatova's lyrics. But perhaps the most regrettable omission of all from the one-volume *History* was the annotated bibliographies; apart from giving the most succinct possible idea for the reader of where things stood when Mirsky began, they contain some of his most acute critical judgements. All these losses were exacerbated when a paperback version of Whitfield's version was issued that further curtails Mirsky's account by terminating at 1900; this became the most accessible version of Mirsky's masterpiece.[95]

AFTER THE *HISTORY*

The *History* put Mirsky incontestably in the position he has never subsequently lost, as the principal intermediary between Russian literature and the English-speaking world. The contemporary reviews of the two volumes ranged between positive and ecstatic. Mirsky even became something of a literary lion. On 30 January 1928 he accepted an invitation to dinner from the London branch of the PEN Club; his letter shows that he had mastered British self-deprecation: 'I feel highly honoured by your invitation to dine at the PEN. I accept it with great pleasure, though also with great misgivings, as I do not feel fit to speak before so distinguished an audience.'[96] On 28 February the Secretary instructed Mirsky that a speech of five minutes would be 'admirable', and on 29 February Mirsky promised not to exceed this limit. On 7 March Mirsky informed Suvchinsky that this meeting, which he said had been held in his honour, had taken place the day before; his speech really had lasted five minutes and was about 'the primacy of being over consciousness, and had an enormous success'. This idea had really struck the English, he told Suvchinsky with barely veiled contempt, so much so that he had been 'asked to take it further!' More tangible acknowledgement by the British cultural establishment soon came his way: Mirsky contributed some articles to the stopgap edition of the *Encyclopaedia Britannica* in 1926;[97] he then duly contributed several entries on his subject to the full 14th edition (1929). Among them is the major article 'Russian Literature'.[98]

It was entirely typical of Mirsky that he did not rest on his laurels and remain within the professional field in which he had made himself such a solid reputation in England and the USA. Instead, in his general intellectual interests and his writing in English, Mirsky turned increasingly to Russian history. In all, forty-five of the total number of items in Mirsky's bibliography, about one-tenth of the total, deal with entirely non-literary subjects, primarily politics and current affairs. Of them, twenty-one were published in the period 1929–32. They include a major article that once more signals Mirsky's acceptance by the English establishment, a contribution to the *Cambridge Medieval History*.[99] Mirsky told Suvchinsky on 4 March 1927 that he was 'struggling' with this piece, and that it would 'come out very weak'; he probably has in mind the way the factual information outweighs the conceptual aspect of his essay. Then there are four books, all of them in English. The seventy-nine-page *A History of Russia* that Mirsky produced for a series published by the amateur Russia-watcher Ernest Benn (London, 1927) is a minor affair; the series in which this book appeared, Benn's Sixpenny Library, was edited by Victor Gollancz, who several years later started his own firm and published Mirsky's book on the intelligentsia of Great Britain.

The other three books Mirsky undertook during his last three years in emigration are much more substantial. Two of them appeared in 1931: *Lenin*, the work Mirsky considered to be of crucial importance in his intellectual development, and *Russia: A Social History*. Mirsky probably began writing this book, one of his biggest, in 1928; it was completed in the spring of 1929, but did not appear until 1931. The preface to *Lenin* is dated 'May, 1930'. When exactly Mirsky translated the two stoutish volumes of Pokrovsky's *Brief*

History of Russia is not clear; they came out in 1933, after he had gone back to Russia. In his surviving letters there is no explicit mention of this project; it would seem from the fact that he attributed some significance to it in his conversion to Marxism that he was busy with it in 1931 and perhaps the first half of 1932.

Notwithstanding his turn to history, Mirsky went on writing about contemporary Russian literature for ten years after he finished his great book. Besides his contributions in Russian on literary subjects to the newspaper *Eurasia* in 1928–9, in these same years he continued his activities as an intermediary between Russian and Western European cultures, and in certain respects expanded them, at the expense of his English-language contributions. We have seen that in England he took an active part in the Tolstoy centenary of 1928; but the special supplement on Tolstoy he edited for the *Slavonic Review* in 1929 was his last major contribution to the School's house journal. In 1930 he published only three items in it, and in 1931, two. His contributions to the *London Mercury* continued unabated until 1930; the later ones include a particularly enthusiastic review article of one of the most important feats of literary research of these years, Helen Waddell's study of the Goliard poets.[100]

The least-known element in Mirsky's writing on literature for the English-speaking public is a series of prefaces he wrote in the late 1920s for various limited editions of Russian classics. These pieces were undertaken, obviously, first and foremost in order to make easy money, but they are by no means perfunctory. For example, the preface Mirsky furnished for an exquisite edition of *The Queen of Spades*, published by one of his close Russian associates in London, is a *tour de force*; it includes some of his boldest generalizations both about Pushkin and about poetry in general:

One feature in Pushkin's style will make him unacceptable as long as romantic standards dominate the Western world. This is his absolute avoidance of metaphor. Ever since the romantic revival metaphor and poetry have been practically identified. But Pushkin was a pre-romanticist. He had not reverted to the primitive mythical mentality which does not distinguish between an object and its image. He had not divorced poetry from reason. For him, as for those great rationalists, Homer and Dante, the *simile* was an instrument good enough to dominate the entire world of images. The simile distinguishes what the metaphor confuses. It is active, where the metaphor is passive: better than anything else it bridges the gulf between poetry and reason. Pushkin never regarded poetry as hostile to reason. . . . But only part of Pushkin's work is inspired by this lofty 'geometrical' conception of poetry as understanding. It is the most important and, alone, answers to the proudest definition that can be given of poetry: a non-Euclidean ethics. If the Russians are justified in placing Pushkin by the side of Homer and Dante, it is on the strength of that small number of poems—*The Gypsies, Mozart and Salieri, The Stone Guest, Rusalka, The Bronze Horseman*, a few lyrics—in which he crystallized his understanding of the tragic.[101]

This book was published by the Blackamore Press, a creation of the remarkable Flora Solomon, who probably made a deeper impression on British society than any other Russian, *émigré(e)* or otherwise, when she reorganized the management style of the Marks and Spencer stores. As business manager of her publishing enterprise she brought in J. E. Pouterman, with Mirsky as chief editor. J. E. (Iosif Efimovich) Pouterman (1885–1940) is one of the most shadowy figures in Mirsky's *émigré* life,[102] but they were obviously frequent companions. Like Mirsky, Pouterman divided his time between London and Paris. He was friendly with Erenburg, and was one of several acquaintances Mirsky had in the world of French journalism; in the 1930s Pouterman edited the left-wing weekly *Lu*. Flora Solomon described her other editor:

In contrast to Pouterman, Dmitri Sviatopolk-Mirsky, son of the liberal politician of Tsarist days, was a rip-roaring *bon viveur* eternally short of the funds to finance his drinking. We met for dinner in Paris while he was working on our handsome edition of Milton's *Brief History of Moscovia* . . . Dmitri had given his family tradition an ironic twist by espousing Communism, and eventually returned to Russia as a Soviet citizen. But at our dinner an excess of wine washed this momentarily out of his system and he reverted to his origins. He startled me by rising shakily from his chair and inviting the entire restaurant to join him in a toast to the dynasty of Romanov! He grieved at the complacency with which the West bore its ignorance of Russian culture and felt a special responsibility for making Pushkin available to the English reader. So we issued a selection of Pushkin's letters, with the master's own drawings reproduced in collotype, as well as a de luxe edition of *The Queen of Spades* bound in goat vellum and priced at ten guineas. I don't recall whether this sold like hot cakes or whether hundreds remained tucked away under Pouterman's bed in Great Russell Street.[103]

Mirsky's supreme achievement as a translator into English also appeared as a limited edition, his version of Gogol's *Diary of a Madman*, published in a sumptuously illustrated edition of only 250 copies by the Cresset Press.[104] One of the least well known but most rewarding of Mirsky's general works on Russian poetry was published as an introduction to a book of translations by the obscure amateur Charles Fillingham Coxwell.[105] But the most original and penetrating of all these pieces is not about literature, but, characteristically for Mirsky's changing interests at this time, about history, an edition—again by the Blackamore Press, as we know—of John Milton's compilatory narrative about Russia, which Flora Solomon particularly remembered.[106]

As Mirsky's academic commitment to England waned, he switched his attention more to the Continent. He made several substantial contributions to a new scholarly periodical, *Slavische Rundschau*, which was launched in 1929. They include a farewell to *émigré* literature in which Mirsky notices the poetry of Poplavsky, which parallels a piece published almost simultaneously in Russian.[107] The connection with the German journal was made via Roman Jakobson, with N. S. Trubetskoy acting as matchmaker.[108] In 1931 Mirsky published the single item among all his writings to appear originally in Italian, a substantial piece on Dostoevsky.[109]

On the Continent, though, apart from his Russian-language activities, which peaked in 1928–9, Mirsky's main involvement was with the French journal *Commerce*, which was published in Paris between 1924 and 1932.[110] Its chief editors were Paul Valéry and Saint John Perse. The sponsor and director was the wealthy American Marguerite, née Chapin (1880–1963), who was married to the dilettante musician Prince Roffredo Bassiano-Caetani (1871–1961) and was a diligent patroness of the arts.[111] Mirsky's involvement began in November 1926, and was made in exchange for Marguerite Bassiano's support for Mirsky's journal *Vyorsts*. The connection with *Commerce* may well originally have been made through André Gide, whom Mirsky probably first met at Pontigny in 1924; their acquaintance continued into the 1930s.

Hélène Izvolsky devoted some space to her dealings with this journal in her maddeningly vague memoirs. In her account of the journal, she says that 'The Russian adviser, Mirsky, came to Versailles as often as he visited Paris. He was still the black-bearded and rather fierce-looking man I had known in uniform. He was now more mature, however, and had acquired prestige which made him resemble a "Byzantine emperor", according to Marguerite Bassiano's enthusiastic opinion.'[112] This coming to Versailles refers to the Bassianos' Sunday receptions; among the people Izvolsky met there were Valéry as the person who presided, Stravinsky, Erik Satie, Prokofiev, Poulenc, Ravel, Dufy, Derain, Horowitz (who played 'Chopsticks' for the guests), Fargue, Julien Benda, and chain-smoking Bernard Groethuysen. It was here that Mirsky maintained the place he had established through his attendance at Pontigny among the élite of the European literary intelligentsia. In his Journal under 26 September 1929, Gide reports a trip to one of the Bassianos' regular open houses; the car mentioned here was one of a chauffeured fleet that was sent out for the guests and later took them home: 'At three-thirty the Princess de Bassiano's motor comes to pick me up and take me, together with Alix Guillain, Groethuysen, and Prince Mirsky, to Versailles, where I spend the rest of the day. I talk with much greater facility than ordinarily, feeling that I am being listened to with affectionate interest.'[113]

Gide was moving to the left politically in roughly the same way as Mirsky, but not so decisively. In his letters to Michael Florinsky, Mirsky goes out of his way to report on Gide, most probably because of Gide's contemporary notoriety as an avowed homosexual and therefore a person of considerable interest to Florinsky. And Dorothy Galton, when talking about Mirsky's summer journeys, several times mentioned that his eventual destination was Le Levandou, in the vicinity of Gide's home. Gide finally became a Communist in 1934 and journeyed to Moscow, and then recanted in his sensational *Retour de l'U.R.S.S.* (Paris, 1936). Mirsky saw Gide at Gorky's funeral in 1936, but the extent of the personal contact between the two in the 1930s is not clear.

The kind of inclusive yet independent-minded self-confidence with which Mirsky wrote the *History* and the essays that followed it was largely lost after his generation, to the immense advantage of certain branches of literary study, but to the detriment of the general historiography of literature, which has become less and less feasible as canonic conviction has wavered and fallen.

Mirsky felt that he belonged to the first generation of genuine literary critics that his nation had brought forth. He consistently sets his face against the sociological critics of the nineteenth century, and his alternative canon of Russian criticism forms an interesting and original selection that has never really been investigated. He declared several times that he considered the only genuine literary critic of his time to have been Konstantin Leontiev (1831–91), whose masterpiece, Mirsky said more than once, was his book on Tolstoy of 1891. After Leontiev, Mirsky particularly admired two lawyers who wrote literary criticism in the 1880s and 1890s. The first of them was S. A. Andreevsky (1847–1920), whose critical essays (1891) were, apart from the work of Leontiev, 'the only work of criticism in the true, European sense of the word, as distinct from party propaganda, that appeared in Russia between the time of Belinsky and that of Merezhkovsky'. The other was Prince A. I. Urusov (1843–1900), who 'was one of the best critics of literature of his time, though all his criticism was contained in conversation and private letters'.[114] The high esteem in which Mirsky holds these gentlemen is quite shocking for a Russian literary intellectual; if Mirsky's princely origin and military connections were not enough to set him apart from his fellows, his positive words about lawyers show how radically his cast of mind diverged from that of the intelligentsia as a whole.

And so Mirsky regarded himself as a pioneer, but not as an isolated voice. Despite everything that has been said about his subjectivity—a quality for which *émigré* and Soviet commentators alike have unanimously hastened to condemn him—Mirsky regarded himself as an objective critic who expressed the communality of literary taste of his generation. He said as much several times: 'I believe that my taste is to a certain extent representative of my literary generation, and that *on the whole* my appreciations will not seem paradoxical or capricious to the competent Russian reader.'[115]

The following passage, written in Russian at exactly the time Mirsky was putting together the first volume of his *History*, is the most revealing statement he ever made about objectivity and subjectivity, for confusing which he has so often been condemned:

The critic must not bother about differences in taste, but attempt to explain the objective (*objective*) value of what is going on around him. This task is hopeless, of course, and practicable only with the coarsest approximation. Every writer has his objective magnitude, his particular amount of power (the eventual coefficient of which depends, of course, not on natural power alone, but also on the way it is applied—that is elementary). This power may be deployed against the grain for me personally. But it is my obligation to measure this power. Instruments to measure it (a 'powerometer' perhaps) have not yet been invented. But empirically, in the end a sort of general *consensus doctorum* comes about that with time acquires greater and perhaps final convincingness. Everyone has the right (and I deploy it in every way I can) not to love Dostoevsky and Chekhov, and to prefer (as I do) Pisemsky and Kushchevsky, say.[116] But to assert that Pisemsky is *greater* than Dostoevsky or Kushchevsky *greater* than Chekhov is as plainly wrong as it would be to say that Brussels has more inhabitants than London. It is from the point of view of this kind of 'powerometer' that I wish to approach contemporary Russian literature.[117]

In all Mirsky's writings, there is not a single item devoted to the exposition of a theoretical position. The nearest he ever came was a review he published in Russian in 1925, at just the same time as he was writing the *History* in English. The review is concerned with the last publications brought out by the Russian Formalist critics as such. Their most enduring works were actually published at this stage, in 1923–4, after the *Sturm und Drang* period of Formalism was over, and when, as Mirsky says here of Shklovsky, 'instead of easy victories over the old social-minded critics from the intelligentsia and the impressionists, he has to defend himself against the much more fearsome enemy of official Marxism'. In this single piece, Mirsky dealt with Eikhenbaum's *Through Literature* and *Lermontov*, Slonimsky's *The Technique of the Comic in Gogol*, Tomashevsky's *Russian Versification*, Tynyanov's *The Problem of Verse Language*, and Zhirmunsky's *Rhyme: Its History and Theory* and *Byron and Pushkin*.

The central theoretical positions of these classic books are formulated by Mirsky with astonishing acuity, and compared and contrasted with each other with equal pithiness. Mirsky pays due tribute to the way these post-Shklovskian scholars had laid the basis for a genuinely historical and also text-based approach to the literary work. The most telling sentence in the piece comes at the conclusion of Mirsky's discussion of Eikhenbaum, keyed by the latter's notion that 'To study an event historically does not at all mean to describe it as a single occurrence'. Mirsky comments:

This historicism, which is so different from the usual kind, brings Eikhenbaum closer to Marxism, with which he is also made akin by his undeviating and simplifying dogmaticism. It hardly needs to be said that this dogmaticism of his is totally *a priori*, and Eikhenbaum does not even attempt to ground it by means of a broad comparative-historical method. And that is not all—he insists that theory must *precede* knowledge, for only then can research bear fruit . . .[118]

Mirsky makes this sentence tail off with suspension points, all the more eloquent because of their extreme rarity in his writing. He has just defined by implication what is strongest in his own best critical writing, and—surely unwittingly—foretold what will make it lose some of its best qualities after he himself became a dogmatic Marxist.

Mirsky's mind was above all analytical and reductive (in the best sense) rather than creative. Throughout his career, he was a practical critic. It is one of the supreme virtues of his work that he always deals directly and unswervingly with actual writing. But it is also quite striking for the modern reader that Mirsky never goes in for the extended analysis of texts. In the whole of his work there is not one example of what we are used to calling a 'close reading' of a particular text. The nearest he gets to this is the nineteen-page analysis of *War and Peace* he published in Russian in 1935.[119] Mirsky's way of dealing with poetry, in particular, is characterized by a swooping down upon the small passages that support a central insight, and there is no concern with arguing the systemic relationships between all the parts and the whole of a particular text. This is not to say that Mirsky was insensitive to literature at the primary, textual level. He certainly was not, as the numerous brilliant observations of particularities attest. But he was more interested in making summarizing judgements on the totality of a work, with evaluating the whole, than in finely detailed analysis. And this is one important reason why his writing retains its vitality, despite the way particular phrases have dated: it is never trivial. Meanwhile, nothing dates so rapidly or definitively as crusading and overarching theoretical stances.

It is not difficult to point to some of the ways in which Mirsky's style changed over the years. The Greek and Latin phrases, and the knowing references to the classics that sometimes choke Mirsky's earlier writings, are weeded out. In his earlier work, he makes some almost manic comparative judgements. Speaking of Valery Bryusov, for example, he writes: 'If a poet at all, he is most of all akin to Ausonius and Claudian, perhaps even Fulgentius, but a Fulgentius bred on Villiers de l'Isle Adam and Verhaeren.'[120] There were very few readers even of Mirsky's own generation who could do anything other than take this sort of thing on trust; the vast majority of later readers have probably just shrugged and sighed for the loss of what they fondly imagine to have been a shared corpus of cosmopolitan literary knowledge. Fortunately, not much of Mirsky's best writing is doomed to be lost on later readers in this kind of way. His comparative judgements are radically toned down as time goes on. But even Mirsky the Soviet Marxist fiercely condemns the monoculturalism of his fellows as a vulgarization of the outlook of the great fathers of Communism. In his writings after the return to Russia, Mirsky freely makes comparisons with various national literatures—now confining himself, though, to the greatest names, writers it is reasonable to expect the average reader to recognize, instead of revelling in his own knowledge of obscure writers as he had done before. And his English style changes. The delight in what the writer imagines to be telling idioms—the most tasteless give-away of the non-native speaker who knows his command to be exceptional—falls away, leaving a pure but impassioned informative clarity, which after 1930 is adulterated by Marxist jargon. The change is even more marked in his Russian.

Perhaps the most salient indicator of change is that Mirsky soon abandoned the sometimes outrageous impressionism of the articles he wrote in the early 1920s. At the beginning he could write, for example, of Fet as 'the astonishing alchemist of *Evening Lights*, every one of which is as a drop of rose-essence, distilled from pounds of rose',[121] or speak of Akhmatova's early poems as 'lyrical epigrams . . . to such an extent saturated with poetical substance that they can be compared only with the bursting shell of an over-ripe pomegranate'.[122] It is clear from Mirsky's essay on Lytton Strachey that at this time he regarded this approach as not only perfectly legitimate, but extremely valuable. He called it 'descriptive criticism', and found it best exemplified in Strachey's remarks on Saint-Simon in his *Landmarks in French Literature* (1912). Mirsky defines descriptive criticism as 'this most difficult kind of criticism, which is not to give an interpretation or a commentary on the author in question, but to describe in words of your own the effect which the writer produces and the way he goes about it'; at its finest, this approach 'bears the same relation to the work described as an engraving to the picture it reproduces'.[123] Mirsky's work is full of this kind of thing, which soon became unfashionable in British academic circles (but remains standard in the work of practising literary critics as well as that of all amateurs) after being ridiculed in I. A. Richards's *Principles of Literary Criticism* (1924).[124] From this 'descriptive criticism' there is an evolution to the language of Mirsky's work after 1929, with its persistent delving into the sociological dimension. The *History of Russian Literature*, fortunately for us, stands at the mid-point of the curve.

One additional factor that affected Mirsky's work was that under Soviet conditions, he usually had much more space at his disposal than was the case in his *émigré* period. He was working for editors who offered ample resources to the right people. The result is the long-windedness that has plagued Soviet criticism since the early 1930s; in this respect, it shared the ponderous deliberateness of political discourse in the Soviet state. Mirsky was never dull before 1932. His writing in English was almost all commissioned and processed by experienced professionals who had a strong commercial interest and an equally strong commitment to intellectual excellence. The specific readership for each undertaking had to be borne in mind. These dimensions were absent when Mirsky was writing in Russian, first in the emigration and then back in Russia. Nobody involved in the operation needed to give much thought to the reader;

guidance came only from those involved in the process of production. And these people were themselves guided by ideological priorities and commitments, voluntarily assumed in the first case and externally imposed in the second. In the first case, a lively if somewhat self-indulgent individualism resulted; in the second, the passage of time has made what was on the whole unread into what is on the whole unreadable.

Notwithstanding the element of eclecticism in his approach to literary history, Mirsky did have a consistent underlying attitude towards literary culture, and this attitude was in turn part of his attitude towards human life in general. It comes to the surface nowhere more categorically than in the following statement, made with reference to Symbolism:

The poetry of the Symbolists as a whole had, for all its great qualities, substantial drawbacks. It was feminine, passive, more receptive than active. It was also on the whole too exclusively musical, and the appeal of its metaphysical subject-matter, apart from its occasional obscurity, was not sufficiently broad.[125]

This statement proceeds from an observation about what happened to the greatest poet of Symbolism at the end of his life:

Blok's genius was essentially feminine and passive, and after this last fitful achievement [*The Twelve*] inspired by the breath of the Revolution there followed in him a reaction of complete impotence and black despair. He lost his momentary faith in the Revolution, and his last years were spent in a state of terrible gloom and emptiness.[126]

A vivid and manifestly lived awareness of this 'terrible gloom and emptiness', which Mirsky often articulates in sexual terms, as something threatening emasculation and impotence, lies at the root of his attitudes, and indeed of the decisions he made about the course of his own life. It is much too simpleminded to write it off as a projection of Mirsky's own inability to be fruitful except in the realm of words; along with it went a thirst for practical action that he did satisfy in life on more than one occasion. The antithesis between fruitfulness and sterility forms one item in a persistent set of biologically imaged oppositions in Mirsky's aesthetic and political thinking, among which the former is positive, the latter negative: the healthy and the diseased, the living and the dead, energy and entropy. This disposition, however, is not equated with anything that can be reduced to some crude 'life-affirming' value, and Mirsky was scathing about the most egregious example of this among the writers of his time:

Lawrence's conception of himself is of a primeval buck for whom the womenfolk of the bourgeoisie, being quite unsatisfied by their decadent weakling men, yearn. He has a characteristic situation which comes again and again in his work—a female member of the aristocracy whose husband is impotent gives herself to a 'man of the people,' who is presented as a hundred-per-cent crude male devoid of all personality, as just so much male sex.[127]

Mirsky thus did not equate positive versus negative with masculine versus feminine in a biological and social sense. Mirsky extends his oppositions into the metaphysical categories of active versus passive, reason versus instinct, voluntarism versus determinism, action versus contemplation, thinking versus meditation. And on occasion he equates them with vitalist, geographical, and political categories: rising and falling lines, West versus East, the Tsar versus Lenin.

For Mirsky the born post-Nietzschean, there was no possible move backwards or forwards into religious faith, the escape route that so many of his contemporaries found that they could or indeed must take. For him, the biological and zoological realm is supreme, and provides the only intellectually respectable sense of continuity and purpose; this was long before popular genetics made such an approach a commonplace. He recognized this attitude in Jane Harrison. Once he had understood and articulated something, there was no point for Mirsky in resting at the point of understanding (nor indeed any psychological possibility of doing so); there always had to be the question of 'what next?' But when he wrote the *History*, he seemed to be content with the wrestling for understanding itself, without having to posit a goal or purpose for the process, and the book therefore has no extrinsic agenda. Five years after he finished the *History*, Mirsky decided that he had understood the ultimate purpose of human activity; the touchstone of his judgement was now centred outside his individual sensibility, and his writing became dogmatic.

5   Writing Russian

In *Foma Gordeiev*, which I consider to be Gorky's masterpiece, there is an unforgettable scene where Foma's father Ignat watches the loss of his ship laden with goods. He knows that his entire fortune will go down with it, but his only feeling is admiration for the beauty of the spectacle. He will have his moment of exultation over his own splendid disaster, for he knows that he has it in him to begin again and build himself up an even greater fortune. (D. S. Mirsky, 1922)

RUSSIA OUTSIDE AND IN

A good number of the front-rank Russian writers and critics active in 1917 emigrated rather than stay on in the Soviet state.[1] There was something of a generational and genre split; on the whole, the older prose writers left, while the younger poets and critics stayed. Among Mirsky's contemporaries who had made a reputation before 1917, Akhmatova, Mandelshtam, and Mayakovsky remained in Russia, for very different reasons. Tsvetaeva left Russia to join her husband in Czechoslovakia in 1922. Pasternak, Viktor Shklovsky, and Count A. N. Tolstoy—the last-named an aristocrat of fairly similar background to Mirsky—went back to Russia in 1923 after spending some time in Berlin.

In August 1922, about 120 key intellectuals and administrators were expelled from Russia after Lenin decided that he could not put up with the potential strength of opposition that they represented.[2] From among these men (all the prime targets were men, but their families were sent out with them), Mirsky soon came into personal contact with Nikolay Berdyaev, Sergey Bulgakov, V. N. Ilin, and Lev Karsavin. The reaction of Mirsky's soon-to-be friend Suvchinsky to the expulsion expresses an irreverent view of these men as sanctimonious failures that was common among his and Mirsky's generation:

When the first group arrived (Frank, Berdyaev, [I. A.] Ilin) it felt as if some sort of *individual* selection of people was going on. All they've done now is simply to transplant from Russia to Berlin—like a piece of turf from one cemetery to another, or like a piece of dead skin—a cultural layer that has completely outlived its time, and for what? So that these people should stand at the head of the emigration, of course, so they should speak for it, and by doing so prevent anything being born that is new and alive, and consequently *dangerous* for the Bolsheviks.[3]

In 1922–3, after the returns and the expulsions, *émigré* culture began to crystallize as a consciously separate formation. Mirsky played an active part in it for several years. At the same time as he was writing on Russian literature for the English readership, he was steadily publishing in Russian for his fellow *émigrés*. As with his critical writing in English, at no time did Mirsky promote Russian literature outside Russia at the expense of the literature on the inside. But at the same time, he did not hesitate to point out the difficulties faced by writers under the new regime, and he could still refer to himself late in 1925 as an 'anti-Communist'.[4]

During the first two or three years of the post-revolutionary emigration, there was no insuperable barrier to communication between the literary intellectuals in emigration and those who had remained behind in Soviet Russia, and each side kept a keen eye on the other. Books could be published simultaneously inside and outside Russia; for a couple of years, 'Berlin–Petrograd', for example, was a common item on title-pages. It was always much easier, though, for those on the outside to get hold of what was published on the inside. Maksim Gorky, who was expelled by Lenin in 1921 but remained fundamentally pro-Soviet, at first thought that the journal he edited from Berlin in 1923–5, to which he gave the hopeful title *Dialogue*, would be admitted into Russia and put on open sale; he was disabused of this idea by 1924.[5] The idea of a permanent rupture was generally accepted only about 1925. The most poignant discussion of it is the lament that Vladislav Khodasevich published in the Paris newspaper *Days*, 'Over There or Over Here?', in which literature on both sides of the divide is said to be seriously infirm.[6]

Evidently, copies of the *London Mercury* carrying Mirsky's 'Russian Letters' reached the most famous literary Anglophile left in the country, Korney Chukovsky, and he wrote an appreciation to Mirsky, whose reply, written on 12 May 1922, has survived. Even allowing for the positive emphasis that would have been inevitable under these circumstances, Mirsky's letter shows that from the very beginning of his time outside Russia he believed that the *émigré* segment of Russian literature was not and could not be sufficient unto itself, much less set out on an independent and autonomous existence. Rather, it was and would remain a subordinate fragment of the literature as a whole, whose centre remained inside Russia. And Mirsky wanted to take part in the work of the centre, not the periphery:

We on this side are dreading that an unbridgeable abyss will open up between us and you. Your letter is a sign that this is not so. Those who have stayed behind in Russia are for us like saints and martyrs for the faith [*podvizhniki*], and consequently, if Russian Culture survives, it will be due to you and your heroic efforts. We are no better than rats who have saved themselves from the ship, while you still might be destined to save the ship itself. . . . [The] Russians here are not up to much economically, and the English are nowhere near as interested in Russian culture as it might seem. . . .

However, something will be done. . . . We will find the opportunity to move the English along in a literary sense.

In general, books from Russia are our daily bread. I enclose my article about the first two volumes of Blok from the 'Times Literary Supplement'.[7] Please give my most sincere greeting to Anna Andreevna [Akhmatova].[8]

And may God grant you strength and success.

D. S.-Mirsky[9]

This would seem to be the contact that led to the most surprising item in Mirsky's bibliography, an essay on contemporary English poetry that was published in Soviet Russia in 1923 in the journal *The Contemporary West*, which was edited by Chukovsky and Evgeny Zamyatin. This was the only piece Mirsky published in Russia between 1911, when his collection of poems came out, and 1932, when he returned from emigration. In his letter to Mirsky, Chukovsky had evidently asked Mirsky to set about the task of publicizing and translating the literature currently being published in Russia. The most immediate result was Mirsky's translation of Zamyatin's story 'The Cave', which soon became a classic of the revolutionary period.[10]

It was in London, rather than on the Continent, that Mirsky made personal contact with the young Soviet prose whose rise he saluted several times shortly after he began his teaching career, as he undertook to do in his letter to Chukovsky. The novelist Boris Pilnyak (1894–1937), who was rapidly making a name for himself as one of the most significant post-revolutionary literary figures after the publication of *The Bare Year* in 1922, left Russia for a four-month trip to England on 1 May 1923. Pilnyak had wangled an official visit to the London trade delegation of the newly recognized state, and off his own bat he attempted to set up a Russian chapter of the PEN Club; the organizers wanted Gorky, but he considered the project too politically sensitive. While Pilnyak was in London, he met Mirsky. Pilnyak reported to Chukovsky from England that in his view Mirsky 'was born a hundred years too late'.[11] In May 1924 Mirsky wrote an introduction to a collection by Pilnyak that was called in English *Tales of the Wilderness*; at this time and also later, he was in general uncomplimentary, arguing that Pilnyak was too undisciplined mentally to be a great writer of prose. It is clear, though, that Mirsky and Pilnyak, however much they might have disagreed with each other, shared a fondness for extended discussion over a bottle, the favoured location being the back room of Mrs Makarova's Russian bookshop near the British Museum.[12]

Apart from this chance contact with a prominent literary Russian, Mirsky tried to keep up with his schoolmate Viktor Zhirmunsky, who had remained in Petrograd, now renamed Leningrad. In a letter to Suvchinsky of 19 December 1924 Mirsky says that he is in correspondence with Zhirmunsky and has been receiving books from him, but that the copy of 'my English Avvakum' (by which Mirsky means the translation by Harrison and Mirrlees with his preface) has been returned stamped 'Non-admis'. No letters from Mirsky have turned up in Zhirmunsky's archive; it may well be that he destroyed anything he had relating to Mirsky after the latter was arrested. But this, and the much more important letter to Chukovsky, constitute the only evidence that has sur-faced so far that Mirsky was in touch with literary people in Russia before he managed to write to Pasternak in 1927.

BOILED LETTUCE

Throughout the 1920s the principal site of Mirsky's *émigré* activities was Paris. The first surviving letter written from France back to England is to Sir Bernard Pares, dated 20 August 1924, and addressed from 214 rue de Bécon, Courbevoie. This is the house that Mirsky's mother and sisters had settled into when they moved from Athens at a date unknown, and it was to serve as Mirsky's Paris base until it was put up for sale after the death of his mother.

The addresses of Mirsky's letters and the announcements in them of his travel plans show that he would make his way to Paris as soon as possible after the end of the university term, and that he would only return to London at the last minute to start his teaching. From Paris, Mirsky ventured far and wide in France; during his first years he was in Quimper in Brittany, Nantes, Cannes, and Normandy. In January 1926 he spent some time in Pau.[13] In August 1927 he stayed with the Bassianos at their villa near the then exclusive Atlantic resort of La Baule-les-Pins, Loire Inférieure. On 23 September 1927, Mirsky wrote to Salomeya Halpern from perhaps the most spectacular hostelry of all those whose stationery he used, the Grand Hôtel du Raisin de Bourgogne in the town of Niort. Vera Traill, who was no stranger to the kitchen, and who once pub-lished a Russian cookbook with her friend Moura Budberg, said:

When he came [to France] with money in his pocket, he was a terrible glutton, terri-bly interested in food, and he would make expeditions. He had the gastronomic guide . . . and he was perfectly capable of taking a trip for just one night, let's say to Lyon, just to taste a special chicken dish. . . . In Paris we went to terribly expensive, spectac-ular restaurants. . . . I remember one of them where we had something I wouldn't know how to cook myself—boiled lettuce. It's the same as spinach but made with lettuce. Anyway, he knew where to go, where the thing to eat was this lettuce.

Marina Tsvetaeva saw all this from a different perspective in a letter to Yury Ivask in June 1934, by which time Mirsky's diet had become rather more austere:

What's my favourite food, you ask. Does it really matter? *I hate kasha*, every sort except the black, and even in Moscow in 1920, the most savage year, *I didn't eat millet*. That aside, I'm very unassuming and simple—I eat everything, and I don't pay much atten-tion to it, which during our friendship made Mirsky heartily disappointed (he was a passionate eater and expert, as very isolated people often are). He took me—in secret, conspiratorially-connoisseurily—round the best restaurants of Paris and London. 'All you do is talk!' he once exclaimed, grief-stricken, 'and you don't care what you're eating—they might as well be serving you *hay*!' Hay maybe, but not millet, though.[14]

'THE POETRY OF WILL AND REASON'

The general evolution of Mirsky's involvement with Russian *émigré* culture is clear-cut: to borrow once more one of his own favourite images, it traced a rising line until 1926, then a plateau until 1929, and after that it fell away steeply. From the time Mirsky arrived on the *émigré* scene in 1922 until the summer of 1926 he was regarded on the whole as a talented but untried younger colleague by the leading lights in the literary emigration. He compelled them to take him seriously, but he then managed to alienate them completely. After 1926 he withdrew further and further from literature, and by the end of 1929 this process was practically complete. He returned to writing literary criticism in Russian only after he arrived back in Moscow in 1932, and then, it would seem, primarily because he was directed to do so rather than by choice. In the interim, during his last three years in emigration, he was writing mainly in English on historical and political subjects.

Mirsky's earliest piece of critical writing in Russian for the *émigré* readership after he came to London turned out to be a non-starter. It was a survey article on the current state of Russian poetry, submitted to *Russian Thought* (*Russkaya mysl'*), the journal edited by P. B. Struve, in June 1922. Soon after this, the journal encountered insuperable financial and organizational problems, and this became the earliest of several articles by Mirsky that were first published only long after his death.[15] In this case, though, there may well have been another reason: a good deal of the factual material in the article, especially its account of which poets were in which places, was rapidly overtaken by events as the division between *émigré* and Soviet literature coalesced. Struve may well have decided that, despite the brilliance of Mirsky's literary judgements, there was too much in the article that events had rendered inaccurate.

The most significant aspect of this article is its bravura tone, which is set by the first sentence: 'For about a quarter of a century now Russian poetry has been experiencing a period of flowering which has taken it from the debased and insignificant situation of the 1890s to its dominant situation of today.' This view contrasts strongly with Mirsky's attitude about five years later, when he saw not just the poetry of his youth, but all Russian literature of that period, as obsessed with death. The article culminates with a discussion of three women poets who lapsed into obscurity soon after the date of Mirsky's article: Anna Radlova, Mariya Shkapskaya, and Irina Odoevtseva. He had probably known Radlova before 1917, and met her again after he went back to Russia; he came to know Shkapskaya in the 1930s; but he never seems to have met Odoevtseva (1895–1991), who emigrated with her husband Georgy Ivanov (1894–1958), and survived long enough to be able in 1987 to go back and die in the city she left seventy years previously, soon before it was renamed once more and became St Petersburg again.

The article's final paragraph presents a conception of poetry that Mirsky was to restate many times in his later writings; he was always on the side of 'will and reason':

Mandelshtam declared that 'Classicism is the poetry of Revolution'. And if by Revolution is understood that which Peter the Great began, there is a certain amount of truth in this. Classicism is active poetry, the poetry of Will and Reason—teleological art, antithetical to Romanticism, which is passive, determinist art.[16]

A LITTLE ANTHOLOGY

On 8 August 1923, at Quimper in Brittany, Mirsky finished the introduction to his Russian-language *The Russian Lyric: A Little Anthology from Lomonosov to Pasternak*, the first book he published after his youthful collection of poems in 1911. The crisp Notes that Mirsky included at the back of his anthology make a highly instructive contrast with those he supplied in the same year as his own anthology was published, 1924, for Maurice Baring's *Oxford Book of Russian Verse*. Writing in English for Baring, Mirsky can take nothing for granted:

Konstantin Konstantinovich Sluchévsky, b. 1837 in St. Petersburg. Served in the Foot Guards and later on in the Civil Service; he was for a long time editor of the official Pravitel'stvennyi Vestnik (Government Gazette). His first poems appeared in 1860, but he was hissed off the literary stage by the Anti-Verse critics and did not appear in book form until 1876. He died in 1904. He is the most remarkable and original poet of an unpoetical period. He had real genius and a wonderfully alert and receptive mind. Much of his best poetry is metaphysical, but he is probably at his best in his 'geographical' poems (especially in his poems of the North of Russia). He was heavily handicapped, for never in any Christian country (except perhaps in America at the same time) was the level of poetical craftsmanship so low as it was in Russia in the last lap of the nineteenth century. His verse is more often than not uncouth and clumsy, but his ideas are always original and stimulating.[17]

Easily recognizable here are some permanent features of Mirsky's evaluative thinking: the evolution of poetry describing a 'falling line', the deleterious effect of 'social' criticism, the importance of work and craftsmanship, the supreme importance of *thought* in poetry. There is even evidence of his peculiar staff officer's fascination with terrain. By contrast, here is Mirsky's note on the same poet from his own anthology; the translation is deliberately literal:

Konstantin Konstantinovich Sluchevsky, b. 1837 in Spb †1904. Sluchevsky was a tongue-tied genius. An insatiable love for the concrete multiplicity of physical existence; a sharp eye, directed all around him; the vigilant work of powerful thought to which the 'light yoke' of ideas is absolutely alien—these could have made of him a poet of the first magnitude. His decadent times denied him the armament he needed. This is Demosthenes with his tongue cut out. Sluchevsky's lofty tongue-tiedness is perhaps his principal attraction but it is indisputably annoying. He liberates himself from it rarely and not always appropriately, and in doing so he lapses (especially in the early poems) into cheap prettiness. His first poems began to appear in the second half of the 1850s, but were hissed at by the critics; from 1860 until 1876 he was silent. In our age when formal tasks are dominant, Sluchevsky has little chance of attracting attention.[18]

This incisive verve, spiked with the occasional bold metaphor, is entirely characteristic of Mirsky's Russian-language criticism. The two notes cover the same ground and are consistent with each other, but the English note primarily imparts information, while the Russian one is above all impressionistically evaluative. Equally instructive is the contrast between Mirsky's notes on those (very few) individual poems that happen to appear in both books. For Blok's 'The Unknown Woman' Mirsky supplies Baring with two short dry sentences: 'The most widely popular of Blok's poems. The scene is a summer resort in the environs of St. Petersburg.'[19] For his Russian readers, Mirsky can display the inwardness of his understanding:

The Unknown Woman, dated 24 March 1906 Ozerki, from *An Unexpected Joy*. An extremely well-known poem. It is central for an entire period; in it some lyric themes intersect that are repeated in different combinations. Here Blok for the first time achieves a synthesis of his dissonances, combining sharp, grotesque naturalism with a romantic melody (the second half); remarkable here is the 'magical', 'forced' disposition of vowels.[20]

The second name in the subtitle of Mirsky's anthology, 'From Lomonosov to Pasternak', was a shocking provocation in a Russian *émigré* publication even before the battle-lines had hardened, because—apart from the obscurity of the little poetry he had published by then—Pasternak had declared allegiance to the Soviets by returning to Russia. Mirsky's subtitle is one of the earliest unambiguous proclamations in Russian literary history of Pasternak's major status.

Mirsky is at his most incisive in discussing what he calls his 'Salon des Refusés'. The poets of the modernist period for whom he finds no place in his anthology seem in part like a deliberate provocation to the emigration, because although he finds room for one poem each by Balmont and Gippius, he does not include Bunin and Khodasevich. Mirsky shows off his insider's knowledge by apologizing for not including some of the cult poets of his generation:

Konevskoy, Dobrolyubov, Komarovsky, and—another pointer towards some sort of personal connection—Elena Guro. But the poet whose absence was most remarked upon, and her omission persistently used as a stick to beat Mirsky with in view of what happened soon after the appearance of the anthology, was Marina Tsvetaeva; it is in this preface that Mirsky used the phrase 'a talented, but hopelessly undisciplined woman from Moscow'.[21]

Tucked away in his note on the second-rate poet Apollon Maikov (1821–97) is a passage in which Mirsky came nearer than anywhere else to defining what he detested most in Russian poetry, an attitude that lies behind all his negative assessments: 'The self-satisfied pomposity of his "concern with ideas" (*ideinost'*), the eclecticism of his taste, the neutrality of his verbal texture make him almost into a blank space for the modern reader. Maikov made entirely real the ideal poet "according to Belinsky" with his "artistry", "thinking in images", and concern for public opinion.'[22] Instead of these qualities, Mirsky admired poets who wrestle with their own thought instead of received ideas, expose 'the resistance of the material' in the linguistic surface of their texts so that the poem is manifestly a thing made, and whose concerns are aristocratically élitist rather than populist.

THE *ÉMIGRÉ* PRESS

Mirsky made his debut in January 1924 in a periodical based in Paris, *The Link* (*Zveno*). This journal was founded as a literary supplement to the leading Russian newspaper in Paris, *The Latest News*, the nominal editor being that of the main paper, P. N. Milyukov, who was joined by the almost equally nominal M. M. Vinaver;[23] the actual work was done by Solomon Vladimirovich Pozner (1876–1946). *The Link* appeared from 1923 to 1928.[24] It carried a wide variety of articles on current literary history. The chief literary critic was Georgy Adamovich, but an increasingly prominent part was played by the highly gifted but wayward Nikolay Bakhtin (1894–1950), who had served a stint in the Foreign Legion. He has remained in relative obscurity, overshadowed by his vaunted younger brother Mikhail.[25] Mirsky gave *The Link* several substantial pieces about current English literature in 1924 and 1925, including what appears to have remained the only serious essay ever written in Russian on the work of Maurice Baring.[26]

In 1925 Mirsky began contributing to the most important Russian 'thick journal' of the inter-war period, *Contemporary Notes* (*Sovremennye zapiski*), which came out regularly from 1921 to the fall of Paris in 1940, edited by a notoriously philistine group of former SRs. Three of his reviews are particularly important. One of them concerns the earliest collected edition of Babel's stories; the others deal with the debuts in prose that had recently been made by the poets Mandelshtam and Pasternak. Mirsky was among the very first critics to argue for the significance of these now long-canonical texts.[27] Besides these, in 1926 he published the first ever article-length assessment in Russian of a long poem by Tsvetaeva.[28] And, as we have seen, he also gave to *Contemporary Notes* a composite review of nine of the classic texts of Russian Formalist criticism that had come out in its final years of glory, 1923–4.[29]

Mirsky's most substantial contribution to *Contemporary Notes* was in fact his first, an obituary of the poet who had been one of the models for his own youthful efforts, Valery Bryusov, who died in October 1924 after spending his last years as a member of the Bolshevik party. Mirsky's obituary culminates with some acid remarks about Bryusov's political opportunism, which in a sense foreshadowed his own ten years later, anticipating some of the charges that would later be made against himself when he declared for the Soviets.

In late 1925 and early 1926 Mirsky also contributed some incisive pieces on current English literature, including articles on Belloc, George Saintsbury, and living poets, to *Days*, the newspaper edited by the former head of the Provisional Government, Aleksandr Kerensky. In 1926 Mirsky also contributed important articles on Tsvetaeva and Esenin to the most explicitly left-wing 'thick journal' of the emigration, *The Will of Russia* (*Volya Rossii*), which was published in Prague for a decade starting in 1922. The Esenin obituary contains one particularly noteworthy passage where Mirsky makes some ominous remarks about the doomed nature of his own generation:

Esenin simply was a poet, while Nadson was not. But their functions within the social organism were similar. Both of them concentrated within themselves, with special power for the average contemporary reader, all the *weakness* and *anguish* of their generation. The manner of death of each is significant—Nadson's tuberculosis and Esenin's noose. The first symbolizes the limpness, powerlessness, and sterility of the 'men of the 1880s'. The second symbolizes the emptiness, the restlessness, the violated state [*ograblennost'*] of our generation. Nadson's was a sickness of power. Esenin's was a sickness of faith. Nadson could not act. Esenin could not believe. Unbelief is the root of Esenin's tragedy.[30]

The most celebrated elegy on Esenin was written by another member of his generation, Mayakovsky. The poem has a closing couplet that became a byword for Communist commitment: 'In this life, to die is nothing hard, / Making life is harder, and by far.' Mirsky's next obituary for a major poet with whom he identified himself was to be about Mayakovsky, with whose own suicide these words took on a ghastly new resonance.

THE WELL-INTENTIONED

Mirsky's final involvement as a contributor to an *émigré* publication edited by someone else came about in 1925–6 in connection with a short-lived and essentially amateur project by another *émigré* prince, Dmitry Alekseevich Shakhovskoy. He published two almanacs whose title uses the adjectival noun often found in the diary of Mirsky's mother, *The Well-Intentioned*. The first of these almanacs brought together in uniquely broad church fashion a number of eminent writers in the emigration who were soon to become irreconcilable enemies and would no longer be seen between the same two covers. In his dealings with Shakhovskoy, Mirsky speaks condescendingly, and as a definite advocate of 'the left' in literature. When he is writing in Russian, as opposed to English, he resists style-editing: 'Do not change particular words, and retain my punctuation as far as possible. I'm afraid that in general the article has come out too political, and what's worse is that it's completely disconnected. *Malheureusement on n'écrit pas ce qu'on veut mais ce qu'on peut.*'

The article concerned was 'On the Current State of Russian Literature', in which Mirsky makes a trenchant statement of general principle and some concise literary assessments. As living classics he cites Akhmatova, Zamyatin, Khodasevich, and A. N. Tolstoy (with some reservation about the last-named). The remaining living writers are then mustered into groups. 'Genuine, fully formed masters' who are continuing to develop include Mandelshtam, Tsvetaeva, Pasternak, and Babel. Those who have stopped developing include Mayakovsky, Aseev, and perhaps Tikhonov. Promising beginners include Artyom Vesyoly and Selvinsky. Worth mentioning in other categories are Leonov, Zoshchenko, Esenin, Pilnyak, Nikitin, perhaps Lidin. The tail-enders in this list are dealt some stinging remarks:

Genuinely talented and clever, but lacking any 'inner content', a journalist and also 'a slave to authority' and, what's worse, to the consumer: Erenburg.

Almost a 'man of genius', but a completely undisciplined[31] journalist who cultivates his indiscipline but is the father of almost all the ideas by which contemporary aesthetics lives: Shklovsky.[32]

Mirsky notes as he goes through these names the high proportion of Jews among them; he uses the term standard in the late Tsarist administration, *inorodtsy*, 'aliens'. He eventually apologizes for the fact that of all the names he lists, only one is 'completely white': he has in mind, of course, Khodasevich. This leads to the second half of the article, which condemns the use of political criteria in judging literature, a sin committed not so much by the Bolsheviks, says Mirsky, as by the emigration.

MIRSKY AND CONSERVATISM

By 4 February 1926, Mirsky had finished his article for the second and final issue of Shakhovskoy's almanac, 'On Conservatism', which, he remarks in his accompanying letter, he hopes 'is not too ill-intentioned'.[33]

'The reader you speak about (there is another kind, but there are fewer of them) is guided by two laws: intellectual laziness and the fear of making a fool of himself. Literature has to keep him occupied and cheer him up, "like tasty lemonade in summer".[34] He is not prepared to expend any effort. Literature, like music in a restaurant or cinema, like the cinematograph, is rest and relaxation. It therefore has to be immediately comprehensible, and to achieve that it has to follow familar models. A small amount of innovation is fine; it stimulates the appetite and tickles the nerves. . . . The educated reader knows that one should take an interest in what is new and that art must renew itself. But he also knows from bitter experience that there are many charlatans and impostors, that he can't distinguish between them and the "real" ones, and it's therefore easy to make a fool of himself by saying that Igor Severyanin is a great poet, while Khlebnikov's a clown. He therefore entrenches himself inside the wholly dependable classics, making common cause with them according to their degree of deadness, or with what look to him like the least innovatory of his contemporaries according to their degree of sclerosis. You musn't reproach the reader for doing this, of course. Too much of his energy goes on following the ups and downs of the stock market, or to earning himself a salary, and there's none left for reading "incomprehensible" poets, as you call them.'
'But they really are incomprehensible.'
'Everything is incomprehensible to someone who hasn't the time to comprehend. Art is the creation of new values. . . .'

This last sentence caught the fancy of Jane Harrison; she wrote from Cambridge on 9 August 1926:

'Art is the creation of new values' [Harrison cites the phrase in Russian] now that is really worth saying & to me the most illuminating thing I have read for a long time with more stuff in it than a whole decade of Pontigny analysis.

I have often wanted to ask you to formulate for me the reactionary and revolutionary element in yr outlook but I did not feel I knew you quite well enough (asking a person to state their opinions is really more intrusive than asking the amount of their income)[35] & now you have done it unasked.

By the next time Mirsky wrote to Shakhovskoy he had delivered his lecture on 'The Ambience of Death in Pre-Revolutionary Russian Literature', which was to become notorious. Mirsky offered this piece to Shakhovskoy for publication in *The Well-Intentioned*, but then evidently changed his mind, and saved it for his own journal, *Vyorsts*, even though it would miss the first issue. The last letter of the correspondence with Shakhovskoy dates from 17 June 1926. Mirsky complained that Shakhovskoy was a bad correspondent—not knowing that during the preceding couple of months Shakhovskoy had gone through the decisive phase of the evolution that led him to choose the path diametrically opposite to the one that Mirsky soon opted for: he gave up the world entirely and went to Mount Athos in order to study to become a priest of the Orthodox Church. He would end up as one of the most eminent clerics of the emigration, known in the highest office he occupied as Archbishop Ioann of San Francisco and the Western United States.

By 1926, the year in which the first volume of his English-language history appeared, Mirsky had thus made an appearance in all the principal periodical publications of the Russian emigration. As a sort of epitaph to this involvement, he then published a harshly critical review of the back issues of *Contemporary Notes* and *The Will of Russia* in the first issue of the journal he founded himself, *Vyorsts*, and left himself with no way back into the mainstream.[36]

THE EURASIAN MOVEMENT

In his dialogue on conservatism, Mirsky set down one particularly significant passage about his relations with his fellows in the emigration:

'Tradition is like Ariadne's thread—once dropped, it cannot be picked up again. One can take one's stand only on a directly precursive tradition that has not yet been broken. Restoration never happens, either in politics or culture. The new must be new, not yesterday's stuff warmed up. It *must* be revolutionary, it must look forward and not back. True, it sometimes dons a mask that's got up to look like the old. But that's only a mask. You mentioned the Eurasians. They have one face but two souls, which "war with each other, alas". If the soul wins that wears the face, they will lose all significance. If the soul wins whose face wears the mask, the soul that is organically related to the future, they will become the greatest cultural force of tomorrow.'

Starting in 1925, Mirsky involved himself more and more deeply with these mask-wearing men who had two souls, the men of the Eurasian movement.[37] The initial contact took place in September 1922, when Mirsky visited Berlin and was introduced to Pyotr Petrovich Suvchinsky, one of the four founders of Eurasianism. Though this impression may be the result of the fact that more evidence concerning it survives than concerning any other—163 letters by Mirsky written between October 1922 and September 1931—Mirsky seems to have formed a closer relationship with Suvchinsky, and for longer, than with any other person he met after he left Russia.

Suvchinsky (1892–1985)[38] was born in Kiev and educated in St Petersburg; he went to the Tenishev school, like Mirsky. He became a musicologist and took part in musical journalism immediately before the First World War; he was then found unfit for military service. In emigration he became an amateur of the arts whose main interest remained music; his practical abilities and/or dedication as pianist and singer never seem to have been sufficient for him to make a career as a performer. Suvchinsky first lived in Sofia, where the Eurasian movement began. He moved to Berlin at some time in 1922, then to Paris in 1925, and remained there to the end of his life.

As soon as Mirsky got back to London from Berlin in the autumn of 1922, with his customary expeditiousness he published three English-language accounts of the Eurasian movement, all of them positive.[39] In a letter of 7 September 1922 to P. N. Savitsky, Suvchinsky claimed Mirsky as a convert, and in 1923 charged him with forming a Eurasian group in England.[40]

The Eurasian movement was a complex and tangled conglomeration of ideas and personalities, policies, theories, and agendas. By the end of the 1920s it had spawned a very substantial body of printed documents. They include a series of collections of articles, several monographs, and a chronicle dealing with the organization's public activities.[41] Eurasianism is best known, indeed almost exclusively known, in its ideological aspect, which has been confidently summarized many times. By far the clearest summary of its ideology in its initial phase (1921-6) is by Mirsky, an article that stands as one of the best examples of his ability to boil down complex notions to their essentials.[42] The article was written in 1926, when Mirsky was feeling maximally benevolent towards the movement and the personalities involved in it, and just at the time when he himself was becoming a leading participant. Several further summaries of Eurasian ideology were made long after the demise of the movement by scholars outside Russia.[43] Until the late 1980s, the movement was not an approved topic of research and discussion inside Russia. After the fall of the USSR, the Eurasians' attempts to conceptualize a post-Communist Russia became of great interest and relevance, and there began a spate of republications[44] and reinterpretations.[45]

The formal beginning of the movement was marked by a collection of ten essays that appeared in Sofia in 1921 under the title *Exodus to the East*, edited and written by four *émigrés* who had landed up there after making their way out of Russia by various routes: Prince Nikolay Sergeevich Trubetskoy (1890–1938), Georgy Vasilievich Florovsky (1893–1979), Pyotr Nikolaevich Savitsky (1894–1968), and, as we know, P. P. Suvchinsky. How exactly the four got together and from whom the original impetus came to produce the book has not yet been clearly related. All four original Eurasians, like Mirsky, were in terms of social and academic background and upbringing metropolitan Russian intellectuals from the *dvoryanstvo*, but they had different areas of specialization. Trubetskoy was the only one of them who had published any significant proto-Eurasian writings before the 1921 collection, and he was clearly the principal ideologue. But he was always a reluctant leader. He was an academic dedicated to research in his specialist subject; in emigration at the University of Vienna he held one of the most prestigious chairs in Slavonic studies, and he was soon to emerge as one of the greatest theoretical linguists of the twentieth century if not of all time.[46] His commitment to his academic work grew stronger as the 1920s went on, and eventually led him to resent the time and energy he was called on to spend on his unruly brainchild, which from his point of view kept on side-slipping into politics and away from the speculative ideas that interested him. It would appear from his earliest writings that as an adolescent, in strong contrast to Mirsky, Trubetskoy conceived a violent antipathy towards Western culture, and British attitudes in particular.

Savitsky was an economist and geographer who had been a favourite pupil of P. B. Struve and had worked with him in the White administration in the Crimea. He responded immediately to Trubetskoy's early publications, and he was to prove the most enthusiastic and persistent proponent of Eurasianism among the original quartet. He was also the most prolific author among them; indeed, he was something of a graphomaniac, and the knotty loquacity of his writings is one factor that has deterred scholars from tackling his archival legacy.[47] Mirsky eventually came to view him as a self-righteous bigot.[48]

Florovsky was an Orthodox theologian, and very soon publicly distanced himself from the movement.[49] Florovsky and Savitsky, however, were brothers-in-law, and apparently retained a close personal relationship. Florovsky was replaced as the Eurasian house theologian by Lev Karsavin (1882–1952), the ballerina Tamara's brother, who suffered all his life from not being as rich and famous as she was.[50] He was one of the group of intellectuals expelled from Russia in 1922, and he became closely involved with Eurasianism when he moved to Paris in 1925. The presence in the same place of Suvchinsky and Karsavin was one factor that altered the centre of gravity of the movement for a while at this point.

Suvchinsky was the least distinguished of the four founders intellectually. He contributed a number of culturological essays to the various Eurasian publications, but none of them really repays careful study because his thought is so slipshod; they consist mainly of verbose emotional gestures. Mirsky's letters to Suvchinsky teem with ever-harsher instructions about how he should tighten up his thinking and clean up his style. Suvchinsky was by nature a parlour intellectual, fond of the sound of his own voice and loving to hold court. How he managed to support himself is an enigma, unless he really did manage to allot himself a salary from Eurasian funds; his third former wife, Vera, contemptuously referred to him as 'a genuine parasite'. He was something of a sexual predator, and he married four times, all the women concerned being between 18 and 22 years old at the time. His fourth marriage, in 1933, was something of a Eurasian dynastic event, to Marianna Karsavina, one of the daughters of the philosopher. Karsavin, incidentally, was conned into thinking that Suvchinsky was a millionaire.

As a body of doctrine, Eurasianism has been much more frequently summarized than critically examined. This is partly because the publications are so extensive, and partly because they are still difficult of access; there does not seem to be a single repository anywhere in the world where all the Eurasian publications can be studied together.[51] The anonymous preface to *Exodus to the East* spelled out the fundamental ideas. The sentence from it that became most famous also marks the limit of the usual notion of what Eurasianism amounted to: 'The Russian people and the peoples of the "Russian world" are neither European nor Asiatic.'

The Eurasian people, one but only one constituent among whom are the ethnic Russians, inhabit that geographically distinctive space which stretches from the Baltic to the Pacific, and from the Arctic to the mountain ranges that provide it with a southern border. In terms of climate and vegetation it is divided into four broad 'flag-like' strips that run east–west; reading from north to south they are made up of tundra, northern forest, steppe, and desert.[52] Eurasian history is essentially the process of human confrontation with and assimilation of this space. This history begins not with Kievan Christianity but with the unfortunately named Tartar yoke, which the Eurasians viewed as a positive phenomenon rather than a catastrophe that gave rise to Russia's notorious 'backwardness'. Under the Mongols the Eurasian space was first brought under unitary rule; it functioned efficiently as a political and economic entity and successfully defended itself against Catholicism and Protestantism and the false beliefs and economic exploitation indivisible from them.

A definition of national identity, subsuming and transcending ethnicity, sprang from the geopolitical basis. The Eurasian mentality, according to *Exodus to the East*, is continental, nomadic, and tolerant in religious affairs. Nevertheless, a central administration came about that gave a coherent political articulation to 'continent Eurasia' as a geographical space, further integrated by growing adherence to the Russian Orthodox Church and the use of the Russian language. The outlook of the people who inhabit the landlocked and featureless expanses of Eurasia was and remained utterly different from that of the peoples who inhabit the regions west of the Elbe, with their peninsulas and islands riven by mountains and short rivers flowing fast to nearby seas. In this setting there developed individualism, participatory democracy, aggressive chauvinism, rapaciously acquisitive materialism, religious intolerance and eventually secularism, and a ruthless hunger for technological development; these attitudes drove the acquisition of sea-borne empires founded on myths of national supremacy and on the enslavement or even extermination of aliens rather than the Eurasian process of comparatively benign enserfment of the native lower orders. The reforms of Peter the Great betrayed the Eurasian idea by importing alien Western concepts and structures of government, leading to a loss of organic unity, a growing alienation between rulers and ruled, and the eventual revenge of the ruled in 1917. The revolution was taken over from the top, however, by fanatical adherents of Marxist Communism, the most obnoxious of all the ideologies that had been foisted on Russia from the West. The Eurasians thus accepted the legitimacy of the Russian revolution, but rejected the legitimacy of Bolshevism.

The four founding ideologues of Eurasianism were all Russian men of the same generation as Mirsky. Like him, they just had time to complete at least a substantial part of their higher education in their native country before historical developments robbed them of the context in which it would have been natural for them subsequently to emerge as leading figures in their chosen fields and perhaps more widely, in political life.[53] Their personal circumstances had been transformed beyond recognition by the events that began in 1914. Instead of being leaders-in-waiting, these men found themselves outcasts in alien societies whose values they found unacceptable.

All along there were really two Eurasias in the thinking of the original group, as is implied by Mirsky's remark about the two souls. They were complementary, and were never really synthesized. The first, associated with Trubetskoy, was an ethnic and cultural construct. The second, developed particularly by Savitsky, was a geopolitical construct. In the second phase of the movement there was an attempt to add a legal arm and what one might call a religious arm, the theory of the 'symphonic personality' as developed by Karsavin. But from the start there was a fatal lack of agreement about the *purpose* of the movement. In a situation where no power was at stake, there was a vacuum at the point where male motivation normally has its roots. Eurasian ideology was in no way less coherent than that of Bolshevism before or after 1917, but there was no equivalent among the Eurasian leaders to Lenin, whose life and soul were dedicated to the cause of revolution and who before 1917 was undeterred by apparent success or failure in the real world—and whose mother supplied him with an allowance that enabled him to devote himself to his obsession. Savitsky was the nearest thing there was to a Eurasian fanatic, but his thoughts and actions seem childish and unfocused compared with the unremitting purposiveness of Lenin.

'A MAN WITHOUT CONVICTIONS'

It is quite clear from his first few letters to Suvchinsky that Mirsky did not share some of the fundamental tenets of Eurasianism in its early form. He made only one contribution to its coterie publications before 1928—the article on Avvakum that is discussed at length in the letters to Suvchinsky of August and October 1924. And it can be seen from subsequent letters that Mirsky's intellectual reservations remained. He was interested in Eurasianism not because he thought it was right but principally because he thought that it was a uniquely dynamic element in what he saw as the stagnant slough of *émigré* thought and politics.

The Eurasians produced enormous amounts of printed paper and no doubt even greater amounts of hot air that has mercifully evaporated. No single individual writing after the demise of the movement can ever actually have read, much less carefully studied, the entire range of published documents engendered by or associated with Eurasianism. Much less has any single person yet studied all the unpublished documents as well. The production of such quantities of what must have been largely unread verbiage was possible because the Eurasians secured for themselves substantial financial backing in Western funds. It was commonly insinuated by the enemies of the Eurasians in the Russian emigration of the 1920s that the movement was in fact a front organization for the Soviet government, and in its pay. This charge was, and remains, unsubstantiated. How the publications before 1924 were financed is not clear, except in the case of the third collection.[54] But what happened then is quite certain. From the Moscow archive materials and the Mirsky letters we know that the Eurasians were financed by the British philanthropist H. N. Spalding.

Henry Norman Spalding (1877–1953) was educated privately and at New College, Oxford; he was a civil servant in the Admiralty from 1901 to 1909, then became a barrister, and made two unsuccessful attempts to enter Parliament. He returned to the Admiralty during the First World War. From the fortune he inherited he was a generous benefactor to the University of Oxford, endowing *inter alia* the Chair of Eastern Religions and Ethics. 'The Spalding money', as the Eurasian officers referred to it, was a gift of £10,000 made to the movement in 1922 or 1923. This was a huge sum; to get some idea of what it was worth, it is enough to recall that in the early to mid-1920s Bernard Pares ran the School of Slavonic Studies with a staff of seven on an annual grant from the UGC of £2,000.

Just before the movement split, Spalding published the most substantial treatment of it to appear in a language other than Russian, and in fact the only such treatment by a non-Russian, which is surprising in view of the geographical distribution of the intellectual emigration, but not surprising in view of the emigration's generally Russia-oriented priorities.[55] Mirsky's reaction to this book in his letter to Suvchinsky of 6 May 1928 was vitriolic:

I got Spalding's book yesterday. I've skimmed it, and it looks like a huge piece of mediocrity [*bol'shoe ubozhestvo*, a favourite phrase of Mirsky's]—it's nothing but the Elder Zosima plus the *Upanishads*. What's worse is that it talks about the necessity for a bloody *coup d'état* when the Communist Party is overthrown. Finally, it is completely impermissible to twist the name 'Eurasian' into 'Europasian'. What a disgrace to renounce one's name just because some petty little wogs in Ceylon call themselves the same thing.

The use of the phrase 'new party in Russia' in Spalding's title proclaims how little the author understood about what was really going on, for there was no 'party' in any substantial sense, and the idea that the Eurasians were based inside Russia was the result of a GPU confidence trick, as we shall see.

In the early 1920s Mirsky was prepared to take the postulates of Eurasianism seriously, but with some real reservations, as prolegomena to a theory of Russian history, and even—before he completely repudiated essentialist and idealist concepts and became a Marxist—a theory of 'the Russian idea'. He stated his position with absolute clarity to Suvchinsky in his second letter, written on 4 December 1922; this is notwithstanding the fact that, as we have seen, Suvchinsky had already claimed him as a convert:

The first thing is that, though I accept absolutely that Russia is a specific cultural-historical type (to use Danilevsky's language), I consider it to be neither absolutely shut off and impenetrable nor absolutely alien to the West. Spengler is accused (and rightly so) of overlooking Christianity, and the same thing should not happen to us, for the West after all is Christian, and with all the conviction I can muster I insist that both Rome and Luther are closer to me than Islam. The Christian world is one thing and Asia another. Just as India and China are closer to each other than either of them is to us. I agree that we (thanks to the Greeks) possess a purer ideal of Christian faith, but I cannot consign St Francis and Pascal to the outer darkness.[56]

Second, and going on from that. I cannot consider Orthodoxy to be the property of the Russian people alone; Orthodoxy was created (in so far as it was created by human beings at all) by the Egyptians, the Syrians, and the Greeks. . . . And no matter how low the faith has sunk in the Balkans, we are nevertheless a *province* of Orthodoxy. . . . In short, the mystical identification of Russia with Orthodoxy I most emphatically do not accept, and in general I do not accept the heresy of being Chosen by God. Let's leave that to the Yids. In all this there is a great danger of relativism, exactly that.

Mirsky adds a postscript to this disquisition that characteristically broadens the horizons of his argument in a way that would not have occurred to many Russians; it is worth remembering that the 'Troubles' were at their height when he arrived in England in 1921: 'In Europe there is another Eurasia, you know—Ireland. It's just as alien to the Germano-Roman world as we are. Which doesn't in the least mean that it's especially close to us.' Suvchinsky kept badgering Mirsky for a contribution to one of the Eurasian publications, but Mirsky fended him off, in the process making one of his most revealing statements about himself, on 11 August 1923:

I'll be happy to write something for you later on, if you're willing to take on someone who's so lacking in seriousness that he's a Eurasian in even years and a European in odd ones. In general, though, I'm a man without convictions, and a born (though not always open) enemy of ideas in general. So just try doing business with me.

Mirsky's only contribution to the coterie publications of the Eurasian movement was an essay on Avvakum, a Russian parallel to the preface he had provided for the Harrison–Mirrlees translation; it displays the same heightened vivacity and resonance compared to the English as do the other writings on the same subject in the two languages.[57] And it contains the most trenchant statement Mirsky ever made of his views on the Russian literary language and how he thought it should be written. He was concerned here not so much with the language of creative writing as with that of journalism and criticism. Mirsky regarded the 'newspaper' Russian of the intelligentsia as degenerate, debased by 'Westernizing' influences and scholasticism, and he constantly promoted a specific succession of writers who in his view remained creatively rooted in the soil of colloquialism: Avvakum, Derzhavin, Field Marshal Suvorov, Admiral Shishkov (Mirsky's admiration for these two non-literary men is entirely characteristic of him), Griboedov, and Leskov. Coming nearer to his own time, Mirsky added two more names to this list, arguing that the literary language

needs to be shaken up and moved along. . . . This is something that has to be done, and everyone has to do it for himself. Everyone must once more come to feel the weight and significance of words, the *resistance of the material*. This is what Tolstoy did in his time. . . . and after him Rozanov did the same. One should not write *like* Avvakum, *like* Tolstoy, *like* Rozanov—one must oneself do the same work that Avvakum, Tolstoy, and Rozanov did.[58]

Mirsky followed this advice in his own written Russian, which has a rugged vitality that his English lacks; he manifestly does not feel 'the resistance of the material' in his second language. Among the Russian creative writers of his own time, Mirsky discerned the linguistic quality he was looking for in one man and woman: Aleksey Remizov and Marina Tsvetaeva.

ALEKSEY REMIZOV

Despite his reservations about an outright Eurasianist contribution, Mirsky had evidently decided by late 1925 that he and Suvchinsky could do business with each other. Remizov and Shestov, two giants of the older generation, were on the scene and unattached. Mirsky and Suvchinsky brought them in, but a serious enterprise eventually coalesced because of the arrival in Paris of a woman of their own generation, the poet Marina Tsvetaeva.

Remizov had a firmly established, though not popular, reputation by the time he left Russia, while Tsvetaeva was not widely known at all. With Remizov, Mirsky concentrated from his earliest years in emigration on transmitting knowledge of his work to the English-speaking public and providing him with a Russian-language outlet for his new writings.[59] With Tsvetaeva, beginning from the time he met her at the end of 1925, Mirsky did the same, but acted primarily as the first serious critic to establish what he saw as her major status with what he knew all too well to be the exiguous Russian reading public of the emigration.

Both Remizov and Tsvetaeva were profoundly innovatory writers, but their originality stemmed not so much from what they had to say, which was fairly unremarkable, but from the way they said it. They were therefore the hardest kind of writer to translate, and at an increased disadvantage in emigration compared with those writers who were stylistically conventional, like Bunin and Aldanov. Neither of them could ever become a really popular writer with foreign readers, but Mirsky exerted mighty efforts to promote them, working in parallel for both the English and the Russians.

Aleksey Remizov (1877–1957) came from a Moscow merchant family; next after Gorky, his were the humblest social origins of anyone Mirsky ever knew well.[60] Remizov was arrested in November 1896 at a Moscow University student demonstration, imprisoned, and then exiled to Penza. He was re-arrested there in 1898 for involvement in revolutionary political activity among railway workers, exiled to Vologda province, and then amnestied by P. D. Svyatopolk-Mirsky in 1903; when he was Minister of the Interior, Mirsky's father also gave Remizov permission to return to Petersburg. Remizov lived in the capital until war broke out in 1914. It was here, as we have seen, that the schoolboy Mirsky was introduced to him and his wife by Mikhail Kuzmin.

Remizov's wife and inseparable companion was Serafima Pavlovna Dovgello (1876–1943). Born in the Chernigov area, she went to the famous Bestuzhev Courses for Women and the Institute of Archaeology in St Petersburg, and she was a pupil of Platonov, the man Mirsky called 'the greatest of our modern historians'.[61] Serafima Pavlovna was a devout Orthodox Christian and also a revolutionary, the favourite 'grandchild' of Ekaterina Breshko-Breshkovskaya, 'the grandmother of the Russian revolution'. Eventually she was arrested. She spent a year in solitary confinement, and was then exiled for three years to Vologda, which is where she met Remizov in 1902; they married in 1903. The marriage was opposed by Serafima Pavlovna's parents, and she was disinherited. The Remizovs had a daughter, Natalya (1904–43), who became estranged from her parents while she was still a girl, lived with Serafima Pavlovna's family, and remained in Russia.

The Remizovs moved to Paris in the autumn of 1923. In the spring of 1924 they moved to the apartment where Mirsky saw most of them, one of the most famous addresses of Russian Paris—the Villa Flore at 24 avenue Mozart, in the swanky 16th arrondissement, where they stayed for three years. Serafima Pavlovna was a massively corpulent woman with a chronic liver complaint, while he was a frail, gnome-like, twisted manikin. She was direct and outspoken, and he was evasive and sly. Both Remizovs, and Aleksey Mikhailovich especially, essentially lived in a fantasy world, invented on the basis of their mutual fascination with the pre-Petrine Russian past. Reality for them came to an end in the late seventeenth century. Remizov started to cultivate his legend as a rejected and misunderstood writer very early; his incorrigible self-pity and self-promotion were weapons for his shameless cadging. He was not seriously interested in politics, but he remained loyal to his early Socialist orientation and never came out publicly with any anti-Soviet views. He thereby earned the suspicion and mistrust of a large segment of the emigration.

The most signal accolade Mirsky bestowed on Remizov was to incorporate him into the advisory board of *Vyorsts* in 1926, along with Tsvetaeva and Lev Shestov, and publish some new writing by him in all three issues of the enterprise. The presence of Shestov on this editorial board was an anomaly for contemporary commentators, who could not see what he had in common with the others. Shestov was in fact a marginal figure, and he remained so.

MARINA TSVETAEVA

Mirsky's most important contribution to the literary life of the Russian emigration was made in connection with Tsvetaeva and her work.[62] And his personal relationship with her was the closest he ever had with a writer, with the possible exception of Remizov. In early December 1925, Tsvetaeva moved to Paris from Prague, where she had been living since 1922. On 16 December 1925 Mirsky told Suvchinsky that he would like to meet Tsvetaeva; the meeting evidently took place soon after Mirsky got to Paris for the ensuing Christmas vacation. His relationship with Tsvetaeva dominated the next six months of his personal life.

From the beginning, Mirsky's relationship with Tsvetaeva involved another of his closest friends, Princess Salomeya Nikolaevna Halpern, née Andronikova (1888–1982). Long afterwards, the Halperns became very friendly with Isaiah Berlin, and he wrote a characteristically scintillating memoir of them.[63] I showed Berlin Mirsky's letters to Salomeya, and his response illustrates very well the dangers of assuming that everybody between whom one can prove acquaintanceship always knows everything their other acquaintances know:

I had no idea that [Mirsky] was so close to Salomé (as I called her)—neither she nor her husband ever mentioned his name to me. I have a notion that their entire White/Red Russian world was locked away, and not a subject for conversation with unsound people like me who were strictly anti-Communist. I have no idea why Salomé was so passionately pro-Soviet—I blame myself for not ever putting the question to her; I cannot think why I did not—but I suppose she was part of the general movement of Eurasia, Suvchinsky, etc., which gravitated in that direction—although Suvchinsky had close relations with Stravinsky, who was rigidly anti-Soviet all his life.[64]

Marina Tsvetaeva's husband, Sergey Yakovlevich Efron (1893–1941), came from two prominent radical intelligentsia families. His father's side of the family is known to all literate Russians because a member of it was responsible for the most comprehensive work of reference published in Russia before 1917—its usefulness continued to grow as the Soviet authorities attempted to replace it, and it is still indispensable—the encyclopedia usually referred to simply as 'Brockhaus–Efron'. On his mother's side Efron was a Durnovo, a family which like the Efrons belonged to the solid radical intelligentsia, but which was more politically active and undeviatingly on the left.

Sergey Efron and Tsvetaeva hardly saw each other between 1916 and 1922.

Quite unlike Mirsky, Efron was an amateur soldier; like many sprigs of the intelligentsia he originally joined up in 1916 as a medical orderly (as did Brecht and Hemingway, and Walt Whitman before them); but he was a front-line officer in the White army. Tsvetaeva and their daughter Ariadna joined Efron in Prague after finding out his whereabouts from Ilya Erenburg. In 1924-6 Efron was one of the editors of an extremely interesting periodical called *By Our Own Paths* (*Svoimi putyami*), the earliest attempt by the younger genera-tion of adult *émigrés* to give expression to their views.

Although Mirsky's more intense relationship was with Tsvetaeva, Efron was named as one of the three editors of *Vyorsts*. The evidence available suggests that he was not a leading policy-maker, but was used as a glorified secretary mainly to provide him with some sort of income. Efron has always, inevitably, been seen through his wife's eyes by people who are primarily interested in her. He is usually written off as a hopelessly idealistic individual who was incapable of 'supporting' her, and who eventually brought about her downfall by selling out to the Soviets. In all this, Tsvetaeva is usually portrayed as a political inno-cent who had no real idea of what her husband was up to. It is sometimes said that he was incapable of earning any money, which is manifestly inaccurate, an allegation enthusiastically promoted by his wife to boost her begging. Efron had a Czech government grant up to the end of 1925. After that he had some income from *Vyorsts* and *Eurasia*; after that he soon started to get money from Soviet sources. He probably actually earned as much as Tsvetaeva, but the handouts from the Halpern–Mirsky source and Raisa Lomonosova were directed primarily to supporting her as a creative artist, and he was a benefi-ciary. Efron's published writings and his letters show him to have been a highly intelligent and perceptive person, if erring on the side of idealism rather than cynicism.

Tsvetaeva's first reading in Paris took place on 6 February 1926, and it was a triumph that she never managed to repeat. By this time Mirsky had gone back to start his teaching term in London, and he was not present. But on 23 January 1926 he had written to Ariadna Tyrkova-Williams enlisting her help in organizing and publicizing a reading by Tsvetaeva in London.[65] He wrote four letters altogether, exploring various possibilities; by 25 February he was able to send her ten tickets for the reading. On 27 February Mirsky published the first substantial article ever to appear about Tsvetaeva in English, in the *New Statesman*, which was edited at the time by Leonard Woolf.[66]

Tsvetaeva was in London from 11 to 25 March 1926. On the day she arrived, she wrote a letter to Suvchinsky for his eyes alone. It contains one of the most startling statements she ever put down on paper about her personal relation-ships and her triadic theory of human relations:

How much I lack an elder in life, and how much at this moment, in London, I miss you! My interlocutor [Mirsky] keeps silent, and so I'm the one who does the talking.

And I have no idea whether what I say goes home or not. After all, I can't see people at all, especially close up,[67] in a relationship I need a firm hand leading me, so that the leitmotif doesn't come from me. And nobody wants (perhaps nobody is able!) to take this upon themselves, they wait for me to *lead*, me, who all my life have been one of the LED! . . . I need the calmness of the other person and the calmness I feel on his behalf. What am I to do with human silence? It oppresses me, deflects me, knocks me down, and I fill it with content that's perhaps completely inappropriate. If he's silent, that means things are bad. What can I do to make it good? I'm becoming unnatural, forced-jolly, completely vacuous, completely concentrated on one concern—not to let the air in the room *be silent*. Yesterday, in the course of a single evening, I expended so much that I feel—and the night didn't help!—completely beggared. The silence of the other person means that I have to expend, for nothing, in vain. The man doesn't talk. Doesn't talk, just looks. And here am I hypnotized by *silence, watching*—and what?—enemy forces!

'I'm a difficult person. Will you be able to stand me for these two weeks?' Long pause. 'What about you standing me?'

I would like simplicity, calm, certitude. But the other is no help, with his immobility challenging me to complexity, confusion, doubt, something obviously not mine, and it's made me feel humiliated, I'm suffering. You know what it's like when there's false air between people? Not reliable, soon to explode.

Ah, I think I get it! I can't stand it when a person is filled *with me*. I can't stand the responsibility. I want him to be *mine, my own*, but not *me*. After all, I don't love myself (personally), I love *what's mine*. Something that coincides with *what's mine*, that's the thing. Otherwise, eventually, it's loneliness, non-meeting, passing by without meeting. If two people come together in a third,—yes. But two people can never meet in one of the two or in each other. X loves Y, and Y loves X = isolation. X loves Y, and Y also Y = isolation. X loves Z and Y loves Z = meeting. Z = his own (for X and for Y), what coincides is that both X and Y are superior.[68]

In 1925, the same year as Tsvetaeva, Konstantin Rodzevich (1895–1988) had moved from Prague to Paris; he became an active Eurasian, and a friend of Mirsky, though not a close one. Rodzevich emigrated from Russia after service in the Civil War, and in Prague in the autumn of 1923 he had a passionate affair with Tsvetaeva, who immortalized it in two of her greatest works, *Poem of the Mountain* and *Poem of the End*. Rodzevich's view of Tsvetaeva, and the views of many other witnesses of their affair, has been amply discussed in the massive biographical literature on Tsvetaeva, and also represented in a few poor words by Rodzevich himself. Many years later, Rodzevich spoke about the relationship between Mirsky and Tsvetaeva in London; the banality of his version of it could not be further from the soaring fancy of hers: 'There was one incident when they were in a restaurant together facing each other across the table. She said something offensive to him and he turned his chair round and sat with his back to her. She often used to demonstrate for us how he did it, and she would tell this story with humour but also with annoyance.'[69]

Tsvetaeva gave her reading at the School of Slavonic Studies on 12 March

1926, the day after she wrote her extraordinary letter to Suvchinsky. Mirsky introduced the reading. Two years later Tsvetaeva recalled the occasion: 'Poems, with an introductory statement by Prince Svyatopolk-Mirsky, of which I understood only my own name, and even that in phonetic transcription into English!'[70] But writing to Suvchinsky on 15 March, she said that Mirsky began by heaping disgrace on Chekhov, who was, he said, more distant from him than some Chinese poet he had never read. She also said that her poems had 'struck home'. Mirsky reported to Suvchinsky on 16 March that the reading had been a success, especially financially.

In this same letter Tsvetaeva reported to Suvchinsky that she had been to see the Golitsyns. She and Mirsky were driven to Chessington by a White Russian veteran called Rastorguev. I talked to 'Rasti' in 1974 and with bated breath asked this unique surviving eyewitness what Mirsky and Tsvetaeva had said to each other during the journey. He replied with considerable satisfaction that they had said nothing in his presence, because he did all the talking himself. Tsvetaeva asked questions about the White army (at the time she was beginning work on *Perekop*, the long poem about the final episodes of the Civil War), and Rastorguev gave her his account of it, while Mirsky sat silently, in a huff, not wanting to dredge up his past.

Towards the end of the time she spent in London, on 24 March 1926, Tsvetaeva wrote to her Czech benefactress, Anna Tesková, that this had been her first two weeks of freedom for eight years:

I'm going back tomorrow. I'm glad, but also sorry. London is wonderful. Wonderful river, wonderful trees, wonderful children, wonderful dogs, wonderful cats, wonderful fireplaces and wonderful British Museum. Not wonderful is only the chill brought in by the ocean. And the dreadful crossing. (I just lay there without raising my head.) I wrote a big article here. I finished it in a week, at home it would have taken six.[71]

The 'big article' was 'Poet on Critic', one of Tsvetaeva's most scathing pieces of invective. Towards the end of it she singles out Mirsky for approval as distinguished from the vast mass of critics by not judging poetry in terms of politics. This was perhaps the highest accolade the critic Mirsky ever received during his lifetime, and from the harshest critic.

FINDING FUNDS

The editors of *Vyorsts*, and especially Mirsky, faced demoralizing difficulties in their struggle to publish literature in Russian when there were not enough customers to make this an economically viable enterprise.[72] These practical difficulties, in addition to the inevitable clashes of personality within the editorial board, led to the closure of the journal after three annual issues, which is by no means an indication of failure. The journal stands as one of the most enduring literary monuments of the prewar Russian emigration; an unusually small proportion of its contents are dross, and it contains several masterpieces. It was Mirsky's finest Russian-language achievement.

The idea of founding a literary journal crops up from time to time in Mirsky's letters to Suvchinsky from the very beginning of their relationship in 1922. Suvchinsky clearly expected Mirsky to find the funding for the enterprise. The immediate stimulus for getting things off the ground was Tsvetaeva's arrival on the Paris scene in December 1925. During the early months of 1926 Mirsky was working out editorial policy and drumming up financial support for the project. He went first to Jane Harrison, who immediately stumped up £50 of the £200 Mirsky reckoned he needed, and recommended several other useful contacts.[73] One of them was Leonard Woolf; in writing to him, Mirsky follows Harrison's advice and presents the enterprise as belonging purely to the realm of aesthetics, and staying out of politics. The letter was written from 15 Torrington Square, London WC1, on 1 February 1926:

I have been writing to Miss Harrison about a plan I have, & she has responded with even more than ordinary kindness & helpfulness. She has also advised me to write about it to you. This is the matter: as you probably know the Russian press outside Russia is entirely under the control of the leaders of the *émigré* political parties, who give their columns to independent & non-political writers (novelists & poets) only in so far as those conform to their political demands. It thus happens that, for instance, the two writers who to my best understanding are the most significant writers outside Russia— Remizov & Marina Tsvetayeva (as well as others of minor but still considerable significance) have practically had their mouths stopped. For their works are either refused publication, or censored in a most ridiculous way. The Russian money available outside Russia is also all at the service of the political parties, and thus Russian Literature abroad is in the same situation as Balaam,—the prophet silenced & the ass alowed to prophecy [*sic*]. I am trying to find money in England for a magazine that would be free from political control, and that might unite under one cover independent writers living in & outside Russia. The main group of contributors here will be Remizov, Shestov, Marina Tsvetayeva and myself, and we hope to have the support of several writers living in [the] USSR, including especially Pasternak, Mandelstam, Babel & Shklovsky.

I would be infinitely grateful to you if you could help me in this affair by your advice. Miss Harrison suggests that Mr. Keynes might take an interest in it. But I do not know him. Do you think it would be possible to approach him about it? He has met Remizov in Paris at Miss Harrison's, and Mrs Keynes[74] (Miss H. tells me) very much took to him. . . .[75]

Keynes did in fact donate £20. Mirsky got another substantial donation from Mrs Meyrisch, the wife of a Luxembourg steel magnate, who was involved in the Pontigny meetings. On 8 February 1926 Mirsky wrote to Suvchinsky about how he saw the publication: it would be an issue of about 240 pages, with a print run of 1,000 or even 2,000 copies. The title was decided upon after some argument between the prime movers. The word *Vyorsts* refers to an Old Russian unit of linear measure, just over one kilometre, and it also refers to the posts that indicated these distances along the sides of the main roads; it has often been translated as 'Mileposts'. Tsvetaeva had published a collection of poetry with this title in two editions in 1922. The inside cover announced that the journal was 'edited by Prince D. P. Svyatopolk-Mirsky, P. P. Suvchinsky, and S. Ya. Efron, with the closest cooperation of Aleksey Remizov, Marina Tsvetaeva, and Lev Shestov'.

'THE AMBIENCE OF DEATH'

Mirsky made his single most controversial contribution to literary polemic in the Russian *émigré* community in connection with the launch of *Vyorsts*. On 5 April 1926, at the same location, 79 avenue Denfert-Rochereau, where Tsvetaeva had given her reading in February, he delivered his lecture on 'The Ambience of Death in Pre-revolutionary Russian Literature'. The occasion was announced as being organized by the editorial board of *Vyorsts*, and it was chaired by Suvchinsky. The lecture was attended by many famous figures who after it were to become Mirsky's implacable enemies; they included Adamovich, Aldanov, Bunin, Gippius and Merezhkovsky, Khodasevich, and Zaitsev. Khodasevich left a description of Mirsky's performance; in an undated letter to Prince Shakhovskoy, he minimizes the number of important people who were there:

Sv. M. just gave a proclamatory lecture; he'd sent out invitations to take part in discussion following it. Of those invited, only Bunin, Aldanov and I turned up. We didn't sit through to the discussion—we left after the lecture, which was rubbish of a kind nobody (even I) expected from Svyat. It was a disaster for him, and Bunin, Aldanov, and I celebrated in a bar.[76]

When the text of the lecture was published the following year in the second issue of *Vyorsts*, Mirsky added a postscript, saying that it aroused

the indignation of the entire *émigré* sinedrion.[77] I can only rejoice in the indignation of the majority of my accusers. As for the epigones and nihilists who take pride in their corpse-like odour, I would not wish to hold any opinions in common with them, and I consider their condemnation the highest form of praise.[78]

Zinaida Shakhovskaya, the sister of the 'well-intentioned' Prince, was present at this occasion; she accompanied the Remizovs. She reports that Mirsky spoke 'with exemplary cleverness', at one point declaring emphatically: 'as the eminent Russian writer Kundyshin once said'. When they were all leaving the building someone asked in confusion: 'Forgive me, Dima, I can't quite seem to recall who Kundyshin was.' 'He wasn't anybody,' said Mirsky solemnly, 'I made him up.'[79]

This address did indeed mark a parting of the ways for Mirsky with the established powers of the emigration; after it, he published nothing in the Russian *émigré* press that was not edited by himself. The first sentence of the piece is categorical: 'The entire literature of the last reign is shot through with a spirit of death and decay.' The subsequent argument, in characteristic fashion for Mirsky's critical writing, images the sociological through the somatic, and contrasts sickness with health. Mirsky explains that he is talking about 'historical death, the death of a cultural formation, the body of culture', and he has in mind what he customarily refers to as 'Petersburg culture', that is, Russian culture from the early eighteenth century to 1917. The culture of the *dvoryanstvo* was mortally wounded by the Decembrist débâcle, and the culture of the intelligentsia that succeeded it was mortally wounded by the rout of the People's Will. By the early twentieth century, says Mirsky, Petersburg culture had an 'upper storey', inhabited by the 'decadents' and the religious philosophers, and a 'lower storey', in which lived the Chekhovian intelligentsia and the revolutionary parties, which had 'lost their soul'. There was no staircase connecting them. The writers of the lower storey, says Mirsky, had no sense of purpose, and the most symptomatic case among them was that of Gorky's 'passionate thirst for truth and tragic inability to find it'. Bunin, Artsybashev, and Andreev were all obsessed by the theme of death. On the upper storey, the 'decomposition of the spirit' that came out of Dostoevsky and Solovyov, the latter with his 'mystical eroticism', degenerated into 'subterranean necrophilia, pathophilia, and a love for non-existence', the latter most strongly expressed in the poetry of Gippius. When the Revolution brought about the historical death of 'Petersburg Russia', the inhabitants of the upper storey 'greeted it like the Juggernaut, with a frenzy of horror and self-destruction'. The tonality of Russian literature began to change; it underwent what Mirsky calls, emphasizing the phrase, a *liberating impoverishment*. In explaining what he means, Mirsky resorts to his pet surgical metaphor:

In literature this was connected with formalism, futurism, and acmeism. The significance of all three lay in their amputation of the spirit, which was so far gone in decomposition that it could not be healed. But *ferrum sanat*, and to save the organism the decomposing spirit was removed. This operation may not have saved us, but had it not happened, it would have been impossible for us to be saved. (Thus, the Revolution itself was a crisis that could have been followed by either death or recovery, but without it recovery was impossible.)[80]

The remaining sentences of 'The Ambience of Death' hint that recovery is in progress, saluting the birth of 'a new phase of the Russian spirit', a 'Renaissance of the Heroic', which has been foreshadowed in the work of Gumilyov, and which can be found at its best in Pasternak and Tsvetaeva, and in 'many of the young writers working in Russia'.[81] This peroration could well be read as a manifesto for what was to come in *Vyorsts*.

Mirsky's lecture and its later publication had unpleasant ramifications. 'The problem of death' and ways of 'overcoming' it formed a substantial element in the intellectual fabric of modernist Russian culture, and were articulated principally in the thought of Nikolay Fyodorov (1828–1903), with which Mirsky toyed when he was a Eurasian and which he then swiftly rejected when he became a Marxist. Though this aspect of his work seems not to have been much remarked upon by his contemporaries or his more recent critics, Fyodorov was manifestly obsessed by the idea of resurrecting the dead as a way of avoiding the necessity for human sexual reproduction, for which he had a pathological aversion—few others have tried to build a philosophical system on loathing for female genitalia. Strikingly, those Russians who became most vehement on the subject of the 'culture of death' in the mid-1920s were themselves physically sterile: Mirsky, Khodasevich, Gippius, and Bunin in the emigration, and Mayakovsky back in Russia. Which of their ways out was the most deplorable: Mirsky's Stalinism, Khodasevich's nihilism, Bunin and Gippius's sour misanthropy masquerading as Christianity, or Mayakovsky's suicide?

VYORSTS

The three issues of *Vyorsts* were fairly standard in terms of the way Russian 'thick journals' and literary almanacs tend to be put together. Poetry and fiction lead the way, followed by critical articles, and then come reviews. The principal formal innovation in *Vyorsts* was to reprint a substantial text as a supplement bound in with each issue. What mattered most about *Vyorsts* was that works by authors resident in the USSR are presented side by side with *émigré* writing, as represented chiefly by Remizov and Tsvetaeva. The marginal place occupied by Shestov's work in the journal is particularly remarkable; he was named as an associate editor, but the only piece by him that appeared in *Vyorsts* was transferred into the first issue from *Contemporary Notes* because of delays in publication by that journal.[82]

The first number of *Vyorsts* occupies 269 closely printed pages of very good quality rag paper, using a bewildering variety of founts and both New and Old orthography. It includes five outstanding items. The first is Tsvetaeva's *Poem of the Mountain*, written in Prague in 1924, and the greatest love poem in twentieth-century Russian literature. After it come nearly 100 pages of miscellaneous literary matter, punctuated by one of the most extraordinary pieces of sentimental whimsy Remizov ever created. Under the title 'In Very Truth', it is an open letter addressed to the writer Mirsky several times said was the greatest of his time, Remizov's old friend Vasily Rozanov, the seventieth anniversary of whose birth fell in 1926, but who had died in 1919. Remizov brings Rozanov up to date on what has happened in Russian culture since then, with heavy emphasis on his own doings.[83] Not too many pages later comes a factually expert and copiously illustrated overview of the music of Stravinsky by Artur Lurie.[84] Lurie continued this survey in the third issue of *Vyorsts* with a piece on Stravinsky's two controversial operas, *Mavra* (1922) and *Oedipus Rex*, which was brand new when Lurie wrote about it in May 1927. Lurie's first essay is followed by some turgid stuff by Suvchinsky and Mirsky's perfunctory 'Poets and Russia'.

After Mirsky's contribution comes a magnificent essay, 'Three Capitals', on the hoary theme of the contrasts between Petersburg, Moscow, and Kiev; this one, though, has never really been bettered. It is signed 'E. Bogdanov', which was a pseudonym adopted for his own good reasons by the religious philosopher Georgy Fedotov (1886–1951), who had left Russia only the year before. And in the reviews section comes Mirsky's devastating survey of *Contemporary Notes* and *The Will of Russia*, which he reads as the sepulchres of the right and left wings respectively of the old Socialist Revolutionary Party. It was in this context that Mirsky delivered an insult that has never been forgotten or forgiven; he describes Vladislav Khodasevich as 'that little subterranean Baratynsky, the favourite poet of everyone who doesn't like poetry'. The supplement to the first issue of *Vyorsts* presented the complete text of *The Life of the Archpriest Avvakum*, which had been specially edited and copied out for the purpose by Remizov.

VLADISLAV KHODASEVICH

Predictably, the first issue of *Vyorsts* was met largely with contempt by the leading lights in *émigré* literature; equally predictably, it was Khodasevich who eventually made the heavyweight pronouncement, prompted by Gippius.[85] Khodasevich's long article in *Contemporary Notes* was the first systematic attempt to destroy the credibility of the man Khodasevich calls 'our worker-peasant prince' by writing him off as a politically motivated opportunist, who would uncritically and unscrupulously say anything whatsoever to promote the Soviet cause; there is a constant insinuation that Mirsky has somehow been bought and is acting under instructions from Moscow.[86] The next public assault on Mirsky of this kind would come from the Soviet dramatist Vishnevsky after Mirsky had returned to Russia, and there is a ghoulish similarity in tone between his article and Khodasevich's. The personal animus in both is unmistakable.

Khodasevich points out that the *émigré* contributors to *Vyorsts* were all against Lenin's revolution when it happened, but insinuates that they were too cowardly to do anything overt: 'One of the editors, S. Ya. Efron, took up arms against it. Where Messrs Suvchinsky and Bogdanov, Prince Trubetskoy, Svyatopolk-Mirsky himself, and the others were at the time—we know not.' This is an obvious provocation, fishing to get Mirsky the proto-Communist to declare his credentials as a White officer, which Khodasevich must have known about full well. Meanwhile, the now whiter-than-white Khodasevich had originally accepted the revolution, and remained in Russia until 1922, working for Soviet institutions.

The editors of *Contemporary Notes* were hesitant about publishing the piece by Khodasevich, and in the event it came out with significant cuts, which have never been described in detail.[87] Whatever these were, there cannot be much doubt about the main reason for the editors' hesitation. In another provocative phrase that was left in the article, Khodasevich accused Suvchinsky of gleefully anticipating a 'good old Russian pogrom'—'which is not very polite in a journal where one of the editors is S. Ya. Efron, and among the contributors are Pasternak, Babel, L. I. Shestov and Artur Lurie'. The editors of *Vyorsts* dealt with this accusation and several others in their indignant repudiation of this slur.[88] All the members of the editorial board of *Contemporary Notes* happened to be Jewish; Khodasevich was the son of a Polish father and a mother who was an ardent convert to Catholicism, the daughter of a notorious Jewish anti-Semite.

Like Mirsky, Khodasevich was a sterile and deeply neurotic man, but unlike Mirsky he always opted to cohabit with women. He reached the age of 40 in 1926; the fount of his superb poetry dried up soon after. The studied Pushkinian form of his poetry articulates one of the most devastating expressions in Russian of the spiritual aridity that Mirsky spoke about so often with reference to postwar Europe.[89] But Khodasevich drew conservative conclusions, while Mirsky did the opposite. Instead of poetry, Khodasevich subsequently gave himself to writing literary journalism of increasing biliousness, and to his obsession with card games. He never wrote literary history on the scale that Mirsky did; instead, he tended to do the opposite and write concise personal memoirs about the writers he had known, and they are among the very best of their kind in Russian. Notwithstanding the radical difference in their politics, Khodasevich's literary views and many particular emphases in them are very similar to Mirsky's, and the acuity of his literary judgement is the equal of Mirsky's; he is the only Russian contemporary besides Gumilyov of whom this can be said. The spectacle of the two most gifted critical minds of the emigration tearing at each other in the way Mirsky and Khodasevich did is one of the most dismal in the unhappy story of Russia Abroad.

Khodasevich's allegations about the editors of *Vyorsts* truckling to the Soviets were countered, unbeknownst to him, from the horse's mouth. The editors of *Vyorsts* sent a copy of the first issue to Russia; to whom it was addressed is not clear, but it came into the hands of the appropriate official, M. Arseniev, Political Editor of the Leningrad branch of the Soviet censorship, Glavlit (Foreign Literature Sub-Section). His report is concise and to the point:

A collection of work by Russian authors, published, so the preface says, for genuinely Russian people presently living outside the country. The entire collection is saturated with an anti-Soviet tendency and with hatred for the Bolsheviks. The collection is alien to our ideology. Conclusion: 'Prohibit'.[90]

COOLING TO TSVETAEVA

Mirsky visited Tsvetaeva in St Gilles-sur-Vie in the Vendée soon after 15 July 1926.[91] By this time, their relationship was starting to cool off; Tsvetaeva was deep into her next obsession after Mirsky, the triangular epistolary relationship with Pasternak and Rainer Maria Rilke that has been extensively documented and discussed.[92] As for Mirsky, this was the time that he was feverishly putting the finishing touches to his *History*. On 30 September 1926 Mirsky wrote one of his best staff officer's dispatches to Suvchinsky:

I was at Shestov's yesterday. He reproached us, and I think he's right, for not paying any attention to the Orthodox philosophers, Berdyaev and so on, and he says that we should at least write something about *The Way*,[93] and about Ilin's book (*Resistance to Evil*).[94] This seems essential to me, but 1) we can't have a Yid writing about it, 2) Ilin and Karsavin don't inspire my trust, and consequently it has to be you that writes it— *tertium non datur*. I've had a letter from Marina where she 1) demands a reply about whether we agree to give her 2,500 francs for *Theseus* and if so when, and if we can't agree we've to pass it on to *The Will of Russia*! I don't think this amount excessive, but this kind of ultimatumish behaviour is completely improper 2) She demands a reply about whether Seryozha [Efron] will be getting 500 francs per month, and if not, she'll get him another position and he'll work for *Vyorsts* only in the time he has free from his duties 3) Finally, she's very much against *Schmidt*.[95]

One other thing—the distribution of *Vyorsts*. It's shamefully badly set up. Efron is an incredible arsehole.

Shortly before he vented his feelings in this way, on 6 September 1926, Mirsky wrote, from what was now after the death of his mother the house he and his sisters owned at Courbevoie, to Salomeya Halpern about Marina Tsvetaeva, and informed her that he was sending some money to the poet at St Gilles. This was the beginning of the financial support system Mirsky and Halpern organized; for six years it constituted the nearest thing Tsvetaeva had to a regular income.

During the winter of 1926–7 Mirsky was putting together what became the second issue of *Vyorsts*. On 23 January 1927 he told Suvchinsky:

I do not wish to continue publishing *Vyorsts* according to the formula as it is now. I wouldn't mind, but two factors get in the way: a growing and completely insuperable revulsion (not in the figurative sense, but simply *inhibitio*, impossibility) towards Efron and Marina. Any dealings with them whatsoever, spoken or written, are complete torture for me. I'm exaggerating a bit, but this is a very serious matter. Secondly, my role as drummer-up of funds is even more revolting for me than having to deal with the Efrons. It's absolutely not my line, and no matter what you might say to me about my obligations and so on, I'm getting totally impotent in this respect—I just can't rise to it [the sexual innuendo is more explicit in Mirsky's Russian]—there's nothing more to say. And so I propose the following scheme: instead of these huge bricks of ours let's publish small collections of articles. I'd say we could bring out the first one by summer, made up of you, me, maybe Fedotov, maybe Karsavin or Shestov . . . not both of them. . . . And a new title (not *Vyorsts*), but we could put *Vyorsts* Publishers on it. What think you?

There were several other reasons for this change in attitude. One of them involved Pasternak. On 12 January 1927 Tsvetaeva wrote a letter to Pasternak accompanying one by Mirsky to the poet, which Mirsky had left with her to send on to Moscow. He was forced to do this because she had refused to give him Pasternak's home address, and she implored Pasternak not to give it him either, but to fob him off with something institutional. Tsvetaeva eventually sent off the letter on 9 February 1927, and added another note:

The last milestone [*versta*] on your road to him: please send your letter to him open, so as to teach the critic hierarchy and the prince, politeness. (A note on Hierarchy: a poet and a critic cannot have a secret from another poet. I never name names, but in a context like that ours sound right.) Your letter to him, the open one, naturally, I shall not read.[96]

The letter sent on to Pasternak by Tsvetaeva was written by Mirsky from his university address in London on 8 January 1927. He enquired whether or not Pasternak had seen *Vyorsts*, and then switches to enthusiastic flattery:

After such material subjects I do not dare to write what I would wish to—of that great attachment that I have long felt towards you as the author especially of *My Sister Life*, a book which is however so bottomlessly full of content that, plunging down into it ever more deeply as I constantly do, I still do not know whether I have reached its final circle and concentration. If I could dare to hope that my evaluation might be of interest to you, I would like also to tell you that there has not been a poet such as yourself in Russia since the Golden Age, and that in Europe now there can be a contest only between you and T. S. Eliot.

I shall ask Marina Ivanovna to send this on to you, but I would be happy if you would reply to me directly at the address above and let me know yours.[97]

It is not difficult to imagine Tsvetaeva's fury when she read Mirsky's letter before sending it on—as she must inevitably have done, despite her assurance to the contrary—and discovering that Eliot rather than she was mentioned as the equal of Pasternak.

On 5 June 1928, writing to Suvchinsky, Mirsky expressed a vigorously coarse reaction to the last book Tsvetaeva published during her lifetime, which had just come out after a long delay; it finally brought together her poetry of the Prague period:

I just received Marina's poems. I reread a lot of them and was deeply moved—what a fucking poet she is, all the same! (*Kakoi vse-taki, ebi ee mat', poet!*) The one bad thing is that she wasn't thrashed enough early enough. These years, 1922–25, are her best. Her rising line continues up to Rodzevich and with Rodzevich it breaks off.[98]

In a letter of 18 June 1928 to Salomeya Halpern, Mirsky says that he had attended a poetry reading the day before, by 'that woman'—Marina Tsvetaeva. This same date is found beneath the dedication to Mirsky in the book he reported on to Suvchinsky, *After Russia*: 'To my dear friend Dmitry Petrovich Svyatopolk-Mirsky, to remind him of *that* Villette, *that* London, and *that* Vendée. Marina Tsvetaeva, Meudon, 17 June 1928.'[99] The dedication is an obvious reproach for what had happened in the preceding two years between the best poet of the emigration and her best critic.

MORE *VYORSTS*

The 285-page second issue of *Vyorsts* is a manifest step down from the luxurious first. It is printed on poor-quality paper that makes it half as thick as the 1926 issue, and it has no illustrations; the first carried excellent glossy portraits of Pasternak and Tsvetaeva (demonstratively on the same page), and also studio portraits of Remizov, Shestov, and Stravinsky. The first eighty-three pages contain Tsvetaeva's verse drama *Theseus*, about which Mirsky and Suvchinsky wrangled painfully with the author, trying to point out that it was far too long for their purposes and that the fee was more than they could afford. They eventually yielded, but Mirsky found Tsvetaeva's insistence hard to forgive.

The vivid phrasing and compressed argument of Mirsky's own essay here, the revised text of the lecture he had given in 1926 on 'The Ambience of Death', make it jump off the crumbling pages to this day, made even more lively by its drab, droning context. At the head of the bibliographical section, Mirsky's survey of current Russian literature is another superb piece of compression; it looks briefly at the recent posthumous edition of Esenin, and then turns to some of the major achievements of Russian fiction of the mid-1920s, all of them by writers resident in Soviet Russia except the first, Maksim Gorky. One sentence in this review of *The Artamonov Business* is of particular interest in view of the fact that less than a year after he wrote it, Mirsky would meet Gorky personally and claim that he had rediscovered Russia in him. Mirsky says that into the characters of Kuzma and Tikhon 'Gorky has poured all the tormented history of his own quest, in its helpless hopelessness the most tragic drama of the Russian soul. There can be no doubt that with this hopeless blundering Gorky carries a cross for all of us, we of little faith, we strutters on the spot, we Khlestakovs of the spirit . . .'.[100]

The most distinctive feature of the 1927 issue of *Vyorsts* was the contributions by a number of non-Russian critics, all of them commissioned by Mirsky and translated by him. His Pontigny colleagues Bernard Groethuysen and Ramón Fernández appear here. The single most remarkable item is an essay by E. M. Forster, 'Contemporary English Literature', the original of which was apparently lost with the archive of *Vyorsts*.[101] Mirsky had originally approached I. A. Richards for a contribution, but he can surely not have been disappointed; the essay may be read as a concise version of Forster's *Aspects of the Novel*, which was among the many classic books of the period that Mirsky reviewed for the *London Mercury*.[102] The substantial review by Mirsky of T. S. Eliot's *Poems, 1905-1925* in the 1927 *Vyorsts*, and several other less significant items, make this issue stand out among the publications of the Russian emigration for its serious and well-informed attention to contemporary non-Russian culture. The Eliot review was the end result of a rather different plan by Mirsky, which he mooted in his letter to Suvchinsky of 11 March 1926: 'I've had the idea of doing a verse translation (*vers libre*, like the original) of T. S. Eliot's long poem *The Hollow Men* (4 pages, about 100 lines), a work of genius in terms of the concentration of its feeling for the death and impotence of post-war Europe, and it really is a very important piece in artistic terms.'[103]

The literary supplement to the 1927 *Vyorsts* is a sixty-page passage from Rozanov's *The Apocalypse of Our Time*. Janko Lavrin, who had been a journalist colleague of Rozanov in St Petersburg, remembered this publication particularly well, though he thought it had been in the 1926 issue. He characterized *The Apocalypse* as 'one of the most biting and vicious attacks on Socialism, Communism and so on', and surmised that when Mirsky reprinted it he can still only have been 'flirting' with Communism.

Mirsky directed a mounting barrage of protests at Suvchinsky while the third issue of *Vyorsts* was being worked out. By 27 May 1927 he was getting desperate; he wrote to Suvchinsky, using his now familiar numbered points:

What to do about *Vyorsts* I don't know. It looks as if I have no options left for raising money. When I ask people about it, their answer is: 1) why do you publish such thick books? 2) why is nobody buying it? I had hoped to sink into *Vyorsts* my part of the proceeds from our house in Asnières [i.e. Courbevoie], but it still hasn't sold, and I don't know when it will. I could contribute from my earnings, but then I'd have to write much more in English than I'm doing now, and this would exclude the possibility of writing for *Vyorsts*. The Eurasian publishing house might advance us a certain amount. You can't deny that *Vyorsts* is serving the Eurasian cause and has done a lot to propagandize Eurasian ideas.

Mirsky had become even more exasperated by 12 June 1927:

I'll do all I can to get out the third issue of *Vyorsts*. But on the following conditions, which are absolute: 1) if you produce an article for it. This is a *sine qua non* and if you don't produce one, there is decidedly nothing I can do; b) if you swear a solemn oath that you will never in any way try to persuade me to continue *Vyorsts* after No. 3. I'm fed up to the back teeth with it. I've got nothing out of it except enormous unpleasantness; none of the contributors interest me at all, apart from you, Avvakum, and Rozanov (and Pasternak, Babel, and others).

This might reasonably be taken to indicate that a breach of relations was imminent, but in fact the opposite happened. Mirsky and Suvchinsky soon made common cause in ventures quite different from those represented by *Vyorsts*.

If the first issue of *Vyorsts* had not been in any real sense 'Eurasian' except for the formal association with the name of Suvchinsky, the contents of the second and third have a much stronger connection with the movement.[104] However, N. S. Trubetskoy appeared in the first two issues, his precise scholarly tone contrasting strongly with his surroundings on these occasions. His essays are both literary rather than linguistic.[105] In the 1926 issue he published his celebrated article on one of the most interesting works of late Old Russian literature, Afonasy Nikitin's *Journey beyond the Three Seas*, attempting to read it as a creative work rather than as a linguistic monument.[106] To the 1927 issue Trubetskoy gave another pioneering study, on the metrics of the Russian folk *chastushka*, based on original material recently brought from Russia whose intermediacy is a puzzle.[107] The Eurasian flavour of *Vyorsts* was intensified not so much by Trubetskoy's contributions as by the articles in the second and third issues by Lev Karsavin. His 'Without Dogma' in the 1927 issue is mainly about the historiographical conceptualization of the Russian Revolution, and it is a very good example of the persistent tendency in Russian high journalism to make enormous generalizations without adducing very much accurate documentation; but it does contain some valuable thoughts about historicism. The 1928 item, 'Russia and the Jews', was prefaced by a cautious note from the editors, and followed by a riposte from A. Z. Shteinberg, and then another piece by him, on Dostoevsky and the Jewish question.[108]

The other surviving patriarch of Eurasianism, P. N. Savitsky, contributed a characteristic 'geographical essay', 'Towards an Understanding of the Russian Steppes', to the third issue of *Vyorsts*. It is so clotted with interpolated quotations, reference material, and unexplained technical terms that it could serve as a useful model of how not to write an article, except perhaps a pseudo-scholarly one. The growing impression that some sort of maniac is at work is confirmed when after nearly thirty double-columned pages of this stuff, there is a precise date of writing following the author's signature. The fact that Savitsky was capable of producing this amount of verbiage is surpassed by his apparent belief that it matters that he did it on 10 May 1927. And after he has signed off, Savitsky opens up again because of two new sources that he had devoured since his first discharge finally petered out.

For the third issue of *Vyorsts*, the editors abandoned the idea of reprinting a substantial text, and instead published three letters written in 1899 by Fyodorov, whose ideas were being taken very seriously at the time by several

Eurasians. A long introduction by one of them, N. A. Setnitsky, attempts to point out the contemporary relevance of this material. Mirsky was to deal with this interest in Fyodorov among the Eurasians when he became a Marxist and came to think of Fyodorov's writings as one of the snares on his way to enlightenment.[109]

The most remarkable contribution to the 1928 *Vyorsts*, though, came from Nikolay Berdyaev, who had published several articles in the immediately preceding years that take a respectful but eventually negative view of Eurasianism. His 'Russian Religious Thought and the Revolution' is an extended and slightly breast-beating historical account of the relations between the Russian intelligentsia and the revolutionary movement, in the spirit of 'where it all went wrong'. The writing is fatally fluent and stylistically flat, with absolutely no sense of 'the resistance of the material' that Mirsky celebrated in the prose he liked. There is no more striking contrast than that between Berdyaev's self-indulgent rambling and Mirsky's crisp and specific discussions of similar subjects.

The principal difference between the last issue of *Vyorsts* and the two that preceded it was announced in the introductory matter: there would be no reprints of literary work originally published in the USSR. The editors claimed that they had achieved the object of their previous policy and compelled the readers outside Russia to take this writing seriously. The most provocative item in the 1926 issue was a reprint of the 1925 Party declaration on literature and the responses to it by a number of eminent writers who included Bely, Veresaev, Leonov, Shklovsky, Pasternak, Pilnyak, and A. N. Tolstoy. There is also a reptilian paragraph by one of Mirsky's future colleagues when he became a Soviet literary critic, G. Lelevich (1901–45); at the time, this Party veteran had already failed as a poet and was becoming a militant proletarianist critic. Khodasevich made great play with all this in his essay in *Contemporary Notes*, alleging that the editors of *Vyorsts* were illustrating their conviction that literary life had now been liberated in Russia, and confronting it with his own material showing that the opposite was the case.

The selections from Soviet fiction in the 1927 issue are magnificent. They include extracts from three of the novels that Mirsky discussed in the bibliographical section of the same issue: Artyom Vesyoly's *Insurrection*, Tynyanov's wonderful historical novel *Kyukhlya*, and Bely's remarkable *Moscow under the Hammer*. Two important names are absent from these lists of Soviet authors. In his letter to Leonard Woolf about the aims of *Vyorsts*, Mirsky specifically mentioned Mandelshtam and Shklovsky as authors he hoped to publish, but they did not appear. The authors selected for reprinting in *Vyorsts* reflect Mirsky's taste, and his critical articles of the mid-1920s are full of praise for these two figures.

Vyorsts was Mirsky's finest contribution to the cultural legacy of the Russian emigration, but it was achieved at the price of tremendous strain. He acted as the staff officer he was trained to be—constantly reassessing the situation, making plans, chivvying his associates to get things moving in the required direction, and threatening disciplinary action when they failed to do so. He got very little support from his co-editors; Suvchinsky in particular was continually letting him down. Tsvetaeva's claim in various letters that it was her husband Efron who bore the main burden of producing *Vyorsts* is yet one more example of her self-aggrandizement, this time vicarious; he seems to have been used only for secretarial work, and Mirsky continually complains about his slackness. Meanwhile, Efron was being paid, while Mirsky was shelling out. The quality of Suvchinsky's individual contributions to *Vyorsts* is truly abysmal, but fortunately there are only two of them. One stroke of good fortune was that Suvchinsky was originally supposed to write on Stravinsky, but Lurie stepped in admirably when Suvchinsky failed to produce.[110]

It is quite clear from Mirsky's letters that hardly any copies of *Vyorsts* were sold to the reading public, and that to the bitter end Mirsky was responsible for finding the money to meet the fees and production costs of the enterprise. There was no chance of the series being sold to readers in Russia. In November 1926 Mirsky considered one obvious way out, analogous to the way later taken by Nabokov—to cross the language barrier, produce an English version of the more important items from the journal, and bring in a representative to handle sales in the USA. He produced the appropriate flyer, but nothing else happened.

On 27 February 1927 Mirsky wrote to Suvchinsky, expressing more strikingly than anywhere else that commitment to concision that makes his own *émigré* writing so bracing:

[You] can't publish a journal that nobody buys—and if, as you assert, everybody *is* reading it, then it's clear that we have to publish it in such a way as the readers can *buy* it, and for this there's one condition, and this is the main thing—to write shorter pieces, which our contributors don't know how to do—and not to print what's not strictly necessary. . . . There's nothing that can't be fitted into 8 pages of our format. . . . Long articles are a holdover from the period when paper and production costs used to be cheap. That kind of writing is like still taking a *dormeuse* from Paris to Berlin.[111] I can't forgive myself that we published *Theseus*. But in any case, if you can, have a word with that woman. I'll write to her and tell her to have a word with you.

MIRSKY AND RELIGIOUS FAITH

Mirsky's dealings with Eurasianism and the Eurasians in 1926–9 constantly confronted him with the problem of religious faith. Adherence to Orthodoxy was a fundamental tenet of Eurasianism; and Suvchinsky was a communicant member of the Church—though his then wife Vera told me that he only went to services to listen to the singing. The religious concerns of Eurasianism came to the surface in the second and third issues of *Vyorsts*, as we have seen, at first in connection with Karsavin and the question of the Jews.

In writing to Suvchinsky, rather than the neutral *evrei* (Jew), Mirsky persistently and naturally uses a word I have unavoidably translated as 'Yid' (*zhid*), which is now as thoroughly taboo in decent Russian company as it is in English. For a man of Mirsky's generation and background this would probably have been a habitual term that did not necessarily imply any animosity or contempt. In this regard as in so many others, Mirsky was something of a special case. In general, in the social circles in which he grew up, and especially in the élite reaches of the officer corps, anti-Semitism was endemic and virulent. It is quite likely that Mirsky was not personally acquainted with anyone Jewish before 1918, just as he was not personally acquainted with any professional women; there was no reason why such people should have crossed his horizon. The one exception can only have been the schoolmate with whom Mirsky made his literary debut, Viktor Zhirmunsky, the son of a prosperous Petersburg laryngologist. In view of all this, Mirsky's subsequent attitude is remarkable, because in his adult life and writings he seems to have been without prejudice. If anything, he was somewhat philo-Semitic. He several times went out of his way to point to the superior cultural achievements of Russian Jewry compared to those of ethnic Russians since 1917; suffice it to mention Pasternak, Mandelshtam, and Babel. There were many others. Mirsky rather blots his copybook writing to Suvchinsky on 4 March 1927 when he observes that 'the only idea of Trubetskoy's about the Yids known to me is that all Yids are exhibitionists, which by the way is true'.[112] But he restores something of his credibility when he responds spiritedly to the manuscript of Karsavin's article on 11 March 1927:

Karsavin's article is not bad either, and mine will be a defence of the Jewish periphery, starting with Philo.[113] Objectively, Karsavin is absolutely wrong when he asserts that the Jews of the periphery are all second-rate, 'except *perhaps* Spinoza' (that 'perhaps' is absolutely ridiculous). In Russia this may be the case (but what about Trotsky and Pasternak, though), but in Europe the entire nineteenth century is full of an absolutely disproportionate amount of Jews 'in leading positions', such as *Marx*, Heine, Disraeli, Lassale, Minkovsky. And at the present time in France and Germany there's more of them perhaps than non-Jews (Bergson, Einstein, Freud, etc.). The periphery is a legitimate and inalienable manifestation of Jewry.

Whatever the case, Mirsky was obviously far too intelligent a person to be a racist. As with everything, the basis of his attitude was intellectual. During his discussions with Suvchinsky about the possible contributions to *Vyorsts* on the Jewish question, he stated: '*In the West* the Jewish question is increasingly being put in purely racial terms, to the exclusion of others. Therefore perhaps it would be better to emphasize that we're talking about the Russian-Jewish question, where putting things in any specifically racial terms is out of date.'

The Russian Orthodox Church in Mirsky's time tended to take a much less rational view of this matter than Mirsky did. Inevitably for a person of his age and social background, Mirsky had been brought up in the Church, and we have seen evidence of his mother's piety, especially with regard to the journey to the new shrine of St Serafim in 1904. All Mirsky's public life before he left Russia, especially his army service, was conducted in a context of ritual observance of the Church's rites. Whether or not Mirsky's short-lived marriage began with a religious ceremony, we do not know. Religious observance was especially prominent in the White army, and formed one of the few elements of a genuinely shared ideology in the movement. In emigration, however, the practice of these observances inevitably loosened. The Church was a prime focus of Russian émigré life in London and Paris; but there is no evidence that Mirsky was a communicant member in London, and very little evidence that he went to services in Paris. The argument with Roger Fry suggests that in 1925 Mirsky was still far from being an atheist; but the exchanges with Shakhovskoy suggest equally strongly that Mirsky viewed the 'dark' side of religion and the Orthodox Church with mounting revulsion. Mirsky dealt with his religious evolution in a curt paragraph of his intellectual autobiography:

Since I was inwardly inclined towards materialism, it was not the religious and mystical side that appealed to me most in Eurasianism, although neither did it repel me. . . . For twenty years my 'reason' succeeded in imposing on my 'heart' an idealist and theological chaos that my common sense refused to take seriously, but which was enough to inhibit any shift in my intellectual conscience.[114]

Mirsky locates the final break at the time *Eurasia* came to an end, in September 1929:

My materialist 'heart' rebelled against this so-called 'reason' which had held it prisoner for nearly a quarter of a century. The chains were worn; it needed only one last effort to break them. Pokrovsky had already swept away a good deal of idealist refuse. I had made contact again with Marx.[115]

6   *Writing Politics*

Any *émigré* intellectual who wishes to remain alive must either lose
his nationality or accept the revolution in one way or another.
(D. S. Mirsky, 1931)

GOING TO GORKY

The final phase of Mirsky's life in emigration began with an event that explicitly raised the idea of his going back to Russia: during the Christmas vacation
of 1927–8 he went with Suvchinsky to visit Maksim Gorky in Sorrento. Many
years later, Suvchinsky told Véronique Lossky: 'One day Mirsky asked me to
go with him, and we spent Christmas at Gorky's. . . . We were followed the
whole time. Gorky tried to persuade us to go to Russia, saying "I'll fix you up",
and he convinced Mirsky and me.'[1] Suvchinsky told me: 'I had known Gorky
back in Petersburg-Petrograd and met him at Shalyapin's. D.P. didn't know
him and asked me to introduce him. I exchanged letters with Gorky and we
got visas through the poet Ungaretti, which at that time was not easy.'[2]

On what basis exactly Gorky promised Mirsky and Suvchinsky that he could
'fix them up' in Russia is a puzzle, because Gorky's own standing at this time
was not at all clear. He had been given his marching orders by Lenin in October
1921 because of the persistent criticism he levelled at the new regime, chiefly
in his journal *Untimely Thoughts*, on the basis of its record in human rights
and freedom of information; he had not been back to Russia since.[3] Gorky lived
at first in Germany; in the spring of 1924 he moved to Sorrento. Mussolini
would not allow him back onto Capri, where Gorky, as a political exile with
a massive international reputation and correspondingly large income, had
created a refuge for the Russian revolutionaries before 1914. In his rented villa
in Sorrento he lived as before with a substantial entourage, which now included
two additions of particular significance: the enigmatic Moura Budberg[4] and
also the more obvious eyes of the NKVD in the form of Gorky's 'secretary',
Pyotr Kryuchkov.

It is clear from Mirsky's letters to Suvchinsky in the run-up to their visit
that Mirsky not only made the necessary arrangements, but also paid
Suvchinsky's expenses. Giuseppe Ungaretti (1888–1970) was employed at the
time in the Ministry of Foreign Affairs in Rome; he was the Italian literary
adviser to *Commerce,* and Mirsky would have known him in that connection.
Mirsky may not have been personally acquainted with Gorky, but the latter
certainly knew who he was. Gorky had noted and commented on the publica-

tion of *Vyorsts* in one of his regular reports about what was going on in Western Europe, a letter of 24 July 1926 to A. K. Voronsky in Moscow:

The editor is Prince Svyatopolk-Mirsky, apparently the son of the one who promised to make a 'spring' in 1901–2. He's a very clever and independent critic who writes superlative characterizations of Zaitsev, Merezhkovsky, Khodasevich and others. There are reprints of Artyom Vesyoly . . . Babel . . . Pasternak. . . . But the Eurasians are in here too—Lev Shestov, Artur Lurie, and, of course, Marina Tsvetaeva and Remizov. It's a princely affair.[5]

In a letter written from Sorrento on 6 January 1928 to the novelist Olga Forsh, Gorky speaks of 'the Eurasian Suvchinsky, who is living at the Minerva[6] together with one of the descendants of Svyatopolk the Accursed'.[7] Since Mirsky was anything but the kind of person who paid visits to celebrities just because they were celebrities, there must have been a weighty reason for his approaching Gorky. He had no illusions whatsoever about the ambiguities of Gorky's personality and political stance; in his writings Mirsky had mercilessly formulated the ethical reservations about him that were standard among the *émigré* intelligentsia:

With an enormous insight into reality, Gorki has no love of truth. And as he has no motive to restrain him from telling half-truths, and insinuating untruths, his essays more often than not become grotesque distortions of reality. This practically nullifies his moral weight in the eyes of all Russians. And it seems Gorki will be richly repaid for his contempt of the Russian people. Even now he is not taken seriously except by foreigners, for the Bolsheviks use him only as a convenient signboard to be contemplated from beyond the pale.[8]

Side by side with remarks of this kind, though, Mirsky had constantly stressed Gorky's pre-eminent status among living Russian writers, and spoken warmly of his efforts to maintain links between the divided worlds of Soviet and *émigré* culture. The obvious reason for going to see Gorky would have been in order to forge such a link, presumably with reference to the Eurasian movement, because at this stage Mirsky did not want to go directly to an official Soviet representative. Meanwhile, several significant but inconclusive pointers suggest that in 1927 the Eurasian leadership did attempt a direct *rapprochement* with the Soviet authorities, as we will see.

To get Gorky back to Russia was an important objective of Soviet policy. Khodasevich observed in 1925: 'The most compromising thing about the Bolshevik paradise is that those who adore it would do anything rather than live there.'[9] He was referring specifically to Erenburg, but Gorky was the prime illustration of this notion in the public mind. After Gorky settled in at Sorrento, a stream of Soviet writers started to visit, always with the permission of their own and the Italian authorities, neither of which was easy to secure. His visitors eventually included several representatives of the new literary élite, both Party members and fellow-travellers: the poets Aseev and

Marshak, the novelists Babel (whose Italian visa was facilitated by Mirsky), Olga Forsh, Vsevolod Ivanov, and Valentin Kataev, and the playwright Nikolay Erdman. In the autumn of 1927 Sholokhov was on his way, but he was refused an entry visa by the Italians. Just before Mirsky and Suvchinsky went to see Gorky, Anastasiya Tsvetaeva had paid him a visit, and towards the end of it she went to see her sister Marina in Paris; there may well have been some direct connection between this visit and that of the two Eurasians.[10]

Also in the autumn of 1927, Gorky was visited by Kamenev, who had just been appointed Soviet Ambassador to Italy;[11] this seems to have been the moment when an agreement was struck that Gorky would come back to Russia. How and when he would come, though, was a ticklish business. For one thing, the state of Gorky's health was more than a politically convenient excuse for his spending at least the winters outside Russia. But the main problem was, of course, the delicate relationship between Gorky and Stalin. Gorky had immaculate credentials as a close personal friend of Lenin, and such people were increasingly felt to be a threat by his successor.

Mirsky expressed the public face of his private feelings about his visit in a letter he wrote to Gorky from London on 2 February 1928:

I have been meaning to write to you ever since I left, and I still can't find the right words to tell you what an enormous blessing our meeting was for me. I probably never will be able to, but I feel that I was not in Sorrento but in Russia, and that this time I spent in Russia really *straightened me out*. There is no other man who could bear Russia within himself like you do, and not only Russia, but also that quality without which Russia cannot exist—humanity. . . . As we were leaving, Suvchinsky said to me 'We never saw Tolstoy, though!' Tolstoy was the only person we could think of. But you are more Russian, you 'represent' Russia, more than Tolstoy did.[12]

Writing a week later, on 9 February 1928, Mirsky put to Suvchinsky a leading question, and answered it himself: 'I keep asking myself what divides us (me) from the Communists? Only first principles.' Mirsky attributed particularly great importance to the visit to Gorky in the account of his intellectual development that he wrote after he had joined the Communist Party in 1931:

Leaving aside the unforgettable impression made on me by the great charmer that was Gorky, this visit was our first direct contact with 'the other side of the barricade' and our first breath of pure materialist air from regions uninfected by the metaphysical miasma we had been breathing.[13]

At the time, though, the thoughts of going back to Russia that Mirsky says were stimulated by the visit to Gorky were left to lie fallow; nearly three years went by before Mirsky next contacted him. As we shall see, Mirsky was not at first thinking in terms of going back for good. In fact, until about a year before he actually left for Moscow, he seems to have conceived the enterprise as a visit and no more. Gorky's example, or perhaps even Gorky's own advice, may have suggested that it would be possible to go and come back.

AMERICA

Instead of turning irrevocably east, Mirsky did the opposite. He finally paid his long-mooted visit to the USA in the summer of 1928, as a result of an invitation from Columbia University that had been brokered by Michael Florinsky. After this visit, Mirsky considered taking up a permanent academic appointment in America. The idea of America had been part of his consciousness since his earliest days in emigration: through the intermediacy of Bernard Pares, whose connections with American Russianists were of long standing, Mirsky's books had found parallel American publishers, and he had contemplated a lecture tour as early as 1924. After Florinsky moved to New York in 1926, one of his first letters sounds Mirsky out about a possible job at Columbia University. Later, Florinsky offered to fix up a lecture tour so that Mirsky could have a look round. On 6 December 1926 Mirsky replied that he would be glad to come, but 'for this I'd like to receive a goodly amount of dollars, since three weeks on the ocean is worth that'. He also said that he could only be released in the summer term. On 14 February 1927 Mirsky told Florinsky that he had had an invitation from Clarence Manning[14] to give a lecture series from 1 to 15 July 1928 for 600 dollars. Very soon after this, though, Mirsky made an abrupt about-turn, telling Florinsky: 'I must say honestly, though, that I absolutely don't want to come to America, and I'll take it on only out of a sense of duty. To hell with it [*Nu ee sovsem*]. I attach three copies of my biography.'

Eventually Mirsky sailed for America on 27 June 1928. Two letters survive that he wrote to Suvchinsky from New York. In the first, he hints that something to do with the Eurasian connection had gone seriously wrong there. Malevsky-Malevich had been active on behalf of the Eurasians, and Mirsky took a dim view of the results:

Unfortunately, I'm not seeing much of the Americans. The Russians are mediocrities, on the whole worse than those in Paris, with a few exceptions. I haven't seen any Eurasians and I think it's not worth it, I can see from here they're mediocrities. Malevsky has debauched himself here to the limit. Perhaps I'll still try and say a few warm words to them.[15]

In the second letter from New York, written on 9 August, Mirsky claims to have established a link with the Department of State and to be trying to fix up a meeting with the head of the Russian section for Suvchinsky or Arapov when that person is next in Paris. Whether anything came of this is unknown, but it seems unlikely that anything did. Mirsky gave three lectures, at Columbia, Cornell, and Chicago. The lecture at the University of Chicago was delivered on 31 July in the Harper Assembly Room, and its subject comes as rather a surprise in the light of the way Mirsky's views were developing at this time: 'Elements of Russian Civilization: Russia and the Orthodox Church'.[16]

EURASIANISM EXPANDS

Meanwhile, at the same time as he was planning his trip to America and writing his major historical works in English, the main concern of Mirsky's practical life increasingly became Russian politics, and in particular the politics of the Eurasian movement. The letters to Suvchinsky show that from about the middle of 1926 Mirsky was constantly offering advice about the policy decisions that were being taken by the Eurasian leadership.

Mirsky was not the only, nor yet the most influential, newcomer to the leadership of the movement at this time. Lev Karsavin became involved with Eurasianism soon after he arrived in Berlin in 1923.[17] Karsavin's candidacy for a leading position in the movement was initially treated with considerable reservation by Trubetskoy and Savitsky, but Suvchinsky apparently convinced them to take him on purely as an expert adviser. In talking about Karsavin in this connection, Suvchinsky uses the current Soviet slang term for an expert, *spets*, which Savitsky thought deeply suspicious when the branch of expertise concerned was religion. Mirsky's reaction to Karsavin was similar, and ominous; he wrote to Suvchinsky on 8 August 1926:

Forgive me, but I can't help sensing in [Karsavin] something that is in the highest degree spiritually unsound . . . —his entire approach is the purest utilitarianism, isn't it? He's a nihilist and a blasphemer, and his very theologizing looks to me like a sort of refined defamation.

The generation that was born in the years of Dostoevsky's evil deeds (*Notes from Underground*, 1864–1881!) will not bring forth sound fruit. And if you take him on purely as a *spets* in theology, isn't that doing things the Latin way? Does Orthodoxy really have any familiarity with this kind of spetsish theologianizing that has no connection with the spiritual essence?

Karsavin moved to Paris in July 1926 and settled in Clamart, where Suvchinsky and also Berdyaev (and later Tsvetaeva) lived. That autumn Karsavin instituted a Eurasian seminar there; it became the ideological engine of the movement. This was the first articulation of the schism between Paris and Prague that was to wreck Eurasianism in 1929.

Three other men became prominent in the Eurasian movement at the same time. Vladimir Nikolaevich Ilin (1890–1974) was another philosopher who had been expelled from Russia in 1922; he had contributed an essay to the Eurasian volume of 1923 on East–West ecclesiastical relations. He was resident in Prague. The legal scholar Nikolay Nikolaevich Alekseev (1879–1964) was also resident in Prague; from 1926 he began publishing essays that attempt to construct a Eurasian theory of the state and law. Finally, Vasily Petrovich Nikitin (1885–1960) began contributing essays to Eurasian publications on the relations between Russia-Eurasia and the Middle East.

The contemporary published documents give no precise indication about how the Eurasian movement was formally managed. Though the *Eurasian Chronicle* contains a good deal of information about various events, there are no systematic reports of when and where meetings were held or how many people attended them, not to mention any financial accounts. It may well be that there was in fact no formally constituted structure, no protocols and formalized proceedings. Some evidence about the high command of the Eurasian movement after 1925, though, has emerged from the previously secret materials that have become available since the downfall of the USSR.

The earliest such documents are two 'Protocols' of March 1923 in which 'the three Ps', as they call themselves—Arapov, Suvchinsky, and Savitsky (who shared the first name Pyotr)—discuss Eurasian publishing policy, and another 'Protocol' of June 1923 in which the same three set out a concise definition of the nature and aims of the movement. Their concluding paragraph is of considerable interest:

In practical matters, the first and foremost essential is circumspection. Effort should be concentrated in the first instance on spreading the spiritual influence of Eurasian ideas in Russia, and in the second, on the creation of a circle of persons spiritually connected with each other and variously gifted in terms of action.[18]

In 1927 Karsavin left Paris to take up a teaching post at the University of Kaunas in Lithuania, but he remained an active Eurasian until the schism of 1929.[19] He lived in Kaunas until 1940, when his university removed to Vilnius. He lost his job after the Soviet occupation in 1945, and was duly arrested on 9 July 1949. He was then interrogated, mainly about the Eurasian movement.[20] He stated that in 1926, when he first became involved, there was a Council (*Sovet*), which consisted of five men. In the order in which Karsavin names them, and which seems to indicate a hierarchy at least in his mind, they were: Trubetskoy, Savitsky, Suvchinsky, Arapov, and Malevsky-Malevich. At a congress in Prague in 1926, this Council chose a four-man Politbyuro—the Soviet-style term is indicative—which consisted of Trubetskoy, Suvchinsky, Malevsky-Malevich, and Arapov. The Council was then expanded; Karsavin himself joined it, but according to his own testimony he soon resigned. Three others joined the Council in or around 1926, precisely at what date Karsavin does not say: they were 'the former Russian consul in Persia, Nikitin; colonel of the Tsar's army Svyatopolk-Mirsky; and the officer Artomonov'. If this statement is accurate, it means that in the run-up to the schism the governing body of the Eurasian movement consisted of eight men, of whom Mirsky was one.

Karsavin himself seems to have been involved only in the public activities of the Eurasians. There was, though, another side to the movement, which Karsavin does not discuss, but which may be inferred from a passage in Mirsky's essay of 1927:

In practical politics the Eurasians condemn all counter-revolutionary activity, not to speak of political terror or foreign intervention. They do not, however, abdicate from making propaganda for their ideas in the U.S.S.R., and signs are not lacking that these ideas are being favourably accepted inside the Union by ever-increasing numbers.[21]

Behind this coy reference to propaganda for their ideas in the USSR there lay in fact an extensive covert operation.

All the published accounts of Eurasianism suggest that it began as a purely intellectual enterprise, but was then hijacked and betrayed in about 1925–6 by politically motivated scoundrels, with Mirsky prominent among them. The story is usually told as a decline and fall from the innocence of the preternatural spiritual quest of the Russian intelligentsia to a Bolshevik-bedevilled mess of cynical politicking.

This interpretation is not seriously defensible. Apart from anything else, the financial support that enabled the Eurasian movement, the 'Spalding money', came from a source whose motivation may not have been purely philanthropic, to say the least, and it was secured not by the Continental intellectuals but, according to most accounts, by Malevsky-Malevich, and negotiated with the aid of Arapov. Malevsky-Malevich and Arapov were quite different from Trubetskoy and Savitsky. They came not from the intelligentsia, but from the executive arm of the old Imperial ruling class. Like Mirsky, they had both been career army officers in crack regiments, and they had served in the high command of the White armies during the Civil War. Exactly how much Mirsky knew about their activity when he wrote the passage about not abdicating from making propaganda in the USSR is unclear, but there is considerable circumstantial evidence to suggest that in fact he knew a great deal.

The role of Savitsky in all this is enigmatic. He was by no means a closeted intellectual of the kind that Trubetskoy made himself out to be.[22] There is abundant evidence to suggest that Savitsky really did believe that the Eurasians could take power in Russia, that he fancied his own chances of assuming a leading position, and that he was deeply involved in political manoeuvring and covert activities. He made at least one covert trip to Russia, in the latter half of January and early February 1927, and boasted about the warmth of his reception, especially the fact that he was able to take Communion at a Moscow church.

The most detailed account published so far of the covert activities of the Eurasians comes from another source that only became available after the collapse of the USSR. On the night of 9/10 October 1939, just over a year after he was repatriated to Russia, Sergey Efron was arrested, and subjected to lengthy interrogation.[23] The main focus was his participation in the Eurasian movement. His captors' task was to build the case that the Eurasians had been a prime focus of anti-Soviet activity in the emigration, and to incriminate everyone who had been involved in it.[24] Efron appears to have conducted himself with immense fortitude under interrogation. There is no reason to suppose that he told anything but the truth as he understood it during his ordeal, which was suspended several times when his mental balance was judged to be disturbed; he was confined for a while in the psychiatric section of the Butyrka Prison after attempting suicide, and he was repeatedly beaten. The contents of these interrogations are grotesque to a degree that makes *Darkness at Noon* seem infantile. Efron repeatedly 'confesses' that he did indeed make contact with various Western intelligence services, but his equally genuine insistence that he did so under instructions from his GPU controller is unacceptable to the NKVD interrogator of 1939, because this aspect of the truth does not fit his brief, which was to prove that Efron was working against the USSR as a hired agent of foreign powers and not on behalf of it as a willing collaborator.

Efron stated that the Eurasians had two principal political goals for the future of Russia: first, the replacement of the economic monopoly of the state by state capitalism; and secondly, the replacement of Communists in the Soviet administrative structure by Eurasian sympathizers. To work for these goals there was a covert wing within the movement in emigration. Its activity was divided into three sectors. The first sector, said Efron, was concerned with the dispatch of Eurasian literature into the USSR, using in part the Polish diplomatic bag. This sector was organized by Konstantin Rodzevich and Pyotr Arapov. The second sector was concerned with sending emissaries into the USSR. This was undertaken through a body that Efron refers to as 'the Trust'. Efron does not immediately say who ran this sector, but from his subsequent answers it is clear that the principal figure involved was also Pyotr Arapov. The task of the third sector, much less covert, was to spread Eurasian propaganda among Russians in France. This activity was organized by Efron himself; he would arrange meetings and discussion sessions, to which Soviet citizens living abroad as well as *émigrés* would be invited.

With the hindsight of seventy years, these goals and methods may seem intrinsically unrealistic, but in fact they represent one particular facet of the extensive practical efforts to undermine the Soviet regime that began in the emigration when the regime itself began, and ceased only with the collapse of the USSR in 1991. From the perspective of the post-Soviet period, one fundamental similarity between the Eurasian programme and that of Stalin's CPSU is more striking than anything else: the Eurasians had no respect for what Mirsky once called 'the paraphernalia of liberal democracy', by which he meant government by popularly elected representatives. Mirsky explained Eurasian thinking on this point as follows:

They have given the name of 'ideocracy' to the system of government they propose. They visualise it as exercised by a unique party united by one idea, but an idea accepted by the symphonic personality of the People. Here again Communism and Fascism have to be regarded as rough approximations to a perfect ideocratic state. The insufficiency of Fascism lies in the essential jejuneness of its ruling idea, which has little content apart from the mere will to organise. The insufficiency of Communism lies in the only too obvious contradiction between a policy that is ideocratic in practice, and the materialist philosophy it is based on, which denies the reality of ideas, and reduces all history to processes of necessity.[25]

In Mirsky's mind, this contradiction was soon to be resolved, as it was for so many others, by an acceptance of Stalin as the embodiment of 'willed necessity' (to cite a standard Soviet definition of freedom); Mirsky thus found a focus for the voluntarist principle that was central to all his positive judgements. But the fundamentally anti-democratic position of Eurasianism made it vitally cognate with the Soviet system, so that the politically minded Eurasians could reasonably think in terms of taking over that system and re-ideologizing it rather than conducting another revolution that involved the masses.

The most intriguing aspect of Efron's deposition of 1939 concerns what he refers to as 'the Trust'. This has long been known to have been the cover-name used for the most successful operation mounted by the Soviet secret service in the 1920s. Its activities have been described several times in English and elsewhere, but the Eurasians make hardly any appearance in these accounts.[26] The Trust was a fictional anti-Soviet organization on Soviet territory invented by the GPU to smoke out, draw in, and eventually control anti-Soviet activity based abroad. The only authoritative account of this organization by someone who was actually involved with it outside Russia was written by S. L. Voitsekhovsky, a former White officer who was in emigration from September 1921 and seems to have become involved in covert activity very soon after that.[27] Voitsekhovsky never makes clear the precise relationship between the émigré monarchist organizations on the one hand and the Eurasians on the other. This would appear to be because for him, as for many others, the relationship never actually was clear at the time. They evidently used the same channels of communication and shared some personnel, principally Pyotr Arapov. Several Russian scholars have stated with great confidence on the basis of archival documents that the Trust in fact penetrated the Eurasian movement via Pyotr Arapov as early as December 1922.[28] Arapov did not simply write letters and send money into Russia; he was also a courier.

Pyotr Semyonovich Arapov remains one of the most enigmatic figures in

Mirsky's life. Apparently a few years younger than Mirsky, he was a nephew of General Vrangel, commanded his personal escort during the Civil War, and earned a reputation for ruthless cruelty. In emigration, he seems to have been prominent in both the militant monarchist and the Eurasian movements. Under interrogation, Sergey Efron said that Arapov told him that he was connected with the intelligence services of Poland, Germany, and perhaps England; and that he had made these connections *at the behest of the GPU*. It seems abundantly clear that Arapov had been a Soviet agent from the start, but his motives and procedures for becoming one have gone with him to his unmarked grave. Suvchinsky and Savitsky knew about his connections with the Trust and his trips to Russia, but they seem to have taken all this at face value.

The nature of Mirsky's relationship with Arapov, and some details of Arapov's activities, can be reconstructed from the many passing references to him in Mirsky's letters to Suvchinsky. Arapov lived with the Golitsyn family, Mirsky's old friends, at Chessington in Surrey. He appears to have had no regular employment, but nonetheless to have been able to travel frequently between England and the Continent without difficulty. Mirsky first came into contact with Arapov late in 1922. The evidence in Mirsky's letters to Suvchinsky about Arapov indicates that Mirsky regarded him as a ruthless, even unscrupulous man of action whose limited intellectual capabilities were an invaluable corrective to the endless theorizing of Savitsky and Suvchinsky. A firm friendship developed between the two men during the 1920s. Mirsky says several times that he misses Arapov badly when the latter is away on his various missions; it can be inferred from Mirsky's letters to Suvchinsky that Arapov went to Russia in February 1925, February 1928, and December 1929. There may well have been other trips; the first of them may have taken place in September 1924.[29]

In strong contrast to his attitude towards Arapov, it is clear from the letters to Suvchinsky that Mirsky soon came to detest the other leading Eurasian who was based in England, Pyotr Nikolaevich Malevsky-Malevich (1891–1974). The latter published *A New Party in Russia* (London, 1928), which Mirsky derided almost as sarcastically as he did Spalding's effort of the same year.[30] The fact that these two books, the only contemporary accounts of the Eurasian movement in a language other than Russian, were published in English in London, suggests that they might have been undertaken as an effort to convince some paymaster of the value that was being obtained for his money. Where Malevsky-Malevich's funding came from is obscure; like Arapov, he seems to have been a frequent international traveller on Eurasian and other business—he was certainly the principal Eurasian connection with the USA— but not to have held any kind of salaried post. Whatever may be the case, Malevsky-Malevich remains the most mysterious figure in the Eurasian high command.

THE NEWSPAPER *EURASIA*

Mirsky was back in London from America on 28 August 1928. In the first fort-night of October he sent off to Suvchinsky in Paris his first contributions to the newspaper that had been proposed in Eurasian circles.[31] Mirsky then wrote an enigmatic letter to Suvchinsky on 16 October in which he outlines a project he calls '*hommage à l'URSS*'. He tells Suvchinsky that John Squire had promised an article on Lenin, and that on Leonard Woolf's advice he had written to Maurice Dobb, Kingsley Martin,[32] and Lowes Dickinson.[33] Mirsky asks Suvchinsky what he should tell 'these gents' about fees. It looks as if this was a plan to get some prominent British left-wingers to write something about Soviet Russia.

Mirsky wrote to Salomeya Halpern from London on 6 November 1928 that he had been impossibly busy with Eurasian business during his recent time in Paris and unable to find the time to see even her. He did find the time to meet Mayakovsky on this occasion, though, and described him in this letter offhand-edly—showing his own customary lack of seriousness towards Halpern—as 'a very serious man'. For the public record he later said something much more substantial:

A future biographer will be faced with establishing to what extent this soul, 'squeezed out' of his work, found its revenge by manifesting itself in life. People who knew Mayakovsky well will perhaps write about this. On people who knew him superficially (like myself) he made, in the last years of his life, an impression of the greatest self-restraint and of feeling a sense of responsibility for every word he said.[34]

This meeting with Mayakovsky undoubtedly fuelled Mirsky's push to have Tsvetaeva's notorious salutation to him published in *Eurasia*.

The salutation itself has a headline in small type that runs over two columns: 'V. V. Mayakovsky in Paris', and beneath it: 'V. V. Mayakovsky is presently a guest in Paris. The poet has given more than one public reading of his work. The editorial board of *Eurasia* offer below Marina Tsvetaeva's salutation to him.' Tsvetaeva's words are set in two vertically parallel columns:

On 22 April 1922, the eve of my departure from Russia, early in the morning, on the completely deserted Kuznetsky I met Mayakovsky. 'Well then, Mayakovsky, what message d'you want me to pass on to Europe?' 'That the truth is over here.'

On 7 November 1928, late in the evening, as I was coming out of the Café Voltaire somebody asked me: 'What d'you say about Russia after hearing Mayakovsky?' —and I replied without hesitation: 'That the power is over there.'

This item was not carried demonstratively on the front page of the first issue of *Eurasia*, as has sometimes been asserted, but as a tiny item squeezed into the top right-hand corner of the back page. This is telling evidence about how few people have actually ever seen the original; a complete run of the newspaper is perhaps the rarest of all Eurasian printed documents.

The first issue begins with an anonymous editorial that takes up half the front page and does not mention Eurasianism by name at all; instead, it speculates about various attitudes towards the Russian revolution and the building of the new Russia. An article by Trubetskoy, 'Ideocracy and the Proletariat', begins at the top of the extreme right-hand column of the first page and continues on the top right-hand third of the second page. Its tone is strongly pro-Soviet, endorsing the dictatorship of the Party. The article continues in the second issue on 1 December. This was to be the only article Trubetskoy contributed to the newspaper. The dominant think-pieces that carry a signature in the first and other early issues are by Karsavin; his 'The Meaning of Revolution' occupies what Russians call the 'cellar' at the bottom of the first and second pages, and spills over onto the third. The middle sections of the paper bring on some much more obscure figures. 'An Assessment of the Economic Situation of the USSR' by A. S. Adler, and 'Points of Departure of Our Politics' by N. N. Alekseev both manage to end on a hyphenated word on page 3 and continue on page 4, but at least they both end there without further spillage. The first issue also contains three anonymous items containing summary information, one concerning economic developments in the USSR, the second concerning major international events, and the third concerning events in the Russian emigration. Nikitin occupies the cellars on pages 5 and 6 with 'The East and Us'. Then, relegated to the back as usual, come cultural affairs. There is a turgid survey article of current French literature over the odd signature 'Ajaxes', which the letters of Mirsky to Suvchinsky reveal to have been a pseudonym used by Malevsky-Malevich. And finally, at the back, comes Mirsky.

At some stage during the early work on the paper, Suvchinsky drafted an article under the title 'The Revolution and Power', which is a kind of pro-Soviet manifesto and eventually appeared in No. 8 on 12 January 1929. The manuscript text was shown to Trubetskoy, who wrote a letter strongly objecting to it. On 1 December 1928 Mirsky wrote to Suvchinsky that he had just seen Malevsky-Malevich, who had shown him Trubetskoy's letter about this article. Mirsky responded:

This is of course a very serious crisis, and in my opinion we should try and deepen it, i.e. go for a final break. It's clear that this is what Trubetskoy wants, and I don't blame him all that much, knowing how much of a burden Eurasianism and politics are for him as a brake on his scholarly activity. But on the other hand we must not allow this completely unpublic-spirited man to put a brake on the work of Eurasianism. In my opinion there can be no question of any kind of 'bans' on the paper by Trubetskoy, nor of a *kurultai* [Eurasian council of state] to wind it up. We must accept the challenge and sever the diseased member (luckily not the prick, as it happens).

The conclusion of Mirsky's argument is outrageous, and typically maximalist: he urges that two of the pillars of the movement be expelled from it:

Meanwhile, this incident demonstrates that the present organisational system of Eurasianism (the 'group of five') is completely unsatisfactory. It is essential to 'democratize' Eurasianism, to make it into a *party*. . . . [We] need a big congress, with the central committee + representatives of the local organisations. There is no need to chase after representation from the USSR (which will in fact be representation by the GPU). The congress must be public (or at least open) and be of an agitational nature. The only alternative is a retreat to intelligentsia positions, turning [the movement] into a purely ideological circle, but even in that case it's essential to distinguish it from the underground. But the thing I do insist on unconditionally is the immediate expulsion of Trubetskoy and Savitsky from Eurasianism, unless of course they *submit unconditionally*. But any more *negotiations* with them are impermissible. I understand that this break will be painful for you, but it's essential, for otherwise Eurasianism is doomed to rot alive. (Each of us rotting individually is enough.) We must acknowledge the position that has already been created (and created by you). Eurasianism is you and the Paris group. There is nothing else worth talking about.

'ARE WE TRYING TO INFLUENCE STALIN?'

The seventh issue of *Eurasia*, published on 5 January 1929, carried Trubetskoy's letter stating that he was leaving the editorial board and the Eurasian movement as a whole. From the tenth issue onwards the newspaper has an increasingly perfunctory feel. It may eventually become possible to establish the authorship of the anonymous articles and those signed by otherwise unknown persons and, in particular, to establish whether or not any of these pieces came from Soviet sources. The letters to Suvchinsky make it clear that even Mirsky did not know who had written some of these items. They are for the most part quite unreadable; hindsight makes them risibly wide of the mark as the pointers to the future they were intended to be—even before Marxist inevitability entered the scene.

The unsigned leaders spelled out an increasingly hard pro-Stalin line, especially in discussing the left-wing and other deviations that had recently rocked the Soviet political boat. A series of anonymous articles on 'The Problem of Ideocracy' began in No. 12, published on 9 February 1929, and went on and on; as we shall see, these articles were written by Suvchinsky, and subjected to increasingly harsh criticism by Mirsky in his letters. The summaries of economic developments and the reports of what was going on in the USSR at the time, though, retain some interest since they manage to maintain a critical edge.

The single fresh voice to appear was that of the only woman to have made a serious contribution to Eurasianism, and then, as we see now, when it was staggering towards its demise: this was Mirsky's *protégée* Emiliya

Emmanuilovna Litauer, who contributed an extensive series of reviews on philosophical topics. They began with a piece on Heidegger's *Sein und Zeit* in No. 2 and went on to tackle some more of the most serious publications in current Continental philosophy; this is technical philosophy on a high level of competence, and it contrasts strongly with the woolly 'philosophizing' of such as Karsavin and Suvchinsky.

The later issues of *Eurasia* did succeed in attracting some advertising, which to the mentality of seventy years later is much more attractive as literary text than the ponderous articles that precede it. The advertisements tout the services of various Russian-speaking lawyers and doctors in Paris, along with some tailors and oculists; as always, the patent medicines are the most arresting items on offer.

On 26 January 1929 Mirsky informed Suvchinsky that he was so busy writing a big book—he was referring to *Russia: A Social History*—that he now had too little time to write serious articles for *Eurasia*. On 13 March 1929 Mirsky tried again for a showdown with Suvchinsky:

When I come over I want to confront directly the question of what we're doing and what we want. It's not a matter of the content of Eurasianism, but the way it impinges on real life. Do we anticipate taking power? Are we educating a younger generation? Are we addressing problems that are of general use for anybody besides ourselves? Are we trying to influence Stalin?

The file that was kept on Mirsky after his arrest states that on 24 April 1929 he took part in a meeting of the Eurasian Council; but what transpired has not been discovered so far. On 14 May 1929 Mirsky wrote one of his most peremptory letters to Suvchinsky, treating him now almost like a child. This is the ultimate example of Mirsky's 'numbered points' procedure. He is reacting to the draft of an article, and begins by objecting to the way Suvchinsky makes his philosophy too overt. This is the beginning of a sustained assault:

Secondly, I object to your manner of philosophizing; in the articles about ideocracy, you've started writing without knowing how you were going to finish. You've been doing your thinking in public. This spadework should be done in private behind closed doors (in the bog, maybe). Thirdly, the philosophical part must be either a) immediately comprehensible, or b) if that is not possible, it must be written in absolutely precise and sustained terminology, and that terminology must be as far as possible 1) uniform, 2) avoid phenomenological language, which is alien to us, and stay close to Hegel, 3) when a new term or one that is not generally understood is introduced, a precise definition must be given immediately (which in the case of new concepts will even precede the appearance of the term itself, thus: this is what we call this process (or these facts)); for example, it took me a long time to understand in which of very many senses you were using the word 'anthropology', 4) if a concept is not absolutely new, then you shouldn't dream up a new word for it, 5) the main thing is to stay completely away from unusual words that do not have an *absolutely precise* meaning.

In August 1929 Mirsky's biography of Lenin was commissioned, and he set to work on the reading that would, as he soon asserted, redefine and clarify his entire attitude, leaving all half-way houses behind. On 1 September he peremptorily told Suvchinsky that with Efron and Rodzevich he had decided to close the newspaper after the next issue. He also emphasized that there was no further reason for him to stay in the same organization as Malevich. It took the rest of the year for the affairs of the newspaper to be wound up.

By the time the newspaper closed, Mirsky had published about forty separate items in it. Not surprisingly, his original role was that of the leading spokesman on literature and culture. His first two contributions appeared together in the back pages of the first issue. One of them is an essay on Tolstoy, a pendant to the magnificent articles in English of 1928, the centenary of Tolstoy's birth, and it concludes with the noblest declaration of his sense of personal ethics that Mirsky ever set down. His familiar emphasis on the creative will is replaced here by a stress on the ethical implications of the passivity he could not tolerate:

Tolstoy's prophetic inspiration was eventually more powerful than the commandments he invented. We do not believe him when he says that to serve the cause of social justice it is better to do nothing. But the fact that each one of us bears within ourselves responsibility for present untruth; that not a single one of our submissions to this untruth is morally indifferent; that he who is not with the truth is against it, and that there can be no neutrality in this argument; that the first obligation of a man and a Christian is his obligation towards the community of his brothers; that any wealth of the one is founded on the poverty of others, and is therefore criminal and ought to be abolished—all this remains true, and it was all said by Tolstoy more loudly, more powerfully, and more pitilessly than by anybody else, and Tolstoy will always remain the Teacher.[35]

The second item by Mirsky in this first issue, though, contrasts strangely with the ringing confidence of the piece on Tolstoy. It is a review of the younger Soviet poet Bagritsky's collection *The South-West*, and is crushed in small type onto the back page underneath Tsvetaeva's greeting. Mirsky singles out and cites one poem from the book as 'not only one of the best lyric poems of the post-revolutionary period, but one that both in terms of its theme and its tone must necessarily be very close for many men of our generation':

> Against black bread and faithful wife
> We've been inoculated by greensickness.
> Our years have been tried by hoof and stone,
> Our fluids suffused with evergreen wormwood,—
> Wormwood that's bitter upon our lips . . .[36]

Mirsky supplied some more pieces to *Eurasia* on literary subjects as 1929 went on, none of them up to his highest standards except for two, which discuss

Khlebnikov and Chekhov.[37] There are two articles, again characteristically on rising Soviet authors—one on Nikolay Tikhonov and the other called 'Prose by Poets', one of his old warhorses. There is also what became almost the final word Mirsky published about Russian *émigré* literature; his opinion corresponds very closely to what he said on the same topic for *Slavische Rundschau*. And there is another interesting piece on literature and cinema.[38]

Mirsky contributed his most significant articles to *Eurasia* on non-literary subjects. They are the most explicitly pro-Soviet items in the newspaper. Mirsky's largest contribution was a doggedly factual thirteen-part series on 'The Nationalities of the USSR'. It reads in fact like a translation of the appropriate parts of his *Russia: A Social History*. In a series of purely political articles Mirsky contributed between January and March 1929 he speaks explicitly as a Eurasian, examining the compatibility of Marxist and other ideas with the standpoint of the movement. They begin with 'The Proletariat and the Idea of Class' on 19 January, continue with 'Our Marxism' on 2 February, 'Three Theses on Ideocracy' on 9 February, 'The Problem of the Difference between Russia and Europe' on 23 February, and culminate with a three-part discussion of 'The Social Nature of Russian Power' that ran to the end of March. In these articles, Mirsky essentially redefines Eurasianism in the spirit of his nascent Marxism; the end result is to present the case that there is no further justification for the independent existence of Eurasianism itself.

The schism in the Eurasian movement, and the political articles Mirsky contributed to the newspaper in 1929, it goes without saying, related to the contemporary events in Russia and elsewhere that made this year a turning-point. In Russia, Stalin decisively consolidated his power. In 1927, he had eliminated the Left Opposition—Trotsky and his followers. In 1928 he conducted the elimination of the Right Opposition, the comrades who had supported him against Trotsky—chief among them Kamenev and Zinoviev, who were soon followed by Bukharin, Rykov, and Tomsky. Stalin then brought back Radek, Zinoviev, and Kamenev, humiliated and cowed. In December 1928 the extension of Soviet power to the countryside, the brutal anti-kulak campaign, began. On the industrial front, the Shakhty trial was mounted at the same time. In February 1929, Trotsky was expelled from the USSR. The collectivization of agriculture and the first Five-Year Plan were pushed ahead. Elsewhere in Europe, the first triumphal Nazi rally was held in Nuremberg as the party's elected representation rose in the Reichstag; the British parliament acquired a precarious Labour majority;[39] and in the USA, on 'Black Thursday', 24 October 1929, the New York stock market collapsed. On 17 October 1929 Mirsky ended a letter to Suvchinsky with an eloquent sentence: 'In my room are installed as the only decorations a World Map (published by Moscow Worker Press) and a portrait of Stalin looking at it.'

On 31 October 1929 Mirsky wrote Suvchinsky what is essentially his farewell to Eurasianism, a letter also tantamount to a farewell to Suvchinsky as a serious ally. The disenchanted attitude towards the USSR here is particularly remarkable; Mirsky had no illusions whatsoever about the way he and the others were viewed by the Soviet authorities. He thinks about his own possible contribution in terms of service, as a subordinate working to external command:

[The] authorities will never agree to let in a group of people who wish to develop a new ideology. . . . [As] a group we can be useful only through what we do here. Only here can we retain the external independence that alone can give us some kind of authority. Over there we can work only as individuals, and then only if we entirely and unconditionally enter the orbit of the C[ommunist] P[arty] (which I personally would agree to do, but I shan't go there for a long time yet because I think there's a greater need for me here, if I'm needed at all). . . . As far as I'm concerned, the ideology of Eurasianism was only a means, a working hypothesis, which has now fulfilled its function. I've said all this (approximately) to Arapov too, and he accuses me of defeatism, *aber ich kann nicht anders.*

In his next paragraph, Mirsky unwittingly foretells his own personal fate; 'to be sent to places far removed' was the Tsarist administration's language for internal exile, and it persisted into the Soviet period:

Going back to practical matters, and once again absolutely condemning the idea of transferring to the Union, at the same time I would very much welcome it if *you made a trip there*, with Arapov or without. With your well-known ability to butter up and charm people, such a trip might bring good results. But of course one can only consider this if there is a favourable solution to our practical problems. Any kind of transition from visit to residence will of course end badly, most likely of all in places more or less far removed.

Mirsky goes on to dismiss the course he was shortly to take:

One could still think about Gorky, but you understand of course that a connection with Gorky can only come about as a result of the liquidation of organized Eurasianism and a transition to a broad alliance of non-party Leninist-Stalinists. I would welcome an alliance of that kind, of course, and there is a place in it for us. But in practice I don't believe in it. Everything that has ever been done on Gorky's initiative has always been afflicted with sterility.

On 11 November 1929 he told Suvchinsky: 'I'm writing to you just after finishing the Leader's October article.[40] I'll read the rest of it on the way to Oxford, where I'm going with Arapov to give a lecture.' This was the occasion when Mirsky was observed by Isaiah Berlin, who gave me a completely different account of what went on that evening from the published account of the meeting. The report in the *Oxford Magazine* summarizes a familiar line of Mirsky's about Pushkin's non-metaphorical style; Berlin, however, insisted that Mirsky was drunk and incapable of coherent speech and thought.[41]

This was probably one of the occasions on which Mirsky stayed with the Spaldings; in the words of the daughter of the family: 'In those days we lived in Shotover outside Oxford & I seem to remember that Prince Mirsky mostly stayed in a cottage, then called Domic [Russian *domik*, 'little house'], with the Narishkins at the bottom of our garden.' This may have been the same visit Miss Spalding was speaking about when she said: 'I certainly remember my parents being much put out when they had invited a number of people to tea to hear, as they expected, Prince Mirsky talking along White Russian lines, to find that over night he had turned Red.'[42]

MIRSKY'S MARXISM

Mirsky actually proclaimed himself a committed Communist in a letter written to Suvchinsky from London two days after the trip with Arapov to Oxford, on 13 November 1929. Two years later he published an account of how his conversion came about. It points to several factors that influenced his decision. In particular, Mirsky named three living men who played a part in converting him to Marxism. Two of them were Russians. The first, as we might expect, was Gorky, whose 'Marxism' was of an extremely peculiar kind, indistinguishable in fact from Nietzscheanism. The second was the historian M. N. Pokrovsky, whose work Mirsky translated, as we have seen. The third was an Englishman, Maurice Dobb (1900–76), lecturer in economics at the University of Cambridge from 1924, and a founder member of the Communist Party of Great Britain in 1920. In Mirsky's reference to Dobb, the use of the word 'realities' is piquant:

The third source of help was a growing acquaintance with Soviet realities—especially with the great economic achievement of the period of recovery. Maurice Dobb's *Economic Developments in Soviet Russia* was of particular assistance. It made me finally understand that the Nep was not transforming Russia into a peasant bourgeois community, but was indeed heading towards Socialism.[43]

On 11 November 1929 in London, after watching *Battleship Potemkin*, Mirsky met Eisenstein and Aleksandrov,[44] and with the latter, as he told Suvchinsky, he had 'a long and interesting conversation—he spoke about Soviet construction, the state farms, and all this in such an encouraging spirit (very concrete) that I was even more confirmed in the general line'. Mirsky's next letter to Suvchinsky, written on 13 November, is characteristically categorical:

Workers of the World, Unite!
That Marxism is correct as a theory of history is for me not conditional but absolute.
. . . I assert the absolute value of Marxism as a historian, and this is my considered and

tested conviction, formed precisely through the study of *pre*capitalist periods. The only matter in which I do not go along with current Marxism is that I do not draw conclusions of a metaphysical nature from the absolute correctness of historical materialism.

The last letter to Suvchinsky of the intensive series that began when Mirsky became seriously involved with Eurasianism in 1926 was written on 22 January 1930. Mirsky tells his friend that he has got down to writing his biography of Lenin. To judge from the remainder of the letter, nothing untoward had happened between the two men. But there was then a sixteen-month break in the correspondence, at least from Mirsky's side; he next wrote to Suvchinsky on 21 May 1931. What went on in the interval is impossible to reconstruct in any detail on the basis of the evidence currently available. Mirsky had nothing further to do with organized Eurasianism, except to pour scorn on it in his account of his conversion to Marxism. But it was in April 1930 that relations between Mirsky and Suvchinsky's wife, Vera, reached a crisis, and the break with Suvchinsky doubtless had something to do with this.

TROUBLE AT THE SCHOOL

In October 1928, just before the launch of *Eurasia*, Dorothy Galton (1901–92) was appointed secretary to Bernard Pares at the School of Slavonic Studies and came into contact with Mirsky.[45] In her published account of her relationship with Mirsky, Miss Galton set down one of the most striking representations we have of Mirsky's social demeanour as it appeared towards the end of the *émigré* period:

His memory was prodigious and he had a profound knowledge of at least four literatures. His post at the School, as all lectureships in those days, only provided a small salary, but he probably earned additional money from his books, lectures and articles; it must have been on the rare occasions that he had such a windfall that he would ask me out to dinner. He loved good food and drink; I have seen him start with oysters and Bass, go on to white and red wine, and end by drinking a quarter-bottle of port, while I sipped a little of the wine. Meanwhile, instead of conversing, he would recite poetry in any of his four languages.[46]

Mirsky's letters to Miss Galton provide ample evidence that during his last years in emigration, after he had made his decisive move to the left, he continued the pattern of life he had established in 1922, supplementing his salary included. The very first of Mirsky's surviving letters to Dorothy Galton, written from the up-market resort of Talloires in Haute Savoie on 20 July 1929, reveals that at some time he had signed up with Gerald Christy's Lecture Agency. Exactly how much work came his way through this organization is not clear, but in a c.v. probably written in 1931 Mirsky states that besides the lectures in America and to the Brontë Society that we already know about, he had lectured at the Royal Society of Literature, the English Association, something called the Ethological Society, the Tolstoy Society, the Philosophical Society (Newcastle upon Tyne), the Literary and Philosophical Society (Hull), 'etc.' Of these occasions, by 'the Tolstoy Society' Mirsky probably means the lecture he gave on critical assessments of Tolstoy at a Tolstoy Memorial dinner on 6 November 1928. He had accepted this assignment on 28 October 1928 from the PEN Club; it was presided over by John Galsworthy.[47] At the time he composed this c.v. Mirsky had in progress a course of lectures on 'Intellectual Europe of the Present Day' at the City Literary Institute. As before, Mirsky was in London only during term-time.

The only doctoral student Mirsky supervised to completion in his last years in London was Elizabeth Hill, who took her undergraduate degree at the School in 1924 and finished her thesis in 1931. Mirsky wrote a preface to her first book.[48] Elizabeth Hill was the only person who gained both undergraduate and graduate degrees in Mirsky's subject during his time at the School. In her words, 'We admired his brain and originality, but he was shy and remote in his dealings with us.'[49]

In the autumn of 1929 Mirsky discouraged E. H. Carr as a potential graduate student. On 1 November, Carr noted in his diary: 'Letter from Pares who wants me "to meet Mirsky" to take Ph.D. degree!' Then, on 19 November: 'Went up to see Mirsky: an amusing talk; he doesn't care whether I take a degree or not.' And finally, on 27 November: 'Mirsky lunched with me: got some interesting details out of him. A strange creature.'[50] Mirsky kept in touch with Carr and wrote a preface, which is very outspoken, to his first book, as he had to Elizabeth Hill's.[51] According to Carr, 'It is quite worthwhile. He said that he had written it because otherwise Pares would have done it, and this would have spoiled the book.'[52]

Mirsky supervised part of the doctoral work of Andrew Guershoon Colin, Bertha Malnick, and Helen Muchnic,[53] all of whom went on to publish significant work in the field of Russian language and literature. But his attitude towards his teaching was becoming more and more casual, as his initial communications with Carr suggest. And his relations with his boss, Bernard Pares, soon began to deteriorate.

The earliest evidence of serious trouble between Mirsky and his Director came soon after the end of the work on *Eurasia*. On 24 January 1930 comes the first of a series of letters to Florinsky that demonstrates just how unsettled Mirsky was becoming; he is still aristocratically arrogant, though, and yet again uses numbered points:

I have suddenly (not altogether suddenly) concluded that I need to move to America. Could you perhaps help me in this, perhaps through the good Shotwell? Most of all I would like a one-year stint at a University so as to have a look round, and then either find something better or come back here. Cohabitation with Pares, *à la longue* (though *non-consommé*) is becoming intolerable. And there are no prospects for anything better.

My communism notwithstanding, I really can't go to the USSR,—I'm socially alien no matter what. There remains America. I very much rely on the assistance of you and Shotwell. I would point out the following: 1) My speciality is *not* literature but history; 2) Most of all I would like to get to Stanford because of the climate (and the proximity of Hollywood), and also it seems they like inviting guest speakers there, and they have a leftish inclination; 3) I absolutely don't want to go to Columbia.

Mirsky followed this up on 30 January: 'I apologise for sticking to you like a leaf in a bathhouse. I have just found out that there is a vacancy at Stanford University for the chair of Russian history. Do you not think that this is the hand of Providence and that I ought to do something?' Five weeks then went by. Mirsky wrote again to Florinsky on 7 March:

My plans for America have been put aside for the time being, it may well be that I'll come to America next summer, since (this is confidential for the time being) California University looks as if they're going to invite me. I've had a massive scandal with Pares that ended with making things up like a lovers' quarrel.

How are your intimate feelings? In all respects I'm in a very indeterminate and transitional state—*l'âge dangereux*. Perhaps by the end of the year things will become clearer.

VERA, AND *LENIN*

The most striking manifestation of this 'dangerous age', or mid-life crisis, concerned Mirsky's personal life. It involved Vera, the wife of his closest friend, Suvchinsky, and took place in the spring of 1930.[54] Vera told me that she had met Mirsky 'as a Eurasian' before she came to Paris, in 1924 or early 1925, and thought about marrying him then. Vera was born in St Petersburg in 1906, the daughter of Aleksandr Guchkov (1862–1936), one of the most colourful politicians of the Duma period of Russian history;[55] his grandfather had been an Old Believer peasant, but his father made a fortune as a Moscow merchant. Vera's mother, who was in her daughter's words 'religious and eccentric', came from the musical Ziloti family; one of her brothers was a famous conductor, the other an admiral. Vera herself was named after her godmother, the great actress and theatrical impresario Vera Kommisarzhevskaya. She attended the Taganskaya *gimnaziya* in Petersburg—one of the top two for girls, according to her own account—before continuing her schooling in the Caucasus after the family fled south in 1917. When they arrived in Berlin, Vera went to the Russian *gimnaziya* that had opened there, one of her classmates and friends being Nabokov's sister Olga. She then went to Berlin University for two years, reading philosophy, but left to get married before taking her diploma. She came to England several times before 1925, on visas arranged by Bernard Pares, who had known her father before the revolution.

Vera married Pyotr Suvchinsky in Paris towards the end of 1925, and after that came to know all the principal Eurasians. She claimed the credit for making Mirsky revise his opinion of Tsvetaeva; and she was present when Mirsky and Suvchinsky met the poet in person at the end of 1925.[56] In the summer of 1928 she spent some time at Pontaillac with Suvchinsky, the Karsavin and Nikitin families, and other Eurasians; it was during this summer sojourn that much of the immediate planning for *Eurasia* must have been done. During this time, on 1 September, Marina Tsvetaeva wrote Vera an extraordinary letter of affection.[57] But Vera was much more fond of Efron than of his wife; and she felt great sympathy for their daughter, Alya, who was six years younger than she was.

Vera kept seven of her letters from Mirsky. They all date from the first half of 1930, and they constitute the only substantial first-hand evidence there is about Mirsky's intimate life where a person of the opposite sex is involved. They are also the only documents that show Mirsky slackening his intellectual control. The first of them dates from 12 March 1930, and was probably written in London. Mirsky refers to Vera's husband Suvchinsky by his pet name, 'Petya':

My dear sweet Vera, I've reread your letter many times, and thought about you weeping as you wrote, and about much more besides, and that night couldn't get to sleep for a long time . . . I mentally wrote you a letter on all these subjects, but [perhaps] it's better that it should remain for the time being unwritten. Now my only task is to live through these sixteen days without loosening my grip and without yielding to provocations (from within myself). I think I'll manage it, thanks specifically to what you call my lack of seriousness but which is in fact my unconscious optimism (purely dialectical, i.e. relating to this specific stage). Yesterday I sent you some very foolish poetry and I'm afraid I overtaxed your patience with it, but really I've been completely obsessed with that rubbish for three days now.

In spite of all that Lenin is progressing well and keeping me going. Up to yesterday the task was overfulfilled by 9%. Without Lenin I don't know what I'd do (and today I'm 11% over).

When he mentions here that 'Lenin' is progressing well, Mirsky refers to the biography of Lenin that he began in August 1929 and finished in May 1930. It is the most dated of all Mirsky's books to read now, its categorical assertion of truth contradicted by the evolution of history since 1930 so comprehensively as to make what Mirsky says verge on the surreal. However, despite the absence of explicit autobiography that characterizes all Mirsky's writings, *Lenin* is at the same time of all his books the one in which his own personality seems to be most profoundly engaged. Lenin had no sympathy for the whining and posturing of the intelligentsia; the fact that they were whining and posturing about such issues as the liquidation of those with whom one does not agree is apparently as unimportant to Mirsky as it was to Lenin. He finds in Lenin what was undoubtedly his own ideal, a synthesis of thought and action, where being is indivisible from consciousness:

Lenin's life was ultimately all action. But, unlike the men of action of previous history, action in him was not dissociated from theoretical knowledge. His political career is explained without omission in his written work. Every one of his acts sprang from knowledge that was organically related to theory. They were not the outcome of those short cuts that go by the name of intuition, but were matured and carried out in the full light of logical consciousness. The complete harmony between action and under-standing which we find in Lenin is the first announcement of a new age, the age of Socialism, whose main characteristic will be the absolute 'transparency' of its activity in the light of its own understanding.[58]

Meanwhile, the man who wrote this paean to the willed suppression of the emotions and inflexible self-dedication to the cause was—for the only time in his life, so far as we know—thrashing about in a paroxysm of self-abasing emotion. The day after his first letter to Vera, he wrote to Michael Florinsky:

Right now my life is taking a highly dramatic turn (not in the political sense) and I am completely unable to foresee how it will develop, but in any case to leave for America would be extremely desirable. Otherwise all I have left is the road to the USSR, which I could easily take tomorrow, but restrain myself for the time being for reasons of a purely personal nature.

In the middle of all this, during the Easter vacation of 1930, in fact in early April, Mirsky made the most spectacular of all the eating trips that we know about, to the Hôtel Terminus, Lyon Perrache. The *Guide Bleu* of the period, his standby in these matters, proclaims it to be: '*établissement de luxe, vieille réputation, spécialité de poulardes à la gelée et de quenelles Morateur*'.[59] By 7 April Mirsky had apparently passed through Paris and seen Vera; he wrote to her on that day from Lyon, practically abandoning punctuation, and making a patheti-cally childish sexual boast:

My dear unique beloved Vera my sweet. Very soon after the train left the girl you liked came up to my window and started smiling at me very charmingly at which I also began smiling at her and then she came and sat down next to me and I had a conversation with her, *je m'imaginais* that she was your representative. I was very happy. But the lady who had been travelling with me on her own at the far end soon started getting so obvi-ously bored and not knowing where to put herself and fidgeting that I felt absolutely awkward and in Dijon just so she wouldn't fidget I bought her *Vu, Cinémonde* and *Détective*,[60] but as for conversing, I didn't do that all the way to Lyon. I even didn't take advantage of the tempting possibility of raping her in a tunnel we were in for a long time. Please *signale ça* to Petya. However, the whole way here I was thinking only of your perfections which more and more amaze and impress me. Really I can't understand how it can be that you exist in the world. Where did you come from? Sweetie?

I had dinner here at Morateur's; he was very gracious and tried to make me get more wine going but I was just as firm as I was yesterday with the Arapovs.[61]

On 10 April 1930 Mirsky wrote again to Vera:

My dear sweetie, I hoped very much to get a letter from you here but so far I haven't. There'll be one more post before I leave, though. What are you doing?—it interests me very much and worries me. As does which way your mind is working (*qui est si grand*).

Today it's very hot the first real hot day (in the sun) although now the clouds seem to be gathering about the Montagne de Lans. Yesterday I had dinner with Sonya and Volodya in a restaurant and had quite a lot to drink. I got so disgusted with myself for being such an abysmal and total drunkard. Sweetie when we live together you must seriously get down to rooting this out because it's unspeakableness and dissipation. You see your presence in itself will make things better.

The next letter to Vera is from St Pierre de Rumilly, dated Friday, 11 April 1930.[62] Mirsky reported to Miss Galton on 14 April from Paris that he would probably not be back in London before later that month. This was the day that Mayakovsky committed suicide; Mirsky was soon to publish his considered thoughts on the matter. On May Day Mirsky wrote from his Gower Street address to Salomeya Halpern a letter whose opening sentences resume the story of his relationship with Vera; by now, it seems, she had left her husband and moved back in with her parents (or one of them; her father had remarried by this time):

My dear, I have to bother you with a request to help fix up a position for Vera Suvchin-skaya. Apart from her completely catastrophic financial position, she is very brought down by her enforced idleness and dependence on her parents. The most desirable thing would be, if possible, to arrange a position as secretary or something like that whereby she could live at the place where she works. It would be especially desirable if it could not be in Paris, or involve taking trips, e.g. chaperoning idiot women from America.

This, then, is how Mirsky the proto-Communist understood the permissible roles of younger women; the awkward praise of her intelligence and abilities that he had expressed in his intimate letters to Vera shortly before he wrote to Salomeya throw his social conventionality into even greater relief. It must have been perfectly obvious to Salomeya that Mirsky was really trying to find a way of detaching Vera from her family and finding her a place in London where they could be together as much as possible.

According to Vera, Mirsky told her that if she did marry him, they would stay in England, because at the time she was not enough of a Communist to be taken to Moscow. She reported her response as: 'I love you, I adore you, I have no better friend, but as for marriage—no.' The insurmountable reason for her refusal, she told me in a few sentences that she would not allow to be recorded, was that Mirsky was sexually impotent. Vera was a vigorous 24 at the time, and Mirsky had just reached 40; she was coming to the end of a love-less first marriage to another Russian *émigré* of Mirsky's age and roughly similar background. She had married Suvchinsky to get away from her parents and had broken off her education; there was no way now she could achieve independence by taking up a profession. This vivacious young woman was born into politics, impatient of intellectuals, not seriously interested in the arts, and in other circumstances would have been immensely well suited for some sort of public career. As things were, the most she was ever able to do before 1939 was become a Communist foot soldier, which inevitably involved her not so much in public affairs as in skulduggery.

From Paris on 22 September Mirsky informed Miss Galton that he would be back in London by the last day of the month. He came back to trouble. A postcard to Miss Galton datestamped in London on 25 October 1930 bears the simple message: 'Pares is a bloody idiot.' On a postcard dated 19 November from somewhere in London Mirsky tells Miss Galton that he had had a most interesting dream the night before, 'consisting of a long conversation with prominent officials of the GPU'.

MAYAKOVSKY

A frustrated love affair with an *émigrée* Russian who refused to go back to Russia with him was one important factor among many that drove Mayakovsky to suicide. Mirsky wrote two obituaries of the poet, one in English and one in Russian. The Russian version is dated 7 November 1930, and is the earliest example of Mirsky dealing with literature in uncompromising Marxist categories. It is structured as an extended comparison between Pushkin and Mayakovsky, the deaths of whom Mirsky takes to have both marked the end of an epoch. The article takes wing when, towards the end, Mirsky starts to look closely at Mayakovsky as a representative of a particular generation, which he calls 'the generation of the 1910s', and among which he implicitly includes himself.

The writers among these people stand in a tight 'genetically antithetical' relationship with Symbolism, argues Mirsky, and they fight against Symbolism on its own ground. They are stronger and more healthy, because they are nearer to the health-giving plebeian soil, but internally they are profoundly cognate with their predecessors. Like them they are individualists, but more active and—again—more healthy. They do not create closed worlds of subjective experience, but assert their right to live in their own way; their time sees the flowering of the Russian bohemia. They go much further than the Symbolists in the individual differentiation of their techniques, in conscious 'originality'. Like the Symbolists they are formalists, but their formalism is more active and materialist; the work of art for them is not an aesthetic (i.e. passively perceptible) 'value', but instead a series of technical processes which culminate in the creation of a material 'thing', which, using Shklovsky's famous phrase, Mirsky refers to as 'the sum of its devices'.[63]

Mayakovsky, says Mirsky, was the most prominent figure in the generation he is talking about. And unlike most of the others, the poet was explicitly on the side of the revolution from the very beginning. But ten years after the revolution, another generation of writers came on the scene who possessed not an individualistic outlook but one for which, as the class society of NEP was overcome by the Great Leap Forward in 1929, the individual could be subordinated to the mass without a legacy of personal anxiety. Mayakovsky understood the necessity for this transition, but committed suicide in a noble act of recognition that he as an incorrigible individualist was incapable of making it:

We do not know the subjective reasons that led Mayakovsky to suicide (and let us hope that we will not find out soon—'the late lamented didn't like that at all'). But the objective meaning of his death is clear: it is an acknowledgement that the new Soviet culture has no need of individualistic literature, which has its roots in pre-revolutionary society.[64]

Mayakovsky, concludes Mirsky, 'laid bare his antique soul only in order to murder it'. His suicide was 'the act of an individualist and at the same time a putting down of individualism. It buried pre-proletarian literature once and for all.'

Seen from the point of view of someone who values literature, this position revalidates individualism, since literature is not possible without it; but Mirsky apparently now believed that literature, as a phenomenon lacking social utility, may wither away unlamented. Six weeks after he said all this, Mirsky finally wrote another letter to Gorky and set in train the events that were to lead to his return to Russia. Nearly three years had elapsed since his visit to Sorrento with Suvchinsky.[65]

SOVIET LITERATURE

Meanwhile, on the real 'literary front' in the real Soviet Russia the public events that led Mayakovsky to commit suicide unrolled. From the beginning of its rule, the Party leadership had issued numerous pronouncements about literature, but it had always stressed that the aesthetic side was not its concern, and apparently meant what it said.[66] The Party leadership also insisted that it did not want to get involved in the administration of the creative arts. After all, it had more weighty matters on hand.

After the Great Leap Forward began in 1929 the Party became aggressively interventionist in cultural affairs. However, the idea of the publicly endorsed professional literary organization, so foreign to accepted notions in the Western world about how cultural activity should properly be conducted, was not a Stalinist innovation in Russia. During the 1920s a succession of such organizations had existed, each bidding for the endorsement by the Party that would bring with it decisive political and economic clout. By 1929 the leading organization in the field was the militantly Marxist Russian Association of Proletarian Writers (RAPP).[67] This was the organization that did most to alienate Mayakovsky.

Its leader acted as Mirsky's mentor in the first years after his return to Russia. Before he was 30 years old, Leopold Averbakh (1903–37) became the single most powerful person in the Soviet literary world. He dressed in a military-style tunic and jackboots, wore a pince-nez, shaved his head so that it glistened like a billiard-ball, could overwhelm anybody by sheer force of oratory, and would unquestioningly do anything the Party told him to; he was the very model of a 1920s Bolshevik functionary. Averbakh belonged to a new élite, but one that made use of the kind of connections that no human system seems able to keep out or down for very long. He came from a prosperous merchant family in Nizhny Novgorod. His mother was the sister of Yakov Sverdlov, Lenin's right-hand man; their brother Zinovy Peshkov was Gorky's stepson. Averbakh's wife was the daughter of another crony of Lenin's, Vladimir Dmitrievich Bonch-Bruevich, who adopted and brought up Averbakh's son when the father was arrested and the mother exiled in 1937. And Averbakh's sister Ida was married to the notorious Genrikh Yagoda (1891–1938), an orphan whom their father had taken in and brought up; he became the head of the NKVD at the start of the purges in 1934.

Averbakh and his buddies wanted to keep RAPP in existence, and have it endorsed by the Party, but Stalin and the Party bosses overruled him. In its last years RAPP was split into two warring factions, and could hardly have been endorsed anyway. Stalin's preference—or that of the key policy-makers in the Party—was for a unitary organization without any formal ties to the recent past, one that could be presented as a consensus arrived at by the mutually hostile groupings, with the Party acting as grand conciliator. It would be a centrist body and eliminate the infighting that had been for many an archaic and undignified feature of the Soviet literary scene in the 1920s; it would reflect the new socialist society in which class conflict was supposed to have been eliminated. Not coincidentally, it would be much easier to control than a variety of squabbling groups. There is no doubt that the majority of the creative intelligentsia welcomed this prospect at the time. Among other things, the material benefits to them promised to be considerable.

GORKY GOES BACK

Stalin needed Gorky more than Gorky needed Stalin: Gorky was the only international cultural star available to the Party whose participation would lend respectability and the appearance of continuity in the national cultural tradition to what was in prospect. There was no doubt whatsoever that in the last analysis Gorky was on the side of the revolution: his interventions in international cultural politics had always been on balance pro-Soviet. He paid the price by, among other things, making himself unelectable for the Nobel Prize for literature; he was by far the most meritorious Russian candidate after the First World War, and the award of it to the relatively paltry *émigré* Bunin in 1933 was commonly regarded at the time, and rightly, as a despicable act of political expediency. Bunin's own relentless lobbying for it alone should have been enough to disqualify him.

Gorky was pitilessly worked on by the Soviet security services while he was living in Sorrento. Yagoda, who became the first truly Stalinist head of them, had, apart from his professional assignment, a personal interest in courting Gorky: he was attracted to Nadya Peshkova, the writer's daughter-in-law. At some time in the late 1920s Gorky was added to the GPU payroll, though just how fully aware he was of the source of the money and perks that came his way is not known.

The pressure on Gorky to come back to Russia increased when his 60th birthday was celebrated in the spring of 1928. On 27 May that year, a few months after Mirsky and Suvchinsky had visited him in Sorrento, Gorky finally agreed to make a summer visit to Russia, and he was duly fêted on a tour of the country in July and August. He was allotted some of the luxury perquisites that had been expropriated from 'has-beens' like Mirsky in 1917–18: the former Ryabushkinsky mansion to live in when he was in Moscow, a palatial dacha in the Crimea, and another dacha at Gorki[68] in the countryside near Moscow. Gorky regularly made grumbling protests against these signs of personal favour, emphasizing to anyone who would listen that 'the people' had bestowed them on him, and that he did not personally own what had been allotted to him in the proletarian paradise. One reason why Gorky decided to go back may well have been financial; his international reputation and sales outside Russia were beginning to slip. It is tempting to speculate about what arrangements were subsequently made for Gorky by the Soviet authorities in the matter of receiving his foreign royalties. Was he deemed to wish to surrender them to the state, in the way that later became standard practice for Soviet figures of international stature in the arts?

In the summer of 1929 Gorky visited Russia again, this time for a longer period. Among other things he made a tour of inspection to Solovki, the pioneering Soviet concentration camp in the far north-west, where he was duly impressed by the success of what he genuinely took to be a rehabilitation programme. It is not clear whether he set eyes on the religious philosopher Father Pavel Florensky or the medieval historian and later Academician Dmitry Likhachov, who were serving sentences in Solovki at the time of his visit. On 15 November 1930 Gorky demonstrated beyond all doubt which side he was on by publishing an article which soon became notorious, entitled 'If the Enemy Does Not Surrender, He Is Exterminated'. This principle soon came to seem like an expression of old-fashioned humanitarianism; the highly placed 'enemies' such as Bukharin, Zinoviev, and Kamenev, who did surrender to Stalin, were exterminated in short order nonetheless.

Gorky went back to Russia for the summer again in 1931, and made his decisive move back to Moscow in the spring of 1932, about six months before Mirsky; the winter of 1932–3 was the last he spent by the Mediterranean. The return of the great man was anticipated and commemorated by a burst of the renaming mania that would become a familiar feature of Soviet life. The old Tverskaya, the premier Moscow thoroughfare heading north-west from the centre, was renamed for Gorky in 1931. In 1932, the fortieth anniversary of Gorky's literary debut, all manner of things were named after him: the city of Nizhny Novgorod, the Literary Institute that was being planned in Moscow by the fledgling Union of Writers, and which admitted its first students in 1933; the Central Park of Culture and Rest in Moscow; and even the Moscow Art Theatre, which Stalin insisted on naming after Gorky despite the much more significant link it had with Chekhov. On 19 May 1933 Gorky returned to the USSR for good.

On 30 December 1930 Mirsky contacted Gorky again after a lapse of nearly three years, to ask for advice about what practical steps to take in order actively to work for the Communist cause.[69] In this characteristically categorical declaration, Mirsky told Gorky that he had now arrived at 'a complete and unconditional acceptance of Communism', and that from now on he wished to 'dedicate what strength I have to the cause of Lenin and the Soviet Republics'. Recent events had convinced him, said Mirsky, that 'there can no longer be any neutrality and half-way houses, and that he who is not with the working class is against it':

[The] more normal way of addressing myself to the Soviet Consulate seems not entirely satisfactory to me, because firstly, I am motivated not by Soviet patriotism but by hatred of the international bourgeoisie and faith in a universal social revolution; and secondly, I have not the slightest wish to be an ordinary Soviet citizen, but instead a worker for Leninism. Communism is more precious to me than the USSR.

Gorky—or one of the people who processed his mail—underlined this last sentence when he read the letter, as well he might. Mirsky undoubtedly meant what he said; this sentence offers one more indication that he was thinking not of moving permanently to Russia, but of working for the cause outside it, perhaps making visits to the homeland. This attitude was soon construed as anti-Soviet.

As a result of Mirsky's appeal for help, Gorky evidently advised him to write to the Central Committee, which Mirsky did, sending his letter via Gorky on 17 February 1931.

MORE TROUBLE WITH PARES

In August 1930, after he had begun writing *Lenin*, Mirsky wrote the preface to his *Russia: A Social History*, the text of which he had finished in the spring of 1929. This book is his most undeservedly neglected work; it still has no serious rivals in English as a compact narrative introduction to the subject, and the vivid account of the multi-cultural empire in which the author grew up is particularly valuable. However, Mirsky himself repudiated the book. He is fully conscious, he says in the preface, of grave defects in it, 'the most serious of which is the absence of a single point of view':

This serious shortcoming is due to the fact that in the course, and under the direct action, of my work, my own historical conception underwent an adjustment, which, at first imperceptible to myself, only crystallized after it was completed. If I now were to rewrite it, it would be more strictly consonant with the conception of historical materialism, and economic facts would have been more consistently emphasised as the one and only protophenomenon of all historical reality.[70]

Mirsky concludes this preface by expressing his thanks to Trubetskoy and Savitsky for their help, with ethnology and linguistics from the former and geography and archaeology from the latter, but now asserts that 'their general views are *toto caelo* removed from mine'.

This move to the left inevitably affected Mirsky's relations with his employer. His letters to Pares show that in 1929 and 1930 Mirsky was still a valued member of the *Slavonic Review* team, consulted as before by Pares for opinions on manuscripts that had been submitted to the journal. However, relations between Pares and Mirsky soon became strained. The following ominous communication came from Pares on 23 January 1931:

I want you to realise that if it was your considered attitude about the *Review* which you were expressing this morning, you put me in a difficult position. The *Review* is part of the most important work of the School and collaboration in it is part of the work of each member of the Staff. We could hardly have a Lecturer in Russian Literature who refused to write for the *Review*. If I had asked you to express my own views in it, you would have every ground for refusal. What I asked you to do was to express your own [views]—however different from or opposite to my own, as I particularly emphasised. Our principle is that all views can be expressed. The Editors cannot of course accept the suggestion that their own should not, or that they should be dictated by anyone else. I can hardly think that you mean that. Please think the matter over and let me hear from you.[71]

Mirsky replied on the same day:

I had to go before finishing our conversation, & I am afraid the reasons I gave you for not being anxious to write a political article for the *Slavonic Review* was not the principal reason why I felt that way. The real reason is that I am well aware of your opinion of me in so far as I hold or express political views. I know that you do not take me seriously (or rather do not take my political views seriously) & that you regard me primarily as an amusing *enfant terrible*. I have no doubt that this view is largely justified, but you will understand that my being aware of this opinion of yours forces me to be very careful about expressing such political views as I hold in your presence or under your auspices. Knowing your attitude it would on my part be a grave lack of respect to the causes with which I sympathise to write about anything directly connected with them in a periodical where I am regarded as primarily an object of mild amusement. In connection with this last phrase please do not think that I am in the least offended: every man deserves the opinions held about him, & your personal attitude towards me has always been one of infinite tact and kindness. The point is that the views I hold—I hold seriously, and to give public expression to them in company where I am not taken seriously would be incompatible with this. I am afraid there is no way out of this situation, for even if you wished you cannot change your opinion of me at a month's notice.

I thought that it would be better to put all this down in writing, as the more dispassionate way. I hope—I am sure—you will not take my letter *en mauvaise part*.

Soon after this, Mirsky sent Pares a contribution to the *Review*—it turned out to be his last—and then on 26 February 1931 he asked Pares for permission to be away for three or four weeks at some time in the next term, probably immediately following the Easter vacation. He promised to give extra teaching to make up, though this involved only two students. What Mirsky was planning to do during his absence is not clear, and certainly, he did not make it clear to Pares—a move guaranteed to put any Head of Department's back up.

The final break with Pares came when Mirsky stepped over the limits of collegiality by publishing a contemptuous review in the *Listener* on 11 March 1931 of Pares's contribution to a series of BBC broadcasts under the general title *The New Russia*.[72]

PAYING OFF TSVETAEVA

At the same time as Mirsky's relationship at work with Bernard Pares was running into trouble, the finale of his most important literary relationship was also approaching. It is clear from his letter to Suvchinsky of 20 May 1929 that Mirsky had agreed to speak at a reading by Tsvetaeva scheduled for five days later.[73] But this plan came to nothing; it would seem from subsequent discussion that Suvchinsky dissuaded Mirsky from speaking, and that as a result he incurred Tsvetaeva's wrath, and this led to further resentment by Tsvetaeva against Mirsky. Mirsky visited the Efrons at some time shortly before 20 September 1930 for two days, and Tsvetaeva describes him as 'gloomy as hell' and 'moaning more than ever'.[74]

Tsvetaeva now thought that Mirsky simply no longer wanted to help her. Writing to Raisa Lomonosova[75] on 10 February 1931, Tsvetaeva complained that Mirsky 'doesn't want to take anything on—there was a time when he was crazy about my poetry, now he's completely cooled off, just as he has towards me as a person—we didn't quarrel, it just went away'.[76] On 13 February 1931 she again lamented the 'cooling off', now citing the first lines of one of her love lyrics:

About DPSM (sounds like an institution, doesn't it?) 'You can't be friends with me, to love me is impossible'—and so it ended, in deliberate indifference and enforced for-getting. He has locked me up tight inside himself, on his visits to Paris he visits every-one except me, and he sees me by chance and with other people around. There was a time when he loved me (I want to put that in parenthesis). I was the first to show him, that is, make him realize, that the Thames at the time of (high or low tide?) flows back-wards. . . . I wandered around London with him for three weeks,—he kept wanting to go to museums, but I wanted to go to markets, to bridges, *under* a bridge. It turned out that I taught him life. And made him bankrupt himself for three wonderful sky-blue (one beige) shirts, which he, out of savage meanness *towards himself*, hasn't forgiven me to this day, but he hasn't worn them out either. At that time he loved Boris [Pasternak] just as madly as he did me, but Boris is a man, and over the hills and far away, so that [love] hasn't changed.

We parted company over Mandelstam's stillborn prose [memoir], *The Noise of Time*, which he adored and I hated, where the only live things are objects and anything that's alive is a thing.

That's how it ended.[77]

Eventually, Tsvetaeva wrote to Anna Tesková on 27 February 1931[78] that she had received 'the final cheque' from Mirsky (it was for £6) on 24 December 1930—and there had been a terrible mistake; she had been given the equiva-lent of £10 in French francs and she had not questioned the amount, think-ing that Mirsky had sent more because the cheque was to be the last—but the bank was now asking her for the difference.

Tsvetaeva was a married woman and a mother; she had two daughters, one of whom died in childhood, and a son. In her private life she acted as a free agent to an extent either desired or managed by few even of the unmarried women of her time, but family considerations weighed heavily in the decisions she made about her life. Mirsky, apart from the fact that he was a man, was never fettered by such concerns; after his mother died in 1926, there were no serious constraints on his personal freedom of action. Tsvetaeva eventually followed her husband and daughter back to Russia, taking her son to what she thought was the best future she could provide for him—in Stalin's Russia. Mirsky's free choice was eventually as fatal as Tsvetaeva's circumscribed choice.

SOKOLNIKOV AND SOVIET CITIZENSHIP

Mirsky had still heard nothing as a result of his appeal to the Central Committee, and he was getting desperate. On 14 March 1931 he wrote to Gorky again, saying that he hoped to accompany him on his next trip to Russia. Two weeks later there had been no reply, and Mirsky wrote yet another anxious letter to Gorky. But at some time in the first fortnight of May, things began moving. The Sokolnikovs—the Soviet Ambassador in Britain and his wife, who had just returned from a visit to Gorky in Sorrento—assured Mirsky that the case was going to be decided in his favour.[79] It was evidently at this point that Mirsky joined the Communist Party of Great Britain; his statement about his conversion was published on 30 June 1931.[80] His first public appearance as a Party member seems to have been made when he gave a lecture on 'Leninism: Theory and Practice' on the evening of Sunday, 21 June 1931 at 71 Park Street, Camden Town.[81]

Does Mirsky's relationship with the Soviet Ambassador mean that he was a collaborator with the Soviet secret service? It is only reasonable to assume that he was. In the first place, Sokolnikov would have been duty-bound to refer Mirsky's application for a visa and a passport to 'the organs', and they would have been duty-bound to consider his potential value to them. But only one unambiguous statement on this matter has been published so far. The high Soviet literary official Ivan Mikhailovich Gronsky (1894–1985) asserted that Mirsky had worked for foreign intelligence services (though at what time he does not say), and adds that Mirsky was very close to Kryuchkov, Gorky's secretary (as his GPU minder was euphemistically called). This implies that Mirsky, like Sergey Efron, had made contact with various Western services under the instructions of the Soviet service.[82] Mirsky's Soviet passport was probably earned at least partly by his agreeing to appear as a propagandist in British universities and elsewhere. Soviet Russian intellectuals used to be fairly sophisticated, for obvious reasons, about collaboration with the secret services; in my experience they always made a careful distinction between informing, or agreeing to disinform, as a 'secret collaborator' (*seksot*), and actually being a paid or hired agent. They regarded the latter kind of person as an infernal creature, but the former simply as someone doing what one had to do. Mirsky would have been in close contact with the Soviet diplomatic staff, and it would have been perfectly normal for him to have been allotted a GPU control, but he was in no sense an intelligence professional.[83]

Mirsky naturally did not mention to Gorky or to his Soviet contacts more generally an additional factor that was recorded by Dorothy Galton, and it undermines any sense of absolute purposiveness in his actions in 1930–2. This was that he applied not only for Soviet citizenship, but—simultaneously—for British citizenship as well.[84] There was no single and logical progression in Mirsky's actions, certainly none over which he had control. He reached a point where he threw rationality to the winds and took a gamble, and his life could have gone in a completely different direction from the one it did if the result of the gamble had been different.

On 17 April 1931 Mirsky wrote to Miss Galton from Paris agreeing to give a lecture to the Fabian Society, of which Miss Galton's father was the secretary, and he also reported that he had just returned from a 'splendid, but unfortunately too short tour in the South'. His health had been giving him some concern lately, he said, but he told Miss Galton on 17 April that his 'neurasthenia' was now better; evidently he was recovering from the emotional stress of the crisis in his relationship with Vera. 'Still,' he added, 'I am rather horrified at the prospect of another term at the School.'

On 21 May 1931, Mirsky wrote his first letter to Suvchinsky since the end of Eurasianism; it was evidently Suvchinsky who took the initiative. In his reply, Mirsky told his old friend that he would be in Paris in early August, dependent on the date of his proposed trip to Moscow. He told Suvchinsky that his Soviet citizenship had been restored, and that he would be glad to see him. This letter was later marked by Suvchinsky as 'the last'.

Mirsky was still at Gower Street on 10 June 1931, as a letter to Salomeya Halpern shows. But on 23 June he wrote yet again to Gorky, now from Paris, fearing that Gorky had 'completely forgotten' him, and making yet more categorical statements of devotion:

Outside the general line of the All-Union Communist Party and the Comintern there is no place for those who do not wish to be the enemies of humanity and culture. And I insist that the cause of Communism has finally and unconditionally flowed into one, and there is neither humanity nor culture outside the Communist revolution.

He also referred to making contact with the French Communist Party, which he had first mentioned as a possibility on 14 May.

On 6 July 1931 Mirsky wrote to Miss Galton saying that he could not after all come to England because of 'unforeseen circumstances' which were keeping him in Paris. On 9 July, he informed her that he was going to speak on that day to the 'returnees' (*vozvrashchentsy*) on 'the political situation in general'. This is another possible indication of an assignment from the Soviet secret services.[85]

On 18 July 1931 Mirsky gave Miss Galton the following momentous information: 'I have just received a letter from the London Embassy that I have been restored in my citizenship. Only the actual passport is not ready yet.' He reported this same information to Gorky on 31 July, declared that he was intending to set off for Moscow by 1 September, and hoped he would arrive in time to see Gorky there. A note at the top of the letter to Dorothy Galton adds:

Of course this is *not for publication* (esp. not for Florinsky). I will probably write to Pares when it [the Soviet passport] materializes. I saw another doctor last Thursday.

He told me that my blood pressure was slightly *below* normal, and that the only thing that is wrong with me is the Great Gut, or whatever it is called in English (*gros intestin*). . . .

According to Suvchinsky, he and Mirsky applied for Soviet citizenship on the same day, but Suvchinsky, to his annoyance, was turned down: 'Now he was a real White Guard. . . . Socially we were identical. But they still gave it him and refused me.'[86] Evidently, the Soviet authorities considered that Suvchinsky would not be of much use to them back in the USSR, while Mirsky, with his high public profile, had great potential as a trophy. Quite apart from his expertise in foreign literatures, his highly articulate ideological commitment was bound to have been attractive.

On 22 July, Mirsky told Miss Galton that he was going to Grenoble on the 27th of the month and would stay there until the 31st. On 9 August he wrote from the Hotel Recamier, Place St Sulpice, enclosing a letter from Pares that has not survived with the rest of the correspondence. Evidently, Pares had refused to vouch for Mirsky's application for further residence in Great Britain. Mirsky reacted by asking:

If Pares would not help, then could your Labour friends help me to get readmitted? Don't you think it rather caddish to connect in this way the refusal to admit him into Russia with the question of my readmission into England? Is that the behaviour of an English gentleman?

On 13 August Mirsky wrote to Gorky to tell him that his intention had been to make a trip to Russia and then return to England for the beginning of the academic session in October 1931, but that as the bearer of a Soviet passport he would not be permitted to come back into the country. Mirsky then speaks to Gorky of enticing prospects for Party work in England, and says he will go from Paris to London and remain in London doing Party work until such time as he is extradited. The Soviet passport led to a final breach of relations with Pares, who, in his own account, agreed that summer to help Mirsky renew his residence permit with the Home Office; he added:

I wrote that I would do so; but the Home Office would certainly require from me a pledge on his behalf that while in England he would not work for the overthrow of our own system of government by violence. To this he did not reply, but on his return he told me he could not give this pledge, so I left his relations with our Home Office to himself.[87]

It is worth recalling just how tense the domestic political situation was in Britain at this time; in progress was the most serious confrontation between Left and Right after the General Strike of 1926. There were two general elections in 1931. As a result of the first, the National Government was formed in August 1931 by Ramsay MacDonald, an event widely interpreted by the Left as proof that a Labour government could not be viable in England, and that

Communism was the only answer; and then there was another election in October. In between came the Invergordon mutiny.

On 11 September Mirsky acknowledged a letter from Gorky:

I shall be very glad to come to Italy and travel with you to Moscow. But will they let me into Italy? It would be very annoying to keep putting off my trip. But I think that I can do some more work in England. Certain prospects have suddenly opened up there of a kind about which one could only have guessed three months ago. I'm going there in the next few days.

Then, on 15 September, he wrote to Miss Galton from Marseilles that he would be in London about 1 October, but 'this depends however on R. P. Dutt whom I want to see on the way in Belgium'. Mirsky upbraided Miss Galton for telling Pares he had not yet got permission to go to Russia, and Miss Galton must have questioned this accusation, for Mirsky wrote again to her from the Recamier on 21 September that he had written to Pares about 10 August that 'owing to your abominable and swinish behaviour I shall have to put off my journey to Moscow'. Pares had replied, Mirsky tells Miss Galton, that

'you need not go out of your way to blackmail me in this kind of way, because I understand from Miss Galton that you have not yet got your permission', which was quite true, but which was no business of his. As a matter of fact I got the papers only the other day, but I shall not be leaving before the end of the [academic] year. When I leave it will be for good.

This is the earliest indication that Mirsky had decided that he would not come back from Russia. In the autumn of 1931 he did indeed manage to arrange an entry permit for England, apparently without Pares's support—Dorothy Galton may well have fixed it through her influential friends, as Mirsky requested. He duly returned to London to begin the 1931–2 academic session, and also to continue his work on behalf of the Communist Party of Great Britain.

TWO VERSIONS OF LIBERATION

Mirsky asked Miss Galton on 21 September 1931: 'Have you seen my article in the [*Nouvelle Revue Française*]? It is making quite a sensation here.' The article he had in mind was his 'Histoire d'une émancipation', in which he gave an account of the ideological evolution that had led up to his conversion to Marxism and joining the Communist Party. It had come out in the September 1931 issue of the journal that Mirsky had perused in Athens a decade before. In the article, Mirsky makes no mention of the various alternative paths that we have seen him considering on his way to his commitment to Communism. Instead, he presents his development as a gradual but consistent shedding of the baggage of his idealist education and habits of thought. He dismisses this education in a few cutting sentences; contemptuously reviews his early respectful attitude towards the first phase of Eurasianism; notes with satisfaction the healthy influence of reading the new Soviet literature and the part *Vyorsts* played in spreading knowledge of it; registers his growing revulsion for the British bourgeoisie, especially during the General Strike; and then turns to the immediate prehistory of his conversion:

Towards 1928 'left Eurasianism' was formed, totally different from the original Eurasianism, and with the journal *Evraziya* as its mouthpiece. If in politics the new journal wanted to adopt bolshevism (or rather that which was least communist in bolshevism, because they supported the rightists against Stalin), its ideology was a completely extraordinary hotchpotch in which a confused idealism proclaiming itself to be Orthodox theology was attempting to unite with a Marxism emasculated of its materialism. . . . Of all Marx's work it was the *Theses on Feuerbach* that absorbed us first and that we liked most. This route into Marxism is doubtless abnormal and was only forced on us by our dear old idealist education, but it is perhaps to be particularly recommended to intellectuals.[88]

Eurasianism came to an end; Mirsky finally rejected the last lingering remnants of religion. He then recounts that he was invited to write his life of Lenin, and testifies to the effect of his preparatory reading:

The months that I spent alone with Lenin were the most important and fruitful of my life. They allowed me finally to emerge from an intellectual adolescence that had been prolonged far beyond natural limits. What Lenin gave me was above all clarity and reality. The idealist servitude of my mind had made the free exercise of my intelligence impossible. . . . Lenin was for me an intellectual liberation, for it was he who made me see reality as it is, not as one would wish it or as one imagined it. And the reality that he made me see was a complex, complete reality, with an infinity of dimensions, in constant movement, but capable of being grasped by the truly free and active mind, the mind that approaches this reality not as a 'disinterested' observer but as a technician who wishes to understand reality only in order to change it, in short—a dialectical reality.[89]

Through Lenin, Mirsky says, he came to Marx, and at that very time world events were proving incontrovertibly that the Marxist analysis was correct: the Five-Year Plan, the agrarian revolution, the end of American prosperity, the beginning of the world crisis of capitalism.

Mirsky's public account of his development, with its gloating self-righteousness typical of Party discourse at the time, was written at almost exactly the same time as a remorseful private statement by Mirsky's exact contemporary and erstwhile comrade, Nikolay Trubetskoy. Princes Mirsky and Trubetskoy were taking stock of what had happened to themselves during the two years that had passed since the downfall of Eurasianism, and both of them speak explicitly of undergoing a personal liberation, but they draw diametrically opposed conclusions from evidence and experience that was in many essential respects identical. Trubetskoy conveyed his conclusions to Savitsky in an agonized letter that took him three days to write, from 8 to 10 December 1930.[90] It is one of the most heartrending documents in Russian intellectual history. Trubetskoy tells Savitsky that he has reviewed his old writings, public and private, and found most of them 'childish'. He has lost the youthful optimism that fuelled Eurasianism. He no longer has the self-confidence that enabled him to write about so many large issues; instead, he is full of scepticism about these things, and begrudges the time they took away from his specialized professional work: 'I have learned to see the fragility and illusoriness of broad generalizations. The soundness of an edifice is more important for me than its grandeur.' He then expresses exactly the same feelings as Mirsky about cultural developments in Russia: that they have made the generation of 1890 into relics of the past, like the Old Believers. 'No matter how much we wish to, we cannot be part of the new proletarian Russian (or proletarian-Eurasian, if you like) culture, and the values we are creating will not become part of it.' These values are the swan-song of pre-revolutionary European-Russian culture, says Trubetskoy. Meanwhile, like Mirsky, in 1930 Trubetskoy asked himself the permanent Russian question, and answered it just as categorically as Mirsky did: 'What to do? I think nothing remains but to venture outside this nationally limited European-Russian culture and (*horribile dictu!*) work for a common European culture that aspires to be called that of common humanity. There is no alternative.' This is already facing in the opposite direction from that of the Eurasian Trubetskoy. But worse is to come:

I would never permit myself to write in German or French about something I didn't know or that I wasn't sure of, because I'm aware of the fact that among the hundred or so specialists who will read what I write there will assuredly be some who will expose me in print. In Russian, meanwhile, more than once have I written irresponsible things, and what is more about questions I am not competent to discuss; you say to yourself 'Never mind, it'll get by!' When I look back now on my past as an author, I regret not so much that I wrote such dilettante works, but that along with them I wrote some valuable things in Russian. . . . If [they] had been written in German or French they would have been of real use.

Mirsky, of course, had acted in exactly the opposite way from Trubetskoy, and with exactly the opposite results: he had published general works in English, and more narrowly specialist works in Russian; and he had achieved an exceptionally positive reputation with his foreign readership and a negative one among his fellow Russians.

Trubetskoy then turned to the Eurasians. He had reached the same conclusion as Mirsky: 'I have become convinced that for [Europe] Communism with all its consequences is unavoidable and essential.' But he had drawn the opposite inference in terms of personal action: not to become involved in Communism, but to withdraw from the political arena, since he could not in good conscience 'preach' that truth, the truth of Communism, which he had understood but with which he could not reconcile himself personally. Both Trubetskoy and Mirsky subsequently acted according to their convictions: Trubetskoy devoted himself to scholarly linguistics and withdrew almost entirely from the Eurasian movement, while Mirsky joined the Communist Party and resigned his academic post. They both saw themselves as anachronisms, or 'relicts'; but while Trubetskoy the academic aristocrat reconciled himself with this and went on constructing 'old cultural values', Mirsky the service aristocrat found a way, as he thought, of subordinating his individuality to the new social demand and contributing, as he thought, to the new values.

WORKING FOR THE CAUSE

On 26 September 1931 from the Hôtel de Lutèce, 17 avenue de Keyser, Antwerp, Mirsky wrote the last of his long series of letters to Suvchinsky. He said that he was there on political business, and that the business was in Brussels. This concerned the Communist Party of Great Britain and the Comintern: the next day Mirsky reports to Miss Galton that he had seen Palme Dutt in Brussels and would see him again that day. Rajani Palme Dutt, the most important British person in the Comintern network, was based in Brussels from 1929 to 1936.[91] Mirsky was no doubt directed to this meeting by the CPGB.

Once back in London, Mirsky began teaching as usual. Bernard Pares's account of subsequent events tries to maintain a dignified tone: 'While still with us, he attacked me violently in the press as a "mouth piece" of reaction. I took his political views as temperamental and did not reply. At the end of the next session he went off to Russia. . . .'[92] Towards the very end of 1931 there was an exchange of letters between Pares and Michael Florinsky. Pares wrote on 16 December:

The Mirsky affair has worked out as you expected. He wrote casually to me from abroad in the summer saying he was going on to a Soviet passport and asking me to arrange his visa at our Home Office. I had meanwhile read his 'Lenin' which, well as it is written, is evidently a most ex-parte statement. I replied saying the Home Office might ask me certain questions, for instance, was he prepared to abstain from agitating, while in England, for an overthrow of our system of government by force. This he did not answer in his reply, which was heated. On his return he refused to give the pledge mentioned above, but said he was leaving us at the end of this *session*, which he wished me to communicate to our Principal (of King's). This interview took place in Seton-Watson's presence. In view of his leaving we decided to take no further step: but since then he has not only done a lot of Communist propaganda here, but has now written a grossly perverted statement with regard to myself calling me 'one of the principal mouth-pieces of Anti-Soviet propaganda' and suggesting that I know nothing of Russia. He had earlier published a scurrilous invective against the 'Oxford and Cambridge blacklegs' who volunteered for public service during our General Strike. You might tell all this to Shotwell.[93]

Pares's recommendation that Florinsky denounce Mirsky to Shotwell prob- ably indicates that Pares had got wind of Mirsky's tentative steps about finding himself a job in America. His further thoughts provide eloquent testimony about just how thin the field of Russian studies was in the English-speaking world in the early 1930s, and about the way appointments were arranged in those easygoing days:

It is all very unpleasant, but the main reason why I am writing is that there will anyhow be a vacancy on our staff next October if not earlier. My own Chair is supposed to cover 'Russian Language, Literature and History' and Mirsky does the literature. This gap must be filled, but it is not necessary that the scope of my Assistant should be defined in the same way as for him. The salary is £325. I am writing to one or two people to ask if they would like to be candidates, and that is why I am writing to you. I understand that your father was Professor of Philology. What are your own record and studies in the field of Literature? We have a separate post for Comparative Slavonic Philology (held by Jopson, who is excellent). Could you more or less cover the litera- ture (up to the standard of an Assistant Lecturer)? Were you appointed, I should of course welcome your cooperation in history. Have you at all followed current contem- porary Russian Literature (in Moscow & abroad)? Don't understate things, but let me know—if you would like to be a candidate—how you stand in these matters and give me your full curriculum vitae with dates.

Florinsky politely declined Pares's invitation: 'I know nothing about philol- ogy, and I have never made any study of Russian literature except what one learns in a *gimnaziya*, which, as you know, is not much. I feel therefore that I would be a most inadequate substitute for Mirsky.' Florinsky is surely not the only person who has entertained the sentiment expressed in this last sentence.

HUGH MACDIARMID

The 'Party work' Pares mentions consisted, at least in its public aspect in England, of speaking at rallies and writing for Communist publications. Mirsky contributed a series of articles to the *Labour Monthly*, which was edited by Palme Dutt. The first two appeared in 1931;[94] two more appeared there in 1932.[95] None of them is concerned with literature. The first of these articles has been recognized as the earliest authoritative presentation for the British Left of the current state of Dialectical Materialism in Soviet Russia after the 'Deborinite' ideological crisis of 1930.[96] It found at least one appreciative reader in Antonio Gramsci, one of Mirsky's most illustrious Communist contemporaries.[97]

In the autobiographical statement not for publication that he made in 1936, Mirsky claimed that he had spoken at about sixty meetings in various parts of England and Ireland, mainly on behalf of the Friends of the Soviet Union.[98] He is known to have spoken on behalf of the Friends of the Soviet Union and the Workers' Educational Association, in Manchester on 12 December 1931, 16 January 1932, and in September 1932; in Edinburgh on 18 December 1931; in Glasgow in February 1932; and in Liverpool in March 1932.[99] Vera Traill expressed the obvious view of what inevitably went on: 'He was a prince, and then he was a Russian by origin, and when he gave Communist speeches at Communist meetings, someone in the crowd would always yell: "If you think it's so marvellous, why don't you go there to your country?"' Vera's version of the cry from the crowd, to which the unregenerate English mind irresistibly supplies a few expletives, was as manifestly unidiomatic as Mirsky's must have been when he gave these grotesque speeches.

At least one English proletarian did attribute to Mirsky a decisive role in the formation of his political views, though. One Sunday morning a certain David Wilson went for a long walk with Mirsky and had his eyes opened to what he describes as the power of the bourgeois press to instil bourgeois opinion into the British proletariat, but their inability to create proletarian opinion.[100]

The most prominent proletarian Mirsky knew at this time was a Scotsman, Hugh MacDiarmid (Christopher Murray Grieve, 1892–1978).[101] MacDiarmid was fond of using Russian sources, and he was dependent on translations into English; among his principal sources were the writings of Mirsky.[102] Direct contact between MacDiarmid and Mirsky was apparently made, by correspondence if not in person, after the Scotsman reviewed *Modern Russian Literature*[103] and *Contemporary Russian Literature*.[104] MacDiarmid's admiration for Mirsky and solidarity with his political development as the 1920s drew to a close were expressed in his dedication of the programmatic *First Hymn to Lenin* (1931) to 'Prince D. S. Mirsky'. This dedication, which has appeared many times in the various republications of MacDiarmid's works, stands as the most enduring testament to the two men's affinities. In a return tribute which many fewer people can have noticed, Mirsky included an item by MacDiarmid in the anthology of modern English poetry which eventually appeared without his name after he was arrested.[105] These lines render into standard literary Russian three stanzas of 'The Seamless Garment', a Scots lyric addressed by MacDiarmid to a cousin who worked at the mill in their native town, Langholm. Eventually, one of MacDiarmid's major later works was dedicated, among others, to Prince Dmitry Mirsky,

> A mighty master in all such matters
> Of whom for all the instruction and encouragement he gave me

I am happy to subscribe myself here
The humble and most grateful pupil.[106]

Mirsky and MacDiarmid were born at opposite ends of the social spectrum, but both came from border country, and both were on active service on foreign soil in the First World War; like most survivors of this conflict, they subsequently wondered what on earth they had been fighting for. In emigration, beginning with some of his earliest publications, Mirsky was involved in the agonized debate about the Russianness of the Russian Revolution;[107] his involvement in the Eurasian movement revived this question. He conceived *Russia: A Social History* with a special emphasis on the nationalities question. In the book he wrote about the British intelligentsia soon after he returned to Russia, though, Mirsky makes no mention of nationalism as a significant element in their views.

Meanwhile, Hugh MacDiarmid was a founder member of the National Party of Scotland in 1928, but he was expelled from it because of his Communist sympathies in 1933. At some time in 1934 he joined the Communist Party of Great Britain.[108] MacDiarmid's involvement with nationalist politics undoubtedly helps to account for Mirsky's reservation about his ideology in a Soviet encyclopedia article of 1933, and also the reference to the poet's 'idealism' in the anthology of 1937.[109] The fact that, for publication in the anthology, Mirsky's translator turned MacDiarmid's Scots into standard Russian is a patent manifestation of the Great Russian chauvinism that was then becoming an important part of the ideology of Stalinism. Mirsky's standard English prose in his translation of a poem by Pushkin was turned into MacDiarmid's self-marginalizing Scots poem 'Why I Became a Scots Nationalist'; then his original Scots poetry about Lenin was translated into standard literary Russian, another language of imperial power.

Between the time he first read it and his arrest, Mirsky was probably too busy to think much about MacDiarmid; but between then and his death in the GULag, Mirsky had ample time to reflect on the now infamous stanza of the poem the Scotsman had dedicated to him in 1931:

> As necessary, and insignificant, as death
> Wi' a' its agonies in the cosmos still
> The Cheka's horrors are in their degree;
> And'll end suner! What maitters't wha we kill
> To lessen that foulest murder that deprives
> Maist men o' real lives?[110]

Mirsky, along with millions of others, certainly came to 'end suner'. The author of this poem, meanwhile, not being a Russian, had nearly fifty years of 'real' life left to reflect on whether or not all this mattered.

THE INTELLECTUAL LEFT

According to some contemporaries, Mirsky's new-found Communism was fanatical. Beatrice Webb reports and then paraphrases his old friend Meyendorff's sad words (it is worth recalling the same man's assertion concerning Mirsky's erstwhile fanatical monarchism):

'We never meet now', for apparently he has a real admiration and liking for the talented and wayward Mirsky; he rejected Kingsley Martin's suggestion that Mirsky's conversion was not sincere—it was all of a piece with his romantic career and his refusal as a young Guards officer to drink the health of the Tsar and consequent dismissal from his regiment. Indeed he said that Mirsky was a little mad and was becoming madder—he feared that there might be some crisis.[111]

Thirty years later, Kingsley Martin declared that 'Marxism, as understood in England, began with the destruction of the Labour Government in 1931 and ended with the Nazi–Soviet Pact in 1939. It was not an aberration of the Left Wing, but a deduction from the facts.'[112] This idea underlies the book Mirsky wrote about the British intelligentsia after he went back to Russia. In its penultimate chapter, dealing with the current state of British science, Mirsky asserts: 'From the autumn of 1931, in all British universities and in wide circles of the left intelligentsia, the study of dialectical materialism began.'[113] The process, he says, was set in train by the political events of 1931, for scientists in particular by the publication of an English translation of Lenin's *Materialism and Empiriocriticism*, and also by 'the arrival of a delegation from the USSR to the International Congress on the History of Science and Technology'.[114] In the very last pages of the book Mirsky finds some hope for the future of Britain:

The interest in the U.S.S.R. is enormous and the interest in marxism is growing. In the course of the 1931–1932 academic year a number of clubs to the left of the reformists were founded. To-day there are, in the London School of Economics, *The Marxist Society*, in Oxford, *The October Club*, while in Cambridge the old *Heretics* now has a marxist leadership and a radically inclined membership.[115]

Much of all this, Mirsky concedes, is transient and superficial, but 'everywhere there is healthy young growth; cadres are already forming'. We know with hindsight that certainly the most effective of these cadres, 'clear that civilisation to-day is inseparable from the task of proletarian revolution', were the ones whose commitment took the form of an agreement to work underground for the Soviets. The spectre of English Marxism has haunted the country ever since; the question of collaboration with the secret service raises a more substantial phantom.

The reference Mirsky makes in *The Intelligentsia of Great Britain* to the reformed Heretics Club in Cambridge is of particular interest. On Sunday, 22 November 1931 Mirsky lectured to the Heretics on Dialectical Materialism.

1. Prince D. P. Svyatopolk-Mirsky the poet, *c.*1911 (G. S. Smith)

2. Prince D. P. Svyatopolk-Mirsky the officer, *c*.1913 (G. S. Smith)

3. D. S. Mirsky with the staff of the School of Slavonic Studies at King's College, 1922–1923. *Front row, l. to r.*: Baron A. F. Meyendorff, Harold Williams, Sir Bernard Pares, Sir Ernest Barker, L. C. Wharton, F. Chudoba, D. S. Mirsky. *Upper row, l. to r.*: Arshak Raffi, R. W. Seton-Watson, D. P. Subotic (Courtesy of the late Dorothy Galton)

4. D. S. Mirsky and the staff of the School of Slavonic Studies at King's College, 1925. *Seated, l. to r.*: Baron A. F. Meyendorff, Sir Bernard Pares, F. Chudoba, R. W. Seton-Watson. *Standing, l. to r.*: D. P. Subotic, L. C. Wharton, Arshak Raffi, D. S. Mirsky, N. B. Jopson, R. Dyboski (Courtesy of the late Dorothy Galton)

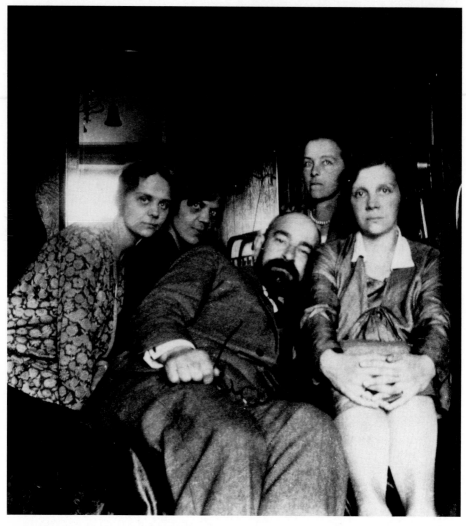

5. D. S. Mirsky with the Shuvalova sisters, Paris, 1920s. *l. to r.*: Olga (Mrs Rodionov), Elizaveta, Mariya (Countess Tolstoy), Aleksandra (Countess Fersen) (Courtesy of Sir Dmitry Obolensky)

6. Detail from 'D. S. Mirsky,
Michael Florinsky, and the
Pidget', by Philip Evergood.
(Whereabouts of original
unknown; copy courtesy of the
late Salomeya Halpern)

7. Dedication to Mirsky by
Marina Tsvetaeva in her *Posle
Rossii* (Paris, 1928). (Courtesy
of the School of Slavonic and
East European Studies,
University of London)

ПОСЛЕ РОССИИ

8. Soviet writers at the Elektrokombinat factory, 1934. Mirsky stands immediately behind the teletype machine; on his right is Leonid Leonov, on his left, Efim Zozulya and Vladimir Lidin (*Literature of the Peoples of the USSR*, 7-8, 1934), (VOKS Illustrated Almanac)

9. Soviet writers meet Romain Rolland, July 1935. *Seated, r. to l.*: Maksim Gorky, Rolland, J. Sadoul; *standing, front row, l. to r.*: A. S. Novikov-Priboy, Lidiya Seifullina, Agniya Barto, Ilya Selvinsky, Marietta Shaginyan, Galina Serebryakova, A. Kurella; *rear row, l. to r.*: Valentin Kataev, Lev Nikulin, Shinko, D. S. Mirsky, A. A. Isbakh, I. S. Novich, I. I. Anisimov, A. Ya. Arosev, Marchenko (*Pravda*, 10 July 1935)

10. D. S. Mirsky at the Minsk Plenum, 1936; caricature by the Kukryniksy, from *Literaturnaya gazeta*, 10 (573), 14 February 1936

11. D. S. Mirsky under arrest, June 1937 (G. S. Smith)

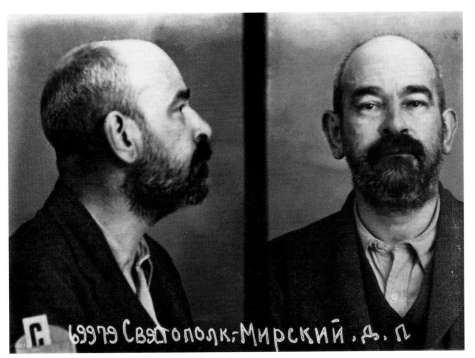

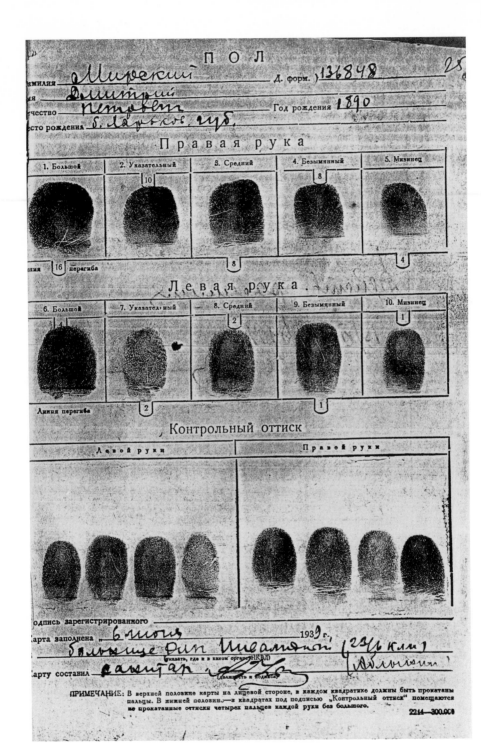

12. Posthumous fingerprints, 6 July 1939 (G. S. Smith)

Several eyewitnesses have described this event, with various degrees of hindsight. Esther Salaman set down her memory of it nearly half a century later:

We knew a good many people in the audience: Desmond Bernal and J. B. S. Haldane, in the front; behind us was Herbert Butterfield, the historian. Mirsky talked of 'the collapse of capitalism', the 'end of Western bourgeois civilisation'. . . . Now Mirsky was disinforming us; but I did not know at the time that he was driven by a desire to go back to Russia. Bernal got up and mumbled complete agreement on Dialectical Materialism. Butterfield asked some pointed questions. . . .

Salaman, who had grown up in Russia, listened with growing resentment. Eventually she blew up, and reproached Mirsky for daring to speak of the death of civilization in Cambridge, where so much pioneering work was going on in the natural sciences. It was, after all, at the Cavendish in 1932 that Rutherford's team discovered the neutron; Cockcroft split the atom at almost exactly the same time as Mirsky gave this talk, and Mirsky's compatriot Pyotr Kapitsa (1894–1984) was still working in the University.[116] Mirsky, though, cheerfully admitted that he knew nothing at all about science. Salaman then

told Mirsky that the Bolsheviks had ruined 'our revolution': by introducing an alien philosophy to Russia. I had not forgotten our hope of a free Russia after the Revolution of 1917, which the Bolsheviks crushed by closing the Constituent Assembly and putting an armed guard outside when they found themselves in the minority. And the slogans! 'Dictatorship of the Proletariat' when there was no proletariat, 'Class war' when there were no classes in Marx's sense.

When there were no more questions Mirsky got up, and made his replies. At the end he said: 'As for the lady's criticism, it's not a matter for argument but for pistols . . .'[117]

Perhaps the most talented younger member of the CPGB in the early 1930s was the poet John Cornford (1915–36), the son of the Cambridge historian of ancient philosophy Francis and his poet wife, Frances. Frances Cornford wrote a letter to her son on Tuesday, 24 November 1931:

We went and heard Prince Mirsky last Sunday night on Dialectical Materialism—the philosophy of Communism. I *longed* for you to be there. Haldane tackling him. But Esther [Salaman] made *much* the best speech and Dadda asked much the best question, which really drew him. I'll have to tell you about it at length. Mirsky can't think much—but he looks like a Byzantine Saint and he believes in Communism like a B. S. in the Trinity—and his smile, when his ugly black-bearded face lights up with belief and hope, is one of the best things I've seen for ages.[118]

This meeting of the Heretics was chaired by the distinguished Germanist Roy Pascal, who recalled it for me more than forty years later. He asserted that Mirsky's lecture was the first time that he and the other young Heretics who had recently radicalized the Club had heard about dialectical materialism from someone who seemed to know what he was talking about. Pascal was certain that Haldane and Bernal were present, also Maurice Cornforth and Hugh

Sykes Davies, and probably also Joseph Needham and David Haden Guest. The moving spirit was Maurice Dobb. Pascal had met Mirsky before in Dobb's rooms in Cambridge, and thought he might have been to a talk on art or literature that Mirsky had given on a previous occasion, when Mirsky 'was very rough indeed to the traditional Cambridge approach to these problems, and he startled us very much with the brusque way in which he dismissed our attitudes, but he was always a very attractive person, a bit eccentric, with a strange whining in his voice whenever he stopped talking and so on, but very charming'.

Pascal took Mirsky as

really a man of ideas. You see, with this passion for culture, for ideas and so on, but very impractical, and I think very impractical about politics . . . he wouldn't understand, but hardly anyone in England understood either . . . however much one tried, one couldn't quite understand what the character of the Party was, and what was the relationship between the Party (the Communist Party, of course) and the ideals which it represented or the proletariat that it represented and so on . . .

The Party cell inside the university was founded by David Haden Guest soon after Mirsky's talk, in April 1932, and Maurice Dobb and J. D. Bernal were among its leading members. Similar cells came into being in the LSE in October 1931 and at University College London at about the same time; the three units made contact with each other in London at Easter 1932, and evolved a plan for coordinating student Communist activities throughout Britain.[119] This was the situation when Mirsky returned to the USSR.

Mirsky's public speaking on behalf of Communist-front organizations continued. On 5 March 1932, the *Morning Post* reported that 'The activities of Prince Mirsky outside his work at King's College are such as to call for the attention of the public.'[120] On 11 March, under the headline 'Mr D. S. Mirsky No Longer Connected with London University', the *Morning Post* carried the following notice:

It was stated at Kings College yesterday that Mr D. S. Mirsky, who had been a lecturer in the School of Slavonic Studies, had recently resigned—although his contract was not due to expire until next July—and that he was no longer connected with the College.

It will be recalled that on March 5 the 'Morning Post' called attention to the Communistic speeches that Mr Mirsky (who was formerly known as Prince Mirsky) had been making up and down the country.

After this unpatriotic activity in Great Britain, Mirsky spoke at two separate conferences in Amsterdam in 1932; the first took place in April.[121] The second was held in late August, and is much better known; it is referred to variously as the 'Anti-War', 'Anti-Military', or 'Peace' Conference, a Comintern exercise masterminded by their propaganda wizard, Willi Münzenberg.[122] The figureheads were billed as Gorky, Romain Rolland, and Henri Barbusse, and the proceedings opened on 27 August. The members of the Soviet delegation, headed by Gorky and Shvernik, were denied visas. This seems to have been the culminating point of Mirsky's involvement with the international Communist movement that was orchestrated by Palme Dutt in Brussels.[123]

WHY MIRSKY WENT BACK

In a letter written on 22 June 1932 to Lady Ottoline Morrell, Virginia Woolf mentions that she must 'tomorrow dine with Mary Hutchinson and go to the Zoo; and on Monday have Mirsky and his prostitute, and on Tuesday dine with Americans . . .'. Woolf's supercilious 'prostitute' refers, of course, to Vera Suvchinskaya.[124] But for herself she noted, in her journal entry for this day:

So hot yesterday—so hot, when Prince Mirsky came . . . but Mirsky was trap mouthed: opened and bit his remark to pieces: has yellow misplaced teeth: wrinkles in his forehead: despair, suffering, very marked on his face. Has been in England, in boarding houses, for 12 years; now returns to Russia 'for ever'. I thought as I watched his eye brighten and fade—soon there'll be a bullet through your head. That's one of the results of war, this trapped cabin'd man.[125]

One question is asked more often than any other about Mirsky's life, for obvious reasons. Why did he go back to Russia? If Virginia Woolf's perception is to be trusted, his decision to go had not brought Mirsky any serenity. Enough has been said so far about Mirsky's character to demonstrate that his actions were not seriously influenced by the drives that are conventionally reckoned to motivate men. He never seems to have done anything for the sake of power, for example, or fame actual or posthumous, or sexual passion—especially the final item in this list.[126] Janko Lavrin asserted, though, in all seriousness, a different sort of physical basis for Mirsky's actions:

Somebody told him—or several people must have told him—that his face was a replica of Lenin's face. It *was* so. And, d'you know, at first glance when you saw him, for the first time, you would have taken or mistaken him for Lenin; and he told me once: 'I'm very proud to resemble Lenin. He has made one of the greatest revolutions in history, and Russia is going to play an enormous part in world history now'. . . . This was in the 20s, long before those bloodbaths of Stalin and so on; he was quite seriously convinced that something enormous would come out of Russia . . . If he *was* a Communist, he was a patriotic Communist, you know. Hoping, d'you know, for the very best as far as his own country was concerned.

The idea that Russian patriotism should lead to a commitment to the Soviet state was utterly inadmissible for Gleb Struve, and he postulated instead a purely psychological basis for Mirsky's actions, which he saw as irresponsible: 'To many people his conversion to Communism . . . came as a surprise. But to some who knew him well this about-face seemed a natural result of his love of intellectual mischief and his instinctive nonconformism, and when in 1932 he went back to Russia, these people confidently predicted that he would end badly.'[127]

The impressions of Lavrin and Struve concur in their implication that rather than by any of the usual considerations, Mirsky's actions were to an extraordinary degree driven by intellectual conviction. This conviction seems to have occupied the space usually shared to a greater or lesser extent by physical and emotional drives. Mirsky did many things for money, but only in order to have enough to supply his immediate needs; he seems to have had no interest in accumulating more. He denigrated his aristocratic origins, but he remained loyal to his parental family for as long as it lasted, and never seems to have wanted to start one of his own, preferring his 'boarding houses' to some alternative such as Virginia Woolf's childless and asexual arrangement. In his eyes, of course, it was she, not he, who was 'trapped, cabin'd'—in English bourgeois society.

Mirsky did have a strong sense of his own dignity, though, and by the end of 1927 the life he was living must constantly have offended it. As a Russian *émigré* he was an embodiment of pitiable failure. As a Russian *émigré* prince he even embodied a standard caricature in the popular mythology of contemporary Western Europe. He had been teaching at the School of Slavonic Studies for five years, and although he had come across a small number of excellent individual students, his work in the classroom was demeaning for a man of his family tradition. He had published what he must have known to have been his best work, the two-volume history of Russian literature. This literature itself, the object of his study and teaching, seemed to be going into decline, and what promising talent did exist was making itself felt in Soviet Russia rather than where he was, on the outside. Mirsky's own efforts to publish new Russian writing outside Russia had been an artistic success, but also an immense burden, because there were simply not enough readers to liberate the enterprise from dependence on private sponsors. The Eurasian movement seemed at first to offer some possibility of genuine creative work, but it proved incapable of being moved on from what Mirsky saw as the pettifogging scruples of the old Russian intelligentsia. And the Eurasians' attempt to establish some sort of footing inside Russia was ignominious. Mirsky had lost his faith in the Orthodox Church and with it one of the central mainstays of Russia Outside Russia. He was accepted on equal terms by the literary élite of England and the other countries of Western Europe, and French cuisine was second to none, but given his character, how long could he have gone on with these pleasant distractions in this cultural wasteland that he considered 'done for'? He toyed with the idea of America, but his one expedition there boded ill. Above all, as someone who was never content to settle for what he had, Mirsky must have felt that he lacked a worthy purpose.

Meanwhile, Stalin was taking his country in hand. Russia had been restored to something closely approximating the borders of Mirsky's youth, when it was at the height of its prosperity and international weight. And it was setting itself up as the country that would lead the world towards the future. Russia was going somewhere. Its leader was the embodiment of that conscious will that Mirsky spoke about so often, while the rest of the world seemed to be going nowhere. And Mirsky's attitude was by no means an isolated case, to say the very least. Here is Hugh Dalton's rehearsal of a view that was commonplace among European intellectuals by the end of 1931:

There was no unemployment in the Soviet Union. Here was no 'industrial depression', no inescapable 'trade cycle', no limp surrender to 'the law of supply and demand'. Here was an increasing industrial upsurge, based on a planned Socialist economy. They had an agricultural problem, we knew, in the Soviet Union, but so had we in the capitalist West, where primary producers had been ruined by the industrial slump. We knew that in Soviet Russia there was no political freedom. But there never had been under the Russian Czars and, perhaps some of us thought, we had over-valued this in the West, relatively to the other freedoms.[128]

Mirsky seems to have been able to live with the inescapable contradiction between Marxist determinism and godless post-Nietzschean willed forging of destiny. Though his knowledge of the rise of Stalinism was abstract, deriving almost entirely from his reading, Mirsky understood perfectly well what was actually going on in Russia. And he had no objection to it in principle, in fact quite the opposite: he had never believed in liberal democracy, with its 'paraphernalia', but instead he respected and argued the necessity for strong, even ruthless, leadership. Though he never explicitly worshipped 'necessary' cruelty to the extent that MacDiarmid and some other admirers of the USSR did, Mirsky evidently considered the inhumanity attendant on the introduction of a new order to be acceptable, and preferable to what he came to see as the protracted death of life under capitalism. Mirsky's disdain for Chekhov, which so many English people have found it so hard to forgive him, was partly based on stylistic grounds; but his most vehement objection was to what he called Chekhov's 'horrid contemptible humanitarianism, pity, contempt and squeamishness towards humankind, and not a single clever thought'.[129] Having condemned Mayakovsky, who, though he had been on the side of the revolution all his conscious life, could not in the end put his and his generation's individualism behind him, Mirsky himself committed suicide, but suicide psychological rather than physical. He attempted to murder his individuality by committing himself to the service of the common cause, as some sort of disembodied agent of History. His return to Russia was the final expression, and also the abnegation, of that 'willed consciousness' he had spoken about so much in his writings about literature. He ended by surrendering his own will to Stalin's.

Some of the Russian intellectuals who stayed in Russia after 1917 did so because they wanted at least to represent the older values of their country in the face of the values of the new regime. Many *émigrés* had left because they thought this cause hopeless, so that the national heritage had to be preserved and defended outside the geopolitical borders until such time as a new regime replaced the Bolsheviks. For Mirsky, though, his country always seems to have retained some supreme significance in and of itself; he was a patriot in a way which is not to be confused with the maudlin nostalgia that was a persistent theme in Russian *émigré* writing, nor with the mystical messianism that was a common attitude among Russian intellectuals of his time. He always felt that what mattered most for his country was necessarily going on inside it, not outside it. He was born a Russian and brought up with the idea of service to his country, and his extraordinarily cosmopolitan education and his exposure to non-Russian societies reinforced rather than weakened his sense of national identity.

There is ample evidence that Mirsky's decision to go back was certainly not rash and impulsive, as has so often been said to be the case. He twisted and turned, considering several radical alternatives to Russia, chief among them a post in America or staying in England with Vera. It was the circumstances of twentieth-century political history, the crudely politicized view of loyalty that closed borders to 'undesirables' of all kinds, that meant that Mirsky's decision to go to Russia, once made, was irreversible; there was no possibility, for example, of making the maximum use of his abilities and coming and going between Russia and the West. Of his contemporaries, only Erenburg came near to achieving this balancing act, and it was done at a terrible cost in terms of personal integrity.

Mirsky's movements during the summer of 1932 can be traced from the postcards he regularly sent to Dorothy Galton in London. He indulged in his customary gastronomic tourism, for the last time. He left Paris for Gibraltar on 15 July, Vera Suvchinskaya taking the same ship from Marseilles. He said he was intending to be in the south of France by about 1 August. He sent another postcard from Seville on 23 July: 'Spain is really too sweet, I don't think I'll get out of it in a hurry. I am flying tomorrow to Madrid.' And again on 25 July: 'Seville is delightful . . . I flew here, at a tremendous height all the time, about 5,000 feet I should say.' The last dated message to Miss Galton from Mirsky the *émigré* was dated 6 August 1932 and sent from the Hôtel Mélodia, par Le Levandou (Var): 'Vera and I are here till next Sunday (7th). On Thursday we shall be in Toulon. On Sunday we shall probably be going to Nice.' Mirsky sailed for Russia from either Le Havre or Marseilles, and arrived in Leningrad by ship in late September.

PART III

Back in Russia, 1932–1939

7 The Rising Line

We may expect an age when the Russian mind, technical and practical in
its practice, will submit its techniques and practices to one ultimate dogma
placed above all questioning. (D. S. Mirsky, 1928)

MANOEUVRING IN MOSCOW

There was much less of potential advantage for Mirsky to return to in the land
of his birth than there had been outside it when he arrived in emigration in
1921. Everything his family owned had been confiscated, and people of his
social background, often referred to as the 'has-beens' (*byvshie lyudi*), were systematically reviled and persecuted. His major work had been published abroad
in English, and was destined to remain unknown in Russia until long after his
death—which was perhaps a good thing, because much of what he had written
even after his conversion was actionable in terms of official Soviet thinking.
Hardly anybody Mirsky had known before going into emigration was in a really
influential position in Soviet Russia. There was no equivalent to Baring in the
literary circles and Pares in the academic world of England; and there was
nothing remotely resembling the family home and alternative society that
awaited Mirsky in France during his vacations. Although Baring and Pares
were much older than he was, their late Victorian mentality was in some ways
closer even to the Marxist Mirsky's than that of the upstarts who were running
the USSR fifteen years after the revolution. Among the patriarchs there,
Mirsky was *persona grata* with one of the grandest, Gorky; but he was only
one of many trying to get past the security-service gatekeepers around him.

There was no Jane Ellen Harrison to come to Mirsky's aid and make useful
introductions; nor could there have been in this overwhelmingly male-
dominated society which was engaged in the steady restitution of the public
and private situations that had been somewhat eroded in the 1920s. Men
monopolized the higher reaches of the public sphere, and women on the whole
settled for rank-and-file public roles and domination of the private sphere.[1] A
regiment of replacements for behind-the-throne women such as Mirsky's
mother was soon in place after 1917.[2] The capital of Stalin's Russia was among
other things an intrigue-ridden hothouse where access and connections were
all-important, and the principal female role, as before 1917, was networking
by wives. Mirsky chose to do without this kind of support. Not that it would
necessarily have done him any good if he had opted for the more conventional
way.

The most remarkable Russian literary wife of this time was Nadezhda Yakovlevna Mandelshtam (1899–1980). In 1930 she had a conversation with the wife of Stalin's most infamous satrap-to-be, Nikolay Ezhov (1894–1939); Mrs Mandelshtam does not reveal Mrs Ezhov's first name. Before the decade was out, both these women became unpersoned widows. ' "It's us Pilnyak calls on", she said. "What about you?" When I indignantly passed this on to M[andelshtam], he tried to calm me down: "Everybody 'calls on someone'. There's no other way, it seems. We do too. On Nikolay Ivanovich [Bukharin]".'[3]

On 3 May 1937, a month before he was arrested—and knowing full well that the noose was tightening—Mirsky wrote a desperately self-exculpatory account of his literary activities since 1932 to the Executive Secretary of the Union of Writers, V. P. Stavsky, which begins:

I arrived in the USSR in 1932 with only a bookish knowledge of Soviet reality and very brief experience of active political work (in the English workers' movement), and my understanding of the literary situation was very poor. In Moscow at first I found myself in the company of the most right-wing writers, ex-Formalists and so on, who knew me from my previous literary activity abroad. This milieu did not satisfy me.[4]

Obviously, anyone Mirsky might have actually named in this context at this time would probably have been put on a list for investigation and arrest in short order. Whom might he have had in mind? Perhaps he was thinking of the seedy literary café society who sat around in the central Moscow hotels. The leading lights of it were Mikhail Svetlov (1903–64) and Yury Olesha (1899–1960). Mirsky knew both of them, and Olesha quite well. Each writer published one outstanding work in the late 1920s—duly acclaimed by Mirsky in his *émigré* writings—and never really managed a follow-up; they soon became career barfly raconteurs, among the first of many such men to take advantage of membership of the Union of Writers as a welfare provision.[5]

As an 'ex-Formalist', the outstanding candidate is Mirsky's schoolmate Viktor Zhirmunsky, who was now a Professor, and heading the Western European sector of the Academy Institute of Russian Literature (Pushkin House) in Leningrad, of which Gorky was the nominal Director. Of all Mirsky's old friends Zhirmunsky was the most supportive, eventually negotiating a position at his Institute and several publishing opportunities. It was apparently Zhirmunsky who told Leonid Chertkov that he had once urged Mirsky to spend less time on public polemic and more on 'serious' (i.e. academic) matters, only to receive the reply: 'D'you think I came back just to talk to you and Tynyanov?'[6]

The literary critic and historical novelist Yury Tynyanov (1894–1943) was just too young to have attended Vengerov's Pushkin seminar at the same time as Mirsky. In a diary entry of 26 April 1935, Korney Chukovsky records a meeting he had just had with Tynyanov, who told Chukovsky that he was very angry with Mirsky, giving a 'wonderful representation' of how Mirsky had come to see him 'straight from London' and showered him with questions: 'You're at the university?' 'No.' 'The Institute for the History of the Arts?' 'No.' 'Where do you lecture?' 'Nowhere', and so on.[7] And then it turned out, says Chukovsky, that Mirsky had published a most malicious review of Tynyanov abroad where among other things he had said that 'Tynyanov's attitude to Soviet power is negative, or something of the sort'.[8] This was a completely unfounded allegation, and it provides a good example of the consequences of the absence of free communication between the USSR and the emigration; almost everything Mirsky had written about Tynyanov had in fact been enthusiastically positive.[9]

Among the Soviet writers with whom Mirsky had had some contact before he came back, potentially the best placed was Boris Pasternak. The letters Mirsky wrote to him beginning in 1927 have yet to be published; but it is clear that Mirsky regularly sent him copies of what he wrote about his poetry, and the poet was very pleased by them.[10] Mirsky called on Pasternak as soon as he got to Moscow, an event which the poet reported to Anna Akhmatova.[11] On the whole, though, Pasternak was a doubtful asset in 1932, and he became even more doubtful later on as he followed his precarious path towards acceptance of the Soviet regime.[12]

In the autobiographical statement for the files of the Academy Institute of Russian Literature that he wrote in June 1936, as potential referees among Soviet writers who could vouch for his activity abroad Mirsky naturally named Gorky in the first place. But then he added three writers who had spent time in Paris: Lev Nikulin, Isaak Babel, and Ilya Erenburg.[13] The name of Lev Veniaminovich Nikulin (1891–1967) does not appear in any documents by or concerning Mirsky during the émigré period. He was a poet, essayist, and novelist who specialized in political themes, and he had very close connections with the secret police. The nature of Mirsky's connection with Nikulin is highly enigmatic.[14] As for Babel, Mirsky had written positively about his work many times, laid the foundation for his reputation in the West, and translated one of his key stories into English.[15] By the time Mirsky returned to Russia, Babel had already begun to 'choose silence'; but he was also driven by his sadistic instincts into playing a high-risk game and 'going to see' various NKVD hitmen in order to 'have a sniff and see what death smells like'.[16] He was to follow Mirsky into oblivion in 1939. Erenburg, who in the 1930s was working in Paris and making only infrequent visits back to Moscow, was in no position to be of assistance to Mirsky; apart from anything else, he had been a schoolboy friend of Bukharin, who was soon to be disgraced. There was one other prominent Soviet writer whom Mirsky had met abroad, but who is significantly absent from Mirsky's list of potential referees: Boris Pilnyak. Soon after returning to Russia from London in 1923, Pilnyak had risen to high office in one of the writers' organizations that preceded the creation of the monolithic Union. In 1932 Pilnyak was still at liberty, but disgraced, and he eventually 'called on'

Ezhov in a rather less agreeable manner than the commissar's wife had in mind when she made her boast to Mrs Mandelshtam.[17]

In Leningrad, Mirsky's former mentor, Mikhail Kuzmin, in his declining years was an even more doubtful connection, especially after homosexuality was criminalized soon after Mirsky returned to Russia.[18] Zhirmunsky got Mirsky to write an internal review of the translation by Kuzmin of Byron's *Don Juan* that occupied a good deal of the poet's time during his last years. Mirsky said a number of nice things about Kuzmin's mastery of verse form, but took the translation to pieces, and it has still not been published in full.[19]

Still on the scene from among Mirsky's old non-aristocratic friends were some lesser mortals. Mirsky told Maurice Baring in his letter of 1920 from Athens that all his friends had been killed in the wars 'except two', but did not specify who they were. The likely candidates are his old schoolmates from the Tenishev *gimnaziya* Aleksey Sukhotin and Kornily Pokrovsky. Both of them were living in Moscow when Mirsky returned. In his autobiographical account of 1936, Mirsky cited Sukhotin and Pokrovsky as people who could vouch for the veracity of his account of his early years.[20] Sukhotin had become a professor at the Moscow State Pedagogical University, and he was a recognized academic linguist. Vera Traill said that Mirsky continued to see him regularly until the end. About Mirsky's relations with Pokrovsky we will discover more shortly.

Mirsky's sisters had been left behind in France. In his autobiographical statement of 1936, Mirsky stated that he corresponded with them 'infrequently'. But when he was required to give details of his family connections after he was arrested in 1937, Mirsky denied their very existence. Also left behind in Paris were Efron, Rodzevich, and Suvchinsky. That Mirsky remained in contact with these three after he went back to Russia is highly improbable. Perhaps Mirsky heard something about his old comrades from Pasternak after the latter got back to Moscow from the Paris congress of writers in June 1935; he was shown round there mainly by Efron and his daughter Ariadna,[21] and Vera Traill told me that she too saw Pasternak on this occasion.

NOT MUCH ROOM OF HIS OWN

When he got back to Moscow, Mirsky lived for a few weeks in the Intourist Hotel, near the centre. Accommodation in the city, which had regained its old capital status in 1918 and was filling up with government, Party, professional, and diplomatic personnel, was already at a premium by the mid-1920s. Soon after the revolution, family houses and larger apartments had been subdivided into what became the standard Soviet family unit in older buildings, a one-room apartment with shared bathroom and kitchen, or *kommunalka*. This is what happened, for example, to the seven-room quarters on the Volkhonka, a street that runs parallel to the river just south-east of the Kremlin, that the Pasternak family and its entourage had lived in from 1911 until they emigrated. The poet settled into the one room of it he was still entitled to when he returned to Moscow with his wife from Berlin in 1923. This was the address Tsvetaeva had refused to divulge to Mirsky in 1927; it probably never struck her that Pasternak's living conditions were significantly more straitened than the ones she moaned about so much to her correspondents from her various Paris lodgings in the 1920s.

As opposed to the *kommunalki*, apartments in purpose-built or renovated buildings had one living room, less often two, and their own separate kitchen and bathroom. After many years of wandering, the Mandelshtams moved into such an apartment in the autumn of 1933 on Nashchokin pereulok in the centre of Moscow; the poet was arrested there twice, first in 1934 and again, for the last time, in 1938. Mikhail Bulgakov was living in the same building at the times Mandelshtam was arrested there. Only the Party high-ups had any more substantial accommodation than this before the mid-1930s (and not many others after that). Mirsky once made the conventional Communist sneer on this subject, but there is no doubt whatsoever that in this case he is clenching his rotten teeth:

But it must not be thought that [the Bloomsburyites] are in the least degree democrats. They see civilisation as the privilege of people who are well brought up and enjoy leisure. Having 'one's own room' in which one can escape from the outer world and its racket is, so we are informed by a book written by Virginia Woolf on the emancipation of women, the first condition of civilised creative work.[22]

One very strong incentive impelling writers to fall in and apply to join the Union of Soviet Writers when the list was opened in 1932 was the opportunity it promised for access to better accommodation. No writer was above this elementary 'material self-interest', including Mirsky. These engineers of human souls, as Stalin soon dubbed them, all seem to have had a sufficiently advanced sense of the importance of their own bodies to feel thoroughly entitled to their privileges. Their jockeying for perks was encouraged by Stalin's keynote declaration in 1931 to the German journalist Emil Ludwig: 'Only people who are unacquainted with Marxism can have the primitive notion that the Russian Bolsheviks want to pool all wealth and share it out equally.'[23] But Mirsky never climbed very far up the Soviet ladder, nor seemed to want to; his living conditions as a parasite upon the workers' paradise did not differ all that much from what Dorothy Galton had called the 'dingy rooms' he had chosen to live in while he was in London.

In Moscow, Mirsky moved from room to room more frequently than he had in London. After February 1933 he had no stable institutional address. This caused him some inconvenience; his letters to Dorothy Galton contain several complaints about mail being delayed or not received because of his changes of address. His most spectacular complaint, though, came after Miss Galton had sent him yet another consignment of books in 'an enormous box full of shavings' which he had had to carry from the Post Office 'all through Moscow'; Mirsky had the temerity to admonish her and order her in future to use small packets that could be delivered to his door.

Just the same as in emigration, there never seems to have been any doubt that Mirsky would live not only in the capital, but right in the centre of it; and this he managed to do until he was arrested. By December 1932 he had moved into Flat 109, 5 Yazykovsky pereulok, where, as we shall soon learn, there was no bathroom. From mid-February 1933 to late May 1934 Mirsky gives his address as Flat 34, 7 Rusakovskaya Street. It was from here that he told Dorothy Galton on 22 October 1933: 'They are building an underground in Moscow. I went down into the shaft the other day. But at home I suffer a great deal from it because a stone-breaking machine stands under my very window & works 24 hours a day.'

BACK TO LITERATURE

On 4 December 1932 Mirsky apologized to Miss Galton, as in so many letters, for not getting in touch earlier, but excuses himself: 'it is so difficult to write letters when one passes one's days in writing other things, till one's bum is numb and one's fingers ache'. There follows a general description of his new situation: 'As you can guess I have got lots of work to do. Literary work is paid for royally, but the Cooperative Publishing Co. are exceedingly niggardly. So that I earn about *thirty* times (no exaggeration) as much when I am working on my own than when I work for them.' Mirsky mentioned in his autobiographical statement of 1936 that he 'had a salaried job' (*nakhodilsya na sluzhbe*) only from October 1932 to May 1933, at the Publishing House of Foreign Workers, where he contributed to the translation of Lenin into English; and after that he existed on his piecework literary earnings alone.[24] Just as in London, he was very successful back in Russia at making a good living for himself with his pen.

The first letter he wrote to Miss Galton in the new year of 1933 was written on 22 January: 'I see a lot of people and drink a lot of vodka, and work a great deal. But I havn't yet been anywhere outside of Moscow, or even seen very much in Moscow except the Electrograd where I have been several times.'[25] Mirsky apologizes for not replying earlier, pleading pressure of translation work. On 19 February he wrote to Gorky, assuring him that he was working hard and satisfactorily, primarily on the translation of Lenin into English, and also on 'the book about England'. The work of translation that Mirsky ended up with when he first got back to Russia was the last he did of this kind to be independently published.[26] The 'book about England' was to become the last of Mirsky's to be published in English during his lifetime, *The Intelligentsia of Great Britain.*

There is a profound difference between the accounts left by the Soviet citizens who observed Mirsky after his return and those of the foreign visitors who happened to do the same. The former are guarded and full of clichés, the latter significantly more frank and lively. His unpersoning in 1937 meant that subsequently, his name was systematically expunged from the record. Relatively few Soviet literati kept diaries; there is nothing that remotely compares with Kuzmin's (let alone the Tsar's or Mirsky's mother's!) for the prerevolutionary period. One individual who did make the attempt to record a bare minimum about his doings was Korney Chukovsky; but even he desisted between 1936 and 1952, too afraid to risk putting anything down on paper. One great exception to this fear of self-incrimination was his daughter Lidiya, one of the bravest of all Russians, who wrote her immortal novel *Sofya Petrovna* closer to the times it describes than any other account of the Great Purge.[27] The most revealing documents of the time for the modern reader are potentially the millions of depositions made by ordinary people to the NKVD, which have scarcely yet begun to be studied in their totality. But despite all this, some of his new colleagues set down their reaction to Mirsky as they saw him soon after his return.

Aleksandr Gladkov[28] saw Mirsky on one of his early visits to the editorial offices of the *Literary Gazette* on 11 November 1932. The occasion was a reading by Mandelshtam, attended, as Gladkov charmingly notes, 'mainly by the maidens from the editorial office' (*redaktsionnye devitsy*). Gladkov reports that 'he is a curiosity: a former prince with a historic name (Svyatopolk Mirsky), a former *émigré*, aesthete, and member of the English Communist Party'.[29] Following the reading there was a discussion full of what Gladkov called 'worthless words about simplicity'; the critic Selivanovsky was banal, and the best speakers, Gladkov thought, were Shklovsky and Mirsky. Aleksey Selivanovsky (1900–38) had immaculate Party credentials; he was one of Pasternak's main baiters during the 1930s, but his attacks earned him the same reward as Mirsky's defence of the poet.

Mirsky was also observed 'immediately after he returned' by Georgy Munblit at a small literary gathering in Moscow where Nikolay Aseev's new poetry was being discussed. Georgy Nikolaevich Munblit (b. 1904) was at the time a literature-struck Komsomol, and he later became a fairly minor Soviet dramatist. On this occasion there was a fierce polemic. Munblit remembered it particularly because Pasternak and Mandelshtam were both present, and Aseev became angry with them for arguing about their own affairs rather than discussing his poetry. Mirsky sat motionless, with his eyes half closed. During the interval Munblit asked him how all this seemed in the eyes of someone who was new to Soviet literary circles. 'Just like it does to you,' replied Mirsky, deadpan.

Munblit goes on to relate how Mirsky rapidly became a fixture on the Moscow literary scene. Every morning he would repair to the café in the National hotel in the centre of Moscow, order a bottle of Borzhom mineral water, and sit there writing, 'biting his moustache and from time to time absent-mindedly sweeping the room with unseeing eyes'.[30] (His eyes had evidently deteriorated; all the pictures of him after 1932 show him wearing horn-rimmed spectacles with round lenses, whereas only one of the émigré pictures shows him with spectacles.) Munblit says that by about midday a circle of habitués would have gathered around Mirsky and a lively, witty conversation would be under way. This circle was a seedbed of literary rumour and opinion. Mirsky sat among it all 'like a cliff washed by the tide'; more often than not he would be silent, occasionally smiling at the jokes. But he was an essential and valued listener: 'his silent, barely noticeable approval' was the best reward one could possibly earn as a young writer. He would sometimes pick up his bottle of Borzhom and move to another table to get on with his writing, because, as Munblit observes, unlike the majority of the lounge lizards at the National he was serious about his work. He was 'isolated, unsociable, self-enclosed, and he had no real friends in Moscow'.[31] One great exception to this was the poet Eduard Bagritsky, whom Munblit and many other enthusiastic Komsomols regarded as the personification of their ideals. Even more important, Bagritsky seemed to trust Mirsky, something that Munblit says happened very rarely.

According to Munblit, Mirsky simply telephoned Bagritsky one day and said he must meet him. Bagritsky was the idol of the up-and-coming younger poets of Moscow. Munblit had known Bagritsky since 1925, when the poet was living out at Kuntsevo along with other members of the 'Odessa mafia', the fairly extensive group of younger Soviet writers who came from the famous southern port city.

Munblit recalled one day at Kuntsevo hearing Bagritsky give a riveting reading of Elizaveta Polonskaya's translation of Kipling's 'Ballad of East and West' and of his own masterpiece, The Lay of Opanas, still unfinished at the time. Polonskaya's translation had been the lead item in that same journal, The Contemporary West, edited by Chukovsky and Zamyatin, where Mirsky had published his extraordinary article on contemporary English literature in 1923. Bagritsky moved into a newly built apartment block in the centre of Kuntsevo in December 1930 and assembled for himself surroundings that (like Remizov's) everyone remembered who spent any time there: simple furniture, an aquarium, a parrot, and a collection of weapons hanging on the wall. One of the weapons was a Cossack cavalry sabre, which apparently only once came into the hands of a man who knew how to use it; and that man was Mirsky, or 'Tsar Dima', as he was nicknamed by Yury Olesha, another principal member of the Odessa mafia. Munblit thought Mirsky had taught at Oxford while he was in emigration; this became a common item in the legend (see Chapter 9 below). Munblit described Mirsky as 'a tall corpulent man in spectacles, with a wedge-shaped beard and permanently unshaven cheeks who externally resembled the Russian writers of the beginning of the century, such as have not been seen for a long time in Moscow'.

MALCOLM MUGGERIDGE

Much less inhibited than the pen-portraits of Mirsky by his new Soviet colleagues are the descriptions of him by two foreigners who saw him at the time. The first of them was Malcolm Muggeridge, who ran into Mirsky at the New Moscow Hotel on 4 October 1932.[32] Mirsky told Dorothy Galton that he was seeing 'Muggeridge, the new Manch[ester] Guard[ian] correspondent, a very good exhibit of the typical Radical intellectual from Oxford (although I do not think he is from Oxford)'. The introduction to Muggeridge must have come about in England through the Webbs; Muggeridge's wife, Kitty, who went with him to Moscow when he was posted there in 1931, was Mrs Webb's niece. The Webbs briefed the Muggeridges before the latter went to Russia; and the two couples met in Moscow in 1932, when the Webbs were making the visit that led to their notorious apologia for Stalinism, published in 1935, Soviet Communism: A New Civilization? (The question mark was dropped from the title of the second edition, published in 1936.)

Muggeridge's diaries afford some of the most penetrating glimpses of Mirsky's early days back in Moscow; and inevitably, they tell us as much if not more about the observer as they do about the observed. As we have seen, the two men met by chance in the first days of October 1932. Muggeridge noted that Mirsky 'is to work on the standard life of Lenin',[33] manifestly misunderstanding the nature of Mirsky's real activity, which was hack translation. Then, Muggeridge records that Mirsky 'looked in' on 28 November, and discussed with him the possibility of sharing a room when Kitty Muggeridge left for England to have her baby. 'I tried to get at his mood,' writes Muggeridge, 'but he gave away nothing. "It is just as I expected to find it", he said. Yet somehow he seemed sadder than when I saw him before. More sombre. I know he is a little mad.'

On 1 December, Muggeridge noted that he let his diary go for three weeks at this point in order to finish his first novel. So the following entry may well summarize a relationship that developed during the course of several unrecorded meetings:

Mirsky is a great puzzle. As time goes on he is less and less eager to see anything of me. This may be because he finds me a bore, or because he is a bit frightened. He would never, of course, say. I don't think he is happy in Russia; but then I doubt if he has ever been particularly happy anywhere. He is difficult to talk to. All the while his eyes move here and there. It might be shiftiness; but I'm sure it's not. His face is full of fanaticism, and sombre.

On the first day of 1933 Mirsky dined at Muggeridge's along with the Chamberlins[34] and someone called Barnes, 'an ill-assorted company', as Muggeridge notes in his diary.

Sonia [Chamberlin] treats Mirsky with exaggerated respect. Mirsky himself sat in glum silence most of the evening. 'Oh, Mr Mirsky', Sonia said, 'We met Sir Bernard Pares in London. He talked a lot about you, and said how sorry he was to lose you from his staff'. 'The bloody liar', Mirsky suddenly interrupted, and then relapsed into silence.[35]

On 13 January 1933 Mirsky met Muggeridge again in order to introduce the journalist to some friends, who are referred to by Muggeridge as 'a Polish writer and his wife', and who lived in an apartment block specially reserved for writers—whether Muggeridge mentions this detail because he thinks it outlandish or enviable, he does not say. The writer spoke French and had a large number of Russian books and some French. He showed Muggeridge some de luxe Soviet editions, which Muggeridge found 'pretentious and tawdry'. He also told Muggeridge that the Soviet censorship was 'not severe'. The Polish writer's wife 'turned on to me a great flood of advocacy of the Soviet Government', which was 'a little embarrassing'. 'The Polish writer was less enthusiastic than his wife; walked nervously up and down the room while he was talking. A Jew, though Mirsky said not. I have an idea that the Jews, with characteristic shrewdness, are beginning to feel that it is time to move on.'[36]

On 16 January 1933, Muggeridge was taken to another party by Mirsky, and met the Jasienskis again, this time in the company of another remarkable foreign sympathizer with the Soviet cause:

It was in the very spacious and, for Moscow, luxuriously furnished flat of Louis Aragon, the French 'Surrealist' poet. I think Mirsky was in love with his girl—Elsa. The Polish writer and his fat wife . . . were there. Elsa is beautiful. . . . When I looked closely at her I saw that she was hard and unhappy. We ate with a great air of joviality, and Mirsky drank a lot of vodka. He grew rather flushed, and more talkative than usual. I was shy and gauche. After supper the Russian took Elsa in his arms and began to kiss her; Aragon walked about uneasily with the familiar strained expression of someone who is jealous but who doesn't believe in jealousy; Mirsky sank into a state of utter gloom; sat on the floor; wouldn't speak or smile. They were a dingy crew, intellectuals who had moved their tents. . . .[37]

The 'girl' being mauled by Mirsky is Elsa Triolet (née Ella Yurievna Kagan, 1896–1970), one of the few Russians to make a reputation as a writer in their second language to rival that of Nabokov. She was the long-time companion of Louis Aragon (1897–1982), who had been a member of the French Communist Party since 1927, and survived much longer than most of his like-minded colleagues.[38] Mme Triolet is best known to literary Russians as the sister of Lilya Brik, whom Elsa introduced to one of her early admirers, the poet Mayakovsky; Lilya became the great love of his life.[39] Mirsky's uninhibited behaviour in the scene with Triolet that Muggeridge records is, as usual, attributable to the amount of vodka he had consumed.

The scene at the Aragon apartment is the last diary entry by Muggeridge that refers to Mirsky. However, Muggeridge reworked this material into a novel which was published soon after he returned to England in disillusionment.[40] The book harnesses the full force of Muggeridge's talent for denigration to express his revulsion for the various foreign visitors who (like the author himself before he came into contact with the reality) have seen Soviet Russia as Utopia and have made pilgrimages to worship at the shrine. This is all fair comment, and for most people it remains politically justified—especially with the benefit of hindsight—but the casual anti-Semitism and anti-Americanism that are continually voiced in the novel make it extremely distasteful reading. The remorseless clarity of Muggeridge's political insight saves the enterprise. Long before the purges of the later 1930s, even before the murder of Kirov, in this novel as in his contemporary reports for the *Manchester Guardian* Muggeridge exposed the authentic anti-humanitarian nature of the Soviet experiment for anyone who would listen. Many would not; Muggeridge's diary of his Moscow days makes clear just how reluctant his editors were to accept the veracity of his reports—about the catastrophic man-made famine in Ukraine, for example.

A character based unmistakably on Mirsky appears towards the end of *Winter in Moscow*; he is given the name 'Prince Alexis'. He is first observed at a party, where

Three of the girls with fringes and high-waisted dresses grouped themselves round Prince Alexis. He looked at them mournfully; a dark-bearded man with a decaying mouth; savage and unhappy and lonely. 'Tell us', the girls chanted together like school-children reciting a multiplication table, 'how you, a prince, an aristocrat, became a Communist'. Prince Alexis made noises in his stomach. . . . 'I'm a Communist because of you', he said savagely.

Muggeridge offers a reconstruction of Mirsky's ideas and motivation:

The Dictatorship of the Proletariat was, to him, a principle; a law, that he believed in because it was exact. He had come to it at last as some debauchees come at last to join a religious order, or as some scientists and philosophers come at last to absorb themselves in the mathematics of the Old Testament. The more he had come to detest human beings the more attractive the Dictatorship of the Proletariat had seemed, because it alone opened out the possibility of clearing the world altogether of human beings and leaving only a principle existing, like electricity, in space. In the beginning was the Word, and in the end the Word, too. He wanted such an end.[41]

The manifestly autobiographical hero of the novel is called Wraithby, and he walks home from the party with Prince Alexis. 'I hate the Dictatorship of the Proletariat,' he observes.

'Don't be a fool,' Prince Alexis said.

'I hate the Dictatorship of the Proletariat,' Wraithby repeated, knowing he was being ridiculous; not minding; 'and so do you.'

Prince Alexis stopped. His voice was pompous and dry. It rolled down the silent street prophesying wrath to come. 'War soon. Europe falling into chaos. All except Russia. Then the great conquest which Marx and Lenin prophesied. Then the final victory.'

After all, Wraithby thought, what is he but a man who's managed to be a parasite in three regimes? Aristocrat under Tzarism. Professor under capitalism. Proletarian man-of-letters under the Dictatorship of the Proletariat.[42]

The speech delivered by 'Prince Alexis' in the Moscow street compels Wraithby to thoughtful silence, and then he turns again to the Prince, and invites him to come in for a nightcap. The prince refuses the drink, but instead asks 'shyly' for a bath, explaining that there was no bathroom where he lived. Wraithby agrees. Afterwards—

He watched Prince Alexis dry himself. His body was white and tender like a boy's. The head; so battered and decayed, did not seem to belong to it; like an old worn hood on a new motor-car. All the wear and tear of living seemed to have gone into the head, leaving the rest of his body fresh and new.

'Do you really believe', Wraithby asked, 'that these awful plays are good; these wretched people happy; these revolting Jews, great leaders and prophets; these decrepit buildings, fine architecture; these dingy slums, new socialist cities; these empty slogans bawled mechanically, a new religion; these stale ideas (superficial in themselves and even then misunderstood), the foundation and hope of the future?'

'You don't understand in the least,' Prince Alexis said, drying himself slowly as though reluctant to cover up his body and leave only his stained head exposed. 'You're a fool. Plays and people and leaders and buildings and slogans have nothing to do with it. They don't matter in the least.'

'What does matter then?'

The bathroom had no windows. Steam hung in it. It might have been a remote cave. Or just space. 'The inevitability of it all. The fact that it had to happen. Forces interacting and producing a resultant force. The fulfilment of the law and the prophets.'

In the beginning was the Word, and in the end the Word, too.[43]

This, then, was the impression the newly returned Mirsky made on a sensitive, politically sophisticated, and newly disenchanted observer. It is the most far-reaching interpretation of the Communist Mirsky's character and mentality to have been ventured, with the possible exception of the description left by Edmund Wilson on the basis of his acquaintanceship with Mirsky in Moscow a little over two years later.

The commitment to Soviet Communism from a belief in the 'inevitability' of the Socialist revolution sounds a familiar note. Nadezhda Mandelshtam devoted one of the most compelling chapters in the first volume of her memoirs, 'Capitulation', to a description and analysis of this mentality among Russians of Mirsky's generation. Her great first book is a tribute to her husband, who was one of them, but one who understood earlier and more profoundly than any other literary intellectual what was going on in Russia, and was organically incapable of taking part in it even if he had wanted to and been allowed to:

It was none other than the people of the twenties who began making a clear-cut distinction between the sheep and the goats, between 'us' and 'them', between those on the side of the 'new' and those who had still not forgotten the most elementary rules of human society. . . . it was actually during the twenties that the entire groundwork was laid down for our future: the casuistical dialectic, the dethronement of values, the will towards unanimity and subordination.[44]

Mirsky was fully aware of what was going on in Russia as the 1920s came to a close and Stalin consolidated his position. But the contemplation of this process from abroad, and the contrast he drew between it and what was happening around him in his places of emigration, made Mirsky into one of the new fanatics. And this, we do well to remember, was before Hitler came to power on 30 January 1933 and set about implementing policies that would convince so many intellectuals that there was no other choice but Stalin.

The nihilistic, anti-humanitarian ground Muggeridge stipulated for Mirsky's commitment to the Communist cause is one of the most devastating things that has ever been asserted about him by any of the people who have claimed to be able to read his mind. Muggeridge may be talking about that same inner void, that incapacity for human contact, which Marina Tsvetaeva discerned in Mirsky and felt so desperately compelled to supply from her own resources when she came to visit him in London in 1926. It may be evidence of that willed suppression of individuality in favour of the collective that the émigré Mirsky spoke of with reference to Mayakovsky and others. But Muggeridge's capitalized 'Word' is a misplaced exaggeration, even as a metaphor; what mattered to Mirsky was never some divine or transcendental Word, but— at least until he was 35—the written words of literature.

Muggeridge's sense that Mirsky had undergone a bitter disillusionment after he arrived in Moscow has been echoed by several other people who saw him there, all of them visitors rather than Soviet citizens. Whatever may have been the case, there would be much greater squalor and humiliation to come than a Moscow flat without bathroom before Mirsky's stained head and white body were laid to rest.

THE GREAT LEAP FORWARD

The Russia to which Mirsky returned from emigration was on its way to becoming what is now thought of as quintessentially Stalin's, after the 'Great

Leap Forward', literally 'Great Breakthrough' (*Velikii perelom*) towards Sovietization in 1929. There will never be agreement about what kind of society
this was intended to be, much less the degree to which it actually was what it
proclaimed itself to be at the top of its voice; nor about the significance of
intention as against expediency and contingency in the creation of it. Nor yet
will there ever be agreement about the extent to which it was a dictatorship by
one man. Except, that is, among Russians, and in my experience, especially
those Russians who actually lived through the Stalin years. For them, the attribution of all crimes to Stalin personally seems to be the most accessible way
to fend off the idea of endemic national connivance and the guilt that is thereby
entailed, and then perhaps to console themselves by resorting to the national
myth that they were destined to suffer, purify themselves, and, Christ-like,
save the world by taking upon themselves the worst ordeals it was capable of
inflicting.[45]

The most distinctive characteristic of Stalinism, at least for the foreigner
who did not experience it directly, lies unmistakably and beyond all revisionism in its totalitarian intent—the forcible creation of a system in which all economic, political, social, and cultural activities would be harnessed towards
achieving goals set by the centre and subject to centralized mechanisms of
control. In Stalin's Russia these goals were formulated by the Party leadership
and its apparatus, articulated by an information system based on monopoly
ownership of the media, and enforced by the most insidious policing system
ever developed. The system of censorship described by Jasienski to Muggeridge as 'not severe' had in fact been continually refined and extended since
the first decrees on the subject immediately after the October revolution, and
Mirsky had commented on this process in some of his *émigré* articles. He had
no illusions about this or anything else that was going on in Soviet Russia. The
central institution of censorship, Glavlit, had been radically reformed by a
decree of 5 October 1930. One of the main aspects of the system that was
singled out for strengthening on this occasion concerned materials coming into
the USSR from abroad.

The system of proscriptive pre-publication censorship was tightened up
again with the decree concerning military secrets of November 1933. The
institutionalization of Socialist Realism soon afterwards brought in a strong
element of prescription to add to the centuries-old Russian practice of pro-
scription.[46] These systems were policed by the Party, and by a centralized internal security service which rapidly became a state within the state, possessing
its own armed forces and having at its disposal a system of concentration camps
that was one of the vital elements in the planned economy and the process of
social engineering.

The security services were aided and abetted, as far as it seems possible to
be sure, by enthusiastic cooperation as much as if not more than by compulsory collaboration, expressed mainly in a system of informing that was offi-

cially regarded as the duty of a good citizen. The denunciation (*donos*) became the most important genre in the creative repertoire of this newly literate society, used for selfish ends as well as idealistic ones. It is irresponsible to talk about all this nowadays without constantly bearing in mind the eventual cost to the Russians in terms of human lives, physical and mental suffering, and moral and ethical degeneration. It adds up to an issue that their government has still not been able to confront, let alone attempt to exorcise or atone for by the institution of due process in identifying, investigating, and putting on trial the surviving perpetrators. There has been no equivalent in Russia for South Africa's Truth and Reconciliation Commission.

At the time, the goals were indubitably seen by a majority of those involved as ultimately benign, if unavoidably harsh (but authentically and laudably 'Russian') in terms of short-run costs; not only in covert informing and denunciation was there more enthusiastic cooperation than submission to coercion. The pre-revolutionary ruling class had been eliminated, and so had the non-Bolshevik and later the anti-Stalin segments among the leaders who had carried this process through. The system of education and training had been radically overhauled, with pre-revolutionary teachers being forced to conform or being discarded, and proletarian and peasant origin taking precedence over other qualifications for access. Across the whole of society, Stalinism offered unprecedented opportunities for young and energetic men to become leaders, and similar women to become their pampered helpmeets. In his day-to-day activities, from 1932 onwards Mirsky's fate was in the hands of men who were as a rule ten years younger than he was, and who until less than a decade before could have aspired at best only to be the servants of him and his like.

The contemporary Soviet media soon began to articulate public triumphalism on an unprecedented scale, with Stalin increasingly identified personally as the genius who was planning, motivating, and leading the giant strides forward that the country was taking. The cult of Stalin is sometimes said to have been initiated by Karl Radek's article 'The Architect of Socialist Society', published in the New Year issue of *Pravda* for 1934.[47] The one literary work that adequately represented the horrific process of social reconstruction, Andrey Platonov's *The Foundation Pit*, written between December 1929 and April 1930, was not published in Russia until 1987; and probably only contemporaries could fully appreciate the veracity of what it has to say.

In the early 1930s a succession of measures tightened up the state control of Soviet society, resulting in a general regimentation that was much more repressive than the case had been even before the abolition of serfdom in 1861. First came labour law: in January 1931 prison sentences were introduced for the violation of labour discipline; in February 1931 compulsory 'labour books' were brought in, with every worker required to register their place of employment; in July 1932 it became legal for state enterprises to transfer workers from one plant to another without their consent; and on 7 August 1932 the death

penalty was introduced for the theft of state or collective property. All this cul-
minated on 27 December 1932, just after Mirsky got back to Moscow, with the
reintroduction of the internal passport. Collective farm workers were not
issued passports, and were thus tied to their place of work unless they were
prepared to risk becoming outlaws. Just as significant were the changes in
Soviet family law as the 1930s went on. The paramount need, in the eyes of
the Party, was for a settled and expanding labour force, and so it was conve-
niently recognized that socialism and the family were in fact natural allies,
and not antagonists, as had previously been the general idea in the revolutionary movement. And so on-demand abortion and easy divorce went out, and
rewards for 'Heroine Mothers' came in.[48]

None of these things can have meant much to Mirsky personally, but they
go to make up one more respect in which he was becoming what the Russians
call a 'white crow' among his fellow intellectuals and Soviet citizens in general.
As they became professionalized and entrenched their privileges in the course
of the 1930s, Mirsky's literary colleagues tended to acquire a plump career wife
in a fur coat, a peasant woman freshly arrived from the countryside to do the
domestic chores, and a peasant nanny to look after the child—usually only one,
and at most two, since the married ladies of the intelligentsia did not go in for
heroine motherhood. And their menfolk spent as much if not more time lobbying to upgrade their square footage and making their reservations for vacations at the Crimean resorts as they did writing. Meanwhile, Mirsky (at least
as Muggeridge saw him at the Aragons') seems to have behaved according to
the old socialist tradition—conducting himself as if women were the common
property of the men and expecting husbands to do their best not to be seen
treating them like chattels. In appearance, too, Mirsky was old-fashioned. Just
as in London, he managed to look distinctively sloppy after he returned to
Moscow, helped by the fact that proletarian and paramilitary chic for men had
now passed out of style, yielding to the ill-tailored suits that were one of the
outward signs of the *embourgeoisement* of the Soviet writer under Stalinism—
the customary absence of a tie being a vestigial nod towards the old ideals.
Mirsky persisted with the Lenin rig: three-piece suit with collar and tie, and
peaked cloth cap. His full black beard made him even more of a white crow.

Much more closely than by the reforms in family law, Mirsky was potentially touched by the criminalization of homosexuality, which came about previously to and independently of the major Stalinist reforms of family law. The
Politbyuro resolved to pass legislation making 'sodomy' illegal, in secret, on
16 December 1933; the government adopted the legislation on 1 April 1934.
The move had been preceded by a roundup of homosexuals in Moscow and
Leningrad in September 1933.[49] The reason seems to have been paranoia about
their loyalty and trustworthiness as servants of the state; according to the standards of the time, Soviet Russia was if anything acting normally in taking the
official view it did.

In addition to mass starvation, one of the most grievous consequences of industrialization and collectivization was the dehumanization of the Party. In the early 1930s it finally degenerated from being a life of service for idealistic volunteers into a haven for careerists. The Party was the weapon of terror used to implement collectivization and industrialization, and its mentality and mode of operation adjusted accordingly. It became in fact not much more in the last analysis than the public face of a private army, i.e. the security organs. Coercion was applied by the Party first and foremost by the leadership against its own members. Until late 1935, however, the times were relatively 'vegetarian', as the Russians say; the times then became carnivorous, and more gluttonous than ever before in Russian peacetime history. The situation was formalized in July 1934 when the old OGPU (General State Political Directorate) was reorganized as the NKVD (People's Commissariat of Internal Affairs), with Genrikh Yagoda as its head. This institution was the direct descendant of the ministry Mirsky's father had briefly headed in 1904–5, but one grown vastly more tentacular and ruthless. The NKVD was now defined as a 'Special Sector' of the Central Committee, making it in effect a unit of Stalin's private secretariat.

The show trial, sometimes thought of as a quintessentially Stalinist measure dreamed up by the abominable Vyshinsky, was in fact a venerable institution by the time Mirsky got back to Moscow. Such trials had been held several times, the first being of a woman, Countess Sofia Panina, the Deputy Minister of Education in the Provisional Government, on 10 December 1917.[50] In 1922 the rump of the Social Revolutionaries were put on trial; in 1928 the Shakhty workers—which is when the ex-Menshevik Vyshinsky made his debut as a prosecutor; then in 1930 came the 'PromPartiya' or 'Industrial Party', proponents of an alternative strategy to the Great Breakthrough; in 1931 the rump of the Mensheviks; and then in 1933 the British engineers from the Manchester firm of Metropolitan Vickers, charged with 'wrecking'. From the expulsion of Trotsky in 1929 until the assassination of Kirov in September 1934 Stalin was exploring various methods of achieving the elimination of dissidents within the party; after that date, physical liquidation was resorted to without compunction.

The most spectacular case at the time Mirsky went back to Russia concerned one of his exact contemporaries, Martemyan Ryutin (1890–1937), a candidate member of the Central Committee from 1927, the only prominent Bolshevik actually to set about organizing practical opposition to Stalin. He was expelled from the Party in September 1930 for expressing his views, and arrested. On 17 January 1931 he was acquitted, released, and re-admitted into the Party. In June 1932 he wrote his 'Appeal to all members of the All-Union Communist Party (Bolsheviks)', and the remarkable 'Ryutin platform' calling for an end to Stalin's leadership. On 23 September 1932 Ryutin was expelled again and arrested. The question of whether or not to execute him was referred to Stalin and the Politbyuro, and the death sentence was supported only by Kaganovich. The grounds were that the execution of Old Bolsheviks for purely political deviation was an unknown practice in Party tradition. On 2 October the 'Ryutin group' was expelled. The ringleaders were given ten years, and twenty-nine other individuals got shorter sentences. As a consequence of the 'exposure' of Ryutin, Zinoviev and Kamenev were exiled to the Urals; they were brought back to the centre in May 1933 and 'surrendered', calling for their fellow oppositionists to cease resistance. On 12 January 1933 the Central Committee passed a resolution on purging the Party, and well over a million members were expelled in the course of the next year.

From 26 January to 10 February 1934 the Party held its XVII Congress, the 'Congress of Victors' that celebrated the first Five-Year Plan and the collectivization of agriculture. The former oppositionists spoke—Zinoviev, Kamenev, Bukharin, Rykov, Tomsky, Preobrazhensky, Pyatakov, Radek, and Lominadze—all of them proclaiming their acceptance of Stalinist orthodoxy. There was a mood of reconciliation—especially, the Party unilaterally claimed, between itself and the people. The simultaneous rise of Nazism was one genuine factor in working for Party solidarity under Stalin at this time, as also was the widely held idea, standard among arguments for the status quo everywhere, that Stalin was the only possible leader the USSR had and that things would fall apart without him. At this conference Stalin proclaimed that 'There is nobody left to beat'; but of the 1,966 delegates who listened in fearful rapture to him saying this, none of them daring to be seen to be the first to stop applauding, 1,108 were to be shot over the next few years. None of the prominent recusants survived.

This was not all due to personal paranoia on the Great Leader's part. Stalin 'had brutalized the Party, but he had not enslaved it'.[51] There was still an element inside the Party leadership that remembered Lenin's dying warning and objected to Stalin's pre-eminence. Kirov and some other leaders were gaining popularity; there was backstage talk of removing Stalin from the General Secretaryship and the possibility of instituting a more moderate leader. And then on 1 December 1934 came the assassination of Kirov, which has now been shown beyond all doubt to have been engineered by Stalin himself. After this, the bacchanalia began. On 17 December 1934 there were denunciations of Zinoviev and his 'anti-Party group', then came the arrest of Zinoviev and Kamenev. On 29 December 1934 Nikolaev and other suspects in the assassination of Kirov were sentenced and shot in short order, the haste being in most people's eyes one very good piece of evidence that Stalin wanted these people out of the way. On 15–16 January 1935 Zinoviev and Kamenev, the so-called 'Moscow centre', were tried in Leningrad. Zinoviev was sentenced to ten years, Kamenev to five. Shortly after this came the trial of the Leningrad NKVD chiefs, the light sentences that resulted usually considered to be evidence of Stalin's protection, evidence of his complicity in Kirov's murder.

NOT A WORD TO MISS GALTON

Needless to say, there is not a word about any of this in Mirsky's letters to Dorothy Galton in London. In his public and private utterances Mirsky maintained the convention of enthusiastic complicity. He had little option: open dissent was tantamount to suicide from about the end of 1934. And silence was just as suspicious as speaking out, if not more so. Mirsky's published work now began to be topped and tailed with ritual enthusiastic endorsement of the Soviet system. He was aware, like everyone else, of course, that his private utterances might well be held against him. For example, he wrote to Dorothy Galton on 22 October 1933 that 'Things are changing here very rapidly. The harvest as I suppose you know was first class and the peasants have sprung into unprecedented wealth.'

Even more significant than this piece of gross disinformation are the resonant silences in Mirsky's letters to Miss Galton, the only continuous link he maintained with the world in which he had spent the 1920s. On the night of 16–17 May 1934, Mandelshtam was arrested. Anna Akhmatova was visiting from Leningrad at the time.[52] The search of the apartment went on for most of the night, watched by the two women, and accompanied by the sound of Hawaiian guitar records from next door, where the poet Kirsanov lived. Osip Mandelshtam was arrested and taken to the Lubyanka for interrogation. Akhmatova and Nadezhda Mandelshtam began frantic lobbying. They got Pasternak to 'call on' Bukharin, and Akhmatova and Pasternak went together to the apartment of the critic Usievich,[53] where they saw the top brass of the nascent Union of Writers. Akhmatova also went to see Pilnyak, believing that he was still a force to be reckoned with. It was on 25 May 1934—the very day that Mirsky wrote his only surviving letter from Moscow to Mandelshtam's old flame Salomeya Halpern, and another letter to Dorothy Galton—that under interrogation Mandelshtam finally wrote out and admitted to having composed what was tantamount to his death warrant, the poem about Stalin for which someone as yet unidentified (almost certainly V. P. Stavsky) had denounced him ('We live without feeling the land 'neath our feet').

On 26 May Mandelshtam was sentenced to exile in Cherdyn, and he left Moscow on 28 May, accompanied by his wife. Soon after, Stalin made his notorious telephone call to Pasternak to enquire why he had asked Bukharin to intervene, and to consult about what to do with Mandelshtam. On the strength of his conversation with Pasternak he decided that Mandelshtam was to be 'isolated, but not eliminated'. Mandelshtam was allowed back to Moscow in May 1937, just before Mirsky was arrested. The poet was finally taken nearly a year after Mirsky, on 3 May 1938, and sentenced on 2 August, but he died before Mirsky. Mirsky never published a single word about Mandelshtam's post-revolutionary writing after he went back to Russia; nor did he about Akhmatova's. Much less did he say anything about them to anyone in his letters. But it is inconceivable that he did not know what was happening to these contemporaries, whose work he had written about so much in former years. The contrast between Mirsky's letters to Miss Galton from Moscow and those he had written to Suvchinsky from London in the 1920s point up vividly the difference between an open society and one where fear is paramount, denunciation officially encouraged as a citizen's duty, and awareness of the secret police is uppermost in everyone's mind.

Contact with the outside had been getting more difficult since the early 1920s. The USSR, increasingly the drum-beating world leader of the Communist International, permitted its citizens to come into contact only with persons and documents which it deemed sufficiently sanitized.[54] Instead of turning outward, it closed its borders and behaved like an international, multicultural concern only in terms of the non-Russian constituent nationalities ideologically imprisoned on the inside. For Mirsky, with his cosmopolitan European education and cultural outlook, the resulting prospect was not good. As a career commodity, a knowledge of Georgian or Armenian, say, very soon became more advantageous than a knowledge of French or English. And the classic canon of these literatures, in which Mirsky had schooled himself since childhood, was out of fashion; it is enough to look through the *Literary Gazette* for the period 1932–5 to see that the leading foreign figures are such as Babbitt, Dos Passos, and Upton Sinclair.

There was still a certain amount of direct personal contact. Some of Mirsky's old acquaintances visited Moscow during the years after 1932. Miss Galton herself visited Moscow twice, accompanying Professor Hyman Levy in 1934 and Sir Bernard Pares at the very end of 1935. When this latter visit was in prospect, Mirsky gave Miss Galton some stern instructions: '*I do not want to see B.P.!* So do not give him my new address or in fact any address (except something absolutely misleading).' However, Miss Galton seems to have insisted on a meeting, and she made Mirsky shake hands with his former boss. Pares recorded: 'We met in Moscow in 1935, on the stairs, so to speak, I coming in and he going out, and had a pleasant chat.'[55] This would have been on Pares's first visit to Soviet Russia, in December 1935,[56] the same visit that is described in Pares's book *Moscow Admits a Critic.* Even the old anti-Bolshevik warrior Pares had reconciled himself to some extent with Stalinism; with precisely the same reasoning as in the years before 1914, he decided that a tyrannical Russia was still a better ally for Britain than a militarized Germany.

Mirsky's letters to Miss Galton record a steady stream of other transitory figures. We shall soon see that after he had been arrested, Mirsky's interrogators were very interested in these people. Mirsky also met some visiting foreigners by teaching in English on various literary subjects. In early 1934 he informed Miss Galton that he had just finished a course of lectures on Soviet literature at something called 'the American Institute' in Moscow. In a postscript he told Miss Galton that he was reading *Lady Chatterley's Lover*, and liked it 'better than I expected from its reputation'. A copy of the book must have been brought in by one of the people Mirsky met, possibly a foreign correspondent. Mirsky apparently felt no inclination to make use of his old comrades in the CPGB, though; he may even have got wind of the attitude towards him that was expressed in a backstabbing official letter to the ideological boss Pavel Yudin in September 1934 by Ralph Fox, the leading literary light among them: 'Of course, as long as you have English "specialists" like Mirsky, things will be in a sorry state.'[57]

Mirsky's letters to Dorothy Galton show that there was no way of acquiring current Western literature in Moscow except by asking for it to be sent or brought privately from abroad, and paid for at source with hard currency. The letters contain extensive and shamelessly peremptory lists of *desiderata* which include such elementary items as the poetry of Hardy and Kipling, and the *Oxford English Dictionary*. On 19 February 1933 Mirsky thanked Miss Galton for sending W. H. Auden's *The Orators* and requested more Auden and also Spender: 'You must try and explain to them, that it is highly important what they are thought about here [*sic*]. And that largely depends on me.' It did indeed largely depend on him; hardly anybody else had access to the newer books in English, and precious few people could understand them. He was also dependent on Miss Galton for information about what was going on in the world, but he could only permit himself to ask about what the hard left-wing press was saying. Mirsky was thus completely cut off from independent information, as was the vast majority of the Soviet population. He was also cut off from some elementary tools of his trade; he asks Miss Galton at various times for things like a good penknife, some blue-black Waterman's ink, and coffee, though of course only 'as much as possible within customs regulations'. And then there was that pair of trousers for his expanding 'waiste'; to go out in, for as we shall see, at home he worked in his dressing gown, no doubt hoping to save the seat of the trousers he had brought with him back to Russia.

Mirsky told Miss Galton in a letter written while he was still at the Intourist Hotel on 19 October 1932 that he was

still in a rather indefinite position. I have got plenty of work, but I do not yet know to what sort of work I will settle down as my main job. I have not seen much of the country yet but have chiefly been seeing people, especially literary people because this is the line of least resistance for me.

This must have been something of a humiliation for Mirsky, perhaps the most proximate reason for the sense of disillusion that Muggeridge perceived in him. He had made a maximal and irreversible demonstration of loyalty, and been rewarded by being put to drudgery as a translator. This situation would change quite rapidly in the months to come, though, and the change would be due quite directly to Gorky, working most of the time through his right-hand man,

Leopold Averbakh. But there was a limit to what Mirsky would be trusted to do.

THE UNION OF WRITERS

Stalin's unmistakable agenda was to make literature an instrument of Party control. The decree of 23 April 1932, a date which Russian intellectuals tend to identify as the beginning of a new age in literature, uses a key word that was to become international in the 1980s, *perestroika*: 'On the Restructuring of Literary Organizations'. The Central Committee announced its intention to create a monolithic Union of Soviet Writers; and it abolished all other organizations in the field of literature. On 15 May an Organizing Committee (*Orgkom*) formally under Gorky's chairmanship was set up to bring the Union into being, and to prepare its founding Congress, about which there was rancorous disagreement before it was finalized as a huge international showpiece with Gorky at centre stage. The decisive meeting in the preparatory process took place about a month after Mirsky got back to Russia, on 26 October 1932. Stalin, Voroshilov, Kaganovich, and other eminent men with significant contributions to make to the wellbeing of Russian culture met for dinner at Gorky's mansion with about fifty writers. This infernal banquet went on until 5 in the morning, and Stalin consumed an entire bottle of brandy after the plentiful wine he took with dinner. The evening had begun, naturally, with vodka and snacks. Several accounts of the proceedings mention the mingling of the two mighty moustaches as by dawn's early light Stalin and Gorky kissed each other goodbye. At what point in the proceedings Stalin made his speech about 'engineers of human souls' and Socialist Realism is not quite clear from the various accounts. But this grotesque occasion can justifiably be seen as the authentic moment of conception of Soviet literature in its Stalinist phase.

The dissolution of RAPP under the decree of April 1932 was the beginning of the end for Averbakh, though for a year or so he remained at the centre of things before being sent away in 1934 to be secretary of the Party committee at Uralmash, the enormous heavy engineering factory that had been founded at Sverdlovsk in the Urals in 1928. This was a demotion: Averbakh was in effect exiled from literature. And his post was no sinecure: he soon complained to Gorky that he was mentally and physically exhausted. Mirsky seems to have formed a warm personal relationship with Averbakh, and went to visit him in Sverdlovsk, perhaps at the behest of Gorky, in the summer of 1935.[58] Unfortunately for Mirsky, this meant that his name was indelibly linked with that of the critic not just as a colleague but as a personal friend; and Averbakh was shortly to be not only disgraced but anathematized.

And so the juggernaut was rolling when Mirsky got back. The most con-

vincing account of what it was like for a member of the literary intelligentsia
to find oneself in its path is by Nadezhda Mandelshtam. The reading at which
Gladkov saw Mirsky on 10 November 1932 was the same occasion that is mentioned by Mandelshtam's widow in her memoirs; written long after the event,
and after many years of struggling to survive and preserve her husband's literary legacy, they are anything but circumspect:

M[andelshtam] imperiously steered his life towards the doom that lay in wait for him.
. . . In the winter of 1932–33, at a reading M[andelshtam] gave at the *Literary Gazette*
offices, Markish suddenly understood everything and declared: 'You are leading yourself by the hand to your own execution.' He was rephrasing Mandelshtam's own lines,
a variant reading of 'I have led myself by the hand down the streets . . .'[59]

THE INTELLIGENTSIA OF GREAT BRITAIN

In October 1933, a year after his return, Mirsky reported to Miss Galton: 'My
occupations are chiefly literary and I have much less to do with politics than I
used to in England. I have written a book on the English intelligentsia and am
preparing another on the literature of the Imperialist bourgeoisie, chiefly in
France and England.' Here we see Mirsky responding to the demands that were
made of him to prove his credentials as a worthy returnee. The second book
he mentions here was never published as such; it ended up as a series of articles in various journals. The first book, though, became for a time his best
known, even more so than the history of Russian literature. However, its notoriety lasted only a couple of years. The original is a shoddily produced and now
extremely rare little item under the title *Intellidzhentsia*, which in the original
Cyrillic is a phonetic representation of an English word originally borrowed
from Russian. Published in Moscow in 1934, the book teems with sneering,
arrogant contempt for the British intellectual élite, and especially the self-
conscious caste that had taken Mirsky to itself during his Bloomsbury years.
The book is far better known in Alec Brown's translation as *The Intelligentsia
of Great Britain*, published in London in 1935 by Victor Gollancz with his
trademark glaring yellow dust-jacket designed by Stanley Morison, the author
described as 'Dmitri Mirsky (*ci-devant* Prince Mirsky)'.

Brown's translation takes many liberties with Mirsky's text, and uses an
English style much less elegant than Mirsky's own. Here is Mirsky warming
up before putting his old Bloomsbury acquaintances to the sword. The first
two paragraphs involuntarily suggest why Mirsky had fitted in so well when
he first arrived in London, and what comes after suggests equally why he found
his new friends irksome:

The basic trait of Bloomsbury is a mixture of philosophic rationalism, political rationalism, estheticism, and a cult of the individuality [*sic*]. Their radicalism is definitely

bourgeois, a product not even of Shaw's new progressivism or the fabians, but of the old bourgeois radicalism and utilitarianism. . . . Bloomsbury liberalism can be defined as a thin-skinned humanism for enlightened and sensitive members of the capitalist class who do not desire the outer world to be such as might be prone to cause them any displeasing impression.

The atmosphere of Bloomsbury is extremely aristocratic, the atmosphere of gentlemen in well-furnished studies. Bloomsburians live amid books, 'great minds' of the past (as assessed according to their outlook, of course), and move in the best intellectual and esthetic circles (as assessed, etc.) of the day. They avoid all the extremes and abnormalities, though they treat everything which is original and 'inspired' with great respect.

Their rationalism and liberalism mark them off very sharply from the common or garden esthetic bohemians of modern times, and also very sharply from the Russian modernism of the opening of the century. Being theoreticians of the passive, dividend-drawing and consuming section of the bourgeoisie, they are extremely intrigued by their own minutest inner experiences, and count them an inexhaustible treasure store of further more minutious inner experiences. They have a high opinion of Dostoievsky and of Freud.[60]

Mirsky is equally scathing about 'The Progressives' (the Fabians, Bernard Shaw, Wells and Chesterton, Keynes, and Russell), other 'Highbrows' besides the Bloomsburyites (D. H. Lawrence and Aldous Huxley, among others), about 'Religion, etcetera', and eventually about 'The Intelligentsia and Science' (Wells again, Malinowski, Russell again, but mainly the popularizers Eddington and Jeans). The book was widely reviewed in England. One of the many indications of how cut off Mirsky became in Moscow is the fact that he had to ask Miss Galton for reports on these reviews; and he pointedly asked her only what the Communist publications had said. The *Daily Worker* was duly appreciative.[61] The burden of the non-Party reviewers' response was that this ingrate had bitten the hand that had fed him, and on the whole the book was soon written off as a piece of Soviet propaganda, the price the author had had to pay for his Soviet passport.[62] This is unfortunate, because the book retains its vituperative vitality even through Alec Brown's translation. Writing twenty years later, Edmund Wilson was much more judicious than the original reviewers:

Yet this bold and brisk Marxist summary of the modern intellectual history of Britain and the United States (for he polishes us off at the same sitting) is rather an able and brilliant book. It is today less annoying than pathetic to read a critic who believes that he has got the key to all the problems of human culture as well as an infallible ferrule with which he can poke into their places all the practitioners of bourgeois letters. . . . Yet there are very good things in this ill-inspired book. I am not sure that there is any other in which a foreigner so well-informed has attempted in so uninhibited and so un-academic a way to run through the main currents and figures of recent English literature and thought.[63]

NEW PROJECTS

The completion of the *Intelligentsia* book was the first watershed in Mirsky's literary life back in the USSR. After this and other publications on intellectual developments outside Russia, Mirsky was invited to participate in some of Gorky's imposing new literary projects, with Leopold Averbakh as his mentor and intermediary with Gorky during the early stages. Before Gorky left Russia in 1921, he had initiated a sweeping series of publications designed to reshape the supply of Russian and foreign literature to meet the needs of the country's new reading public. Most of these projects ran into the sand after Gorky left; the New Economic Policy fragmented the Bolshevik publishing effort, and the Party had other things on its mind. As part of his return to stewardship of Soviet literature, Gorky's name was used in connection with a vast new series of broadly designed publishing initiatives that far exceeded his efforts immediately after the revolution.

Just how far Gorky himself initiated and controlled these projects is not entirely clear. There were in fact far too many of them for any one person to have overseen in any detail, whatever their capacity for hard work—and Gorky's capacity, like Mirsky's, was formidable. (His routine was to rise at six, swallow two raw eggs and some coffee, and then stay at his desk until two in the afternoon, when he took lunch; but unlike Mirsky, he chain-smoked, despite the tubercular condition that was his stated reason for living in Italy.) The projects were actually developed by Gorky in consultation with a large number of advisers. In the last letter he wrote to Gorky before coming back to Russia, on 10 July 1932, Mirsky put to Gorky a proposal for a grand encyclopedia that would represent the Communist point of view in a manner accessible to the working class outside the USSR, and defuse the impact of such popular authors as H. G. Wells, and particularly his widely read *The Work, Wealth, and Happiness of Mankind*.[64] Nothing seems to have come directly out of Mirsky's proposal.

The projects that Gorky did push through were designed to shape the literary visage of the newly proclaimed socialist society in which class war had been superseded. The regime now wished to present the country as a multinational but socially and culturally monolithic union that was thoroughly modern. It was also a state that was now no longer an international pariah, but instead a major world power with an unprecedented role to play as the cultural flagship of 'progressive humanity', the one state that had the power and authority to come to the aid of the underprivileged of the world—including writers who were persecuted in their own countries. In addition to all this, the literacy programme of the 1920s had immeasurably expanded the number of readers inside Russia. Stalin outlined some of this thinking in one of his bluff, matey letters to Gorky, written on 12 November 1931 as part of his effort to get the 'living classic' on side in Russia:

Things are going not badly here. In both the industrial and agricultural sectors of the economy there is indubitable progress. Let them all over there in Europe cat-call that medieval stuff they keep dredging up about the 'collapse' of the USSR as loud as they want. They won't change our plans or what we're doing by one iota. The USSR will become a first-class country with the most massive, technically equipped industrial and agricultural production. Socialism is invincible. There will be no more '*poverty-stricken*' Russia. It's finished! There will be a powerful and plentiful *advanced* Russia.[65]

Beginning in the late 1920s, considerable resources were allotted to the 'cultural front', and it inevitably sprouted a bureacratic jungle of officials, committees, lobbying activities, and documentation for making and administering the allocations.[66] The Union of Writers rapidly became a privileged enclave within the privileged hierarchy of Soviet institutions, an elephantine, heavily male-dominated, inward-looking pressure group, with its own facilities that were accessible only to its members and their dependants. And one of its principal functions, as with all other Soviet institutions, was as a listening-post for the secret police.

The Union soon acquired its own newspaper, the *Literary Gazette*. The first new journals published under Gorky's aegis were socio-political disinformation sheets: the mendacious *Our Achievements* began in January 1929, *Abroad* in 1930, and in the same year *The USSR Constructs*, with Mikhail Koltsov's name added to Gorky's on the masthead. *Our Achievements* used two outstanding talents of Mirsky's generation, the ex-Futurist Aleksandr Rodchenko (1891–1956), whose photographs perfectly catch the official concept of gargantuan goal-directed mass activity, and the graphic designer El Lissitsky (1890–1941). *Abroad* is a key case study in inter-war propaganda techniques; the similarities between it and its contemporary Nazi analogues are very striking. It was designed to feed the Soviet citizen (whose freedom to travel was limited administratively as well as economically) with information from the foreign press, chiefly the Russian *émigré* newspapers and journals, with appropriate commentaries. During 1932 Gorky's correspondence contained a series of directives about it. On 19 December he wrote to Koltsov from Sorrento:

Excellent idea to do an article on *émigré* poetry. This poetry is pessimistic through and through,—I attach some samples, clipped from the *jubilee*, 50th issue of *Contemporary Notes*, and this 'jubilee' aspect needs to be emphasized. But at the same time I think you need to draw the attention of our poets to the slickness, the skill, with which the *émigrés* can turn sow's dung into silk purses [*kozeiki*], while our lads turn the most excellent material into verbal sow's dung.[67]

The point Gorky makes here comes up time and time again in Mirsky's writing about Soviet poetry: the content is right, but the stylistic presentation is primitive, and the educational level of writers needs to be raised as a matter of priority. In this same letter, not for the first time, Gorky advises Koltsov to make use of Mirsky for this journal, and in fact he did contribute one piece, about Middleton Murry. An oral history series with the same broad orientation as *The USSR Constructs* and conceived on a similarly enormous scale, the 'History of the Factories', was projected in 1931 and began to appear in July 1933.

Then there were Gorky's more specifically literature-oriented projects. In April 1930 the first issue of *Literary Schooling* (*Literaturnaya uchoba*) was published in Leningrad; it transferred to Moscow in 1935 and came out regularly until 1941. In January 1931 came the first issue of *Literature of the World Revolution*, published simultaneously in Russian, German, French, and English. In 1933 its name was changed to *International Literature*. In June 1932 the monthly *Children's Literature* began publication. In June 1933 came the first issue of the monthly *Literary Critic*, which in the words of the last literary encyclopedia to be published before the collapse of the USSR 'was founded during the period of struggle against RAPP methodology. It made pronouncements against *vulgar sociology*. It strove for the assimilation of classical aesthetics and the creation of a new socialist aesthetics';[68] despite all this, it was still closed down in 1940.

These periodicals were accompanied by some new series of books in the literary field, all of them attributed to initiatives by Gorky. In 1931 plans were announced for, and in late April 1933 there appeared the first volume in, the 'Poet's Library' (*Biblioteka poeta*), perhaps the most grandiose enterprise of them all, and certainly the most valuable in terms of eventual achievement. Leonid Tchertkov has suggested, on the basis of archive materials, that this series was the result of a suggestion made to Gorky by Mirsky, but this matter has never been thoroughly investigated.[69] The idea was to give the new Soviet reader reliably edited texts, with scholarly preface and annotation, of an approved canon of Russian poetry, including both individual authors and chronological or ideological groupings.

In May 1933 came the first issue of an annual series bearing as its title the number of the current year since the revolution; *The Year XVI* was the first, in 1933. The series continued until 1955, when it was renamed and reorganized as *Our Contemporary*. In 1934 the Union was allotted its own new publishing house, 'Soviet Writer', a Leningrad branch being added to the Moscow headquarters later in the 1930s.[70] The Academia publishing house had been founded as a private undertaking in Petersburg in 1922 and made its name as a top-end literary imprint especially treasured for its graphic design; the series was nationalized and brought to Moscow, and went on bringing out translations of classic fiction.

For once not directly connected with Gorky were two other grand projects of the 'Great Breakthrough' year. The irregular series for publishing literary documents to high academic standards, *Literary Heritage*, began in October

1931; it stayed in existence under its original editor until, defunded in the post-Soviet period, it was left to stagger on towards its 100th huge volume. Another massive project began in 1929, a new and emphatically Soviet *Literary Encyclopedia*. It was never completed, and it had a curious publishing history, as we will soon see.

'Comrade Mirsky' the Soviet critic, now definitively without a title or double-barrelled surname, began to appear regularly in the new Gorky-sponsored publications soon after he arrived in Moscow, and in the course of the next three years his work was featured in all those that were just mentioned. An article by Mirsky appeared in the very first issue of *Literary Critic*, for example. Mirsky's debut in the *Literary Gazette* was actually made before he arrived in Russia physically: it was a concise version of his confessional 'Story of a Liberation', summarized from the *Daily Worker*, and published in Moscow on 29 February 1932. Mirsky's first article after he arrived in Moscow was published in the *Literary Gazette* on 29 October 1932, and he became a very frequent contributor during the next four years. Mirsky wrote excellent prefaces for two Academia translations of English classics, *Robinson Crusoe* (1934) and *Peregrine Pickle* (1934-5); the latter piece was subjected to a viciously negative review.[71]

Significantly, nothing by Mirsky ever appeared in the venerable journal *The New World*, which was in the hands of the younger Party cadres. One of Mirsky's fallings-out with powerful literary figures occurred, as we shall see later, when he refused to take part in another of Gorky's grand projects, for a series of books designed to be read by agricultural workers. More significant than difficulties of this kind is the fact that, although Mirsky was used as a contributor, he was never invited into the control room—the editorial board—of any of the purely literary publications; in this respect once again, he was held at arm's length by his new bosses.

All these initiatives were instruments of the control system operated by the Party and enforced by the NKVD. Their educational function, while not inconsiderable and in many cases long-lasting, was always firmly subordinate to the political in the mind of the establishment. They were all funded by the state, and had to compete for their subsidies in the five-year planning system, the priorities and criteria of which were primarily political, and set centrally. Being 'an organ of the Union of Writers' or 'under the Union of Writers' meant that the Union executive had the formal right to appoint the holders of the key posts of the publication concerned. But these key posts were on the *nomenklatura*, which meant that nominations to them were made by the Party, as indeed were the nominations to the top posts in the Union itself. The cells formed by the Party members were ever-present in all levels of these enterprises, frantically trying to wring what they thought their superiors wanted out of the recalcitrant 'masses' of rank-and-file staff. This situation was the main reason why Mirsky was never much more than an ordinary contributor.

Mirsky had been a member of the Communist Party of Great Britain, and he could have expected to be transferred into membership of the CPSU, the 'conscious avant-garde' of Soviet society, with the opportunity to contribute at the cutting edge to 'the vital work of construction', and be included in the attendant access, privileges, and civic obligations. This did not happen, though. Mirsky had been 'restored in his Soviet citizenship', but he was clearly given to understand that he remained an outsider. Membership of the Party during the 1930s certainly carried with it no invulnerability from even minor forms of unpleasantness; in fact, the opposite was the case, since during the 1930s the Party in the first instance directed its 'vigilance' against itself. But Mirsky ran afoul of the highly placed Party members about ten years or so younger than himself, men to whom his background was alien, offensive, and unredeemable. The most signal indication of Mirsky's outsider status was that he was not made a delegate to the founding Congress of the Union of Writers. He had been accepted as a member of the Union on 4 June 1934, fairly well down the list, in a kind of runners-up section after the Moscow top brass and the national republic brass.[72]

As we have seen, Mirsky told Dorothy Galton soon after he got back to Russia that his concerns had shifted back to literature from the political matters that had dominated his last years in England, that he was having discussions in literary circles, and that literary work was 'the line of least resistance'. He had said to Gorky before he returned that he was not interested in purely literary work, especially in an academic or teaching capacity. His words to Miss Galton are tantamount to an admission of defeat. He had declared several times from 1928 onwards that he considered Soviet literature to be played out. His most sweeping statement on this general theme was made in 1931, when he proclaimed that in the USSR

the victorious proletariat is building a socialist society, which aims to do away with capitalist commodity production, and thus with the necessity of cheap production, which results in the divorce of utility from beauty. But it is still far from that goal, and the function of art there is still much the same as in a capitalist country—a release for maladjusted energy. The working class and that part of the technical intelligentsia which is most organically allied with it have full opportunities to devote all their best energies to practical projects. Only the constructive 'engineering arts', like architecture and the films, are flourishing. Bolshevik art is utilitarian, and even so it is almost exclusively the field of the second-rate, for only the second-rate are not engaged in the vital work of construction. As long as the present conditions last, it is idle to expect 'great literature' from the Soviet Union. What literature is produced will be valuable for the social information it gives, not for the 'values' it creates.[73]

This is the attitude behind Mirsky's indignant rhetorical question about coming back to Russia only in order to converse with the likes of Zhirmunsky and Tynyanov.

THE WHITE SEA CANAL

Meanwhile, not always entirely repressing the view that he was involved with something 'second-rate', and applying his usual high level of 'maladjusted energy', Mirsky got on with making a contribution to Soviet literature, but in its least academic aspects. During the initial organizing period of the Union, Gorky's commission sent out 'brigades' of writers from Moscow into the provinces. Pasternak managed to get himself sent to Georgia instead of the Ukraine, where he was originally assigned, and thus began the activity as a translator from Georgian that first signalled his acceptance of Stalin and his regime.[74] On 19 February 1933, writing to Gorky, Mirsky said that he was 'seeing a lot of Averbakh', and also that he was hoping to go to Central Asia for about two months in April, in order to write about it 'for the English'. On 2 May he told Gorky he was leaving the next day for Central Asia, with Bruno Jasienski and also perhaps the young poet Vladimir Lugovskoy (1901–57; he succumbed to alcoholism after several spells in the camps). This journey took Mirsky to Tashkent and Stalinabad. On 22 October he summed up to Miss Galton: 'I travelled a lot last summer: I went to Central Asia as far as the Afghan frontier & the outskirts of the Pamir, & then to the White Sea to the new Canal which was built under the direction of the GPU.' In March 1934 he made a visit to the massive iron mine at Vysokie Gory in the Urals. These expeditions had literary consequences, as they were meant to.

To spearhead the industrialization of the economic system under the Great Leap Forward, three projects in particular were conceived that were supposed in addition to demonstrate to the depression-ridden outside world that the planned economy of the USSR could outdo not only them, but any previously known system of management. They were: the colossal dam on the Dnepr, known as 'Dneprostroi'; the biggest steel works in the world and its satellite city at Magnitogorsk, 'Magnitostroi'; and the canal to link the Baltic and White seas, 'Belomorstroi'.[75] The White Sea Canal became the next major abomination of early Stalinism after collectivization. Under the supervision of the GPU, the project used convict labour almost entirely, and the death rate averaged about 10,000 per month. No mechanized equipment and very little concrete was allowed to be used in the construction; the materials had to be 'won' on site. The canal was finished inside the twenty months demanded, and triumphantly reported to Yagoda by Semyon Firin, the GPU commander of the enterprise, on May Day 1933. Stalin, Kirov, Voroshilov, and Yagoda sailed down it that July. A widely circulated image of this visit was produced by one of the top artists to the court of Stalin, D. A. Nalbandyan; Yagoda soon had to be painted out of it when he fell from power.[76] In economic terms, the project was a monumental waste of time, money, and human lives. The propaganda aim seems to have been achieved in at least two foreign minds (or perhaps they had one between them): Sidney and Beatrice Webb devoted three glowing pages to Belomorstroi, concluding with a piece of *echt*-Fabian Pecksniffery: 'It is pleasant to think that the warmest appreciation was officially expressed of the success of the GPU, not merely in performing a great engineering feat, but in achieving a triumph in human regeneration.'[77]

The collective production of the book celebrating the White Sea–Baltic Canal was proudly announced on its introductory pages as an example of 'shockwork' tempi on the cultural front. The first editorial meeting concerning the project took place on 13 August 1933; on 17 August a delegation of 120 writers went to the site of the canal. On 29 August the *Literary Gazette* ran a two-page spread in which the major authors gave a concise account of their contributions (Mirsky did not appear). On 10 September the plan of the book was drawn up and the writers given their assignments; on 20 October the series of collective discussions of the manuscript began and continued at a rate of one every three days; on 28 November the composition of the book began; and on 12 December the manuscript was delivered to the printer. (The photography and layouts were by Rodchenko.) On 20 January 1934 the advance copies appeared, the mass edition following on 15 April.[78] The book was dedicated by the Organizing Committee of the Union of Soviet Writers on behalf of the authors to the XVII Congress of the CPSU 'as a token of the readiness of Soviet writers to serve the cause of Bolshevism and struggle by means of their creative work on behalf of the teachings of Lenin and Stalin and for the creation of a classless society'.

Mirsky's contribution to this book represents the point in the trajectory of his literary career furthest away from the slim volume of fugitive poetry with which it began in 1911. He was one of a seven-man team that contributed the sixty-page chapter called 'The GPU, the Engineers, the Project'; his 'brigade' is listed as 'S. Budantsev, N. Dmitriev, M. Kozakov, G. Korabelnikov, D. Mirsky, V. Pertsov, Ya. Rykachev, and V. Shklovsky'.[79] The vituperative pages devoted to it by Solzhenitsyn make further discussion of this monstrous book superfluous. Fortunately, Mirsky's name seems to have meant nothing to the great dissident, and he is spared the scorn heaped on the other eminent Soviet writers who were involved.[80]

Mirsky's behaviour during the journey to the White Sea Canal was witnessed by a former street urchin called Aleksandr Avdeenko (b. 1908), the youngest writer involved in the enterprise—his construction novel *I Love* had not yet come out in book form at the time. Avdeenko was drafted in from Magnitogorsk, and on the train journey to Moscow every station he passed through was crowded with hungry people begging for bread, a sight that haunted him during the ensuing days of privileged gluttony. The participants assembled at the Writers' Club in Moscow; they included just about every famous name in Soviet literature. Among them were the poets Bezymensky, Vera Inber, Utkin, and Pavel Vasiliev; the novelists Ilf and Petrov, Vsevolod Ivanov, Jasienski, Leonov, Pilnyak, Seifullina, Sobolev, Trenyov, and Zoshchenko; the dramatists

Kirshon and Pogodin; and the three-man team of caricaturists known as the Kukriniksy. When the group had assembled, they were harangued by Kirpotin, Secretary of the Organizing Committee of the Union of Writers, and Semyon Firin. The writers were then bussed to the Leningrad station, where a train of gleaming first-class carriages awaited them. It was at this point, Avdeenko observes, that total Communism began, in the form of as much free food and alcoholic drink as the participants could consume. The party journeyed overnight to Leningrad.

Avdeenko shared a compartment with Mirsky and another critic, Selivanovsky—the one who had reportedly made banal remarks about Mandelshtam's new poetry in 1932. The young novelist listened in amazement as the two critics traded quotations from 'world poetry'. When they had had their fill of this game, they toasted each other, and then Mirsky turned to Avdeenko, apologized for keeping him awake, and asked him about his background. Avdeenko told him he came from the Donbass, and Mirsky gave him a mini-lecture about it and then another one about Magnitogorsk, larded with amazingly accurate factual information even though he had never been to these places himself. By way of explanation Mirsky asserted: 'The Earth is my planet, and I am obliged to know it. Especially my own country.'[81] The group spent the next day in Leningrad, visiting the Hermitage and Peterhof and then sitting down to a Rabelaisian feast in a private room at the Astoria; it was, says Avdeenko, as if the pictures in the Hermitage had come to life. Did Mirsky tell his companions about his previous sojourns in these places? Perhaps about his drunken foray on horseback into the Winter Palace, where the Hermitage is located?

The next day, the team poured itself into another train and set off northwards for the canal. During their trip along the 120-odd miles of the canal itself (they were not allowed to get off the boat), the writers put questions to Firin, who gave affable and assured answers. Mirsky kept silent, but eventually, when everybody else had finished, he spoke up. He asked Firin if there was any precedent for this enterprise, and was assured that there was none, either in Russia or anywhere else in the world—and what is more, the White Sea project had cost the state considerably less than the Suez and Panama canals, for example, had cost their ruthlessly exploitative capitalist backers. Mirsky asked how these savings had been achieved, and was told by Firin:

'On account of radically cutting down construction time. On account of good labour organization. On account of the enthusiasm of the army of canal workers, enthusiasm that was conditioned by the fact that these people from the labour camps were offered the opportunity to take a full part in this grandiose work of construction.'

'And probably also on account of unpaid labour?'

'Of course. People undergoing punishment are not paid wages. That's been the way throughout the civilized world since time began. Any further questions?'

'What's the point of the secrecy? Why was this heroic canal-building epic kept secret from the nation and the entire world for two years?'

'In actual fact the White Sea project wasn't kept secret in the literal sense of the word. It's just that the newspapers and radio didn't happen to say anything about it.'

'Why was that?'

'The wise advice of Comrade Stalin was to keep quiet about it for the time being.'[82]

Mirsky's insistent questioning made the assembled writers feel awkward. Though Avdeenko does not spell this out, here after all was a former prince, the son of a head of the secret police and Minister of the Interior under the old regime, interrogating the No. 2 man in the Soviet security service about state secrets and even bringing up the name of the Leader, whom Firin had personally shown round his canal not a month before! Mirsky's companions tried to avoid him after this discussion. But Mirsky kept seeking out Avdeenko and launching into conversations in which he took Avdeenko into his confidence. Avdeenko did not welcome this attention at all; he certainly had no desire, as he says, to see 'our life' through 'Mirsky's spectacles'. Avdeenko reconstructs one such conversation, which begins when Mirsky senses Avdeenko's feeling of alienation from him, and issues a challenge:

'You don't approve of my curiosity, it seems?'

'You spent a long time away from the motherland and because of that you perceive many things—what's the precise word—in your own way.'

'Surely it's no bad thing to perceive life independently, without being told how to by someone else, without having to keep an eye out for the pointing finger?'

'That's not what I said.'

'Yes you did. The words were different, but they meant precisely that. And you're not the first. It really makes me feel sad. More than that—it alarms me. I may turn out to be a fish out of water [ne ko dvoru]. It'll be very, very sad if that happens. I fell in love with Lenin. I fell in love with the new Russia. There's a lot I like about what's been done and is being done. But there's a lot I don't understand. There's quite a few things that Lenin wouldn't have approved of if he'd still been alive. The saddest thing is that I can clearly see shortcomings, miscalculations, mistakes, omissions, and sometimes even arbitrariness,[83] but your eyes have got used to the big defects and the small ones too and they don't notice them. Many people get offended when you rub it in about their mistakes. For example, you can only see the canal as a great miracle, and you can't see the other side of the coin.'

'What other side of the coin?'

'Everywhere you go here, some secret has been hidden. Under every dam. Under every lock. In the destiny and the labour of each and every soldier in the canal army. If it had suited fate to make me younger and put me in your enviable place, as a young writer, d'you know what I'd do? I'd write a story called "The Secret of the Three Letters".'[84]

I look disapprovingly at the former prince and do not hide my challenge:
'What secret? Everything's out in the open, they're showing us everything.'
'There's a good deal that I haven't figured out. This grandiose waterway with its bridges, reservoirs, locks, and dams is the same as Magnitka—one of the new wonders of the socialist world. If . . .'
'What d'you mean, "if"?'—came off my tongue before I could stop it.
'If the White Sea Project is exactly and only what it seems to us to be.'
'But how could it be something different?' I asked in confusion.
His reply was calm and somehow sad:
'Perhaps, dear chap, perhaps. People are capable of setting up not only miracles, but all sorts of cunning traps as well, for their fellows and for themselves. All sorts of things have happened in history. More often than not, great national disasters have begun from the good intentions and assurances of the great men of this world.'
'I don't understand what you're talking about.'
Mirsky laughed, gnashing teeth that were worn down almost to the roots.
'D'you think *I* know why I'm holding forth at you like this? There's only one thing I'm certain about: just make sure you don't complain to any of the writers or chekists that this former prince is tempting you away from the straight and narrow.'[85]

This is the most eloquent testimony we have to Mirsky's lack of sensitivity to his own position in his new surroundings. Perhaps at this stage, as a known confidant of Gorky and Averbakh, he was simply over-confident. In other societies this behaviour could perhaps be ascribed to personal ineptness, but in Stalin's Russia it was much more serious. This conversation with Avdeenko is also the most substantial interaction that has been recorded between Mirsky and a member of the proletariat that was supposed to be the new ruler of his country. There is no way of knowing if these words, on either side, are more reliable as evidence than the conversation of nearly ten years before that Roger Fry reconstructed. If the two reported dialogues are compared, it is not difficult to perceive that Mirsky speaks the same language as the English aesthete and despite their intellectual disagreements is recognized by him as a kindred soul, while Avdeenko the Russian prole comes from a completely alien social and intellectual dimension. Written long after the event, this is also the most graphic record we have of Mirsky's disillusion after his return to Russia. When Mirsky talks about the 'secrets' under every dam and lock, he unmistakably has in mind human corpses. His final words about mankind's intentions undercut completely his reported words to Muggeridge about the inevitability and inscrutability of the historical process.

In the English-language version of the White Sea Canal book, the contribution of Mirsky's brigade was split into two: 'The Big House at the Corner of Lubyanka' and 'The GPU Men'.[86] The editor of the English version was Amabel Williams-Ellis. She was the sister of John Strachey, and visited Russia with him early in 1928; she later joined the editorial board of *Left Review*, and would probably therefore have known Mirsky personally. Williams-Ellis appears to have been the only British delegate to the I Congress of Soviet Writers in August 1934. Like many of the leading artefacts of the Stalin period, the White Sea book had a fairly short shelf life in Russia; it was 'unmasked' in 1937 and withdrawn from circulation, mainly because Yagoda had become an enemy of the people, and he was one of the main heroes of the book. Worst of all, Averbakh's name appears as an editor alongside those of Gorky and Firin.

HISTORY OF THE FACTORIES

Mirsky took a prominent part in another grandiose project undertaken on the initative of Gorky, the 'History of the Factories'. This was intended to get the workers themselves to set down their own stories about their working lives in the revolutionary era. In March 1934 Mirsky made a visit to the massive iron mine at Vysokie Gory in the Urals to subedit the manuscripts that had been submitted by the workers there. A detailed report on how this book was produced, and an impressively concise theoretical and practical justification of the idea of collective authorship, was made at the II Plenum of the Union of Writers in Moscow, in March 1935, by the most prominent writer involved, the novelist Vsevolod Ivanov.[87] Mirsky, who was present at this meeting, is not mentioned in Ivanov's account, even though he is named on the book's title-page as co-editor. But then, neither is Leopold Averbakh, who was in charge of the whole enterprise in its initial stage; by this time he had been unpersoned. Unlike the White Sea Canal book, says Ivanov, which had been produced by thirty-six writers—admittedly of varying levels of achievement and experience—the Vysokie Gory book was actually 'written by the masses'.

In May 1933 a month-long series of conferences was organized to which workers were invited to bring their memoirs; prizes were given for the best efforts. The first prize was a trip to Moscow to present the finished manuscript text of the collective book to Gorky in person. The complete draft was discussed on New Year's Eve; it was confirmed, and a delegation presented it to Gorky on 20 January 1934.

The total number of authors involved in the Vysokie Gory project was eventually 100. The workers were instructed to write the way they spoke. Ivanov thought that the book demonstrated the immense growth of cultural consciousness in the workers as a result of the revolution; the book was above all 'joyful'; and he considered that the workers' own knowledge of their jobs that comes through in their accounts makes the efforts of professional writers look primitive. This was said in the context of the drive to get out 'production novels' by the professional writers of the Union describing the achievements of the First Five-Year Plan.

However, what was really going on may be inferred from the statement made at the same Plenum by one of Mirsky's most interesting contemporaries, Mariya Shkapskaya. Before the revolution she had qualified as a doctor in Paris, where she had been sent to keep her out of political trouble; inevitably, she made friends with Ilya Erenburg there. She had been a very significant poet in her younger years, but in the early 1920s she turned to journalism in the service of the Party.[88] Shkapskaya was involved in writing the history of the Karl Marx (formerly Lessner) factory in Leningrad; her brigade began its work on May Day 1933. She reported to the II Plenum:

I'll give you as an example one old worker, Gondukov. He told us in great detail about the struggle the old Lessner workers conducted in the factory and on the street just before 1917. Anyway, he enumerated countless sallies onto the streets, strikes, arrests, searches and other details of that struggle and then got to the February days, the moment when the women workers burst in on them in the factory shouting 'Revolution!' 'I'—says Gondukov—'ran up to Kadatsky, who was working on the next lathe to mine, and I yelled: "Vanya, let's go, it's the revolution!" And Gondukov added immediately: 'That's understandable—after all, the revolution broke out suddenly, of its own accord, nobody had ever seen anything like it before.'

Shkapskaya comments:

This is a typical misconception about the elemental nature of the revolution. Willy-nilly one had to intervene and help [the worker] cross that final bridge that remained uncrossed in his consciousness—from a knowledge of events to an understanding of them. He was himself one of those who had made the revolution, carried it on his shoulders and day after day watched the Party preparing it. It follows that empirically he knew that it was not in the least elemental, but didn't know how to call this by its real name. You should have seen his delight when he was helped to draw this conclusion. What does this mean, comrades? It means that not only did we have to describe our hero, but also to a certain extent to educate him, to re-create him—or rather, to put the finishing touches to the creation of him, to unfold before him that historic role he had played in the workers' movement.[89]

This is a textbook illustration of Stalinist democracy at work, and an eloquent application of the anti-socialist, anti-realist theory of literary representation that underlay the method of Socialist Realism. Shkapskaya was one of the Party representatives among the writers, historians, and Komsomols who were involved in this project along with Mirsky; they began by attending a seminar on the workers' movement at the Communist Academy, so as to get their ideology straightened out.[90]

RETURNEES

In his early years in Moscow, Mirsky continued to intercede on behalf of certain friends he had left behind after he had converted to Communism and been accepted as a Soviet citizen. On 9 March 1934 he wrote to Gorky asking him to help in the case of Emiliya Litauer, who was now working in Paris for the International Organization of Revolutionary Writers (MORP). Litauer, a former pupil of Heidegger and the only female contributor to *Eurasia*, was now in her early 30s, an extremely gifted philosopher. Mirsky told Gorky that Litauer wanted to come back to Russia, but was getting no support from her home organization, the French Communist Party. Mirsky's request was eventually granted, with the inevitable consequence: Litauer arrived back in Russia in 1936, and was kept in virtual seclusion. Whether or not she saw Mirsky is unknown. She was sometimes in Marina Tsvetaeva's company after the poet returned in 1939. Arrested on the same day as Tsvetaeva's daughter Ariadna Efron, 27 August 1939, she was interrogated—no doubt with the aid of the depositions Mirsky had given after he was arrested two years earlier—and eventually shot on 27 August 1941.

The same thing would undoubtedly have happened to Suvchinsky if the authorities had restored him in his Soviet citizenship. As we know, he applied in Paris on the same day as Mirsky, but was turned down. Mirsky pleaded for him in a letter to Gorky of 13 August 1931, but nothing seems to have happened as a result.

The other principal who escaped with her life from Mirsky's sponsorship was Vera Suvchinskaya, the last person to see Mirsky before he got on the boat for Leningrad. Now determined to come back to Russia, she was held back among other things by the fact that her eminently counter-revolutionary father was still very much alive and politically active. Mirsky got on to Gorky about her too in a letter he wrote on 19 February 1933, saying among other things that he could vouch for her 'as well as I can for myself'. Vera came to Moscow on an Intourist visit 'for 10 days or 2 weeks' at some time in 1935. When she joined the French Communist Party is not clear, but Sergey Efron testified that he recruited her for the GPU in 1932.[91] She eventually arrived for good in 1936, with results we shall soon see.

LITERARY CRITICISM

To his evident annoyance as expressed in his letters to Dorothy Galton, Mirsky was unable to go away for the summer in 1934 in his customary manner because the founding Congress of the Union of Writers was in prospect. His letters at the time show that he confidently expected to take part in it. The Congress was originally supposed to take place the year before, but the infighting among the various groupings and regroupings of the Organizing Committee caused considerable delays.[92] The Congress was eventually held from 17 August to 1 September 1934 in Moscow. The verbatim transcript of the proceedings, with its huge statistical supplement, was soon published. At the back is the list of delegates to the congress, and Mirsky's name is not among them. He may have attended some sessions, but he did not speak. In fact, he seems to have left for Georgia while the Congress was in progress—whether bidden or unbidden, remains to be discovered.[93]

However, Mirsky devoted a good deal of time and effort to attending meetings of the various sections of the Union of Writers, spoke frequently on these occasions, and became a very active current contributor to the literary press. His industry was if anything more remarkable once he got started in Russia than it had been in England. The five Soviet years (1932–7) account for just over one-quarter of his lifetime total of about 400 publications.[94] No longer was he spending much time and energy on translation.[95] In 1934 he published twenty-four substantial articles, and then no fewer than forty-one in 1935 (not for nothing, it seems, was this the year when the Stakhanovite movement started). There is nothing among all this about Russian *émigré* literature; in all Mirsky's writing about poetry after 1932, there is not a single mention, to choose the most obvious example, of Marina Tsvetaeva.

Mirsky unfailingly published something on every single topic that was tabled by the rolling Party directives of the 1930s—'formalism', 'quality', 'professional mastery', the literatures of the national republics, and so on. On the first of these subjects he set the ball rolling with an extremely learned contribution that begins with the art of the Stone Age, touches on the entire history of Western literature, and has much to say about the development of the private market in pictorial art. Eventually, Mirsky deplores what he sees as a reactivization of formalist tendencies in recent Soviet literature, centred on the 'cult' of Proust and Joyce.[96] Buried among all this heavy stuff are some items in which Mirsky's literary judgement enters into a productive dialectic with his hard-line Marxist categories. Some of these were very serious contributions on subjects where Mirsky has remained unsurpassed in Russian criticism.

Perhaps the best piece of all, in some ways superior to anything Mirsky had written before 1929, was his long introductory essay on Baratynsky, written for the 'Poet's Library' edition. Here, the sociological, psychological, and aesthetic dimensions mesh with and illuminate each other. Mirsky submitted this article in February 1934.[97] Shortly before, he had written a couple of stinging reviews about the quality of the earliest books in the new poetry series and also the Academia series.[98] On the same high level is the most sustained piece of analysis Mirsky ever published about a single work of literature, the text concerned being *War and Peace*.[99] Significantly, this essay was written as a preface to an edition of the novel to be published by Goslitizdat, but Lebedev-Polyansky, the chief editor of the literary classics department, turned it down without explaining why. Gorky then sent it to the *Literary Contemporary*, telling the editor, Nakoryakov, that the piece was 'fresh, structured not in a clichéd way, and it talks in a correct way about the fundamental contradiction of Tolstoy— lord and peasant combined in one person'.[100]

Besides the acerbic comments he had made in *The Intelligentsia*, Mirsky kept up a steady stream of articles on English literature during his Moscow years. He wrote substantial prefaces to prestigious editions of works by Defoe, Shelley, Kipling, Aldous Huxley, and others. In his introduction to Huxley's *Point Counter Point*, Mirsky draws on his first-hand knowledge of the British literary and intellectual circles that are satirized in the novel, identifying the prototypes of the characters to the accompaniment of remarks as caustic as those in *The Intelligentsia of Great Britain*. He also wrote an article covering the whole of recent English literature for the *Granat* encyclopedia, a publication that retained its a-Soviet character longer than practically any other survival from the pre-revolutionary period. This was the last of Mirsky's many magisterial survey articles.[101] And, following on from the articles he had written in Russian while he had been in England, but now working from his hard-line Marxist point of view, Mirsky commented on current trends in English poetry. He took a patronizingly disdainful view of what he wrote off as the childish pseudo-Marxist antics of the Auden group, and became ever more scathing about what he saw as Eliot's emergence as a spokesman of right-wing obscurantism.

Pride of place among Mirsky's Soviet works on English literature in terms of physical size and continuing value is held by the *Anthology of Modern English Poetry* that he prepared for publication, bringing together a splendid team of translators and calling into play all the knowledge he had accumulated about English poetry to inform his Introduction and Notes. The translators Mirsky used in his anthology were all based in Leningrad, and he set up the project during a visit there in September 1935. The finished anthology was in the process of publication when Mirsky was arrested; in order to save the enterprise, his name was completely removed from the book and replaced by that of M. Gutner, one of his team of translators.[102] Gutner, a young scholar who was soon killed in the Second World War, was made immortal through this deception.

Mirsky's last book, of over 450 pages, with his magisterial twenty-page introduction (over Gutner's name), is still the best anthology in Russian of English poetry from the mid-Victorian period to the 1930s, and it has been massively influential. The standard of the verse translations is unusually high; among them there are some real masterpieces, such as the translation of Wilfred Owen's 'Strange Meeting' by Mikhail Zenkevich. A translator is credited for each individual text, with the striking exception of the half-dozen translations from D. H. Lawrence, where no credit is given; it is tempting to think that these exceptionally accurate and sensitive versions are in fact by

Mirsky himself. Along with many other major figures—Hopkins, Yeats, Masefield, James Joyce, not to mention the generous selection from T. S. Eliot—this anthology introduced the poetry of W. H. Auden to the Russians, and it was here, over twenty years later, that Joseph Brodsky first came across the poet who became his idol, without ever knowing who was really responsible for this revelation.[103] The book is equally a silent monument to Dorothy Galton, who supplied the raw materials for it out of a combination of political conviction and personal devotion to the compiler.

The ideological screens that Mirsky erects fore and aft of his Soviet publications do not obscure the continuing acuity of his literary judgement. This is particularly true with reference to what he said about James Joyce in pioneering articles of 1933 and 1935, and about Eliot all the way through. These writers are routinely presented as ideologically hostile to the USSR and as symptomatic of the degeneration of capitalism in the period after the First World War, but there is never any suggestion that they are anything but writers of the first artistic magnitude. This excess of fidelity to his literary judgement got Mirsky into trouble again, because in Moscow it could easily be presented as kowtowing to the lackeys of the bourgeoisie. These writings about contemporary English literature, which represent an important strand in its reception history in Russia, constitute the most thoroughly forgotten segment of Mirsky's published work, and undeservedly so.[104]

The lists of *desiderata* appended to Mirsky's letters to Dorothy Galton mention some of the basic materials for two substantial articles he wrote for the earliest major reference work of the Stalin period, the *Literary Encyclopedia*. The first of these, on Realism, was one of the most important theoretical statements on this subject to appear at the time when official Soviet literary policy on the subject of Socialist Realism was being formulated.[105] The other big article Mirsky supplied for the *Encyclopedia* was on Romanticism.[106] The volume in which this article was to appear, the tenth in a projected twelve-volume set, suffered the same fate as the majority of its editorial board: it disappeared from history. The reason may have had something to do with the fact that this particular volume should have contained the article on 'Stalin, I. V.', and nobody could or would produce anything suitable. Unfortunately, a series of articles under the general heading 'Russian Literature', written by the cream of living Soviet literary scholars, and a good deal more that would have been of great interest, went down with this same ship. For reasons nobody has yet explained, a proof copy of the book survived, and it was eventually spirited out of Russia and published in Munich in the last year of Soviet power.

The last major project for a work of reference that Mirsky undertook at this time was also destined to appear only many years after he wrote it. In three or four of his letters Mirsky asks Miss Galton for materials connected with his work on the Baroque in English literature. This was needed for a collectively written history of the literatures of Western Europe under the editorship of

Mirsky's old schoolmate Viktor Zhirmunsky. The resulting article would have been the earliest substantial study of the subject in Russian if it had appeared in good time. Fortunately, the manuscript survived in Zhirmunsky's archive, and the piece was published fifty years after Mirsky's arrest. It is a magnificent feat of compression, logical organization, and literary insight. It was no longer the first treatment of the subject by the time it came out, but it had still not been surpassed.[107]

Among the substantial works of a non-literary nature that Mirsky was involved with at this time was the English–Russian dictionary he edited jointly with A. D. Miller.[108] Only the first edition carries Mirsky's name; after his arrest, the book was reprinted many times under Miller's alone. Like Mirsky's *History*, from which several publishers must have made a small fortune in royalties they have never had to pay out, the *Dictionary* enriched somebody else.

These various projects were for the most part non-controversial, at least when they were conceived; they did not involve issues where core matters of Party policy were involved. Mirsky showed that he was willing and able to buckle down and deliver the goods in the new conditions. The collective book on the White Sea Canal marked the apogee of Mirsky's activities after his return in terms of non-literary affairs; and the articles for the various literary reference works undertaken in the same years occupy a similar position with regard to Mirsky as an acknowledged leading Soviet authority on English literary history and European literary theory. After these projects, and not entirely of his own volition, he increasingly turned his attention to the current literary scene in the Soviet Union, now working not as a member of an establishment-sponsored collective but as an increasingly marginalized individual. The consequences were soon to be very discomfiting for him, and before very much longer they were disastrous.

8 The Falling Line

Spender is gripped by an obsession—the obsession of the 'independence' of the artist, of the necessity for him to fight shy of all party allegiance for fear of forfeiting his inner freedom. . . . One of the manifestations of this obsession is his obstinate care to retain all the appearances of the bourgeois intellectual, of a gentleman conducting a gentlemanly discussion with other gentlemen who have every right to their own opinions and prejudices. (D. S. Mirsky, 1936)

'BETTER THAN IN PARIS AND LONDON'

On 19 February 1934 Mirsky informed Dorothy Galton that 'Edward Bagritsky, one of our two or three finest poets, and about my best friend in Moscow has just died. This is a very bad blow to poetry here, and to me personally.' Mirsky published four articles in memory of Bagritsky.[1] This abundance points up the fact that he wrote nothing to commemorate three other important poets whose work he had proclaimed in earlier years: Maksimilian Voloshin (1877–11 August 1932), Andrey Bely (1880–8 January 1934),[2] and the pre-revolutionary poet he had known best, Mikhail Kuzmin (1872–1 March 1936). Back in Paris, Tsvetaeva wrote something substantial about all three of them, even though Voloshin was the only one she had met more than once. Her essays about them form part of the extraordinary autobiographical prose she embarked on in the 1930s, none of which Mirsky can have read.[3]

Bagritsky's death marked a turning-point in Mirsky's fortunes. After it came a succession of polemics whose fallout in the noisome atmosphere of the times eventually choked him. Practically everyone who observed Mirsky after the middle of 1935 emphasized his isolation. By this they did not necessarily mean an absence of personal friends; in Soviet conditions this was an unreliable observation anyway, because people tended not to talk to one person about their private relations with another, for obvious reasons. In Moscow Mirsky behaved as he had in London and spent the vast bulk of his time in solitary reading and writing. Those who have spoken about his isolation were pointing first and foremost to political alienation and lack of patronage, having nobody to 'call on'—a situation that became critical after Gorky died on 18 June 1936.

Mirsky's health had declined after he came back to Russia. Alcohol was the most obvious cause of the problem. Soviet literary life in the 1930s was emphatically a drinking culture, as was Russian male life in other spheres, and so things have remained. On 27 March 1936 Mirsky wrote to Dorothy Galton: 'Intourist are selling now their stock of foreign wines for Soviet money & you can imagine what a severe strain this has been on my budget (which *néanmoins* is going strong).' At least once during his time in emigration he had attempted to swear off drink, as we know, and in one of his abject letters of 1930 to Vera Suvchinskaya he had childishly implored her to control his habit. He made another attempt to go dry after he went back, perhaps because the Intourist wines had turned out to be duds; on 14 June 1936 he told Miss Galton: 'My latest is that I have abandoned alcoholic drink, quite; for how long is another question. But the funny thing is that it came quite naturally, *"simple comme bonjour"*, and that I have not the slightest wish to break my abstinence.' But the abstinence cannot have lasted long. Describing Mirsky's state of mind when she arrived in Moscow in the autumn of 1936, Vera—now according to her own account a blindly enthusiastic young Communist—said: 'He was in a pretty nasty state, and he was drinking a very great deal. We used to meet every day. I told him he had been demoralized by bourgeois democracy, and he told me I was a fool and I understood nothing. Of course, it was he who was right, not I.'

I asked Vera about Mirsky's statement to Miss Galton that he had given up drink, and without much difficulty at that, and she responded with a mixture of astonishment and indignation: 'He *never* gave up drinking . . . *I*'ve never seen him give up drinking. He wasn't an *alcoholic*, I mean he just liked drinking . . .' And she proceeded to give evidence that in her view demonstrated that Mirsky was not an alcoholic—to the effect that he did not regularly go off on binges lasting several days, during which time he would be incommunicado and incapable of work. Most non-Russians, however, would regard his behaviour as unmistakably that of an alcoholic.

Soon after Mirsky got back to Russia, another health problem came up. On one of his first trips away from Moscow, to the Pamirs in the summer of 1933, he contracted malaria. Writing to Miss Galton just before he reported Bagritsky's death, on 29 January 1934, Mirsky complains that he was not as well as he should be, because of 'that damned malaria'. And on 25 June: 'The weather is beastly, and I have again got malaria, though I thought I had been cured of it. A terrible nuisance.' However, on this same day—the day Mandelshtam confessed—Mirsky replied to a letter he had received from Salomeya Halpern. He made light of his infirmity, and capped it with a typical alcoholic's plea, the import of which he would betray when the Intourist cellar went on sale: '[Apart] from the malaria I feel much better than in Paris and London, which I ascribe partly to vodka, which is much more beneficial than wine.' Mirsky was just short of 48 years old when he was arrested in June 1937, but he was already considerably debilitated.

FIVE CONFRONTATIONS

From about the middle of 1934 Mirsky's writing turned increasingly towards current Soviet literature and literary policy.[4] He soon touched on five topics that led him into rankling clashes with authority. They were, in the chronological order in which they arose: eighteenth-century Russian literature; the work of the novelist Aleksandr Fadeev; the reception of Western European literature in the USSR, especially James Joyce; current Soviet poetry, chiefly Boris Pasternak and poets of the younger generation; and the literary significance in the Soviet era of Pushkin.[5]

The seriousness of these topics had very little to do with the intrinsic importance of the literary issues involved, something to do with their political resonance as defined by the literary leadership's current priorities, and even more to do with the Party status of Mirsky's opponents. The people opposed to Mirsky were nominally professional writers or scholars, but in reality they were for the most part men of above-average pushiness who, after earning their Party spurs, often on the fronts of the Civil War, had been rushed through a token education and then pitchforked into the rapidly expanding party and government machine. The only criterion they really understood was the one they had been taught—political expediency. The intellectual level of the arguments that got into print is on the whole abysmal; the oral proceedings were probably worse. What passed for debates were in fact for the most part mere sloganeering. There is next to no verbal felicity, inventiveness, or humour.[6]

What did these men actually believe they were doing when they railed at each other with such vehemence? There is very little contemporary informal evidence with which to contextualize the surviving printed texts. Perhaps these documents will have some value eventually as material for the study of mass psychosis, recording the flailings of men enmeshed in a system from which fear has dispelled trust. Among them there must have been the same proportion of honest and sincere enthusiasts as among any other sample of any given profession at any given time. And there would inevitably have been the usual proportion of intelligent and gifted individuals. But the circumstances were such as to produce extraordinarily rapid rewards for careerism, if only in the very short run. Those who succeeded were the ones whose creative and contemplative instincts were subordinate to their political instinct, which is perfectly normal, but which in Stalin's Russia had life-threatening implications. They behaved like bullies in a school playground. The dominant gang in the playground, the Party leadership, did its best to keep the others in terrified fealty, building up myths of rival gangs. These rivals were referred to in the Party slang of the time by the bogey-word 'group' (*gruppa*), which was replaced by the actual equivalent of 'gang' (*banda*) when the people concerned had been officially 'unmasked' by the security organs. The Party isolated and crushed an unending series of these groups and gangs, enhancing its own mystique of vigilant control.

A hierarchical, bureaucratic system had been set up to run the country at the Party's behest, with Party fractions in all its institutions. Men were appointed to operate this system. They had to be seen to be frenetically active. The system followed the Party's initiatives in generating issues (each with an appropriate slogan) to argue about and give the appearance of purposeful activity. As we have seen, a panoply of journals and series had been set up, and their pages had to be filled, or else there would be reprisals for not fulfilling the plan—or, even worse, for 'wrecking' (*vreditel'stvo*). Hardly anybody can ever have attempted to read this stuff apart from the professionals involved in producing it. The result was double-think, conspiratorial collusion with which could not be acknowledged—even surreptitiously, after the usual safety-valve fashion of less repressive societies. The last thing possible under this system was to stay at home and concentrate on genuine creative writing or thinking (as Mirsky had done all his working life), or to contemplate fundamentals— unless one happened to be in the circumstances of Mikhail Bakhtin, who was arrested in 1929 and spent many years in internal exile dialoguing and polyphonizing mainly with himself, far away from the Moscow madhouse.

THE SOVIET PUSHKIN

In April 1933 Mirsky contributed to a discussion put on by the Academy Institute of Russian Literature (Pushkin House) in Leningrad. The subject was eighteenth-century Russian literature, which has always been a stepchild of scholarship. Mirsky briskly disposes of it in the third chapter of his *History*, which occupies about thirty pages of the 380 in the one-volume edition. The published version of his Leningrad paper, which appeared in an early issue of *Literary Heritage*,[7] is one of the most doctrinaire pieces ever written about the subject. Mirsky's essay excoriates the work published by the Leningrad scholars in their attempt to inject some vitality into the subject during the 1920s, and argues for what was coming to be called the 'vulgar Marxist' line in which sociology is paramount, with the various aspects of the literary process narrowly understood as determined by particular class elements. Mirsky calls for most attention to be devoted to the 'democratic' forces in the literature of the period, that is, work by authors from non-gentry social backgrounds. Little is left standing of eighteenth-century Russian literature if one proceeds in this way. But Mirsky's cosmopolitan education gave him an edge in what he had to say about the problem of imitativeness, the most vexed issue involved in the subject. This was to become a liability as Stalinist chauvinism (called at the time 'national/folk feeling', *narodnost'*) became entrenched. So too, less predictably, was Mirsky's rigidly class-based analysis, since the official campaign against 'vulgar sociology' was primarily meant to warn people that it was not acceptable to analyse Soviet society using Marxist categories, since in theory, class-against-class antagonism had been left behind. In truth, of course, the potential productivity of such analysis was rising rapidly with the embourgeoisement of Stalinist society.

Mirsky's opponents in the discussion of eighteenth-century literature were formidable. They included two academic heavyweights, the Old Bolshevik V. A. Desnitsky (1878–1958) and G. A. Gukovsky (1902–50); the former was one of the most senior figures in the Institute, the latter its most brilliant young Turk—for all his precociousness, he was born just too late to have been a Formalist, but he eventually suffered a worse fate than most of them nonetheless.[8] The Party clout on this occasion was provided by an academic nonentity called Sergievsky, who published a vicious denunciation of Mirsky, to which Mirsky replied, complaining bitterly of being misquoted and misunderstood.[9] For all the bad feeling aroused, though, the confrontation was a blow-up in a backwater; no really influential people were involved and the subject was of secondary importance. This was not the case with the argument about Pushkin which came up the following year, and was still going on when Mirsky was arrested.

Mirsky's 'The Problem of Pushkin' was published in an issue of *Literary Heritage* that came out soon after his article on the eighteenth century.[10] Just as he had in the latter case, Mirsky laid waste recent Soviet work on Pushkin, emphasizing in particular its 'national narrowness', which he saw as symptomatic of a wider problem: 'We do not have a single history of European literature that includes Russian literature, nor a history of Russian literature that sees it as part of European literature.'[11] This was bad enough, but Mirsky proceeded to make things worse. He looked at Pushkin from a pan-European perspective, and declared not only that the Russian did not measure up to other national poets, but that his significance was limited to Russia—unlike that of Gogol and Tolstoy, for example (at the time, Dostoevsky could no longer be mentioned in Soviet Russia in the same breath as other nineteenth-century giants). Even worse than this, Mirsky asserted that in his socio-political views and behaviour, Pushkin 'capitulated to autocracy', with the result that his entire work is 'permeated with servility' (*lakeistvo*). This was fighting talk of a very serious order; it soon became a pretext for accusations of near high treason.

The Aesopian resonance of Mirsky's remarks, coming at the time when the cult of Stalin was warming up and literature was being organized to serve the state, is fairly obvious. But the central difficulty was that here, as in other essays written at this time, Mirsky had the gall to articulate an old-fashioned Marxist class consciousness just at the moment when Stalinist ideology was playing this down in order better to appropriate the cultural legacy of imperial Russia. These statements were to be used as ammunition when people sniped at Mirsky later on. At the time, the most detailed riposte was published by one of

Mirsky's old schoolmates, Vasily Gippius; it is a reasoned piece that continually acknowledges the merits of Mirsky's literary insight. Gippius's principal
objections concerned not demonstrable errors, but that Mirsky had taken the
argument too far. Again, Mirsky's maximalism, his impatient urge to push
things to the logical limit, was the root of the trouble.[12]

Despite these unpleasant clashes, Mirsky continued to maintain good
working relations with the Academy Institute. The autobiographical statement
of 1936 that has been cited many times earlier was written for Mirsky's
appointment as a Senior Research Fellow there, evidently a non-residential
position. Gorky was the nominal head, but the basis for the appointment was
Mirsky's relationship with his old classmate Viktor Zhirmunsky, who was in
charge of the Western Literature section of the Institute—a very fraught
assignment indeed as Stalinist chauvinism gathered strength. Zhirmunsky
continued to bring Mirsky to Leningrad, and to invite him as a contributor to
various academic projects. A notice in the newspaper *Literary Leningrad* for
14 January 1936 announced that a paper by Mirsky under the title 'Russian
Literature as Part of World Literature' would be delivered that evening at the
Mayakovsky House of Writers. On 29 May that year he told Miss Galton that
he would be reading a paper on the English metaphysical poets at the Academy
Institute on 3 June that year, believing that it would be the first ever given in
the country on the subject.

Mirsky undertook three major projects based in Leningrad. The first was
his anthology of English poetry in translation, which he managed to finish
before he was arrested. Mirsky mentioned the other two to Miss Galton on
30 June 1936: 'I have signed a contract to write a life of Pushkin and after that
I will devote myself mainly to English literature. A collective history of English
literature is being prepared. Besides that I am preparing a work on English
literature between 1600–1660.' The fruit of these undertakings withered on
the tree. Part of the Pushkin book was written, and its serial publication was
under way when Mirsky was arrested. As we have seen in the previous chapter,
the substantial historical survey of English Baroque poetry that Mirsky wrote
for Zhirmunsky would have been the very first serious discussion of this topic
to be published in Russian if it had come out when it was supposed to.

VSEVOLOD VISHNEVSKY

As we know, Mirsky was one of very few people in the Soviet literary world in
the 1930s who had any up-to-date knowledge of Western literature, especially
current English and American writing. One of the cardinal problems that faced
the founders of Soviet literary policy concerned the proper way to deal with
this body of material. In one sense, they did not need to bother: there were
tight controls on what came in from abroad, and foreign currency was needed

to pay for it. There was as yet no broadcasting into the USSR from beyond its borders to provide alternative sources of information to the print media. But in any case, very few people in Russia at the time were capable of reading modern English literature in the original. Chukovsky, Marshak, and Ivy Litvinov could manage English literature up to about the First World War. Besides them, there were a few younger people, prominent among them Ivan Kashkin (1899–1963) in Moscow, and in Leningrad Mirsky's acquaintance Valentin Stenich (1898–1939), the ill-starred would-be translator of *Ulysses*, both of whom were interested in Anglo-American modernism and had the linguistic equipment to take it on.[13]

There was also a cohort of French and German Communist sympathizers who used to be invited to come and drink at the fount of progressive humanity (and report to 'the appropriate organs'), people like Aragon and Triolet.[14] Erenburg functioned as a coordinator of this activity. But there was nobody else in Moscow who had actually met T. S. Eliot and was capable of understanding his work first-hand and also translating it, as Mirsky could. Needless to say, the number of native speakers in the anglophone countries at the time who could 'get at' (as Jane Ellen Harrison liked to say) Akhmatova, Pasternak, Mandelshtam, or Tsvetaeva in the original could be counted on the fingers of one hand.

The old educated classes of Russia, who knew French as a matter of course and who were beginning to take up English in a serious way from late in the nineteenth century, had been exterminated, exiled, or disgraced in the first decade after the revolution. The lingua franca of the international Communist movement was German, and German—officially considered to be the language not of literature but of technological progress and efficiency—remained the first foreign language of the Soviet educational system before the Second World War. It was only long after Mirsky's death that English became the first foreign language of the USSR's Russian speakers; for those with any other mother tongue, the obligatory first foreign language was Russian.

And still, the Soviet reader had to be given some instruction on what was going outside the country, which claimed to be in the vanguard of world culture, if it were not to appear to international observers to be the closed society it was in fact. The interpretation of this material had to be controlled. This gave rise to a lasting situation whereby there was much more writing about European modernism by a few privileged experts than there was reading of its texts by the general public. The original materials were simply not accessible to the average reader; as we have seen, even Mirsky, a professional critic who in addition was one of the few people who had access to foreign currency, had to order books privately from a source outside the country. There was no question of writing about Western literature in terms of literary merit; from 1932 it was axiomatic that Soviet literature was superior, because it emanated from the most advanced civilization in the world, and the most that could be done was to create a canon of acceptable foreign writers for internal consumption. The eventual result was the peculiar roster of modern English literature that Soviet citizens regarded as canonical, and which evoked wonderment at meetings with English native speakers, very few of whom had even heard of Richard Aldington, say, let alone read his novels.[15] It goes without saying that loyal Soviet citizens used to recoil from the canon of modern Russian literature proffered in Western universities and more widely in translations into English. But the Soviet policy was remarkably successful; to this day, even well-educated Russians commonly believe that they know English literature better than the English do, or at least know a better version of it.

The business of translation had to be organized and controlled, like all the other areas of literary endeavour under Stalinism. Immediately after the revolution, Gorky had initiated the grandiose 'World Literature' translation project in Petrograd; Chukovsky and Gumilyov had been leading lights in this enterprise. It ran into the sand when Gorky left the country. After the formation of the multinational USSR in 1924, the task of translation from and into the various constituent literatures became more vital than translation from the literatures of Western Europe and the USA. This area eventually developed into one of the most monstrous extravagences of the Soviet system.[16] Soon after the formation of the translation sector of the Writers' Union, there was a violent polemic about the relative merits of the two natural and inevitable approaches to the problem of translation: faithfulness either to the original or to the receiving culture. The official line soon condemned 'literalism' (i.e. faithfulness to the original) in favour of 'adequate' or 'equivalent' translation, that is, creating a matching work of art in the target culture, a doctrine that licensed the artistically impoverished but politically acceptable nature of the results. The first conference of Soviet translators met in the wake of the first Congress of Writers, from 3 to 7 January 1935 in Moscow. A conference on literature for children followed later that same month. These activities were to become the two principal 'feeding-troughs' (as Soviet professionals used to call them) from which not only hacks but many talented but a-Soviet writers were able to sustain themselves in subsequent years.

One of the most problematical authors facing the decision-makers in all this was James Joyce. Everybody was vaguely aware that he was regarded by the Western cultural élite as an outstanding novelist; everyone knew about his outsider's stance towards the Western cultural establishment, about his anti-clericalism and his contempt for British imperialism.[17] All this, and the fact that Joyce was censored in Western Europe, made his work a tempting exhibit for the Soviet system. But unfortunately he was not in any acceptable sense a realist, and so he could not be dished up to the Soviet reader without considerable hedging. Mirsky was the first Soviet critic to point these things out; his general conclusion was that Joyce was of little relevance for Soviet culture, from the point of view of both producers and consumers.[18] The polemic about

Joyce in which Mirsky was involved was conducted in a situation where very few of the participants had actually read *Ulysses*, to say nothing of *Finnegans Wake*.[19] Mirsky's adversaries had read at the most the chunk that he translated himself (brilliantly) in his first article on the subject, and two chapters from Stenich's translation, to which Mirsky supplied an introduction.[20]

On this issue Mirsky soon came into conflict with the playwright Vsevolod Vishnevsky (1900–52), the most unlikely champion that Joyce can ever have had. Vishnevsky was a bullying thug of a kind all too common in the Stalinist literary establishment. He had been a left-wing member of RAPP, and had belonged to the hard-line faction Litfront in 1930. Vishnevsky's speciality became national defence literature. He was deeply involved with the military wing of the intelligence services, became a leading light in the literary organization of the armed forces (LOKAF), and for many years played the role of premier civilian spokesman for the Soviet military.

Vishnevsky made the following entry in his diary for 5 November 1935: 'The prince has turned into a boor and must be put in his place. . . . I had attacked him in *Literary Critic* (1933) in my article "Know the West" and there is profound antipathy between us.'[21] The article Vishnevsky refers to is rivalled only by the one Khodasevich wrote about *Vyorsts* as the most sustained attempt that was made during his lifetime to destroy Mirsky as a literary critic.[22] It portrays him as an arrogant and ignorant newcomer on the critical scene who sets about sorting things out when the job had been taken care of long before by seasoned veterans like Vishnevsky himself. A good proportion of the article is concerned with establishing Vishnevsky's own credentials, displaying his manifest inferiority complex with regard to Mirsky's competence in English. Vishnevsky involuntarily exposes the shakiness of his own position; among other things, he evidently did not know of Mirsky's acquaintanceship with Yury Olesha, which seems to have been close:

Orientation can be very useful, and if Mirsky tried a bit of it, he would be able to make correct use of his knowledge of literature and the English language. Mirsky must have noticed that here in Russia it is customary to conduct polemic using a businesslike and proper tone. Possibly Mirsky will take the trouble simply to have a chat with a few Soviet writers about the West. Possibly, things like the difficulty of climbing up to the fifth floor of the writers' building where I live have prevented Mirsky having a chat with me about certain topics in military literature. And nobody is barring his way, for example, to a writer like Yury Olesha. . . . If Mirsky won't risk talking to Olesha, who is also working in a profound and original way on the problem of the West, I can give him a bit of help.

I've talked with Olesha (there is such a way of finding out people's views; so far Mirsky seems to be unfamilar with it). Here is a transcript of this conversation: 'I consider the movement represented by Joyce and Dos Passos to be progressive. True, I haven't read *Ulysses*, but Stenich, who is translating this book, has given me a keen idea of it. Dos Passos, I think, is taking further some of Tolstoy's devices.'

The derisory level of argumentation was neither here nor there, for Vishnevsky had entrenched himself in the literary bureacracy. He was a member of the Credentials Committee of the Union before the founding Congress, and it could well have been he who blackballed Mirsky as a delegate. There was no way out of this situation. Vishnevsky is now known to have been one of the most enthusiastic denouncers of his fellow writers to the security organs; the topics and names that would have come up if Mirsky had accepted his invitation to a fifth-floor conversation would certainly have been passed on to 'the proper quarter' (*kuda sleduet*), and only prejudiced Mirsky's dubious standing still further.[23]

ALEKSANDR FADEEV

Even at this early stage in the history of Stalinist culture and his own career, Aleksandr Fadeev (1901–56) was a heavyweight; that he should already be such in his early 30s was nothing unusual for the times, as we shall see again and again in encountering the people in authority who crossed Mirsky's path. Fadeev had been a member of the Party since 1918. He had an immaculate record in the Civil War, had been wounded in the armed suppression of the Kronstadt rising in 1921, and had then become a full-time Party worker. In 1927 he published his autobiographically based novel about the Civil War, *The Rout*, which instantly became a classic of Soviet literature and remained so until the end of the Communist regime. Mirsky had written about it several times in emigration. He referred to it in the late 1920s as a work that had been overtaken by subsequent developments, but in his intellectual autobiography of 1931 he accorded it a very important place:

Other transforming influences came from the direction of the USSR. In first place came Soviet literature: by 1927–28 a new wave, this time entirely proletarian, was beginning to roll back the formalist and semi-bourgeois literature of the men of 1921–22. Above all, it was Fadeev's remarkable novel *Rout* (*Razgrom*), a magisterial study of communist ethics and psychology, which made an ineffaceable impression on me.[24]

In the late 1920s Fadeev came to occupy a prominent place in RAPP; in terms of his social origins he was more genuinely proletarian than most other members. As a long-term Party member and official with an acknowledged Communist classic to his credit, he was tailor-made for high office in the new Union of Writers. On 6 May 1933 the draft Statute of the Union was published and the membership list opened. Fadeev's official standing may be judged from the fact that on the pages of *Pravda* he published a leading article on the draft Statute of the Union, jointly written with Pavel Yudin.[25] Among other policies, Fadeev and Yudin demanded the firm establishment of

Socialist Realism as 'the basic method of Soviet artistic literature and literary criticism'; this is one of the earliest published references to this notorious formula.[26] All the organizing committees for the founding Congress of the Union met in Moscow on 16–17 July 1933, and it was Fadeev who gave the principal report. The part Fadeev played in the Union during the purge years is still not entirely clear. But it is now thought that he started acting as the right-hand man of General Secretary Stavsky as early as 1936, and that he was deeply involved in the purges from the very beginning.[27] Clearly, Fadeev was one of the last people Mirsky should have crossed.

In June 1934, in the *Literary Gazette*, no less, Mirsky published an article called 'Intention and Fulfilment'. It contains a withering analysis of Fadeev's most recent and still incomplete novel *The Last of the Udege*, and ends with a categorical conclusion: 'Maturing with the epoch, Soviet literature has reached its present high level without the participation of Fadeev. In order to reach this level, Fadeev faces an enormous amount of work, and his first step will probably be to recognize that *The Last of the Udege* is a mistake in artistic terms.'[28] The Udege are a Siberian people; the point of Fadeev's novel was to show them being carrot-and-sticked into the high civilization of Soviet Communism. The first part of the novel was published in 1930, and the second, which is the part Mirsky attacked, in 1933. In the letter to Stavsky that he wrote just before his arrest, Mirsky gave a circumstantial account of how he came to write the offending article. He defends himself by pleading that he was conned:

In the early summer of 1934 Jasienski, whom I had not seen for a fairly long while before that, came to see me and struck up a conversation to the effect that a general demobilization and movement to the right was under way in literature, and that it should be resisted. He cited *The Last of the Udege* as an example of how moral problems were usurping political problems, and persuaded me to write an article about this novel. Since this was the first time I had ventured official criticism of a major writer who was a member of the Party, I wanted to try it out on my comrades who were members, and I read it to Korabelnikov and Jasienski. It did not satisfy them; they found it not pointed enough. I was weak enough to give in to them and revise it. In its final form it was edited in detail by Korabelnikov, with whom I was never close personally.[29]

Manifestly unspoken here is the part, if any, that Gorky played in starting this business; the circumstances were particularly fraught in the run-up to the founding Congress. On 27 June 1934 Yudin, in his official capacity as Party secretary in the Union's Organizing Committee, wrote a letter to the highest political authorities—Stalin, Kaganovich, and Zhdanov—expressing dissatisfaction with the recent contents of the *Literary Gazette*. The letter specifically mentioned Mirsky's article on *The Last of the Udege*, and stated that 'What the ex-Vrangel officer and ex-White *émigré* Mirsky (formerly Prince Svyatopolk-Mirsky) is doing ... is tantamount to drumming Comrade

Fadeev out of Soviet literature. . . . On Mirsky's part this is arrogance, to say the least. . . .'[30]

Mirsky's article was thus taken to be not only a personal assault on a trusted Party stalwart, but an assault on the official aims set by the Party and State authorities in cultural affairs. The article elicited a good deal of comment and led to some savage infighting. On 22 July the *Literary Gazette* printed a grovelling retraction of Mirsky's piece. One of the main points of Mirsky's argument had been that Fadeev was seeking to win back the favour of the intelligentsia, whom he had offended by painting the intellectual Meichik in *The Rout* as weak and vacillating.[31] Mirsky was therefore coming at Fadeev from the left; but several defenders of Fadeev took the opportunity to point out that this former White Guard officer had little standing from which righteously to find fault with people who had been loyal Communists since the Civil War. Gleb Struve asserts that as a result, 'For a time Mirsky's name disappeared from the *Literary Gazette*',[32] but this is not in fact the case: the rapturous article on Sholokhov's *Virgin Soil Upturned* that Mirsky published there as soon afterwards as 24 July was obviously an attempt to smooth over the mistake. The day before it appeared, *Pravda* published an article by Yudin demanding that the Party members get their line dominant in the Union of Writers. Mirsky's article on *The Last of the Udege* was called 'an irresponsible outburst by a man whom it costs nothing to pitch a talented proletarian writer out of literature'.[33]

Mirsky continues his account to Stavsky in 1937:

When the articles by Comrade Yudin and especially Comrade Kosarev appeared,[34] I understood them as a condemnation only of certain incorrect conclusions in the article and wanted to come out with an acknowledgement that they were incorrect. Jasienski tried to persuade me not to, saying 'Just wait a bit and you'll see that it'll be acknowledged as correct.'

Then Gorky intervened, and in a big way; whether or not he had seen Yudin's letter or not is not clear, but on 2 August he wrote to Stalin, expressing a lack of confidence in 'Yudin's group', and asserting bluntly: 'I consider Mirsky's evaluation of *The Last of the Udege* to be absolutely correct.'[35] Three days after Gorky stepped in, Yudin spoke to the meeting of critics that preceded the founding Congress and declared: 'It is impermissible to write in this way about any writer who has contributed something distinctive to Soviet literature. It is impermissible to allow people like Comrade Mirsky to decide the fate of Fadeev as a writer.'[36] Mirsky's own retrospective account of this meeting continues:

In his speech at the conference of critics before the Congress Korabelnikov responded negatively about this article, which had after all been edited by him; Jasienski spoke in my defence but did not say that what I had said was correct, just talked about my right to my own opinion about Fadeev's novel. . . . It was precisely the conduct of

Korabelnikov and Jasienski in this matter that implanted in me a profound mistrust for all kinds of advice and all attempts to direct me, which to a significant extent created that isolation in which I find myself now.[37]

On 24 January 1935 Gorky spoke out again in favour of Mirsky on the pages of *Pravda*:

Dm. Mirsky, an extraordinarily literate person, a wise critic, a member of the English Communist Party, was absolutely right when he indicated in print that *The Last of the Udege* did no credit to Soviet literature. This judgement is universally accepted, there is nothing offensive in it, and the author himself knows that the book is a very bad one. But Dm. Mirsky permitted himself to be born into this world of noble parents, and this has been enough to make people yell at him: 'How can he, a man guilty of this incorrect birth, criticize a book written by a member of the Communist Party?' . . . One needs to remember that Belinsky, Chernyshevsky, and Dobrolyubov were the sons of priests, and one could name several dozen sincere and important revolutionaries who were the children of bourgeois parents, but who have gone down in revolutionary history as the most honest of warriors and true comrades of [Vladimir] Ilich [Lenin].[38]

Fadeev himself seems to have been prepared to forgive and forget; on 10 April 1935 in a letter to one of his best friends, the poet Lugovskoy (with whom Mirsky had taken his trip to Central Asia), he delivered himself of a positive opinion of Mirsky as a critic, referring particularly to his enormous erudition.[39]

Fadeev had the reputation of being personally close to Stalin. Throughout his career he demonstrated unswerving obedience and devotion to the Leader. Eventually, in 1946, he became General Secretary of the Union of Writers. In 1956, with Stalin's reputation officially denounced by the Party, and after the first amnesty of political prisoners, confronted at literary gatherings by the silently eloquent faces of those few fortunate writers whose arrest warrants he had signed who had escaped execution and survived the camps, the vodka-sodden Fadeev committed suicide. Many literary people thought it was the first decent thing he had done in his entire life; but it is clear from his dealings with Mirsky that he had some respect for talent.[40]

POLYCRATES' RING

Korney Chukovsky was in Moscow at the time Gorky made his first public defence of Mirsky, and he records in his diary that he met Mirsky on 25 January 1935 when he lunched at the National Hotel. Gorky's defence of him in *Pravda* the day before came up in conversation. Chukovsky asked Mirsky if he was pleased. Mirsky's reply was even more gnomic than usual: 'Polycrates' ring.'[41]

The story of Polycrates comes from Herodotus. King Polycrates, who ruled during the fourth century BC, was successful in whatever he did. Thinking that Polycrates was tempting fate and needed to experience unhappiness to appreciate his luck, the king of Egypt advised him to dispose of his most precious possession. Polycrates threw his ring into the sea. A week later the ring was found inside a fish that had swallowed it, and returned to Polycrates. Soon afterwards the Persian satrap Oroit lured Polycrates into his power and had him hanged upside down.[42]

Whether or not Chukovsky grasped the implications of Mirsky's remark at the time is not clear. He goes on:

I find him extraordinarily nice. Broad education, sincerity, literary talent, the most absurd beard, absurd bald head, a suit that though it's English is unkempt, worn, and baggy, and a peculiar manner of listening—after every phrase uttered by the person he's talking to he utters a sympathetic 'ee-ee-ee' (a pig-like squeal in the throat)—in all this there's something amusing but endearing. He's got very little money, he's a convinced democrat, but from his high-born forebears he's inherited a taste for good food. He's ruining himself with his gluttony. Every day he parks his poverty-stricken little fur hat and his dog-fur-lined overcoat with the doorman at the National, goes into the opulent restaurant there, and never leaves behind him less than 40 roubles (since he doesn't just eat, he drinks as well) and he tips the waiter 4 roubles and the doorman 1.[43]

It was probably a year later, in 1936, that Mirsky's unregenerate tipping habits were also observed by John Lehmann, who seems to have been the only Bloomsburyite to have visited the motherland of socialism:

In my Moscow hotel I used sometimes after dinner (which means round about midnight)[44] to meet Prince Mirski, whom I had known slightly in London before he made his gesture of return to Russia. In spite of his conversion to Bolshevism, he could not rid himself entirely of the Old Adam: he used to give huge tips to the waiters (many of whom were themselves weary relics of the *ancien régime*) with an aristocratic disdain for the change, and conversed freely about literature in Bloomsbury terms. I remember talking with him one night about Zoshchenko, Olyesha, and other Soviet writers who seemed not to care overmuch for the fatuous dictators of Socialist Realism. 'Yes, it still goes on', he said in a rather gloomy undertone. 'But I wouldn't like to say how long our political leaders will stand for it.'[45]

THE II PLENUM OF 1935

Mirsky published an article in the *Literary Gazette* on 28 December 1934 complaining about the poor showing criticism had received at the founding Congress.[46] He may well have been voicing a view that the leadership shared, or perhaps Gorky had suggested the idea, because the second plenary meeting of the Union of Writers was duly held in Moscow from 2 to 7 March 1935, its principal topic announced as the state of literary criticism. It was preceded by a meeting of the Union's Presidium at which two of the principal speeches intended for the Plenum, by Bespalov and Afinogenov, were discussed. It was at this same meeting that Pasternak made an extraordinarily negative speech about the present state of Soviet literary criticism.[47] Mirsky's December article anticipates many of the major issues that were discussed at the Plenum. It is worth dwelling on what happened at this meeting, for three reasons. First, it gives a very good idea of the general state of Mirsky's specialist field at the time he was most active in it. Secondly, it may serve as an example of the kind of meeting that Mirsky spent a good deal of time attending in 1935–6. Most adults are familiar with the way bureaucracies function, and in particular the way their minions conduct formal meetings, but there has been no real equivalent elsewhere for the ponderous grinding of the Soviet machine, especially in its Stalinist phase, peculiarly compounded as its public proceedings were from ritual self-congratulation and licensed self-criticism, with a minimum of hard facts and practically no autonomy for individuals. Thirdly, this particular occasion has attracted curiously little attention from literary historians, including even those who have attempted detailed accounts of the early history of the Union of Writers. This is readily understandable in terms of the limits of human intellectual forbearance. Very few people can ever have waded through the 714 closely-printed large-format verbatim proceedings of the founding conference (which, like the White Sea Canal book, was rapidly withdrawn because of the prominent contributions by such as Bukharin and Radek); even fewer can ever have found the stamina to go on and tackle the record of the next big occasion of this kind, which fills 517 admittedly smaller but still forbiddingly dense pages.

The proceedings of the II Plenum were published very expeditiously.[48] The meeting was conducted by the bloated, owl-bespectacled alcoholic A. S. Shcherbakov, the manifest hand of Stalin in the Union's business.[49] One of the first motions he put to the Plenum was to welcome an equally odious fellow apparatchik to the presidium: A. I. Stetsky.[50]

The opening speech was delivered by Gorky himself, an indication of the meeting's status. His remarks were blunt and crude. He endorsed the self-congratulatory Party line about the current state of Soviet politics and society as promulgated at the XVII Party Congress. After this, though, his remarks about current state of Soviet literary culture were almost entirely negative. Indeed, they would have been regarded as actionable coming from almost anyone else; only Gorky and a few foreign fellow-travellers had a mandate to speak like this.

Gorky declared that he had read the speeches that were about to be read (which takes some believing), and he condemned them as excessively theoretical. He demanded that instead of all this rhetoric, simple questions be asked, such as: 'Why is our literature backward? Why is our playwriting weak?'—and why, with the twentieth anniversary of the Revolution fast approaching and needing to be celebrated in an appropriate way (we know how in fact it was celebrated, the year in question being 1937), the new Soviet reality was still not being reflected in the literature that was being produced. 'People are not working hard, and they're working badly to boot,' he concluded.

Shcherbakov then took over and announced that there would be four major items on the agenda. Three of them would be reports. First, Ivan Mikhailovich Bespalov would speak on 'The Situation and Tasks of Soviet Criticism'.[51] Bespalov's report would be followed by two papers from practising writers: the prominent novelist Marietta Shaginyan (1888–1982) on 'What the Writer Expects from Criticism', and the playwright Aleksandr Afinogenov on 'Theatrical Criticism'.[52] The second major item would be by one I. I. Mints, who would report on behalf of the editorial committee of the project to write the history of the Civil War. The third, with which we are familiar already, would be a similar report by Vsevolod Ivanov on behalf of the editorial board of the 'History of the Factories' project. Fourthly and finally, Shcherbakov himself would speak to the confirmation of the plan of work by the directorate of the Union of Writers for the year 1935.

It would seem from all this that the main purpose of the Plenum was to mop up the issues that had slipped off the agenda of the founding Congress, and it is tempting to think that the reasons for the omissions had more to do with haste and administrative incompetence than calculated disparagement. Planning the early gatherings of the Union must have been a nightmare, with novice administrators learning on the job and things going wrong all over the place. Mirsky's absence from the founding Congress may even have been caused by his section of the proceedings being shunted off the agenda from sheer lack of time.

The agenda as announced by Shcherbakov was not clearly followed during the actual meeting. The reports by Bespalov, Shaginyan, and Afinogenov were duly delivered, one after the other. Bespalov's speech amounts to about 14,000 long Russian words, and is a model of Stalinist cultural discourse, following a paradigm that was repeated thousands and thousands of times at formal meetings. It begins with a roll-call of 'achievements', as per the latest pronouncements of the Central Committee. These achievements represent an overcoming of 'well-known' deviations and mistakes; but certain 'shortcomings' remain, and so what needs to be done is . . . — followed by an agenda which the audience was supposed to rush away and get down to. The main shortcoming identified by Bespalov was that the critics were not doing their job in explicating all the wonderful literary material that was being produced by the writers for the Soviet masses. Neither—and here comes the standard note of menacing 'vigilance'—were they condemning certain writers whose work was objectionable to the Party.

Shaginyan closed the first day. Instead of going for the critics, she weighed in with some devastating criticism of two of her fellow novelists: Erenburg for *The Second Day*, and Mirsky's colleague Jasienski for *A Man Changes His Skin*. This was the novel that drew on the research trip the author had made to

Central Asia in the company of Mirsky in 1933.[53] Shaginyan's purpose was to demonstrate that the professional critics were incompetent at literary analysis, and she offered a model of what they *should* have said about Jasienski's book, asserting that it was badly written, mangled in design and execution because of the author's revisions between serial and book publication, and so on. The third keynote report was Afinogenov's speech, on theatre criticism; it opened the second day of the Plenum on 3 March. Then came a rambling series of speeches from the floor. These proceedings took up seven sessions (duly punctuated by ten-minute breaks for the benefit of the nicotine addicts), and ended with the morning session (it began at 10.30, no doubt to allow for hangovers) on 7 March. On the evening of 5 March the proceedings were peremptorily wound up to allow for a concert by some Karelian folk singers,[54] after which the writers repaired to the House of Cinema, where—no doubt a blessed relief—they watched two foreign films, which are unfortunately not identified in the published proceedings.

The speakers from the floor were called in no particular order, and several of them complain about being unprepared or inappropriately placed. Their contributions blunder about among the issues that had been broached by the principal speakers, the one partial exception being that what looks like a structured climax had been arranged for the sixth session, when there was a concentration of local critical heavyweights; it took place on the evening of 5 March before the folk singers and films. This was when Mirsky was given the floor. Towards the end of this session Shcherbakov came in with the heavy Party line, which would have formed the logical climax to the proceedings; but then on the morning of 6 March four more speakers were allowed to take the floor, one of them being Samuil Marshak. After a total of fifty-two people had spoken, the chairman put a motion to terminate the discussion, even though over sixty more people still had their names down to speak. This motion was carried by acclamation from the presidium, and then yet two more speakers were allowed to reply to personal attacks that had been made on them in the preceding discussion. Finally, Afinogenov, Shaginyan, and Bespalov were given the opportunity to deliver concluding remarks; the two writers were acerbic about the things the critics had said, but Bespalov tried to strike a statesman-like note, becoming even more stilted than in his opening speech.

The critics who gathered at this Plenum embodied Mirsky's professional field in year two of its full Sovietization. The entire current roster was on display; and the difference between it and its equivalent five years earlier is very instructive.[55] The senior figure present at the Plenum of March 1935—he was just over 40 at the time—was Viktor Shklovsky, one of Soviet literature's most miraculous survivors, the only founding Formalist to remain in tolerably good odour throughout the Stalin period. But gone were the old guard who had 'overcome' Shklovsky and his Formalist comrades and struggled to establish Marxist literary criticism and history in the 1920s. The most eminent figures among them happened to have died just in time—Vladimir Fritshe (1870–1929), Pavel Sakulin (1868–1930), Pyotr Kogan (1872–1932), and Vyacheslav Polonsky (1886–1932). Some other recent stars had been extinguished by other means. Aleksandr Voronsky (1884–1943), the first great journal editor of the post-revolutionary period with *Red Virgin Soil*, had been anathematized as early as 1927 and banished to Siberia, though not placed under arrest. At the time of the Plenum Voronsky had been allowed back to Moscow again, and much of what he had once advocated became official Union policy. He was never re-admitted into a responsible position, though; instead, he plodded on in obscurity before being duly arrested in 1937.[56] Another absentee was the former pride of the Communist Academy, Bespalov's disgraced teacher Valerian Pereverzev.[57]

The person most spectacularly absent from the Plenum, of course, was Mirsky's mentor Leopold Averbakh. Almost all the critics who spoke at the Plenum owed their early careers to Averbakh, Pereverzev, or Voronsky, and to Averbakh in particular—they had all been involved in the White Sea Canal project under his editorship, for example. During Bespalov's opening survey these erstwhile giants were accorded curt anathematization, followed by the occasional vicious side-swipe during the discussion from the floor. They were on the Party's list for licensed abuse, and not to abuse them was therefore potentially suspicious; the sure sign that they were now beyond rational discussion was that their surnames had already been suffixed to form minatory collective nouns to stand for the obnoxious words and deeds now officially associated with their bearers: *averbákhshchina*, *perevérzevshchina*, *vorónshchina*.

The limelight at the conference was held by the men in their 30s who had emerged as the victors from the polemics that had raged in the period before 1932. These polemics were constantly referred to at the Plenum by another minatory noun, *gruppóvshchina*, 'the time of squabbles between the groups' which had preceded the all-wise solution announced by the Central Committee resolution of 23 April 1932. These men formed Mirsky's peer group after his return to Russia. The majority of them, like Mirsky, were living their last few years in freedom or on this earth.

In the morning session on 7 March, after fifteen speeches had already been made, Vsevolod Vishnevsky peddled his warmongering stuff with the same relish as at the I Congress the year before. The highlight of his (justifiably, as things turned out) alarmist revelations about the Japanese military build-up was that their soldiers were being trained to eat kasha instead of rice so they would be able to forage locally when they invaded Russian territory. Eventually, Shcherbakov delivered the final motion, proposing the texts of resolutions on the main subjects covered at the conference, before he called on Gorky to close the proceedings. The texts of the resolutions form a series of appendices to the published record of the Plenum.

The part of this welter of verbiage that directly concerned Mirsky was the criticism of poetry. The critics were chary of addressing this topic because, as we know, Bukharin had spoken about it at the founding Congress the previous year, and the political charge was therefore high. In the last few words of his keynote address, Bespalov turned to poetry, and made a reference to Mirsky's article of 5 February,[58] citing his remarks about the work of the poet being less regular than that of the prose writer, professional poets therefore having more free time than other writers, and that working in journalism was good for prose writers but bad for poets. Bespalov turned all this into a clumsy threat about Soviet poets idling away their time. Subsequently, Selivanovsky ticked Mirsky off for the *Literary Gazette* article in which he had come out for Adalis's collection *Power* as a model for the future development of Soviet poetry.[59] This was relatively lightweight stuff.

As we have seen, Mirsky got his chance to speak on his own account at the evening session on 5 March.[60] Without saying anything directly about Pasternak himself, Mirsky made some criticism of Erenburg's interpretation of Pasternak's work. Erenburg, he declared, lacked an understanding of Marxism, and furthermore—this was a really underhand allegation—was compromised by his long-standing friendship with Bukharin and his demonstrative closeness to him at the founding Congress.[61] The main purpose of Mirsky's speech, however, was to mount a defence of Soviet criticism; he insisted that by and large the critics were more cultured than the writers—with the strong implication that this was not saying very much. In particular, Mirsky singled out Georgy Lukács and his colleagues at the Communist Academy for their excellent work on the historical novel.[62]

Much more serious than anything that Mirsky said himself during the Plenum was the prominent place Shcherbakov gave to an attack on him very near the beginning of his summing-up. His argument was a model Stalinist syllogism: since at the I Congress Zhdanov had stated that Soviet literature was 'the most ideologically aware, the most advanced, and the most revolutionary' in the world, and since criticism was a part of Soviet literature, then Mirsky must have been making a mistake when he said that writers ignore critics and that criticism had lost its former political authority. Mirsky's name was mentioned by another principal speaker, Vsevolod Ivanov, in the course of a speech that is on a significantly higher intellectual level than the others that were delivered on this occasion. Ivanov objected to Mirsky's characterization of writers as ignorant of Marxist-Leninist theory, and said he thought Mirsky's speech in this respect exhibited—here he used a somewhat old-fashioned word—*komchvanstvo* ('Commieswank'), a remark that evoked 'laughter'. This is an example of what became a commonplace view of Mirsky as a has-been who was now *plus royaliste que le roi*. Ivanov also said he thought Mirsky simply didn't know many writers—which was broadly true, because he spent his time writing about them rather than hobnobbing with them; in addition, he seems to have preferred poets to writers of prose like Ivanov.

In his concluding speech Gorky once more came to Mirsky's defence. 'Mirsky's opinion about poets doing newspaper work has been cited, about its harmful influence on them. I think Mirsky is right as far as major poetic talents are concerned. It is of course inefficient [!] to squander talent of this kind on feuilletons, music-hall chansonettes, and in general on trifles . . .'[63] However, Gorky was mainly concerned to draw attention to the rising level of triviality in Soviet culture—a point that was worth making, even though it was usually laced with a good deal of élitist and fogeyish contempt for the genuinely popular entertainment that was coming in as part of the embourgeoisement of the culture.

The Plenum then turned to discuss the literary coverage of the Civil War. It is tempting to wonder what might have gone through Mirsky's mind when he heard the following words, spoken by a certain Eideman:

Writers have failed to grasp so important an element of the civil war of 1918–20 as the wholesale, totally undisguised, deranged and savage terror of the dying classes, terror that very often recalled the fearsome final chapters of the Paris commune. Even today as I stand on this platform I can still hear the glassy ringing against the telegraph poles made by the stiff-frozen bodies of the Red Army men, partisans, Communist workers, and simply honest folks, who had been strung up by Denikin when we were advancing on Kharkov. I remember this very well.[64]

Several things happened soon after this Plenum which set the proceedings in some sort of perspective. On 7 April 1935 liability to the death penalty for various civil crimes, such as industrial espionage, was extended down to 12-year-olds. And just over a fortnight after that, on 23 April, Ambassador William Bullitt threw the notorious party at the American Embassy to which Bulgakov was invited after Bullitt had seen his play *The Days of the Turbins*; this party was the prototype for Satan's ball in *The Master and Margarita*. Mirsky may well have been there too; he gave lectures from time to time to visiting American students.[65] Then, in early June, came a spectacular fall: one of Stalin's closest cronies, Avel Enukidze (b. 1877), was denounced for immoral conduct and expelled from the Central Committee and the Party. In the publicity following this event, the newspapers carried attacks accusing Enukidze of harbouring enemies of the people, such as 'former princes, ministers, courtiers, Trotskyites, etc.'.[66] Who were these 'former princes', one wonders? After this, the period from July 1935 to August 1936 was relatively quiet; it is remembered by Russians who lived to tell the tale as a year of nervous calm before the ultimate storm. Enukidze languished for more than two years; he was executed on 30 October 1937.

After the founding Congress of the Union of Writers in 1934, the next was not held until 1954, the year after Stalin's death. The Union's day-to-day affairs were in the hands of the Directorate, a politically driven body that liaised closely with the Central Committee of the Party. The plenum became the routine form of stocktaking, when the Directorate displayed to the political leadership that it was doing the job they required of it. Mirsky was to attend another plenum, the Third, less than a year after the Second. The baleful question of how seriously to take what was said at these meetings is unanswerable. One comes away with the impression that the non-Party participants were licensed to indulge themselves in public advocacy of their pet causes and institutions, and then the Party heavyweights laid down the law and got on with the agenda that was set before the meeting, irrespective of anything that had been said from the floor. All this is standard practice for ideologically driven conferences, political, religious, and financial, in all cultures; but only in Stalin's Russia did physical extermination hover so heavily in the wings.

PASTERNAK AND SOVIET POETRY

At the 1935 Plenum, Mirsky spoke primarily as a critic of poetry. In the first half of 1935 he established himself as the leading critic in this field, publishing a series of articles in the central press; the first of them had already appeared by the time of the Plenum. He may well have been redeployed (*pere-broshen*, in the militarized parlance of the Writers' Union) into the sector of poetry criticism by Gorky in the autumn of 1934.[67] After the fuss caused by the argument about Fadeev, it probably seemed politic to shift Mirsky out of the field of prose.

Poetry, however, was no less of a minefield. Gorky was incontestably the No. 1 prose writer, but after the suicide of Mayakovsky and the death of Bagritsky there was a vacancy for Poet No. 1. Of the poets who qualified for the position on literary merit, Akhmatova not only had been subjected to an unspoken ban since 1925, but was anyway a manifestly a–Soviet figure, and a woman to boot. Mandelshtam started writing poetry again in 1931 after a long silence, but he was soon given to understand that his contribution was not required in the new Russia. The obvious candidate for the position of Poet No. 1 was Pasternak. But no matter how hard Pasternak had tried to Sovietize himself, he was after all a sprig of the pre-revolutionary intellectual élite, Jewish, foreign-educated, with parents and sisters living abroad, and he was not a member of the Party. He famously claimed that he had been 'born again' in 1931–2, but nobody really understood the rather more accessible poetry he started writing then, even among his fellow professionals. When Pasternak wrote prose or tried to explain himself through public speaking, he tended to become even more opaque. His speech to the founding Congress of the Union of Writers is a case in point. Among right-thinking Communists this lofty complexity and intangibility created the distinct impression that the author was suspiciously a-Soviet, or perhaps even subversively anti-Soviet. The problem of poetry soon became the problem of Pasternak, and Mirsky became embroiled in another welter of animosities.

There was another very serious difficulty. The principal speech about poetry at the founding Congress, as we know, happened to have been delivered by Bukharin—who knew considerably more about the subject than Karl Radek did about James Joyce, for example, and who shared some of the old intelligentsia's piety towards the practitioners. The keynote of his speech was a constant refrain in Gorky's articles too: 'quality' (*kachestvo*), which soon became a heavily loaded concept. For how could quality be achieved, when practically all the models worthy of respect were by ideologically unacceptable poets writing before 1917? Mirsky and many other Soviet critics were to wrestle desperately with this problem in the next few years. Bukharin endorsed Pasternak as Poet No. 1, but for the reasons just listed, this was unacceptable in Party circles. The eventual answer, since no living No. 1 was forthcoming, was to sanitize the dead Mayakovsky and use him instead. This was announced by Stalin in his famous statement of 5 December 1935, thereby letting Pasternak off the hook, for which he was duly grateful.[68] Mirsky was one of the first critics to respond to the Leader's canonization of Mayakovsky.[69]

Mirsky addressed Bukharin's speech in the course of a general survey called 'Problems of Poetry' that he published early in February 1935, just before the Plenum.[70] He put distance between himself and Bukharin's position, claiming that it had licensed an excess of emotional lyricism at the expense of ideas. This was to become Mirsky's calling-card, and it evoked a good deal of resentment, for some influential people naturally drew the conclusion that he was calling them wet and stupid. Mirsky's stance in 1935, it should be noted, is entirely consistent with that of his principal writings on the subject in emigration, where he had written of 'the poetry of will and reason' as the best.

In this article Mirsky also referred to a current scandal in Moscow literary circles. Late in January 1935, there took place what seems to have been the first case of an expulsion from the Union of Writers. The member concerned was the poet Pavel Vasiliev, who was prodigiously talented but unreliable (to use a word favoured by men in suits). There had been a constant row about his work since Gorky had condemned him in the summer of 1934 for 'hooliganism'. The precise nature of the incident that took place early in 1935 could never be spelled out in print, given Soviet conventions, but the main offence was known to have something to do with drunkenness—not the licensed behind-closed-doors swilling that was characteristic of all levels of Soviet male society, but riotous behaviour and falling down incapable in the street, which was not. Vasiliev was a virulent anti-Semite, and in public one day in a drunken rage he physically assaulted a fellow poet, Jack Altauzen (1907–42; he was killed in one of the battles for Kharkov). Mirsky's line on this 'hooliganism' was that the cultural level of young poets needed to be raised in order to counter the 'kulak tendency' exemplified by Vasiliev's behaviour. The raising of poetic culture would be possible, said Mirsky in the kind of clotted phrase that now crops up more and more in his writing, only by means of 'a repudiation of the epigonic exploitation of outdated versificatory norms and an incorporation of the achievements of Symbolism and Futurism', i.e. learning from the enemy.

It was at this point that the Plenum took place, with the opportunities it offered for indignant rebuttals. Mirsky's articles on current poetry continued to appear after it. He retaliated against Selivanovsky and Surkov, who had attacked him at the Plenum, calling for poetry that made 'great lyrical generalizations'.[71] This article centres on a problem that was to exercise Soviet criticism for ever after: the proper place of the lyric hero in Soviet poetry, that is, the individual versus the collective.[72] Mirsky made a classic statement here, typical of his work at this point:

Not all poetry and not all lyric poetry has to have a lyric hero. The 'lyric hero' (i.e. the author's 'I' as the subject of lyric biography) is first and foremost characteristic of bourgeois poetry. In pre-bourgeois poetry as often as not it is absent. And in the classic poetry of the ascendant bourgeoisie and bourgeois democracy the poet was often able to forswear the lyric hero and become a lyric voice which is the direct lyric expression of his epoch and class. Schiller's philosophical lyrics are of this kind, so is the poetry of Whitman, the second American revolution's poet of genius,[73] and so is a significant part of the best revolutionary-democratic poetry, Barbier's *Iambes* for example. . . . The dominance of the lyric hero in Soviet poetry for such a long time, including its best poets (Mayakovsky, Bagritsky), may be explained precisely by the persistent domination of the theme of 'me and the revolution'. With the growth of proletarian poetry and the transition of Soviet literature to a higher—socialist—level, the lyric hero is experiencing a crisis and even exhibiting a tendency to disappear.[74]

On 15 April 1935 came the first of a pair of survey articles by Mirsky about the Soviet poetry published during 1934 in which he argued that the non-Russian part of it was in a healthier state than the Russian, thanks to the excellent recent translations of Georgian poets by Pasternak and Tikhonov.[75] The second article dealt with current Leningrad poetry, and is not much more than a list of names.[76] When Mirsky was dutifully going through these second-raters, did his thoughts turn to the two figures from his past whom he knew full well to be the greatest living poets of the former capital, Anna Akhmatova and Osip Mandelshtam? Did he know where Mandelshtam was? There can be no doubt that he did know.

On 27 April 1935 the Critics' Section of the Union held a 'Discussion of Literary Conclusions of 1934'. At this meeting, Mirsky referred to Mayakovsky's famous phrase and stated that 'Poets do not have the right to step on the throat of their own song', and defended Zabolotsky's new long poem 'The Triumph of Agriculture'. He was thoroughly told off by yet another young whelp, A. K. Tarasenkov (1909–1956), who ran the criticism section of the *Banner*. Tarasenkov told him that 'You are excessively liberal, Comrade Mirsky', that his opinion of Zabolotsky's poetry, the influence of which was 'rotten and harmful', was 'extraordinarily incorrect', and finally:

It seems to me that Comrade Mirsky is profoundly wrong in ascribing any particular artistic fertility to Zabolotsky. His influence is harmful, insulting to our poetry, and is hindering very many young poets from seeing the genuine greatness, seriousness, and profundity of the world, which is what he ought to be depicting in his creative work.[77]

In the middle of May 1935 there was another meeting of the Presidium of the Union of Writers at which poetry was discussed. Pasternak made one more of his astonishing speeches, full of barely comprehensible qualifications, but unmistakably declaring among other things that individual poems could not express a particular 'class ideology'.[78] Once again, whether or not Mirsky was present on this occasion is not clear; but he was certainly in close touch with Pasternak at this time.[79]

EDMUND WILSON

After the indignity with the stonebreaker under his window in Rusakovskaya Street, in the early summer of 1934 Mirsky had moved nearer the middle of town, into a building on the major thoroughfare leading north-west from the Red Square, the old Tverskaya, which had recently been renamed Gorky Street after his patron. He lived at Flat 68 in the building of the same number. Though centrally situated, this was no luxury quarters. For a start, the location was too far north to be a really prestigious address; anyone who was anyone lived down the hill towards the Kremlin at No. 25 ('Herzen House', where a number of prominent writers resided) and lower. Edmund Wilson visited Mirsky at No. 68 in the summer of 1935. Twenty years later he published the most substantial and also the most vivid piece of personal reminiscence we have about Mirsky.[80]

Wilson (1895–1972) was similar to Mirsky in some important ways, but radically different in others. He came from the American upper middle class and had an élite education. Like Mirsky, he was usually impatient to be getting on with his work, and did not make small talk; in conversation he would lecture, not discuss. He too was a serious drinker. His political evolution took him from aestheticism to left-wing political commitment; largely because of the Wall Street crash and subsequent economic depression, in 1931 he became a 'progressive', but he never actually joined the Communist Party.[81] Wilson did his best to be cosmopolitan, though compared to Mirsky he was a mediocre linguist.

Wilson's account of his first visit to Mirsky on Gorky Street will strike a chord in all foreign Russianists, evoking that awful sinking feeling one has while searching for an address in the bowels of a big Moscow building with endless dank internal courtyards:

I found Mirsky, when I first went to call on him, in antique and rather shabby surroundings . . . The address I had took me, I found, through a dark and narrow passage that was cluttered by a secondhand bookstall. I came out into a cobbled court . . . and had to penetrate beyond that to a second one. . . . I located Mirsky's door on the stairway of one of the entrances. It was covered—I supposed, for warmth—by what I took to be a piece of old carpet. This muted my attempt to knock, so I tried turning the bell, which did not seem to ring. Though he had made an appointment with me, I decided he had not yet come in, so went away to kill time for an hour. . . . When I returned, I worked the bell in the other direction, and this time I heard it ring. The door was opened, and I saw before me, standing immobile and very erect, a tall, bearded, bald, and bespectacled man who stared at me without shaking hands. He invited me in, however, and apologised for receiving me in his dressing-gown, in which, he said, he always worked.[82]

Mirsky seemed very ill at ease, as well he might. Wilson 'learned later that, returning to Russia, he had insisted on only one thing: that he should have a room to himself'. Virginia Woolf's advice had not gone unnoticed, it seems; but Mirsky's insistence had not got him very far. The flat where Wilson visited him was not his; he had made an arrangement to occupy one of its two rooms while the tenant was away. On 24 May 1934 Mirsky wrote to Dorothy Galton from there:

I have moved to the centre of the town . . . The room is worse, and the other room is occupied by a lady who translates Shakespeare, & is the wife of two men, one of whom is a very old friend of mine, but absent building a railway in Bashkiria. She is a bore, which is a bore, considering the very great proximity. . . . Fortunately she lives permanently in Leningrad & is here only because of *Romeo & Juliet*.

The 'lady who translates Shakespeare' was Anna Dmitrievna Radlova (née Darmolatova, 1891–1949). This particular letter to Miss Galton was written about a week after Radlova's brother-in-law, Osip Mandelshtam, had been arrested. Radlova was a graduate of the exclusive Bestuzhev Courses for Women in St Petersburg, and may well have known Mirsky before 1917. Her translations of *Othello*, *Romeo and Juliet*, *Richard III*, and *Macbeth* were published in one volume in 1935; her translation of *Hamlet* appeared in 1937. Her second husband was the eminent Leningrad theatre director Sergey Ernestovich Radlov (1892–1958).[83] The other husband and 'very old friend' was the man in whose flat Mirsky and Radlova were camping out, one of his old schoolmates, Kornily Pokrovsky.[84] The dedicatee of Kuzmin's 'Lazarus' had become a railway engineer. The statement that he was 'absent in Bashkiria' immediately suggests a coded reference to the GULag, but this was apparently not the case. However, Pokrovsky came to a different sort of bad end. The Radlovs were on holiday together in Sochi when Pokrovsky hanged himself in

Moscow in the summer of 1938—perhaps in the very apartment that Anna had shared with Mirsky.

Wilson said that Mirsky's appearance in the summer of 1935 'had something of Kropotkin, something of Edward Lear', and duly noted his oriental eyes and hideous teeth. Mirsky

would offset the bristling and slant-eyed mask appearance that recalled the Muscovite tsars by a giggle that suggested Edward Lear and was not always the proper accompaniment for the conventional Communist sneer. Or Kropotkin would come to the fore, and, warmed by the good cheer, his dark eyes would melt and glow with an emotional sensibility and idealism that had something quite guileless and touching.[85]

During the time Wilson spent in Moscow, Mirsky disappeared for three weeks; it turned out that he had been to Tashkent. Wilson supposed that he had been given a low-grade assignment in order to humiliate him, but the effect had actually been to cheer Mirsky up immensely; he had in fact been giving lectures on Russian literature to local officials, and seemed to feel that he had been doing something in which he believed and which was of use to the state.

Wilson does not mention the most notable literary event that took place while he was in Moscow; it is inconceivable that he and Mirsky did not discuss it. This was the International Congress in Defence of Culture that met in Paris from 21 to 25 June. The preparations for it were extremely fraught, with the literary authorities in Moscow spending a good deal of effort getting agreement with the Central Committee about which Soviet authors to send.[86] At the last moment Pasternak and Babel were added to the delegation; Pasternak made a non-speech which was greeted with rapturous acclaim, and for which he was not punished as soon as he got back, but which was used in evidence against him shortly thereafter. Pasternak was in a state of almost gibbering terror while he was abroad.[87] The person he opened his heart to during this trip was none other than the dreaded Shcherbakov, with whom he shared a cabin on the sea journey back to Russia. This marked the height of Pasternak's attempts to join in with the Sovietization of literature; after Shcherbakov was replaced by Stavsky, the poet withdrew from public life.

On 9 July 1935 Mirsky was summoned along with about twenty other Soviet writers to meet Romain Rolland at Gorky's dacha; they included Kataev, Seifullina, Selvinsky, Shaginyan—and two novelists whom Mirsky had known in the West, Lev Nikulin and Galina Serebryakova ('Mrs Sokolnikoff'). All of them could apparently manage to make themselves understood in French. Rolland praised Mirsky's book on Lenin, but Mirsky said he would not have written it now since he had subsequently 'moved forward'.[88]

Edmund Wilson thus saw Mirsky when he was at the height of his official acceptance as a Soviet critic. The summer of 1935 was the last he had of his customary travel and intense writing. He had less than two years of liberty left.

'PARALYSIS OF THE WILL'

At the end of September 1935 Mirsky moved to the address at which he was arrested, Flat 125 (soon afterwards renumbered 22), 7 Bolshoy Karetny pereulok, further out from the centre than before, but not by very much. He reported to Dorothy Galton that the room was on the fifth floor and had no lift, but commanded a splendid view over northern Moscow. After a year living here, he was to complain to the Union of Writers about how difficult it was to work in his room, one of a set of four that made up a *kommunalka* with shared bath and kitchen. Vera Traill said that Mirsky did not want her to see the conditions he was living in, and did not visit his room. Most survivors of the time say they lay awake listening to the lift. One can imagine the occupants of Mirsky's building in 1937 listening to try and make out on which floor the footsteps in the night would stop, and perhaps taking a last look at the splendid northerly view.

Though the clouds were gathering around him, Mirsky continued to be sent on official trips by the Union of Writers. On 12 May 1935 he told Dorothy Galton he was leaving the next day for Stalinabad (now Dushanbe); this journey, as we know from Wilson's testimony, was postponed until the summer. On 9 December Mirsky told Miss Galton that he had just been in the Donbass at a Congress of Beginning Writers, which was 'very interesting, but very tiring, especially the train'.

Mirsky's article 'Pasternak and the Georgian Poets' appeared in the *Literary Gazette* on 24 October 1935; it was part of a rising level of discussions of Pasternak's work late that year.[89] In June he had spoken of Pasternak's work as an exemplification of a 'disappearing' tendency in the present-day lyric, a 'poetry of exclusive, refined sensations, a poetry of the impressionistic mythologization of the external world, a poetry of nuances and moods'.[90] Mirsky now motivated his rapturous acclamation of Pasternak's work by reference to the specificities of its civic position, its independence in principle, and its refusal to take part in 'time-serving opportunism'. This article contains some penetrating insights into Pasternak's own poetry, because Mirsky is arguing mainly about whether or not he 'remained himself' when translating or subordinated himself to the style of the poet he was working on:

One sometimes hears the opinion that Pasternak writes Russian like a foreigner. This is total nonsense. Pasternak writes Russian like a poet, i.e. not as the slave of the language but its master. . . . Mayakovsky puts words into unusual contexts but never loses sight of or allows one to forget their original colouring. The element of contrast (between a vulgar conversational word and an elevated lyrical intonation, for example) plays a primary role in Mayakovsky's style. Pasternak has none of this. He as it were proclaims equal rights for all the words in the language, their identical suitability for all intonations. Mayakovsky's style 'sounds' at its fullest against the background of the poetry that precedes him. Pasternak writes as if nobody before him had ever written anything in Russian.[91]

At this stage, in the late autumn of 1935, there took place an incident which was probably a carry-over from Mirsky's old assignment to prose. Yet another of Gorky's grandiose publishing schemes proposed a series of Russian literary classics of special interest to collective farm workers; the person put in charge of it was Vladimir Yakovlevich Zazubrin.[92] At an editorial meeting on 13 November Mirsky was allotted the preface to the works of Pisemsky. He came late to this meeting, and attempted to get a clear idea of what kind of prefaces were required. Zazubrin summarized Gorky's directive, which amounted to saying that the prefaces should be political rather than literary. He describes the effect of this in reporting back to Gorky on 15 November:

D. P. Mirsky reacted to this very sharply; he took my words as a direct personal insult and announced: 'I cannot do business with you. I refuse. I can't do it like that. I can only write about the author and his works, putting them at the basis of everything.' Begging his pardon—I think Mirsky is happier with formal than with sociological analysis. Good luck to him. Somebody else can do the commentary for the Pisemsky.

There seemed to be some threat that some of the other critics would follow Mirsky's line, but they came round after further discussion, and eventually Mirsky was the only one who refused to take part in the new series.[93] This incident was no doubt made known to the Union authorities as further evidence of Mirsky's unreliability.

Mirsky then went back to Pasternak and other poets. On 28 January 1936 he published an article in *Izvestiya* called 'On Soviet Poetry', in which he defended Pasternak's translations of three Georgian poets. On the very same day, *Pravda* carried the infamous article by David Zaslavsky slandering Shostakovich, 'A Mess, Not Music' ('*Sumbur vmesto muzyki*'), a landmark sally in the onslaught against formalism, a term that would be used increasingly to condemn practitioners of the arts in the USSR. The witch-hunt for it in literature began soon after the condemnation of Shostakovich, and dominated critical discourse during 1936, rivalled only by the escalating problem of how to celebrate the forthcoming Pushkin centenary. Mirsky had published one of the keynote articles on the subject of formalism some time before it became Official Target No. 1.[94]

The arguments about Pasternak came to a head at the next Plenum of the Union of Writers, the Third, which took place in February 1936 in Minsk. On 10 February there was a very fraught argument about poetry, centring on Pasternak, who was present.[95] Mirsky made his speech on 14 February. He began by trying to restrict himself to a discussion of the poets of Georgia, but then he declared that he 'felt himself compelled to respond to the demagogic sallies of the "komsomol" poet [Bezymensky] who wishes to strike Pasternak out of Soviet literature'. Mirsky concludes his response:

And I can tell you, Comrade Bezymensky—the poetry of Pasternak plays a greater role in the propaganda of Soviet culture, in capturing for us the best part of the Western intelligentsia, than the poetry of Bezymensky. (Applause.) *Voice from the presidium*: 'That's arguable, though.' *Second voice from the presidium*: 'That's unarguably wrong.'[96]

This statement was singled out for repudiation in a leader in the *Literary Gazette* on 16 February. Mirsky, it said, had made a digression from his main theme in order to assert the international significance of Pasternak as an individual poet, irresponsibly omitting the broader context. Mirsky had called attention to the rapturous reception accorded Pasternak at the Paris conference, 'not understanding that in the person of Pasternak the congress was greeting all Soviet poetry, the entire Soviet Union, and Pasternak as one poet from our great country'.[97]

The Minsk plenum was soon denounced by the Party watchdogs. At a meeting of the Party fraction of the Directorate of the Union of Writers on 1 March 1936, the poet I. S. Fefer stated that 'even a critic as confused [the Shostakovich adjective, *sumburnyi*] as Mirsky has not been repudiated. . . . I consider that Mirsky has made too many mistakes for the representatives of the criticism section to rest on their laurels and consider the job done.'[98] The ensuing discussions opened on 10 March.[99] Stavsky was reported in the *Literary Gazette* on 15 March as criticizing Mirsky for praising the poet Petrovsky.[100] *Izvestiya* stated on 14 March: 'Yesterday at the Union of Soviet Writers the discussion about formalism in literature continued. Speeches were made by Comrades Pasternak, Vera Inber, A. Bogdanov, D. Mirsky, V. Kirpotin, A. Surkov, G. Munblit. There will be a further continuation of the discussion on 16 March.'[101]

When the discussion of formalism was continued, Mirsky said something that goes to the heart of his personality and attitudes. He reveals here exactly what he thought formalism was; and in doing so he hinted at his personal demons in the shape of that ambience of death he had once discerned in the culture of his youth:

Formalism remains the principal survival of decadent-bourgeois culture, constituting as it does that final phase in which the content of culture is reduced to a minimum, and where no integral world-view remains, but only its relics—devastation and nihilism. Historical Formalism arose on the ruins of the last integral bourgeois world-view in our literature, the ruins of symbolism. Symbolism itself was not formalist, for its formalist tendencies were saturated with particular content. Formalism, though, by its very nature does not have a world-view, and therefore formalism is a phenomenon which in essence is profoundly anti-cultural, because it is a denial of what gives culture unity, a denial of a philosophical outlook on the world.[102]

Mirsky's first letter of 1936 to Miss Galton, written on 27 March, refers to a peculiar mental state which is without doubt attributable to the tremendous stress he had been subjected to for several months. But it may also stem from a recognition by Mirsky that there was now in fact a vacuum at the centre of his being, if there had not been before.

It is absolutely inexplicable why I have not written to [you] yet. The only explanation is that I am contracting a sort of paralysis of the will which makes it terribly difficult for me to undertake anything at all. It has become easier for me to write a volume than to write a letter because the effort is the same, but the result in prospect much greater, and that has its influence. I hope I shall recover some time, especially when I get out of Moscow, which I am doing tomorrow. Tomorrow morning I leave for Odessa & there I intend to stay till the end of April.

The journey to Odessa was manifestly an attempt to escape and lie low, away from the gathering storm of criticism—though Mirsky must have had some sort of official backing to be able to make the trip. In all probability, he applied for the funds to work on his biography of Pushkin, and specifically to do some on-the-spot research into Pushkin's 'Southern period'. He told Miss Galton later on that he had informed nobody in Moscow of his whereabouts during his sojourn in Odessa. On 11 May Mirsky reported to Miss Galton from Odessa that he was leaving for Kiev and Moscow, after spending six weeks away, and then on 29 May that he had returned to Moscow to find about fifty or sixty books stolen from his library—including 'some of the best; also some of the English—all Auden, Spender, & Day Lewis & Eliot's *Rock* (the Anglo-Catholic play). Strange thieves to steal such stuff.' Soon after he got back to Moscow from Leningrad, Mirsky made his first visit to Golitsyno, where a vacation facility for writers had just been opened on the estate where he had spent a good deal of time with his friends before 1917.

Until the summer of 1936 Mirsky had Gorky as his protector. Supreme figurehead though he was, Gorky was by no means omnipotent. There was constant opposition to his policies, as we have seen. Mirsky may indeed have become 'the actual mouthpiece of Gorky's assessments',[103] Gorky's object being 'the neutralization of the people put up by the party-bureaucratic apparatus' and to nudge the agenda of the Union towards the discussion of problems specific to artistic creation rather than concentrating on bureacratic and narrowly political issues.[104] But after Gorky's death, Mirsky was dreadfully vulnerable. He had made some powerful enemies who had scores to settle and the wherewithal to settle them.

On 30 June Mirsky reported to Miss Galton that he was again at the Writers Union rest-home at Golitsyno. He comments on the current news; Gorky had died on 18 June. Mirsky writes: 'Poor Gorky! I had not seen him since last summer. The funeral was very grand. Stalin carried the urn; André Gide spoke from Lenin's tomb (besides Molotov and others).' Still at Golitsyno on 5 July, Mirsky says that he was 'again very badly rifled the other day & about two dozen books disappeared. I have set the militia going. The loss includes Blake, the Nonesuch Press edition, which is a great pity, as I believe it is very difficult to get.' Mirsky remained at Golitsyno until 1 August; this was the last time he went away for the summer.

Mirsky did not have to wait long for the first public attack on him after the death of Gorky. It was a denunciation called 'The Critic Mirsky Sets Some Records', and must have been ordered from on high, because the author was David Zaslavsky, the same budding expert in the genre who had been hired to destroy Shostakovich at the beginning of the year; what is more, it was published in *Pravda*, on 28 August 1936. The article concentrated on what Mirsky had said about Pushkin, alleging that his retractions of his mistakes had been irresponsible and insincere. Mirsky responded with a classic piece of Soviet self-criticism in which he admitted the charges, promised that he had now got the point about vulgar sociology and formalism, and expressed the hope that in future he would be able 'to give the multi-million Socialist readership a correct understanding of their great poet'.[105]

Soon afterwards Vera Suvchinskaya arrived in Moscow, apparently for good; her father had died earlier in 1936. Vera told me that in Moscow she was employed as a translator, and she recalled working on some children's books; Mirsky gave her 'masses' of translations to do. Vera soon got married, to an expatriate Communist called Robert Traill, who worked on the *Moscow Daily News*. Traill left for the war in Spain in January 1937, leaving Vera pregnant, and he was soon killed in action.[106]

A Commission to write a new Constitution had been set up in February 1935, the principal authors involved being Bukharin and Karl Radek. That what became known as the Stalin Constitution was impending was announced in June 1936. Mirsky contributed to the promotional hoo-hah one of his most abysmal pieces of writing, 'On the Great Charter of the Peoples: The Constitution of Victory', published on 20 July.[107] The new Constitution was promulgated on 27 November. Vera recalled Mirsky's private reaction:

I'm in rapture, a Communist one hundred per cent, and I remember sitting on the floor at my friends' place and listening to that Georgian voice on the radio for an hour and a half explaining about all sorts of freedoms, democratic rights, and so on. As far as I remember it was in the evening; anyway, the next day I had dinner with Mirsky and his face was completely distorted, and he said: 'Surely you understand that it's a *diabolical* lie!' I was a Communist, remember, and naive, and a complete idiot. I told him he should be ashamed, that he was demoralized . . .

In one of the most telling juxtapositions of the Stalin period, the public exultation in 1936 about the Constitution, with its various guarantees about the inviolability of the person and so on, went on at the same time as executive acts that were to deprive a larger number of persons of their freedom, and their lives, in a shorter time than ever before. On 24 August 1936, after remarking on the unusual heat Moscow had been experiencing that summer, Mirsky enquires of Miss Galton: 'What do you say to this business of Trotsky and the rest of them? One good thing is that he will lose what little credit he retained with the stupid intellectuals of the west.' He is referring to the show trial of Zinoviev and Kamenev, which opened in Moscow on 19 August. The confessions had been laboriously extracted and the sentences decided before the trial began.[108] Those on trial were accused of plotting at the behest of Trotsky the murder of Stalin, Voroshilov, Kaganovich, Kirov, Ordzhonikidze, Zhdanov, Kossior, Postyshev, and others. Statements made at the trial by the accused implicated just about every other prominent surviving Old Bolshevik: Tomsky, Bukharin, Rykov, Radek, Pyatakov, Serebryakov, and Sokolnikov were alleged to have been involved in these plots. Vyshinsky made his statement on 21 August, and summed up on 22 August. Sentences were passed on 24 August, and carried out in the next few days.

Robert Conquest observes that outside Russia, 'The truth could be deduced, but it could not be proved. Few cared to hear it, given the more evident menace of Fascism.'[109] Bukharin and Rykov were not proceeded against for the moment. But Sokolnikov was arrested on 26 August and immediately started to confess.[110] Pyatakov, who had been in contact with the Paris Eurasians in the late 1920s, was arrested on 12 September, and Radek ten days later. Ezhov became Head of the NKVD on 30 September 1936, succeeding Yagoda. Preparations started on the case against the 'Reserve Centre' allegedly headed by Pyatakov.

'TRAGIC EVENTS'

In October 1936, when all this was brewing, Stavsky sent a letter to the literary critics of Moscow and Leningrad, asking them about the present situation of their field and their own current work. Mirsky replied on 28 October:

This is in reply to yours of 20 X 36. At present I am working on a biography of Pushkin, which I have to submit on 15 February to 'Lives of Remarkable People'.[111] Certain chapters from it will appear in advance in *The Star*, the first two in the January issue. One is finished, the other still being written.

Unfortunately, besides that I still have an earlier piece of work on my hands. I am finishing editing an Anthology of English poetry for Goslitizdat in Leningrad. This is nearing completion, but is being held up because of the translators. Apart from that, under the terms of a long-standing obligation by 15 December I have to submit an article about Franco-Russian literary relations for the French issue of *Literary Heritage*.[112] This earlier commitment is to a certain extent holding back my work on the Pushkin biography.

Apart from that I have received an invitation from the Literary Agency to write an article in English for the Pushkin jubilee.[113] I am thinking of accepting it.

On the whole, nothing is getting in the way of my work at the moment apart from my living conditions. [!] I had been hoping to move to new quarters by the beginning of November, but this has once more been put off by a month. (And perhaps more?) The flat I occupy at present is extremely cramped, noisy, and overcrowded and it is extremely difficult to work here. This too puts a brake on my productivity. . . .[114]

In a letter he wrote six weeks later, on 12 December 1936, Mirsky presses Miss Galton for information about the abdication crisis in England, describing it as 'a bit of comic relief in the midst of all the tragic events going on'. This phrase was probably not even intended to hint at what was happening all around Mirsky in Stalin's Russia, but with the benefit of hindsight, as with much else in the letters to Miss Galton, Mirsky's words take on a chilling note of irony.[115]

On 23 January 1937 the trial of the 'Anti-Soviet Trotskyite Centre' began in the October Hall in central Moscow. The principals were Pyatakov, Radek, Sokolnikov, and Serebryakov. They were charged with organizing acts of sabotage in various economic enterprises, in order to undermine industrialization and collectivization; and with espionage on behalf of the Germans and Japanese. On 26 January, Mirsky did what he could to stave off his own downfall by publishing an article in the Literary Gazette under the title 'Alien Rubbish', exulting in the trial and impending execution—before sentence had been passed—of Pyatakov, Radek, Sokolnikov, and the others. It stands at the opposite end of Mirsky's career as a publishing writer from his ecstatic contribution to the schoolboy journal about the radiant future. The thirty years of Russian history that elapsed between the two pieces had changed the nature of public discourse; there had been plenty of righteous indignation in the pre-revolutionary press, but in general, people tended not to gloat about the sufferings of the politically oppressed:

After Zinoviev and Kamenev it would seem difficult to astonish us with new records for vileness, treachery, and malice. But Pyatakov, Radek, Sokolnikov, and the others outdo everything we have seen so far. Language refuses to characterize these people because it lacks a word that would plumb the depths of human degradation that have been exposed! We speak of 'Judas Trotsky', but the legendary Judas was an innocent simpleton by comparison with this.

The article goes on in this vein for eleven more paragraphs, with the exclamation marks coming thicker and thicker. Eventually, Mirsky winds up: 'Our country is cleansing itself of this alien rubbish. The poisonous serpents have been caught and will be exterminated. Our Stalinist home, soundly built as it is, will be cleansed of them.'[116] And 'cleansed' it was indeed. All the principals were immediately shot except for two: Sokolnikov and Radek, who had co-operated enthusiastically under interrogation; they survived in prison to be murdered by their cell-mates in May 1939.

On 18 February 1937 one of Stalin's closest associates, 'Sergo' Ordzhonikidze (who had once been arrested when the gendarmes were under the command of Mirsky's father), committed suicide. And finally, on 26 February, Bukharin and Rykov were arrested. At a Plenum of the Central Committee in February and March, Stalin's despotism became an absolute autocracy as he made the final steps in subordinating the organs of investigation to his personal control.[117] There was a purge of Yagoda's cadres in the NKVD; and Vyshinsky purged the apparatus of the Procuracy. Robert Conquest comments: 'Russians who had thought that the country was already in the grip of terrorists were now to see what terror really meant.'[118]

In *Pravda* on 25 February, Jack Altauzen described Mirsky as 'the voice of Bukharin' because he had 'allegorically' spoken against political poetry; another critic, Abram Lezhnyov, who like Mirsky had not long left to live, repeated this charge on 28 February. In the *Literary Gazette* on 5 March, N. G. Plisko (1903–41; he was killed in the first battle for Moscow) damned Mirsky as 'an aesthete of a critic'. In all probability, there was personal animus behind this phrase, because in the autumn of 1935 Mirsky had published a contemptuous critique of Plisko's introductory article to the first substantial edition of Mayakovsky's poetry, turning the whole thing into a potential nightmare for 1937 by citing the following sentence as the only really indubitable thing Plisko had said: 'His [Mayakovsky's] work passes the test when one approaches it from that apex of world-wide criteria that was mentioned at the Congress of Writers by N. I. Bukharin.'[119]

Several meetings of Moscow writers about this time happened to be attended by the American writer Joshua Kunitz,[120] who had been opposed to RAPP and had once been expelled from the American Communist Party for saying so at the wrong moment, only to be reinstated in 1932. Edward Brown told me that Kunitz briefed him about the events in Moscow:

He reported to me about the writers' meetings at which Averbakh, Libedinsky, Kirshon and other RAPP leaders were accused of various crimes. It was his account of the meeting at which Mirsky was attacked that I used in the book.[121] He seemed to me an honest and reliable witness, even though still hopelessly committed to the Communist cause (though he said he was not, at that time, a member). He still seemed to believe when I spoke to him in 1949 what he had believed on the night of that meeting in 1937, namely that Averbakh and his henchmen were surely traitors and rightly attacked as such, but that a 'bad mistake' was being made about Mirsky, who was an innocent man. He wanted to tell the truth about him and tried to get the floor, but Stavsky, he told me, came down to him from the podium and said simply: 'Ne nado' ['Better not']. I'm not sure [Kunitz] ever realized how carefully prepared and orchestrated the attacks had been, and that intervention by him would have been absurd, and dangerous.[122]

The occasion described here may have been the general meeting of Moscow writers held on 3 April at which Mirsky made a confession, saying in particular that his views on Fadeev's literary development had been mistaken, and also that his assertion about Pushkin's 'servility' had also been wrong. This was referred to in the report on the meeting published in the *Literary Gazette* on 6 April.

It would be natural to suppose that at least some of the material incriminating Mirsky would have come from the interrogation of the other writers who were being mopped up at this time. The principal one among them, as we know, was Leopold Averbakh, who was arrested on 4 April 1937; he was sentenced to death on 14 June, but not executed until 14 August 1939.[123] However, among the documents pertaining to Mirsky's rehabilitation is a summary of Averbakh's case which states that Mirsky does not appear in Averbakh's depositions. It seems likely that the primary incriminating material was put together from the confessions extracted during the interrogations of Pyatakov and others of his 'gang' that began in December 1936.

The last letter in the Galton correspondence is dated 2 May 1937, one month before Mirsky was arrested.

I am really astonished at what a bloody blighter I am! I received the books you sent me ages ago & never wrote about it. It turns out that the Studio people are not contemplating a new edition of my book but only at selling it a cheaper price (2/6) so revisions are out of question & the whole business has no importance of principle, as we say here.

The book in question was Mirsky's *Lenin*. News had reached him some time before that a new cheap edition was planned, and Mirsky wrote frantically to Dorothy Galton trying to get her to stop it: 'You know there are passages in the book which may have been all right in 1931 but have become impossible in 1937.' Mirsky no doubt squirmed when he recalled that the book contained sentences such as the following: 'To-day, when Lenin has become the hero and beacon of the revolutionaries of all the world, while Trotsky has fallen into political nonentity, one is rather inclined to forget and belittle the part played by him during the critical years that saved the Soviet Republic.'[124] Anyway, Mirsky's sense of relief can only have been of small comfort. His last letter continues:

I am leaving for Leningrad & will write to you again before long (really!). Your government *are* swine. I think even Pitt & Canning & Palmerstone [*sic*] must turn in their graves at the sight of the abject depths British Imperialism has come to.

Well, *à tantôt*,
D. Mirsky

One of the books you bought for me is defective (16 pages missing, & 16 pages occurring twice over). Do you think they would exchange it for a good copy if I sent it back? The publishers are Longmans.

The day after he set down this studied triviality, Mirsky wrote to Stavsky trying to save his neck. The letter begins: 'My connection with Averbakh and the Averbakhites distorted my entire trajectory as a Soviet writer. The unmasking of the Trotskyite essence of *averbakhshchina* and the real face of Averbakh himself compels me to render an account both to myself and to the Soviet literary public in this connection.' Then follow the paragraphs describing Mirsky's early years after his return that were cited earlier, culminating in

Mirsky's account of how he was set up by Korabelnikov and Jasienski at the critics' forum that preceded the I Congress in 1934. Mirsky concludes:

After all this business I began to distance myself from the Averbakhites, though I did not terminate my personal relations with Averbakh, and went to see him at Uralmash. But I avoided talking to him about my literary work. I began seeing Jasienski only on rare occasions, and only on his initiative.

I consider it necessary to state that my article about Pushkin which contains the theses that have been so justly condemned was written early in 1934, before the article on Fadeev, and although they had no direct input whatsoever, it was written under the general influence of the 'left-wing' phrases of the Averbakhites.

I also consider it necessary to state that my inner reaction against Averbakhism that began at the end of 1934 led me in part to make mistakes of the opposite (formally the opposite) kind, which bespeak themselves in some of the articles on poetry I published in 1935 and my speech at the Minsk plenum.

Anyway, I had liberated myself from the influence of Averbakhian ideas by the beginning of 1935, but my connection with them diverted me from my path, and I carry the grave consequences with me to this day. However, I fully understood the negative significance of this connection only recently, after my conversation with Comrade Fadeev (in early March) and it is only very recently indeed that I have understood on what a dangerous path I was standing.

I firmly hope that the Directorate of the Union of Soviet Writers will not refuse me the specific help that will enable me to straighten out my literary path and liquidate the negative results both of my connection with Averbakhism and with my previous biography.

Eleven days after he had kissed the rod in this manner, on 14 May 1937, Mirsky wrote to Stavsky again, asking him to put the problem of his relations with Averbakh and his 'group' on the agenda of the Union's Directorate.[125] Some days before this, there had been a meeting of the Party Committee of the Moscow organization of the Union of Writers, which was reported in the *Literary Gazette* on 15 May.[126] There had also been a meeting of the Secretariat. During this meeting, Stavsky drew a clear line between the case of Mirsky and that of 'the presence in the leadership of people who were closely connected with Averbakh and who aided and abetted him'. However, he also asserted that Mirsky's conduct should be condemned, and especially the writing of 'insincere' articles—but with that the matter should be considered closed. This did not satisfy Yudin and his faction; Yudin published an article in the *Literary Gazette* in which Mirsky was damned as a 'Wrangelite' and 'White Guard'.[127] Mirsky spoke in his own defence at a meeting of the 30-man Presidium, arguing against Yudin's allegations. Yudin was supported by the powerful Lakhuti,[128] who spoke against Stavsky's proposal to censure Mirsky and then consider the matter closed. The Secretariat accepted Stavsky's formulation. However, in the report of this decision, the political blackening reappeared: 'the Presidium of the USW issued a decision condemning the conduct of Mirsky, who for the benefit of the Trotskyite-Averbakhite gang wrote articles damaging to Soviet literature'.[129] Mirsky was clearly too deeply compromised to escape.

The Great Purge rolled on. Now came the turn of the army high command: these were almost all younger men of Mirsky's generation who had first made their names fighting on the other side from him in the Civil War. On 27 May 1937 they arrested Marshal Mikhail Tukhachevsky, who began his military career as a Guards officer in 1912. On 29 May they took Marshal Ieronim Uborevich, who in 1921 had put down the Antonov revolt, the most spectacular peasant protest against Bolshevik power; and on 30 May they took another hero of the Civil War, Marshal Iona Yakir. On 31 May General Yan Gamarnik, the head of the Red army's political section, knowing that he would probably be next on the list, committed suicide in a public park, and on 6 June he was subjected to public vilification for doing so. On the night of 11/12 June 1937 Tukhachevsky, Uborevich, and Yakir were executed.

God only knows what Mirsky went through in the weeks and days before they came for him during the night of 2–3 July 1937. It must have been a relief when they finally came up the stairs, climbing up past all those five floors. After they took him away, he ceased to exist for the outside world, except as a legend.

9   End of the Line

Inscription

All that I longed for, all I suffered—
The gold of my nocturnal dreams,
The love, the malice, and the legend
Of my so recent olden days.

I would not wish the world to slander
That which has dwelt within my soul,
I would not wish the world to force me
To feel ashamed of what I've done.

I would not wish the fruits of silence
Before a neutral judge to stand—
The febrile rant, the dreams exquisite
Of this inconstant soul of mine.

(Prince D. P. Svyatopolk-Mirsky, 1906)

But pity is a noble and a manly feeling, and in no wise relaxing. (D. S. Mirsky, 1921)

LEGENDS

There are individuals in all human societies who become legendary: thoughts and deeds are attributed to them by popular invention, embroidered, and passed on through various channels. Soviet society was particularly active in creating legends. The reasons are not far to seek. The public media were efficiently censored, and very little of normal human interest could be written about or permanently recorded in other publicly accessible ways. For reasons as much to do with long-standing notions of propriety as with official censorship, information about such matters as the private lives of eminent individuals was never committed to print. But people naturally speculated about these things, and the smallest scraps of information were transformed into full-blown narratives. They were added to as they passed from narrator to narrator. And these legends were believed; indeed, some of them continue to be believed after history has provided evidence to refute them. They then, according to one theory, become myths: stories which are not believed to be true, but which are discussed as if they were.[1] Mirsky soon became a legend, and then something of a myth.

Vera Traill was supposed to see him for dinner as usual on 3 June 1937, and he did not turn up. She received a telephone call the next day from Aleksey

Sukhotin, who told her that Mirsky had been arrested. She set about trying to get Mirsky released, going so far as to write a letter to Ezhov protesting his innocence. She was called to two interviews with Ezhov in his Kremlin office; soon afterwards, she was instructed to leave for Paris without delay. According to other versions of these events, this was a cover story, and Vera had in fact been brought to Moscow in the first place by the GPU, had even undergone some training at one of their institutions, had married Robert Traill at their behest in order to obtain a British passport, and was then sent to Paris as a courier.[2]

Vera returned to Paris in mid-September 1937 and gave birth to her daughter by the now deceased Robert Traill. In October she had a letter from Sukhotin saying that Mirsky was 'finished', but that he had nonetheless asked Sukhotin to send him some books. Sukhotin also said that the letter was completely calm, as if nothing terrible had happened, so that Mirsky's conditions at least at the beginning of his time in prison were not all that appalling. When Hitler's army invaded France, Vera was arrested as a member of the French Communist Party, and interned in the Rieucros concentration camp for women, in the *département* of Lozère, between Vichy and Marseilles.[3] She was extracted from there by A. J. Halpern, and admitted to England on the basis of her British passport. She left France on the day the Nazis invaded Russia, 22 June 1941. After this, Vera only heard rumours about what had happened to her friend. In the extraordinary story of her life, the involvement with Mirsky, while much more than an episode, faded into the background as she developed new contacts and interests; but she never forgot him.

Dorothy Galton never forgot Mirsky either; most immediately, on 21 October 1937 she reported to Michael Florinsky, without revealing any source for her information: 'Yes, I have every reason to believe that Mirsky really is in trouble this time. There have been so many cries of "Wolf!" in his case that people don't believe the stories any more. But I have definite proof that something is wrong.'[4]

Sir Bernard Pares visited Moscow again in August 1939. He went to look for Mirsky, and 'found his quarters were sealed up; he was evidently in prison. I heard of him later as exiled to Siberia and conducting a provincial paper there, and again later that he had died in conditions of starvation. It was a thousand pities that his shining intellect should be lost.'[5]

P. N. Savitsky, Mirsky's old adversary from the Eurasian movement, remained in Prague, and was duly arrested when the Soviet army liberated that city in 1944. He was sent to the GULag. When he was amnestied in 1956 he went back to Prague, and tried to renew his old academic and personal contacts. He told another veteran Eurasian, N. N. Alekseev, that in the camps he had looked out for people who had seen Mirsky in the last days of his life, and had found two. One was a peasant from the Bobrinsky family estate near Tula, who had tried to care for Mirsky (he ended as he began!), and had heard him give forty-five lectures on Pushkin, all from memory. The second was a certain

V. S. Bunyaev, a Reader in Western Literary History at Leningrad University, who after Mirsky's death (according to Bunyaev, in April 1941) inherited the manuscript of Mirsky's last book, 'Russian Poetry from Pushkin to Fet', which had been written in the GULag.[6] No trace of this manuscript has ever come to light.

For many years after Mirsky's death, though, nothing was known for sure about what had happened to him. He had no relatives living in the USSR who would have learned of his death in the usual way for people in their position, that is, by having their aid parcels refused by the prison authorities.

Apparently the first attempt to discover something about Mirsky through official channels was made by Professor Francis J. Whitfield in the late 1940s, when at the request of Alfred H. Knopf he undertook the one-volume edition of Mirsky's history of Russian literature. The Soviet Embassy in Washington, however, was unable to give him any information. Robert M. Glauber, the Knopf editor responsible for this book, approached Vladimir Nabokov about endorsing it, but he refused, with the best of motives:

Yes—I am a great admirer of Mirsky's work. In fact, I consider it the best history of Russian literature in any language including Russian. Unfortunately I must deprive myself of the pleasure of writing a blurb for it, since the poor fellow is now in Russia and compliments from such an anti-Soviet writer as I am known to be might cause him considerable unpleasantness.[7]

Nearly twenty years after Mirsky's arrest, Edmund Wilson commented: 'I have been told that Mirsky . . . was always in love in the most romantic fashion, and that an unwise affair in Moscow supplied one of the pretexts for banishing him.'[8] Apart from this, which seems to be pure fantasy on someone's part and wishful thinking on Wilson's, Wilson understood far more than most about what had really happened, and said it in his article about Mirsky: that he had lost the support of Gorky; that people as outstanding as he were the natural prey of the mediocrities that were taking over Soviet literature; and that Mirsky lacked the self-restraint to avoid falling foul of these mediocrities. Later, Wilson came by a letter dated 1 May 1952, written by 'a Russian D[isplaced] P[erson] in Europe' to 'one of Mirsky's friends'. Wilson appended a translation of this letter.[9] The original Russian text was eventually published by the émigré poet and literary scholar George Ivask in 1977.

The letter records that on 3 October 1937 a detachment of political prisoners arrived from Moscow at a transit camp on the way to Vladivostok, and some of them were put in the same hut as the author of the letter. One of them was Mirsky. The DP conversed with him during this time, and reported: 'During our conversations the prince didn't say much, but he did not refuse to state his opinion on the subject of Maksim Gorky. He said that Maksim Gorky was incapable of being an indifferent observer of bloody arbitrary rule.'[10] On 27 October 1937, the letter goes on, the detachment left Vladivostok and arrived on 4 November 1937 at Magadan. After that Mirsky and the DP were sent to different camps. Then, in December 1938, the DP got frostbite in his feet and was sent to a camp for invalids twenty-three kilometres from Magadan. He there met some people from the Moscow group, and they told him that Mirsky was in the same camp, in the hospital. He was reported to be violently insane. Several weeks later, he was informed by an orderly that 'Prince Svyatopolk-Mirsky was dead. I suppose that this was the end of January 1939.'[11]

The most extended retelling of the Mirsky legend written in Russia was published abroad in 1977 by Anatoly Krasnov-Levitin, the heroic religious dissenter, who expended a good deal of time and effort trying to piece together the stories of people who had disappeared. Krasnov-Levitin believed among other things that Mirsky had taught at Oxford, and that his *Lenin* had been written for an Oxford University competition for the best biography of the subject. The most specific part of his testimony concerns the circumstances of Mirsky's death:

In 1949 I happened to meet Sergey Vladimirovich Gruzinov, an old Moscow doctor, in the internal prison at the Lubyanka. . . . In 1938 he was working as a doctor in a camp hospital. One day an old (or prematurely aged) man came in who was suffering from dystrophy (acute emaciation) and chronic diarrhoea. This man was in fact Dmitry Mirsky. There was an incident as soon as he entered the hospital: the criminals stole his pince-nez and 'literary notes'. (He had found the strength to write something even in those conditions.) Dr Gruzinov came into the hut and said: 'If the pince-nez and manuscript are not returned within half an hour, I will immediately sign out for work ten men from the right side and ten from the left.' The pince-nez and notes were found in short order. Gruzinov's story went on as follows: 'One evening I was making my rounds with two orderlies. Suddenly a figure in his underwear jumps out and goes down on his knees: "Sergey Vladimirovich, save me! I'm dying!" I glanced down and saw that it was Mirsky. I laughed and went on my way.' (Such were the cruel habits of the camps—he found it possible to laugh, but after all he was not a bad man, even a good one, and he too later died in prison.) An hour later they reported to him that Mirsky had died.[12]

As we shall soon see, the accounts by the DP and Krasnov-Levitin are accurate in many respects, and they represent the reality of Mirsky's last days in a way that the bare facts of the official record leave to the imagination.

Mirsky was officially unpersoned, like countless others who suffered his fate during the Purges. In unofficial speculation, Mirsky's fate was sometimes juxtaposed with that of Mandelshtam, who, as we know, was first arrested on 14 May 1934. He was re-arrested on 2 May 1938, and taken to the Lubyanka. On 9 May he became File No. 16023 at the Butyrka. He was sentenced on 2 August to five years in a corrective labour camp. On 7 September he departed from Moscow by train. Nadezhda Mandelstam was told that later 'He was with Svyatopolk-Mirsky, who became completely emaciated almost straight away, and soon died also.'[13]

Mirsky's name surfaced in one famous Soviet literary scandal in the early 1950s. The story is told in the following way by the novelist and literary historian Grigory Svirsky:

After Stalin's death Georgy Malenkov, who was at the time the de facto head of the government, delivered at a routine plenum an enormous speech about everything: agriculture, Korea, and, of course, literature. On this occasion he brought forth one of the 'golden words' of Marxist aesthetics—on the problem of the typical. 'The typical', he announced from the platform, 'is a political problem. . . .'

The new phrase was immediately seized on by the ideological apparatus, repeated endlessly in the newspapers, taken as a subject for academic dissertations, and then suddenly it was discovered that this phrase 'had been coined by Prince Svyatopolk-Mirsky and published in the old *Literary Encyclopedia*, which had been acknowledged to be ideologically unsound and inimical. . . . The stolen bottom of the "bottomless wisdom" of the Central Committee had suddenly been exposed. . . .'.[14]

Mirsky's name comes up in Russian literary gossip in connection with this incident more often than anything else.[15] The occasion concerned was actually the XIX Congress of the Party, which was held while Stalin was still alive (though indisposed on the day in question), and Malenkov's speech was published in *Pravda* on 6 October 1952. Malenkov's speech-writer in fact plagiarized Mirsky's article 'Realism';[16] the phrase he used actually says 'the problem of typicality is always a political problem', which makes some sense in the context of Mirsky's carefully documented article, but in Malenkov's speech was reduced to a slogan.

In 1982 Gleb Struve referred to 'a certain well-known Soviet literary scholar who himself spent a long time in Kolyma but never met Svyatopolk-Mirsky there'. The person concerned, whom Struve could not name at the time, was the much-persecuted Yu. G. Oksman.[17] Struve paraphrases his words:

[Mirsky] grieved endlessly about his turn to the new faith and his coming to Russia, cursed Communism, made fun of his illusions. He spoke a lot about his plans for a history of Russian poetry, and believed he would remain alive. He died in torment, from a particular kind of pellagra (the three Ds, dystrophia, dementia, and something else besides). Near the end of his life, before his illness, he was working as a watchman at some kind of workshops.[18]

When I asked her about Mirsky's death, Vera Traill uttered a mounting cry of pain and despair:

I think he perished fairly soon, about two years later. . . . People said that he did not live long and that he perished in terrible conditions. At this point there are contradictory rumours—some people said he was in Alma-Ata, others that he was in Siberia, and yet others that he had gone mad. The only thing I've seen in print is Edmund Wilson's article. . . . I'm telling you that I really never had a closer friend, and to say that I wish to know how he died . . . what's important for me is that he's not here, and I'm sure it was terrible, and I can't help him, and *I don't want to know*, and it's the same for all the people I've lost, I've lost absolutely everybody, in the war in Spain, or in the Soviet Union, or in the Resistance—*La Résistance, dans le Maquis*, in France,—and the people you could call the friends of my youth, I've got none of them, none came out alive . . . apart from Rodzevich . . . he was in a terrible camp, he was in Buchenwald . . . he survived. But he's no longer my friend. And everyone, absolutely *everyone*, who really did play some part in my life, there's none of them left.

Mirsky's name was restored to the public record in 1967, when a short article on him appeared in one of the landmark literary works initiated under the Khrushchev Thaw, the *Shorter Literary Encyclopedia,* the general editor of which was Mirsky's old adversary from the Plenum of 1935, Aleksey Surkov. The article ends with a sentence that is repeated hundreds and hundreds of times in the nine volumes of this work: 'In 1937 was illegally repressed; rehabilitated posthumously.'[19] Nothing written by Mirsky seems to have been published in the USSR between 1937 and the abbreviated republication of his 1929 article on Pirosmani in the regional *Literary Georgia* by Leonid Tchertkov in 1971.[20]

Although the correct years for Mirsky's birth, arrest, and most importantly death were given in Tchertkov's encyclopedia entry, legends about these events persisted.

REHABILITATION

Soon after Stalin's death in 1953 the Party revised its line on the significance of the Leader and his times, and adopted the view that his purges had been a deviation that afflicted 'the conscious avant-garde of society', i.e. its own members. At this as at other times, the Party had little or no regard for the vast majority of the population. And it was not led to doubt the legitimacy of the position it had arrogated to itself in 1917. It rehabilitated its own members in the first instance, but always selectively, and permitted public reference to them. This process picked up momentum in 1956. But fairly soon after that it began to falter, and it petered out almost completely in the Brezhnev period.[21] The rank-and-file victims remained in oblivion, and the computation of reliable statistics and personal case histories about them was not encouraged. The situation changed radically soon after Gorbachev came to power in 1985; for example, Bukharin was rehabilitated in January 1988, and Ryutin in June that year, but nothing like full disclosure had been achieved by the time the USSR ceased to exist.

There has been very little systematic investigation of the mechanism of rehabilitation in the post-Stalin period. One small piece of evidence is contained in a letter from the oppressed novelist Vasily Grossman, written to his friend, the poet and translator Semyon Lipkin, in September 1956:

I went to the Union [of Writers]. I handed Azhaev[22] a petition that a commission should be set up that would in the name of the Union initiate proceedings for the rehabilitation of writers who perished who have no relatives. I named A. Lezhnyov, Pilnyak, And[rey] Novikov, and Svyatopolk-Mirsky. The proposal had a sympathetic reception, and Azhaev promised to discuss it in the Secretariat.[23]

However, no commission was set up; nothing happened until the Gorbachev period.

Mirsky's elder sister, Sonya, went back to Russia at some time soon after the Second World War, along with her husband and her younger sister, Olga. Sonya at first lived in Kharkov, but moved nearer to Moscow when she was widowed. In December 1961, the post-Stalin rehabilitations had been in progress for some years, and Sonya decided that the times had changed enough for something to be done about her brother's memory. She wrote to Rudenko, Procurator-General of the USSR, on what looks like a scrap of squared paper from a school exercise book:[24]

I request you to re-examine the case of my brother, Mirsky Dm. P., Dmitry Petrovich (date of birth 1890), who was arrested in Moscow in 1937 and, according to information in my possession, died in imprisonment in 1939. If possible I request he be rehabilitated.

S. Pokhitonova

This humble petition generated a printed form headed 'Secret' under the internal letterhead of the KGB, the current metamorphosis of the organ that had brought Mirsky to his end. It is addressed to the Investigative Division, 1 Section, KGB, by one Kremlyov, and entitled DEMAND for Checking via the Central Operational-Documentary Card Index of the Investigative Division of the Ministry of Internal Affairs, the purpose being 're-examination of the case'. It was signed by Head of 1 Division Zagvozdin in February 1962. A scrawled Certificate dated 23 February attached to the form gives the bare facts of Mirsky's arrest, sentence, and death, the number of his file, and its location. This led to a two-page Certificate that summarizes the information we will soon see in Mirsky's KGB file. At the end of February Zagvozdin wrote a series of letters, all headed 'Secret', giving the bare facts of Mirsky's case and asking for further information, to the directors of the principal relevant repositories of historical information in Moscow. Academics, Soviet and foreign, who worked (or tried to work) on literary materials held at these places in the 1960s and 1970s will be wryly amused but not surprised by the speed and efficiency with which they jumped to it at the behest of the KGB.

The Central State Archive produced four responses from its holdings, all headed 'Secret'. The first of them contains information gleaned from the Archive's holdings on the Russian emigration. Zagvozdin is informed—as if he needed to know—that according to holding No. 1513, item 1, file 12, page 17 verso [!] in the documents pertaining to the Staff of the IV Infantry Division of the interned troops of the Volunteer Army in Poland in 1920, Captain Svyatopolk-Mirsky is mentioned as having the right to be reimbursed for personally owned horses surrendered to Poland. The second document from the Central Archive is infinitely more serious. It contains material from 'the card index of the French police held in the Special Archive of the Central Directorate of Archives of the Council of Ministers of the USSR'—how the Soviets came by this source boggles the imagination. This information includes some details about Mirsky's short-lived marriage (which can only have come from a Russian informer who was very close indeed to Mirsky personally), and about his life in emigration; this information has been incorporated into the account given in Chapter 3.

Two further certificates were produced from the special reserve. The first of them summarizes the holdings of the French police files on the Eurasian organization and especially the Clamart group. The second appendix draws on material from 'II Division, General Staff of bourgeois Poland' and gives a few more titbits of information about the Eurasians. The authors state: 'No information has been discovered on the "School of Slavonic Languages" and the journal *Slavonic Review*.' They conclude: 'The archive possesses no information concerning Svyatopolk-Mirsky D. P. having belonged to the agency of the English intelligence organs.'

The head of the secret section of the Lenin Library, A. Khalanskaya, one of the very few women who composed any of the documents in Mirsky's file, reported that the open stacks of the library held only two works by the critic, the Russian original of *The Intelligentsia of Great Britain*, and the preface to the 1934 translation of Smollett's *Peregrine Pickle*. This probably meant that Mirsky's other Soviet-published works had been removed from the open shelves to Khalanskaya's secret repository after his arrest—or possibly destroyed.

These gaps were filled by a densely informative communication dated 28 March 1962 from N. Rodionov, the chief of the Central State Archive for Literature and Art, an institution notorious for its exquisitely obstructionist attitudes during the Soviet years. Rodionov gave Comrade Zagvozdin a concise list of Mirsky's contributions to journals and newspapers, and his major articles in various collections, and concluded by citing the reference to Mirsky's 'psychological restructuring' in Gorky's letter of 20 February 1932 to Romain Rolland.[25]

The connection with Gorky is documented in a response from another lady, S. S. Zimina, the head of the Gorky Archive, which is housed in the Academy Institute of World Literature, yet another institution that bears Gorky's name.

She reported on 11 April 1962 that her archive contained seventeen letters by Mirsky to Gorky dating from 1928 to 1934, and also the manuscripts of three articles, all of which bore corrections and comments by Gorky. Zimina attached typed copies of:

the 8 most characteristic letters of D. P. Mirsky to A. M. Gorky; a photocopy of a secretarial typescript of the single letter of Gorky to him; TASS Foreign Information Bulletin[26] for 4 July 1931 about Mirsky's article 'Why I Became a Marxist', published in the *Daily Worker*; and a copy of this article which was prepared for A. B. Khalatov, the Director of GIZ [the State Publishing House].

Meanwhile, one Captain Evstifeev was combing the KGB archives and producing reports in diligent-schoolboy longhand on the persons whose names appeared in Mirsky's file. He summarized the file on Pavel Nikolaevich Tolstoy, which in its turn mentions Mirsky; we learn from this that Tolstoy was sentenced to execution by shooting on 6 July 1941 and that his case was annulled on 22 September 1956.[27] On 7 March 1962 Evstifeev wrote two separate one-page reports on Bernard Pares, both saying that Mirsky's name does not appear in the KGB holdings on Mirsky's former boss. The next day Evstifeev summarized the file on Averbakh, noting that he was sentenced to death by shooting on 14 June 1937 and that his case was annulled on 29 May 1961; he reports that Mirsky's name does not appear in Averbakh's depositions. On 10 March 1962 he wrote a couple of pages on Bruno Jasienski, summarizing his case and noting that he was sentenced to death by shooting on 17 September 1938, that his case was annulled on 24 December 1955, and that Mirsky does not appear in his depositions either. That Mirsky does not appear in these files is strange, to say the least.

Next, the officer who initiated the search, Major Kremlyov, composed one more certificate 'based on the archive files kept in the Registration and Archive Division of the KGB'. This includes some unique details, such as the exact date—1 September 1931—on which Mirsky was granted Soviet citizenship. It then turns to Bernard Pares, who is characterized as a 'major intelligence officer' (*krupnyi razvedchik*). His meeting with Mirsky in Russia in 1936 is noted; it is stated that Mirsky 'had a very cold conversation' with him on that occasion—someone had evidently been observing them and reporting. Kremlyov further reports that there are 'reference materials' on M. Baring, among others, but there is no information on Mirsky's contacts with these people 'in terms of espionage activity'.

As a result of all this comes a typed Conclusion. Its preamble states that Major Kremlyov has examined the materials in file No. 258079, gives the dates of Mirsky's arrest and sentence, and continues:

There are no objective proofs in the file that confirm MIRSKY's culpability. . . . Analysis of the materials of the criminal case and additional checking has shown that MIRSKY D. P. was arrested and found guilty without foundation.

Mirsky had not concealed the fact that he had served in the White army, there had been no confirmation of his involvement with espionage, Averbakh and Jasienski had been rehabilitated, and Mirsky had worked honestly as a Soviet journalist; and therefore, Kremlyov concludes,

I would be of the opinion that a petition be instituted re the introduction according to the procedure laid down by law of a protest with the object of the repeal of the resolution of the Special Conclave of 28 July 1937 concerning MIRSKY (SVYATOPOLK-MIRSKY) D. P. and the quashing of the case against him on the grounds of the absence of *corpus delicti*.

This document generated a form headed 'Military Tribunal of the Moscow Military District', dated 9 June 1962, and addressed to the Chief of the Documentary and Archive Section of the KGB, city of Moscow, with copies for information to the Head of the Information Department, MVD of the RSFSR, and to the Military Procurator of the Moscow Military District. The body of the document reads (the printed rubrics are indicated with italics):

Together with the original of the determination of the Military Tribunal of the Moscow Military District No. I-461 of 31 May 1962 I forward the file concerning the accused MIRSKY (Svyatopolk-Mirsky) Dmitry Petrovich, born 1890, for further safe keeping.

According to the file data MIRSKY D. P. died in his place of confinement [*v mestakh zaklyucheniya*] on 6. 9. [*sic*] 1939. Before his arrest MIRSKY was without family members.

A certificate concerning the rehabilitation of MIRSKY has been dispatched to his sister, citizen POKHITONOVA S. P., Flat 12, 12 Zhugin St, Ivanovo.

The form is signed by Lieutenant-Colonel (Judiciary) N. Sokolov, Deputy President of the Military Tribunal of the Moscow Military District.

After nearly a quarter of a century as an unperson in his native land, Mirsky thus returned to the historical record.

PERSONAL FILES

Until fairly recently, the vast mass of the Russian people only had access to rumour and legend in the cases of those purge victims whom Party policy had not deemed it expedient to discuss after their rehabilitation. Discussion of the cases that were mentioned remained very cautious, clouded in evasive formulas and clichés. Outside Russia, things were different. Some foreign victims survived the camps, got out of Russia, and told their stories. The most eloquent among them were the future Prime Minister of Israel, Menachim Begin, and the once enthusiastic German Communist Elinor Lipper.[28] Some Russians, outstanding among them Evgeniya Ginzburg and Varlaam Shalamov, survived and wrote their stories; their work was published in the West. Robert Conquest's *The Great Terror* collated a considerable amount of precise information that has since been corroborated time and time again by the revelations coming from Russia; one remarkable manifestation of the glasnost period was the serialization and then hardback publication of Conquest's work in the then USSR. The much-resisted publication in Russia in 1991 of the indigenous attempt to place things on the record, which had led to its author's exile in 1974—Aleksandr Solzhenitsyn's *GULAG Archipelago*—was perhaps the surest sign that some things had radically changed.

During the years immediately preceding the downfall of the Soviet regime and since then, the determination of certain individuals and organizations in Russia to commemorate its victims, and in particular the victims who had not been members of the Party, led to a certain amount of access being granted to the archives of the secret police and the camp system relating to the Stalin period. Documents from these archives began to seep into print from about 1987. As a result, precise information has been made public about certain prominent victims of the purges. Among the first writers whose files were made available and partly published, notably in the illustrated weekly *Ogonyok* by Vitaly Shentalinsky of the Union of Writers, were Babel, Klyuev, and Mandelshtam. A comparison of these documents with those in Mirsky's files shows that Mirsky's case was entirely standard; the same procedures, institutions, and pro forma documents occur in all of them.[29]

Apart from what it made public about the fates of these individual cases among the millions of victims, the verbatim publication of these files testified to something that was not fully appreciated before: the monstrous bureaucratic punctiliousness of the Soviet punitive system. As one sardonic parody popular among Soviet writers went: 'We were born to turn Kafka into reality.' The victims of the Purges were not consigned to oblivion. Instead, they were scrupulously documented. This system of accounting provided work for many thousands of investigators, interrogators, guards, stenographers, archivists, and clerks; perhaps this is the only way a state can maintain full employment if it has a literate population. To realize that the millions of documents they produced (and the written denunciations that lay behind many of them) were among the first fruits of the great Soviet drive for mass literacy is even more depressing than to reflect that the aesthetic goal of literacy in Stalin's Russia was Socialist Realism.

I have been fortunate enough to secure a copy of Mirsky's files through the kind offices of the staff of the Main Information Centre of the Ministry of Internal Affairs of the Russian Federation (GITs MVD RF), who made these documents freely available to the Research Centre archives of the Moscow Memorial Society, the driving force in the restitution of the Purge victims' memory. The documents pertaining to Mirsky's case are in two sets. The first of them, GUGB NKVD (Main Directorate for State Security, People's Commissariat of Internal Affairs, a set of initials we will encounter repeatedly in what follows) archive file No. 258079, is concerned with Mirsky's arrest, interrogation, and sentencing, followed by his rehabilitation, and is preserved in

Moscow. The second, Personal File No. 136848, also holds some documents concerning the arrest and sentencing, but is mainly concerned with events between then and the death of the subject, and is held in Magadan. The reason for this separation is that Mirsky was dealt with in turn by the two appropriate subdivisions of the principal organ involved with penal administration, the NKVD. The prosecution of political offences was the responsibility of GUGB, while the labour camps were the responsibility of GULag (Main Administration for the Camps). Taken all together, the documents in Mirsky's files offer a substantial record of what happened to Mirsky in the last two years of his life.

The contents of Mirsky's files as they have reached me leave the story of his case incomplete in many respects. Only an unrestricted investigation of the KGB archives, more than the work of one lifetime, would enable the full story to be told and set in its proper context. Mirsky's case impinges upon and in certain particulars is probably contingent upon those of other people who were arrested at about the same time, and so far only a very small number of these people have been traced and material on them released. Even more important, we have had no access so far to the workings of the higher levels of the security apparatus in such a way as would enable us to understand the internal connections between the various cases in train at the relevant time, and the way that broad policy decisions and general executive orders led to action in the case of particular individuals and groups of individuals.

ATTEMPTED RE-ARREST

One further significant aspect of Mirsky's immediately posthumous existence emerges from his files. It is appalling to say so, but his death was actually timely: it saved him from being brought back from the GULag to Moscow for a second interrogation and—with gruesome irony—an almost certain death sentence. The trigger document for this is a Resolution in the Moscow file. At the top left-hand side of the first page is a typed annotation: 'I confirm. People's Commissar of Internal Affairs of the USSR, Commissar of State Security 1st Rank L. Beria', 'October 1939' (the day of the month has not been filled in). The pencil scrawl alongside it says 'Conf. 21/X' with two capital letters that appear to be the initials of Beria himself. The resolution was composed by Junior Lieutenant of State Security A. Ivanov, Investigator, of the Investigation Section, GUGB NKVD, and it states that he has examined the materials on Svyatopolk-Mirsky, Dmitry Petrovich. He gives a summary of the case against Mirsky from the Lubyanka file, with the additional detail that Mirsky came to the USSR 'with the collusion of the former chargé d'affaires in England the Trotskyite SOKOLNIKOV'. Ivanov writes that on 10 October 1939 he established that the investigative branch of the NKVD has received materials that 'reveal a new aspect of the anti-Soviet activity of SVYATOPOLK-MIRSKY'.

These materials stem from the interrogation of the 'spy for French intelligence TOLSTOY Pavel Nikolaevich' on 7 August 1939 and the depositions in Tolstoy's own hand of 5 October 1939. In these depositions, Tolstoy states that he was a member of the 'anti-Soviet Eurasian organization', from which a group split off in 1929 of persons 'who apparently having adopted the Soviet platform, formed a bloc with the Trotskyites who were in France and England and in particular with PYATAKOV and SOKOLNIKOV, and continued to engage in anti-Soviet activity'. Mirsky was one of the leaders of the 'left' Eurasians, alleges Tolstoy, and 'in 1932 under orders from the Eurasian organization and the Trotskyites he came to the USSR in order to establish connections with Trotskyites resident in the USSR'.

In addition, the document goes on, the Investigative Section possesses information that there is at present in the USSR a whole group of former *émigrés* who were members of the Eurasian organization and who then returned to the USSR 'as persons who had demonstrated their "loyalty" to Soviet power, but in reality . . . are conducting anti-Soviet activity'. On this basis, Ivanov has resolved 'that SVYATOPOLK-MIRSKY Dmitry Petrovich should be dispatched by convoy to the Investigative Section GUGB NKVD from SEVVOSTLAG and produced as an accused under Art. 58 para. 1a of the Criminal Code of the USSR'. Paragraph 1a of Article 58 refers to the ultimate capital crime: high treason. In the late 1930s, persons convicted under it were shot immediately after sentence was pronounced.

This new proceeding against Mirsky was undoubtedly connected with the principals in the case that was then being concocted against several of his former associates from the Eurasian movement, of whom P. N. Tolstoy was only one. Ariadna Efron was arrested on 27 August 1939; after multiple interrogations accompanied by physical torture, she 'confessed' on 27 September. The order for the arrest of Marina Tsvetaeva's husband, Sergey Efron, was signed on 2 October 1939 and confirmed by Beria on 9 October; Efron was brought in the following day. Emiliya Litauer, whose return in 1936 Mirsky had facilitated, had been arrested on the same day as Ariadna Efron.

The directive of October 1939 was evidently correlated with a form entitled 'Memorandum' from SEVVOSTLAG at Nagaevo addressed to GUGB NKVD USSR, Moscow, with 'Secret' scrawled at the top, and the date 20 June 1939. It gives Mirsky's particulars; the rubric *Departed* is filled in to read '6 June 1939. Died'.

Mirsky apparently rested in peace for about a decade after the move to re-arrest him had been frustrated by his death. His case was then checked in the last months of Stalin's lifetime. In the Moscow file is a typed Certificate headed *Top Secret*, dated 23 January 1953. The body of the document summarizes Mirsky's case and concludes with two paragraphs describing the depositions of P. N. Tolstoy. The final sentence concedes, with incontestable logic: 'In view of his death on 6 June 1939 while serving his punitive sentence in a camp, he was not produced to face criminal charges.'

After this, Mirsky's case 'rested' once again.

ARREST

To ask why, as opposed to how, Mirsky was arrested is fairly pointless as an exercise in rational enquiry. He was one individual victim of the most acute phase of the most sustained campaign of terror that has ever been conducted by a government against its own people in peacetime, the subsequent efforts of Mao Tse-tung and Pol Pot notwithstanding. A recent Russian computation based on archival materials, somewhat suspicious in its precision, asserts that over the period 1921–53, sentences were pronounced against 4,060,306 persons for political crimes.[30] The total for 1937, the peak year, was 790,665; of them, 353,074 were sentenced to capital punishment, and 429,311 to camps and prisons. Of these persons, 688,000 were sentenced by a Special Conclave (OSO), an institution usually referred to by Russians of a certain age as a *troika* or three-man kangaroo court; these bodies had been established according to decrees of 10 July and 5 November 1934. They dealt with 'cases for which the evidence was not sufficient for turning the defendant over to a court'.[31] Approximately 90 per cent of the original (1932–4) membership of the Union of Soviet Writers was arrested at this time, something like 2,000 individuals, and Mirsky was one of approximately 1,500 of them who, according to the best-informed commentators, died in prison or camp before completing their sentences or as a result of re-sentencing.[32] In these circumstances, survival would have been remarkable, and, heartless though it may seem to say so, the reasons for the survival of any individual would form a more significant object of enquiry than the reasons for that person's arrest.

The earliest document in Mirsky's files, the trigger for everything that follows, is a typed Certificate dated 5 May with the words *Top Secret* at the upper right corner, signed at the end by one Minaev, Deputy Chief, III Section GUGB NKVD, Commissar (3rd Class) of State Security. This document states that 'it has been established' that Mirsky was involved

in White *émigré* circles in London and Paris [and] was closely connected with known English intelligence agents, B. PARES in particular, and was a teacher of Russian history in the so-called institute of 'Slavonic Languages', which was in fact a school for English intelligence. It is known from Mirsky's words that he is acquainted with English spies who have travelled to Moscow.

According to agency information MIRSKY in Paris had illegal consultations with PYATAKOV while the latter was Trade Representative in France. At these consultations the question was discussed of the possible creation of 'a bloc between the rightists in the Communist Party and the Eurasians'.

A suspicious connection has been established between MIRSKY and persons connected with English intelligence.

MIRSKY is marked down for arrest.

The reference to Mirsky's own words here, if it does not refer to material cited in a denunciation or by an informant, means that at some point he must have been detained for questioning by the NKVD. On 24 March 1937 in a letter to Dorothy Galton Mirsky assured her that 'the scare report is groundless as you were right to guess'. This would appear to be a reference to his being detained, and his denial if anything confirms that fact.

Scrawled across the typed words of Minaev's report are two instructions in the thick pencil that the NKVD executive officers seem to have preferred, both saying 'Proceed to Arrest'. The report of 5 May leads to a printed form filled out on 15 May by Assistant Chief Mulyarov of 5 Division, III Section, GUGB NKVD, who states that he has examined the relevant material and assured himself that Mirsky, Dmitry Petrovich (the printed rubrics will be cited in italic, as before) *has been sufficiently exposed in re* 'he has served in British intelligence and conducted active intelligence work on the territory of the Soviet Union'. Mulyarov determines that 'Citizen Mirsky D. P.' *is to be produced as an accused under article* 58(6) *of the Criminal Code, and as the measure for interdiction of evasion of investigation and trial is to be selected* 'to be kept under guard'. The infamous Article 58 of the Criminal Code is the one dealing with political crimes. It had twelve paragraphs, beginning, as we know, with Treason against the Motherland.[33] At the bottom of the form is Mirsky's signature acknowledging that the contents were announced to him on 15 June 1937. The 'relevant material' Mulyarov has examined, apart from the evidence that led to the typed report of 5 May, must have consisted of statements mentioning Mirsky that had been made during the interrogation of other persons.

The trigger document took some time to be acted upon, for the next document in the file is another printed form, Warrant No. 2140, dated 2 June 1937, issued to one Sergeant Nikitin and requiring him to arrest Mirsky and carry out a search; the Warrant has a stub with the same date, addressed to *Commandant, Reception of Arrested Persons* instructing him to *receive the arrested person* Svyatopolk-Mirsky Dmitry Petrovich, *docket no.* 33. After this comes the first page (only) of the protocol relating to the arrest and search. The bulk of the document consists of a numbered inventory of items 'seized for delivery to GUGB'. It lists Mirsky's passport, Writers' Union membership card, Moscow residence permit, accreditation as a correspondent of *Moscow News*, Litfond membership card, medical card for the Kremlin hospital, and so forth, and then as item 15: 'Various correspondence and letters in Russian and a foreign language'. Heavily underlined by some reader of the file are items 18,

'Field Regulations of the Red Army of Workers and Peasants', and 19, 'Maps of the Communications and Economic Installations of the Moscow and Leningrad oblasts and the Far East region'. Mirsky's youthful interest in terrain and his staff officer's training seem to have stayed with him to the end, and they now gave rise to suspicion.

There are also two printed receipt forms, both dated 3 June 1937. They list a number of valuables that were confiscated from Mirsky, which include: Promissory Notes of the 2nd Five-Year Plan (fourth year) to the value of 2,200 roubles; £30 sterling in three notes; and a number of savings bank books, with balances totalling over 5,000 roubles. (Mirsky's boast to Dorothy Galton about his earning power had not been idle; but in Soviet Russia, there was not much he could do with his money. When Mandelshtam was arrested for the last time, he had a total of 36 roubles 28 copecks on him, and that was probably borrowed.) The last item in the first list is a pocket watch (without cover) No. 292844 in yellow metal. The second receipt lists a pen 'with eternal nib', scissors, a wallet in yellow leather, a tie, braces, garters, a key, a file, a pillow, and eight individually itemized postage stamps with a total value of about five roubles. Following these forms comes a handwritten note by Mirsky dated 5 August 1937, that is, after he had been interrogated and sentenced, headed 'Power of Attorney', addressed to the Commander of the Butyrka Isolator, and stating: 'Having no relatives, I grant the Commander of the Butyrka Isolator the right to receive the money, securities, and objects listed in Receipt No. 501 of 3 June 1937 and request them to be transferred to my name in the office of the Butyrka Isolator.'

Mirsky was photographed, either at Reception or when he arrived at the Butyrka, full face and right profile; this item, with his full surname and initials and the number 69979 in white ink at the bottom, accompanied his file when he was sent to the GULag. Next in the sequence is a handwritten note: 'Request arrestee Svyatopolk-Mirsky Dmitry Petrovich be placed in Butyrka Prison, Assigned to 5 Div. 3 Sect. GUGB Comrade Mulyarov, Commence New File.'[34] This is amplified in a printed form.

Then comes the first of several personal particulars forms to be found in Mirsky's files. The first page has been rubber-stamped: 'According to Card Index of Section 8, GUGB NKVD, No data', evidently a routine cross-check to ascertain whether or not the arrested man was already attested in NKVD files.[35] The form itself is filled out in Mirsky's own hand. He gives his basic biographical particulars under eight routine headings. Then come the leading questions; Mirsky gave a false answer to the last of them:

9. *Social Origin (Type of Occupation of Parents and their Property Position):* Landowner (Father a general, Minister of Internal Affairs 1904–1905).

10. *Social Position (Type of Occupation and Property Status of Arrested Person). a) Before the Revolution:* Student, officer (1912–13 and 1914–17). *b) After the Revolution:* Writer.

11. *Education (General and Special):* Higher (historical, philological faculty).

12. *Party Membership (Past and Present):* Non-Party. Was a member of the British Communist Party 1931–32.

13. *Nationality and Citizenship:* Soviet.

14. *Category of Military Registration/Reserve and Where Registered:* Excused due to Age.

15. *Service in White and Other C[ounter]-R[evolutionary] Armies, Participation in Gangs and Risings against Soviet Power (When and in What Capacity):* Served in Denikin's Army March 1919–February 1920.

16. *Subjected to Punitive Measures under Soviet Power: Criminal Record, Arrest, etc. (when, by what Organ, and for What Cause):* Not subjected.

17. *Family (Close Relatives, their Names, Addresses, and Occupations):* No relatives.

On 5 June 1937 in the Butyrka Prison Mirsky was fingerprinted, on the appropriate form, which includes instructions to the operator on how to do the job. This document, like his photograph, went with him to the GULag. Interrogation had probably already begun by this date. What that was like at this time has also been described, harrowingly, by Conquest.[36] It has also been described by Evgeniya Ginzburg, who was brought in to the Butyrka in July 1937 after being arrested and interrogated in Kazan; in her unforgettable account she mentions particularly the sweltering weather at this time, so hot that the asphalt was runny.[37] At the Lubyanka, where Mandelshtam was interrogated in 1938, conditions were reasonable: the prisoners were two to a cell and had their own cots, a toilet with a cover, and even toilet paper. In the Butyrka, where Mirsky was, the cells were stuffed full, there were plank beds but only enough for a few inmates, a barrel stood in one corner, and there was no privacy whatsoever.

INTERROGATION

The records of Mulyarov's interrogations present in my copy of the Moscow file occupy fourteen pages in longhand, with running heads at the left hand side, 'Question' followed by 'Answer'.[38] Mirsky's signature is appended to each answer. The procedure was evidently for a stenographer to take down the interrogation as it proceeded, a fair copy then to be made and given the prisoner to read, with him required by signing to indicate his acceptance of the veracity of the record.[39] The Moscow file contains an incomplete transcript of three interrogations.

In the copy of the Magadan file that I have seen there is for some reason a single Butyrka Prison form requiring an arrested person to be summoned for interrogation. It has been filled out with Mirsky's name, a note of whose nominal roll he is accountable to, and his cell number (26b); the interrogation is stated as beginning at 1.25 (a.m., of course) and ending at 3.30, the interrogation lasting 2.05 (hours). It is no longer astonishing to discover that the form (how many millions of them were filled out between 1936 and 1939?) is even signed by the guard who brought Mirsky from his cell for interrogation (Alekseev?) and the guard who took him away afterwards (Bobintsev?). The request was issued by Mulyarov; a pencilled note gives the date 22/VI/37.

Aleksandr Biryukov, who evidently saw the complete file in Magadan, says that Mirsky was actually interrogated nine times during the course of six weeks, that the first interrogations took place on 2, 3, 4, and 9 June, that they were conducted by Mulyarov, and that the longest of them, the third (on 4 June), lasted 5 hours 40 minutes. After this, Mirsky was interrogated mainly by one Sosin.[40] In view of the fact that Mirsky was arrested on 3 June, and that Mulyarov filled out his Protocol that same day, however, the first interrogation would seem to have taken place on this date, and Biryukov's account to be unreliable in respect of this detail. The missing interrogations were no doubt removed from Mirsky's file in connection with an enquiry into some related subject, and not restored to it. Quite possibly there is a separate 'Eurasian' file in existence somewhere.

At what was apparently his first interrogation, the transcript of which is not dated, Mirsky was required to give a detailed account of his participation in the Civil War and the events following the defeat of Denikin's army. This information has been incorporated into the account of Mirsky's life at that time in Chapter 3 above. Mirsky then testifies that he was brought to England by Maurice Baring. Asked how he knew Baring, he says that they met at his parents' home, but that he had not seen him since before 1914. Then he tells the story of how he was given his post at London University: 'at the invitation of Professor B. Pares', whom he met in 1907 when Pares interviewed his father. Mirsky gives a short account of Pares's career. He is cross-questioned about Pares's 'active work against the Soviet Union', and replies:

He had constant contacts with the leadership of the White emigration, in particular with the Cadets, the Octobrists, and some Tsarist ministers, Kokovtsev for example, with whom he conducted active propaganda against the Soviet Union in his journal *The Slavonic Review*. At the same time he communicated anti-Soviet materials to English conservatives, Churchill in particular. During the parliamentary elections of 1924 Pares offered his services to Churchill in supplying him with anti-Soviet materials.

The interrogation continues as follows:

Q: What do you know about Pares's activities in connection with the British 'Intelligence Service'?
A: Pares's activity in connection with the 'Intelligence Service' consisted in training military intelligence cadres in a teaching capacity at the school 'of Slavonic languages' which he headed, [cadres] seconded there from the military Ministries of England.

Q: What do you know about Pares's work in connection with the 'Intelligence Service' against the Soviet Union?

A: This activity is not known to me.

Q: Are you familiar with the aims and tasks of the school 'of Slavonic languages'?

A: Yes, I know that the school 'of Slavonic languages' is an instrument of British policy. The School sets itself the following tasks:

1. Strengthening the influence of British imperialism in the Slavonic countries.

2. Propagandizing the Slavonic states in England and stimulating interest in these countries among British citizens.

Both these tasks were included in the functions of the Central European section of the school, headed by Seton-Watson. In the Russian section, headed by Pares, before the Revolution his goal was to promote the penetration of British imperialism in Russia. After the Revolution his goal was the restoration of positions that had been lost, and in connection with this, the struggle against Soviet Power. Apart from this, the Russian section put on courses where the Russian language was taught to officers seconded from the War Ministry.

Q: What were these courses, and how do you know about them?

A: I know about these courses as a teacher of the Russian language. I was required to teach Russian to officers seconded from the military Ministries. These courses were not permanent. They were attended on average by 8–10 persons, who studied Russian in addition to their other duties. Some of these officers then returned to their units, and others went to Riga or other countries bordering the USSR.

Q: For what purposes did the officers on these special courses study the Russian language?

A: It was said officially that Russian would give them an advantage in their service careers.

Q: And unofficially?

A: One might suppose that the people who studied Russian were military intelligence cadres who were working against the Soviet Union, both on the inside and the outside.

Mirsky then says that the officers lodged in Riga with Russian *émigré* families. Asked to name these men, he offers 'Bannerman, Levy, Cambie', is told to remember some more names, and undertakes to do so at the next session. Mirsky is then told to name the intelligence agents with whom he has had contact in Russia; he begins by denying that he met any such people, but the interrogator presses him, and Mirsky concedes:

Of the intelligence people to whom I taught Russian I have seen none here, but in May 1937 I had meetings in Leningrad and Moscow with one Englishman who could be in intelligence. This person was not among my pupils.

Q: Who is this person and on what basis do you declare that he could be a spy?

A: The name of this Englishman is Carr. He is a writer. He has written two books, on Dostoevsky and Herzen.[41] I met Carr in Leningrad at the Astoria Hotel, and in Moscow several times at the National Hotel. When I asked him what he was doing in the Soviet Union he told me that he was writing a biography of Bakunin.[42] At that time Carr was working at the War Ministry as some sort of official. I knew that

Carr was interested in things Russian and knew Russian well. On the basis of what I have just said I suppose that Carr could be in intelligence.

Q: What was the basis of your meetings with Carr?

A: In London I saw Carr once or twice. If my memory serves, our meeting had to do with a review I had written of his book.[43] In Russia I spoke with him once when we met in Leningrad.

Q: Do you know who Carr saw in Moscow and Leningrad?

A: No, I do not.

Q: Apart from Carr, with whom in the Soviet Union have you had occasion to meet among people you know to be in intelligence, or with persons you suspect of being involved with English intelligence?

A: In Moscow in 1935 I had a meeting with Pares, who was mentioned earlier. . . . Of others involved with English intelligence I saw the Englishman Norman B. Jopson. I met Jopson in 1936 in Leningrad and later in Moscow.

Q: On what basis do you suspect Jopson of being involved with English intelligence?

A: I know that during the imperialist war Jopson was a military censor working on the perlustration of correspondence passing through London in the little-known European languages. . . . My suspicion that he was a spy arose after a conversation I had with the writer Olesha, to whom I introduced Jopson, and on whom he made the impression of being a spy.

Q: Do you know the reasons why Jopson came to the Soviet Union?

A: He told me that he had come out of curiosity, as a tourist.

Q: What do you know about Jopson's contacts, both in the Soviet Union and in London?

A: In Moscow I don't know. In London Jopson was in contact with his colleagues at the school of 'Slavonic languages' where he worked as a teacher. Apart from that he had many acquaintances among foreigners of the so-called lesser nationalities.

Q: Who else do you know of the people involved with the British intelligence organs?

A: I know no such people.

Mirsky was then asked to supply the names of the families in Riga who had offered Russian lessons to British officers, and he volunteered several: 'the Baranovs. I knew Baranov's sister, Olga Petrovna Zykova, who lived in London'; Nina Davis, *née* Khrushcheva, by her first marriage, Kleinmikhel; and 'Varvara Dmitrievna Volkova, an *émigrée* and former landowner'. Asked whether he knew these people personally, he said that he was 'well acquainted with Davis-Khrushcheva before 1914' but had not seen her since then, and that 'I knew Volkova from London'. The interrogation continues:

Q: We know that when you were in London you conducted active work against the Soviet Union. Make a statement about this anti-Soviet work, how and with whom you carried it out.

A: My actions were anti-Soviet, but they did not take an active form. The anti-Soviet activity amounted to the publication of articles in *Contemporary Notes* and the *Slavonic Review*.

Q: The investigation is for the moment not interested in the publication of articles. Make a statement about your work against the USSR in connection with British intelligence.

A: I state that I did not conduct active practical work against the Soviet Union in terms of espionage. In connection with my work at the school of Slavonic Languages I had occasion to come into daily contact with military intelligence personnel who were involved with intelligence work against the USSR. Their espionage activity, and equally the activity of the directors of the institution, and Pares in particular, are unknown to me.

Interrogation continued on 22–3 June 1937. Mirsky was asked if he had recalled the names of any more British officers, and replied: 'No, I have not, but I know their faces well and I could recognize some of them.' Asked yet again to name British intelligence personnel with whom he had contact in Moscow, Mirsky names 'Stafford Talbot, in connection with whom there may be suspicions that he is an intelligence person':

Q: Who is Talbot and how do you know him?
A: Talbot is the former co-owner of capitalist undertakings in Russia, and presently is the editor and publisher with his partner Parker of the *Russo-British Trade Gazette*. I met Talbot soon after I arrived in London in 1921–22.
Q: On what basis do you suspect Talbot of being involved in English intelligence?
A: I have no concrete basis.
Q: Your answers do not correspond to the real state of affairs. Tell us the whole truth about your own intelligence activity and also about the activity of those spies you have named and who are well known to you—Jopson, Talbot, and others.
A: I never engaged in any intelligence activity. The activity of Talbot, Jopson, and others is unknown to me.

The proceedings were then switched to Mirsky's involvement with Eurasianism. The interrogator soon got to the main point:

Q: Are you acquainted with the enemy of the people Pyatakov, who has now been executed?
A: No, I am not.
Q: Did you know that Pyatakov was connected with the leaders of the *Eurasia* group?
A: I know of the meetings Pyatakov had with Suvchinsky, one of the principal leaders of the Eurasians.

Mirsky was then pressed to describe these meetings, and stated that he knew of them only at second hand. The real danger of this line of enquiry soon emerged, and Mirsky incriminated himself by admitting that he had failed to report what he knew to the authorities:

Q: Did you speak to representatives of Soviet power about the fact, which was known to you, that Pyatakov had had discussions with Suvchinsky?
A: I completely forgot about this, since Pyatakov's discussions with Suvchinsky had no consequences.
Q: That is not true. You remembered this fact perfectly well. If you were an honest man, you would have communicated this to the organs of Soviet power when Pyatakov was put on trial. Why did you not do this?

A: Even at the time of the trial I didn't remember it.

Q: So you have a bad memory, do you?

A: Yes.

Q: Stop pretending. You have a good memory and we suggest that you tell the truth. Why, when it was quite apparent to you that Pyatakov was an enemy of the people, did you not communicate to the appropriate organs of Soviet power the fact that you knew about the discussions between Suvchinsky and Pyatakov and the connection of the latter with the 'Eurasians'?

A: It never entered my head, since I had forgotten about it.

Q: You concealed it, just as you are concealing the English intelligence people you know and your activity on behalf of British intelligence. Once again—give us an account of your work for the 'Intelligence Service'.

A: I never engaged in work for the 'Intelligence Service'.

Q: At the last interrogation you made a deposition that you taught the Russian language to military intelligence cadres. Apart from this you stated that you suspected certain Englishmen of being spies. Did you communicate this information to representatives of Soviet power?

A: I confess, I concealed this.

Having achieved his primary aim by securing an admission of guilt, the interrogator twists the knife:

Q: What were your aims in concealing from the organs of Soviet power your work in the school of English intelligence and persons who could be suspected of espionage?

A: I had no aims whatsoever.

Q: That is not true. If you had honestly come over to the side of Soviet power, the first thing you would have done is make a statement about your work for English intelligence, in particular as a language teacher for military intelligence cadres. Why did you conceal this until after you had been arrested?

A: I did not realize the significance that this could have.

Q: You concealed it, just as you are now concealing from this investigation your work for English intelligence on the territory of the USSR. Give true depositions about your work for the English in the USSR.

A: I state once again that I carried out no work for English intelligence in the Soviet Union.

When the interrogation resumed on 29 June, Mulyarov concentrated on Mirsky's literary activity, and in particular his relations with Leopold Averbakh, who had been arrested on 4 April 1937, as we know. This constitutes the third and final interrogation of which the record survives in my copy of the Moscow KGB file. Mirsky essentially recapitulates what he had written about to Stavsky: that he met Averbakh in October 1932 and saw him regularly until March 1936, but did not subsequently break off relations with him. The basis of the relations was purely literary, says Mirsky, and it was some time before he realized that Averbakh 'was not the Bolshevik he was trying to show himself to be in my eyes'. This serves to establish a case of guilt by association:

Q: What caused you to change your attitude with regard to Averbakh?

A: My attitude towards Averbakh changed in 1935, and the cause of this was firstly that I came to understand the nature of his intrigues in striving for leadership in literature, and then especially my trip to Uralmash, where I realized that he was still trying to gain power in literature and in essence was contesting the authority of the factory director. After this I regarded him as an unprincipled careerist.

Q: That is not true. We know that you never changed your attitude towards Averbakh. You are well aware of the c[ounter]-r[evolutionary] convictions and feelings of Averbakh. The investigation puts it to you to give a true deposition on what your c-r connection with Averbakh was really about.

A: I had no c-r connection with Averbakh. In 1932 Averbakh informed me about kulak sabotage in the C[entral] C[aucasus] region. From my conversations with Averbakh on this subject I understood that he was gratified that the Party was resorting to repressive measures in the countryside. This is the only occasion on which Averbakh was frank with me and I could have drawn a conclusion about his c-r feelings.

Q: This Averbakh of yours expressed his c-r convictions very frequently. It is being put to you yet again: make a statement about Averbakh's c-r convictions, which were known to you.

A: They are not known to me.

Q: How could they be not known to you when on Averbakh's instructions you conducted counter-revolutionary activity?

A: I conducted no c-r activity on Averbakh's instructions. Encouraged by the Averbakhites Jasienski and Karabelnikov I wrote an article about Fadeev's *The Last of the Udege* which included some crudely inaccurate evaluations of Fadeev. This was the only case in which I turned out to have been a tool of Averbakh.

Q: What other work did you carry out on Averbakh's instructions?

A: None.

Q: Why did the Averbakhites settle specifically on you to be their accomplice?

A: Because they knew that I was under the influence of Averbakh.

Q: In what way were you worked on by Averbakh, Jasienski, and other like-minded people?

A: They urged me in every way not to confine myself to narrowly literary questions. To be more active politically, to respond more to current problems. Knowing that Fadeev was struggling against *averbakhshchina*, Jasienski put it to me that I should make a statement against Fadeev's novel, in which he was apparently substituting ethical problems for political ones. I accepted Jasienski's suggestion and wrote the article you know about.

Q: From your answer it is clear that you were recruited by the Averbakhites.

A: In this particular case, yes.

Q: You were recruited by the Averbakhites in more than just this particular case. What other tasks did you carry out for the Averbakhites?

A: I was recruited by the Averbakhites, but apart from writing the article against Fadeev I carried out no other tasks.

There follows a single sheet in Mirsky's hand giving a deposition about the contacts between Pyatakov and Suvchinsky, repeating and slightly enlarging on the facts he had given under interrogation, and concluding: 'I was against this [making *Evraziya* a mouthpiece of the right opposition]; I considered it essential to support fully the general line of the Communist Party in the sphere of economic policy.'

SENTENCE

It took about a month for the investigating authorities to come to a recommendation. Three officers then signed a typed document on plain paper, headed 'Accusatory Conclusion'. It summarizes the findings of the investigation under four subject heads: service in the White army, teaching Russian to intelligence officers, concealing the latter activity from the Soviet authorities, and conducting terrorist work in close contact with the unmasked enemies of the people Averbakh, Jasienski, and others. Mirsky is said to have confessed his guilt. The three signatories recommend that the file be presented for inspection by an OSO. By the time Mirsky was sentenced, most of the cases concerned seem to have been tried *in absentia*.

Mirsky was lucky in one respect: when he was sentenced, an OSO did not have the formal right to impose the death penalty. This power was granted very shortly after the investigation of his case, on 30 July 1937, on personal instructions from Stalin.[44] The Conclave's judgement, neatly typed on the appropriate half-page-size form, stamped with the NKVD seal and signed by the Responsible Secretary to the Conclave, is dated 28 July 1937. Mirsky was sentenced for suspected espionage to eight years' confinement in corrective labour camp, the sentence to run from 2 June 1937, and an instruction is given to deposit the file in the archive. Eight years was the normal sentence at this time for Suspicion of Espionage, a crime described by Robert Conquest as 'an offence perhaps unique in the world's legal history'.[45]

A second half-page form dated 7 August from GUGB Section 8 addressed to Comrade Captain Popov, NKVD, Commandant of the Butyrka Prison, instructs him to dispatch Mirsky by the first available convoy to Nagaevo Harbour into the jurisdiction of the Head of the Directorate, North East Camps Directorate (SEVVOSTLAG NKVD), the date of dispatch to be confirmed by 15 August 1937. The prisoners were transported in goods trains fitted out with rough plank beds and a communal toilet barrel, by rail right across the Trans-Siberian to Vladivostok; then by sea via the southern tip of Sakhalin, with the holds containing the prisoners battened down because of the proximity to Japanese waters, then into the Sea of Okhotsk, making port at Magadan. Mirsky sailed on the *Kulu*; it carried an average consignment of 3,000–4,000 prisoners per trip. The voyage took from five to thirteen days.[46]

Many accounts have survived of the transit camps near Magadan on the way to the Kolyma goldfield. Very few people survived of those who were sent on into the interior, to Kolyma proper; this was tantamount to a death sentence.

During the years 1932–53, three million people died in Kolyma; the year 1938, which Mirsky spent entirely in the environs of Magadan, was the worst for casualties.[47]

THE GULAG

The second segment of Mirsky's documentation is Personal File No. 136848, which was kept by the GULag administration from the day of his sentence to the day of his burial.[48] From this segment we discover in some detail what happened to Mirsky after he arrived in the Far East.

Prisoner [Z/K] Mirsky was registered under the jurisdiction of the SEVVOSTLAG NKVD on 24 September 1937, and sent to a sub-camp at Atka, which is near the southern end of the Kolyma mountain range about 100 km inland from Magadan. Mirsky's personal file contains details of his work performance from then on. He was initially assigned to logging. His first three-month assessment sheet states that he worked ninety-two days but fulfilled his norm only by 40 per cent in October 1937, and then by 50 per cent in November and December. His performance and personal conduct were described as 'unsatisfactory'; he did not participate in 'mass-cultural work', though. This last item is of some interest in view of the persistent rumours that Mirsky gave lectures on the history of Russian poetry in the GULag, and even that he managed to produce a draft of a substantial book on this subject.

With the new year 1938, things went from bad to worse. From January to the end of March Mirsky managed only thirty-nine days' work because of illness, which was described as 'simulated' on his report. He was transferred from logging to duty as a watchman, and from June to September 1938 completed ninety-two days' labour, carried out in a way described as satisfactory, but with the additional remarks: 'Avoids physical work, and has a disdainful attitude to it.' His report for the last three months of 1938 says that he has failed to carry out instructions and has often been asleep on the job.

Mirsky was classified as medically unfit for work on 8 February 1939, and the doctors' report mentions myocarditis, oedema, and frostbite in one toe of the right foot. His last work assessment sheet, covering January to March 1939, states that no days have been worked, that he has not been permitted to take part in cultural and educational activities, but that his behaviour has been satisfactory and that he has kept himself clean.

Soon afterwards Mirsky was admitted to the hospital of the camp Invalidnaya, 23 km along the main route from Magadan.[49] What these 'hospitals' actually were we know well from the memoirs of survivors; they were in fact just another ordinary hut, but equipped with a stove and a wooden floor. There were no medicines, and very few medical instruments; the privileged personnel spent most of their time sitting around playing cards. To be admitted into hospital, as we know particularly poignantly from accounts of the last days of Mandelshtam, was like being put in the GULag equivalent of a hospice. Mirsky was now, to use the prison slang that Solzhenitsyn's *Ivan Denisovich* made common currency in Russian, a 'goner' (*dokhodyaga*). He died in this hospital on 6 June 1939. The death certificate diagnoses enterocolitis, chronic inflammation of the kidneys, and also decompensated myocarditis; the cause of death is given as enterocolitis. The dead man was fingerprinted (right and left hands) on the appropriate form by medical orderly Ablynin. The last document in Mirsky's GULag file is an 'Attestation of Burial' scrawled in pencil on a scrap of paper. It states that Z/K Mirsky Dmitry Petrovich P[ersonal] F[ile] 136848 was buried by duty commander Bolotnikov, the aforesaid medical orderly Ablynin, and the camp elder (*starosta*) Biryukov on 7 June 1939, 800 metres east of the command house, at a depth of 1.5 metres, 'his head pointing west'. This last detail is enigmatic, unless for some reason it is meant to indicate deliberate contradiction of Russian Orthodox ritual.

This is how Comrade Prince D. S. Mirsky, aristocrat of critics, came to his final rest. At some time in the future, perhaps, some way will be devised of setting up, in his own country, a memorial worthy of him. In the meantime, this book may serve as a temporary marker.

Notes

INTRODUCTION

1. In referring to Mirsky's publications in footnotes, I have indicated the relevant form of his name in cases where it appears as something other than 'D. S. Mirsky' or 'D. S. Mirski'.
2. Prince D. S. Mirsky, *Contemporary Russian Literature, 1881–1925* (London and New York, 1926); *A History of Russian Literature: From the Earliest Times to the Death of Dostoyevsky (1881)* (London and New York, 1927); D. S. Mirsky, *A History of Russian Literature*, ed. and abridged by Francis J. Whitfield (London, 1949).
3. *Geschichte der russischen Literatur*, trans. Georg Mayer (Munich, 1964); *Storia della letteratura russa*, trans. Silvio Bernardini (Milan, 1965); *Histoire de la littérature russe*, trans. Véronique Lossky (Paris, 1969).
4. *Istoriya russkoi literatury. S drevneishikh vremen do 1925 goda* (London, 1992). The superb translation is by Ruf' Zernova.
5. 'Histoire d'une émancipation', *Nouvelle Revue Française* 216 (1 Sept. 1931), 384–97. For a translation into English, see 'The History of an Emancipation', in *Uncollected Writings on Russian Literature* (Berkeley, Calif., 1989), 358–67.
6. 'Why I Became a Marxist', *Daily Worker* 462 (30 June 1931), 2; 'Istoriya odnogo osvobozhdeniya', *Literaturnaya gazeta* 10(178) (29 Feb. 1932), 2.
7. Akhmatova chooses to mention this crucial work not just because of the chronological coincidence; see Peter Ulf Møller, *Postlude to the Kreutzer Sonata: Tolstoy and the Debate on Sexual Morality in Russian Literature in the 1890s* (Amsterdam, 1989), and the discussion by Catriona Kelly, *A History of Russian Women's Writing, 1820–1992* (Oxford, 1994), 127.
8. For publication details of these and other letters, see Bibliography, Section 2.
9. Vitaly Shentalinsky, *The KGB's Literary Archive: The Discovery of the Ultimate Fate of Russia's Suppressed Writers* (London, 1995), 14.
10. D. Mirsky, *Literaturno-kriticheskie stat'i* (Moscow, 1978). This book has a bio-bibliographical introduction by M. Ya. Polyakov (pp. 5–18).
11. V. V. Perkhin, 'Odinnadtsat' pisem (1920–1937) i avtobiografiya (1936) D. P. Svyatopolk-Mirskogo', *Russkaya literatura* 1 (1996), 235–62.
12. V. V. Perkhin, *Russkaya literaturnaya kritika 1930-kh godov: Kritika i obshchestvennoe soznanie epokhi* (St Petersburg, 1997); Perkhin's views were first presented as an introduction to his pioneering republication of some essays by Mirsky that first appeared outside Russia; see 'O D. P. Svyatopolk-Mirskom', in D. P. Svyatopolk-Mirsky, 'Literaturno-kriticheskie stat'i', *Russkaya literatura* 4 (1990), 120–7.
13. Ol'ga Kaznina, *Russkie v Anglii: Russkaya emigratsiya v kontekste russko-angliiskikh literaturnykh svyazei v pervoi polovine XX veka* (Moscow, 1997).
14. Nina Lavroukine and Leonid Tchertkov, *D. S. Mirsky: Profil critique et bibliographique* (Paris, 1980).
15. René Wellek, *A History of Modern Criticism, 1750–1950*, vii: *German, Russian, and Eastern European Criticism, 1900–1950* (New Haven, Conn., and London, 1991), 348–53. This account is perfunctory, and riddled with elementary mistakes of fact.
16. Mirsky is not mentioned, for example, in the otherwise fairly comprehensive survey by Victor Terras, 'Russian Literary Criticism', in Harry Weber (ed.), *The Modern Encyclopedia of Russian and Soviet Literature*, v (Gulf Breeze, Fla., 1981), 1–19. The single exception to the general neglect is R. H. Stacy, *Russian Literary Criticism: A Short History* (Syracuse, NY, 1974), in which Mirsky's name looms large.
17. For guidance on the uses and abuses of Bakhtin, see Carol Adlam, 'In the Name of Bakhtin:

Appropriation and Expropriation in Recent Russian and Western Bakhtin Studies', in Alastair Renfrew (ed.), *Exploiting Bakhtin* (Strathclyde, 1997), 75–90.

1. TWO NAMES

1. See Geoffrey Hosking, *Russia: People and Empire* (Cambridge, Mass., 1998). For the social history of Russia to 1905, apart from the writings of Mirsky see esp. Sir Donald Mackenzie Wallace, *Russia* (2 vols., London, etc., 1905); also valuable is Bernard Pares, *A History of Russia* (New York, 1926). My copy of this book carries the inscription: 'May 25, 1926. To Prince Dmitry Svyatopolk-Mirsky, grateful for generous help. B. P.' The pages dealing with the period 1890–1914 were uncut when I acquired the book. The account of Russia during their youth written by a close friend of Mirsky is still valuable: M. T. Florinsky, *The End of the Russian Empire* (New York, 1961).
2. For an account of pre-revolutionary social structure which stresses the lack of hard-and-fast boundaries between these groups, see Elise Kimerling Wirtschafter, *Social Identity in Imperial Russia* (De Kalb, Ill., 1997).
3. Maurice Baring, 'The Nobility', in *The Mainsprings of Russia* (London, 1914), 92. For a detailed study, see Dominic Lieven, *Russia's Rulers under the Old Regime* (London, 1989).
4. Baring, *The Mainsprings of Russia*, 183–215; Harold Williams, *Russia of the Russians* (London, 1914), 127–37.
5. Ibid. 130.
6. Baring, *The Mainsprings of Russia*, 213.
7. Prince D. S. Mirsky, *Contemporary Russian Literature, 1881–1925* (London, 1926), 284.
8. 'The Peasants after the Emancipation', in D. S. Mirsky, *Russia: A Social History* (London, 1931), 254–6.
9. The life of the peasantry during Mirsky's youth was described on the basis of scrupulous fieldwork by a remarkable contemporary: Olga Semyonovna Tian-Shanskaia, *Village Life in Late Tsarist Russia*, ed. David L. Ransel, trans. David L. Ransel with Michael Levine (Bloomington and Indianapolis, 1993). The discussion of peasant drinking habits (ch. 7) provides a valuable perspective on Mirsky's 'weakness'.
10. D. S. Mirsky, *A History of Russian Literature* (London and New York, 1949), 261.
11. On this change in attitude, see Leopold Haimson, 'The Problem of Social Identities in Early Twentieth-Century Russia', *Slavic Review* 47 (1) (1988), 1–20.
12. Orlando Figes takes this as the starting-point for his grandiose study of the revolutionary process in Russia, *A People's Tragedy: The Russian Revolution 1891–1924* (London, 1996).
13. Williams, *Russia of the Russians*, 53 ff.
14. Bernard Pares, *My Russian Memoirs* (London, 1931), 54–5; on the cultural issues involved, see Barbara Heldt, ' "Japanese" in Russian Literature: Transforming Identities', in Thomas Rimer (ed.), *A Hidden Fire: Russian and Japanese Encounters, 1868–1926* (Stanford, Calif., 1995), 171–83.
15. Mirsky, *Russia: A Social History*, 269.
16. There is an expert account of this process and the contemporary Russian press in general by Harold Williams, who was a professional journalist, in *Russia of the Russians*, 99–126.
17. See Jeffrey Brooks, *When Russia Learned to Read: Literacy and Popular Literature, 1861–1917* (Princeton, NJ, 1985), and the contributions by Louise Reynolds, Cathy Popkin, Steve Smith, Catriona Kelly, Rosamund Bartlett, and Linda Edmondson in pt. 2, 'Cultural Transformation in Late Imperial Russia', in Catriona Kelly and David Shepherd (eds.), *Constructing Russian Culture in the Age of Revolution: 1881–1940* (Oxford, 1998), 55–224.
18. See Bernice Glatzer Rosenthal (ed.), *The Occult in Russian and Soviet Culture* (Ithaca, NY, 1997).
19. For a concise historical survey of these issues, see Charles E. Timberlake, 'Introduction: Religious Pluralism, the Spread of Revolutionary Ideas, and the Church–State Relationship

in Tsarist Russia', in Charles E. Timberlake (ed.), *Religious and Secular Forces in Late Tsarist Russia: Essays in Honor of Donald W. Treadgold* (Seattle and London, 1992), 3–29.

20. As opposed to qualifications in the liberal professions, outstanding technical and scientific expertise was highly marketable, as witness the spectacular careers in the USA of two of Mirsky's most illustrious contemporaries, the aerononautical engineer Igor Sikorsky (1889–1972) and the electronics engineer Vladimir Zworykin (1889–1982).

21. For some judicious weighing of this problem, see on the one hand Paul Dukes, 'Russian Imperialism, 1894–1917', in his *A History of Russia, c.882–1996*, 3rd edn (Basingstoke, 1998), 173–202, and on the other Richard Pipes, 'Reflections on the Russian Revolution', in his *Russia under the Bolshevik Regime* (New York, 1993), 490–512.

22. See Lev Nikolaevich Tolstoy, *Polnoe sobranie sochinenii*, cx (Moscow, 1958), 251–6.

23. Mirsky once narrated this episode as follows: '[The] Mongols, led by Genghiz-khan's grandson, Batû, reappeared this side of the Urals. After conquering the kingdom of Bulgar, they invaded Russia (1238), sacked Vladimir, and utterly defeated the Suzdal princes on the Sit'.' Prince D. S. Mirsky, *A History of Russia* (London, 1928), 10. He provides a footnote to the word 'princes': 'After the second quarter of the thirteenth century the title of *knyaz'*, cheapened by infinite subdivision and multiplication, ceases to be rendered into Latin by *rex*, and becomes mere *dux*.'

24. Mirsky refers to the Polish military leaders Jan Karol Chodkiewicz (1560–1621), who distinguished himself in campaigns against the Swedes and the Turks, and King Jan III Sobieski (ruled 1674–96), who prevented the Turks from capturing Vienna in 1683.

25. Reprinted in D. S. Mirsky, *Stikhotvoreniya: Stat'i o russkoi poezii* (Berkeley, 1997), 78.

26. Prince D. S. Mirsky, *Pushkin* (New York and London, 1926), 1.

27. P. D.'s patronymic was given wrongly in the standard pre-revolutionary biographical dictionary as 'Danilovich', and this mistake has been repeated constantly since.

28. Matitiahu Mayzel, 'The Formation of the Russian General Staff, 1880–1917: A Social Study', *Cahiers du Monde Russe et Soviétique*, 16 (1975), 302. See also Peter Kenez, 'A Profile of the Pre-Revolutionary Officer Corps', *California Slavic Studies* 7 (1973), 121–58; John Bushnell, 'The Tsarist Officer Corps, 1881–1914: Customs, Duties, Inefficiency', *American Historical Review* 86 (1981), 753–80.

29. See W. C. Fuller, *Civil–Military Conflict in Imperial Russia, 1881–1914* (Princeton, NJ, 1985).

30. Mirsky, *A History of Russia*, 53–4.

31. See Hans Rogger, 'Corridors of Power: The Tsar's Ministers', in his *Russia in the Age of Modernisation and Revolution, 1881–1917* (London and New York, 1993), 27–43. There is an instructive table showing ministerial tenure in Bernard Pares, *A History of Russia* (London, 1926), 509–13.

32. See Lili Dehn, *The Real Tsaritsa* (London, 1922).

33. Gosudarstvennyi Arkhiv Rossiiskoi Federatsii, Moscow (hereafter GARF), *fond* 1729, *opis'* 1, *list* 31. The identity of these people, whose surname was Mirsky and not Svyatopolk-Mirsky, is a puzzle.

34. See V. V. Perkhin, 'Odinnadtsat' pisem (1920–1937) i avtobiografiya (1936) D. P. Svyatopolk-Mirskogo. K nauchnoi biografii kritika', *Russkaya literatura* 1 (1996), 257.

35. On Svyatopolk-Mirsky's activities in Vilna, see Theodore R. Weeks, 'Defining Us and Them: Poles and Russians in the "Western Provinces", 1863–1914', *Slavic Review* 53 (1) (1994), 38–9. For Svyatopolk-Mirsky's report on the Jewish question, see 'Vsepoddanneishii doklad ministra vnutrennikh del P. D. Svyatopolk-Mirskogo (24 noyabrya 1904 g.)', in *Reka vremen: Kniga istorii i kul'tury*, vol. 5 (Moscow, 1996), 216–62; a translation is appended to Pawel Korzec, 'Three Documents of 1903–6 on the Russian Jewish Situation', *Soviet Jewish Affairs* 2 (2) (1972), 75–95.

36. See Dorothy Atkinson et al. (eds.), *Women in Russia* (Stanford, Calif., 1977); for guidance on subsequent work, see Rochelle Ruthchild, *Women in Russia and the Soviet Union: An Annotated Bibliography* (New York, 1994), and Mary F. Zirin, *Women, Gender, and Family in the Soviet Successor States and Central/East Europe: A Bibliography* (Altadena, Calif., 1996).

37. See Richard Stites, *The Women's Liberation Movement in Russia: Feminism, Nihilism, and Bolshevism 1860–1930*, 2nd edn (Princeton, NJ, 1991).

38. After he went back to Russia, Mirsky knew two such doctors, women of exactly his own age, but by that time they had both become professional writers: Elizaveta Polonskaya (1890–1969) and Mariya Shkapskaya (1891–1952). For information on these and other women writers mentioned below, see Charlotte Rosenthal, Marina Ledkovsky, and Mary Zirin, *A Dictionary of Russian Women Writers* (Westport, Conn., 1994).

39. See Christine Ruane, *Gender, Class, and the Professionalization of Russian City Teachers, 1860–1914* (Pittsburgh, 1994). For the situation of the professions in general, see Harley Balzer (ed.), *Russia's Missing Middle Class: The Professions in Russian History* (Armonk, NY, 1996).

40. See Catherine A. Schuler, *Women in the Theatre: The Actress in the Silver Age* (London, 1996).

41. See Laurie Bernstein, *Sonia's Daughters* (Berkeley and Los Angeles, 1995).

42. For an incisive discussion of the 'women's realm' in Russia at this time, and of its representation in literature, see Catriona Kelly, 'Configurations of Authority: Feminism, Modernism, and Mass Culture, 1881–1917', in her *A History of Russian Women's Writing, 1820–1992* (Oxford, 1994), 121–80. For a wide-ranging survey of the representation of women in Russian culture, with excellent bibliography, see Rosalind Marsh, 'An Image of their Own? Feminism, Revisionism and Russian Culture', in Rosalind Marsh (ed.), *Women and Russian Culture: Projections and Self-Perceptions* (New York and Oxford, 1998), 2–41.

43. Mirsky, *A History of Russian Literature*, 440. For the intellectual background to Mirsky's ideas of the feminine and the masculine, see Linda Edmondson, 'Women's Emancipation and Theories of Sexual Difference in Russia, 1850–1917', in Marianne Liljeström, Eila Mäntysaari, and Arja Rosenholm (eds.), *Gender Restructuring in Russian Studies* (Tampere, 1993), 39–52.

44. Lara is the heroine of Pasternak's *Dr Zhivago*; Margarita of Bulgakov's *Master and Margarita*; Nadezhda Yakovlevna Mandelshtam (1899–1980) was the widow of the poet for many more years than she was his wife, wrote two volumes of memoirs about him, and was responsible for saving his later poetry from oblivion.

45. Pares, *My Russian Memoirs*, 137.

46. D. S. Mirsky, 'Some Remarks on Tolstoy', reprinted in *Uncollected Writings on Russian Literature*, ed. G. S. Smith (Berkeley, Calif., 1989), 307.

47. 'Dnevnik kn. Ekateriny Alekseevny Svyatopolk-Mirskoi za 1904–1905 gg', *Istoricheskie zapiski* 77 (1965), 236–93. The diary was passed on to the relevant archive by Mirsky's younger sister, Olga, after she returned to Russia; it is the only family document to have been published.

48. Ibid. 258.

49. Ibid. 254.

50. The ordinary Jews of Kharkov did not survive the Second World War. Kharkov (Kharkiv) is now the second city of independent Ukraine, but its population remains predominantly Great Russian by language and culture.

51. Mirsky provides a lucid explanation of these and other issues in Russo-Ukrainian relations in his 'The Ukraine', *Quarterly Review* 239 (1923), 318–35; see also Chapter 3 below.

52. *A History of Russian Literature*, 360. Mirsky cites Constance Garnett's translation.

53. See Nina Lavroukine, 'Maurice Baring and D. S. Mirsky: A Literary Relationship', *Slavonic and East European Review* 62 (1) (1984), 25–35.

54. Maurice Baring, *The Puppet Show of Memory* (London, 1922), 386–7.

55. In almost all published sources, Mirsky's date of birth is given as 15 (27) Aug. 1890. The correct date was established on the basis of several different archival sources by V. V. Perkhin; see 'K istorii aresta i reabilitatsii D. P. Svyatopolk-Mirskogo (po arkhivnym materialam)', *Russkaya literatura* 1 (1997), 223.

56. 'Avtobiografiya D. P. Svyatopolk-Mirskogo', in V. V. Perkhin, 'Odinnadtsat' pisem

(1920–1937) i avtobiografiya (1936) D. P. Svyatopolk-Mirskogo', *Russkaya literatura* 1 (1996), 257.

57. Mirsky himself once offered a definition of this word as it was understood during his time: '"Byt" is the life of a definite community at a definite time in its individual, as opposed to universally human, features.' 'Introduction' to Boris Pilniak, *Tales of the Wilderness* (London, 1924), p. xi.

58. Mirsky's inside leg measurement would seem to have been rather important here, but presumably his sense of decorum prevented him mentioning it to Miss Galton.

59. Marina Tsvetaeva reportedly got Mirsky to sit in her kitchen grinding coffee, which he did 'humbly', and which made him 'almost happy'; Elena Izvol'skaya, 'Ten' na stenakh (O Marine Tsvetaevoi)', *Opyty* 3 (1954), 156.

60. Luciani, a Corsican, Moscow correspondent of *Le Temps* in the early 1930s; see Malcolm Muggeridge, *Chronicles of Wasted Time*, i: *The Green Stick* (London, 1972), 237.

61. GARF, *fond* 1729, *opis'* 1.

62. On this general subject, see Harvey Pitcher, *When Miss Emmie was in Russia: English Governesses Before, During and After the October Revolution* (London and Toronto, 1977).

63. Prince D. S. Mirsky, 'Through Foreign Eyes: An Address Delivered at the Annual Meeting of the Brontë Society', *Brontë Society Publications* 6 (33) (1923), 147–8.

64. GARF, *fond* 1729, *opis'* 2, *edinitsa khraneniya* 392, fo. 1.

65. Mirsky proudly recorded that 'the present writer, when a small boy, had the privilege of being introduced to Grigori Alexandrovich Pushkin' (the third child and second son of the poet, 1835–1905); *Pushkin* (London, 1926), 195.

66. This uncle and other relatives mentioned in this letter appear to be on the mother's side of the family.

67. Mirsky wrote a poem about this house, dated 'Pokrovskoe, 1907'; exposed when the fir trees shielding it fell into a ravine, and then boarded up, the house seemed to the poet a funerary monument jealously guarding the ghosts of the past. See *Stikhotvoreniya: Stat'i o russkoi poezii*, 63.

68. GARF, *fond* 1729, *opis'* 2, *edinitsa khraneniya* 392, fo. 1.

69. See Robert L. Nichols, 'The Friends of God: Nicholas II and Alexandra at the Canonization of Serafim of Sarov, July 1903', in Timberlake, *Religious and Secular Forces in Late Tsarist Russia*, 207–29. On the saint, see A. F. Dobbie-Bateman, *St Seraphim of Sarov: Concerning the Aims of the Christian Life* (London, 1936). Revd Dobbie-Bateman (1897–1974) was a pupil of Mirsky in London; on him, see G. S. Smith, *The Letters of D. S. Mirsky to P. P. Suvchinskii* (Birmingham, 1995), 216.

70. Miss Trend's brother, the prolific and versatile hispanist J. B. Trend (1887–1958), was a Fellow of Christ's College, Cambridge, and eventually professor of Spanish in that university; his *Calderón* appeared in the same Routledge series, 'The Republic of Letters', as Mirsky's *Pushkin*; and his *Manuel de Falla and Spanish Music* was reprinted in the same series from Knopf as Mirsky's *A History of Russian Literature from the Earliest Times to the Death of Dostoyevsky (1881)*. The family came from Southampton, where the father was a medical doctor and Justice of the Peace. Vera Traill told me that Mirsky kept in touch with Miss Trend during his time in London.

71. Considerably later, his mother's diary records that Dim fell ill with stomach poisoning on 14 Jan. 1905; on this occasion he was treated by no less a personage than one of the Tsar's doctors, L. D. Bertenson.

72. Mirsky, *Pushkin*, 205–6.

73. The mother also had her own cultural pursuits: in Aug. 1902 Dim tells his father that she is excavating a burial mound.

74. Mirsky, *Pushkin*, 176. Mikhail Zagoskin (1789–1852) published this novel in 1829.

75. Mirsky, *A History of Russian Literature*, 115.

76. The Dowager Empress characteristically uses French; her son and his wife preferred English as their polite language.

77. She uses the word *proizvol*, identified by contemporary commentators such as Maurice Baring as the single most obnoxious characteristic of the tsarist regime.
78. 'Dnevnik kn. Ekateriny Alekseevny Svyatopolk-Mirskoi', 240.
79. Broadly the same interpretation was offered by one of Svyatopolk-Mirsky's most thoughtful colleagues: see D. N. Shipov, *Vospominaniya i dumy o perezhitom* (Moscow, 1918), 581–7.
80. 'Dnevnik', 258. It is not apparent from her diary whether Ekaterina Alekseevna considered that she as a woman might 'participate in lawmaking', by being entitled to vote, for example.
81. Bernard Pares, *Russia and Reform* (London, 1907), 499.
82. See Alexander Kaun, 'Maxim Gorky and the Tsarist Police', *Slavonic Review* 8 (24) (1930), 648–9. Tolstoy wrote to Svyatopolk-Mirsky on 6 May 1901 pleading for the alleviation of Gorky's conditions while in prison; see *Polnoe sobranie sochinenii*, lxxiii/lxxiv (Moscow, 1954), 69–71. Mirsky's classmate Viktor Zhirmunsky has been reported as saying that their school sent a delegation to protest to the authorities about the imprisonment of Gorky in 1905; see Leonid Tchertkov, 'L'Œuvre de jeunesse', in Nina Lavroukine and Leonid Tchertkov, *D. S. Mirsky: Profil critique et bibliographique* (Paris, 1980), 12.
83. On the history and nature of the *zemstvo*, see Baring, *The Mainsprings of Russia*, 116–26; he translates the term as 'county council'.
84. 'Dnevnik', 256.
85. Igor Vinogradoff, unpublished letter to G. S. Smith, 13 Feb. 1974.
86. Idem, unpublished letter to G. S. Smith, 26 Feb. 1974.
87. See 'The Ninth of January and the Battleship Potemkin', in M. N. Pokrovsky, *Brief History of Russia*, trans. D. S. Mirsky (2 vols., London, 1933), ii, 101–42.
88. 'Dnevnik', 280.
89. Ibid. 282.
90. The sons of Ekaterina Alekseevna's sister-in-law, Nina Den, Dmitry and Nikolay, were in the navy and fought in the battle of Tsushima; Nikolay was killed on the battleship *Alexander III*.
91. See P. P. Gaidenko, '"Konkretnyi idealizm" S. N. Trubetskogo', in S. N. Trubetskoy, *Sochineniya* (Moscow, 1994), 3–41; and Martha Bohachevsky-Chomiak, *Sergei N. Trubetskoi: An Intellectual among the Intelligentsia in Prerevolutionary Russia* (Belmont, Mass., 1976).
92. 'Dnevnik', 285.
93. Ibid. 286.
94. Ibid.

2. TWO CALLINGS

1. Harold Williams, *Russia of the Russians* (London, 1914), 413.
2. Maurice Baring, *Landmarks in Russian Literature* (London, 1910; repr. London and New York, 1960), 125–6.
3. Translated from *Linguaphone Conversational Course: Russian*. Recorded by Dimitri Svjatopolk-Mirskij et al. (London, n.d.), 41.
4. See G. S. Smith, 'D. S. Mirsky: Two Letters to Elizaveta Polonskaia (1935, 1936) on Translating Kipling and Christina Rossetti', *Slavonic and East European Review* 73 (3) (1995), 490–8.
5. G. S. Smith, 'Jane Ellen Harrison: Forty-Seven Letters to D. S. Mirsky, 1924–1926', *Oxford Slavonic Papers*, n.s. 28 (1995), 90; she is speaking *à propos* the acknowledgement in D. S. Mirsky, *Contemporary Russian Literature, 1881–1925* (London and New York, 1926), p. xi.
6. Ibid. 67. This passage is preserved unaltered in Mirsky, *A History of Russian Literature* (1949), 343.
7. This was a certain Miss Avery, who came to the Guchkovs after being with the Golitsyns.
8. Edmund Wilson once alleged that Mirsky made a sweeping dismissal of the work of Henry

James, but admitted to Wilson privately that he had only ever read *The Ambassadors*; 'Comrade Prince', *Encounter* 5 (1) (1955), 11.

9. V. V. Perkhin, 'Odinnadtsat' pisem (1920–1937) i avtobiografiya (1936) D. P. Svyatopolk-Mirskogo', *Russkaya literatura* 1 (1996), 257.

10. The most serious segment of Mirsky's *Stikhotvoreniya* (St Petersburg, 1911), 'Odes', is dedicated to Sukhotin, and so (simply as 'A. S.') is the first book Mirsky published in emigration, *Russkaya lirika: Malen'kaya antologiya ot Lomonosova do Pasternaka* (Paris, 1924).

11. Tolstoy's secretary D. P. Makovitsky recorded on 21 Apr. 1905: 'L. N. said that Sukhotin's 15-year-old son, a *gimnaziya* student, was editing a journal in Petersburg. Svyatopolk-Mirsky's 11-year-old son has written for it "A Psychological Study", about the state of Balmashov's soul when he was facing execution': see *U Tolstogo 1904–1910. 'Yasnopolyanskie zapiski' D. P. Makovitskogo. Kniga pervaya, 1904–1905* (Moscow, 1979), 253 (*Literaturnoe nasledstvo*, 85). No publication by Mirsky corresponding to this 'debut' has come to light.

12. Modern Greek 'free, unmarried'; Byzantine Greek 'a gentleman'; Ancient Greek 'free, a freeman'. Mirsky no doubt wanted to convey something of all these things.

13. Eleutheròs, 'Proshlo to vremya', in K. I. Azbelev and Ya. Ya. Polferov, *Zven'ya: Literaturno-khudozhestvennyi sbornik* (St Petersburg, 1906), 32.

14. See Boris Gasparov, 'Introduction', in Boris Gasparov, Robert P. Hughes, and Irina Paperno (eds.), *Cultural Mythologies of Russian Modernism: From the Golden to the Silver Age* (Berkeley, Calif., etc., 1992), esp. 1–2.

15. Mirsky explains this word as 'roughly, "vital sap"': *A History of Russian Literature*, 473. Sergey Mitrofanovich Gorodetsky (1884–1967) published two collections in 1907. *Yar* was the first; the other was called *Perun*, after the Slavonic god of thunder. He was the first of the 'back to the Slavonic pagan roots' poets taken up by the avant-garde intelligentsia in the years before 1910 (Stravinsky's *Firebird* was to come in 1910, *Petrushka* in 1911, *The Rite of Spring* in 1913). Written out as a poet with his two collections of 1907, Gorodetsky remains in literary history as the author of one of the Acmeist manifestos, a document containing some curious passages about potency and other masculine virtues in literary texts, which may have helped to form Mirsky's critical vocabulary. Gorodetsky survived in the USSR and eventually earned undying contempt for two main reasons: he was the failed hack who published a sickening denunciation of his disgraced former fellow-Acmeist Akhmatova in 1936; and for the delectation of Stalin he converted the libretto of Glinka's *A Life for the Tsar* into *Ivan Susanin* (1937–44).

16. *Blok v neizdannoi perepiske i dnevnikakh sovremennikov* (Moscow, 1982) (*Literaturnoe nasledstvo*, 92, Book III. *Aleksandr Blok. Novye materialy i issledovaniya*, 272).

17. Ibid.

18. Mirsky, *A History of Russian Literature*, 456–7.

19. Kuzmin disguised his true age in order to avoid call-up for the First World War; his date of birth is given in most reference works as 1875.

20. When the author sold his papers to the State Literary Archive in 1934, the diary was passed on to the NKVD and served as a checklist for rounding up the Leningrad literary bohemia. On the general subject of diaries during the period of Mirsky's youth, see N. A. Bogomolov, 'Dnevniki v russkoi kul'ture nachala XX veka', *Tynyanovskie chteniya* 4 (Riga, 1990), 152–4.

21. See John Malmstad, 'Mikhail Kuzmin: A Chronicle of His Life and Times', in Mikhail Kuzmin, *Sobranie stikhov*, ed. J. E. Malmstad and V. F. Markov (Munich, 1977), iii. 9–319; J. Malmstad (ed.), *Studies in the Life and Work of Mixail Kuzmin* (Vienna, 1989); N. A. Bogomolov and Dzhon E. Malmstad, *Mikhail Kuzmin: Iskusstvo, zhizn', epokha* (Moscow, 1996); N. A. Bogomolov, *Mikhail Kuzmin: Stat'i i materialy* (Moscow, 1995); M. A. Kuzmin, *Stikhotvoreniya*, ed. N. A. Bogomolov (St Petersburg, 1996).

22. Kuzmin's retrospective view of the Tower is especially valuable; see Mikhail Kuzmin, *Dnevnik 1934 goda* (St Petersburg, 1998), 66–112. For a more indulgent contemporary view of Ivanov, see Bernard Pares, *My Russian Memoirs* (London, 1931), 132. Pares was a paying guest at the Tower in Mar. 1907 (because it was opposite the Duma building), and was kept awake by 'the eccentric novelist' Kuzmin's piano playing. This redoubtable Englishman was

not really at home: 'They begged me not to sing [Harrow school songs, no doubt] when I was in my bath in the morning, because that was the time when they were just going to bed.' For a judicious assessment of Ivanov, see Pamela Davidson, 'Introduction', in her *Viacheslav Ivanov: A Reference Guide* (London, etc. 1996), pp. xv–xxix; the annotated bibliography of this book provides Mirsky's assessments of Ivanov with an instructive context.

23. N. A. Bogomolov, in Kuzmin, *Stikhotvoreniya*, 701.

24. Williams, *Russia of the Russians*, 320. Note the word 'barbarous'.

25. Sudeikin left Glebova and emigrated with the actress Vera Shilling; she later married Igor Stravinsky. See *The Salon Album of Vera Sudeikina-Stravinsky*, ed. and trans. John E. Bowlt (Princeton, NJ, 1995).

26. For an interpretation of this reception, see Laura Engelstein, *The Keys to Happiness* (Ithaca, NY, 1992), 397.

27. Bogomolov, *Mikhail Kuzmin*, 67–98. On the intellectual constructions associated with these aspects of sexuality in early twentieth-century Russia, see especially Olga Matich, 'Dialectics of Cultural Return: Zinaida Gippius' Personal Myth', in Gasparov et al., *Cultural Mythologies of Russian Modernism*, 52–72, and eadem, 'The Symbolist Theory of Love: Theory and Practice', in Irina Paperno and Joan Delaney Grossman (eds.), *Creating Life: The Aesthetic Utopia of Russian Modernism* (Stanford, Calif., 1994), 24–50.

28. For these diary entries, see Bogomolov, *Mikhail Kuzmin*, 106–114.

29. Naumov was an officer cadet (*yunker*) at the Engineering Academy; see ibid. 128 ff., 247.

30. Val'ter Fedorovich Nuvel' (1871–1949) had been a leading light in the 'World of Art' movement (he was the secretary of Diaghilev's Russian Ballet), and was one of Kuzmin's closest friends; for their relationship, see esp. 'Perepiska s V. F. Nuvelem', ibid. 216–304.

31. Mirsky, *A History of Russian Literature*, 474.

32. This is Sergey Abramovich Auslender (1888–1943), who left the VII Petersburg *gimnaziya* in 1906 and went on to the university, attending Vengerov's Pushkin seminar in 1908 and 1909; he left in 1910 without taking a degree. His mother by her first marriage was Kuzmin's sister Varvara Alekseevna Moshkova, a schoolteacher. Auslender was the author of prose and dramatic 'stylizations', which Mirsky evidently did not consider sufficiently important to merit inclusion in his discussion of this tendency; see ibid. 473–5.

33. Aleksey Remizov (1877–1957) was married to the palaeographer Serafima Pavlovna Remizova-Dovgello (1876–1943); Mirsky was to visit them often in Paris in the 1920s, and did more than any other critic to foster Remizov's reputation outside Russia; see Chapter 5 below.

34. See A. V. Lavrov, *Andrey Bely v 1900-e gody* (Moscow, 1995), 196–201, 203–6. This book, notwithstanding its russocentrism, is the most authoritative available short guide to the major issues in 'high' Russian literature during Mirsky's youth. For an expert survey in English, see Avril Pyman, *A History of Russian Symbolism* (Cambridge, 1994).

35. The study of this subject was pioneered in Simon Karlinsky, 'Russia's Gay Literature and History (11th–20th Centuries)', *Gay Sunshine* 29–30 (1976), 1–7. See also Jane T. Costlow, Stephanie Sandler, and Judith Vowles (eds.), *Sexuality and the Body in Russian Culture* (Stanford, Calif., 1993), esp. the editors' introduction (1–38); and Rosalind Marsh (ed.), *Gender and Russian Literature: New Perspectives* (Cambridge, 1996), esp. Marsh's introduction (1–37).

36. Veronika Losskaya, *Marina Tsvetaeva v zhizni* (Tenafly, NJ, 1989), 143.

37. Miss Galton means Sonya, the elder sister, with whom she was friendly.

38. Mirsky wrote a very positive review of Praz's classic study of morbid sexuality, *La carne, la morte e il diavolo nella letteratura romantica* (Milan and Rome, 1930; known in English as *The Romantic Agony*), in the *London Mercury* 24 (1931), 190–1, the last of his many contributions to this journal.

39. Dorothy Galton, unpublished letter to G. S. Smith, 25 Jan. 1974.

40. D. S. Mirsky, *Uncollected Writings on Russian Literature*, ed. G. S. Smith (Berkeley, Calif., 1989), 60.

41. Mirsky, *A History of Russian Literature*, 327.

42. This is a literal translation of Mirsky's Russian; this word remained standard for 'homosexual' until recently, and otherwise sophisticated Russians were not concerned about its etymological meaning.

43. Mirsky, *A History of Russian Literature*, 422.

44. See V. V. Rozanov, *Literaturnye izgnanniki*, i (St Petersburg, 1913), 324–6.

45. 'O sovremennom sostoyanii russkoi poezii', reprinted in Mirsky, *Uncollected Writings*, 111. On 19 Dec. 1912 Sergey Gorodetsky spoke on 'Symbolism and Acmeism' at the 'Stray Dog' cabaret in Petersburg. Gumilyov is reported to have contributed to the ensuing discussion the idea that acmeism 'promotes the masculine tendency in poetry as opposed to the feminine stream that symbolism promoted': see R. D. Timenchik, in N. S. Gumilyov, *Pis'ma o russkoi poezii* (Moscow, 1990), 289. This is a striking anticipation of an opinion later expressed by Mirsky; perhaps it was a commonplace.

46. See Bogomolov and Malmstad, *Mikhail Kuzmin*, 9–125, and esp. 136–8, citing Kuzmin's own account of his taste at this time in his letters to V. V. Ruslov of 15 Nov. and 8–9 Dec. 1907; see also Bogomolov, *Mikhail Kuzmin*, 203–4, 210.

47. For a sophisticated account of the history and theory of Acmeism, see Justin Docherty, *The Acmeist Movement in Russian Poetry: Culture and the Word* (Oxford, 1995).

48. 'Some of those [revolutionaries] who derived from the militant group of *The Will of the People* set about the organization of a Socialist Revolutionary Party, quite distinct from the Social Democrats and more in consonance with the earlier traditions of the opposition to the government. The S. R's, as they were called to distinguish them from the S. D's, concentrated their attention not on the workmen but on the peasantry, from contact with whom they derived as much as they gave, including a strong impress of Russian, as distinct from international, patriotism': Bernard Pares, *A History of Russia* (London, 1926), 404.

49. 'In 1905, like the other symbolists, [Vyacheslav Ivanov] did homage to the Revolution, and, in common with the young poet and Revolutionary George Chulkóv, he became the prophet of a new Revolutionary philosophy, which received the name of mystical anarchism. It preached the "non-acceptance of the world" and the revolt against all external conditions, towards a complete freedom of the spirit. This mystical anarchism proved ephemeral . . .': Mirsky, *A History of Russian Literature*, 449.

50. Colonel Pavel Ivanovich Pestel (1793–1826), 'the strongest character and biggest brain among the [Decembrist] conspirators and the head of their Southern Society': Mirsky, *Pushkin* (London, 1926), 48. Pestel was one of the five Decembrists who were hanged.

51. See Bernice Glatzer Rosenthal (ed.), *Nietzsche in Russia* (Princeton, NJ, 1986), and *Nietzsche and Soviet Culture: Ally and Adversary* (Cambridge, 1994). The editor's introduction to the latter (pp. 1–32) is an especially valuable guide to the subject.

52. On the reception of Bergson in Russia, see Elaine Rusinko, 'Acmeism, Post-symbolism, and Henri Bergson', *Slavic Review* 41 (1982), 495–510. The proto-Marxist Mirsky once made a pointed aside: 'the attraction [Jane Ellen Harrison] felt for Bergsonism, a philosophy that seems so unacceptable to us to-day but which was so natural and so useful in dissolving the moral smugness of nineteenth-century capitalism and transferring it into the Waste Land of the capitalism of today': D. S. Mirsky, *Jane Ellen Harrison and Russia* (Cambridge, 1930), 17.

53. Mirsky, 'The Story of a Liberation', *Uncollected Writings on Russian Literature*, 362.

54. On this movement, see Nicholas Zernov, *The Russian Religious Renaissance of the Twentieth Century* (Oxford, 1963); on Bulgakov, see Judith Deutsch Kornblatt and Richard F. Gustafson (eds.), *Russian Religious Thought* (Madison, Wis., 1996), and Catherine Evtuhov, *The Cross and the Sickle: Sergei Bulgakov and the Fate of Russian Religious Philosophy* (Ithaca, NY, 1997).

55. Nikolai Berdyaev, 'Russkaya religioznaya mysl' i revolyutsiya', *Versty* 3 (1928), 40.

56. See in particular Mirsky, *A History of Russian Literature*, 418–24.

57. 'The Exodus to the East', *Russian Life* 1 (1922), 211.

58. Cited by Perkhin, 'Odinnadtsat' pisem (1920–1937)', 259.

59. Leonid Tchertkov, 'L'Œuvre de jeunesse', in Nina Lavroukine and Leonid Tchertkov,

D. A. Mirsky: profil critique et bibliographique (Paris, 1980), 12, citing Mirsky's university dossier from Gosudarstvennyi Istoricheskii Arkhiv Leningradskoi oblasti, *fond* 14, *opis'* 3, *edinitsa khraneniya* 52715.

60. S. A. Vengerov (ed.), *Pushkinist: Istoriko-literaturnyi sbornik*, i (St Petersburg, 1914), 238. The seminar list for 1908 also includes Sergey Auslender and Vasily Gippius.

61. Prince D. S. Mirsky, *Pushkin* (London and New York, 1926), 231. A little earlier, Mirsky had been even more categorical about this edition: 'a monster . . . everything can be found there except understanding of Pushkin' ('Five Russian Letters', repr. in *Uncollected Writings on Russian Literature*, 49).

62. For a general study of the Russian army in Mirsky's time, see Bruce W. Menning, *Bayonets before Bullets: The Imperial Russian Army, 1861–1914* (Bloomington, Ind., 1992).

63. Hélène Izvolsky, *No Time to Grieve* (Philadelphia, 1985), 80. The strong implication here is that Mirsky was one of Izvolsky's dancing partners, which should be seen in the light of something that Vera Traill told me about Mirsky: he was tone-deaf, in fact 'the most unmusical person I've met in my life'. Vera went on to say that Mirsky was badly coordinated physically; he lurched rather than walked, and tended to swing his left and right arm and leg together rather than in balancing opposition to each other. Since his father was the chief of gendarmes, she said, he was excused marching when he was in the army, which was all to the good, because he was incapable of marching in step.

64. For example, Orlando Figes speaks of 'the usual complement of dim and hedonistic Guards officers' accompanying Nicholas II on his travels in 1890: *A People's Tragedy: The Russian Revolution 1891–1924* (London, 1996), 18.

65. L. N. Tolstoy, *Polnoe sobranie sochinenii*, xxxii (Moscow and Leningrad, 1933), 49. Boris Pasternak identified Mirsky with Nekhlyudov, the hero of this novel; see below, Chapter 8, n. 79. Perhaps having in mind passages of this kind, Mirsky noted that *Resurrection* 'has often been used to prove that Tolstoy's genius declined after he became a preacher': *A History of Russian Literature*, 306.

66. See Peter Kenez, 'A Profile of the Prerevolutionary Officer Corps', *California Slavic Studies* 7 (1973), 121–58.

67. Mirsky, *A History of Russian Literature*, 388. This book made a great impression on Mirsky; on 17 Oct. 1929 he wrote to Suvchinsky that he was rereading it, 'and I'm amazed how well I know this book, almost by heart, i.e. I remember each episode as if it were alive, the only thing I can't remember is their sequence'.

68. Perkhin, 'Odinnadtsat' pisem', 257, citing Mirsky's unpublished university record (see n. 59 above).

69. Mikhail Ivanovich Rostovtsev (Rostovtzeff, 1870–1952) taught Latin at St Petersburg University, beginning in 1904; after emigrating he was in London for two years. He was awarded an honorary D.Litt. by the University of Oxford in Feb. 1918. In 1920 he moved to the University of Wisconsin, and he was appointed Sterling Professor of Ancient History and Archeology at Yale in 1925. See M. A. Wes, *Michael Rostovtzeff: Historian in Exile* (Stuttgart, 1990).

70. Harold Williams provided a superbly observed portrait of St Petersburg society at this time: 'In the Chief City', in *Russia of the Russians*, 389–424.

71. The most lucid account of these issues known to me is M. L. Gasparov, 'Antinomichnost' poetiki russkogo modernizma' (1992), repr. in his *Izbrannye trudy* (3 vols., Moscow, 1997), ii: *O stikhakh*, 434–55. The thrust of Gasparov's argument concerns the simultaneity of the Russian reception of French Parnassianism and Symbolism, yet another manifestation of the 'speeded up' development of Russian literature that often elided what were in Western Europe successive and antagonistic movements.

72. Reprinted in D. S. Mirsky, *Stikhotvoreniya: Stat'i o russkoi poezii*, compiled and ed. G. K. Perkins and G. S. Smith (Berkeley, Calif., 1997), 17–78.

73. See Denis Mickiewicz, '*Apollo* and Modernist Poetics', *Russian Literature Triquarterly* 1 (1971), 226–61.

74. Repr. in N. S. Gumilyov, *Pis'ma o russkoi poezii* (Moscow, 1990), 116–17. R. D. Timenchik's

superb notes to this edition offer a good deal of touching information about Gumilyov's pitiful victims; many of them became real victims in the ensuing decade, as did Gumilyov himself.

75. See 'Poet o kritike', in Marina Tsvetaeva, *Sobranie sochinenii v semi tomakh* (Moscow, 1997), vol. v, pt. 1, p. 274.

76. Mirsky, *Stikhotvoreniya: Stat'i o russkoi poezii*, 64.

77. Ibid. 73.

78. On the role of Tsarskoe in Russian literature, see Erikh Gollerbakh, *Gorod muz: Tsarskoe selo v poezii* (Leningrad, 1927), and Lev Loseff and Barry Scherr (eds.), *A Sense of Place: Tsarskoe selo and Its Poets* (Columbus, Ohio, 1993).

79. Mirsky, *A History of Russian Literature*, 448.

80. Prince Ivan I of Moscow (ruled 1325–40), nicknamed 'Moneybag' (*Kalita*), collaborated with the Tartars and was rewarded with the seal of pre-eminent office; the Moscow principality retained this status until 1703, when St Petersburg became the capital of the Russian state.

81. The answer is Honolulu, on Oahu. Captain Cook named the islands after his patron in 1778; the name was changed to Hawaii when the USA annexed them in 1898. Mirsky's anachronism was probably deliberate.

82. S. K. Makovsky, *Na parnase serebryanogo veka* (Munich, 1961), 225–50.

83. 'Recent Developments in Poetry: Poetry and Politics', repr. in Mirsky, *Uncollected Writings on Russian Literature*, 62.

84. Kn. D. Svyatopolk-Mirsky, 'Pamyati gr. V. A. Komarovskogo', *Zveno*, 22 Sept. 1924, 2, partly repr. in V. A. Komarovsky, *Proza i stikhi*, ed. Yury Ivask and W. Tjalsma (Munich, 1978), 23–4. This remained the only serious work on Komarovsky until he was 'rediscovered': see V. N. Toporov, 'Dve glavy iz istorii russkoi poezii nachala veka: I. V. A. Komarovsky. II. V. K. Shileiko (K sootnosheniyu poetiki simvolizma i akmeizma)', *Russian Literature* 7 (1979), 249–326. Tomas Venclova has published the only study that vies with Mirsky's for subtlety and insight: see Loseff and Scherr, *A Sense of Place*, 261–75.

85. Vladimir Pyast, *Vstrechi* (Moscow, 1929), 139.

86. See G. S. Smith, 'The Poetry and Verse Theory', in John E. Malmstad (ed.), *Andrei Bely, Spirit of Symbolism* (Ithaca and London, 1987), 242–84.

87. On the discussion following this paper, see O. A. Kuznetsova, 'Diskussiya o sostoyanii russkogo simvolizma v "Obshchestve revnitelei khudozhestvennogo slova" (Obsuzhdenie doklada Vyach. Ivanova)', *Russkaya literatura* 1 (1990), 200–7.

88. See esp. A. L. Ospovat and R. D. Timenchik, *'Pechal'nu povest' sokhranit'* . . .' (Moscow, 1987), 172–215.

89. Tchertkov, 'L'Œuvre de jeunesse', 12, is definite about Mirsky's participation in a literary society in Petersburg; so is the author of the first essay on Mirsky published in Russia after his rehabilitation, M. Ya. Polyakov, 'Literaturno-kriticheskaya deyatel'nost' D. Mirskogo', in D. Mirsky, *Literaturno-kriticheskie stat'i* (Moscow, 1978), 5; and so is T. Krasavchenko, *Russkoe zarubezh'e: Zolotaya kniga emigratsii. Pervaya tret' XX veka* (Moscow, 1997), 419; but all three state, wrongly, that the society concerned was the Society for Free Aesthetics (*Obshchestvo svobodnoi estetiki*), which was in fact a Moscow body; see Jane A. Sharp, 'Redrawing the Margins of Russian Vanguard Art', in Costlow et al., *Sexuality and the Body*, 97–123. Vyacheslav Ivanov delivered his (as some people think) epoch-making statement 'The Precepts of Symbolism' in Mar. 1910 first to the Moscow society and then to the Petersburg one; the text was published in *Apollo*, May–June 1910, 5–20. Blok's addendum, 'On the Current Situation of Russian Symbolism', follows it (pp. 21–30).

90. British Library, Add. MS 49,604, 'Letters of Prince D. P. Svyatopolk-Mirsky to Sir B. Pares, 1922–1931', fo. 1.

91. Tchertkov, 'L'Œuvre de jeunesse', 12.

92. Anna Akhmatova, *My Half Century*, ed. Ronald Meyer (Ann Arbor, Mich., 1992), 93. The first-hand discussions of the history of Acmeism collected in this book provide a salutary antidote to those of scholars writing retrospectively.

93. On the activities of the Guild, see Docherty, *The Acmeist Movement in Russian Poetry*, 72–90.
94. D. S. Mirsky, *Russia: A Social History* (London, 1931), 274.

3. TWO ARMIES

1. 'Contemporary Movements in Russian Literature', repr. in D. S. Mirsky, *Uncollected Writings on Russian Literature*, ed. G. S. Smith (Berkeley, Calif., 1989), 258. On the attitudes of the literary intelligentsia to the war, which were much more complex than Mirsky has space to suggest here, see Ben Hellman, *Poets of Hope and Despair: The Russian Symbolists in War and Revolution (1914–1918)* (Helsinki, 1995).
2. In fact, Mirsky's words read uncannily like a maximally conflated synopsis of the greatest literary work about the men of Russia during the First World War, Aleksandr Solzhenitsyn's *Krasnoe koleso* (*The Red Wheel*); see *Sobranie sochinenii* (20 vols., Vermont and Paris, 1978–91), vols. xi–xx (1983–91). This gigantic narrative abounds in characters, events, and opinions that illuminate Mirsky's life and thinking. In particular, the central hero of the work, Colonel Vorotyntsev, who would have been born in about 1875, is made to exemplify the role of younger General Staff officers in the army of 1914.
3. Prince D. S. Mirsky, *A History of Russia* (London, 1928), 73.
4. Hélène Izvolsky reported that Mirsky was one of the few Guards officers who survived the disastrous battle of Tannenberg, but her memory for chronological details is demonstrably imprecise with respect to numerous assertions in her memoirs; see *No Time to Grieve* (Philadelphia, 1985), 66.
5. V. V. Perkhin, 'Odinnadtsat' pisem (1920–1937) i avtobiografiya (1936) D. P. Svyatopolk-Mirskogo', *Russkaya literatura* 1 (1996), 259.
6. *Beatrice Webb's Diaries 1924–1932*, ed. Margaret Cole (London, 1956), 300–1.
7. Perkhin, 'Odinnadtsat' pisem', 257.
8. Leonid Tchertkov, 'L'Œuvre de jeunesse', in Nina Lavroukine and Leonid Tchertkov, *D. S. Mirsky: profil critique et bibliographique* (Paris, 1980), 13. However, one of the documents in Mirsky's rehabilitation file (see Chapter 9 below) says that he was also in Paris at some time in 1916.
9. Edmund Wilson, 'Comrade Prince', *Encounter* 5 (1) (1955), 12. Incidentally, Vladimir Nabokov's father when leader of the KD Party also refused to drink the health of the Tsar: Vladimir Nabokov, *Drugie berega* (New York, 1954), 169.
10. Mirsky, *A History of Russia*, 73. The most active planner of a *coup d'état* was Aleksandr Guchkov, Vera's father; eventually he was one of the two ministers who travelled to the wayside halt of Dno to receive the instrument of abdication from Nicholas.
11. Matitiahu Mayzel, 'The Formation of the Russian General Staff, 1880–1917: A Social Study', *Cahiers du Monde Russe et Soviétique* 16 (1975), 321.
12. D. S. Mirsky, 'The Exodus to the East', *Russian Life* 1 (1922), 210. Mirsky has in mind Voloshin's poem of 23 Nov. 1917, 'Mir' ('S Rossiei koncheno . . .'); see Maksimilian Voloshin, *Stikhotvoreniya i poemy* (St Petersburg, 1995), 219. Voloshin here speaks of the Mongols rather than the Japanese. I have not been able to trace the source of the remark by Merezhkovsky.
13. Mirsky, *A History of Russia*, 75.
14. Prince D. S. Mirsky, 'Through Foreign Eyes: An Address delivered at the Annual Meeting of the Brontë Society', *Brontë Society Publications*, 6 (33) (1923), 148.
15. D. S. Mirsky, 'The Ukraine', *Quarterly Review* 239 (Apr. 1923), 318–35.
16. The novelist and journalist Ilya Erenburg (1891–1967) was the only Russian writer of their generation whose first-hand knowledge of contemporary cultural life outside Russia could rival Mirsky's. Erenburg's foreign world was as much French as Mirsky's was English. Precisely when, where, and how Erenburg and Mirsky knew each other will probably never be satisfactorily elucidated. In answer to my question about their relationship, Vera Traill said

they were good friends. The most complete account of Erenburg's life is Joshua Rubenstein, *Tangled Loyalties: The Life and Times of Ilya Erenburg* (London and New York, 1996); Mirsky does not appear. The exact time Erenburg was in Kharkov in 1918 is not clear from Rubenstein's account of this period, which was indeed one of 'tangled loyalties' (pp. 50–61).

17. See D. S. Mirsky, 'Recent Developments in Poetry: Poetry and Politics', repr. in *Uncollected Writings on Russian Literature*, 66, and also Ronald Vroon, '*Puti tvorchestva*: The Journal as a Metapoetic Statement', in Kenneth N. Brostrom (ed.), *Russian Literature and American Critics* (Ann Arbor, Mich., 1986), 219–39.

18. *Uncollected Writings on Russian Literature*, 84; the book was eventually published in Sofia in 1920, which Mirsky learned about only after making his first reference to it in 1921.

19. Ibid. 50. The book has never been published in full. The author is that same Beletsky who came to visit Kuzmin's cousin Sergey Auslender in St Petersburg when Mirsky was a university student.

20. Mirsky, 'The Ukraine', 331–2. Khristian Georgievich Rakovsky (1873–1941), a Bulgarian by birth, was Lenin's representative in the south-west and then chairman of the provisional revolutionary government of the Ukraine. He became Soviet ambassador in London in 1923 and moved to Paris in 1925. A friend of Trotsky, he was expelled from the Party in 1927 and arrested in 1934.

21. V. V. Perkhin, 'K istorii aresta i reabilitatsii D. P. Svyatopolk-Mirskogo (po arkhivnym materialam)', *Russkaya literatura* 1 (1997), 223–4.

22. For a masterly overview of the events of the Civil War, see Orlando Figes, *A People's Tragedy: The Russian Revolution 1891–1924* (London, 1996), esp. 589–720.

23. A good idea of the complexity of the situation concerning the Cossacks in the Civil War may be gained from Peter Holquist, ' "Conduct Merciless Mass Terror": Decossackization on the Don, 1919', *Cahiers du Monde Russe* 38 (1 and 2) (1997), 127–62.

24. 'Literature and Politics, 1917–1925', repr. in Mirsky, *Uncollected Writings on Russian Literature*, 195.

25. Prince D. S. Mirski, 'Russia in Literature', *Literary Review* [of *The New York Times*], 2 Sept. 1922, 921.

26. D. S. Mirsky, 'Mikhail Sholokhov', *Literaturnaya Gazeta* 93 (409), 24 July 1934, 2–3.

27. Prince D. S. Mirsky, 'Babel', *The Nation and the Athenæum*, 23 Jan. 1926, 581–2.

28. 'The Literature of the Emigration', repr. in Mirsky, *Uncollected Writings on Russian Literature*, 85. This passage contains the most comic lapse of all in Mirsky's published English, an attempt at an equivalent of Russian *obezoruzhennyi*, 'disarmed': 'a piercingly tragic, and at the same time gloriously humorous narrative of the retreat of the almost armless defendants to the Roumanian frontier' (ibid.).

29. Cited in Ariadna Tyrkova-Williams, *Cheerful Giver* (London, 1935), 231.

30. Bernard Pares was in close touch with Kolchak at this time; see *My Russian Memoirs* (London, 1931), 524–46.

31. Tyrkova-Williams, *Cheerful Giver*, 235.

32. C. E. Bechhofer, *In Denikin's Russia* (London, 1921), 96.

33. *Farewell to the Don: The Journal of Brigadier H. N. H. Williamson*, ed. John Harris (London, 1970), 33.

34. Bechhofer, *In Denikin's Russia*, 97. What 'disease' meant, and in particular the disease that Mirsky contracted, is spelled out by Brig. Williamson: 'Whilst typhus normally resulted from bites from lice on dirty bodies, it more or less died out by the spring but there were still many cases of it which were usually fatal and frequently resulted in homicidal mania and sometimes caused nurses to be killed by patients' (*Farewell to the Don*, 104).

35. Mirsky, 'The Ukraine', 333.

36. Williamson, *Farewell to the Don*, 207.

37. Ibid. 207–8.

38. Mirsky's rehabilitation file says that he crossed into Poland in Mar. 1920, and that he was then in Greece up to and including Mar. 1921; see Chapter 9 below.

39. See Chapter 7 below for some suggestions about who these two exceptions might have been.

40. Cited in Nina Lavroukine, 'Maurice Baring and D. S. Mirsky: A Literary Relationship', *Slavonic and East European Review* 62 (1) (1984), 27.
41. D. S. Mirsky, *Lenin* (London, 1931), 145.
42. 'Recent Books on Russia', *The Listener* 2 (18 Dec. 1929), 825.
43. Gumilyov fought with distinction as a cavalryman, and was on active service from Aug. 1914 to Mar. 1916 (he was a *vol'noopredelyayushchiisya*, as Mirsky had been when he first went into the army in 1911). He became an NCO, but in Oct. 1916 he failed the examination for promotion to commissioned rank because of his incompetence in foreign languages. See I. A. Kurlyandsky, 'Poet i voin', in *Nikolai Gumilev: Issledovaniya i materialy: Bibliografiya* (St Petersburg, 1994), 254–98.
44. Vladimir Pyast, *Vstrechi* (Moscow, 1929), 145.
45. 'S mirom derzhavnym ya byl lish' rebyacheski svyazan': see O. Mandel'shtam, *Stikhotvoreniya* (Leningrad, 1974), 151.
46. Olga's husband came to the throne in 1863 and was assassinated in 1913.
47. Mirsky, 'Through Foreign Eyes', 148.
48. Maurice Baring, *Landmarks in Russian Literature* (London, 1910); the book was translated into Russian as *Vekhi russkoi literatury* (Moscow, 1913).
49. 'Five Russian Letters: I. Introductory', repr. in Mirsky, *Uncollected Writings on Russian Literature*, 46–7.
50. Lavroukine, 'Maurice Baring', 29.
51. Prince D. S. Mirsky, *Pushkin* (London and New York, 1926), 168–9.
52. 'The Story of a Liberation', cited here from the translation in *Uncollected Writings on Russian Literature*, 358.

4. WRITING ENGLISH

1. See Dorothy Brewster, *East–West Passage: A Study in Literary Relationships* (London, 1954); the relevant parts of Brewster have been superseded by W. Gareth Jones (ed.), *Tolstoi and Britain* (Oxford and Washington, DC, 1995), Patrick Waddington (ed.), *Ivan Turgenev and Britain* (Oxford and Washington, DC, 1995), and W. J. Leatherbarrow (ed.), *Dostoevskii and Britain* (Oxford and Providence, RI, 1995).
2. Nabokov's only serious rival in this respect was Elsa Triolet, whose second language was French; see Elizabeth Klosty Beaujour, *Alien Tongues: Bilingual Russian Writers of the 'First' Emigration* (Ithaca, NY, and London, 1989). On Triolet and Mirsky, see Chapter 7 below. Usually considered to stand outside serious literature, though, is Ayn Rand (1905–82), who was born and brought up in St Petersburg and emigrated in 1924; her novels, written in English, have been more successful commercially than Nabokov's.
3. Arkhiepiskop Ioann Shakhovskoy, *Biografiya yunosti: Ustanovlenie edinstva* (Paris, 1977), 201–3.
4. For a statistical analysis of Mirsky's publications by language and date, see G. S. Smith, 'D. S. Mirsky, Literary Critic and Historian', in D. S. Mirsky, *Uncollected Writings on Russian Literature*, ed. G. S. Smith (Berkeley, Calif., 1989), 29–35.
5. For a general introduction to the post-1917 Russian emigration, see Marc Raeff, *Russia Abroad: A Cultural History of the Russian Emigration, 1919–1939* (New York and Oxford, 1990); notwithstanding its amerocentricism, W. Chapin Huntingdon's *The Homesick Million: Russia-out-of-Russia* (Boston, 1933) retains considerable value. Sir John Hope Simpson, *The Refugee Problem: Report of a Survey* (London, etc., 1939) includes a chapter on the Russian emigration (pp. 62–116), and a passage on Russian refugees in England (pp. 339–40). The first instalment of the invaluable 'Chronicle' that Bernard Pares published throughout the 1920s gives 2 million as the number of Russian currently living abroad: *Slavonic Review* 1 (2) (1922), 235.
6. It is customary to refer to the post-revolutionary Russian *émigrés* as 'the First Wave', to

those who emigrated after the Second World War as 'the Second Wave', and to those who emigrated in the 1970s and 1980s as 'the Third Wave'. For some carefully assembled statistics and a useful chronology, see John Glad, *Conversations in Exile* (Durham, NC, and London, 1993); the Russian version of this book, *Besedy v izgnanii* (Moscow, 1991), contains additional material.

7. See Aleksandr Usakov, 'Gallipoli: Die weiße Armee in den Lagern', in Karl Schlögel (ed.), *Der große Exodus: Die russische Emigration und ihre Zentren 1917 bis 1941* (Munich, 1994), 21–42, and Nur Bilge Criss, 'Istanbul: Die russischen Flüchtlinge am Bosporus', ibid. 42–63.

8. Aleksandr Yakovlevich Galpern (A. J. Halpern, 1879–1956) was a legal adviser to the British Embassy in pre-revolutionary Petersburg; Maurice Baring acknowledges his assistance with the relevant chapter of *The Mainsprings of Russia* (London, 1914). He emigrated to England, where his legal career flourished. Halpern and his wife, Salomeya, were close friends of Mirsky during the 1920s; on her, see Chapter 5 below.

9. Kropotkin was originally a professional geographer; the writings by him and his peers in the great age of Russian geography during the last 35 years before 1914 were among Mirsky's favourite reading, and provided him with a rich source of metaphor.

10. See D. S. Mirsky, *A History of Russian Literature from the Earliest Times to the Death of Dostoevsky (1881)* (London and New York, 1927), 371.

11. D. S. Mirsky, *Jane Ellen Harrison and Russia* (Cambridge, 1930), 7.

12. John Carswell, *The Exile: A Life of Ivy Litvinov* (London, 1983), 61.

13. See Monica Partridge, 'Russians, Russian Literature, and the London Library', in *Rossiya, zapad, vostok: Vstrechnye techeniya: K 100-letiyu so dnya rozhdeniya akademika M. P. Alekseeva* (St Petersburg, 1997), 340–51.

14. 'I even heard an intelligent Englishwoman married to a commissar make fun of him as "Comrade Prince"': Edmund Wilson, 'Comrade Prince', *Encounter* 5 (1) (1955), 16.

15. See Andrew Boyle, *The Climate of Treason* (rev. edn, London, 1980).

16. On Zamyatin in England, see Ol'ga Kaznina, *Russkie v Anglii* (Moscow, 1997), 199–226.

17. See Richard Garnett, *Constance Garnett: A Heroic Life* (London, 1991); for a critical assessment of Garnett's translations, see Rachel May, *The Translation in the Text: Reading Russian Literature in English* (Evanston, Ill., 1994). For an astute Russian critique of one work, *The Brothers Karamazov*, see A. N. Nikoliukin, 'Dostoevskii in Constance Garnett's Translation', in Leatherbarrow, *Dostoevskii and Britain*, 207–27. On Garnett's Russian contacts in England, see Barry Hollingsworth, 'The Society of Friends of Russian Freedom: English Liberals and Russian Socialists, 1890–1917', *Oxford Slavonic Papers* n.s. 3 (1970), 45–64.

18. On the Russian emigration in England, see Ol'ga Kaznina, *Russkie v Anglii* (Moscow, 1997); this book contains a section devoted to Mirsky (pp. 119–55). The most substantial single book on the history of the Russian emigration lacks a chapter on England: Schlögel, *Der große Exodus* (Munich, 1994). The 'centres' concerned are Sofia, Belgrade, Riga, Tallinn, Helsinki, Warsaw, Prague, Berlin, Paris ('Die Hauptstadt der russischen Diaspora'), Rome, Harbin, Shanghai, and New York.

19. The data are summarized and tabulated in Raeff, *Russia Abroad*, 203; see also Huntingdon, *The Homesick Million*, 19.

20. See E. B. Kudryakova, *Rossiiskaya emigratsiya v Velikobritanii v period mezhdu dvumya voinami* (Moscow, 1995).

21. See Gleb Struve, *Russkaya literatura v izgnanii* (2nd edn, New York, 1984), 24–9; Robert C. Williams, *Culture in Exile: Russian Emigrés in Germany, 1881–1941* (Ithaca, NY, and London, 1972).

22. See Robert H. Johnston, *New Mecca, New Babylon: Paris and the Russian Exiles, 1920–1945* (Kingston and Montreal, 1988).

23. On Williams, see Ariadna Tyrkova-Williams, *Cheerful Giver* (London, 1935); Irene Zohrab, 'From New Zealand to Russia, to England: A Comment on Harold W. Williams and His Relations with English Writers', *New Zealand Slavonic Journal* (1985), 3–15; and ead., 'The

Place of the Liberals among the Forces of the Revolution: From the Unpublished Papers of Harold W. Williams', ibid. (1986), 53–82.

24. On Williams, and also Bernard Pares, in the context of anglophone Tolstoyism, see R. F. Christian, 'The Road to Yasnaya Polyana: Some Pilgrims from Britain and Their Reminiscences', in Jones, *Tolstoi and Britain*, 185–216.

25. The counterpart of Williams in England was Isaak Vladimirovich Shklovsky (1865–1935), who published under the pseudonym 'Dioneo'. He came to England as a political exile in 1896; from then until 1917 he was the English correspondent of several leading Russian newspapers (see Kaznina, *Russkie v Anglii*, 89–91). For a fleeting reference to a meeting between Shklovsky and Mirsky on 6 Dec. 1921, see ibid. 123.

26. Tyrkova-Williams, *Cheerful Giver*, 72.

27. Florinsky is not to be confused, if humanly possible, with three eminent older contemporaries: the theologian and priest Georgy Florovsky (1893–1979); his less famous elder brother, the historian Anton Florovsky (1884–1968); and finally another theologian and priest, Pavel Florensky (1882–1943).

28. Vinogradoff (1854–1925), an eminent professor of medieval history at Moscow University, was invited to England by like-minded liberals when he ran into trouble with the authorities; in 1903 he was appointed Professor of Jurisprudence at Oxford University. There was no serious question of his going back to Russia after 1917. His son's words about the family of Mirsky's mother were cited in Chapter 1.

29. The ABC tea-rooms were a modestly priced but respectable London chain. Count Michael Karolyi frequented them at about this same time; he reports that a fish-and-chip dinner could be had for one shilling and sixpence, and that a meal costing half a crown (two shillings and sixpence, one-eighth of a pound) was an extravagance: *The Memoirs of Michael Karolyi: Faith without Illusion* (London, 1956), 197. Dorothy Galton worked as Karolyi's secretary before she joined the School of Slavonic Studies. For Karolyi's account of a dinner in Paris in the late 1920s attended by Mirsky and also Aleksandr Kerensky, see ibid. 222; here, Karolyi says of Mirsky: 'A refugee from the Soviets, he nourished a deep, Dostoievskian dislike of the West, where he was obliged to dwell.'

30. Patrick Howarth, *Squire: 'Most Generous of Men'* (London, 1963); for Mirsky's first meeting with Squire, see p. 138.

31. *The Letters of Dorothy L. Sayers. 1899 to 1938: The Making of a Detective Novelist*, ed. Barbara Reynolds (London, 1995), 173. Sayers was involved at this time with the prolific novelist, essayist, and translator John Cournos (1881–1966), who was taken from Russia to America by his parents in 1891. From 1912 to 1930 he lived mainly in England, and wrote several successful novels about his experiences as an immigrant to the USA. Cournos spent part of 1917 in Petrograd as a member of the Anglo-Russian Commission, and later worked for the Foreign Office and Ministry of Information. In Petrograd he got to know Korney Chukovsky, Aleksey Remizov, and Fyodor Sologub, whom he was later to translate, along with several other modernists. Some aspects of his relationship with Mirsky are mentioned in passing in the letters to Suvchinsky, but Cournos's *Autobiography* (New York, 1935; repr. New York, 1978) does not mention Mirsky. However, in the preface to his notoriously inadequate translation of Andrey Bely's *Petersburg* he writes, speaking of himself in the third person: 'Secondly, and foremost, he is obligated to his friend, Prince Dmitry Svyatopolk Mirsky ("Damn my title!" he once wrote the translator), for pointing out to him the essential beauties of Biely's novel during a weekend with me at Oxford. This is but a slight token to his memory. He was a great man and a lovable one, and a good friend. He is the author of the best history of Russian literature in any language, a work written in English': 'Introduction', in Andrei Biely, *St Petersburg* (New York, 1959), p. xviii.

32. D. S. Mirsky, *The Intelligentsia of Great Britain*, trans. Alec Brown (London, 1935), 126–7.

33. Emma Letley, *Maurice Baring: A Citizen of Europe* (London, 1991), 195.

34. On Vogel, see Richard Davies and G. S. Smith, 'D. S. Mirsky: Twenty-Two Letters (1926–34) to Salomeya Halpern; Seven Letters (1930) to Vera Suvchinskaya (Traill)', *Oxford Slavonic Papers* n.s. 30 (1997), 110.

35. Bernard Pares, *A Wandering Student* (Syracuse, NY, 1947), 292.
36. On Meyendorff, see the obituary by Helen Rapp, *Slavonic and East European Review* 42 (99) (1963–4), 440–2. He published a richly annotated book which has unfortunately been completely forgotten: *The Background of the Russian Revolution* (London, 1929).
37. The references are preserved in British Library Add. MS 49,604, 'Letters of Prince D. P. Svyatopolk-Mirsky to Sir B. Pares, 1922–1931'.
38. Dorothy Galton, 'Sir Bernard Pares and Slavonic Studies in London University, 1919–39', *Slavonic and East European Review* 46 (107) (1968), 482.
39. Mirsky apparently borrowed this word from the title of a book by Andrey Bely, written in 1917 and published in Berlin in 1922; it means 'speech that has sound but no sense', or perhaps 'speaking in tongues'.
40. Prince D. S. Mirsky, 'Through Foreign Eyes', *Brontë Society Publications* 6 (33) (1923), 152.
41. See Dorothy Galton, 'The Anglo-Russian Literary Society', *Slavonic and East European Review* 48 (111) (1970), 272–83.
42. See the report in *Slavonic Review* 1 (3) (1923), 703.
43. Ibid. 704.
44. An abstract of this lecture is given ibid. 3 (7) (1924), 240.
45. Ibid. 6 (16) (1927–8), 213. On Miss Webb, see G. S. Smith, 'Jane Ellen Harrison: Forty-Seven Letters to D. S. Mirsky 1924–1926', *Oxford Slavonic Papers* n.s. 28 (1995), 80.
46. Published as 'Contemporary Movements in Russian Literature'; repr. in Mirsky, *Uncollected Writings on Russian Literature*, 258–82.
47. On Harrison's life, see Jessie Stewart, *Jane Ellen Harrison: A Portrait from Letters* (London, 1959); Sandra J. Peacock, *Jane Ellen Harrison: The Mask and the Self* (New Haven, Conn., and London, 1988); for Harrison's contribution to scholarly anthropology, see Robert Ackermann, *The Myth and Ritual School: J. G. Frazer and the Cambridge Ritualists* (London, 1991), esp. 67–127.
48. The novelist Helen Hope Mirrlees (1887–1978) read classics with Harrison at Newnham, and later published several novels, of which Mirsky especially valued *Lud-in-the-Mist*. She received a diploma in Russian from the École des Langues Orientales in 1919. On her, see Peacock, *Jane Ellen Harrison*, esp. 109–15.
49. Mirsky, *Jane Ellen Harrison and Russia*, 6.
50. Ibid. 3–4.
51. Cited in Stewart, *Jane Ellen Harrison*, 155.
52. Cited in Mirsky, *Jane Ellen Harrison and Russia*, 16.
53. 'Preface', in *The Life of the Archpriest Avvakum by Himself. Translated from the Seventeenth Century Russian by Jane Harrison and Hope Mirrlees, with a Preface by Prince D. S. Mirsky* (London, 1924), 7–30. Through his maternal grandmother's family Mirsky claimed descent from the Old Believers Princess Feodosiya Prokopievna Morozova and her sister Evdokiya Prokopievna Urusova, who famously gave succour to Avvakum in 1664, and were exiled to the monastery at Pechersk. In *A History of Russian Literature from the Earliest Times to the Death of Dostoevsky*, Mirsky included a translation of the beginning of the passage from Avvakum's epistle referring to his ancestors (p. 41), but did not mention his kinship.
54. Postcard of 29 Aug. 1924, cited in Smith, 'Jane Ellen Harrison: Forty-Seven Letters', 63.
55. On the Bloomsbury of Mirsky's time, see Hermione Lee, *Virginia Woolf* (London, 1996).
56. 'A Dialogue on Mount Pentelicus', first published in *The Times Literary Supplement*, 11–17 Sept. 1987, 989.
57. 'The first time I met Mirsky was in Paris, in Jane Harrison's flat. . . . She liked Mirsky and enjoyed talking to him, and he, I felt, sat at her feet': Leonard Woolf, *An Autobiography* (2 vols., Oxford, etc., 1980), ii: *1911–1969*, 204.
58. 'Kot' (1882–1954) came to London in 1911 as a political refugee, and worked in an office in High Holborn that provided translations and certifications of Russian legal documents. He got to know John Middleton Murry, became a friend of D. H. Lawrence in 1914, fell hopelessly and unrequitedly in love with Katherine Mansfield, and eventually made contact with the Woolfs. Koteliansky was the leading figure among a group of less

mightily industrious translators who took over the now significantly less mighty prose heritage of Russian literature where Constance Garnett and Aylmer Maude left off. On his literary relationships in England, see John Carswell, *Lives and Letters: A. R. Orage, Katherine Mansfield, Beatrice Hastings, John Middleton Murry, S. S. Koteliansky, 1906–1957* (London and Boston, 1978).

59. Esther Salaman, 'Prince Mirsky', *Encounter* 54 (1) (1980), 94.
60. On the contents of this book, see Smith, 'Jane Ellen Harrison: Forty-Seven Letters', 74–9.
61. See Wendy Rosslyn, 'Boris Anrep and the Poetry of Anna Akhmatova', *Modern Language Review* 74 (1979), 884–96
62. See G. S. Smith, *The Letters of D. S. Mirsky to P. P. Suvchinskii* (Birmingham, 1995), 224.
63. On Mirsky's contacts with Forster and Eliot, see Chapter 5 below.
64. There is still no systematic study of the relationships between Russian *émigré* writers and the literatures of the non-Russian countries, particularly with regard to translation out of and into Russian. The only real exception concerns Nabokov: see Brian Boyd, *Nabokov: The Russian Years* (Princeton, NJ, 1991).
65. See *Paul Desjardins et les décades de Pontigny: études, témoignages et documents inédits, présentés par Anne Heurgon-Desjardins, Préface d'André Maurois* (Paris, 1964).
66. The historian of science and philosophy Koyré (1892–1964) was born in Taganrog; he studied with Husserl at Göttingen, and then with Bergson in Paris. He achieved greater eminence as an academic in France than any other Russian *émigré*, eventually becoming Director of Studies at the École des Hautes Études and editor of *Recherches Philosophiques*.
67. Shakhovskoy, *Biografiya yunosti*, 201.
68. The text of the dialogue, drawn from Fry's archive, was first published in Denys Sutton's preface to *The Letters of Roger Fry* (2 vols., London, 1972), i. 74–80. Fry's impressions of what went on at Pontigny are recorded in a letter to Helen Anrep of 29 Aug. 1925: ibid. ii. 577–9.
69. There is perhaps a more private element than usual in Mirsky's inclusion in his Russian anthology of the poem 'Winter Train (Sudden Snow)' by Innokenty Annensky, a proponent of stoic resignation before the nightmare of human life; its final couplet represents this attitude with a truly horrendous metaphor: 'And steadfastly the rotten tooth must / Chew through the cold stone.'
70. Woolf, *Autobiography*, ii. 202. Woolf adds a footnote to the phrase 'shark or crocodile' about one occasion when he was travelling on the south coast of Ceylon and the train passed a platform on which lay dozens of dead sharks: 'On each dead face there was this sinister grin. Talking to Mirsky in a London sitting-room, as he suddenly turned his head to say something and there was a glint of teeth and smile, I was back in Ceylon twelve years ago in the railway carriage looking at the rows of dead, smiling sharks.'
71. Galton, 'Sir Bernard Pares', 487.
72. Maurice Baring, *The Mainsprings of Russia* (London, 1914), 245.
73. Mirsky was used as a reviewer for *The Listener*: see 'Three Views of Russia', *Listener*, 11 Mar. 1931, 418; 'An Uncompromising Utopian' (a review of R. Fülöp-Miller's *New Light on Tolstoy*), ibid., 8 July 1931, 54; and 'Reporting on the New Russia', ibid., 9 Dec. 1931, 1009. On the first of these items, which aroused the indignation of Bernard Pares, see Chapter 6 below.
74. Galton, 'Sir Bernard Pares', 483.
75. See David Bethea, *The Shape of Apocalypse in Russian Literature* (Princeton, NJ, 1989).
76. 'O sovremennoi angliiskoi literature (Pis'mo iz Londona)', *Sovremennyi zapad* 2 (1923), 148. The simplified form of Mirsky's name appears here for the first time in a Russian publication.
77. Mirsky, *Jane Ellen Harrison and Russia*, 5.
78. See British Library, Add. MS 49,604, 'Letters of Prince D. P. Svyatopolk-Mirsky to Sir B. Pares, 1922–1931'.
79. See Mirsky's letter to Shakhovskoy of 23 Nov.: Shakhovskoy, *Biografiya yunosti*, 203.
80. Mirsky, 'Pushkin', repr. in *Uncollected Writings on Russian Literature*, 119.

81. Two years before writing this part of the history, Mirsky published what was at the time the most substantial treatment of the history of Old Russian literature in English: 'Old Russian Literature: Its Place in the History of Civilisation', *Slavonic Review* 3 (7) (1924), 74–91. This essay would have formed an ideal introductory chapter to the first volume of his *History*, in which discussion of the older period is severely curtailed, and was perhaps originally written for inclusion in that book.

82. D. S. Mirsky, 'Russian Literature since 1917', *Contemporary Review*, Aug. 1922, 205.

83. Mirsky, *Jane Ellen Harrison and Russia*, 11. Mirsky delivered a broadside against this concept in 1924: '[Aksakov] seems to come as an antidote to the current opinions on the "message of Russia," to all the loose talk and looser ideas on the imaginary thing our friends over the Channel call *l'âme Slave*. After the effeminate graces of Turgenev, the destructive logic of the Tolstoite Tolstoy, the sublimely grotesque vistas of Dostoyevsky, the relaxing and melancholy sweetness of Chekhov, the rude brutality of Gorky, Aksakov comes as a relief and a breath of fresh air. Pending the time when English readers will find themselves prepared to taste of Russia's ripest and choicest fruit—the poetry of Pushkin—Aksakov, together with that more familiar (and, after all, greater) book *War and Peace*, may stand as an eloquent reminder, that Russia is not the exact synonym of either morbidity, or insanity, or barbarism.' Prince Mirsky, 'Introduction', in Aksakov, *Chronicles of a Russian Family* (London and New York, 1924), 5.

84. Mirsky supervised the early stages of the first serious study of this phenomenon, the Ph.D. thesis of Helen Muchnic, eventually published as *Dostoevsky's English Reputation, 1881–1936* (Northampton, Mass., 1939).

85. Rosa Newmarch, *Poetry and Progress in Russia* (London and New York, 1907).

86. Mme N. Jarintzoff, *Russian Poets and Poems* (Oxford, 1917). This book has a sensible preface by Neville Forbes, who rather holds his nose about the contents of it.

87. 'Introduction: Russian Fiction since Chekhov', in Boris Pilniak, *Tales of the Wilderness* (London, 1924), p. vii.

88. Mirsky, *Contemporary Russian Literature*, p. viii.

89. 'The Revival of Russian Fiction', *The Nation & the Athenæum*, 14 Mar. 1925, 811.

90. Ibid.

91. Mirsky, *A History of Russian Literature* (1949), 490–1.

92. Ibid. 211.

93. Isaiah Berlin, 'A View of Russian Literature' (a review of Marc Slonim, *The Epic of Russian Literature*), *Partisan Review* 17 (6) (July–Aug. 1950), 617–23. The lordly lack of specific examples makes this peroration tantalizingly vague: '[Mirsky's] judgements were recklessly personal, and his facts and dates sometimes inaccurate. He lavished magnificent encomia upon authors, who, for reasons not always clear, delighted or excited him, and launched violent personal attacks on writers both great and small, men of genius and forgotten hacks, who happened to bore or annoy him. . . . He was not a systematic critic, and there are large and capricious omissions in his work; but his confidence in his own literary insight was unbounded and, armed with it, he succeeded in rescuing various authors from undeserved oblivion, and in introducing figures hitherto little known outside Russia in a manner which arrested the attention of Western readers to their great and abiding profit' (pp. 617–18).

94. The major missing segments were reprinted in Mirsky, *Uncollected Writings on Russian Literature*, 156–202.

95. D. S. Mirsky, *A History of Russian Literature from Its Beginnings to 1900* (New York, 1958).

96. Unpublished letter, Harry Ransome Humanities Research Center, University of Texas at Austin.

97. 'Russian Literature', a survey of developments since 1910, in *Encyclopaedia Britannica: The Three New Supplementary Volumes constituting with the Volumes of the Latest Standard Edition the Thirteenth Edition* (London and New York, 1926), iii. 435–9; Mirsky's 'Chekhov' appears in i. 572–3 of the same edition.

98. D.S.M., 'Russian Literature', *Encyclopaedia Britannica*, 14th edn, xix. 751–8. Mirsky also

contributed 'Ukrainian Literature', and individual articles on Dostoyevsky, Gorky, Tolstoy, Turgenev, and others.

99. Prince D. S. Mirsky, 'Russia, 1015–1462', *The Cambridge Medieval History*, vii (Cambridge, 1932), 599–631.

100. 'The Wandering Scholars', *London Mercury* 16 (1927), 409–16.

101. D. S. Mirsky [*sic*], 'Preface', in Alexander Pushkin, *The Queen of Spades. Engravings in Colour by A. Alexeieff, Preface by Prince D. Sviatopolk-Mirsky* [*sic*] (London: Blackamore Press, 1928), 13–14. The translation is by J. E. Pouterman and C. Bruerton. Some passages of Mirsky's essay match exactly the corresponding parts of an untitled essay in French: see *Commerce* 16 (1928), 85–97, which was reprinted in *Pouchkine, 1837–1937. Textes recueillis et annotés par J.-E. Pouterman* (Paris, 1937), 125–34.

102. On Pouterman, see Davies and Smith, 'D. S. Mirsky: Twenty-Two Letters to Salomeya Halpern', 113.

103. *Baku to Baker Street: The Memoirs of Flora Solomon by Herself and Barnet Litvinoff* (London, 1984), 141.

104. *The Diary of a Madman by Nicolas Gogol. Translated by Prince Mirsky, illustrated with acquatints by A. Alexeieff* (London, 1929).

105. 'Introduction', in C. Fillingham Coxwell, *Russian Poems* (London, 1929), pp. xvii–xxii.

106. 'Introduction', in *A Brief History of Muscovia and of Other Less-known Countries lying eastward of Russia as far as Cathay. Gather'd from the Writings of several eye-witnesses by John Milton. To which are added other curious documents, with an Introduction by Prince D. S. Mirsky* (London, 1929), pp. ix–xxvi. The 'other curious documents' include principally a forged 'Declaration' by Tsar Aleksey Mikhailovich that was discovered in the British Museum by Baron Meyendorff.

107. 'Die Literatur der russischen Emigration', *Slavische Rundschau* 1 (1929), 290–4; cf. 'Zametki ob emigrantskoi literature', *Evraziya*, 5 Jan. 1929, 6–7.

108. Jakobson's programmatic article for the first issue of *Slavische Rundschau*, which he never reprinted, is brilliantly analysed in N. S. Avtonomova and M. L. Gasparov, 'Yakobson, slavistika i evraziistvo: Dve kon"yunktury, 1919–1953', *Novoe literaturnoe obozrenie* 27 (1997), 87–91.

109. 'Il posto del Dostojevskij nelle letteratura Russa', *La Cultura* 2 (1931), 100–15.

110. See Sophie Levie, *Commerce, 1924–1932: une revue internationale moderniste* (Rome, 1989), esp. 'D. S. Mirsky et la littérature russe', 198–204.

111. On Mirsky's relations with the Bassianos, see Smith, *The Letters of D. S. Mirsky to P. P. Suvchinskii*, esp. 192.

112. Hélène Izvolsky, *No Time to Grieve* (Philadelphia, 1985), 167.

113. *The Journals of André Gide*, trans. and annotated by Justin O'Brien, iii: *1928–1939* (New York, 1949), 62.

114. See 'The Literary Lawyers', in Mirsky, *A History of Russian Literature*, 343–5. Mirsky says nothing about the source of his information about Urusov.

115. Mirsky, *Contemporary Russian Literature*, p. ix.

116. Mirsky's *A History of Russian Literature from the Earliest Times to the Death of Dostoevsky (1881)* ends with Kushchevsky, who was born in 1847 and died in 1876 after 'years of hopeless struggle against starvation, undermined by drink and consumption'. 'Kushchevsky's delicacy of touch is unique in Russian literature. For liveliness and lightness of humour [*Nicholas Negorov*] has no equals' (pp. 369–70); see also *A History of Russian Literature*, 287–8.

117. 'O nyneshnem sostoyanii russkoi literatury', repr. in Mirsky, *Uncollected Writings*, 222–3.

118. Kn. D. Svyatopolk-Mirsky, 'Izdaniya rossiiskogo instituta istorii iskusstv', *Sovremennye zapiski* 24 (1925), 436.

119. 'Voina i mir', repr. in Mirsky, *Uncollected Writings on Russian Literature*, 339–57.

120. *Uncollected Writings on Russian Literature*, 52.

121. Ibid. 46.

122. Prince D. S. Mirski, 'A Russian Poetess', *Outlook*, 18 Mar. 1922, 218.

123. Prince D. S. Mirsky, 'Mr. Lytton Strachey', *London Mercury* 8 (43) (May 1923), 177.
124. In Feb. 1926 Mirsky tried to enrol Richards as a contributor to the journal *Vyorsts*, but he declined, and Mirsky secured E. M. Forster instead; see Chapter 5.
125. Prince D. S. Mirsky, *Modern Russian Literature* (London, 1925), 109.
126. Ibid. 108.
127. Mirsky, *The Intelligentsia of Great Britain*, 121.

5. WRITING RUSSIAN

1. On Russian literature of the first emigration, see principally Gleb Struve, *Russkaya literatura v izgnanii*, 2nd edn (New York, 1984); Simon Karlinsky and Alfred Appel, Jr. (eds.), *The Bitter Air of Exile: Russian Writers in the West, 1922–1972* (Berkeley, Calif., 1977); Temira Pachmuss, *A Russian Cultural Revival: A Critical Anthology of Emigré Literature before 1939* (Knoxville, Tenn., 1981); Robert H. Johnston, *'New Mecca, New Babylon': Paris and the Russian Exiles, 1920–1945* (Kingston and Montreal, 1988).
2. On this deportation, see Mikhail Geller, ' "Pervoe predosterezhenie"—udar khlystom', *Vestnik russkogo khristianskogo dvizheniya* 127 (1978), 187–232.
3. P. P. Suvchinsky, letter to N. S. Trubetskoy, 25 Nov. 1922; 'Pis'ma P. P. Suvchinskogo–N. S. Trubetskomu (1922–1924)', in *Rossiiskii arkhiv: Istoriya otechestva v svidetel'stvakh i dokumentakh XVIII–XX vv.*, v (Moscow, 1994), 478.
4. See the penultimate paragraph of 'O nyneshnem sostoyanii russkoi literatury', repr. in D. S. Mirsky, *Uncollected Writings on Russian Literature*, ed. G. S. Smith (Berkeley, Calif., 1989), 229.
5. Vladislav Khodasevich saw a good deal of Gorky in the early 1920s, co-edited the journal *Dialogue*, and lived in his household from Oct. 1924 to Apr. 1925; see 'Gor'ky', in Vladislav Khodasevich, *Koleblemyi trenozhnik* (Moscow, 1991), 353–74.
6. 'Tam ili zdes'?', repr. in Vladislav Khodasevich, *Sobranie sochinenii*, ed. John Malmstad and Robert Hughes, ii: *Stat'i i retsenzii, 1905–1926* (Ann Arbor, Mich., 1990), 364–8.
7. Anon., 'Alexander Blok', *The Times Literary Supplement*, 13 Apr. 1922, 242.
8. Mirsky had published 'A Russian Poetess', *Outlook*, 18 Mar. 1922, 217–18; in the first issue of the School of Slavonic Studies' journal he reviewed the three most recent collections by Akhmatova: *Slavonic Review* 1 (1) (1922), 690–1.
9. V. V. Perkhin, 'Odinnadtsat' pisem (1920–1937) i avtobiografiya (1936) D. P. Svyatopolk-Mirskogo', *Russkaya literatura* 1 (1996), 241–2.
10. *Slavonic Review* 2 (4) (1923), 145–53.
11. On Pilnyak's visit to and literary representations of England, see Ol'ga Kaznina, *Russkie v Anglii: Russkaya emigratsiya v kontekste russko-angliiskikh literaturnykh svyazei v pervoi polovine XX veka* (Moscow, 1997), 316–37.
12. See Stephen Graham, *Part of the Wonderful Scene: An Autobiography* (London, 1964), 291.
13. Mirsky's friend Hélène Izvolsky lived with her invalid mother in Pau in the early 1920s, and this may have been a visit to them.
14. Marina Tsvetaeva, *Sobranie sochinenii v semi tomakh* (Moscow, 1995), vii. 392–3.
15. 'O sovremennom sostoyanii russkoi poezii', repr. in Mirsky, *Uncollected Writings on Russian Literature*, 87–117.
16. Ibid. 117.
17. *The Oxford Book of Russian Verse. Chosen by the Hon. Maurice Baring* (Oxford, 1924), 204.
18. Kn. D. Svyatopolk-Mirsky, *Russkaya lirika* (Paris, 1924), 191.
19. *The Oxford Book of Russian Verse*, 206.
20. Mirsky, *Russkaya lirika*, 197. Ozerki is the name of the summer resort referred to in the English note. *An Unexpected Joy* (*Nechayannaya radost'*) is the title of the cycle of lyrics in which 'The Unknown Woman' was included by Blok.
21. Mirsky, *Russkaya lirika*, p. xii ('*talantlivaya, no beznadezhno raspushchennaya moskvichka*').

The second adjective also means 'debauched' or 'dissipated', and indicates someone who takes liberties with themselves and others.

22. Ibid. 184.
23. On the great lawyer, politician, and Jewish activist M. M. Vinaver (1862–1926), see H. M. Winawer (ed.), *The Vinaver Saga* (London, 1994), 275–413.
24. See Oleg Korostelev, 'Parizhskoe "Zveno" (1923–1928) i ego sozdateli', in M. Parkhomovsky (ed.), *Russkoe evreistvo v zarubezh'e*, i (6) (Jerusalem, 1998), 177–201.
25. For studies of Nicholas Bakhtin and his work, see the introduction and annotation to Galin Tihanov, 'Nikolay Bakhtin: Two Letters to Mikhail Lopatto (1924) and an Autobiographical Fragment', *Oxford Slavonic Papers* n.s. 31 (1998), 68–86.
26. D. S. Mirsky, 'Novoe v angliiskoi literature: Moris Bering', *Zveno*, 11 Aug. 1924, 3.
27. Kn. D. Svyatopolk-Mirsky, 'I. E. Babel', *Rasskazy*', repr. in *Uncollected Writings on Russian Literature*, 203–5; 'O. E. Mandel'shtam, *Shum vremeni*', repr. ibid. 208–10; 'B. L. Pasternak, *Rasskazy*', repr. ibid. 206–7. The Mandelshtam book was reviewed at the same time by two of the best critics of the emigration, Konstantin Mochulsky in *The Link* and Vladimir Veidle in the newspaper *Days*; their articles were reprinted, together with Mirsky's, and with an informative introduction by K. Polivanov, as 'Trizhdy uslyshannyi shum: Retsenzii na knigu "Shum vremeni"', *Literaturnoe obozrenie* 1 (1991), 55–8.
28. 'M. I. Tsvetaeva, *Molodets. Skazka*', *Sovremennye zapiski* 27 (1926), 567–72; Mirsky published a parallel review in English: *Slavonic Review* 4 (1926), 775–6.
29. Kn. D. P. Svyatopolk-Mirsky, 'Izdaniya rossiiskogo instituta istorii iskusstv', *Sovremennye zapiski* 24 (1925), 434–8.
30. 'Esenin', repr. in Mirsky, *Uncollected Writings*, 211–12. Mirsky's English-language obituary is much less emotional and personal: see 'S. A. Esenin', *Slavonic Review* 4 (12) (1926), 706–7.
31. Mirsky uses the adjective *raspushchennyi*, which he famously applied to Tsvetaeva.
32. 'O nyneshnem sostoyanii russkoi poezii', 225–6.
33. Kn. D. Svyatopolk-Mirsky, 'O konservatizme: Dialog', *Blagonamerennyi* 2 (1926), 208. This piece, uniquely among Mirsky's writings, is in dialogue form.
34. Mirsky was inordinately fond of quoting this line from Derzhavin's ode 'Felitsa' (1782), sometimes substituting the adjective 'sweet' for the original 'tasty'.
35. Harrison no doubt had in mind inherited income, the possession of which she seems, like Virginia Woolf, to have regarded as a precondition for the intellectual life; it was certainly a precondition for her own.
36. '*Sovremennye zapiski, 1–26 (1920–1925); Volya Rossii, i (1922, 1925, i 1926, 1–2)*', *Vyorsty* 1 (1926), 206–10.
37. For a general account of Mirsky's dealings with the movement, but written before the publication of Mirsky's letters to Suvchinsky, see Ol'ga Kaznina, 'D. P. Svyatopolk-Mirsky i evraziiskoe dvizhenie', *Nachala* 4 (1992), 81–8.
38. For a well-disposed view of Suvchinsky, see Vadim Kozovoï's introductory article to 'Iz perepiski B. Pasternaka i P. Suvchinskogo', *Revue des Études Slaves* 58 (4) (1986), 637–48.
39. 'The Exodus to the East', *Russian Life* 1 (1922), 210–12; 'Two Aspects of Revolutionary Nationalism', ibid. 5 (1922), 172–4; 'A "Eurasian" Manifesto', *The Times Literary Supplement*, 1 July 1922, 350.
40. See Kaznina, 'D. P. Svyatopolk-Mirsky i evraziiskoe dvizhenie', 81.
41. After *Exodus to the East* (*Iskhod k vostoku*, Sofia, 1921) came *On the Paths* (*Na putyakh*, Berlin, 1922) and *Russia and the Latin World* (*Rossiya i latinstvo*, Berlin, 1923), both substantial collections of articles. There were three issues in the series under the title *Evraziiskii vremennik* (Berlin, 1923 and 1925; Paris, 1927); and ten of the chronicle *Evraziiskaya khronika*: nos. 1 and 2 (Paris-Berlin, 1925); nos. 3–6 (Prague, later Paris, 1925); nos. 7–9 (Paris, 1927); and no. 10 (Paris, 1928).
42. 'The Eurasian Movement', repr. in Mirsky, *Uncollected Writings on Russian Literature*, 237–45.
43. Struve, *Russkaya literatura v izgnanii*, 40–9; Otto Böss, *Die Lehre der Eurasier* (Wiesbaden, 1961); N. V. Riasanovsky, 'The Emergence of Eurasianism', *California Slavic Studies* 4

(1967), 39–72; Georges Nivat, 'La "fenêtre sur l'Asie" ou les paradoxes de l' "affirmation eurasienne"', *Rossiya/Russia* 6 (1988), 81–93.

44. See *Evraziya: Istoricheskie vzglyady russkikh emigrantov* (Moscow, 1992); *Puti Evrazii: Russkaya intelligentsiya i sud'by Rossii* (Moscow, 1992); *Rossiya mezhdu Evropoi i Aziei: Evraziiskii soblazn* (Moscow, 1993); *Evraziiskaya perspektiva* (Moscow, 1994); *Mir Rossii- Evraziya: Antologiya* (Moscow, 1995); *Russkii uzel evraziistva: Vostok v russkoi mysli: Sbornik trudov evraziitsev*, ed. Sergey Klyuchnikov (Moscow, 1997); Petr Savitsky, *Konti- nent Evraziya* (Moscow, 1997); and the reprint of *Iskhod k vostoku* (Moscow, 1997).

45. S. M. Polovinkin, 'Evraziistvo i russkaya emigratsiya', in N. S. Trubetskoy, *Istoriya: Kul'tura: Yazyk* (Moscow, 1995), 731–62; Yu. K. Gerasimov, 'Religioznaya pozitsiya evra- ziitsev', *Russkaya literatura* 1 (1995), 159–76; S. Polovinkin, 'Evraziistvo', in *Russkaya filosofiya: Malyi entsiklopedicheskii slovar'* (Moscow, 1995), 172–8; A. V. Antoshchenko, 'Spory o evraziistve', in *O evrazii i evraziitsakh* (Petrozavodsk, 1997), 7–43; O. S. Shirokov, 'Problema etnolingvisticheskikh obosnovanii evraziistva', in *Iskhod k vostoku* (Moscow, 1997), 4–42.

46. On Trubetskoy's life and thought, see Anatoly Liberman, 'Introduction: Trubetzkoy as a Literary Scholar', in N. S. Trubetzkoy, *Writings on Literature*, ed., trans., and introduced by Anatoly Liberman (Minneapolis, 1990), pp. xi–xlvi; id., 'Postscript', in N. S. Trubetz- koy, *The Legacy of Genghis Khan and Other Essays on Russia's Cultural Identity*, ed., and with a postscript, by Anatoly Liberman (Ann Arbor, Mich., 1991), 295–375; and *N. S. Tru- betskoy i sovremennaya filologiya* (Moscow, 1993).

47. For Savitsky's views on the development of Eurasianism during the period of Mirsky's involvement, see his 'V bor'be za evraziistvo: polemika vokrug evraziistva v 1920-kh godakh', in *Tridtsatye gody* (Paris, 1931), 1–52 (*Utverzhdenie evraziitsev*, 7), published under the pseudonym 'Stepan Lubensky'. Savitsky was deported from Prague to the USSR in 1945 and sent to the GULag; amnestied in 1956, he returned to Prague and died there. On his geographical theory of Eurasia, see esp. M. Bassin, 'Russia between Europe and Asia: The Ideological Construction of Geographical Space', *Slavic Review* 50 (1) (1991), 1–17.

48. For a view of Savitsky as a prophet of genius and a major figure in twentieth-century geo- political theory and the theory of 'the conservative revolution', see A. Dugin, 'Evraziiskii triumf', in Savitsky, *Kontinent Evraziya*, 433–53.

49. On Florovsky's life, see Andrew Blane, 'A Sketch of the Life of Georges Florovsky', in *Georges Florovsky: Russian Intellectual and Orthodox Churchman* (Crestwood, NY, 1993), 11–217; this book also contains a bibliography of Florovsky's writings. On Florovsky's departure from Eurasianism, see particularly the letter from Suvchinsky to Trubetskoy of 27 Feb. 1923: 'Pis'ma P. P. Suvchinskogo–N. S. Trubetskomu (1922–1924)', 479–81.

50. See A. Shteinberg, *Druz'ya moikh rannikh let (1911–1928)* (Paris, 1991), 198; this sibling rivalry became especially acute when in the early 1920s Erik Pommer used Tamara for the leading role in his film *Kraft und Schönheit* and she became a household name.

51. An excellent bibliography is A. V. Antoshchenko and A. A. Kozhanov (eds.), *O Evrazii i evraziitsakh (Bibliograficheskii ukazatel')* (Petrozavodsk, 1997).

52. Mirsky expounds Eurasian geopolitical ideas, with excellent maps, in his *Russia: A Social History* (London, 1931). For the geopolitics of 'Eurasia' written without reference to Russian sources and Russian Eurasian theory, and based instead on the theories of Mackinder and others that may have influenced Savitsky, see Stuart Legg, *The Heartland* (New York, 1970).

53. It is worth remembering that among the close contemporaries of Mirsky were Dwight D. Eisenhower (1890–1969), Charles de Gaulle (1890–1970), Ho Chi Minh (1890–1969), Jawa- harlal Nehru (1889–1964), and Adolf Hitler (1889–1945). In Stalin's entourage, Mirsky's closest contemporary was Vyacheslav Molotov (1890–1986), who got his first big Moscow job in 1930.

54. Pyotr Arapov secured the money to publish *Rossiya i latinstvo* (Berlin, 1923) from a lady he had seduced. See 'Pis'ma P. P. Suvchinskogo–N. S. Trubetskomu (1922–1924)', 477; the

same article contains as a supplement the publishing agreements made by the Eurasians in 1923, but in Feb. 1924 Suvchinsky told Trubetskoy that the coffers were empty.

55. *Russia in Resurrection: A Summary of the Views and of the Aims of a New Party in Russia. By an English Europasian* (London, 1928).

56. As an afterthought, Mirsky inserted the name 'Serafim' (St Serafim of Sarov) between those of St Francis and Pascal. His point here exactly anticipates one of the major conclusions of Otto Böss: cf. *Die Lehre der Eurasier*, 76.

57. 'O moskovskoi literature i protopope Avvakume (Dva otryvka)', repr. in Mirsky, *Uncollected Writings on Russian Literature*, 145–55.

58. Ibid. 154.

59. See esp. Irene Zohrab, 'Remizov, Williams, Mirsky and English Readers (with some Letters from Remizov to Ariadna Tyrkova-Williams and Two Unknown Reviews)', *New Zealand Slavonic Journal* (1994), 259–87. Zohrab established that the earliest post-revolutionary article in English about the writer, 'Alexei Remizov', *The Times Literary Supplement*, 21 Feb. 1924, was jointly written by Mirsky and Harold Williams.

60. On Remizov's life, see Horst Lampl, 'A. M. Remizov: A Short Biographical Essay (1877–1923)', and Natalya Reznikova, 'Alexei Remizov in Paris (1923–1957)', *Russian Literature Triquarterly* 19 (1986), 7–60, 61–92.

61. Mirsky, *A History of Russian Literature* (1949), 22.

62. See G. S. Smith, 'Marina Tsvetaeva i D. P. Svyatopolk-Mirsky', in Robin Kemball et al. (eds.), *Marina Tsvetaeva: Actes du I Colloque Marina Tsvetaeva* (Bern, 1991), 192–206. This article was written in 1982, and traces the history of Mirsky's published responses to Tsvetaeva's work, which will not be summarized here; instead, attention will be drawn to materials that have become available since that time.

63. 'Aleksandr i Salomeya Gal'perny', in Mikhail Parkhomovsky (ed.), *Evrei v kul'ture russkogo zarubezh'ya: Sbornik statei, publikatsii, memuarov i esse*, i: *1919–1939 gg.* (Jerusalem, 1992), 229–41. Berlin asserts in passing here that A. J. Halpern was a British intelligence agent.

64. Sir Isaiah Berlin, unpublished letter to G. S. Smith, 20 Mar. 1996.

65. See G. S. Smith, 'D. S. Mirsky: Four Letters to Ariadna Tyrkova-Williams (1926), with an Unknown Review by Ariadna Tyrkova-Williams (1924)', *Slavonic and East European Review* 71 (3) (1993), 482–9.

66. 'Marina Tsvetaeva', repr. in Mirsky, *Uncollected Writings on Russian Literature*, 217–21.

67. Tsvetaeva is talking partly here about her short-sightedness, which was acute; she refused to wear glasses.

68. Tsvetaeva, *Sobranie sochinenii v semi tomakh*, vi. 315–16.

69. Veronika Losskaya, *Marina Tsvetaeva v zhizni* (Tenafly, 1989), 143.

70. Tsvetaeva, *Sobranie sochinenii v semi tomakh*, vi. 317.

71. Ibid. 345.

72. For a summary of these problems, see Marc Raeff, 'The Gutenberg Galaxy: Publishing in Alien Lands', in *Russia Abroad: A Cultural History of the Russian Emigration, 1919–1939* (New York and Oxford, 1990), 73–94.

73. 'Jane Ellen Harrison: Forty-Seven Letters to D. S. Mirsky, 1924–1926', *Oxford Slavonic Papers* n.s. 28 (1995), 86–7.

74. Lydia Lopokova; on her, see Jane Ellen Harrison's letter to Mirsky of 29 Jan. 1926.

75. Unpublished letter, Leonard Woolf Papers, University of Sussex Library.

76. Arkhiepiskop Ioann Shakhovskoy, *Biografiya yunosti: Ustanovlenie edinstva* (Paris, 1978), 193.

77. Mirsky uses the Greek form of this word, usually represented in English as 'Sanhedrin', the supreme council of the Jews in Biblical Jerusalem; the equivalent in the Russian Bible is the richly ironic *sovet*. Bulgakov also uses the Greek form in the second chapter of *The Master and Margarita*.

78. 'Veyanie smerti v predrevolyutsionnoi literature', repr. in Mirsky, *Uncollected Writings on Russian Literature*, 236.

79. Zinaida Shakhovskaya, *Otrazheniya* (Paris, 1975), 25.
80. Mirsky, *Uncollected Writings on Russian Literature*, 236.
81. Georgy Adamovich was present at Mirsky's lecture, and wrote a letter to *The Link* protesting particularly about the pro-Soviet tone of Mirsky's coda (*Zveno* 169, 25 Apr. 1926); Mirsky replied, emphasizing that his chief example was Gumilyov, who was in no sense Soviet: Kn. D. Svyatopolk-Mirsky, 'Pis'mo v redaktsiyu', *Zveno* 172, 16 May 1926, to which is appended a riposte by Adamovich.
82. G. S. Smith (ed.), *The Letters of D. S. Mirsky to P. P. Suvchinskii 1922–31* (Birmingham, 1995), 183.
83. In passing, Remizov mentions the recent three-evening celebration of Shestov's 60th birthday (Shestov had a considerable private income, and could afford to put on this sort of thing). The third, 'philosophical' evening was attended by Berdyaev, Vysheslavtsev, Efron, Ilin, Pozner, Lazarev, Lurie, Suvchinsky, Mirsky, Fedotov, and Mochulsky ('Stepun didn't come!'); Remizov entertained them with a three-hour reading of *The Life of Archpriest Avvakum* without an interval: Aleksey Remizov, ' "Voistinu" ', *Vyorsty* 1 (1926), 83.
84. Artur-Vintsent Lurie (1892–1966) was a composer; he is most famous for being another man besides Boris Anrep whom Akhmatova refused to follow into emigration. On him, see B. Kats and R. Timenchik, *Akhmatova i muzyka* (Leningrad, 1989).
85. See Zinaida Gippius, *Pis'ma k Berberovoi i Khodasevichu*, ed. Erika Freiberger Sheikholeslami (Ann Arbor, Mich., 1978), 43.
86. Vladislav Khodasevich, 'O "Verstakh" ', repr. in Vladislav Khodasevich, *Sobranie sochinenii* (2 vols., Ann Arbor, Mich., 1990), ii. 408–17.
87. M. V. Vishnyak, *'Sovremennye zapiski': Vospominaniya redaktora* (Bloomington, 1957), 140–6. The essentially decent and long-suffering philistine Vishnyak recoils here from the intemperate feuding of his literary colleagues. He contentedly points out (p. 146) that the principal contributors to *Vyorsts* soon returned to *Contemporary Notes*: Shestov and Tsvetaeva sooner, Remizov later. The devious Remizov, however, actually wrote Vishnyak a letter distancing himself from Mirsky and Suvchinsky before the text of Mirsky's lecture was published.
88. For documentation and discussion of this incident, see the annotation by John Malmstad and Robert Hughes in Khodasevich, *Sobranie sochinenii*, ii. 544–9. The most significant outcome of it was an astonishing letter written by Tsvetaeva to Suvchinsky and Karsavin on 9 Mar. 1927 about Sergey Efron and Jewish identity.
89. See G. S. Smith, 'The Versification of V. F. Xodasevič, 1915–1939', in Thomas Eekman and Dean S. Worth (eds.), *Russian Poetics: Proceedings of the International Colloquium at UCLA, September 22–26, 1975* (Columbus, Ohio, 1982), 373–92.
90. Cited from an unpublished document in the Suvchinsky archive in Vadim Kozovoï, 'Pis'ma Mariny Tsvetaevoi', 203–4.
91. See Tsvetaeva's letter to Salomeya Halpern, 12 Aug. 1926, *Sobranie sochinenii v semi tomakh*, vii. 101.
92. See Reiner Maria Ril'ke, Boris Pasternak, and Marina Tsvetaeva, *Pis'ma 1926 goda* (Moscow, 1990).
93. Mirsky refers to the journal edited by Berdyaev, which began publication in Paris in 1925 and continued until the outbreak of the Second World War. The early issues were reviewed by V. Sezeman: *Versty* 2 (1927), 275–80, and 3 (1928), 175–81. For dealings between the Eurasians and Berdyaev in the period before the publication of *The Way*, see 'K istorii evraziistva: 1922–1924 gg.', *Rossiiskii arkhiv: Istoriya otechestva v svidetel'stvakh i dokumentakh XVIII–XX vv.*, v (Moscow, 1994), 489–91.
94. I. A. Il'in, *O soprotivlenii zlu siloyu* (Berlin, 1925). This reasoned refutation of Tolstoy's pacifism and non-resistance to evil was inspired by what Ilin saw as the disastrous consequences of that doctrine in revolutionary Russia; it was later read with great interest by Aleksandr Solzhenitsyn.
95. On Tsvetaeva's reaction to Pasternak's poem *Lieutenant Schmidt*, see particularly her letter

to Pasternak of 1 July 1926, in which she describes its hero as 'an *intelligent*, not a sailor' (*Pis'ma 1926 goda*, 159).

96. Tsvetaeva, *Sobranie sochinenii v semi tomakh*, vi. 269.

97. Cited in Lazar' Fleishman, 'Iz pasternakovskoi perepiski', *Slavica Hierosolymitana* 5 and 6 (1981), 535–41.

98. Mirsky is referring to *Posle Rossii* (Paris, 1928), published after considerable delay by his friend J. E. Pouterman.

99. Library of the School of Slavonic and East European Studies, University of London.

100. Kn. D. Svyatopolk-Mirsky, 'Kriticheskie zametki', *Versty* 2 (1927), 257.

101. A back-translation into English of this essay by G. S. Smith is cited and discussed in Evelyn Hanquart, 'Forster on Contemporary English Literature', *Aligorh Journal of English Studies* 5 (1) (1980), 102–9.

102. Untitled composite review, *London Mercury* 17 (1927), 208–10. Forster was working at the time on his Clark Lectures (Jan.–Mar. 1927), which were rewritten and published as *Aspects of the Novel*.

103. *The Hollow Men* (1925) was included in Eliot's *Poems: 1909–1925*. A translation by Ivan Kashkin, 'Polye lyudi', was included in Mirsky's *Antologiya novoi angliiskoi poezii* (Leningrad, 1937), 352–6.

104. John Cournos, reviewing the third issue, said: 'This is the organ of the Eurasians, who are extreme Nationalists and hold that Russia is a separate cultural entity': *Criterion* 8 (30) (Sept. 1928), 182–3.

105. See Anatoly Liberman, 'Introduction: Trubetzkoy as a Literary Scholar', in N. S. Trubetzkoy, *Writings on Literature* (Minneapolis, 1990), pp. xi–xlvi.

106. For a translation, see N. S. Trubetskoy, *Three Philological Studies* (Ann Arbor, Mich., 1963), and Ladislav Matejka and Krystyna Pomorska (eds.), *Readings in Russian Poetics: Formalist and Structuralist Views* (Cambridge, Mass., and London, 1971), 199–219.

107. See M. L. Gasparov, 'K geografii chastushechnogo ritma', in his *Izbrannye trudy*, iii: *O stikhe* (Moscow, 1997), 279–89.

108. On this episode, and the friendly relations and radical differences of opinion about Judaism and Othodoxy that had preceded it for many years, see A. Shteinberg, 'Lev Platonovich Karsavin', in his *Druz'ya moikh rannikh let (1911–1928)* (Paris, 1991), 193–217.

109. For a brief but usefully contextualized view of Fyodorov's significance, see Irene Masing-Delic, 'The Transfiguration of Cannibals: Fedorov and the Avant-Garde', in *Laboratory of Dreams: The Russian Avant-Garde and Cultural Experiment* (Stanford, Calif., 1996), 17–36.

110. Alternatively, Suvchinsky's failure to produce a contribution may have led to the insertion of a very interesting article that is not listed in the contents and has consequently been omitted from bibliographies: Vladimir Dukel'sky, 'Dyagilev i ego rabota', *Vyorsty* 3 (1928), 251–5, datelined 'London, 1927'. In his American identity as Vernon Duke, Dukelsky (1903–69) made a greater contribution to Western popular culture than any other Russian of the emigration (with the possible exception of Ayn Rand); he was the composer of 'I Can't Get Started with You', 'April in Paris', 'Cabin in the Sky', and other standards.

111. A *dormeuse* is a heavy horse-drawn carriage equipped with beds, the predecessor of the railway sleeping-car.

112. Trubetskoy published his views on this subject later, sharply criticizing Nazi theories: 'O rasizme', *Evraziiskie tetradi* 5 (1935), 43–54.

113. Mirsky did not produce this article, in which he proposes to discuss the Alexandrian philosopher Philo Judaeus (*c*.20 BC–*c*. AD 50); later in this letter he mentions among more famous men Herman Minkowski (1864–1909), the Russian-born mathematician who studied and taught in Germany. In speaking of the 'periphery', Karsavin has in mind secularized persons of Jewish origin living outside the principal European area of Jewish settlement.

114. Mirsky, *Uncollected Writings on Russian Literature*, 362.

115. Ibid. 366.

6. WRITING POLITICS

1. Cited in Veronika Losskaya, *Marina Tsvetaeva v zhizni* (Tenafly, 1989), 196.
2. Cited in G. S. Smith, *The Letters of D. S. Mirsky to P. P. Suvchinskii* (Birmingham, 1995), 2.
3. On Gorky's life, see Geir Kh'etso [Kjetsaa], *Maksim Gor'ky: Sud'ba pisatelya* (Moscow, 1997).
4. On Budberg, see Nina Berberova, *Zheleznaya zhenshchina* (New York, 1981).
5. *M. Gor'ky i sovetskaya pechat'*, ed. A. G. Dementiev et al. (2 vols., Moscow, 1964), i. 40 (*Arkhiv M. Gor'kogo*, 10). By 'princely' Gorky probably means something like 'magnanimously hospitable'.
6. The Minerva was a boarding-house opposite Gorky's villa, run by one Signora Cacace. Her surname sounds to the Russian ear like a neologism meaning 'shittier', and it entered the language of Gorky and his circle; see Vladimir Khodasevich, 'Gor'ky', in *Koleblemyi trenozhnik* (Moscow, 1991), 358–60.
7. *Gor'ky i sovetskie pisateli* (Moscow, 1963), 602. The annotation to this letter (603) contains one of the very few references to Mirsky published in the USSR in the 40 years following his death, and gives his date of death as 1937.
8. 'The Literature of Bolshevik Russia', repr. in D. S. Mirsky, *Uncollected Writings on Russian Literature*, ed. G. S. Smith (Berkeley, Calif., 1989), 70. For a fuller discussion of Mirsky's published opinions of Gorky, see Ol'ga Kaznina and G. S. Smith, 'D. S. Mirsky to Maksim Gor'ky: Sixteen Letters (1928–1934)', *Oxford Slavonic Papers* n.s. 26 (1993), 87–92.
9. Khodasevich, *Sobranie sochinenii* (2 vols., Ann Arbor, Mich., 1983), ii. 535.
10. See Anastasiya Tsvetaeva, *Vospominaniya*, 3rd edn (Moscow, 1983). Tsvetaeva (1894–1993) remained in Moscow when her sister emigrated; she 'sat' in the GULag from 1937 for ten years, then in internal exile, and finally returned to Moscow in 1959.
11. Kamenev (1883–1936) was expelled from the Party as a Trotskyite in Dec. 1927, but re-admitted after denouncing Trotsky the next year, only to be expelled again in 1934.
12. Kaznina and Smith, 'D. S. Mirsky to Maksim Gor'ky', 93.
13. 'The Story of a Liberation', in Mirsky, *Uncollected Writings on Russian Literature*, 364.
14. Clarence Augustus Manning (1893–1972) was Professor of Russian at Columbia University in Mirsky's time.
15. Malevsky-Malevich seems to have made his first address on behalf of the Eurasians in New York on 2 Jan. 1926: see *Evraziiskaya khronika* 4 (1926), 48–50.
16. University of Chicago, *Weekly Calendar*, 29 July–4 Aug. 1928. The university archivists at Cornell and Columbia have not been able to trace any information about the subjects of Mirsky's talk at their institutions.
17. For summary information on Karsavin's life and work, see *Bibliographie des œuvres de Lev Karsavine. Établie par Aleksandre Klementiev, Préface de Nikita Struve* (Paris, 1994). On Karsavin's role in the Eurasian movement, see Claire Hauchard, 'L. P. Karsavin et le mouvement eurasien: de la critique à l'adhésion', *Revue des Études Slaves* 68 (3) (1996), 360–5.
18. Cited in 'K istorii evraziistva. 1922–1924 gg.', in *Rossiiskii arkhiv: Istoriya otechestva v svidetel'stvakh i dokumentakh XVIII–XX vv.*, v (Moscow, 1994), 494.
19. There is no evidence for the assertion (see *Lev Karsavine: Bibliographie*, 13) that in 1927 Karsavin turned down an offer made by Mirsky to take up a post at Oxford; this is one of many mysterious references to Mirsky's having some sort of Oxford association while he was in England. The offer may have had something to do with H. N. Spalding, who lived at Shotover Cleve near Oxford, rather than with the University of Oxford.
20. See S. S. Khoruzhy, 'Karsavin, evraziistvo i VKP', *Voprosy filosofii* 2 (1992), 84–7. See also A. B. Sobolev, ' "Svoya svoikh ne poznasha": Evraziistvo, L. P. Karsavin i drugie', *Nachala* 4 (1992), 49–58.
21. 'The Eurasian Movement', repr. in *Uncollected Writings on Russian Literature*, 245.
22. Trubetskoy was something of a whited sepulchre, though; the letters he wrote to his close friend Roman Jakobson during the early years of the Eurasian movement show that he slyly

relished the potential political resonance of his publications. See especially the letters of 1922 in *Trubetzkoy's Letters and Notes. Prepared for publication by R. Jakobson with the assistance of H. Baran, O. Ronen and M. Taylor* (The Hague, 1975).

23. The last interrogation took place on 5 July 1940, but Efron was pronounced guilty only on 6 July 1941, and then was not executed until 16 Oct. 1941.

24. The materials on this subject that beyond reasonable doubt once existed in Mirsky's GPU files, consisting of the transcripts of those interrogations at which certain aspects of Eurasianism were discussed, have been removed, probably to use against Efron and the others who came back at about the same time as Mirsky (who had been arrested more than two years before Efron was repatriated). Efron's depositions have not been published in full; for extracts and summary, see M. Feinberg and Yu. Klyukin, 'Po vnov' otkryvshimsya obstoyatel'stvam', in *Bolshevo: Literaturnyi istoriko-kraevedcheskii al'manakh* (Moscow, 1992), 145–66, and Irma Kudrova, *Gibel' Mariny Tsvetaevoi* (Moscow, 1992), 95–156.

25. Mirsky, 'The Eurasian Movement', 244.

26. Geoffrey Bailey, *The Conspirators* (London, 1971); Christopher Andrew and Oleg Gordievsky, *KGB: The Inside Story of Its Foreign Operations from Lenin to Gorbachev* (London, etc., 1990), 43–114. See also A. V. Sobolev, 'Polyusa evraziistva', *Novyi mir* 1 (1991), 180–2.

27. S. L. Voitsekhovsky, *Trest* (London, Ont., 1974). Andrew and Gordievsky seem not to have known about this book. Voitsekhovsky apparently knew Bailey's book, but manifestly did not understand very much of what it has to say. There is also a fictionalized Soviet account of the Trust, based on conversations with Langovoy, the chief agent involved: Lev Nikulin, 'Mertvaya zyb'', *Moskva* 6 (1965), 5–90, and 7 (1965), 47–141. On Mirsky's acquaintanceship with Nikulin, see Chapter 7 below.

28. A. V. Sobolev, 'Knyaz' N. S. Trubetskoy i evraziistvo', *Literaturnaya ucheba* 6 (1991), 127.

29. See Suvchinsky's letter to Trubetskoy of 7 Oct. 1924: 'K istorii evraziistva', 487–8.

30. 'Col. Peter Malevsky Malevitch stayed with us often when my father was writing that book. I think he did something to inspire it' (Anne Spalding, unpublished letter to G. S. Smith, 5 Nov. 1974).

31. On the editorial disagreements before and during the establishment of the newspaper, see Irina Shevelenko, 'K istorii evraziiskogo raskola 1929 goda', *Stanford Slavic Studies* 8 (1994), 376–416.

32. Kingsley Martin (1897–1969) taught at the London School of Economics from 1923 to 1927, worked on the *Manchester Guardian* from 1927 to 1931, and then edited the *New Statesman and Nation* from 1932 to 1962.

33. Galsworthy Lowes Dickinson (1862–1932) was a Fellow of King's College, Cambridge, and a part-time lecturer at the London School of Economics.

34. D. Svyatopolk-Mirsky, 'Dve smerti: 1837–1930', repr. in *Stikhotvoreniya: Stat'i o russkoi poezii* (Berkeley, Calif., 1997), 135.

35. D. Svyatopolk-Mirsky, 'O Tolstom', repr. in Mirsky, *Uncollected Writings on Russian Literature*, 293.

36. D. S. Mirsky, '*Yugo-zapad* V. Bagritskogo', repr. in *Stikhotvoreniya: Stat'i o russkoi poezii*, compiled and ed. G. K. Perkins and G. S. Smith (Berkeley, Calif., 1997), 110.

37. D. Svyatopolk-Mirsky, 'Khlebnikov', repr. in *Uncollected Writings on Russian Literature*, 294–7; 'Chekhov', repr. ibid. 298–302.

38. D. Svyatopolk-Mirsky, 'Literatura i kino', *Evraziya* 15 (2 Mar. 1929), 6; Mirsky also reviewed Pudovkin's film *Potomok Chingiskhana*, *Evraziya*, 20 Apr. 1929, 8 (this film is known in English as *Storm over Asia*).

39. Mirsky published two articles about these developments: 'Posle angliiskikh vyborov', *Evraziya* 29 (22 June 1929), 4, and 'Pervye shagi "rabochego" kabineta v Anglii', *Evraziya* 31 (13 July 1929), 5.

40. I. V. Stalin, 'God velikogo pereloma: K XII godovshchine Oktyabra', published in both *Pravda* and *Izvestiya* on 7 Nov. 1929; see I. V. Stalin, *Sochineniya* (13 vols., Moscow, 1946–51), xii (1949), 118–35.

41. For Berlin's account, see Smith, *The Letters of D. S. Mirsky to P. P. Suvchinskii*, 223–4.
42. Anne Spalding, unpublished letter to G. S. Smith, 29 Aug. 1974.
43. 'Why I Became a Marxist', *Daily Worker* 462 (30 June 1931), 2.
44. Grigory Vasilievich Aleksandrov (1903–84), Eisenstein's assistant on his first four films, travelled abroad with him during 1929–31, and later became a very successful Soviet director.
45. Dorothy Galton, 'Sir Bernard Pares and Slavonic Studies in London University, 1919–39', *Slavonic and East European Review* 46 (107) (1968), 481–91.
46. Ibid.
47. *Slavonic Review* 7 (20) (1929), 512.
48. 'Introduction', in *Dostoevsky's Letters to His Wife*, trans. Elizabeth Hill and Doris Mudie (London, 1930), pp. ix–xiv.
49. Elizabeth Hill, unpublished letter to G. S. Smith, 31 Jan. 1974. Hill (1900–96) was born in St Petersburg, and taught at Cambridge from 1936 until her retirement in 1968 from the Chair of Slavonic Studies, to which she had been elected in 1948.
50. Unpublished diary entry, E. H. Carr archive, King's College, Cambridge; I am grateful to Jonathan Haslam for this reference.
51. 'Preface', in E. H. Carr, *Dostoevsky (1821–1881): A New Biography* (London, 1931), unpaginated.
52. E. H. Carr, unpublished letter to G. S. Smith, 1 Feb. 1974.
53. Guershoon's thesis was eventually published as *Certain Aspects of Russian Proverbs* (London, 1941). Bertha Malnick's first book offers a highly informative but now embarrassingly uncritical introduction to the Russia Mirsky went back to: *Everyday Life in Soviet Russia*, with drawings by Pearl Binder (London, 1938). On Helen Muchnic, see Chapter 4 above, n. 84.
54. For detailed information about Vera's life and the Russian texts of her letters to Mirsky, see Richard Davies and G. S. Smith, 'D. S. Mirsky: Twenty-Two Letters (1926–34) to Salomeya Halpern; Seven Letters (1930) to Vera Suvchinskaya (Traill)', *Oxford Slavonic Papers* n.s. 30 (1997), 91–122.
55. There is a vivid representation of Guchkov and his political activities, particularly his plan for a *coup d'état* in 1916, in Aleksandr Solzhenitsyn's *Krasnoe koleso* (*The Red Wheel*).
56. See Irma Kudrova, 'Vera Treil, urozhdennaya Guchkova: Po materialam doprosov na Lubyanke', *Russkaya mysl'* 4068 (9–15 Mar. 1995), 11–12. It is clear from this article that Vera repeated to Kudrova many of the things she had said in her interviews with me.
57. Vera gave me this letter, one of the few personal documents that survived her mother's *auto-da-fé* after her daughter was arrested in 1940, in the course of our interviews in 1974. I duly gave it to Leeds Russian Archive, and it was first published without permission in Russia: see *Zvezda* 10 (1992), 34–6, and again in Marina Tsvetaeva, *Sobranie sochinenii v semi tomakh* (Moscow, 1995), vii: *Pis'ma*, 181.
58. D. S. Mirsky, *Lenin* (Boston and London, 1931), 190.
59. *Vallée du Rhône: Cévennes* (Paris, 1927), 10. Morateur, at 3 rue du Président Carnot, was the premier eating-place in the city.
60. Hélène Izvolsky worked for the Paris weekly *Détective* as an investigative journalist; among other cases, she was assigned the kidnapping of General Kutepov, but 'The police were as confounded as I was. I found the "case of the vanishing General" so scary that I turned it over to a reporter with stronger nerves than mine': *No Time to Grieve* (Philadelphia, 1985), 175. General A. P. Kutepov (1882–1930), on whose staff Mirsky had served when Kutepov's army captured Oryol at the height of the White success in the Civil War, in emigration became the president of the Russian General Military Union (ROVS), the principal ex-servicemen's organization and a prime target of GPU counter-intelligence. Kutepov was kidnapped on the street in Paris in broad daylight on 26 Jan. 1930, and never seen again.
61. This is chronologically the last reference in Mirsky's correspondence to Pyotr Arapov. Which other Arapov was present on this occasion I do not know; perhaps it was Pyotr Arapov's brother Kirill. It is possible that Pyotr was repatriated because he had something

to do with the abduction of General Kutepov. There is also a private reason for Mirsky's mentioning Arapov to Vera. During our conversations in 1974, Vera told me that there had been two great loves in her life. One was Bruno von Salemann, a German Communist she met in France during the early part of the Second World War; the other was Pyotr Arapov. I never discovered when her affair with Arapov took place, and what relationship if any it had to her feelings for Mirsky in 1930. On Vera's affair with von Salemann, see her novel *The Cup of Astonishment* (London, 1944), published under the pseudonym 'Vera T. Mirsky'.

62. This village in Haute Savoie was the location of the Château d'Arcine, a boarding-house and sanatorium run by the Shtrange family, who were Russians and Communist sympathizers; they went back to Russia after the Second World War. Sergey Efron went there on 23 Dec. 1929, after a recurrence of his tuberculosis. See Davies and Smith, 'D. S. Mirsky: Twenty-Two Letters', 118.

63. 'Dve smerti: 1837–1930', repr. in Mirsky, *Stikhotovoreniya: Stat'i o russkoi poezii*, 127.

64. Ibid. 134.

65. On 7 Sept. 1932 Gorky sent a copy of Mirsky's essay to Stalin, saying that his opinion of it would be important in connection with setting up the proposed Literary Institute. Stalin seems not to have replied. See '"Zhmu vashu ruku, dorogoi tovarishch"', *Novyi mir* 9 (1998), 170.

66. For an expert examination of this question, see Karl Aimermakher [Eimermacher], 'Sovetskaya literaturnaya politika mezhdu 1917-m i 1932-m', in *V tiskakh ideologii: Antologiya literaturno-politicheskikh dokumentov, 1917–1927* (Moscow, 1992), 3–61.

67. The most instructive treatment of the period leading up to the reform of 1932 is still Edward J. Brown, *The Proletarian Episode in Russian Literature, 1928–1932* (New York, 1953); it has been supplemented by the previously secret documentation in D. L. Babichenko (ed.), *'Schast'e literatury': Gosudarstvo i pisateli* (Moscow, 1997).

68. The name means 'Hillocks', and is unrelated etymologically to Gorky's pseudonymous surname, which means 'The Bitter One'.

69. See Kaznina and Smith, 'D. S. Mirsky to Maksim Gor'ky: Sixteen Letters (1928–1934)'.

70. D. S. Mirsky, *Russia: A Social History* (London, 1931), p. ix.

71. 'Letters of Prince Svyatopolk-Mirsky to Sir B. Pares, 1922–1931', British Library, Add. MS 49,604.

72. Dorothy Galton said that this review was the real reason for the break between Mirsky and Pares: see 'Sir Bernard Pares and Slavonic Studies', 487.

73. In a letter to Sergey Efron of 19 May 1929 that has been preserved with the letters to Suvchinsky, Mirsky writes: 'I consider it a great honour to speak at M[arina] I[vanovna's] evening, but I'm afraid that 1) I'll speak badly; 2) my participation will keep many people away. No?'; see Smith, *The Letters of D. S. Mirsky to P. P. Suvchinskii*, 217.

74. Davies and Smith, 'D. S. Mirsky: Twenty-Two Letters', 176.

75. Raisa Nikolaevna Lomonosova (1888–1973) was the wife of the railway engineer Yury Vladimirovich Lomonosov (1876–1952), who decided to stay in the West rather than going back to the USSR in 1927; her primary residence was in England. Lomonosova furnished material assistance to both Pasternak and Tsvetaeva. She seems not to have been personally acquainted with Mirsky, even though he is mentioned in her correspondence with the two poets. On Lomonosova, see the annotation by Richard Davies to 'Pis'ma Mariny Tsvetaevoi k R. N. Lomonosovoi (1928–1931 gg.). Publikatsiya Richarda Devisa, podgotovka teksta Lidii Shorroks', *Minuvshee* 8 (1989), 208–73. The texts of the letters and some annotations are repr. in Tsvetaeva, *Sobranie sochinenii v semi tomakh*, vii. 313–47.

76. 'Pis'ma Mariny Tsvetaevoi k R. A. Lomonosovoi', 244; see also Tsvetaeva, *Sobranie sochinenii*, vii. 328.

77. 'Pis'ma Mariny Tsvetaevoi k R. A. Lomonosovoi', 247; Tsvetaeva, *Sobranie sochinenii*, vii. 330.

78. Ibid. vi. 392.

79. G. Ya. Sokolnikov (1888–1939) was appointed Soviet ambassador to London in 1929 as a

result of his opposition to Stalin. Mirsky was invited to a PEN monthly dinner at the Garden Club, Chesterfield Gardens, on 1 Mar. 1932, presided over by Louis Golding, with 'Mrs Sokolnikoff' as the guest of honour (unpublished letters to D. S. Mirsky from the Secretary of London PEN Club, Jan. 1932, Harry Ransome Humanities Research Center, University of Texas at Austin). Sokolnikov's wife was the prominent historical novelist Galina Serebryakova (1905–80), who among other things worked on her life of Marx while she was in London. Serebryakova and Mirsky saw each other back in Russia; they were among the group of writers invited out to Gorky's country house to meet Romain Rolland on 9 June 1935; see Chapter 7 below. Serebryakova survived 17 years in the GULag, and achieved notoriety when she made a pro-Stalin speech at the XX Party Congress in 1956, when Stalinism was officially 'unmasked'.

80. 'Why I Became a Marxist', *Daily Worker*, 30 June 1931, 2.

81. See announcements in the *Daily Worker*, 17 June 1931, 2, and 20 June 1931, 2.

82. I. M. Gronsky, 'Beseda o Gor'kom: Publikatsiya M. Nike', *Minuvshee* 10 (1990), 71.

83. A fleeting reference in a letter of 8 Oct. 1936 to Dorothy Galton suggests that Mirsky might have known Samuil Borisovich Kagan, the Soviet resident in Britain who controlled the 'climate of treason'; on Kagan, see Andrew Boyle, *The Climate of Treason*, rev. edn (London, 1980). In his autobiographical statement of 1936, as someone who could vouch for his activities before he returned to Russia Mirsky gave the name of one A. F. Neiman, who was attached to the Soviet Embassy; again, the nature of their contacts remains to be discovered (see V. V. Perkhin, 'Odinnadtsat' pisem (1922–1937) i avtobiografiya (1936) D. P. Svyatopolk-Mirskogo', *Russkaya literatura* 1 (1996), 259).

84. Galton, 'Sir Bernard Pares and Slavonic Studies', 485. Vera Traill told me the same thing.

85. Mirsky means the Union of Returnees (*Soyuz vozvrashchentsev*), set up in Paris by the Soviet authorities to stimulate and control pro-Soviet sentiment among the emigration; Sergey Efron later worked for this organization.

86. Cited in Losskaya, *Marina Tsvetaeva v zhizni*, 196.

87. Sir Bernard Pares, *A Wandering Student* (Syracuse, NY, 1948), 291.

88. Mirsky, *Uncollected Writings on Russian Literature*, 364–5.

89. Ibid. 366–7.

90. For the text of this letter, see O. A. Kaznina, 'N. S. Trubetskoy i krizis evraziistva', *Slavyanovedenie* 4 (1995), 89–95.

91. See John Callaghan, *Rajani Palme Dutt: A Study in British Stalinism* (London, 1993), 128–72.

92. Pares, *A Wandering Student*, 291.

93. Unpublished letter, Michael Florinsky Deposit, Bakhmeteff Archive, Columbia University; the reply from Florinsky is from the same source.

94. D. S. Mirsky, 'Bourgeois History and Bourgeois Materialism', *Labour Monthly* 13 (7) (1931), 453–9; 'The Philosophical Discussion in the C.P.S.U. in 1930–31', ibid. 13 (9) (1931), 649–56.

95. D. S. Mirsky, 'The Outlook of Bertrand Russell', *Labour Monthly* 14 (1932), 113–19 (a review of *The Scientific Outlook*); 'Mr Wells Shows His Class', *Labour Monthly* 14 (1932), 383–7 (a review of *The Work, Wealth, and Happiness of Mankind*).

96. Jonathan Rée, *Proletarian Philosophers: Problems in Socialist Culture in Britain, 1900–1940* (Oxford, 1984), 71–2.

97. Gramsci (1891–1937) had been in prison since 1926; he was not in Stalin's GULag, though, but in a prison of Mussolini's, where conditions were not dissimilar from those the leading Russian revolutionaries had enjoyed before 1917. Gramsci wrote to Tatyana, the sister of his Russian wife, Yulka, from Turi prison on 3 Aug. 1931: '[It] is quite surprising how ably Mirsky has made himself master of the central nucleus of Historic Materialism, displaying in the process such a lot of intelligence and penetration. It seems to me that his scientific position is all the more worthy of note and of study, seeing that he shows himself free of certain cultural prejudices and incrustations which infiltrated the field of the theory of history in a parasitic fashion at the end of the last century and the beginning of this one,

in consequence of the great popularity enjoyed by Positivism': *Gramsci's Prison Letters*, trans. and introduced by Hamish Hamilton (London, 1988), 153–4.

98. See Perkhin, 'Odinnadtsat' pisem (1922–1937) i avtobiografiya (1936)', 258.

99. See Nina Lavroukine and Leonid Tchertkov, *D. S. Mirsky: profil critique et bibliographique* (Paris, 1980), 41.

100. See Leopold Labedz, 'Isaac Deutscher's "Stalin": An Unpublished Critique', *Encounter* 52 (1) (1979), 68.

101. On Mirsky and MacDiarmid, see G. S. Smith, 'D. S. Mirsky and Hugh Mac-Diarmid: A Relationship and an Exchange of Letters (1934)', *Slavonica* 2/3 (1996–7), 49–60.

102. See Peter McCarey, *Hugh MacDiarmid and the Russians* (Edinburgh, 1987).

103. C. M. Grieve, 'Modern Russian Literature', *New Age* 37 (8) (25 June 1925), 92; the review is hostile, especially with reference to Mirsky's comments on Chekhov.

104. C. M. Grieve, 'Contemporary Russian Literature', *New Age* 40 (1) (4 Nov. 1926), 9. Here, MacDiarmid is almost entirely positive: 'a model book of its kind. . . . These 330 pages have a readability and, indeed, a raciness any literary historian might envy. I know no parallel to his feat.'

105. M. Gutner (ed.), *Antologiya novoi angliiskoi poezii* (Leningrad, 1937), 392.

106. Hugh MacDiarmid, *In Memoriam James Joyce: From a Vision of a World Language* (Glasgow, 1955); see *The Collected Poems of Hugh MacDiarmid* (2 vols., Manchester, 1993), ii. 736.

107. 'Two Aspects of Revolutionary Nationalism', *Russian Life* 5 (1922), 172–4; 'Russian Post-Revolutionary Nationalism', *Contemporary Review* 124 (1923), 191–8.

108. MacDiarmid was expelled from the Communist Party for nationalist deviation in 1938, and rejoined it—as usual for him, against the grain—in 1956. In between, he rejoined the Scottish National Party (as it had then become) in 1942, and left it in 1948.

109. In an article whose date of writing is unclear, Mirsky described MacDiarmid as 'A radical and Scottish nationalist in politics, a confused vitalist in philosophy': 'Angliiskaya literatura', in *Entsiklopedicheskii slovar' russkogo bibliograficheskogo instituta Granat*, 7th rev. edn, supplementary vol. i (Moscow, 1936), cols. 434–5.

110. *The Collected Poems of Hugh MacDiarmid*, i. 298.

111. *Beatrice Webb's Diaries, 1924–1932*, ed. Margaret Cole (London, 1956), 301. On 7 Jan. 1932 Mirsky informed Miss Galton that the Webbs had invited him for a weekend, and commented: 'This is rather amusing (the idea rather than the fact).'

112. Kingsley Martin, *Father Figures: A First Volume of Autobiography, 1897–1931* (London, 1966), 201.

113. D. S. Mirsky, *The Intelligentsia of Great Britain*, trans. Alec Brown (London, 1935), 205.

114. This delegation to the International History of Science Congress, held in London in the summer of 1931, also visited Cambridge; among its members was Nikolay Bukharin. See Gary Werskey, *The Visible College* (London, 1978), and *Science at the Crossroads: Essays by N. I. Bukharin and Others*, 2nd edn (London, 1971).

115. Mirsky, *The Intelligentsia of Great Britain*, 235–6.

116. See J. W. Boag, P. E. Rubinin, and D. Schoenberg (eds.), *Kapitza in Cambridge and Moscow: Life and Letters of a Russian Physicist* (Amsterdam, 1990).

117. Esther Salaman, 'Prince Mirsky', *Encounter* 54 (1) (1980), 93–4. True to his officer's code, Mirsky doubtless means that the appropriate response would be to call out the lady's husband for allowing her to speak in this way in public.

118. *Understand the Weapon, Understand the Wound: Selected Writings of John Cornford, with some Letters of Frances Cornford*, ed. Jonathan Galassi (Manchester, 1976), 143.

119. Bruce Page, David Leitch, and Phillip Knightly, 'The Cambridge Marxists', in *Philby: The Spy who Betrayed a Generation*, rev. edn (London, 1977), 64–70.

120. Cited in Lavroukine and Tchertkov, *Mirsky*, 41.

121. Mirsky reported to Dorothy Galton that he spoke in Amsterdam on 18 Apr., on what occasion he does not say.

122. On Münzenberg (1889–1940), see Stephen Koch, *Double Lives: Stalin, Willi Münzenberg and the Seduction of the Intellectuals* (London, 1996).
123. Mirsky and Dobb made some sort of proposal to the Comintern about setting up a special section for intellectuals: see Callaghan, *Rajani Palme Dutt*, 133.
124. *The Sickle Side of the Moon: The Letters of Virginia Woolf, v: 1932–1935*, ed. Nigel Nicolson and Joanne Banks (London, 1979), 71.
125. Virginia Woolf, *A Writer's Diary: Being Extracts from the Diary of Virginia Woolf*, ed. Leonard Woolf (London, 1953), 181–2.
126. A persistent rumour insists that there was more to Mirsky's private life than the relationship with Vera Suvchinskaya: 'his unsuccessful marriage to Vera Nikolaevna, Countess Buxhoeveden, which is what drove him to take that desperate deranged step with regard to the "Soviet paradise". I knew Vera Nikolaevna personally, and I know from her personally about these circumstances. She blamed herself for his downfall; every time the conversation turned to "Dima" she would say that she alone was to blame for the fact that he totally gave himself over to those monsters': unpublished letter by Marina Ledkovsky to Olga Kaznina, 10 June 1994, quoted with permission.
127. Gleb Struve, *Russian Literature under Lenin and Stalin, 1917–1953* (London, 1972), 270.
128. Hugh Dalton, *The Fateful Years* (London, 1957), cited in Kingsley Martin, *Editor* (London, 1968), 60. Dalton visited the USSR in 1932, and he was not alone; indeed, 'The entire British intelligentsia has been in Russia this summer', declared Kingsley Martin: *Low's Russian Sketchbook. Drawings by Low, text by Kingsley Martin* (London, 1932), 9. Dalton is mentioned among other leading left-wing politicians as a person to contact in Mirsky's letter to Suvchinsky of 18 Oct. 1928.
129. Letter to Suvchinsky, 8 Oct. 1924. The phrase in Russian is: *Gadkaya prezritel'naya gumannost', zhalost', prezrenie i brezglivost' k chelovechestvu, ni odnoi umnoi mysli.*

7. THE RISING LINE

1. See Barbara Evans Clements, *Bolshevik Women* (Cambridge, 1997), and Beth Holmgren, *Women's Works in Stalin's Time* (Bloomington, 1993), esp. 1–26. For the effect on literature, see Catriona Kelly, 'Class War and the Home Front: From the Revolution to the Death of Stalin (1917–1953)', in her *A History of Russian Women's Writing, 1820–1992* (Oxford, 1994), 227–48.
2. On these women, see Larisa Vasil'eva, *Kremlevskie zheny* (Moscow, 1992).
3. Nadezhda Mandel'shtam, *Vospominaniya* (New York, 1970), 119–20. Anna Larina, the second wife and subsequently official widow of Nikolay Ivanovich Bukharin (1888–1938), the most literary of all the Old Bolshevik bosses, survived to see him rehabilitated in 1988, and even published her memoirs.
4. V. V. Perkhin, 'Odinnadtsat' pisem (1920–1937) i avtobiografiya (1936) D. P. Svyatopolk-Mirskogo', *Russkaya literatura* 1 (1996), 253.
5. Mirsky several times praised Svetlov's famous poem 'Grenada'; see e.g. *Stikhotovoreniya: Stat'i o russkoi poezii*, compiled and ed. G. K. Perkins and G. S. Smith (Berkeley, Calif., 1997), 201. Mirsky dwelt on Olesha's failure to follow up *Envy* (1928) in an article written after his return, 'Yury Olesha', *Literaturnaya gazeta* 69 (385) (2 June 1934), 2. Mirsky's interrogations reveal that he knew Olesha well enough to introduce Norman Jopson to him (see Chapter 9 below). Olesha recorded one particular altercation with Mirsky, which is not dated, in his jottings: see *No Day without a Line: From Notebooks by Yury Olesha*, ed., trans., and with an Introduction by Judson Rosengrant (Evanston, Ill., 1998), 126. Here, Mirsky is said to have struck Olesha with his stick after the latter denied the existence of the ancient world; the pair were reconciled over wine and Caucasian chicken.
6. Leonid Tchertkov, 'L'Œuvre du retour', in Nina Lavroukine and Leonid Tchertkov, *D. S. Mirsky: profil critique et bibliographique* (Paris, 1980), 45.

7. The Institute for History of the Arts was the bastion of Formalism (for Mirsky's review of its most famous publications, see Chapter 4 above, n. 118); it was purged in 1930, and Tynyanov may well have thought Mirsky was indulging in provocation.

8. Korney Chukovsky, *Dnevnik 1930–1969* (Moscow, 1994), 126.

9. See inter alia 'The Present State of Russian Letters', repr. in D. S. Mirsky, *Uncollected Writings on Russian Literature*, ed. G. S. Smith (Berkeley, Calif., 1989), 255–6. Soon after his return to Russia, however, Mirsky called Tynyanov 'second-rate' as a historical novelist; see D. Mirsky, 'Za khudozhnika-istorika', *Oktyabr'* 7 (1934), 222–3; Chukovsky perhaps misremembered a response to this latter publication.

10. For Pasternak's reaction to these missives in his letters to members of his family, see Boris Pasternak, *Pis'ma k roditelyam i sestram* (2 vols., Stanford, Calif., 1998), per index. In particular, Mirsky sent a copy of his *Encyclopaedia Britannica* article of 1929 to Pasternak, who boasted about the positive reference to himself in a letter of 27 February 1930 to Vissarion Sayanov, the editor of the Leningrad journal *The Star*: see B. L. Pasternak, 'Pis'ma k V. M. Sayanovu', *Ezhegodnik rukopisnogo otdela Pushkinskogo doma na 1977 god* (Leningrad, 1979), 197. A. V. Lavrov's note on this letter (198) constitutes one of the earliest objective references to Mirsky in the USSR after his rehabilitation. Mirsky had a cordial relationship with Sayanov, probably not without Pasternak's intermediacy: see Perkhin, 'Odinnadtsat' pisem', 245–6.

11. Letter by Pasternak to Akhmatova of 19 Oct. 1932, in *Iz istorii sovetskoi literatury 1920–1930-kh godov* (Moscow, 1983), 659–60.

12. See Lazar' Fleishman, *Boris Pasternak v tridtsatye gody* (Jerusalem, 1984). This book set a new standard for the interpretation of Soviet literary history in the 1930s. Fleishman's findings have been amply supported during the 1990s by publications of hitherto secret documents; see esp. D. L. Babichenko (ed.), *'Schast'e literatury': Gosudarstvo i pisateli 1925–1938: Dokumenty* (Moscow, 1997). Some points of detail in Fleishman's account have been amplified on the basis of archive materials by K. M. Polivanov, 'Zametki i materialy k "politicheskoi" biografii Borisa Pasternaka (1934–1937)', *De Visu* 4 (1993), 70–9.

13. Perkhin, 'Odinnadtsat' pisem', 259.

14. It is clear from his travel writings that Nikulin was in France in 1928, and in Spain in 1929, but his accounts of what he was doing are so politically correct (for the Khrushchev period) that very little useful information can be derived from them. He was clearly up to something other than simple tourism. See Lev Nikulin, *Lyudi i stranstviya: Vospominaniya i vstrechi* (Moscow, 1962). Nikulin was the author of a fictionalized account of the 'Trust' (see Chapter 6 above).

15. I. E. Babel, 'The Story of My Dovecote', *Slavonic and East European Review* 10 (28) (1931), 1–11. Mirsky had also reprinted the Russian text of this story in *Vyorsts*.

16. Mandel'shtam, *Vospominaniya*, 341.

17. For an account of Pilnyak's last years, see Gary Browning, 'From Accusation to Arrest', in his *Boris Pilniak: Scythian at a Typewriter* (Ann Arbor, Mich., 1985), 51–76.

18. For a contextualized view of this development, see Mark Banting, Catriona Kelly, and James Riordan, 'Sexuality', in Catriona Kelly and David Shepherd (eds.), *Russian Cultural Studies: An Introduction* (Oxford, 1998), 311–51.

19. For the first complete publication of this review and a discussion of its significance, see Mirsky, *Stikhotvoreniya: Stat'i o russkoi poezii*, 288–94.

20. Perkhin, 'Odinnadtsat' pisem', 259.

21. Fleishman, *Boris Pasternak v tridtsatye gody*, 256.

22. Dmitri Mirsky, *The Intelligentsia of Great Britain*, trans. Alec Brown (London, 1935), 114.

23. Cited in David Lane, 'Social Classes and Equality', in R. W. Davies (ed.), *The Soviet Union*, 2nd edn (Boston, etc., 1989), 81.

24. Perkhin, 'Odinnadtsat' pisem', 258.

25. The Electrograd was the major engineering factory in Moscow, officially regarded as a model enterprise.

26. In June 1936 Mirsky was engaged on a translation of *Paradise Lost* into Russian for the

Academia publishing house, but it seems not to have been completed; see Perkhin, 'Odin-nadtsat' pisem', 259.

27. On Chukovskaya (1907–96), see Holmgren, *Women's Works in Stalin's Time*. Chukovskaya's diary is significantly less guarded than her father's, especially on the subject of Anna Akhmatova.

28. This is not the famous Soviet novelist Fyodor Gladkov (1883–1958), but the much more obscure playwright (b. 1912), whose most interesting work is his *Meetings with Pasternak*, trans. Max Hayward (London, 1977).

29. Aleksandr Gladkov, 'Iz poputnykh zapisei', *Voprosy literatury* 9 (1976), 184. Leonid Tchertkov cites a long extract from a letter Gladkov wrote to him about his relationship with Mirsky, including a meeting with Mirsky and Olesha, both in their cups, in the Aurora (now Budapest) restaurant just before Mirsky was arrested: see Tchertkov: 'L'Œuvre du retour', 49–50.

30. G. Munblit, *Rasskazy o pisatelyakh*, 2nd rev. edn (Moscow, 1976), 36.

31. Ibid. 37.

32. *Like It Was: The Diaries of Malcolm Muggeridge*, selected and ed. John Bright-Holmes (London, 1981), 24. Malcolm Muggeridge (1903–90) was a Cambridge graduate; on his life, see Richard Ingrams, *Muggeridge: The Biography* (London, 1995). Muggeridge made several references in his writings to his acquaintanceship with Mirsky at this time; see esp. *Chronicles of Wasted Time*, i: *The Green Stick* (London, 1972), 236–9.

33. Muggeridge, *Like it Was*, 24.

34. Muggeridge refers to these people as 'Cholerton'; but he obviously has in mind the *Christian Science Monitor* Moscow correspondent William Henry Chamberlin (1897–1969) and his Russian-born wife, Sonia (1891–1968). In his *Russia's Iron Age* (London, 1935) Chamberlin gives a vivid journalistic account of the USSR during the period 1929–34; his *Confessions of an Individualist* (New York, 1940), 63–86, 136–59, and 182–201, contain a more personal view. Neither account mentions Mirsky. For Muggeridge's impressions of the Chamberlins, see *Chronicles of Wasted Time*, i. 232–3, 240–2.

35. Muggeridge, *Like it Was*, 60.

36. Ibid. 64. This 'Polish writer', whose name Muggeridge obviously cannot remember, may easily be identified as Bruno Jasienski (1901–38), who left Poland for Paris in 1925 and joined the Communist Party. He was extradited from France because his novel *I Burn Paris* was deemed to be subversive. Jasienski came to Moscow in 1929; he became the secretary of the International Association of Worker Writers and edited a Polish-language newspaper. He joined the CPSU in 1930. In the same year Jasienski began writing his works in Russian rather than Polish or French. He was a member of the Organizing Committee of the Union of Writers, and a founder member of its Directorate. He eventually published a number of significant novels that satisfactorily expounded the current Party line when they came out but soon became involuntarily dissident documents when the line changed. Like most of the other refugee intellectuals in Stalin's Russia, Jasienski fell victim to the Great Purge; he was arrested soon after Mirsky, on 31 July 1937. After extensive interrogation and an appeal against the use of 'illegal methods' during it, Jasienski was, according to some sources, shot on 17 Sept. 1938. He remained an unperson until the first wave of rehabilitations after the death of Stalin, on 24 Dec. 1955; as a Party member he was rehabilitated much more speedily than the 'civilian' Mirsky.

37. Muggeridge, *Like it Was*, 65.

38. Mirsky published a generally favourable review of Aragon's novel *Les Cloches de Bâle* (Paris, 1934): 'Bazel'skie kolokola', *Literaturnaya gazeta* 171 (487) (22 Dec. 1934), 3.

39. See Elizabeth Klosty Beaujour, *Alien Tongues: Bilingual Russian Writers of the 'First' Emigration* (Ithaca, NY, 1989); and Lachlan Mackennon, *The Lives of Elsa Triolet* (London, 1992).

40. Malcolm Muggeridge, *Winter in Moscow* (London, 1934); on Mirsky, see pp. 222–7.

41. Ibid. 223–4.

42. Ibid. 225.

43. Ibid. 226-7.
44. Mandel'shtam, *Vospominaniya*, 175-6.
45. Mirsky's attitude to this myth before he became a Stalinist was cited in Chapter 5: 'Let's leave that to the Yids.'
46. See G. S. Smith, 'Literature and the Arts,' in R. W. Davies (ed.), *The Soviet Union*, 2nd edn (Boston, etc., 1989), 155-69. The standard Western accounts of Socialist Realism in literature are somewhat vitiated by being confined to discussion of the major prose genres, and by taking the 'method' seriously in aesthetic terms, a procedure that rightly evoked and evokes ribald wonderment among Soviet and ex-Soviet writers. In her *Socialist Realism: An Impossible Aesthetic?* (Stanford, Calif., 1992), Régine Robin captures something of the eyewash-saturated nature of contemporary discussions of the subject.
47. For a concise summary of the career and writings of Radek (1885-1939) and some previously unknown evidence concerning his relations with the literary world, see Boris Frezinsky, 'Literaturnaya pochta Karla Radeka', *Voprosy literatury* 3 (1998), 278-316.
48. See Mary Buckley, 'The Family, Divorce, Abortion and Motherhood', in her *Women and Ideology in the Soviet Union* (Ann Arbor, Mich., 1989), 128-36. Despite the campaign against it, abortion remained the primary method of birth control in the USSR.
49. See Banting et al., 'Sexuality'.
50. See Adele Lindenmeyr, untitled note, *Women East-West* 49 (1997), 2.
51. Robert Conquest, *The Great Terror: A Reassessment* (London, 1990), 31.
52. See Anna Akhmatova, *My Half Century*, ed. Ronald Meyer (Ann Arbor, Mich., 1992), 101-2.
53. Elena Feliksovna Usievich (1893-1968), one of very few prominent female literary critics of the time, was a Party member of long standing who travelled back to Russia from political exile with Lenin in the famous sealed train; she appears to have survived the Purges unscathed. On her activities, see V. V. Perkhin, *Russkaya literaturnaya kritika 1930-kh godov* (St Petersburg, 1997), esp. 169-71.
54. A revealing document in this connection is the appeal made to the Central Committee on 22 Apr. 1932 by the official bard of the Party, Demyan Bedny (who lived in the Kremlin), to be allowed to continue his subscription to some of the major Russian-language *émigré* serials: see Babichenko, '*Schast'e literatury*', 117-18.
55. Bernard Pares, *A Wandering Student* (Syracuse, NY, 1948), 291.
56. Ibid. 327.
57. Fox was writing to complain about the irregular and inefficient contacts between the British section of Writers International and the Moscow centre, the International Association of Revolutionary Writers; see *Iz istorii mezhdunarodnogo ob"edineniya revolyutsionnykh pisatelei (MORP)* (Moscow, 1969), 391.
58. Perkhin, 'Odinnadtsat' pisem', 255.
59. Mandel'shtam, *Vospominaniya*, 165. The line comes from a variant of Mandelshtam's 'Ya budu metat'sya po taboru ulitsy temnoi' (1925). The Yiddish poet Perets Davidovich Markish (1895-1952) survived the purges of the 1930s only to be executed along with the other members of the Yiddish sector of the Union of Writers during Stalin's final paroxysm. In 1936 Mirsky said: 'Soviet Jewish poetry possesses a poet of all-Union and therefore world significance, Perets Markish, whose enormous epic power we may perceive so far only dimly through the small extracts from his long poem about the Dneproges that have been translated into Russian': *Stikhotvoreniya: Stikhi o russkoi poezii*, 281. Markish was the only man who visited Nadezhda Mandelshtam after her husband was arrested in May 1934.
60. Mirsky, *The Intelligentsia of Great Britain*, 112-14.
61. T. A. Jackson, 'Mirsky Dissects Our Intelligentsia', *Daily Worker*, 15 May 1935.
62. This is broadly speaking the main point made by Ivor Brown, *Observer*, 6 Apr. 1935; John Cournos, *Yale Review* n.s. 25 (Winter 1936), 425; Malcolm Cowley, *New Republic* 84 (23 Aug. 1935), 14; Raymond Mortimer, *New Statesman and Nation* 9 (420) (23 Mar. 1935); V. S. Pritchett, *Christian Science Monitor*, 8 May 1935, 11; Edward Shanks, *Sunday Times*,

6 Apr. 1935; and Stephen Spender, *Spectator* 154 (22 Mar. 1935), 498; Spender's review is generally the most positive.

63. Edmund Wilson, 'Comrade Prince', *Encounter* 5 (1) (1955), 11.

64. Olga Kaznina and G. S. Smith, 'D. S. Mirsky to Maksim Gor'ky: Sixteen Letters (1928–1934)', *Oxford Slavonic Papers* n.s. 26 (1993), 100–1. For Mirsky's review of this book, see Chapter 6 above.

65. 'Zhmu vashu ruku, dorogoi tovarishch', *Novyi mir* 9 (1997), 183.

66. Babichenko, *'Schast'e literatury'*, contains some fascinating documents in which officials of the Union request financial allocations for their activities from State and Party bodies.

67. M. *Gor'ky i sovetskaya pechat'*, i (Moscow, 1964), 239.

68. V. M. Kozhevnikov and P. A. Nikolaev (eds.), *Literaturnyi entsiklopedicheskii slovar'* (Moscow, 1987), 195.

69. Tchertkov, 'L'Œuvre du retour', 45.

70. The gigantic State Publishing House for Artistic Literature (GIKhL) was founded in 1930 on the basis of the old 'Land and Factory' house, which had been the headquarters of 'proletarian' literature during the 1920s.

71. S. Petrov, review of T. Smollett, *Sobranie sochinenii* (Moscow, 1934), *Khudozhestvennaya literatura* 12 (1935), 57–9.

72. See the announcement in *Literaturnaya gazeta* 71 (387) (1934), 1. The first list of admissions was published on 14 May 1934; it begins with the members of the Membership Commission itself: Gorky, Yudin, Pavlenko, Afinogenov, Vsevolod Ivanov, Fyodor Gladkov, Aseev, and Fedin. The remaining 12 include Bezymensky, Jasienski, Kirshon, and Ilf and Petrov. Fadeev, Demyan Bedny, and Stavsky headed the second list (15 May), which also included Pilnyak, Pasternak, and Tikhonov. The third list came out on 17 May, bringing the total to 90. The order of acceptance does not seem to correspond with the eventual order of membership numbers. The lists of acceptances are accompanied by fairly long lists of rejections; evidently, in view of the privileges in the offing, some ordinary people chanced their arm.

73. 'Books and Films in Russia', repr. in Mirsky, *Uncollected Writings on Russian Literature*, 327.

74. Fleishman, *Boris Pasternak*, 112–52.

75. See Loren R. Graham, *The Ghost of the Executed Engineer: Technology and the Fall of the Soviet Union* (Cambridge, Mass., and London, 1993), 49–65.

76. For a reproduction of the adjusted image, see Archie Brown, Michael Kaser, and G. S. Smith (eds.), *The Cambridge Encyclopedia of Russia and the Former Soviet Union* (Cambridge, 1994), 111.

77. Sidney and Beatrice Webb, *Soviet Communism: A New Civilisation?* (2 vols., London, 1935), ii. 591.

78. See Mikhail Geller, *Kontsentratsionnyi mir i sovetskaya literatura* (London, 1971), 133–57, esp. 151.

79. M. Gor'ky et al. (eds.), *Belomorsko-Baltiiskii kanal imeni Stalina: Istoriya stroitel'stva* (Moscow, 1934), 67–130. On Mirsky's dealings with Korabelnikov, Pertsov, and Shklovsky, see Chapter 8 below. Shklovsky's brother Vladimir was a prisoner working on the Canal, and the two met during the writer's visit.

80. Aleksandr Solzhenitsyn, *Arkhipelag GULag*, iii and iv (Paris, 1974), 79–102.

81. Aleksandr Avdeenko, 'Otluchenie', *Znamya* 3 (1989), 12. Elsewhere in this account, Avdeenko gives a vivid account of the I Congress of Writers and literary life in the later 1930s. He was denounced and expelled from the Party in 1940, but survived service as a war correspondent and was reinstated in 1944.

82. Ibid. 17–18.

83. Mirsky uses the same word, *proizvol*, that his mother had used in her diary to indentify the most objectionable aspect of the Tsarist regime; see Chapter 2 above.

84. Mirsky means 'BBK', the abbreviation for 'Baltic–White Sea Canal'; that he should have meant 'GPU' is too much to believe.

85. Avdeenko, 'Otluchenie', 18.

86. *The White Sea Canal: Being an Account of the Construction of the New Canal Between the White Sea and the Baltic Sea* (London, 1935).

87. *Vtoroi plenum pravleniya Soyuza sovetskikh pisatelei SSSR, mart 1935g. Stenograficheskii otchet* (Moscow, 1935), 403–8.

88. See Barbara Heldt, 'Motherhood in a Cold Climate: The Poetry and Career of Maria Shkap-skaya', in Jane Costlow, Stephanie Sandler, and Judith Vowles (eds.), *Sexuality and the Body in Russian Culture* (Stanford, Calif., 1993), 237–54.

89. *Vtoroi plenum*, 453.

90. Ibid. 454.

91. Irma Kudrova, 'Poslednee "delo" Sergeya Efrona', *Zvezda* 10 (1992), 129.

92. See Vl. Voronov, 'Pervyi s″ezd pisatelei', in *Pervyi vsesoyuznyi s″ezd sovetskikh pisatelei 1934, Stenograficheskii otchet: Prilozheniya* (Moscow, 1990), 3–8.

93. According to a note he left in the visitors' book, Mirsky was in Tbilisi from 27 Aug. to 11 Nov. 1934, staying at the home of Titsian Tabidze, who was away at the time; see Galina Medzmariashvili, *Salomeya Andronikashvili na fone svoego pokoleniya* (Moscow, 1998), 5–6.

94. See G. S. Smith, 'An Annotated Bibliography of D. S. Mirsky's Writings, 1932–1937', in *Uncollected Writings on Russian Literature*, 68–85.

95. In 1936 Mirsky revised Yu. P. Anisimov's translation of *Othello*, of which he had a high opinion; see Perkhin, 'Odinnadtsat′ pisem', 250–1; it was performed at the Theatre of Realism in Moscow, directed by N. P. Okhlopkov (1900–67). Mirsky wrote to Galton on 27 Mar. 1936: 'I have just been recasting a new version of *Othello* and I find that writing blank verse as good as anyone's is very easy. I think I am going to turn poet.'

96. D. Mirsky, 'O formalizme', in M. Gor′ky et al. (eds.), *God shestnadtsatyi: Al′manakh vtoroi* (Moscow, 1933), 490–517.

97. 'Baratynsky', repr. in Mirsky, *Stikhotvoreniya: Stat′i o russkoi poezii*, 243–80; see also Mirsky's letter to Vissarion Sayanov of 12 Feb. 1934, in Perkhin, 'Odinnadtsat′ pisem', 245–6.

98. 'Novye izdaniya starykh poetov: Stat′ya 1-ya', *Literaturnaya gazeta* 43 (534) (4 Aug. 1935), 2–3; 'Novye izdaniya starykh poetov: Stat′ya 2-ya', ibid. 44 (535) (9 Aug. 1935), 2–3.

99. 'Voina i mir', repr. in Mirsky, *Uncollected Writings on Russian Literature*, 339–57.

100. Letter of 30 Jan. 1935; *M. Gor′ky i sovetskaya pechat′*, i (Moscow, 1964), 310.

101. 'Angliiskaya literatura', in *Entsiklopedicheskii slovar′ bibliograficheskogo instituta Granat*, dopolnitel′nyi tom 1 (Moscow, 1936), cols. 403–43.

102. M. Gutner (ed.), *Antologiya novoi angliiskoi poezii* (Leningrad, 1937). On Mirsky's dealings with the poet and translator Elizaveta Polonskaya concerning this project, see G. S. Smith, 'D. S. Mirsky: Two Letters to Elizaveta Polonskaia (1935, 1936) on Translating Kipling and Christina Rossetti', *Slavonic and East European Review* 73 (3) (1995), 490–8.

103. See Joseph Brodsky, 'To Please a Shadow', in his *Less Than One: Selected Essays* (London, 1986), 357–83. Brodsky believed that the book really was edited by Gutner, even though Mirsky's authorship was widely known in Soviet literary circles; see also 'W. H. Auden', in Solomon Volkov, *Conversations with Joseph Brodsky* (New York, etc., 1998), 129. There might have been an earlier meeting between Auden and Brodsky if history had taken a dif-ferent course: on 25 Jan. 1934 Auden, through Dorothy Galton, sent some books to Moscow and also asked for a job teaching English in the USSR; see Charles Osborne, *WHA: The Life of a Poet* (New York and London, 1979), 103–4. Mirsky is not identified in this source, but the person in Moscow concerned can only be he.

104. The reception of current Western literature in the USSR during the Stalin period has still to be adequately described and discussed; despite the forbidding deadweight of dogma and outright falsification, and the debilitating isolation from direct knowledge, there were still some critics and scholars who, like Mirsky, did what they could in good faith to inform the Soviet reader.

105. D. Mirsky, 'Realizm', in *Literaturnaya entsiklopediya*, ix (Moscow, 1935), cols. 548–76. On the subsequent history of this article, see Chapter 9 below.

106. D. Mirsky, 'Romantizm', ibid. x (Munich, 1991), cols. 17–39.
107. 'Barokko v angliiskoi literature', in D. S. Mirsky, *Stat'i o literature* (Moscow, 1987), 21–70. Two typescript synopses on this subject by Mirsky have survived in Zhirmunsky's archive: one for a book called *Seventeenth-Century English Literature*, St Petersburg, PFA RAN, *fond* 1001, *opis'* 4, *edinitsa khraneniya* 51; and a synopsis called 'The Baroque in English Literature (Theses)', ibid., *edinitsa khraneniya* 50.
108. A. D. Miller and D. P. Mirsky (eds.), *Anglo-russkii slovar'* (Moscow, 1936).

8. THE FALLING LINE

1. D. S. Mirsky, 'Eduard Bagritsky', *Literaturnaya gazeta* 23 (338) (26 Feb. 1934), 2; 'Pamyati Bagritskogo', *Khudozhestvennaya literatura* 3 (1934), 1–2; 'Ob Eduarde Bagritskom', repr. in *Stikhotvoreniya: Stat'i o russkoi poezii*, compiled and ed. G. K. Perkins and G. S. Smith (Berkeley, Calif., 1997; hereafter *SSRP*) 162–76; 'Eduard Bagritsky', repr. ibid. 177–86.
2. The provocatively a-Soviet obituary of Bely jointly published by Pilnyak, Pasternak, and Sannikov caused a scandal that helped seal the fate of Pilnyak; see Lazar' Fleishman, *Boris Pasternak v tridtsatye gody* (Jerusalem, 1984), 154–8.
3. Mirsky is mentioned in one of these pieces, practically the only living person to be so honoured. Tsvetaeva is speculating about the referents of a salon romance in folkloric style about the return of a bridegroom, and eventually she gives up: 'Anyway, for a romance they were strange words, and as Svyatopolk-Mirsky used to say, "I'm getting lost in guesses"': 'Mat' i muzyka', an essay written in the summer of 1934 and published the following year; see Marina Tsvetaeva, *Sobranie sochinenii v semi tomakh* (Moscow, 1997), v, pt. 1, 22. The expression that Tsvetaeva recalled (*teryayus' v dogadkakh*) is a standard phrase in literary Russian, but Mirsky does seem to have been fond of it; see his letters to Suvchinsky of 12 Dec. 1926 and 22 Nov. 1927.
4. For details, see G. S. Smith, 'An Annotated Bibliography of D. S. Mirsky's Writings, 1932–1937', in *Uncollected Writings on Russian Literature*, ed. G. S. Smith (Berkeley, Calif., 1989), 368–85.
5. Mirsky's part in these controversies was first remarked on by Gleb Struve, whose summaries of the published documents are remarkably acute: see *Soviet Russian Literature* (London, 1935), *25 years of Soviet Literature* (London, 1944), *Soviet Russian Literature, 1917–1950* (London, 1951), and *Russian Literature under Lenin and Stalin, 1917–1953* (London, 1972), esp. 270–329.
6. In private discourse, however, irreverent wit seems to have persisted, even in the worst years; see in particular Natal'ya Sokolova, 'Iz starykh tetradei, 1938–1941', *Voprosy literatury* 2 (1998), 356–65, and the student skit by B. Pines, Yu. Levin, and I. Frenkel', 'Dantes vystrelil: Fantasticheskaya povest'', *Zvezda* 8 (1994), 194–202, in which Mirsky makes an appearance.
7. 'O nekotorykh voprosakh izucheniya russkoi literatury XVIII v.', *Literaturnoe nasledstvo* 9/10 (1933), 501–9. This article was the subject of what appears to be the earliest published discussion of Mirsky's work after he was rehabilitated: see P. N. Berkov, *Vvedenie v izuchenie istorii russkoi literatury XVIII veka* (Leningrad, 1964), 196–203. Mirsky is taken to task here for vulgar Marxism by a surviving vulgar Marxist, but primly now, instead of in the violent, denunciatory style of the 1930s.
8. The Formalists, who by that time had voluntarily rather than by compulsion abandoned the extremism of their early work, escaped arrest during the Great Purge; they were publicly humiliated and deprived of their academic jobs as Jews rather than Formalists during the anti-Semitic purge of academic life in Leningrad by Andrey Zhdanov in the late 1940s. Gukovsky was first exiled and then arrested, and died of a heart attack at the Lubyanka while awaiting interrogation.

9. 'Otvet I. Sergievskomu i V. Desnitskomu', *Literaturnoe nasledstvo* 19/21 (1935), 645–9; Desnitsky had the final word, though, and at greater length: see ibid. 617–44.

10. D. Mirsky, 'Problema Pushkina', *Literaturnoe nasledstvo* 16/18 (1934), 91–112; there is a partial translation of this article in D. J. Richards and C. R. S. Cockrell (eds.), *Russian Views of Pushkin* (Oxford, 1976), 163–9.

11. Mirsky, 'Problema Pushkina', 95.

12. See Vas. Gippius, 'Problema Pushkina (po povodu stat'i D. Mirskogo "Problema Pushkina")', *Vremennik Pushkinskoi komissii* 1 (1936), 253–61. In his turn, Gippius was taken to task for the weakness of this article, by the same critic who had savaged Mirsky in the controversy about the eighteenth century; see I. Sergievsky, 'Pushkinskii vremennik', *Literaturnaya gazeta*, 26 Feb. 1936.

13. The only meeting between Stenich and Mirsky that I have been able to fix took place in Moscow on 16 Sept. 1935: G. S. Smith, 'D. S. Mirsky to Dorothy Galton: Thirty-Nine Letters from Moscow (1932–1937)', *Oxford Slavonic Papers* n.s. 29 (1996), 116. On Stenich, see Pasternak's letter to Raisa Lomonosova of 22 Nov. 1932, in Christopher Barnes and Richard Davies, '"Neotsenimyi podarok": Perepiska Pasternakov i Lomonosovykh (1925–1970)', *Minuvshee* 16 (1994), 198; and L. F. Katsis, 'V. Stenich: stikhi "russkogo dendi"', *Literaturnoe obozrenie* 5/6 (1996), 65–6. Stenich's end was particularly lamentable; after his arrest, 'for a packet of cigarettes [he] would sign any sort of testimony': see Nikolay Zabolotsky, 'The Story of My Imprisonment', trans. Robin Milner-Gulland, in *Selected Poems*, ed. Daniel Weissbort (Manchester, 1999), 208.

14. Aleksandr Gladkov has left a vivid account of the motley colony of foreign cultural figures in Moscow during the late 1920s and early 1930s; besides Aragon, they included a German thespian referred to simply as 'Fritz'; one Friedrich Wolf; the Hindu poet and dramatist Es-Habib Wafa; the Turkish artist Abi; the Japanese critic Saki Sano; the American Communist ballerina 'Jenny', who married the Soviet dramatist Afinogenov; the Chinese Emi Sao; and the Hungarian poet Antal Gadasz. There was a club for political *émigrés*, directed by Friedrich Platen, who came to Russia in the sealed train with Lenin: 'Iz poputnykh zapisei', *Voprosy literatury* 9 (1976), 184–5.

15. Mirsky was in at the beginning of the Soviet canonization of Aldington (1892–1962), including nine poems by him in his anthology of modern English verse—more than any other poet except Browning, Hardy, and Yeats—and also supplying a preface to the translation of Aldington's novel *The Colonel's Daughter* (Moscow, 1935).

16. There is still no adequate study of this activity. Legends about it were rife in the USSR, their principal focus being the creation of Russian 'translations' from non-existent 'originals' in obscure languages.

17. See 'Odisseya russkogo "Ulissa"', *Inostrannaya literatura* 1 (1990), 172–92, a wide-ranging discussion about the reception of Joyce in Russia involving such experts as Neil Cornwell, Ekaterina Genieva, and Emily Tall.

18. 'Dzhems Dzhois', *God shestnadtsatyi: Al'manakh pervyi* (Moscow, 1933), 428–50, trans. in *International Literature* 1 (1934), 92–102. At the I Congress of Writers, no less a person than Karl Radek made some provocative statements about Joyce; he (or his ghost-writing minion) had clearly read Mirsky's article.

19. A complete translation of *Ulysses* into Russian was only published in 1995, after endless compromises. On the history of Joyce translation in Russia, see Neil Cornwell, *James Joyce and the Russians* (Basingstoke and London, 1992), and for the story of the eventual publication of *Ulysses*, see idem, 'More on Joyce and Russia: or *Ulysses* on the Moscow River', *Joyce Studies Annual 1994* (Austin, Tex., 1994), 175–86.

20. 'Ob "Ulisse"', *Literaturnyi sovremennik* 11 (1935), 115–33. The translation was of part ii, chs. 1 and 2 of *Ulysses*. On the history of this translation, see Cornwell, *James Joyce and the Russians*, 107–27.

21. Cited from V. Vishnevsky, *Stat'i, dnevniki, pis'ma* (Moscow, 1961), 322, in Lazar' Fleishman, *Boris Pasternak v dvadtsatye gody* (Munich, 1980), 268.

22. Vs. Vishnevsky, 'Znat' zapad!', *Literaturnyi kritik* 7 (1933), 80–95.

23. For a spine-chilling example of Vishnevsky's self-serving style of denunciation masquerading as Party duty, in this case calculated to destroy S. B. Reizin, the editor of the Leningrad journal *The Banner*, see Vishnevsky's letter to V. P. Stavsky of 20 Nov. 1937 in D. L. Babichenko (ed.), *'Schast'e literatury': Gosudarstvo i pisateli 1925–1938: Dokumenty* (Moscow, 1997), 256–63. However, Vishnevsky made a substantial monthly donation to Mandelshtam while the poet was in exile in Voronezh; see Nadezhda Mandel'shtam, *Vospominaniya* (New York, 1970), 280.

24. 'The History of a Liberation', in Mirsky, *Uncollected Writings on Russian Literature*, 364. Mirsky declared at a public meeting in Paris in 1928 that he would give the whole of Bunin for just *The Rout*; see Mark Slonim, 'O Marine Tsvetaevoi', *Novyi zhurnal* 104 (1971), 158. At this same meeting, according to Slonim, Mirsky also said that nobody would be reading Chekhov in ten years' time.

25. Yudin (1899–1968) was a Central Committee apparatchik who had absolutely no connection with literature; he had been inserted as the leader of the Party fraction in the Organizing Committee of the Union of Writers.

26. *Pravda*, 8 May 1934, 2, cited in Fleishman, *Boris Pasternak v tridtsatye gody*, 193.

27. See John and Carol Garrard, *Inside the Soviet Writers' Union* (London, 1990), 52–3, 56–8. Vladimir Petrovich Stavsky (1900–43; he was killed on active service) was another party apparatchik, but he had a tenuous literary connection, having served as Secretary of RAPP from 1928 to 1933. He was General Secretary of the Union of Writers from 1936 to 1941.

28. D. Mirsky, 'Zamysel i vypolnenie', *Literaturnaya gazeta* 80 (396), 24 June 1934, 2–3.

29. V. V. Perkhin, 'Odinnadtsat' pisem (1920–1937) i avtobiografiya (1936) D. P. Svyatopolk-Mirskogo', *Russkaya literatura* 1 (1996), 253. G. M. Korabelnikov (1905–96) was expelled from the Union of Writers in 1937 and re-admitted in 1949, apparently after surviving a spell in the camps. He had been in the same 'brigade' as Mirsky for the White Sea Canal project. Mirsky was to take a similar line about the Fadeev business when he was interrogated: see Chapter 9 below.

30. Cited from previously unpublished sources by Perkhin, 'Odinnadtsat' pisem', 255.

31. An assessment included by Mirsky at about the same time in the only article he published in England after going back to Russia reads like a military charge sheet: 'Meichik, the individualist, the young man brought up on "human values", dreaming of abstract heroism, but afraid of blood and incapable even of keeping himself tidy in bush warfare, or properly looking after his horse—an ineffectual individualist, who from sheer discouragement and offence becomes a traitor': see 'Tendencies of the Modern Russian Novel', repr. in *Uncollected Writings on Russian Literature*, 330.

32. Struve, *Russian Literature under Lenin and Stalin*, 270.

33. Quoted in Fleishman, *Boris Pasternak v tridtsatye gody*, 193.

34. I have been unable to trace the second of these articles. Kosarev was the head of the Komsomol.

35. See *Literaturnaya gazeta*, 10 Mar. 1993, 6.

36. Cited in Perkhin, 'Odinnadtsat' pisem', 255.

37. Ibid. 253. I have discovered no further information about Mirsky's relationship with the Jasienskis, except that in the summer of 1936, M. Kanavez (the secretary of the high Party official Raskolnikov) met Mirsky at Leonov's, and Mrs Jasienski was also present: see M. Kanavez, 'Moya zhizn' s Raskol'nikovym', *Minuvshee* 7 (1989), 95–6.

38. M. Gor'ky, 'Literaturnye zabavy', in his *O literature* (Moscow, 1935), 357. For an argument that Gorky was trying to reconcile Stalin and the oppositionists at this time, see Robert Conquest, *The Great Terror: A Reassessment* (London, 1991), 73.

39. See E. Bykova-Lugovskaya and M. Nogteva, '"Nad zemlei vstayushchii Orion": Perepiska V. Lugovskogo s A. Fadeevym', *Literaturnoe obozrenie* 7 (1981), 111: 'But if a book [-carrying] camel [*knizhnyi verblyud*] like Mirsky has given [your] work its due, that means it really must be *good!*'

40. Fadeev was a confidant of Boris Pasternak, his neighbour in the writer's village Peredelkino;

Pasternak evidently regarded him as an honest and sincere person rather than a cynical careerist.

41. K. Chukovsky, *Dnevnik 1930–1969* (Moscow, 1994), 119.

42. Ibid. 482. Schiller's ballad about Polycrates' ring was translated into Russian by Zhukovsky; see 'Polikratov persten'' (1831), in V. A. Zhukovsky, *Stikhotvoreniya* (Leningrad, 1956), 422–5.

43. Chukovsky, *Dnevnik 1930–1969*, 119–20.

44. The echo of Thelonius Monk is surely unintentional.

45. John Lehmann, *The Whispering Gallery: Autobiography I* (London, 1955), 293. Mirsky reviewed Lehmann's collection *The Noise of History* (London, 1934), in *Internatsional'naya literatura* 8 (1935), 174–5, giving him some haughty advice about how to turn himself into a real revolutionary poet. He also included a poem by Lehmann in his anthology of 1937.

46. D. S. Mirsky, 'Politika i estetika (K plenumu pravleniya SSP. Obsuzhdaem voprosy kritiki)', *Literaturnaya gazeta* 17 (490), 28 Dec. 1934, 2.

47. K. M. Polivanov, 'Zametki i materialy k "politicheskoi" biografii Borisa Pasternaka (1934–1937)', *De Visu* 4 (1993), 71–2.

48. *Vtoroi plenum pravleniya Soyuza sovetskikh pisatelei SSSR, mart 1935g. Stenograficheskii otchet* (Moscow, 1935).

49. Shcherbakov (1901–45) was a Party apparatchik pure and simple. He had first worked at local level under his brother-in-law, the dreaded Andrey Zhdanov (1896–1948). When he was put in charge of the new Secretariat of the Union of Writers in 1934, Shcherbakov had no experience of literature, professional or amateur; he was not even a delegate to the founding Congress. Nadezhda Mandelshtam recognized in him the earliest example of a new type of high Soviet official, the 'grandee' (*vel'mozha*), who expected explicit deference and always spoke *de haut en bas*; see her *Vospominaniya*, 147–8.

50. Stetsky (1896–1939) had been a Party activist since his youth; he had supported Bukharin in the power wars of the late 1920s, but emerged unscathed to become in 1930 the head of the Culture and Propaganda Department of the Central Committee, i.e. the biggest boss in the field, compared with whom the officials of the Writers' Union were minnows. He was shot before he had much opportunity to enjoy his perks.

51. Bespalov (1900–37) served on the editorial boards of several central journals, and in 1934 became chief editor of the principal literary publishing house, Goslitizdat. He was soon to be rewarded with one of the new writers' apartments in Lavrushensky pereulok; Mirsky failed to get one. Bespalov was executed soon after being arrested: see Perkhin, 'Odinnadtsat' pisem', 251.

52. Afinogenov (1904–41) was killed by a bomb that fell on the Central Committee building in Moscow while he was completing the documentation for his posting to Washington as head of the Soviet Office of Information. He had been expelled from the Party in 1937 and rehabilitated after a 'confession' in 1938; he was never arrested.

53. On this novel, see Mikhail Geller, *Kontsentratsionnyi mir i sovetskaya literatura* (London, 1971), 184, and Struve, *Russian Literature under Lenin and Stalin*, 287.

54. 'The Karelians of Russia were not ethnologically different from their kinsmen over the Swedish border, and have preserved much of their national inheritance even better than the Finns of Finland; the Finnish epic *Kalevala*, for instance, was extant only in Russian Karelia when it was written down by Lönnrot in the eighteen 'thirties': D. S. Mirsky, *Russia: A Social History* (London, 1931), 154.

55. On these changes of personnel, see the works of Gleb Struve (n. 5 above), and also Harriet Borland, *Soviet Literary Theory and Practice during the First Five-Year Plan, 1928–1932* (New York, 1950), Herman Ermolaev, *Soviet Literary Theories, 1917–1934: The Genesis of Socialist Realism* (Berkeley and Los Angeles, Calif., 1963), and particularly Hans Günther, *Die Verstaatlichung der Literatur: Entstehung und Funktionsweise des sozialistisch-realistischen Kanons in der sowjetischen Literatur der 30er Jahre* (Stuttgart, 1984); Mirsky figures prominently in the latter book.

56. On Voronsky, see Robert Maguire, *Red Virgin Soil: Soviet Literature in the 1920s* (Princeton, NJ, 1968).
57. The writings of Pereverzev (1882–1968; he survived the camps) became the byword for the 'vulgar sociology' in literary theory and criticism that was ritually denounced from the early 1930s, with Bespalov taking the lead. On Pereverzev, see Galina Belaya, *Don-Kikhoty 20-kh godov: 'Pereval' i sud'ba ego idei* (Moscow, 1989), esp. ch. 9, and V. P. Rakov, 'O V. F. Pereverzeve: po-novomu', in *Kontekst 1992* (Moscow, 1993), 221–50.
58. 'Voprosy poezii', repr. in *SSRP*, 188–95.
59. *Power* (1934) by 'Adalis' (Adelina Efron, 1900–69) was concerned, like much of her work, with Central Asia.
60. For Mirsky's speech, which is untitled, see *Vtoroi plenum*, 294–8.
61. There is a substantial quotation from the passage on Pasternak in this speech in Fleishman, *Boris Pasternak v tridtsatye gody*, 243.
62. Whether or not Mirsky ever met Lukács privately during the time they coincided in Moscow—the Hungarian was there from 1933 to 1945—is a moot point. They took part in at least one official meeting together, when Lukács's draft for his entry on 'The Novel' for the *Literary Encyclopedia* was discussed in Dec. 1934. Lukács's speech was published in *Literaturnyi kritik* 2 (1935), 214–20; Mirsky's discussion of it, one of the strongest of his Soviet publications, follows immediately (pp. 221–3). The debate continued in the next issue of the journal. Mikhail Bakhtin certainly knew these publications: see Galin Tihanov, 'Bakhtin, Lukács, and German Romanticism: The Case of Epic and Irony', in C. Adlam et al. (eds.), *Face to Face: Bakhtin in Russia and the West* (Sheffield, 1997), 274–5; and idem, 'The Novel, the Epic and Modernity: Lukács and the Moscow Debate about the Novel (1934–35)', *Germano-Slavica* 10 (2) (1988), 29–42.
63. *Vtoroi plenum*, 500–1.
64. Ibid. 432.
65. The director of these operations was Stephen Duggan, who had helped to organize Mirsky's visit to the USA in 1928.
66. Conquest, *The Great Terror*, 77.
67. There is some evidence that, about this time, Mirsky went beyond simply writing about current poetry and tried to organize a circle of young poets. Nearly 60 years after the event, Lev Ozerov reported: 'It was the middle of the 1930s. Prince Dmitry Petrovich Svyatopolk-Mirsky got us together, a few beginning writers of verse, and from among us with commanding decisiveness singled out Semynin': 'Flamandskoe pero Petra Semynina', *Arion* 3 (1994), 106. The poet on whom Mirsky's choice fell, Pyotr Semynin (1909–83), was extremely talented and original, but was not a self-promoter and was never noticed by the powers-that-be, which probably prolonged his life considerably. It is interesting that, in characterizing Semynin's work, Ozerov asserts that his lyric poetry not only worked on the emotions but also made the reader think. This was exactly the principal quality that Mirsky was soon to call for in his articles in 1935 and 1936. Mirsky discusses Semynin's earliest published work in 'Zametki o stikhakh', repr. in *SSRP*, 228–9.
68. See Polivanov, 'Zametki i materialy', 73.
69. 'The lofty evaluation accorded Mayakovsky by the leader of our country must be thought through by Soviet literary public opinion in the most profound and responsible manner': D. S. Mirsky, 'O sovetskoi poezii', repr. in *SSRP*, 285.
70. 'Voprosy poezii', repr. ibid. 188–95.
71. 'Nam nuzhna poeziya bol'shikh liricheskikh obobshchenii', repr. ibid. 196–203.
72. The classic treatment of this theme in Russian is Lidiya Ginzburg, *O liricheskom geroe* (Leningrad, 1974).
73. Here Mirsky recapitulates the central thesis of his 'Poet amerikanskoi demokratii', which first appeared as an introduction to Korney Chukovsky's translation of *Leaves of Grass* (*List'ya travy*, Leningrad, 1935, 9–30). Mirsky here asserts: 'Whitman is the last great poet of the bourgeois epoch of mankind, the last in the series that begins with Dante.' This article was translated by B. G. Guerney and published in the leading left-wing journal of

America, *Critics Group Dialectics* 1 (1937), 11–29, and translated again by Samuel Putnam in Gay Wilson Allen (ed.), *Walt Whitman Abroad* (Syracuse, NY, 1955), 169–86.

74. *SSRP*, 199.

75. 'Stikhi 1934 goda: Stat'ya 1-ya', repr. in Mirsky, *Literaturno-kriticheskie stat'i* (Moscow, 1978), 240–52. On or around 8 Apr. 1935 Mikhail Bulgakov and his wife heard Pasternak reading his translations from the Georgian poets; Mirsky may well also have been present.

76. 'Stikhi 1934 goda: Stat'ya 2-ya', *Literaturnaya gazeta* 23 (514) (24 Apr. 1935), 2–3.

77. Fleishman, *Boris Pasternak v tridtsatye gody*, 246.

78. See Polivanov, 'Zametki i materialy', 72.

79. In mid-April 1935 Mirsky was invited to a reception for Gordon Craig at Meyerhold's apartment. Among the other guests were Prokofiev and Pasternak. When Pasternak reported this occasion to his parents, he said that Mirsky now repudiated him with the same warmth with which he had once acknowledged him: 'he is a member of the English Communist Party, and I must rightly seem to him to be someone who has not justified the hopes placed in him and also an uninteresting vulgarian', adding that Mirsky is 'a perfect Nekhlyudov, springing out from Tolstoy's works with all his complex and morally strained biography': see Boris Pasternak, *Pis'ma k roditelyam i sestram* (2 vols., Stanford, Calif., 1998), ii. 123; for the context, see Christopher Barnes, *Boris Pasternak: A Literary Biography*, ii: *1928–1960* (Cambridge, 1998), 102. Nekhlyudov, a black-bearded ex-Guards officer prince whose first name is Dmitry, is the hero of two works by Tolstoy. Pasternak no doubt has in mind the novel *Resurrection* (1900), the title of which refers to Nekhlyudov's moral regeneration; Pasternak's father had illustrated Russian and English editions of the novel. It is indicative that a fellow Russian should compare Mirsky to a character out of Tolstoy, while non-Russians like Edmund Wilson and Leonard Woolf sought analogies in Dostoevsky.

80. Edmund Wilson, 'Comrade Prince', *Encounter* 5 (1) (1955), 10–20.

81. On Wilson and the American hard Left, see Sam Tanenhaus, *Whittaker Chambers* (New York, 1997).

82. Wilson, 'Comrade Prince', 13.

83. Besides his own theatre, from 1931 to 1934 Sergey Radlov directed what was soon to become the Kirov. Just before he was sacked, Radlov commissioned Prokofiev's *Romeo and Juliet*, which eventually (after many setbacks) was performed by the Bolshoi; Radlov continued to work on it with the composer in 1935.

84. Mikhail Kuzmin, *Stikhotvoreniya*, ed. K. A. Bogomolov (St Petersburg, 1996), 776.

85. Wilson, 'Comrade Prince', 13.

86. See Fleishman, *Boris Pasternak v tridtsatye gody*, 236–66, and Polivanov, 'Zametki i materialy', 72–3; some internal documents appear in Babichenko, *'Schast'e literatury': Gosudarstvo i pisateli 1925–1938*, 87–97. On Erenburg's involvement, see ' "Poshli tolki, chto den'gi moskovskie . . .": Pis'ma Il'i Erenburga Mikhailu Kol'tsovu 1935–1937 godov', *Novyi mir* 3 (1999), 174–5. It was at this conference that pressure was put on the Soviet government to release Victor Serge, whose life was a mirror image of Mirsky's. Serge was born in the same year as Mirsky, but in the alternative aristocracy of the Russian political emigration in Belgium; he became an active revolutionary himself when he was still a teenager. After serving a prison term in France, in 1919 he went in triumph to Petrograd and dedicated himself to the revolution. He was back in Western Europe, working for the Comintern, from 1922 to 1926; Berlin in Sept. 1922 is the one place Mirsky might conceivably have set eyes on him. Convinced that the revolution had been betrayed by the emerging Stalin faction, Serge sided with the Trotskyist opposition, and was imprisoned again in 1928, then sent into internal exile in Central Asia; in the interim he had published several books abroad, not being allowed to publish in the USSR. He was allowed to leave the USSR in 1936. After years of intense political activity in Europe—directed against Hitler, Stalin, Trotsky, and world capitalism all at the same time—he was finally allowed to go to Mexico, where he died in 1947. Serge's memoirs, written in 1942–3, resonate against Mirsky's story at every turn: 'The men of my generation—those born around 1890—above all the Europeans among them, cannot help the sensation of having lived on a frontier where one world ends and

another begins. The passage from one century to another was a giddy one. I remember my astonishment as a child when I saw the first "horseless carriages" pass in the street. The motor car was being born. I was a news-vendor during the first aeroplane rally organized in France. . . . I knew domestic lighting by paraffin, then by gas, since electricity still penetrated only into wealthy homes. . . . Before the First World War I knew a buoyant Europe, optimistic, liberal and crudely dominated by money. We reached our twenties as young idealistic workers, and we were angry and desperate . . . Suddenly the Europe of revolutions was born at Petrograd. Our Red soldiers chased the generals' bands across all Europe and all Siberia. . . . We revolutionaries, who aimed to create a new society, "the broadest democracy of the workers", had unwittingly, with our hands, constructed the most terrifying State machine conceivable; and when, with revulsion, we realized the truth, this machine, driven by our friends and comrades, turned on us and crushed us. . . . May the passion, the experience and even the faults of my fighting generation have some small power to illumine the way forward!': Victor Serge, *Memoirs of a Revolutionary 1901–1941*, trans. Peter Sedgwick (Oxford, 1963), 379–82.

87. Raisa Lomonosova met Pasternak in London when he was on his way back to Moscow, and wrote to her husband on 6 July 1935: 'The day before yesterday Pasternak arrived with a group of others. He's in a dreadful moral and physical state. The whole situation is sadistic-absurd. . . . To live in eternal fear! No, better to be a lavatory cleaner.' Quoted in Christopher Barnes and Richard Davies, ' "Neotsenimyi podarok": Perepiska Pasternakov i Lomonosovykh (1925–1970)', *Minuvshee* 16 (1994), 378. Some previously unpublished information about this occasion can be found in Barnes, *Boris Pasternak*, ii. 104–6.

88. See Aleksandr Biryukov, *Poslednii Ryurikovich* (Magadan, 1991), 51. Mirsky was defensive because the book contains some favourable remarks about Trotsky; see below.

89. See Fleishman, *Pasternak v tridtsatye gody*, 267. Incidentally, in a volume of previously secret documents concerning the interventions of the Party in literature there is a letter from an NKVD informer, one O. Voitinskaya, written 'before 15 March 1938' and preserved in the Central Committee archive. Beginning with the usual formula, 'I consider it my Party duty to report . . .', Voitinskaya denounces several prominent literary figures, and then, in an aside, says: 'In Georgia everything was entrusted to Pasternak and Mirsky, who were closely connected with the group of the spy Yashvili. One could cite numerous examples': D. L. Babichenko (ed.), *'Literaturnyi front': Istoriya politicheskoi tsenzury 1932–1946 gg. Sbornik dokumentov* (Moscow, 1994), 32.

90. 'Voprosy poezii: Stat'ya 3-ya', repr. in *SSRP*, 209. There was a carping review of this article by the junior critic N. Maslin, 'Dekadenty ili klassiki', *Literaturnyi sovremennik* 9 (1935), 163–7.

91. 'Pasternak i gruzinskie poety', repr. in *SSRP*, 214.

92. Zazubrin (1895–1938) fought on both sides in the Civil War; he later became a novelist, specializing in agricultural themes. His date of death bespeaks his fate. One of the works selected for publication in this series was Tyan-Shanskaya's study of the peasantry in the pre-revolutionary period, of which David Ransel writes that it was 'lost sight of by all but a few specialists in ethnography and the history of peasant institutions': 'Introduction', in Olga Semyonovna Tian-Shanskaya, *Village Life in Late Tsarist Russia* (Bloomington and Indianapolis, 1993), p. xvii. Gorky regarded this as an essential work; it was scheduled as no. 7 in the series, but eventually was not published.

93. See M. Gor'ky i sovetskaya pechat', i (Moscow, 1964), 420–3.

94. 'O formalizme', in M. Gor'ky, L. Averbakh, et al. (eds.), *God shestnadtsatyi: Al'manakh vtoroi* (Moscow, 1933), 490–517.

95. See Fleishman, *Boris Pasternak v tridtsatye gody*, 302 ff.

96. Ibid. 312.

97. Cited ibid. 318.

98. See Perkhin, 'Odinnadtsat' pisem', 251.

99. Fleishman, *Boris Pasternak v tridtsatye gody*, 326. These measures were immediately preceded by the anathematizing of Bulgakov on the basis of his play *Molière*, which was taken

off on 9 Mar. 1936. Not coincidentally, the greatest work of Soviet Socialist Realism, Prokofiev's *Peter and the Wolf*, was written in Moscow in Apr. 1936 and first publicly performed on 2 May 1936.

100. Perkhin, 'Odinnadtsat' pisem', 251.
101. Cited in Fleishman, *Boris Pasternak v tridtsatye gody*, 328.
102. D. S. Mirsky, 'Na dva fronta: Iz rechi tov. D. Mirskogo', *Literaturnaya gazeta* 17 (580) (20 Mar. 1936), 2.
103. Fleishman, *Boris Pasternak v tridtsatye gody*, 160.
104. Ibid. 186.
105. D. Mirsky, 'Pis'mo v redaktsiyu', *Literaturnaya gazeta* 50 (613), 10 Sept. 1936, 6.
106. On Robert Traill, see Richard Davies and G. S. Smith, 'D. S. Mirsky: Twenty-Two Letters (1926–34) to Salomeya Halpern', *Oxford Slavonic Papers* n.s. 30 (1997), 97.
107. D. S. Mirsky, 'O velikoi khartii narodov: Konstitutsiya pobedy', *Literaturnaya gazeta* 41 (604) (20 July 1936), 2.
108. See Conquest, *The Great Terror*, 87 ff.
109. Ibid. 108.
110. See Biryukov, *Poslednii Ryurikovich*, 51, citing the confession of Sokolnikov from *Sudebnyi otchet po delu antisovetskogo trotskistskogo tsentra* (Moscow, 1937), 234, about recruiting like-minded people abroad.
111. This was originally the title of a series that eventually included 60 biographies, published by F. F. Pavlenko in St Petersburg from 1890 to 1907. The Soviet successor was initiated by Gorky in 1933, and it has continued into the post-Soviet epoch. The two chapters Mirsky mentioned were indeed published before his arrest, but the book never appeared and was in all probability never finished.
112. Mirsky's piece seems never to have been published, and not to have survived in manuscript. The edition it was commissioned for is arguably the finest single achievement of Soviet comparative literary scholarship, the monumental *Russkaya kul'tura i Frantsiya* (3 vols., Moscow, 1937–9), representing issues 29–34 of *Literary Heritage*, and amounting to about 2,500 large-format pages with copious illustrations.
113. The centenary of Pushkin's death in 1937 was marked by a relentless drive to assimilate the poet into the Soviet canon. Mirsky mentioned this particular commission to Dorothy Galton on 29 May 1936, asking her in his usual way to send him the materials that would enable him to write it.
114. Perkhin, 'Odinnadtsat' pisem', 252.
115. Mirsky was arrested the night before the Windsors got married.
116. D. Mirsky, 'Chuzherodnyi sor', *Literaturnaya gazeta* 5 (641) (26 Jan. 1937), 6.
117. Conquest, *The Great Terror*, 179.
118. Ibid. 181.
119. 'Klassik sovetskoi poezii Mayakovsky V. V.', repr. in *SSRP*, 238.
120. Mirsky published a very positive review of Kunitz's *Russian Literature and the Jew* among other books in *London Mercury* 20 (1929), 533–5.
121. See E. J. Brown, *The Proletarian Episode in Soviet Literature, 1928–1932* (New York, 1953), 225, and note on 285: 'According to the verbal account given me by a man who was present at this meeting, Mirsky, because of his many contacts with foreigners, was publicly accused of hostility to the Soviet Union and possible spying and treason. According to this account, he did indeed but weakly defend himself, for he was extremely agitated at the time.'
122. Idem, unpublished letter to G. S. Smith, 20 Oct. 1982.
123. On these events, see Fleishman, *Boris Pasternak v tridtsatye gody*, 406.
124. *Lenin* (Boston and London, 1931), 152–3.
125. Perkhin, 'Odinnadtsat' pisem', 256.
126. Ibid.
127. See *Literaturnaya gazeta*, 26 Apr. 1937.
128. Abolgasem Akhmedzade Lakhuti (1887–1957) was a Persian revolutionary and poet who lived in Russia from 1922; he held both government and Writers' Union posts.
129. Perkhin, 'Odinnadtsat' pisem', 256–7.

9. END OF THE LINE

1. The indispensable guide to this complex of issues is Ronald Hingley, 'Communication Devices', in his *The Russian Mind* (London, etc., 1977), 52–101.
2. Irma Kudrova, 'Vera Treil, urozhdennaya Guchkovoi: Po materialam doprosov na Lubyanke', *Russkaya mysl'* 4068 (9–15 Mar. 1995), 11–12. When she was interrogated, Ariadna Efron stated that Vera was summoned to Moscow by the authorities to discuss her future work for the foreign department of the NKVD: see Irma Kudrova, 'Poslednee "delo" Sergeya Efrona', *Zvezda* 10 (1992), 129.
3. She published an autobiographical novel about this experience, under an eloquent pseudonym: Vera T. Mirsky, *The Cup of Astonishment* (London, 1944). The book was favourably reviewed by George Orwell; see Richard Davies and G. S. Smith, 'D. S. Mirsky: Twenty-Two Letters (1926–34) to Salomeya Halpern', *Oxford Slavonic Papers* n.s. 30 (1997), 97.
4. Cited in G. S. Smith, 'The Correspondence of D. S. Mirsky and Michael Florinsky, 1925–32', *Slavonic and East European Review* 72 (1) (1994), 138–9.
5. Bernard Pares, *A Wandering Student* (Syracuse, NY, 1948), 291.
6. Undated letter, Prague, Slavonic Library at Clementinum, P. N. Savitsky Archive, first published in D. S. Mirsky, *Stikhotvoreniya: Stat'i o russkoi poezii*, compiled and ed. G. K. Perkins and G. S. Smith (Berkeley, Calif., 1997), 13.
7. Vladimir Nabokov, *Selected Letters 1940–1977*, ed. Dimitri Nabokov and Matthew J. Bruccoli (London, 1990), 91.
8. Edmund Wilson, 'Comrade Prince', *Encounter* 5 (1) (1955), 15.
9. See idem, *Letters on Literature and Politics, 1912–1972*, ed. Elena Wilson (London, 1977), 576–7 (letters to Gleb Struve of 5 Sept. 1955 and Elizabeth Schouvalov of 25 Mar. 1955).
10. Yu. Ivask, 'O smerti knyazya Svyatopolka-Mirskogo', *Novyi zhurnal* 127 (1977), 291; Wilson's translation of this letter is completely misleading. For another version of this and other legends about Mirsky's death, see Lev Mnukhin, 'Legendy i byl': Eshche raz o gibeli knyazya D. P. Svyatopolk-Mirskogo', *Russkaya mysl'* 4129 (6–12 June 1996), 10; 4130 (13–19 June 1996), 10; and 4131 (20–6 June 1996), 10.
11. Wilson, 'Comrade Prince', 20.
12. A. Krasnov-Levitin, *Likhie gody 1925–1941* (Paris, 1977), 317–18. Some details in this account may also be found in Edvin Polyanovsky, *Gibel' Osipa Mandel'shtama* (St Petersburg and Paris, 1993).
13. Nadezhda Mandel'shtam, *Vospominaniya* (New York, 1970), 402.
14. Grigory Svirsky, *Na lobnom meste* (London, 1979), 200–1.
15. See e.g. Anna Berzer, *Proshchanie* (Moscow, 1990), 202; Anatoly Gladilin, *The Making and Unmaking of a Soviet Writer* (Ann Arbor, Mich., 1979), 23; Abram Terts (Andrey Sinyavsky), *Spokoinoi nochi* (Paris, 1985), 328–9 (Richard Lourie's translation of this passage completely reverses the sense of the original; see Abram Terts, *Goodnight! A Novel*, New York, 1989, 270–1); and Aleksandr Zhovtis, *Nepridumannye anekdoty: Iz sovetskogo proshlogo* (Moscow, 1995), 30–1.
16. D. Mirsky, 'Realizm', *Literaturnaya entsiklopediya*, ix (Moscow, 1935), 548–76.
17. Oksman (1895–1970) had been a member of Vengerov's Pushkin seminar before 1917; he was appointed Vice-Chairman of the Academy Institute of Russian Literature (Pushkin House) in Leningrad in 1933, and would certainly have known Mirsky in this capacity. Oksman was arrested in 1936 and spent a decade in the GULag, after which he was in exile in Saratov until 1958, when he went back to Leningrad. See Elena Dryzhakova, 'The Fifties in Transition: A. S. Dolinin and Yu. G. Oksman, Our Remarkable Teachers', *Oxford Slavonic Papers* n.s. 18 (1985), 120–49. Oksman also told Ivanov-Razumnik about Mirsky, saying that he died of starvation at Nagaevo in either 1939 or 1940; see R. Ivanov-Razumnik, *Pisatel'skie sud'by* (New York, 1951), 22.
18. Cited in Gleb Struve, 'Predislovie', in D. S. Mirsky, *Russkaya lirika* (repr. of the anthology of 1924, New York, 1979), 28.

19. L. N. Chertkov, 'Mirsky, Dmitry Petrovich', in *Kratkaya literaturnaya entsiklopediya*, iv: *Lakshin–Muranovo* (Moscow, 1967), col. 861.

20. 'Niko Pirosmanishvili', *Literaturnaya Gruziya* 7 (1971), 11–12, originally published in *Evraziya*, 27 Apr. 1929, 7.

21. Borys Levytsky's meticulous book summarizes official disclosures in the Soviet press up to 1974: *The Stalinist Terror of the Thirties: Documentation from the Soviet Press* (Stanford, Calif., 1974).

22. Vasily Ivanovich Azhaev (1915–68) wrote one very successful novel before becoming Secretary of the Union of Writers in succession to Stavsky.

23. Semen Lipkin, *Zhizn' i sud'ba Vasiliya Grossmana* (Moscow, 1990), 33.

24. This document and most of the others from Mirsky's Moscow file that are translated in what follows here were published independently by V. V. Perkhin, 'K istorii aresta i reabilitatsii D. P. Svyatopolk-Mirskogo (po arkhivnym materialam)', *Russkaya literatura* 1 (1997), 220–37.

25. In this letter, Gorky tells Rolland that 'there have been several interesting cases of psychological reconstruction: for example, Count Stenbock-Fermor, the legatee of rich Ural manufacturers, and a Guards officer in Wilhelm II's army, has joined the German Communist Party along with a dozen other officers; Prince Svyatopolk-Mirsky, the son of the former Minister of Internal Affairs, has also proclaimed himself a Communist; and the son of Prince Khilkov, who lives in Belgium, a former officer and now a miner, has suddenly broken all connections with the emigration. However, these isolated cases of moral rebirth do not yet permit, of course, serious conclusions to be drawn.' Cited in *Literaturnoe nasledstvo*, 70 (Moscow, 1963), 618. Khilkov may well have been the person Mirsky interceded for in his letter to Gorky of 14 May 1931.

26. This was the restricted publication referred to colloquially as 'Black TASS'.

27. Pavel Nikolaevich Tolstoy (born *c.*1905) was a sociable person with a wide acquaintance in the Paris *émigré* community. He returned to Russia in 1933 and lived for about a year with his relative, the 'Red Count' A. N. Tolstoy, in Detskoe selo (the former Tsarskoe), then in 1934 moved to Moscow and worked in the All-Union Society for Cultural Links (VOKS). This was an NKVD assignment. Tolstoy was arrested in late June 1939, and 'confessed'. From then on he was used to confront other prisoners, including Sergey Efron. In May 1940 Tolstoy tried to retract his depositions, but he reconfirmed them after further treatment by the interrogators.

28. Menachim Begin, *White Nights: The Story of a Prisoner in Russia* (London, 1957); Elinor Lipper, *Eleven Years in Soviet Prison Camps* (London, 1951).

29. For a concise introduction to these kinds of files, see Peter B. Maggs, *The Mandelstam and 'Der Nister' Files: An Introduction to Stalin-Era Prison and Labor Camp Records* (Armonk, NY, and London, 1996).

30. V. P. Popov, 'State Terror in Soviet Russia, 1923–1953 (Sources and their Interpretation)', *Russian Social Science Review* 35 (5) (1994), 48–70.

31. Robert Conquest, *The Great Terror: A Reassessment* (London, 1991), 284.

32. Ibid. 297, quoting *Literaturnaya gazeta*, 28 Dec. 1988.

33. For Solzhenitsyn's corrosive account of this Article, see *The GULag Archipelago*, pt. iii, ch. 10.

34. The conditions in the Butyrka at this time have been graphically described by Robert Conquest: see *The Great Terror*, 264–70.

35. Mirsky had in fact been listed as a suspect before, in Mar. 1934, when he was one of the 36 persons said to require further investigation in connection with the 'Slavists Affair' of 1933–4, in which a leading figure was his friend N. N. Durnovo; see F. D. Ashnin and V. M. Alpatov, *'Delo slavistov': 30-e gody* (Moscow, 1994), 78.

36. Conquest, *The Great Terror*, 277–82.

37. See Evgenia Ginzburg, *Journey into the Whirlwind* (New York and London, 1967), chs. 25–8.

38. In her analysis of the interrogation of Sergey Efron, Irma Kudrova, basing herself on her own ordeal in the 1960s, declared that the protocol 'incorporated hardly a tenth of what

had been said, and then in the investigator's own formulations'; it omitted all the countless tactics such as the mockery and slander of loved ones calculated to make the suspects lose their sense of reality. See Irma Kudrova, 'Poslednee "delo" Sergeya Efrona', *Zvezda* 10 (1992), 112–30.

39. When Gary Powers was interrogated at the Lubyanka in 1960, the procedure was still the same. Powers objected to initialling each page of the transcript of his interrogation, on the grounds that it was in Russian, which he could not understand, and he was told: 'That does not matter. It is required.' See Francis Gary Powers with Curt Gentry, *Operation Overflight: The U-2 Pilot Tells His Story for the First Time* (New York, etc., 1970), 125.

40. Aleksandr Biryukov, *Poslednii Ryurikovich* (Magadan, 1991), 54–5.

41. Edward Hallett Carr, *Dostoyevsky (1821–1881): A New Biography* (Boston and New York, 1931), which has a preface by Mirsky. The book on Herzen is *The Romantic Exiles: A Nineteenth-Century Portrait Gallery* (London, 1933).

42. E. H. Carr, *Bakunin* (London, 1937).

43. Mirsky is probably thinking of his preface to Carr's *Dostoevsky*.

44. Conquest, *The Great Terror*, 286.

45. Ibid. 285.

46. See Robert Conquest, *Kolyma: The Arctic Death Camps* (London, 1978); here, this ship is first reported in use in May 1938.

47. Conquest, *Kolyma*, 227.

48. This file was located, studied, and first published in part by Aleksandr Biryukov in his *Poslednii Ryurikovich* (Magadan, 1991), 47–61; for a summary based on another copy of the file see G. S. Smith, 'What Happened to D. S. Mirsky?', *British East–West Journal* 98 (1994), 10–11.

49. Lipper (*Eleven Years*, 92) mentions the hospital at kilometre 23. She also mentions Atka several times.

Bibliography

1. D. S. MIRSKY: UNPUBLISHED WRITINGS

Angliiskaya literatura XVII v., St Petersburg, PFA RAN, V. Zhirmunsky, *fond* 1001, *opis'* 4, *edinitsa khraneniya* 51

'Barokko v angliiskoi literature (tezisy)', St Petersburg, PFA RAN, V. Zhirmunsky, *fond* 1001, *opis'* 4, *edinitsa khraneniya* 50

Correspondence with Secretary, London PEN Club, Harry Ransome Humanities Research Centre, University of Texas at Austin

Letter to Leonard Woolf, 1 Feb. 1926, Leonard Woolf Papers, the University Library, University of Sussex

'Letters of Prince D. P. Svyatopolk-Mirsky to Dorothy Galton, 1929–1937', British Library, Add. MS 49,530 (Letters 1929–Sept. 1932 unpublished; for published letters, see Section 2 below)

'Letters of Prince D. P. Svyatopolk-Mirsky to Sir B. Pares, 1922–1931', British Library, Add. MS 49,604

Letters to Prince P. D. Svyatopolk-Mirsky, Moscow, GARF, *fond* 172, *opis'* 2, *edinitsa khraneniya* 392

2. D. S. MIRSKY: PUBLISHED CORRESPONDENCE

DAVIES, RICHARD, and SMITH, G. S., 'D. S. Mirsky: Twenty-Two Letters (1926–34) to Salomeya Halpern; Seven Letters (1930) to Vera Suvchinskaya (Traill)', *Oxford Slavonic Papers* n.s. 30 (1997), 91–122

KAZNINA, OLGA, and SMITH, G. S., 'D. S. Mirsky to Maksim Gor'ky: Sixteen Letters (1928–1934)', *Oxford Slavonic Papers* n.s. 26 (1993), 87–103

PERKHIN, V. V., 'Odinnadtsat' pisem (1920–1937) i avtobiografiya (1936) D. P. Svyatopolk-Mirskogo', *Russkaya literatura* 1 (1996), 235–62

SHAKHOVSKOY, ARKHIEPISKOP IOANN, 'D. P. Svyatopolk-Mirsky', in *Biografiya yunosti: Ustanovlenie edinstva* (Paris, 1978), 197–217

SMITH, G. S., 'The Correspondence of D. S. Mirsky and Michael Florinsky, 1925–1932', *Slavonic and East European Review* 72 (1) (1994), 115–39

—— 'Four Letters of D. S. Mirsky to Ariadna Tyrkova-Williams (1926) with an Unknown Review by Ariadna Tyrkova-Williams', *Slavonic and East European Review* 71 (3) (1993), 482–9

—— 'D. S. Mirsky and Hugh MacDiarmid: A Relationship and an Exchange of Letters (1934)', *Slavonica* 2/3 (1996/7), 49–60

—— 'D. S. Mirsky to Dorothy Galton: Thirty-Nine Letters from Moscow (1932–1937)', *Oxford Slavonic Papers* n.s. 29 (1996), 93–131

—— 'Jane Ellen Harrison: Forty-Seven Letters to D. S. Mirsky, 1924–1926', *Oxford Slavonic Papers* n.s. 28 (1995), 62–97

—— *The Letters of D. S. Mirsky to P. P. Suvchinskii, 1922–31* (Birmingham, 1995)
—— 'D. S. Mirsky: Two Letters to Elizaveta Polonskaia (1935, 1936) on Translating Kipling and Christina Rossetti', *Slavonic and East European Review* 73 (3) (1995), 490–8

3. D. S. MIRSKY: PUBLISHED WRITINGS

Abbreviations:

SSRP   *Stikhotvoreniya: Stat'i o russkoi poezii*
UWRL   *Uncollected Writings on Russian Literature*

'Aleksei Remizov', *The Times Literary Supplement*, 21 Feb. 1924 (anonymous; co-authored with Harold Williams)
'Alexander Blok', *The Times Literary Supplement*, 13 Apr. 1922, 242 (anonymous)
'Angliiskaya literatura', in *Entsiklopedicheskii slovar' bibliograficheskogo instituta Granat*, dopolnitel'nyi tom 1 (Moscow, 1936), cols. 403–43
Anglo-russkii slovar', ed. A. D. Miller and D. S. Mirsky (Moscow, 1936)
Antologiya novoi angliiskoi poezii, ed. M. Gutner (Leningrad, 1937) (Mirsky's name deleted)
'Avtobiografiya D. P. Svyatopolk-Mirskogo', in V. V. Perkhin, 'Odinnadtsat' pisem (1920–1937) i avtobiografiya (1936) D. P. Svyatopolk-Mirskogo', *Russkaya literatura* 1 (1996), 257–9
'Babel', *The Nation & the Athenæum*, 23 Jan. 1926, 581–2
'Baratynsky', in E. A. Baratynsky, *Polnoe sobranie stikhotvorenii* (Moscow, 1936), pp. v–xxxiv; repr. in *SSRP*, 243–80
'Barokko v angliiskoi literature', in *Stat'i o literature* (Moscow, 1987), 21–70
'Bazel'skie kolokola' (review of Louis Aragon, *Les Cloches de Bâle*), *Literaturnaya gazeta* 171 (487) (22 Dec. 1934), 3
'Books and Films in Russia', *Yale Review* 20 (3) (1931), 472–87; repr. in *UWRL*, 312–27
'Bourgeois History and Bourgeois Materialism', *Labour Monthly* 13 (1931), 453–9
'Chekhov', *Evraziya* 31 (13 July 1929), 5–6; repr. in *UWRL*, 298–302
'Chuzherodnyi sor', *Literaturnaya gazeta* 5 (641) (26 Jan. 1937), 6
'Contemporary Movements in Russian Literature', in William Rose and J. Isaacs (eds.), *Contemporary Movements in European Literature* (London, 1928), 151–75; repr. in *UWRL*, 258–82
Contemporary Russian Literature, 1881–1925 (London and New York, 1926)
'Die Literatur der russischen Emigration', *Slavische Rundschau* 1 (1929), 290–4
'Dve smerti, 1837–1930', in *Smert' Vladimira Mayakovskogo* (Berlin, 1931), 47–66; repr. in *SSRP*, 123–36
'Dzhems Dzhois', in *God shestnadtsatyi: Al'manakh pervyi* (Moscow, 1933), 428–50; repr. in *Literaturno-kriticheskie stat'i*, 281–307
'Eduard Bagritsky', *Literaturnaya gazeta* 23 (338) (26 Feb. 1934), 2
'Eduard Bagritsky', *Literaturnaya gazeta* 9 (500) (15 Feb. 1935), 3; repr. in *SSRP*, 177–86
'Emily Brontë', *London Mercury* 7 (37) (1922), 266–72

'Esenin', *Volya Rossii* 5 (1925), 75–80; repr. in *UWRL*, 211–16

'Eurasian Manifesto, A', *The Times Literary Supplement*, 1 July 1922, 350 (anonymous)

'Eurasian Movement, The', *Slavonic Review* 6 (17) (1927), 311–19; repr. in *UWRL*, 237–45

'Exodus to the East, The', *Russian Life* 1 (1922), 210–12

'Five Russian Letters', *London Mercury*, 1920–2; repr. in *UWRL*, 45–86

Geschichte der russischen Literatur, trans. Georg Mayer (Munich, 1964)

Histoire de la littérature russe, trans. Véronique Lossky (Paris, 1969)

'Histoire d'une libération', *Nouvelle Revue Française* 216 (1 Sept. 1931), 384–97. Trans. as 'The Story of a Liberation' in *UWRL*, 358–67

History of Russia, A (London, 1928)

History of Russian Literature, A: Comprising a History of Russian Literature and Contemporary Russian Literature, ed. and abr. Francis J. Whitfield (London and New York, 1949)

History of Russian Literature from Its Beginnings to 1900, A (New York, 1958)

History of Russian Literature from the Earliest Times to the Death of Dostoevsky (1881), A (London and New York, 1927)

'Il posto del Dostojevskij nelle letterature russa', *La Cultura* n.s. 2 (1931), 100–15

Intelligentsia of Great Britain, The, trans. Alec Brown (London, 1935)

'Introduction', in *A Brief History of Muscovia and of Other Less-known Countries lying eastward of Russia as far as Cathay. Gather'd from the Writings of several eye-witnesses by John Milton. To which are added other curious documents, with an Introduction by Prince D. S. Mirsky* (London, 1929), pp. ix–xxvi

'Introduction', in Aksakov, *Chronicles of a Russian Family* (London and New York, 1924), 5–13

'Introduction', in *Dostoevsky's Letters to His Wife*, trans. Elizabeth Hill and Doris Mudie (London, 1930), pp. ix–xiv

'Introduction', in *Russian Poems*, trans. C. Fillingham Coxwell (London, 1929), pp. xvii–xxii

'Introduction: Russian Fiction since Chekhov', in Boris Pilniak, *Tales of the Wilderness* (London, 1924), pp. vii–xxxi

'Istoriya odnogo osvobozhdeniya', *Literaturnaya gazeta* 10 (178), 29 Feb. 1932, 2

Istoriya russkoi literatury s drevneishikh vremen do 1925 goda, trans. Ruf' Zernova (London, 1992)

'Izdaniya rossiiskogo instituta istorii iskusstv', *Sovremennye zapiski* 24 (1925), 434–8

Jane Ellen Harrison and Russia (Cambridge, 1930)

'Khlebnikov', *Evraziya*, 19 Jan. 1929, 6; repr. in *SSRP*, 112–17

'Klassik sovetskoi poezii Mayakovsky V. V.', *Khudozhestvennaya literatura* 9 (1935), 7–10; repr. in *SSRP* 235–42

'Kriticheskie zametki', *Versty* 2 (1927), 255–62

Lenin (Boston and London, 1931)

'Literatura i kino', *Evraziya* 15 (2 Mar. 1929), 6

'Literature of Bolshevik Russia, The', *London Mercury* 5 (27) (1922), 2276–85; repr. in *UWRL*, 68–81

Literaturno-kriticheskie stat'i (Moscow, 1978)

'Mikhail Sholokhov', *Literaturnaya gazeta* 93 (409), 24 July 1934, 2–3

Modern Russian Literature (London, 1925)

'Moim kritikam', in *Vremennik pushkinskoi komissii* 1 (Moscow and Leningrad, 1936), 262–4

'Mr Lytton Strachey', *London Mercury* 8 (43) (May 1923), 175–84

'Mr Wells Shows His Class', *Labour Monthly* 14 (1932), 383–7

'Na dva fronta: Iz rechi tov. D. Mirskogo', *Literaturnaya gazeta* 17 (580) (20 Mar. 1936), 2

'Nam nuzhna poeziya bol'shikh liricheskikh obobshchenii', *Literaturnaya gazeta* 17 (508) (24 Mar. 1935), 2; repr. in *SSRP*, 196–203

'Niko Pirosmanishvili', *Evraziya*, 27 Apr. 1929, 7; repr. in *Literaturnaya Gruziya* 7 (1971), 11–12

'Novoe v angliiskoi literature: Moris Bering', *Zveno*, 11 Aug. 1924, 3

'Novye izdaniya starykh poetov: Stat'ya 1-ya', *Literaturnaya gazeta*, 43 (534) (4 Aug. 1935), 2–3

'Novye izdaniya starykh poetov: Stat'ya 2-ya', *Literaturnaya gazeta* 44 (535) (9 Aug. 1935), 2–3

'Ob Eduarde Bagritskom', *Literaturnaya ucheba* 5 (1934), 31–42; repr. in *Literaturno-kriticheskie stat'i*, 225–39

'Ob "Ulisse"', *Literaturnyi sovremennik* 11 (1935), 115–33

'O. E. Mandel'shtam, *Shum vremeni*', *Sovremennye zapiski* 25 (1925), 541–3; repr. in *UWRL*, 209–10

'O formalizme', in M. Gor'ky, L. Averbakh, et al. (eds.), *God shestnadtsatyi: Al'manakh vtoroi* (Moscow, 1933), 490–517

'O konservatizme. Dialog', *Blagonamerennyi* 2 (1926), 87–93

'Old Russian Literature: Its Place in the History of Civilization', *Slavonic Review* 3 (7) (1924), 74–91

'O moskovskoi literature i protopope Avvakume (Dva otryvka)', *Evraziiskii vremennik* 4 (1925), 338–50; repr. in *UWRL*, 145–55

'O nekotorykh voprosakh izucheniya russkoi literatury XVIII v.', *Literaturnoe nasled-stvo* 9/10 (1933), 501–9

'O nyneshnem sostoyanii russkoi literatury', *Blagonamerennyi* 1 (1926), 90–7; repr. in *UWRL*, 222–9

'O sovetskoi poezii', *Izvestiya* 24 (28 Jan. 1936), 2; repr. in *SSRP*, 281–7

'O sovremennoi angliiskoi literature (Pis'mo iz Londona)', *Sovremennyi zapad* 2 (1923), 139–50

'O sovremennom sostoyanii russkoi poezii', with a Preface by G. P. Struve and After-word by G. S. Smith, *Novyi zhurnal* 131 (1978), 79–110; repr. in *UWRL*, 87–117

'O Tolstom', *Evraziya* 1 (24 Nov. 1928), 6–7; repr. in *UWRL*, 288–93

'Otvet I. Sergievskomu i V. Desnitskomu', *Literaturnoe nasledstvo* 19/21 (1935), 645–9

'Outlook of Bertrand Russell, The', *Labour Monthly* 14 (1932), 113–19

'O velikoi khartii narodov: Konstitutsiya pobedy', *Literaturnaya gazeta* 41 (604) (20 July 1936), 2

'Pamyati Bagritskogo', *Khudozhestvennaya literatura* 3 (1934), 1–2

'Pamyati gr. V. A. Komarovskogo', *Zveno*, 22 Sept. 1924, 2; partial repr. in V. A. Komarovsky, *Proza i stikhi*, ed. Yury Ivask and W. Tjalsma (Munich, 1978), 23–4

'Pasternak i gruzinskie poety', *Literaturnaya gazeta* 59 (550) (24 Oct. 1935), 2; repr. in *SSRP*, 211–22

'Pervye shagi "rabochego" kabineta v Anglii', *Evraziya* 31 (13 July 1929), 5 ('D. P.')

'Philosophical Discussion in the C.P.S.U. in 1930–1931, The', *Labour Monthly* 13 (1931), 649–56

'Pis'mo v redaktsiyu', *Zveno* 172, 16 May 1926

'Poet amerikanskoi demokratii', in Uolt Uitman, *List'ya travy*, ed. and trans. Kornei Chukovsky (Leningrad, 1935), 9–30; trans. B. G. Guerney, 'Walt Whitman, Poet of American Democracy', *Critics' Group Dialectics* 1 (1937), 11–29; trans. Samuel Putnam, in Gay Wilson Allen (ed.), *Walt Whitman Abroad* (Syracuse, NY, 1955), 169–86

'Poeziya Red'yarda Kiplinga', *Znamya* 9 (1935), 242–56; repr. in *Literaturno-kriticheskie stat'i*, 308–26

'Politika i estetika (K plenumu pravleniya SSP: Obsuzhdaem voprosy kritiki)', *Literaturnaya gazeta* 17 (490) (28 Dec. 1934), 2

'Posle angliiskikh vyborov', *Evraziya* 29 (22 June 1929), 4 ('D. P.')

'Potomok Chingizkhana', *Evraziya* 20 (20 Apr. 1929), 8

'Predislovie', in R. Kipling, *Rasskazy* (Moscow and Leningrad, 1936), 7–19

'Preface', in E. H. Carr, *Dostoevsky (1821–1881): A New Biography* (London, 1931), unpaginated

'Preface', in *The Life of the Archpriest Avvakum by Himself. Translated from the Seventeenth Century Russian by Jane Harrison and Hope Mirrlees* (London, 1924), 7–30

'Present State of Russian Letters, The', *London Mercury* 16 (93) (1927), 275–86; repr. in *UWRL*, 246–57

'Problema Pushkina', *Literaturnoe nasledstvo* 16/18 (1934), 91–112

'Proshlo to vremya', in K. I. Azbelev and Ya. Ya. Polferov, *Zven'ya: Literaturno-khudozhestvennyi sbornik* (St Petersburg, 1906), 32

'Pushkin', *Slavonic Review* 2 (4) (1923), 71–84; repr. in *UWRL*, 118–31

Pushkin (London and New York, 1926)

'Realizm', in *Literaturnaya entsiklopediya* (10 vols., Moscow, 1930–9), ix (1935), cols. 548–76

'Recent Books on Russia', *The Listener*, 18 Dec. 1929, 825

'Reporting on the New Russia', *The Listener*, 9 Dec. 1931, 1009

Review of Anna Akhmatova, three books, *Slavonic Review* 1 (1) (1922), 690–1

Review of B. L. Pasternak, *Rasskazy*, *Sovremennye zapiski* 25 (1925), 544–5; repr. in *UWRL*, 206–7

Review of I. E. Babel', *Rasskazy*, *Sovremennye zapiski* 26 (1925), 485–8; repr. in *UWRL*, 203–5

Review of John Lehmann, *The Noise of History*, *Internatsional'naya literatura* 8 (1935), 174–5

Review of M. I. Tsvetaeva, *Molodets: Skazka*, *Slavonic Review* 4 (12) (1926), 775–6

Review of M. I. Tsvetaeva, *Molodets: Skazka*, *Sovremennye zapiski* 27 (1926), 569–72; trans. Paul Schmidt, in Simon Karlinsky and Alfred Appel, Jr. (eds.), *The Bitter Air of Exile* (Berkeley, Calif., 1977), 88–93

Review of O. E. Mandel'shtam, *Shum vremeni*, *Sovremennye zapiski* 25 (1925), 541–3; repr. in *UWRL*, 208–10

'Revival of Russian Prose Fiction, The', *The Nation & the Athenæum*, 14 Mar. 1925, 811–12

'Romantizm', in *Literaturnaya entsiklopediya* (Munich, 1991), x, cols. 17–39

Russia: A Social History (London, 1931)

'Russia in Literature', *Literary Review* (of *The New York Times*), 2 Sept. 1922, 921

'Russia, 1015–1462', in *The Cambridge Medieval History*, vii (Cambridge, 1932), 599–631

'Russian Literature', in *Encyclopaedia Britannica: The Three New Supplementary Volumes constituting with the Volumes of the Latest Standard Edition the Thirteenth Edition* (London and New York, 1926), iii. 435–9

'Russian Literature', in *Encyclopaedia Britannica*, 14th edn (London and New York, 1929), xix. 751–8

'Russian Literature since 1917', *Contemporary Review*, Aug. 1922, 205–11

'Russian Poetess, A', *Outlook*, 18 Mar. 1922, 218

'Russian Post-Revolutionary Nationalism', *Contemporary Review* 124 (1923), 191–8

Russkaya lirika: Malen'kaya antologiya ot Lomonosova do Pasternaka (Paris, 1924)

'S. A. Esenin', *Slavonic Review* 4 (12) (1926), 706–7

'Stikhi 1934 goda: Stat'ya 1-ya', *Literaturnaya gazeta* 21 (512) (15 Apr. 1935), 4–5; repr. in *Literaturno-kriticheskie stat'i*, 240–52

'Stikhi 1934 goda: Stat'ya 2-ya', *Literaturnaya gazeta* 23 (514) (24 Apr. 1935), 2–3

Stikhotvoreniya, 1906–1910 (St Petersburg, 1911); repr. in *SSRP*, 17–78

Stikhotvoreniya: Stat'i o russkoi poezii, compiled and ed. G. K. Perkins and G. S. Smith (Berkeley, Calif., 1997)

Storia della letteratura russa, trans. Silvio Bernardini (Milan, 1965)

'Story of a Liberation, The', see 'Histoire d'une libération'

'Tendencies of the Modern Russian Novel', in Hugh Walpole (ed.), *Tendencies of the Modern Novel* (London, 1934), 101–19; repr. in *UWRL*, 328–38

The Diary of a Madman by Nicolas Gogol. Translated by Prince Mirsky, illustrated with acquatints by A. Alexeieff (London, 1929)

'Three Views of Russia', *Listener*, 11 Mar. 1931, 418

'Through Foreign Eyes: An Address delivered at the Annual Meeting of the Brontë Society', *Brontë Society Publications* 6 (33) (1923), 147–52

'Two Aspects of Revolutionary Nationalism', *Russian Life* 5 (1922), 172–4

'Ukraine, The', *Quarterly Review* 239 (Apr. 1923), 318–35

Uncollected Writings on Russian Literature, ed. with Introduction and Bibliography by G. S. Smith (Berkeley, Calif., 1989)

'Uncompromising Utopian, An' (review of R. Fülöp-Miller, *New Light on Tolstoy*), *Listener*, 8 July 1931, 54

Untitled review, *London Mercury* 8 (43) (May 1923), 218

Untitled speech, in *Vtoroi plenum pravleniya Soyuza sovetskikh pisatelei SSSR, mart 1935g. Stenograficheskii otchet* (Moscow, 1935), 294–8

Untitled speech, *Literaturnyi kritik* 2 (1935), 221–3

'V. Ya. Bryusov', *Sovremennye zapiski* 22 (1924), 414–26; repr. in *UWRL*, 132–44

'Veyanie smerti v predrevolyutsionnoi literature', *Versty* 2 (1927), 247–54; repr. in *UWRL*, 230–6

'Voina i mir', *Literaturnyi sovremennik* 11 (1935), 115–33; repr. in *UWRL*, 339–57

'Voprosy poezii', *Literaturnaya gazeta* 7 (498) (5 Feb. 1935), 2; repr. in *SSRP*, 188–95

'Voprosy poezii: Stat'ya 3-ya', *Literaturnaya gazeta* 35 (526) (24 June 1935), 5; repr. in *SSRP*, 203–9

'Wandering Scholars, The', *London Mercury* 16 (1927), 409–16

'Why I Became a Marxist', *Daily Worker* 462 (30 June 1931), 2

'*Yugo-zapad* V. Bagritskogo', *Evraziya*, 24 Nov. 1928, 8; repr. in *SSRP*, 108–112
'Yury Olesha', *Literaturnaya gazeta* 69 (385) (2 June 1934), 2
'Za khudozhnika-istorika', *Oktyabr'* 7 (1934), 221–4
'Zametki o stikhakh', *Znamya* 12 (1935), 231–6; repr. in *SSRP*, 223–30
'Zametki ob emigrantskoi literature', *Evraziya*, 5 Jan. 1929, 6–7
'Zamysel i vypolnenie', *Literaturnaya gazeta* 80 (396), 24 June 1934, 80

4. UNPUBLISHED SECONDARY SOURCES

ALEXANDER, TANIA, Letter to G. S. Smith, 7 Feb. 1994
BERLIN, ISAIAH, Letter to G. S. Smith, 20 Mar. 1996
BROWN, E. J., Letter to G. S. Smith, 20 Oct. 1982
CARR, E. H., Letter to G. S. Smith, 1 Feb. 1974
FLORINSKY, MICHAEL, Letters to Sir Bernard Pares, Bakhmeteff Archive, Columbia University
GALTON, DOROTHY, Interview with G. S. Smith, Leeds Russian Archive, MS 900. 1/3
HILL, ELIZABETH, Letter to G. S. Smith, 31 Jan. 1974
LAVRIN, JANKO, Interview with G. S. Smith, Leeds Russian Archive, MS 900/4
LEDKOVSKY, MARINA, Letter to Ol'ga Kaznina, 10 June 1994
PARES, SIR BERNARD, Letters to Michael Florinsky, Bakhmeteff Archive, Columbia University
PASCAL, ROY, Interview with G. S. Smith, Leeds Russian Archive, MS 900/5
SPALDING, ANNE, Letters to G. S. Smith, 29 Aug. 1974, 5 Nov. 1974
SVYATOPOLK-MIRSKAYA, PRINCESS S. P., Letters to Prince P. D. Svyatopolk-Mirsky, Moscow, GARF, *fond* 172, *opis'* 2, *edinitsa khraneniya* 392
TRAILL, VERA, Interviews with G. S. Smith, Leeds Russian Archive, MS 901/1–3
VINOGRADOFF, IGOR, Letters to G. S. Smith, 13 and 26 Feb. 1974

5. PUBLISHED SECONDARY SOURCES

ACKERMANN, ROBERT, *The Myth and Ritual School: J. G. Frazer and the Cambridge Ritualists* (London, 1991)
ADLAM, CAROL, 'In the Name of Bakhtin: Appropriation and Expropriation in Recent Russian and Western Bakhtin Studies', in Alastair Renfrew (ed.), *Exploiting Bakhtin* (Strathclyde, 1997), 75–90
AIMERMAKHER (EIMERMACHER), KARL, 'Sovetskaya literaturnaya politika mezhdu 1917-m i 1932-m', in *V tiskakh ideologii: Antologiya literaturno-politicheskikh dokumentov, 1917–1927* (Moscow, 1992), 3–61
AKHMATOVA, ANNA, *My Half Century*, ed. Ronald Meyer (Ann Arbor, Mich., 1992)
ANASTAS'EV, N., 'Prisutstvie kritika', in D. S. Mirsky, *Stat'i o literature* (Moscow, 1987), 3–19
ANDREW, CHRISTOPHER, and GORDIEVSKY, OLEG, *KGB: The Inside Story of Its Foreign Operations from Lenin to Gorbachev* (London, etc., 1990)

ANTOSHCHENKO, A. V., 'Spory o evraziistve', in Antoshchenko and Kozhanov (eds.), *O evrazii i evraziitsakh*, 7–43

——and KOZHANOV, A. A. (eds.), *O Evrazii i evraziitsakh (Bibliograficheskii ukazatel')* (Petrozavodsk, 1997)

ASHNIN, F. D., and ALPATOV, V. M., *'Delo slavistov': 30-e gody* (Moscow, 1994)

ATKINSON, DOROTHY, et al. (eds.), *Women in Russia* (Stanford, Calif., 1977)

AVDEENKO, ALEKSANDR, 'Otluchenie', *Znamya* 3 (1989), 5–73

AVTONOMOVA, N. S., and GASPAROV, M. L., 'Yakobson, slavistika i evraziistvo: Dve kon″yunkury, 1919–1953', *Novoe literaturnoe obozrenie* 27 (1997), 87–91

BABEL, I. E., 'The Story of My Dovecote', trans. D. S. Mirsky, *Slavonic and East European Review* 10 (28) (1931), 1–11

BABICHENKO, D. L. (ed.), *'Literaturnyi front': Istoriya politicheskoi tsenzury 1932–1946* (Moscow, 1994)

——(ed.), *'Schast'e literatury': Gosudarstvo i pisateli 1925–1938: Dokumenty* (Moscow, 1997)

BAILEY, GEOFFREY, *The Conspirators* (London, 1971)

BALZER, HARLEY (ed.), *Russia's Missing Middle Class: The Professions in Russian History* (Armonk, NY, 1996)

BANTING, MARK, KELLY, CATRIONA, and RIORDAN, JAMES, 'Sexuality', in Kelly and Shepherd (eds.), *Russian Cultural Studies*, 311–51

BARING, MAURICE, *Landmarks in Russian Literature* (London, 1910; repr. London and New York, 1960)

——*The Mainsprings of Russia* (London, 1914)

——*The Puppet Show of Memory* (London, 1922)

BARNES, CHRISTOPHER, *Boris Pasternak: A Literary Biography*, ii: *1928–1960* (Cambridge, 1998)

——and DAVIES, RICHARD, '"Neotsenimyi podarok": Perepiska Pasternakov i Lomonosovykh (1925–1970)', *Minuvshee* 16 (1994), 150–208

BASSIN, M., 'Russia between Europe and Asia: The Ideological Construction of Geographical Space', *Slavic Review* 50 (1) (1991), 1–17

BEAUJOUR, ELIZABETH KLOSTY, *Alien Tongues: Bilingual Russian Writers of the 'First' Emigration* (Ithaca, NY, 1989)

BECHHOFER, C. E., *In Denikin's Russia* (London, 1921)

BELAYA, GALINA, *Don-Kikhoty 20-kh godov: 'Pereval' i sud'ba ego idei* (Moscow, 1989)

BERBEROVA, NINA, *Zheleznaya zhenshchina* (New York, 1981)

BERDYAEV, N., 'Russkaya religioznaya mysl' i revolyutsiya', *Versty* 3 (1928), 40–64

BERKOV, P. N., *Vvedenie v izuchenie istorii russkoi literatury XVIII veka* (Leningrad, 1964)

BERLIN, ISAIAH, 'Aleksandr i Salomeya Gal'perny', in Mikhail Parkhomovsky (ed.), *Evrei v kul'ture russkogo zarubezh'ya: Sbornik statei, publikatsii, memuarov i esse*, i: *1919–1939 gg.* (Jerusalem, 1992), 229–41

——Letter to G. S. Smith, 2 Nov. 1993, cited in Smith, *The Letters of D. S. Mirsky to P. P. Suvchinskii*, 223–4

——'A View of Russian Literature' (review of Marc Slonim, *The Epic of Russian Literature*), *Partisan Review* 17 (6) (July–Aug. 1950), 617–23

BERNSTEIN, LAURIE, *Sonia's Daughters* (Berkeley and Los Angeles, Calif., 1995)

BERZER, ANNA, *Proshchanie* (Moscow, 1990)

BETHEA, DAVID, *The Shape of Apocalypse in Russian Literature* (Princeton, NJ, 1989)
Bibliographie des œuvres de Lev Karsavine. Établie par Aleksandr Klementiev, Préface de Nikita Struve (Paris, 1994)
BIRYUKOV, ALEKSANDR, *Poslednii Ryurikovich* (Magadan, 1991)
BLANE, ANDREW, 'A Sketch of the Life of Georges Florovsky', in Blane (ed.), *Georges Florovsky: Russian Intellectual and Orthodox Churchman* (Crestwood, NY, 1993), 11–217
BLOK, A. A., *Zapisnye knizhki, 1901–1921* (Moscow, 1965)
Blok v neizdannoi perepiske i dnevnikakh sovremennikov (Moscow, 1982)
BOAG, J. W., RUBININ, P. E., and SCHOENBERG, D. (eds.), *Kapitza in Cambridge and Moscow: Life and Letters of a Russian Physicist* (Amsterdam, 1990)
BOGOMOLOV, N. A., 'Dnevniki v russkoi kul'ture nachala XX veka', *Tynyanovskie chteniya* 4 (1990), 152–4
——*Mikhail Kuzmin: Stat'i i materialy* (Moscow, 1995)
——and MALMSTAD, DZHON E., *Mikhail Kuzmin: Iskusstvo, zhizn', epokha* (Moscow, 1996)
BOHACHEVSKY-CHOMIAK, MARTHA, *Sergei N. Trubetskoi: An Intellectual among the Intelligentsia in Prerevolutionary Russia* (Belmont, Mass., 1976)
BORLAND, HARRIET, *Soviet Literary Theory and Practice during the First Five-Year Plan, 1928–1932* (New York, 1950)
BÖSS, OTTO, *Die Lehre der Eurasier: Ein Beitrag zur russischen Ideengeschichte des 20. Jahrhunderts* (Wiesbaden, 1961)
BOYD, BRIAN, *Nabokov: The Russian Years* (Princeton, NJ, 1990)
BOYLE, ANDREW, *The Climate of Treason*, rev. edn (London, 1980)
BREWSTER, DOROTHY, *East–West Passage: A Study in Literary Relationships* (London, 1954)
BRODSKY, JOSEPH, *Less than One: Selected Essays* (London, 1986)
BROOKS, JEFFREY, *When Russia Learned to Read: Literacy and Popular Literature, 1861–1917* (Princeton, NJ, 1985)
BROWN, E. J., *The Proletarian Episode in Soviet Literature, 1928–1932* (New York, 1953)
BROWN, IVOR, Review of D. S. Mirsky, *The Intelligentsia of Great Britain, Observer*, 6 Apr. 1935
BROWNING, GARY, *Boris Pilniak: Scythian at a Typewriter* (Ann Arbor, Mich., 1985)
BUCKLEY, MARY, *Women and Ideology in the Soviet Union* (Ann Arbor, Mich., 1989)
BUSHNELL, JOHN, 'The Tsarist Officer Corps, 1881–1914: Customs, Duties, Inefficiency', *American Historical Review* 86 (1981), 753–80
BYKOVA-LUGOVSKAYA, E., and NOGTEVA, M., '"Nad zemlei vstayushchii Orion": Perepiska V. Lugovskogo s A. Fadeevym', *Literaturnoe obozrenie* 7 (1981), 107–12
CALLAGHAN, JOHN, *Rajani Palme Dutt: A Study in British Stalinism* (London, 1993)
Cambridge Encyclopedia of Russia and the Former Soviet Union, The, ed. Archie Brown, Michael Kaser, and G. S. Smith (Cambridge, 1994)
CARR, E. H., *Bakunin* (London, 1937)
——*Dostoyevsky (1821–1881): A New Biography* (Boston and New York, 1931)
——*The Romantic Exiles: A Nineteenth-Century Portrait Gallery* (London, 1933)
CARSWELL, JOHN, *Lives and Letters: A. R. Orage, Katherine Mansfield, Beatrice Hastings, John Middleton Murry, S. S. Koteliansky, 1906–1957* (London and Boston, 1978)
——*The Exile: A Life of Ivy Litvinov* (London and Boston, 1983)

CHAMBERLIN, W. H., *Confessions of an Individualist* (New York, 1940)
——*Russia's Iron Age* (London, 1935)
CHERTKOV, L. N., 'Mirsky, Dmitry Petrovich', in *Kratkaya literaturnaya entsiklopediya*, iv: *'Lakshin–Muranovo'* (Moscow, 1967), col. 861
CHUKOVSKY, K., *Dnevnik 1901–1929* (Moscow, 1991)
——*Dnevnik 1930–1969* (Moscow, 1994)
——'Uolt Uitman', in his *Sobranie sochinenii v 6 tt.*, iii (Moscow, 1966)
CLEMENTS, Barbara Evans, *Bolshevik Women* (Cambridge, 1997)
CLOWES, EDITH, *The Revolution in Moral Consciousness: Nietzsche in Russia, 1890–1914* (De Kalb, Ill., 1988)
CONQUEST, ROBERT, *Kolyma: The Arctic Death Camps* (London, 1978)
CORNWELL, NEIL, *James Joyce and the Russians* (Basingstoke and London, 1992)
——'More on Joyce and Russia: or *Ulysses* on the Moscow River', *Joyce Studies Annual 1994* (Austin, Tex., 1994), 175–86
COSTLOW, JANE T., SANDLER, STEPHANIE, and VOWLES, JUDITH (eds.), *Sexuality and the Body in Russian Culture* (Stanford, Calif., 1993)
COURNOS, JOHN, *Autobiography* (New York, 1935; repr. New York, 1978)
——'Introduction', in Andrei Biely, *St Petersburg* (New York, 1959), pp. vii–xviii
——Review of D. S. Mirsky, *Russia: A Social History*, *Criterion* 11 (42) (Oct. 1931), 131–3
——Review of D. S. Mirsky, *The Intelligentsia of Great Britain*, *Yale Review* n.s. 25 (Winter 1936), 425
——Review of *Versty 3*, *Criterion* 8 (30) (Sept. 1928), 182–3 ('J. C.')
COWLEY, MALCOLM, Review of D. S. Mirsky, *The Intelligentsia of Great Britain*, *New Republic* 84 (23 Aug. 1935), 14
Cultural Mythologies of Russian Modernism: see under Gasparov et al.
DAVIDSON, PAMELA, 'Introduction', in *Viacheslav Ivanov: A Reference Guide* (London, etc., 1996), pp. xiv–xxix
DEHN, LILY, *The Real Tsaritsa* (London, 1922)
Der große Exodus: see under Schlögel
Dictionary of Russian Women Writers, ed. Marina Ledkovsky, Charlotte Rosenthal, and Mary Zirin (Westport, Conn., and London, 1994)
DOBBIE-BATEMAN, A. F., *St Seraphim of Sarov: Concerning the Aims of the Christian Life* (London, 1936)
DOCHERTY, JUSTIN, *The Acmeist Movement in Russian Poetry: Culture and the Word* (Oxford, 1995)
DOMBROVSKY, YURY, 'Pis'mo Sergeyu Antonovu', *Grani* 111–12 (1979), 518–27
DRYZHAKOVA, ELENA, 'The Fifties in Transition: A. S. Dolinin and Yu. G. Oksman, Our Remarkable Teachers', *Oxford Slavonic Papers* n.s. 18 (1985), 120–49
DUGIN, A., 'Evraziiskii triumf', in Petr Savitsky, *Kontinent Evraziya* (Moscow, 1997), 433–53
DUKEL'SKY, VLADIMIR, 'Dyagilev i ego rabota', *Versty* 3 (1928), 251–5
DUKES, PAUL, *A History of Russia, c.882–1996*, 3rd edn (Houndmills, 1998)
EDMONDSON, LINDA, 'Women's Emancipation and Theories of Sexual Difference in Russia, 1850–1917', in Marianne Liljeström, Eila Mäntysaari, and Arja Rosenholm (eds.), *Gender Restructuring in Russian Studies* (Tampere, 1993), 39–52
ENGELSTEIN, LAURA, *The Keys to Happiness: Sex and the Search for Happiness in Fin-de-Siècle Russia* (Ithaca, NY, 1992)

[Erenburg, I.,] '"Poshli tolki, chto den'gi moskovskie . . .": Pis'ma Il'i Erenburga Mikhailu Kol'tsovu 1935–1937 godov', *Novyi mir* 3 (1999), 164–75

ERMOLAEV, HERMAN, *Soviet Literary Theories, 1917–1937: The Genesis of Socialist Realism* (Berkeley and Los Angeles, Calif., 1963)

Evraziiskaya perspektiva (Moscow, 1994)

Evraziistvo: Formulirovka 1927 goda (Prague, 1927)

Evraziistvo: Opyt sistematicheskogo izlozheniya (Paris, 1926)

Evraziya: Istoricheskie vzglyady russkikh emigrantov (Moscow, 1992)

EVTUHOV, CATHERINE, *The Cross and the Sickle: Sergei Bulgakov and the Fate of Russian Religious Philosophy* (Ithaca, NY, 1997)

Farewell to the Don: The Journal of Brigadier H. N. H. Williamson, ed. John Harris (London, 1970)

FEINBERG, M., and KLYUKIN, YU., 'Po vnov' otkryvshimsya obstoyatel'stvam', in *Bolshevo: Literaturnyi istoriko-kraevedcheskii al'manakh* (Moscow, 1992), 145–66

FIGES, ORLANDO, *A People's Tragedy: The Russian Revolution 1891–1924* (London, 1996)

FLEISHMAN, LAZAR', *Boris Pasternak v tridtsatye gody* (Jerusalem, 1984)

——'Iz pasternakovskoi perepiski', *Slavica Hierosolymitana* 5 and 6 (1981), 535–41

——HUGHES, R., and RAEVSKAYA-HUGHES, O. (eds.), *Russkii Berlin, 1921–1923* (Paris, 1983)

FLORINSKY, MICHAEL, *The End of the Russian Empire* (New York, 1961)

FLOROVSKY, G. V., 'Evraziiskii soblazn' (1928); repr. in *Rossiya mezhdu Evropoi i Aziei* (Moscow, 1993), 237–65

——'Okameneloe beschuvstvie (Po povodu polemiki protiv evraziistva)', *Put'* 2 (1926), 128–33

FOX, RALPH, Letter to P. F. Yudin, in *Iz istorii mezhdunarodnogo ob"edineniya revolyutsionnykh pisatelei (MORP)* (Moscow, 1969), 391

FREZINSKY, BORIS, 'Literaturnaya pochta Karla Radeka', *Voprosy literatury* 3 (1998), 278–316

FRY, ROGER, Dialogue with D. S. Mirsky, cited in Denys Sutton, 'Preface', in *The Letters of Roger Fry* (2 vols., London, 1972), i. 74–80

FULLER, W. C., *Civil–Military Conflict in Imperial Russia, 1881–1914* (Princeton, NJ, 1985)

GAIDENKO, P. P., '"Konkretnyi idealizm" S. N. Trubetskogo', in S. N. Trubetskoy, *Sochineniya* (Moscow, 1994), 3–41

GALTON, DOROTHY, 'Sir Bernard Pares and Slavonic Studies in London University, 1919–39', *Slavonic and East European Review* 46 (107) (1968), 481–91

——'The Anglo-Russian Literary Society', *Slavonic and East European Review* 48 (111) (1970), 272–83

GARNETT, RICHARD, *Constance Garnett: A Heroic Life* (London, 1991)

GARRARD, JOHN and CAROL, *Inside the Soviet Writers' Union* (London, 1990)

GASPAROV, BORIS, 'Introduction', in Gasparov et al. (eds.), *Cultural Mythologies of Russian Modernism*, 1–16

——HUGHES, ROBERT P., and PAPERNO, IRINA (eds.), *Cultural Mythologies of Russian Modernism: From the Golden to the Silver Age* (Berkeley, Calif., etc., 1992)

GASPAROV, M. L., 'Antinomichnost' poetiki russkogo modernizma' (1992), in his *Izbrannye trudy* (3 vols., Moscow, 1997) ii: *O stikhakh*, 434–55

——'K geografii chastushechnogo ritma', in his *Izbrannye trudy* (Moscow, 1997) iii: *O stikhe*, 279–89

GELLER, MIKHAIL, *Kontsentratsionnyi mir i sovetskaya literatura* (London, 1971)

——'"Pervoe predosterezhenie"—udar khlystom', *Vestnik russkogo khristianskogo dvizheniya* 127 (1978), 187–232

GERASIMOV, YU. K., 'Religioznaya pozitsiya evraziitsev', *Russkaya literatura* 1 (1995), 159–76

GIDE, ANDRÉ, *The Journals of André Gide*, trans. and annotated by Justin O'Brien, iii: *1928–1939* (New York, 1949)

GINZBURG, EUGENIA, *Journey into the Whirlwind*, trans. Paul Stevenson and Max Hayward (New York and London, 1970)

GINZBURG, LIDIYA, *O liricheskom geroe* (Leningrad, 1974)

GIPPIUS, VAS., 'Problema Pushkina (po povodu stat'i D. Mirskogo "Problema Pushkina")', *Vremennik Pushkinskoi komissii* 1 (1936), 253–61

GLAD, JOHN, *Conversations in Exile* (Durham, NC, and London, 1993)

GLADILIN, ANATOLY, *The Making and Unmaking of a Soviet Writer* (Ann Arbor, Mich., 1979)

GLADKOV, ALEKSANDR, 'Iz poputnykh zapisei', *Voprosy literatury* 9 (1976), 168–215

——*Meetings with Pasternak*, trans. Max Hayward (London, 1977)

GOLLERBAKH, ERIKH, *Gorod muz: Tsarskoe selo v poezii* (Leningrad, 1927)

Gor'ky i sovetskie pisateli (Moscow, 1963)

[Gor'ky, Maksim,] '"Zhmu vashu ruku, dorogoi tovarishch": Perepiska Maksima Gor'kogo i Iosifa Stalina', *Novyi mir* 9 (1997), 167–92; ibid. 9 (1998), 156–78

GOR'KY, M., et al. (eds.), *Belomorsko-Baltiiskii kanal imeni Stalina: Istoriya stroitel'stva* (Moscow, 1934)

GORYAEVA, T. M., 'Sovetskaya politicheskaya tsenzura (Istoriya, deyatel'nost', struktura)', in *Isklyuchit' vsyakie upominaniya ... Ocherki istorii sovetskoi tsenzury* (Minsk and Moscow, 1995), 13–64

GRAHAM, LOREN R., *The Ghost of the Executed Engineer: Technology and the Fall of the Soviet Union* (Cambridge, Mass., and London, 1993)

GRAHAM, STEPHEN, *Part of the Wonderful Scene: An Autobiography* (London, 1964)

Gramsci's Prison Letters, trans. and introd. Hamish Hamilton (London, 1988)

GRIEVE, C. M.: see under MacDiarmid

GRONSKY, I. M., 'Beseda o Gor'kom: Publikatsiya M. Nike', *Minuvshee* 10 (1990), 64–87

GUERSHOON, ANDREW COLIN, *Certain Aspects of Russian Proverbs* (London, 1941)

GUMILEV, N. S., *Pis'ma o russkoi poezii*, ed. R. D. Timenchik (Moscow, 1990)

GÜNTHER, HANS, *Die Verstaatlichung der Literatur: Entstehung und Funktionsweise des sozialistisch-realistischen Kanons in der sowjetischen Literatur der 30er Jahre* (Stuttgart, 1984)

HAIMSON, LEOPOLD, 'The Problem of Social Identities in Early Twentieth-Century Russia', *Slavic Review* 47 (1) (1988), 1–20

HANQUART, EVELYN, 'Forster on Contemporary English Literature', *Aligorh Journal of English Studies* 5 (1) (1980), 102–9

HAUCHARD, CLAIRE, 'L. P. Karsavin et le mouvement eurasien: de la critique à l'adhésion', *Revue des Études Slaves* 68 (3) (1996), 360–5

HELDT, BARBARA, '"Japanese" in Russian Literature: Transforming Identities', in

Thomas Rimer (ed.), *A Hidden Fire: Russian and Japanese Encounters, 1868–1926* (Stanford, Calif., 1995), 171–83

HELDT, BARBARA, 'Motherhood in a Cold Climate: The Poetry and Career of Maria Shkapskaya', in Costlow et al. (eds.), *Sexuality and the Body in Russian Culture*, 237–54

HELLMAN, BEN, *Poets of Hope and Despair: The Russian Symbolists in War and Revolution (1914–1918)* (Helsinki, 1995)

HINGLEY, RONALD, *The Russian Mind* (London, etc., 1977)

HOLLINGSWORTH, BARRY, 'The Society of Friends of Russian Freedom: English Liberals and Russian Socialists, 1890–1917', *Oxford Slavonic Papers* n.s. 3 (1970), 45–64

HOLMGREN, BETH, *Women's Works in Stalin's Time* (Bloomington, Ind., 1993)

HOLQUIST, PETER, '"Conduct Merciless Mass Terror": Decossackization on the Don, 1919', *Cahiers du Monde Russe et Soviétique* 38 (1 and 2) (1997), 127–62

HOSKING, GEOFFREY, *Russia: People and Empire* (Cambridge, Mass., 1998)

HOWARTH, PATRICK, *Squire: 'Most Generous of Men'* (London, 1963)

HUNTINGDON, W. CHAPIN, *The Homesick Million: Russia-out-of-Russia* (Boston, 1933)

IL'IN, I. A., *O soprotivlenii zlu siloyu* (Berlin, 1925)

INGRAMS, RICHARD, *Muggeridge: The Biography* (London, 1995)

ISAEV, I. A., 'Utopisty ili providtsy?', in *Puti Evrazii: Russkaia intelligentsiia i sud'by Rossii* (Moscow, 1992), 3–26

Iskhod k vostoku (Sofia, 1921; repr. Moscow, 1997)

Isklyuchit' vsyakie upominaniya . . . Ocherki istorii sovetskoi tsenzury (Minsk and Moscow, 1995)

IVANOV-RAZUMNIK, R., *Pisatel'skie sud'by* (New York, 1951)

IVASK, YU., 'O smerti knyazya Svyatopolka-Mirskogo', *Novyi zhurnal* 127 (1977), 290–2

Iz istorii mezhdunarodnogo ob"edineniya revolyutsionnykh pisatelei (MORP) (Moscow, 1969)

IZVOLSKY, HÉLÈNE, *No Time to Grieve* (Philadelphia, 1985)

——[Elena Izvol'skaya] 'Ten' na stenakh (O Marine Tsvetaevoi)', *Opyty* 3 (1954), 152–9

JACKSON, T. A., 'Mirsky Dissects Our Intelligentsia', *Daily Worker*, 15 May 1935

JARINTZOFF, N., *The Russians and Their Language* (London, 1916)

——*Russian Poets and Poems* (Oxford, 1917)

JOHNSTON, ROBERT H., *'New Mecca, New Babylon': Paris and the Russian Exiles, 1920–1945* (Kingston, Ont., 1988)

JONES, W. GARETH (ed.), *Tolstoi and Britain* (Oxford and Washington, DC, 1995)

'K istorii evraziistva: 1922–1924 gg.', *Rossiiskii arkhiv: Istoriya otechestva v svidetel'stvakh i dokumentakh XVIII–XX vv.*, v (Moscow, 1994), 475–89

KANAVEZ, M., 'Moya zhizn' s Raskol'nikovym', *Minuvshee* 7 (1989), 95–6

KARLINSKY, SIMON, 'Russia's Gay Literature and History (11th–20th Centuries)', *Gay Sunshine* 29 and 30 (1976), 1–7

——and APPEL, ALFRED, JR. (eds.), *The Bitter Air of Exile: Russian Writters in the West, 1922–1972* (Berkeley, Calif., 1977)

KAROLYI, MICHAEL: see *Memoirs of Michael Karolyi*

KATS, B., and TIMENCHIK, R., *Akhmatova i muzyka* (Leningrad, 1989)

KATSIS, L. F., 'V. Stenich: Stikhi "russkogo dendi"', *Literaturnoe obozrenie* 5 and 6 (1996), 65–6

KAUN, ALEXANDER, 'Maxim Gorky and the Tsarist Police', *Slavonic Review* 8 (24) (1930), 636–61

KAZNINA, OL'GA, 'D. Svyatopolk-Mirsky i evraziiskoe dvizhenie', *Nachala* 4 (1992), 81–8

——'N. S. Trubetskoy i krizis evraziistva', *Slavyanovedenie* 4 (1995), 89–95

——*Russkie v Anglii: Russkaya emigratsiya v kontekste russko-angliiskikh literaturnykh svyazei v pervoi polovine XX veka* (Moscow, 1997)

KELLY, CATRIONA, *A History of Russian Women's Writing, 1820–1992* (Oxford, 1994)

——and SHEPHERD, DAVID (eds.), *Russian Cultural Studies: An Introduction* (Oxford, 1998)

KENEZ, PETER, *Civil War in South Russia, 1919–1920* (Berkeley, Calif., etc., 1977)

——'A Profile of the Pre-Revolutionary Officer Corps', *California Slavic Studies* 7 (1973), 121–58

KH'ETSO, GEIR [GEIR KJETSAA], *Maksim Gor'ky: Sud'ba pisatelya* (Moscow, 1997)

KHODASEVICH, VLADISLAV, 'Gor'ky', in *Koleblemyi trenozhnik* (Moscow, 1991), 353–74

——'K istorii vozvrashchenchestva', ibid. 430–3

——'Literatura v izgnanii', in *Literaturnye stat'i i vospominaniya* (New York, 1954), 255–71

——'O "Verstakh"', *Sovremennye zapiski* 29 (1926), 433–41; repr. in John Malmstad and Robert Hughes (eds.), *Sobranie sochinenii, ii: Stat'i i retsenzii, 1905–1926* (Ann Arbor, Mich., 1990), 408–17

——'Tam ili zdes'?'; repr. in John Malmstad and Robert Hughes (eds.), *Sobranie sochinenii, ii: Stat'i i retsenzii, 1905–1926* (Ann Arbor, Mich., 1990), 364–8

KHORUZHY, S. S., 'Karsavin, evraziistvo i VKP', *Voprosy filosofii* 2 (1992), 84–7

KLYUCHNIKOV, SERGEI (ed.), *Russkii uzel evraziistva: Vostok v russkoi mysli: Sbornik trudov evraziitsev* (Moscow, 1997)

KOCH, STEPHEN, *Double Lives: Stalin, Willi Münzenberg, and the Seduction of the Intellectuals* (London, 1996)

KOMAROVSKY, V. A., *Proza i stikhi*, ed. Yury Ivask and W. Tjalsma (Munich, 1978)

KORNBLATT, JUDITH DEUTSCH, and GUSTAFSON, RICHARD F. (eds.), *Russian Religious Thought* (Madison, Wis., 1996)

KOROSTELEV, OLEG, 'Parizhskoe "Zveno" (1923–1928) i ego sozdateli', in M. Parkhomovsky (ed.), *Russkoe evreistvo v zarubezh'e*, i (6) (Jerusalem, 1998), 177–201

KORZEC, PAWEL, 'Three Documents of 1903–6 on the Russian Jewish Situation', *Soviet Jewish Affairs* 2 (2) (1972), 75–95

KOZHEVNIKOV, V. M., and NIKOLAEV, P. A. (eds.), *Literaturnyi entsiklopedicheskii slovar'* (Moscow, 1987)

KOZOVOÏ, VADIM, Untitled introductory article, 'Iz perepiski B. Pasternaka i P. Suvchinskogo', *Revue des Études Slaves* 58 (4) (1986), 637–48

KRASAVCHENKO, T. N. 'Mirsky, Dmitry Petrovich', in *Pisateli russkogo zarubezh'ya (1918–1940): Spravochnik* (2 vols., Moscow, 1994), ii. 114–19

——'Mirsky, Dmitry Petrovich', in *Russkoe zarubezh'e: Zolotaya kniga emigratsii: Pervaya tret' XX veka* (Moscow, 1997), 419–22

KRASNOV-LEVITIN, A., *Likhie gody 1925–1941* (Paris, 1977)

KUDROVA, IRMA, *Gibel' Mariny Tsvetaevoi* (Moscow, 1992)

——'Poslednee "delo" Sergeya Efrona', *Zvezda* 10 (1992), 112–30

KUDROVA, IRMA, 'Vera Treil, urozhdennaya Guchkova: Po materialam doprosov na Lubyanke', *Russkaya mysl'* 4068 (9–15 Mar. 1995), 11–12

KUDRYAKOVA, E. B., *Rossiiskaya emigratsiya v Velikobritanii v period mezhdu dvumya voinami* (Moscow, 1995)

KURLYANDSKY, I. A., 'Poet i voin', in *Nikolai Gumilev: Issledovaniya i materialy: Bibliografiya* (St Petersburg, 1994), 254–98

KUZMIN, M. A., *Dnevnik 1934 goda* (St Petersburg, 1998)

——*Stikhotvoreniya*, ed. K. A. Bogomolov (St Petersburg, 1996)

KUZNETSOVA, O. A., 'Diskussiya o sostoyanii russkogo simvolizma v "Obshchestve revnitelei khudozhestvennogo slova" (Obsuzhdenie doklada Vyach. Ivanova)', *Russkaya literatura* 1 (1990), 200–7

LABEDZ, LEO, 'Isaac Deutscher's "Stalin": An Unpublished Critique', *Encounter* 52 (1) (1979), 65–82

LAMPL, HORST, 'A. M. Remizov: A Short Biographical Essay (1877–1923)', *Russian Literature Triquarterly* 19 (1986), 7–60

LANE, DAVID, 'Social Classes and Inequality', in R. W. Davies (ed.), *The Soviet Union*, 2nd edn (Boston, etc., 1989), 78–89

LAVROUKINE, NINA, 'Maurice Baring and D. S. Mirsky: A Literary Relationship', *Slavonic and East European Review* 62 (1) (1984), 25–35

——and TCHERTKOV, LEONID, *D. S. Mirsky: profil critique et bibliographique* (Paris, 1980)

LAVROV, A. V., *Andrey Bely v 1900-e gody* (Moscow, 1995)

LAVROV, V. A., '"Dukhovnyi ozornik": K portretu knyazya D. P. Mirskogo—kritika i istorika literatury', in *Peterburgskii tekst: Iz istorii russkoi literatury 20–30-kh godov XX veka* (St Petersburg, 1996), 136–47

LEATHERBARROW, W. J. (ed.), *Dostoevskii and Britain* (Oxford and Providence, RI, 1995)

LEE, HERMIONE, *Virginia Woolf* (London, 1996)

LEGG, STUART, *The Heartland* (New York, 1970)

LEHMANN, JOHN, *The Whispering Gallery: Autobiography I* (London, 1955)

LEHOVICH, DIMITRY V., *White against Red: The Life of General Anton Denikin* (New York, 1974)

LETLEY, EMMA, *Maurice Baring: A Citizen of Europe* (London, 1991)

The Letters of Dorothy L. Sayers: 1899 to 1936: The Making of a Detective Novelist, ed. Barbara Reynolds, Preface by P. D. James (London, 1995)

LEVIE, SOPHIE, *Commerce, 1924–1932: une revue internationale moderniste* (Paris, 1989)

LEVYTSKY, BORYS, *The Stalinist Terror of the Thirties: Documentation from the Soviet Press* (Stanford, Calif., 1974)

LIBERMAN, ANATOLY, 'Introduction: Trubetzkoy as a Literary Scholar', in N. S. Trubetzkoy, *Writings on Literature*, ed., trans., and introd. Anatoly Liberman (Minneapolis, 1990), pp. xi–xlvi

——'Postscript: N. S. Trubetskoy and His Works on History and Politics', in N. S. Trubetskoy, *The Legacy of Genghis Khan and Other Essays on Russia's Identity*, ed. and with a postscript by Anatoly Liberman (Ann Arbor, Mich., 1991), 295–375

LIEVEN, DOMINIC, *Russia's Rulers under the Old Regime* (London, 1989)

——*Nicholas II: Twilight of the Empire* (New York, 1994)

Life of the Archpriest Avvakum by Himself, The. Translated from the Seventeenth Century Russian by Jane Harrison and Hope Mirrlees (London, 1924)

LINDENMEYR, ADELE, Untitled note on early Soviet show trials, *Women East–West* 49 (1997), 2

Linguaphone Conversational Course: Russian, recorded by Dimitri Svjatopolk-Mirskij, Formerly Lecturer in Russian, King's College; Basil Timotheieff, B.D., M.A.I.; Serge Ivanoff, L. ès Sc.; Mme Ivanoff; Mme Timotheieff and I. Potiekhin (London, n.d.)

LIPKIN, SEMEN, *Zhizn' i sud'ba Vasiliya Grossmana* (Moscow, 1990)

Literaturnyi entsiklopedicheskii slovar': see under Kozhevnikov and Nikolaev

LOSEFF, LEV, and SCHERR, BARRY (eds.), *A Sense of Place: Tsarskoe selo and Its Poets* (Columbus, Ohio, 1993)

LOSSKAYA, VERONIKA, *Marina Tsvetaeva v zhizni* (Tenafly, NJ, 1989)

Low's Russian Sketchbook: Drawings by Low, Text by Kingsley Martin (London, 1932)

LUKÁCS, GEORG, Untitled speech, *Literaturnyi kritik* 2 (1935), 214–20

M. Gor'ky i sovetskaya pechat', ed. A. G. Dementiev et al. (2 vols., Moscow, 1964)

MACDIARMID, HUGH, *The Collected Poems of Hugh MacDiarmid* (2 vols., Manchester, 1993)

——[C. M. GRIEVE] Review of D. S. Mirsky, *Contemporary Russian Literature*, *New Age* 40 (1) (1926), 9

——Review of D. S. Mirsky, *Modern Russian Literature*, *New Age* 37 (8) (1925), 92

MACKENNON, LACHLAN, *The Lives of Elsa Triolet* (London, 1992)

MAGGS, PETER B., *The Mandelstam and 'Der Nister' Files: An Introduction to Stalin-Era Prison and Labor Camp Records* (Armonk, NY, and London, 1996)

MAGUIRE, ROBERT, *Red Virgin Soil: Soviet Literature in the 1920s* (Princeton, NJ, 1968)

MAKOVSKY, S. K., *Na parnase serebryanogo veka* (Munich, 1961)

MALEVSKY-MALEVICH, P., *A New Party in Russia* (London, 1928)

——(ed.), *Russia U.S.S.R.: A Complete Handbook* (New York, 1933)

MALMSTAD, JOHN, 'Andrey Bely and Serafim of Sarov', *Scottish Slavonic Review* 14 (1990), 21–59, and 15 (1990), 59–102

——'Mikhail Kuzmin: A Chronicle of His Life and Times', in Mikhail Kuzmin, *Sobranie stikhov*, ed. J. E. Malmstad and V. F. Markov (3 vols., Munich, 1977), iii. 9–319

——(ed.), *Studies in the Life and Work of Mixail Kuzmin* (Vienna, 1989)

MALNICK, BERTHA, *Everyday Life in Russia* (London, 1938)

MANDEL'SHTAM, NADEZHDA, *Vospominaniya* (New York, 1970)

MANDEL'SHTAM, O., *Stikhotvoreniya* (Leningrad, 1974)

MARSH, ROSALIND, 'An Image of Their Own? Feminism, Revisionism and Russian Culture', in Rosalind Marsh (ed.), *Women and Russian Culture: Projections and Self-Perceptions* (New York and Oxford, 1998), 2–41

——'Introduction', in Marsh (ed.), *Gender and Russian Literature*, 1–37

——(ed.), *Gender and Russian Literature: New Perspectives* (Cambridge, 1996)

MARSHALL, BILL, *Victor Serge: The Uses of Dissent* (Oxford, 1992)

MARTIN, KINGSLEY, *Editor* (London, 1968)

——*Father Figures: A First Volume of Autobiography, 1897–1931* (London, 1966)

MASING-DELIC, IRENE, 'The Transfiguration of Cannibals: Fedorov and the Avant-Garde', in *Laboratory of Dreams: The Russian Avant-Garde and Cultural Experiment* (Stanford, Calif., 1996), 17–36

MASLIN, N. 'Dekadenty ili klassiki', *Literaturnyi sovremennik* 9 (1935), 163–7

MATICH, OLGA, 'Androgyny and the Russian Silver Age', *Pacific Coast Philology* 14 (1979), 42–50

—— 'The Symbolist Theory of Love: Theory and Practice', in Irina Paperno and Joan Delaney Grossman (eds.), *Creating Life: The Aesthetic Utopia of Russian Modernism* (Stanford, Calif., 1994), 24–50

MAY, RACHEL, *The Translation in the Text: Reading Russian Literature in English* (Evanston, Ill., 1994)

MAYZEL, MATITIAHU, 'The Formation of the Russian General Staff, 1880–1917: A Social Study', *Cahiers du Monde Russe et Soviétique* 16 (1975), 291–321

MEDZMARIASHVILI, GALINA, *Salomeya Andronikashvili na fone svoego pokoleniya* (Moscow, 1998)

Memoirs of Michael Karolyi, The: Faith without Illusion (London, 1956)

MENNING, BRUCE W., *Bayonets before Bullets: The Imperial Russian Army, 1861–1914* (Bloomington, Ind., 1992)

MEYENDORFF, A. F., *Background of the Russian Revolution* (New York, 1929)

MICKIEWICZ, DENIS, '*Apollo* and Modernist Poetics', *Russian Literature Triquarterly* 1 (1971), 226–61

MILIUKOV, P. N., 'Eurasianism and Europeanism in Russian History', in *Festschrift Th. G. Masaryk zum 80. Geburtstag*, i (Bonn, 1930), 225–36

Mir Rossii-Evraziya: Antologiya (Moscow, 1995)

MIRSKY, VERA T. [VERA TRAILL], *The Cup of Astonishment* (London, 1944)

MNUKHIN, LEV, 'Legendy i byl': Eshche raz o gibeli knyazya D. P. Svyatopolk-Mirskogo', *Russkaya mysl'* 4129 (6–12 June 1996), 10; 4130 (13–19 June 1996), 10; 4131 (20–26 June 1996), 10

MØLLER, PETER ULF, *Postlude to the Kreutzer Sonata: Tolstoy and the Debate on Sexual Morality in Russian Literature in the 1890s* (Amsterdam, 1989)

MORTIMER, RAYMOND, Review of D. S. Mirsky, *The Intelligentsia of Great Britain, New Statesman and Nation* 9 (420) (23 Mar. 1935)

MUCHNIC, HELEN, *Dostoevsky's English Reputation, 1881–1936* (Northampton, Mass., 1939)

MUGGERIDGE, MALCOLM, *Chronicles of Wasted Time*, i: *The Green Stick* (London, 1972)

—— *Like It Was: The Diaries of Malcolm Muggeridge*, selected and ed. John Bright-Holmes (London, 1981)

—— *Winter in Moscow* (London, 1934)

MUNBLIT, G., *Rasskazy o pisatelyakh*, 2nd rev. edn (Moscow, 1976)

NABOKOV, VLADIMIR, *Drugie berega* (New York, 1954)

—— *Selected Letters 1940–1977*, ed. Dmitri Nabokov and Matthew J. Bruccoli (London, 1990)

NEWMARCH, ROSA, *Poetry and Progress in Russia* (London and New York, 1907)

NICHOLS, ROBERT L., 'The Friends of God: Nicholas II and Alexandra at the Canonization of Serafim of Sarov, July 1903', in Timberlake (ed.), *Religious and Secular Forces in Late Tsarist Russia*, 207–29

NIKOLIUKIN, A. N., 'Dostoevskii in Constance Garnett's Translation', in Leatherbarrow (ed.), *Dostoevskii and Britain*, 207–27

NIKOL'SKAYA, T. L., 'Emotsionalizm', *Russian Literature* 20 (1986), 61–70

NIKULIN, LEV, *Lyudi i stranstviya: Vospominaniya i vstrechi* (Moscow, 1962)

—— 'Mertvaya zyb'', *Moskva* 6 (1965), 5–90, and 7 (1965), 47–141

NIVAT, GEORGES, 'La "fenêtre sur l'Asie" ou les paradoxes de l'"affirmation eurasienne"', *Rossiya/Russia* 6 (1988), 81–93

'Odisseya russkogo "Ulissa"', *Inostrannaya literatura* 1 (1990), 172–92

OLESHA, YURY, *No Day without a Line: From Notebooks by Yury Olesha*, ed., trans., and with an Introduction by Judson Rosengrant (Evanston, Ill., 1998)

OSBORNE, CHARLES, *WHA: The Life of a Poet* (New York and London, 1979)

Oxford Book of Russian Verse, The, chosen by Maurice Baring (Oxford, 1924)

OZEROV, LEV, 'Flamandskoe pero Petra Semynina', *Arion* 3 (1994), 106

PACHMUSS, TEMIRA, *A Russian Cultural Revival: A Critical Anthology of Émigré Literature before 1939* (Knoxville, Tenn., 1981)

PAGE, BRUCE, LEITCH, DAVID, and KNIGHTLEY, PHILLIP, *Philby: The Spy Who Betrayed a Generation*, rev. edn (London, 1977)

PARES, BERNARD, *A History of Russia* (New York, 1926)

——*A Wandering Student* (Syracuse, NY, 1947)

——*Moscow Admits a Critic* (London, 1936)

——*My Russian Memoirs* (London, 1931)

——*Russia and Reform* (London, 1907)

PARTRIDGE, MONICA, 'Russians, Russian Literature, and the London Library', in *Rossiya, zapad, vostok: Vstrechnye techeniya: K 100-letiyu so dnya rozhdeniya akademika M. P. Alekseeva* (St Petersburg, 1997), 340–51

PASTERNAK, B. L., Letter to Anna Akhmatova, 19 Oct. 1932, in *Iz istorii sovetskoi literatury 1920–1930-kh godov* (Moscow, 1983), 659–60

——*Pis'ma k roditelyam i sestram* (2 vols., Stanford, Calif., 1998)

——'Pis'ma k V. M. Sayanovu: publikatsiya A. V. Lavrova', in *Ezhegodnik rukopisnogo otdela Pushkinskogo doma na 1977 god* (Leningrad, 1979), 193–202

Paul Desjardins et les décades de Pontigny (études, témoignages et documents inédits), ed. Anne Heurgon-Desjardins, Preface by André Maurois (Paris, 1964)

PEACOCK, SANDRA J., *Jane Ellen Harrison: The Mask and the Self* (New Haven, Conn., and London, 1988)

PERKHIN, V. V., 'K istorii aresta i reabilitatsii D. P. Svyatopolk-Mirskogo (po arkhivnym materialam)', *Russkaya literatura* 1 (1997), 220–37

——'O D. P. Svyatopolk-Mirskom', in D. P. Svyatopolk-Mirsky, 'Literaturno-kriticheskie stat'i', *Russkaya literatura* 4 (1990), 120–7

——'Odinnadtsat' pisem (1920–1937) i avtobiografiya (1936) D. P. Svyatopolk-Mirskogo', *Russkaya literatura* 1 (1996), 235–62

——*Russkaya literaturnaya kritika 1930-kh godov: Kritika i obshchestvennoe soznanie epokhi* (St Petersburg, 1997)

Pervyi vsesoyuznyi s"ezd sovetskikh pisatelei 1934: Stenograficheskii otchet: Prilozheniya (Moscow, 1990)

PETROV, S., Review of T. Smollett, *Sobranie sochinenii* (Moscow, 1934), *Khudozhestvennaya literatura* 12 (1935), 57–9

PINTNER, WALTER, 'The Burden of Defense in Imperial Russia, 1725–1914', *Russian Review* 43 (1984), 231–59

PITCHER, HARVEY, *When Miss Emmie Was in Russia: English Governesses Before, During and After the October Revolution* (London and Toronto, 1977)

POKROVSKY, M. N., *Brief History of Russia*, trans. D. S. Mirsky (2 vols., London, 1933)

POLIVANOV, K. M., 'Trizhdy uslyshannyi shum: Retsenzii na knigu "Shum vremeni"', *Literaturnoe obozrenie* 1 (1991), 55–8

——'Zametki i materialy k "politicheskoi" biografii Borisa Pasternaka (1934–1937)', *De Visu* 4 (1993), 70–9

POLOVINKIN, S. M., 'Evraziistvo', in *Russkaya filosofiya: Malyi entsiklopedicheskii slovar'* (Moscow, 1995), 172–8

——'Evraziistvo i russkaya emigratsiya', in N. S. Trubetskoy, *Istoriya: Kul'tura: Yazyk* (Moscow, 1995), 731–62

POLYAKOV, M. YA., 'Literaturno-kriticheskaya deyatel'nost' D. Mirskogo', in D. Mirsky, *Literaturno-kriticheskie stat'i* (Moscow, 1978), 5–18

POLYANOVSKY, EDVIN, *Gibel' Osipa Mandel'shtama* (St Petersburg and Paris, 1993)

POPOV, V. P., 'State Terror in Soviet Russia, 1923–1953 (Sources and Their Interpretation)', *Russian Social Science Review* 35 (5) (1994), 48–70

POWERS, FRANCIS GARY, with GENTRY, CURT, *Operation Overflight: The U-2 Pilot Tells His Story for the First Time* (New York, etc., 1970)

PRITCHETT, V. S., Review of D. S. Mirsky, *The Intelligentsia of Great Britain, Christian Science Monitor*, 8 May 1935, 11

Puti Evrazii: Russkaya intelligentsiya i sud'by Rossii (Moscow, 1992)

PYAST, VLADIMIR, *Vstrechi* (Moscow, 1929)

PYMAN, AVRIL, *A History of Russian Symbolism* (Cambridge and New York, 1994)

RAEFF, MARC, *Russia Abroad: A Cultural History of the Russian Emigration, 1919–1939* (New York and Oxford, 1990)

RAPP, HELEN, Obituary of A. F. Meyendorff, *Slavonic and East European Review* 42 (99) (1963–4), 440–2

RÉE, JONATHAN, *Proletarian Philosophers: Problems in Socialist Culture in Britain, 1900–1940* (Oxford, 1984)

REMIZOV, ALEKSEY, 'Esprit', *Sovremennye zapiski* 23 (1925), 87–112

——'"Voistinu"', *Versty* 1 (1926), 82–6

REZNIKOVA, NATALYA, 'Alexei Remizov in Paris (1923–1957)', *Russian Literature Triquarterly* 19 (1986), 61–92

RIASANOVSKY, NICHOLAS V., 'The Emergence of Eurasianism', *California Slavic Studies* 4 (1967), 39–72; repr. in *Exodus to the East: Forebodings and Events: An Affirmation of the Eurasians* (Idyllwild, Calif., 1996), 115–42

RIL'KE, RAINER MARIA, PASTERNAK, BORIS, and TSVETAEVA, MARINA, *Pis'ma 1926 goda* (Moscow, 1990)

ROBIN, RÉGINE, *Socialist Realism: An Impossible Aesthetic?* (Stanford, Calif., 1992)

ROSENTHAL, BERNICE GLATZER (ed.), *Nietzsche in Russia* (Princeton, NJ, 1986)

——(ed.), *Nietzsche and Soviet Culture: Ally and Adversary* (Cambridge, 1994)

——(ed.), *The Occult in Russian Literature* (Ithaca, NY, 1997)

Rossiya mezhdu Evropoi i Aziei: Evraziiskii soblazn (Moscow, 1993)

ROSSLYN, WENDY, 'Boris Anrep and the Poetry of Anna Akhmatova', *Modern Language Review* 74 (1979), 884–96

ROZANOV, V. V., *Literaturnye izgnanniki*, i (St Petersburg, 1913)

RUANE, CHRISTINE, *Gender, Class, and the Professionalization of Russian City Teachers, 1860–1914* (Pittsburgh, 1994)

RUBENSTEIN, JOSHUA, *Tangled Loyalties: The Life and Times of Ilya Erenburg* (London and New York, 1996)

RUBENSTEIN, ROBERTA, 'Genius of Translation', *Colorado Quarterly* 22 (3) (1974), 359–68

RUSINKO, ELAINE, 'Acmeism, Post-symbolism, and Henri Bergson', *Slavic Review* 41 (1982), 495–510

Russia in Resurrection (London, 1928): see under Spalding

RUTHCHILD, ROCHELLE, *Women in Russia and the Soviet Union: An Annotated Bibliography* (New York, 1994)

SALAMAN, ESTHER, 'Prince Mirsky', *Encounter* 54 (1) (1980), 93–4

Salon Album of Vera Sudeikina-Stravinsky, The, ed. and trans. John E. Bowlt (Princeton, NJ, 1995)

SAVITSKY, PETR, *Kontinent Evraziya* (Moscow, 1997)

——[Stepan Lubensky] 'V bor'be za evraziistvo: polemika vokrug evraziistva v 1920-kh godakh', in *Tridtsatye gody* (Paris, 1931), 1–52

SCHLÖGEL, KARL (ed.), *Der große Exodus: Die russische Emigration und ihre Zentren 1917 bis 1941* (Munich, 1994)

SCHULER, CATHERINE A., *Women in the Theatre: The Actress in the Silver Age* (London, 1996)

Science at the Crossroads: Essays by N. I. Bukharin and Others, 2nd edn (London, 1971)

SERGE, VICTOR, *Memoirs of a Revolutionary 1901–1941*, trans. Peter Sedgwick (Oxford, 1963)

SERGIEVSKY, I., 'Po povodu stat'i D. Mirskogo', *Literaturnoe nasledstvo* 9 and 10 (1933), 510–12

——'Pushkinskii vremennik', *Literaturnaya gazeta*, 26 Feb. 1936

SETON-WATSON, HUGH, *The Russian Empire 1801–1917* (Oxford, 1967)

SEZEMAN, V., Reviews of *Put'*, *Versty* 2 (1927), 275–80, and 3 (1928), 175–81

SHAKHOVSKAYA, ZINAIDA, *Otrazheniya* (Paris, 1975)

SHANKS, EDWARD, Review of D. S. Mirsky, *The Intelligentsia of Great Britain*, *Sunday Times*, 6 Apr. 1935

SHARP, JANE A., 'Redrawing the Margins of Russian Vanguard Art', in Costlow et al., *Sexuality and the Body*, 97–123

SHENTALINSKY, VITALY, *The KGB's Literary Archive: The Discovery of the Ultimate Fate of Russia's Suppressed Writers* (London, 1995)

SHEVELENKO, IRINA, 'K istorii evraziiskogo raskola 1929 goda', *Stanford Slavic Studies* 8 (1994), 376–416

SHIPOV, D. N., *Vospominaniya i dumy o perezhitom* (Moscow, 1918)

SHIROKOV, O. S., 'Problema etnolingvisticheskikh obosnovanii evraziistva', in *Iskhod k vostoku* (Moscow, 1997), 4–42

SHTEINBERG, A., *Druz'ya moikh rannikh let (1911–1928)* (Paris, 1991)

SIMPSON, SIR JOHN HOPE, *The Refugee Problem: Report of a Survey* (London, etc., 1939)

SLONIM, MARK, 'O Marine Tsvetaevoi', *Novyi zhurnal* 104 (1971), 143–76

SMITH, G. S., 'An Annotated Bibliography of D. S. Mirsky's Writings, 1932–1937', in Mirsky, *Uncollected Writings on Russian Literature*, 368–85

——'D. S. Mirsky, Literary Critic and Historian', in Mirsky, *Uncollected Writings on Russian Literature*, 19–43

——'Literature and the Arts', in R. W. Davies (ed.), *The Soviet Union*, 2nd edn (Boston, etc., 1989), 155–69

——'Marina Tsvetaeva i D. P. Svyatopolk-Mirsky', in Robin Kemball et al.

(eds.), *Marina Tsvetaeva: Actes du 1 Colloque Marina Tsvetaeva* (Bern, etc., 1991), 192–206

SMITH, G. S., 'The Poetry and Verse Theory', in John E. Malmstad (ed.), *Andrey Bely: Spirit of Symbolism* (Ithaca, NY, and London, 1987), 242–84

—— 'The Versification of V. F. Khodasevič, 1915–1939', in Thomas Eekman and Dean S. Worth (eds.), *Russian Poetics: Proceedings of the International Colloquium at UCLA, September 22–26, 1975* (Columbus, Ohio, 1982), 373–92

—— 'What Happened to D. S. Mirsky?', *British East–West Journal* 98 (1994), 10–11

SOBOLEV, AL'BERT, 'Knyaz' N. S. Trubetskoy i evraziistvo', *Literaturnaia ucheba* 6 (1991), 121–30

—— 'Polyusa evraziistva', *Novyi mir* 1 (1991), 180–2

—— '"Svoya svoikh ne poznasha": Evraziistvo, L. P. Karsavin i drugie', *Nachala* 4 (1992), 49–58

SOKOLOVA, NATAL'YA, 'Iz starykh tetradei, 1938–1941', *Voprosy literatury* 2 (1998), 356–65

SOLOMON, FLORA, *Baku to Baker Street: The Memoirs of Flora Solomon by Herself and Barnet Litvinoff* (London, 1984)

SOLZHENITSYN, ALEKSANDR, *Arkhipelag GULag*, iii–iv (Paris, 1974)

—— *Krasnoe koleso*, in *Sobranie sochinenii* (20 vols., Vermont and Paris, 1978–91), xi–xx (1983–91)

[SPALDING, N.,] *Russia in Resurrection: A Summary of the Views and the Aims of a New Party in Russia. By an English Europasian* (London, 1928)

SPENDER, STEPHEN, Review of D. S. Mirsky, *The Intelligentsia of Great Britain*, *The Spectator* 154 (22 Mar. 1935), 498

STACY, R. H., *Russian Literary Criticism: A Short History* (Syracuse, NY, 1974)

STALIN, I. V., 'God velikogo pereloma: K XII godovshchine Oktyabra', in *Sochineniya* (13 vols., Moscow, 1946–51), xii (1949), 118–35

STEWART, JESSIE, *Jane Ellen Harrison: A Portrait from Letters* (London, 1959)

STITES, RICHARD, *The Women's Liberation Movement in Russia: Feminism, Nihilism, and Bolshevism 1860–1930*, 2nd edn (Princeton, NJ, 1991)

STRUVE, G. P., 'Predislovie', in D. P. Svyatopolk-Mirsky, *Russkaya lirika: Malen'kaya antologiya ot Lomonosova do Pasternaka* (repr., New York, 1979), 7–29

—— *Russian Literature under Lenin and Stalin, 1917–1953* (London, 1972)

—— *Russkaya literatura v izgnanii*, 2nd edn (New York, 1984)

—— *Soviet Russian Literature* (London, 1935)

—— *Soviet Russian Literature, 1917–1950* (London, 1951)

—— *25 Years of Soviet Literature* (London, 1944)

SUVCHINSKY, P. P., Letter to G. S. Smith, 23 July 1974, in *The Letters of D. S. Mirsky to P. P. Suvchinskii*, 2–3

[——] 'Pis'ma P. P. Suvchinskogo N. S. Trubetskomu (1922–1924)', *Rossiiskii arkhiv: Istoriya otechestva v svidetel'stvakh i dokumentakh XVIII–XX vv.*, v (Moscow, 1994), 475–89

SVIRSKY, GRIGORY, *Na lobnom meste: Literatura nravstvennogo soprotivleniya (1946–1976 gg.)* (London, 1979)

[SVYATOPOLK-MIRSKAYA, E. A.,] 'Dnevnik kn. Ekateriny Alekseevny Svyatopolk-Mirskoi za 1904–1905 gg.', *Istoricheskie zapiski* 77 (1965), 255

[SVYATOPOLK-MIRSKY, P. D.,] 'Vsepoddanneishii doklad ministra vnutrennikh del P. D.

Svyatopolk-Mirskogo (24 noyabrya 1904 g.)', in *Reka vremen: Kniga istorii i kul'tury*, Kniga 5-ya (Moscow, 1996), 216–62

TANENHAUS, SAM, *Whittaker Chambers* (New York, 1997)

TERRAS, VICTOR, 'Russian Literary Criticism', in Harry Weber (ed.), *The Modern Encyclopedia of Russian and Soviet Literature*, v (Gulf Breeze, Fla., 1981), 1–19

TERTS, ABRAM [ANDREI SINYAVSKY], *Goodnight! A Novel*, trans. Richard Lourie (New York, 1989)

——*Spokoinoi nochi* (Paris, 1985)

THOMAS, HUGH, *John Strachey* (London, 1973)

TIAN-SHANSKAIA, OLGA SEMYONOVNA, *Village Life in Late Tsarist Russia*, ed. David L. Ransel, trans. David L. Ransel with Michael Levine (Bloomington and Indianapolis, 1993)

TIHANOV, GALIN, 'Bakhtin, Lukács, and German Romanticism: The Case of Epic and Irony', in C. Adlam et al. (eds.), *Face to Face: Bakhtin in Russia and the West* (Sheffield, 1997), 273–98

——'Bakhtiny v Anglii: Dopolneniya k biografii N. M. Bakhtina i k istorii retseptsii M. M. Bakhtina', in *Tynyanovskii sbornik*, vyp. 10 (Moscow, 1998), 591–8

——'Nikolay Bakhtin: Two Letters to Mikhail Lopatto (1924) and an Autobiographical Fragment', *Oxford Slavonic Papers* n.s. 31 (1998), 68–86

——'The Novel, the Epic and Modernity: Lukács and the Moscow Debate about the Novel (1934–35)', *Germano-Slavica* 10 (2) (1998), 29–42

TIMBERLAKE, CHARLES E., 'Introduction: Religious Pluralism, the Spread of Revolutionary Ideas, and the Church–State Relationship in Tsarist Russia', in Timberlake (ed.), *Religious and Secular Forces in Late Tsarist Russia*, 3–29

——(ed.), *Religious and Secular Forces in Late Tsarist Russia: Essays in Honor of Donald W. Treadgold* (Seattle and London, 1992)

TOLSTOY, L. N., *Polnoe sobranie sochinenii* (Moscow, 1928–64)

TOLSTOY, N. I., 'N. S. Trubetskoy i evraziistvo', in N. S. Trubetskoy, *Istoriya: Kul'tura: Yazyk* (Moscow, 1995), 5–28

TOPOROV, V. N., 'Dve glavy iz istorii russkoi poezii nachala veka: I. V. A. Komarovsky. II. V. K. Shileiko (K sootnosheniyu poetiki simvolizma i akmeizma)', *Russian Literature* 7 (1979), 249–32

Tridtsatye gody: Utverzhdenie evraziitsev, vii (Paris, 1931)

TRUBETSKOY, N. S., *Istoriya: Kul'tura: Yazyk* (Moscow, 1995)

[——] *The Legacy of Genghis Khan and Other Essays on Russia's Identity*, ed., and with a postscript, by Anatoly Liberman (Ann Arbor, Mich., 1991)

——*Trubetzkoy's Letters and Notes. Prepared for publication by R. Jakobson with the assistance of H. Baran, O. Ronen and M. Taylor* (The Hague, 1975)

——'O rasizme', *Evraziiskie tetradi* 5 (1935), 43–54; repr. in *Trubetzkoy's Letters and Notes*

——'Predislovie', in G. Uells, *Rossiya vo mgle* (Sofia, 1920), pp. iii–xvi; repr. in *Istoriya: Kul'tura: Yazyk* (Moscow, 1995), 458–66

[——] *Writings on Literature*, ed., trans., and with an introduction by Anatoly Liberman (Minneapolis, 1990)

TSVETAEVA, ANASTASIYA, *Vospominaniya*, 3rd edn (Moscow, 1983)

TSVETAEVA, MARINA, 'Mat' i muzyka', in Marina Tsvetaeva, *Sobranie sochinenii v semi tomakh* (Moscow, 1997), v (1), 10–31

TSVETAEVA, MARINA, 'Pis'ma M. I. Tsvetaevoi iz arkhiva P. P. Suvchinskogo', *Revue des Études Slaves* 24 (2) (1993), 197–217; rev. text, *Novyi mir* 1 (1993), 197–217; repr. in *Sobranie sochinenii v semi tomakh* (Moscow, 1997), vi. 314–33

——'Poet o kritike', in Marina Tsvetaeva, *Sobranie sochinenii v semi tomakh* (Moscow, 1997), v (1), 274–96

TYRKOVA-WILLIAMS, ARIADNA, *Cheerful Giver* (London, 1935)

Understand the Weapon, Understand the Wound: Selected Writings of John Cornford, with Some Letters of Frances Cornford, ed. Jonathan Galassi (Manchester, 1976)

USTINOV, A. B., 'Delo detskogo sektora Gosizdata 1932g.: Predvaritel'naya spravka', in *Mikhail Kuzmin i russkaya kul'tura XX veka* (Leningrad, 1990), 125–36

U Tolstogo 1904–1910. 'Yasnopolyanskie zapiski' D. P. Makovitskogo. Kniga pervaya, 1904–1905 (Moscow, 1979)

VASIL'EVA, LARISA, *Kremlevskie zheny* (Moscow, 1992)

VENGEROV, S. A. (ed.), *Pushkinist: Istoriko-literaturnyi sbornik*, i (St Petersburg, 1914)

Vinaver Saga, The, ed. H. M. Winawer (London, 1994)

VINKOVETSKY, ILYA, 'Eurasianism in Its Time: A Bibliography', in *Exodus to the East: Forebodings and Events: An Affirmation of the Eurasians* (Idyllwild, Calif., 1996), 143–74

VISHNEVSKY, Vs., 'Znat' zapad!', *Literaturnyi kritik* 7 (1933), 80–95

VISHNYAK, M., *Gody emigratsii 1919–1969: Parizh–N'yu-Iork: Vospominaniya* (Stanford, Calif., 1970)

——'*Sovremennye zapiski': Vospominaniya redaktora* (Bloomington, Ind., 1957)

VOITSEKHOVSKY, SERGEY L., *Trest: Vospominaniya i dokumenty* (London, Ont., 1974)

VOLKOV, SOLOMON, *Conversations with Joseph Brodsky: A Poet's Journey through the Twentieth Century* (New York, etc., 1998)

VOLOSHIN, MAKSIMILIAN, *Stikhotvoreniya i poemy* (St Petersburg, 1995)

VORONOV, VL., 'Pervyi s"ezd pisatelei', in *Pervyi vsesoyuznyi s"ezd sovetskikh pisatelei 1934: Stenograficheskii otchet: Prilozhenie* (Moscow, 1990), 3–8

VROON, RONALD, '*Puti tvorchestva*: The Journal as a Metapoetic Statement', in Kenneth N. Brostrom (ed.), *Russian Literature and American Critics* (Ann Arbor, Mich., 1986), 219–39

Vtoroi plenum pravleniya Soyuza sovetskikh pisatelei SSSR, mart 1935g. Stenograficheskii otchet (Moscow, 1935)

WADDINGTON, PATRICK (ed.), *Ivan Turgenev and Britain* (Oxford and Providence, RI, 1995)

WALLACE, SIR DONALD MACKENZIE, *Russia: New and Enlarged Edition: Revised, Re-Set, and in Great Part Re-Written* (2 vols., London, etc., 1905)

WEBB, BEATRICE, *Beatrice Webb's Diaries 1924–1932*, ed. Margaret Cole (London, 1956)

WEBB, SIDNEY, and WEBB, BEATRICE, *Soviet Communism: A New Civilization?* (2 vols., London, 1935)

WEEKS, THEODORE R., 'Defining Us and Them: Poles and Russians in the "Western Provinces", 1863–1914', *Slavic Review* 53 (1) (1994), 26–40

WELLEK, RENÉ, *A History of Modern Criticism, 1750–1950*, vii: *German, Russian, and Eastern European Criticism, 1900–1950* (New Haven, Conn., and London, 1991)

WERSKEY, GARY, *The Visible College* (London, 1978)

WES, M. A., *Michael Rostovtzeff: Historian in Exile* (Stuttgart, 1990)

The White Sea Canal: Being an Account of the Construction of the New Canal between the White Sea and the Baltic Sea. By L. Auerbach et al., ed. A. Williams-Ellis (London, 1935)

WILLIAMS, HAROLD, *Russia of the Russians* (London, 1914)

WILLIAMS, ROBERT C., *Culture in Exile: Russian Émigrés in Germany, 1881–1941* (Ithaca, NY, and London, 1972)

WILSON, EDMUND, 'Comrade Prince', *Encounter* 5 (1) (1955), 10–20

—— *Letters on Literature and Politics, 1912–1972*, ed. Elena Wilson (London, 1977)

WIRTSCHAFTER, ELISE KIMERLING, *Social Identity in Imperial Russia* (De Kalb, Ill., 1997)

WOOLF, LEONARD, *An Autobiography*, ii: *1911–1969* (Oxford, etc., 1980)

WOOLF, VIRGINIA, 'A Dialogue upon Mount Pentelicus', *The Times Literary Supplement*, 11–17 Sept. 1987, 989

—— *A Writer's Diary: Being Extracts from the Diary of Virginia Woolf*, ed. Leonard Woolf (London, 1953)

—— *The Sickle Side of the Moon: The Letters of Virginia Woolf*, v: *1932–1935* (London, 1979)

ZABOLOTSKY, NIKOLAY, 'The Story of My Imprisonment', trans. Robin Milner-Gulland, in *Selected Poems*, ed. Daniel Weissbort (Manchester, 1999), 203–16

ZERNOV, NICHOLAS, *The Russian Religious Renaissance of the Twentieth Century* (Oxford, 1963)

ZHOVTIS, ALEKSANDR, *Nepridumannye anekdoty: Iz sovetskogo proshlogo* (Moscow, 1995)

ZIRIN, MARY F., *Women, Gender, and Family in the Soviet Successor States and Central/East Europe: A Bibliography* (Altadena, Calif., 1996)

ZOHRAB, IRENE, 'From New Zealand to Russia, to England: A Comment on Harold W. Williams and his Relations with English Writers', *New Zealand Slavonic Journal* (1985), 3–15

—— 'Remizov, Williams, Mirsky and English Readers (with some Letters from Remizov to Ariadna Tyrkova-Williams and Two Unknown Reviews)', *New Zealand Slavonic Journal* (1994), 259–87

—— 'The Place of the Liberals among the Forces of the Revolution: from the Unpublished Papers of Harold W. Williams', *New Zealand Slavonic Journal* (1986), 53–82

Index